Professional
ADSI
Programming

Simon Robinson

Wrox Press Ltd. ®

Professional ADSI Programming

Published by Wrox Press Ltd
Arden House, 1102 Warwick Road, Acock's Green, Birmingham B27 6BH, UK
Printed in USA
ISBN 1-861002-26-2

Trademark Acknowledgements

Wrox has endeavored to provide trademark information about all the companies and products mentioned in this book by the appropriate use of capitals. However, Wrox cannot guarantee the accuracy of this information.

Credits

Author
Simon Robinson

Additional Code
Kjell Tangen

Managing Editor
Chris Hindley

Development Editor
John Franklin

Editors
Jeremy Beacock
Lisa Stephenson
Andrew Tracey

Project Manager
Sophie Edwards

Index
Alessandro Ansa

Technical Reviewers
Robert Chang
Michael Corning
John Granade
Steven Hahn
Andy Harjanto
Todd Mondor
Lucas Mueller
Jon Pinnock
Gavin Smyth
Arthur Wang
Mark Wilcox

Design / Layout
Tom Bartlett
Mark Burdett
Will Fallon
Jonathan Jones
John McNulty

Illustrations
William Fallon
Jonathan Jones

Cover Design
Chris Morris

About The Author

Simon lives in Lancaster, in the North West of England, where he shares a house with some students.

He first encountered serious programming when doing his PhD in physics (mathematical modeling of superconductors). He would program in FORTRAN when his supervisor was watching (physics lecturers like FORTRAN) and C when he wasn't. The experience of programming was enough to put him off computers for life, and he tried to pursue a career as a sports massage therapist instead until he realized how much money was in programming and wasn't in sports massage therapy.

He then spent a year writing some very good cardiac risk assessment software but he and his business partner never got round to selling it to anyone. Finally, driven by a strange lack of money, he looked for a - whisper the word quietly - job. There followed about 18 months working for Lucent Technologies in Welwyn Garden City, UK. He left Lucent in June 1999 in order to take up a career writing.

Simon has a strong academic background with a number of published papers in scientific journals and now has over 10 years experience with programming in many different environments, covering everything from directories to components to numerical simulations. He's also been responsible for setting up the highly successful 'COMFest' regular informal meetings of COM Developers in the UK.

You can visit Simon's website at http://www.SimonRobinson.com.

Acknowledgements

Oh blimey. Where do I begin? There's so many people who directly or indirectly contributed to this book.

Let's do this roughly chronologically, which means the first two people on this list are two guys I've not only met, but have shared a house with for well over a year: **Ian Martin** and **Steve Marple**. They were responsible for getting me into Windows and PCs. So I guess if it wasn't for them you certainly wouldn't be reading this now. It was just over 3 years ago that the bits for my first PC arrived and I made the transition from unix. While I was picking up the RAM modules and saying 'What do dis bit do?' they patiently put it all together. (Well actually patiently's not the word. As I recall they were so keen to play with the bits of hardware that I hardly got a look in.) Thanks to their influence I rapidly progressed from my previous C++ experience to MFC and ATL, which was what lead to me learning ADSI and writing this book. They also made sure my PC had *Transport Tycoon* installed, which probably set back my career by about 3 months, but we'll quietly drop that subject won't we.

Moving on to more recent matters, there've been many people who've helped directly or indirectly with the book. **John Franklin** at Wrox Press for having the confidence to get the whole project started in the first place. Also to Lucent Technologies, particularly **Kit Ruparel**, for allowing me to write part of the book while working for them (besides being a great boss to work for).

The editors **Jeremy Beacock, Lisa Stephenson** and **Andrew Tracey** have been great (believe me – I've seen the hours they worked to bring this book out promptly). And the reviewers who – besides making my life hell for a month or so by painstakingly taking every sentence to bits and picking out anything that was even slightly out of place. (**Jonathan Pinnock**: You are evil).

Andy Harjanto at Microsoft deserves a special mention for patiently answering a lot of queries. Various explanations throughout the book owe their origins to emails from Andy.

Now let's move on to the list servers. One of the best ways to explore new and undocumented technologies is to share experience with other developers over the Internet. As a result there's a lot of people who I have to thank for helping me discover various nuances of ADSI and COM – most of whom I've never actually met.

My understanding of ADSI security owes a lot to a period of joint experimentation with **Tobias Loecke**, and my research on LDAP was helped by **Dina** (**Konstantina Papayannaki**). Where have you disappeared to Dina? By the way, any of you guys who are getting mentioned, feel free to drop me a photo sometime. I'd like to know what most of you look like! More recently, **Mark Wilcox** answered a few last minute queries about LDAP. Thanks also to **Kjell Tangen** for writing and making publically available the `IDispatchImplEx<>` and `CComTypeInfoHolderEx<>` templates which I picked up on and decided would make a very useful example in Chapter 9. (Yes, I did get Kjell's permission first!)

Then there's **Richard Anderson**, - about the only Internet person I have met. Thanks for a lot of discussions about various aspects of COM and Windows. And for giving me lots of sleepless nights picking bits of code apart. Richard, you're not quite as evil as Jon Pinnock - but it's a close call.

Look, after all these people, there are a couple of pages somewhere in the book that are mine. Honest. I just can't remember off-hand which ones...

Last of all, I'd like to thank all the people from the Welwyn Garden City 18-Plus group. These people have between them contributed precisely **nothing** to this book. But they threatened to beat me up and call me horrible names if I didn't acknowledge them. So to Becky, Jackie, Julie, Lowri, Sue, Suzy, Tom, Tom and Wendy – thank you! Your wonderful contribution was truly appreciated. Love, Simon xx.

Table of Contents

Chapter 2: Simple ADSI Clients   59

Chapter 3: Further Inside ADSI   105

Section 2: Applying ADSI   161

Chapter 4: Your Computer Network and ADSI   165

Chapter 5: Common Administrative Tasks with Active Directory and WinNT   205

Chapter 6: ADSI and BackOffice: Exchange Server, IIS, Site Server — 257

Chapter 7: Searching

Chapter 8: Security   335

Chapter 9: Writing a Provider   401

Chapter 10: LDAP   477

Chapter 11: Advanced ADSI Topics   507

Section 3: Writing Directory Enabled Applications   531

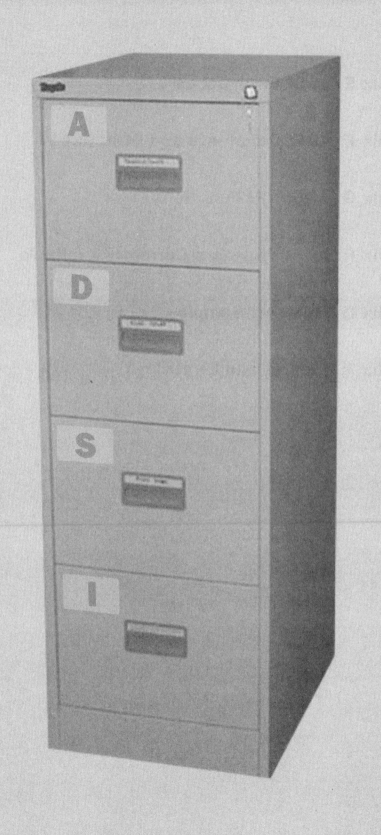

Introduction

Windows 2000 is just around the corner, and with it a new buzzword: **Directory Enabled Applications**. Microsoft is relentlessly pushing its goal of making applications as simple for the end user as possible, and that means big changes are coming for the way that applications share and access data with each other and with the operating system. In short, if any item of data is likely to be of interest to more than one application, then it should be stored in a directory. And by directory I don't just mean a folder in your file system – I'm talking about a specialized database.

The directory should have a single, unified means of access from different applications, and – at least in Windows - the recommended means of access is through the **Active Directory Services Interfaces** (**ADSI**).

This book may have the name ADSI on the cover, but it's also about more than that. It's about writing commercial applications that will look professional and meet the expectations of your end-users in the days of Windows 2000.

Primarily we are going to cover ADSI and directory programming. But if you are to write software that continues to meet your users' increasingly sophisticated expectations for ease of use, common user-interfaces, and ease of installation, as well as meeting the Windows Logo requirements, then you will also need to know about some other technologies – notably **Microsoft Management Console** (MMC), the **Windows Installer**, and **Windows Management Instrumentation(WMI)**. This book covers those areas as well.

With the adoption of Active Directory in Windows2000, there is likely to be some merging of the knowledge required by developers and administrators. Topics such as security and how WindowsNT manages domains on your network are areas that have traditionally been left to systems administrators, but which developers are increasingly going to need to understand in order to write software that looks and feels professional.

This book is aimed at developers who are familiar with programming in their own language, but who want a sufficient understanding of directories and administration to be able to code up software that smoothly integrates with the new technologies in Windows 2000. Because of this I tend to assume you have a good knowledge of developer topics – for example, I'm assuming a reasonable grasp of what COM is about. I'm not going to assume you're as familiar with administrative topics. When it comes to explaining, for example, how Windows 2000 domains or Kerberos security works, I start from scratch.

As far as language is concerned, I've presented examples in C++, VB, VBA and ASP (using VB Script). I've got no language bias other than wanting to use whichever language is most appropriate for the particular task at hand. Although many of the tasks are duplicable in each language, as we shall see, each language has particular roles to play when using ADSI.

What's in this Book

This book covers the following topics (not necessarily in this order):

Directories

- ❑ What directories are and how they are structured.
- ❑ DITs (directory information trees).
- ❑ How schemas work.
- ❑ The Lightweight Directory Access Protocol (LDAP)

ADSI

- ❑ The ADSI COM interfaces
- ❑ Writing ADSI clients
- ❑ Writing ADSI providers
- ❑ Using ADSI with ADO

Your computer network

- ❑ Active Directory
- ❑ Windows domains in Windows 2000.

BackOffice Components that use directories:

- ❑ The Exchange Server Directory
- ❑ The Internet Information Server (IIS) metabase

Windows objects you can Control using ADSI

- ❏ User, Group and Computer Accounts
- ❏ NT Services
- ❏ File Shares
- ❏ Print queues

Security

- ❏ Authentication and Authorization with ADSI
- ❏ How the Kerberos security protocols work

LDAP

Microsoft Management Console

Windows Installer

Windows Management Instrumentation

- ❏ Including WBEM (the web based enterprise management standard) and CIM (the common information model)

As you can see, that's a pretty wide list, covering not just ADSI itself, but all the important related technologies that are worth knowing in order to use ADSI effectively. During the book, we'll develop one large project, an ADSI provider, the *StarRaiders* provider, which lets you access a directory of information about pop stars. That project occupies the whole of Chapter 9. Other than that, there is one medium sized project, an MMC snap-in to manage StarRaiders. The other code samples are mostly small, although several of them are still quite useful ones that allow you to examine objects in directories. One of the strengths of ADSI is that it allows you to develop some very powerful applications and scripts without having to write much code.

Is This Book For You?

So you want to learn ADSI? You are an experienced VB Script, VBA, VB or VC++ programmer, and you've heard that Windows 2000 is going to be based around this great new thing called Active Directory. You know that it'll be a store for all the useful information on your network. You know that ADSI, the Active Directory Services Interface, is going to be the recommended way of accessing that data. You know that, even more than that, ADSI is intended to be the standard for accessing any directory, be it your Exchange Database, your IIS metabase, your company phone directory, or whatever.

In short, this book is for you if:

- ❏ You are an experienced developer
- ❏ You know at least the basics of COM

❑ Either you don't know anything about ADSI, Active Directory, or directories in general, or you know a little but want to know more

❑ You've heard of LDAP, but want to know how it fits in

It doesn't matter what language you program in. ADSI is implemented as a set of COM objects, which means it can be used by any COM-aware language – and I *do* swap between languages quite a bit in this book. That means you will need to be comfortable with at least *seeing* bits of sample code in languages other than your first language – even if you don't understand every line of the samples.

You will also need a passing familiarity with COM – enough to understand what an interface is and how to call up and use COM objects. C++ developers will also need to be comfortable with using ATL to write COM clients and servers. But I don't assume you're an expert COM guru, and where ADSI providers need to use more advanced COM features, such as Monikers, or where you need to dive in and understand some of the internals of ATL, I do go over what you need.

Chapter Breakdown

The book is organized into three parts.

ADSI Basics

The first section of introduces directories in general and ADSI.

Introduction

You're reading this one now! It tells you what the book's about and explains a bit about the history of directories, X500 and LDAP. You can spot the fact that I personally am primarily a C++ developer from the fact that the chapters are zero-indexed.

Chapter 1- Introduction to ADSI

This is the real introduction to ADSI. We look in detail at the kinds of problems that ADSI is designed to solve, and how easy ADSI makes it to unify access to different types of data. Then we go through the structure of ADSI-compatible directories. We cover aspects such as schemas, and we do a brief overview of Active Directory. There's no coding in this chapter. The aim is to get you sufficiently up to speed with the concepts behind ADSI to be comfortably able to start learning to use the ADSI interfaces.

Chapter 2 - Simple ADSI Clients

This is where we start writing ADSI clients. That means learning to use the ADSI interfaces. This chapter aims to get you to the point where you know enough ADSI to write clients that can do some of the most common tasks – browsing a directory and getting and setting properties. This means the chapter has three main topics: we go over the range of interfaces available so you get an idea of what interfaces you need to do what. We look in detail at the two core interfaces of IADs and IADsContainer. And we start to delve into the theory of how and why ADSI works the way it does.

Chapter 3 - Further Inside ADSI

This takes up where Chapter 2 leaves off and looks under the hood of ADSI – covering how and why many of the other interfaces work. Amongst other things we'll cover how ADSI handles schemas, groups, and how you can access the property cache directly. By the time you've finished this chapter you will have a very good grounding in the basic structure of ADSI – although we won't have applied the knowledge yet to different directories.

Applying ADSI

After understanding the basics, we'll move onto applying your new knowledge, by looking at particular ADSI functions and applications.

Chapter 4 - ADSI and Your Network

This chapter is about using ADSI to access resources on your network. You do this using either Active Directory or the ADSI WinNT provider. In this chapter, we'll look the overall directory structure that you'll see using either of these techniques – and the various peculiarities of these directories that you'll need to be aware of. We also study the basic background of how Windows domains work – with the emphasis on Windows 2000 and Active Directory.

Chapter 5 - Common Administrative Tasks with Active Directory and WinNT

Following on from Chapter 4 we'll apply our knowledge of ADSI to actually accessing network resources. We systematically go over the different objects on your network that you can access using ADSI: User, computer and group accounts, NT Services, File Shares and the File Service, and Print Queues and Print Jobs. For each one we run through common tasks you'll want to do with that type of object and show how to carry out those tasks using ADSI. We also provide the necessary background of how the objects themselves work.

Chapter 6 - ADSI and BackOffice: Exchange Server and IIS

We continue our application-centric approach by looking at two directories which are commonly accessed using ADSI: the Exchange Server Directory and the IIS Metabase. I don't assume you know anything about these BackOffice components, but briefly get you up to speed on what they can do, then show you how you can conveniently manage their respective directories using ADSI. We also briefly mention the other large Microsoft directory you can manage using ADSI: the Site Server Membership Directory.

Chapter 7 - Searching

Searching in ADSI is a topic all its own, and not just because its ADSI interfaces implement searching in a different way to almost all the rest of the ADSI functionality. Not only that, but the way you'd do searching from C++ is completely different from the way you'd do it in VB and scripting languages. In C++ we'll use the ADSI interface `IDirectorySearch`. This interface is not directly available to VB and scripting languages, which instead use the ADO provider for ADSI. This chapter goes through both techniques, as well as showing how to use Microsoft's `adsvw.exe` browser tool to search from a user interface (as opposed to programmatically). ADSI's way of doing searches also owes a fair bit to its LDAP heritage – which means where necessary we'll go over some of the LDAP background, such as the workings of LDAP search filters.

Chapter 8 - Security

In this chapter we look at how an ADSI client can authenticate itself to a provider, and also how ADSI providers implement security – and the ADSI security interfaces that allow you to set and view who is allowed to do what to directory objects. This leads us naturally on to how Windows 2000 (and NT) implement security using Access control lists and Access control entries. In order to gain the necessary background, this means going into the basics of NT security. We finish with a look at the Kerberos security protocol used by Windows 2000.

Chapter 9 - ADSI Providers

Up to now we've learned how to code up ADSI clients that use the services of providers that Microsoft and ISVs have written for us. This chapter covers the flip side of the coin: ADSI providers. We learn how to write ADSI providers using ATL by writing one: the StarRaiders provider, which allows access to a directory of Pop Stars, and which we use in some of the samples throughout this book.

To some extent, writing an ADSI provider with ATL is just writing a COM server with ATL – and I assume in this chapter you can already do that. The emphasis here is on picking out the aspects of coding ADSI providers which require more advanced knowledge of either COM/ATL or of the ADSI specifications So we'll cover areas such as Monikers, dispid-encoding, writing enumerators, and some of the subtleties of type libraries.

Theoretically, this is probably one of the hardest chapters – writing providers does require more in-depth knowledge of COM than writing clients – but by the end of the chapter you should have a pretty good grasp of how to write your own ADSI providers.

Chapter 10 - LDAP

This chapter dives behind the scenes a bit. ADSI owes a lot of its design to its LDAP inheritance, and LDAP in turn owes a lot to its original X500 inheritance. Here we look in a bit more depth at the theory of LDAP, and at the how to use the LDAP C API. We also develop a sample project that you can use to browse Active Directory or other LDAP directories directly using the Microsoft LDAP API.

Chapter 11 - Advanced ADSI Topics

At this point we've covered most of the ADSI topics, and we're going to wrap up our examination of ADSI with a lightening tour of the more advanced topics. We explore how you can use a provider to reverse engineer the calls a client makes, and so find out what some of Microsoft's clients expect providers to be able to do. We'll briefly discuss using connections carefully to improve performance of ADSI clients. But the bulk of the chapter is devoted to the subject of ADSI extensions – a topic that requires more advanced COM knowledge (of aggregation) than other areas of ADSI. Extensions are a powerful technique that allow you to add to the functionality of the providers available on your system, and we'll develop an extension that shows how to do this.

Part 3. Writing Directory Enabled Applications

Having looked at ADSI in depth, in the final section of the book I'm going to broaden the scope to look at what you need to create and deploy a professional ADSI application. As such, we'll be looking at several fairly heterogeneous topics, including...

Chapter 12 - Microsoft Management Console

In this chapter we go over what the MMC console and snap-ins actually are, and how the relevant COM interfaces are designed. We explain some of the C++ classes written for ATL that help you write snap-ins, show you how to write a snap-in using ATL, and go on to develop an administration snap-in for the StarRaiders provider.

Chapter 13 - The Windows Installer

The first thing about your application that most of your customers are going to see is how to install it – and the Windows Installer is great for making sure that that is a pleasant experience! We go over what the Windows Installer is and what benefits it will bring. We cover the features Windows 2000 expects an installation package to handle, examine the installer's architecture, then go on to develop a small installation package for StarRaiders.

Chapter 14 - WMI and the CIM Repository

Most applications need to be managed at some point, and WMI is Microsoft's attempt to ensure that other applications have a unified way of being managed – by storing management and configuration data in a special directory called the WMI repository. Making your applications WMI-compliant will be a Windows Logo requirement in Windows 2000. This chapter explains how the CIM repository works and shows you how to use it.

PART 4. Appendices

Appendices

A   Sources of Information

B   Useful RFCs

C   Using VARIANTS from C++ with ADSI

D   ADSI Interface Summary

E   ADSI Error Codes

F   ADSI Constants

G   ADSI API Functions

H   ADSI Providers Currently Available

I   Microsoft Samples

J   Support and Errata

What You Need To Use This Book

As always, this depends to some extent on which bits of the book you're interested in.

If you're prepared to skip all the sections about Active Directory (note that Active Directory is NOT the same thing as ADSI – it's one of the directories you can access using ADSI), then you can get away with using **NT4** or even Windows 95 or 98. (I haven't tested most of the samples on Windows 95 or 98, but in principle ADSI is available for these operating systems, so the ADSI clients and the StarRaiders provider should work without too many modifications!). But if you want the full benefit of the book then you'll need to be running Active Directory – which means having a computer in a domain with a domain controller running **Windows 2000**.

You will definitely need:

❑ The development environment for your preferred language –**Visual Studio 6** or later. VB Programmers may be able go get away with VB 5, but the samples have not been tested on that platform. C++ programmers must have Visual Studio 6. Of course, if you want to program in VBA, a simple install of Microsoft Office will do!

❑ An installation of **ADSI 2.5** or later. This is automatically with Windows 2000, and you can download it from Microsoft's web site for other Win32 operating systems.

❑ An installation of the **ADSI 2.5 SDK,** which you can download from Microsoft's web site.

You'll need these products if you want to run the sample code for the appropriate bits of the book, but they are not needed other than for the chapters in which they are specifically discussed.

❑ **Exchange Server 5.5** or later

❑ **IIS Server 4**, or later

❑ **MMC** 1.1 or later

❑ The Windows Installer

❑ WMI and the WMI SDK

Version of Windows Used

All the code samples in this book were developed using Windows 2000 Beta 3. Microsoft claim that there are going to be very few or no differences between W2K Beta 3 and the final version of Windows 2000, so in general everything in the book should still be correct when Windows 2000 actually ships – but obviously, bear in mind that there may be small changes.

I've pointed out where there are significant differences between Windows 2000 on the one hand, and NT 4, and Windows 95/98 on the other hand.

Conventions Used

I have used a number of different styles of text and layout in this book to help differentiate between different kinds of information. Here are some of the styles you will see, and an explanation of what they mean:

> These boxes hold important, not-to-be forgotten, mission-critical details, which are directly relevant to the surrounding text.

Background information, asides and references appear in text like this.

❑ **Important words** are in a bold font

❑ Words that appear on the screen, such as menu options, are in a similar font to the one used on screen, for example, the File menu.

❑ Keys that you press on the keyboard, like *Ctrl* and *Enter*, are in italics.

❑ All filenames, function names and other code snippets are in this style: DblTxtBx

Code that is new or important is presented like this:

```
Private Sub Command1_Click

    MsgBox "The Command1 button has been clicked!"

End Sub
```

Whereas code that we've seen before or has less to do with the matter being discussed looks like this:

```
Private Sub Command1_Click

    MsgBox "The Command1 button has been clicked!"

End Sub
```

Source Code

All the projects that are given in this book can be downloaded from Wrox's web site at http://www.wrox.com.

Tell Us What You Think

We at Wrox hope that you find this book useful. You are the one that counts and we'd really appreciate your views and comments on this book. You can contact us either by email (feedback@wrox.com) or via the Wrox web site.

The Introduction (Reprise)

If you've got this far, then you've presumably read the quick summary of what the book covers – the stuff you can look at in the shop to decide if the book's got roughly what you want to know about in it. What I'm going to do now is two things.

Firstly, I'll explain in a bit more detail why:

❑ directories are important

❑ you're really going to have to learn ADSI sooner or later...

Secondly, I'm going to go into some of the background that you might find useful. Not so much about ADSI itself – I'll cover that in Chapter 1 – more the history of directories and LDAP (the Lightweight Directory Access Protocol), and related standards in general. We'll go into more detail about LDAP in Chapter 10. For now, if you've vaguely heard terms like X500, directories and LDAP being bandied about but have very little idea what they mean, then this introduction should enlighten you...

Directories and Windows 2000

Directories and Directory Enabled Applications are two key concepts that are going to be very important when Windows 2000 is released. And they are concepts that application developers are going to have to get familiar with pretty quickly in order to continue writing good commercial-grade applications that look and feel up-to-date, and which have all the features end-users are going to expect.

Does your application need to be installed (come on – have you ever known a full-scale application that doesn't have to be installed on some server somewhere, even if – in the case of web applications – the client is not aware of the installation process?) Then you'll almost certainly need to check out the Windows 2000 installer API. Does it need to know about resources etc. on your local network? Then you'll probably need to use Active Directory. Does it create or use any central store of information to look up data? Then you may be needing to look at directories and ADSI. (As we'll discuss in Chapter 1, although relational databases such as SQL server are powerful in their own field, they are not really the right solution if you want a directory of objects you want to look up, as with, for example, network resources). Would it make your application more useful if this information store was also available to other applications? If so, then using ADSI is looking more and more like your best choice! Does your application have configuration options that an administrator would need to access? If so, then you're heading into MMC snap-in and CIM repository territory.

Let's be honest. There's a new operating system coming out, and that means a lot of new technologies to learn. The upside to it is that once you've learned them, you'll find you need to write less code, because a lot more parts of your applications will be handled for you automatically by software that Microsoft have written for you. The downside is you'll have to take the time out to learn all the new technologies. But if you don't, you'll find your software is no longer matching up to the new, higher expectations of users as to how applications will behave.

This is first and foremost a book about ADSI – the Active Directory Services Interfaces – Microsoft's shiny new COM-based technology aimed at letting you access any directory. The technology that Microsoft will do for directories what OLE DB and ADO have done for relational databases and other data stores. But as we've discussed we don't just cover ADSI itself. We also look at the related technologies that will be useful for writing directory enabled applications in Windows 2000.

The Beginning

The beginning's always a good place to start, isn't it? Well I guess for this book the beginning happened soon after Microsoft had started plugging ADSI, when my boss at work gave me a new project to do: learn what this funny new technology was about so I could write an ADSI-compliant phone directory for the phones our company produced. Or perhaps the beginning happened sometime later when the research had been largely completed and I dropped an email to John Franklin at Wrox suggesting that there was this great technology that was really useful and no-one had written any books about it. Why didn't I write one? I'm not sure what state of mind John was in that day but I got an email back saying 'yes, please...'

Seriously, this book exists because I spent several very frustrating months in the early days of ADSI trying to learn to write ADSI clients and providers with nothing to learn from but MSDN, a couple of the Microsoft samples, and – later on - the newly started up ADSI listserver at the 15Seconds.com web site. You know what MSDN is like don't you? It's great if you already know how to do something in principle but just need to check the parameters you pass to this function. But it's not exactly a tutorial guide. And at the time, the ADSI documentation was only at an early beta version anyway, and had a *lot* of gaps. I really needed a book about ADSI when I was learning it, but there wasn't one. Wrox has since then published a couple of other books that cover aspects of ADSI from different angles, but at the time those books had yet to be published. And because there weren't any ADSI books, it took me a lot longer to learn what I needed. You're luckier than me because you've got my book to read.

Let's start by looking at some of the background to directories...

What's a Directory? The Phone Book Example

Qualitatively, we're all vaguely familiar with what a directory is, aren't we? It's quite simply a way of looking up information. The obvious example is the phone book, which, despite being one of the oldest directories around, actually illustrates quite a few of the concepts in modern computer directories – for which reason I'm going to look at it in some detail for the next few paragraphs. So let's go through some of the properties of phone directories:

❏ **Look-up Frequency**
The information tends to get looked up a lot more often than it's changed: telephone numbers usually stay the same for quite a long time. Of course, that's just as well. If telephone numbers changed as often as people wanted to find them out, there wouldn't be much point in producing a book that listed them all! The fact that the book is useful and cost-effective after all the effort involved getting it printed depends on the fact that the information in it will be used millions of times by millions of people before it becomes sufficiently out of date that it needs to be reprinted. Similarly, a computer directory is optimized for efficient read-access.

❏ **Browsing and Searching**
I don't know about other countries, but here in the UK, we get two main types of telephone directories. One of them is just called the Phone Book. It's printed on white paper, and contains the phone numbers of everyone in your local area – including all the private household phones and all the business phone numbers (but not mobiles), listed in alphabetical order. The second one is called the Yellow Pages, and is traditionally printed on yellow paper. It's devoted to businesses, and it's organized differently – it's sorted into business categories. Within each business category, all the companies are listed in alphabetical order.

There's quite a big difference in concept here. When my bicycle gets a puncture, I don't need to know the names of any cycle repair shops in the area. I just go to the Yellow Pages, look up under 'Cycle Shops', and see which ones look suitable. In other words, I can **search** for an entry.

I can't do that with the White Pages. Suppose I want to look up the number of my friend (I wish!) Michael Jackson. The point is I have to know his name. There's no special category in the Phone Book, '*friends of Simon Robinson*' that I can use to search for my friend's numbers. That's not really a problem for me, as I (hopefully) know all my friends' names, but it would be a serious problem looking up businesses, if I couldn't search by category. I don't know the names of all the cycle shops round here – my bike doesn't break down often enough – that's why the yellow pages is so useful.

In computer directory parlance, reading through the directory by the names of the entries is known as **browsing**. The phone book tradition has entered computer terminology as well. Directories set up to allow searching are often known as **yellow pages**. Those that aren't are called **white pages**.

❏ **Properties**
There are several bits of information when you look up an entry in the phone book. Besides the name, there's a telephone number, and quite often there's an address too. In fact, when you think about it, it's really these three bits of information that define each entry. It's the same in a computer network directory: each entry is represented by a number of bits of information. Each of these bits of information is called either a **property** or an **attribute** (depending on your preference – both names are in common use), and each property has a name and a value. For example, my entry has a property called *address*, which has the value of **Street Name**, Lancaster, UK. If you're looking up in a phone directory, you don't really think about names of properties, as it's obvious which bit of information is the name and which is the address. But the concept is still there.

❏ **Tree Structure**
Directories don't necessarily have to, but often do, have a tree structure, in which entries contain sub-entries and so on. You can see this to some extent in phone directories, where you first have to choose the area you live in, and pick the appropriate phone book for that area. Then you can look for the entry in that phone book. You could even go one stage further, and argue that you have to pick the right country first, and get hold of the phone books for that country, then find the right book. You've also – at least in the UK – got to decide whether you are looking for home or business number.

❏ **Multi-Valued Properties**
How many businesses have more than one phone number? Some of the bigger ones, especially Government authorities, have a whole page in the phone book devoted to listing the numbers of each possible department I might want to contact (but often, incidentally, oddly missing the one department I **do** want to contact). Similarly, in computer directories, properties can be multi-valued: they can have more than one value.

I guess you could argue I'm pushing the analogy a bit far here. A page of numbers of company departments might be better compared to an entry in the directory that has a complete subtree beneath it containing other sub-entries. But, hey, it's only an analogy anyway! It makes its point.

I could go on, but I'm sure you get the idea. (I'm also sure you'd never realized before how amazingly interesting telephone directories could be).

Directories and Your Computer

The phone book is a traditional example, but computers need to store a lot more information than phone numbers. The most obvious example, and the one most often quoted for computers, is network resources. As soon as you start connecting computers together into networks, you will want your users to start sharing facilities. It's a lot cheaper to have just one printer which everyone in the office can use, rather than buying a separate one for each machine. That means that every computer on the network has to have some means of locating the printer. Likewise for fax machines, common shared files, and every other resource that more than one person might need.

In order to make all this information easily accessible, it ideally needs to be stored in a central directory. That has long been the approach of Novell, with the NDS Directory Service. Unix systems too, are well catered for, and there have been various third party directories on the market for some years, such as Banyan's StreetTalk, and more recently, Netscape's Netscape Directory Server (this one's aimed at storing more general information, not just network resources).

Up until now, there has not been any comparable directory actually integrated into the Windows family operating systems. The closest Microsoft has come, workgroups and later NT domains, do allow sharing of resources, and some degree of centralized administration as well as good security controls to be put into place to protect data and resources. But these do not come close to the full functionality of directories – a fact which has often been blamed for the lack of adoption of NT as the operating system of choice in many medium and large scale enterprises.

According to Microsoft this all going to change when Windows 2000 comes out. Active Directory will form the centralized directory for local networks and domains, and it does have some pretty sophisticated functionality. We'll discuss Active Directory in depth later, but for the moment, I want to look at the requirements of directories in general.

One important point is that it's not just hardware that needs to be referenced. These are, after all, the days of distributed applications and DCOM. In principle, a COM client application can decide it needs the services of some server, which might be installed on a remote computer. This is a very powerful approach to computing, but up until now has been restricted by the fact that there is no directory to show what COM components are available where, and what interfaces they expose. This means that even though the COM server can be located anywhere, some registry entries still need to be present on the client machine to describe the server, and a suitable proxy needs to be present to allow data to be marshaled.

This does restrict the power of DCOM. Not only that, but we are increasingly moving into a model in which a systems administrator might install some shiny new bit of software, and want anyone on the system to be able to install and use it. This really means we need a central network directory to store information about the software packages and components that are available, so that client machines can simply obtain the software from the central server. At present, the nearest equivalent is often some administrator, at worst wandering round the company offices with the CDs for the software, or at best having to install it in some central location, then email everyone to tell them which folder they can download it from. This is a problem that clearly needs a central directory (along with the Windows Installer) to solve

In this discussion I've concentrated heavily on network resources, but that's not the only area where directories can be useful. All organizations are likely to want to store information about their employees and customers, and provide suitable security access controls around the information. Then there are email addresses. At the heart of Exchange Server is a directory which stores information about the people whose email accounts are handled by that server. There's a similar need in Internet Information Server. The information about how your web site is structured – or even which web sites you're hosting – has to go *somewhere*! Directories can literally store anything that is going to be useful.

In this book, I've chosen a directory of pop stars, my so-called *StarRaiders* provider, as the example that we are going to develop throughout the book. This is partly because I wanted to get away from the traditional network resource/employee database examples that are so often quoted, and show you just how varied the information stored can be. But mostly because I have to admit I find pop stars a much more interesting subject than fax machine and printer addresses. I may be a computer programmer, but I'd like to think I've still got some sense of the real world.

Directories vs DataBases

If you've done any work with databases, you might be wondering why I'm going on about directories as this great new idea, when surely I'm just describing databases? What's the point of inventing ADSI when SQL has been around and very successful for years? The answer is that there is a conceptual difference between a directory and a database, though it is to some extent vague, and not too well defined. Directories and Databases are different animals, although there is a fuzzy area in the middle where you could argue that some, for want of a better phrase, 'information stores' could be categorized either way.

Directories can in some ways be thought of as big sets of information to be looked up. The telephone directory is in many ways the perfect example of this – each number is changed infrequently, and looked up very frequently. It doesn't matter too much if some copies of the information get a bit out of date, as long as there is some way of getting the up-to-date information. (For example, if the number in your phone book is wrong, you can just ring Directory Enquiries, where the bang-up-to-date copy of the directory is held). This analogy is actually closer than you might think. Active Directory is stored on one or more domain controllers, and works by periodically propagating updates amongst the domain controllers. This means that some of them may at any given time hold data that is a few minutes out of date. Active Directory has been designed to tolerate this.

Contrast that, say, with transactions going through your bank account. The information here has to be dead accurate. All changes have to be tightly controlled and monitored, to make sure that incomplete updates are rolled back to avoid corrupting the database. (You'd be a bit miffed off if the amount of that check you wrote to the shop that sold you your new car got deducted from your bank account, but then the computer crashed before it had a chance to pay the amount into the shop's bank account). Also, your bank account probably has frequent updates (whenever you write a check), but its status isn't really checked much more often than the rate at which changes are made to it. This kind of information is the province of databases, not directories.

The History of Directories

X500

The importance of directories to computers was realized very early on, and one of the first attempts at a standard was X500. This was formalized between 1984 and 1994, and it laid down the kind of structure that a directory should have. I say, directory, singular, because the designers of X500 correctly foresaw that computers across the world would get linked together, and were already starting to think in terms of a single global directory. The kind of directory that would let you find what you were looking for anywhere in the world.

To some extent, you can see what they were thinking of when you think how you use – say – a search engine to locate internet sites related to your favorite topic, although this search isn't using X500. Tying into this idea, one of the main features of X500 was that it provided for localized management of different parts of the directory, rather than one central body controlling everything. If – for the sake of argument – you regard the Internet as a big directory, then you can see that this is exactly how the Internet works. While there might be bodies like Internic that control domain names and suchlike, but in the end, provided I don't break my contract with my Internet Service Provider, what information goes on my web site is entirely up to me. I manage that little bit of the Internet. Locally.

The X500 standard is related to the directory itself. It defines the rules that determined how the information should be structured– how restrictions should be imposed on data types to ensure only sensible data got stored (the **schema**). X500 also laid down the idea of a tree structure, in which information would be managed locally.

A standard for a directory would be of limited value if there wasn't a reasonably standard way of getting to the information. For that reason, another standard was introduced at about the same time, the **Directory Access Protocol** (**DAP**). DAP defined the kinds of operations that could be carried out on the directory, and was very comprehensive. As it turned out - too comprehensive for the capabilities of computers at the time. Although some trial directories were successfully implemented using X500 and DAP, it was apparent that the software required to fully implement DAP could not be easily and cheaply accommodated on the PCs of a few years ago. Which is why LDAP came along.

LDAP v2

LDAP is the **Lightweight Directory Access Protocol**, and is a subset of DAP. The first significant version was LDAP v2, which is defined – literally – in RFC 1777.

> *If you've never encountered RFCs before, they are Requests for Comments. They are presented as draft outlines of proposed standards for adoption on the Internet, the text of which is made available on the Internet. After a reasonable period of testing and comments by interested parties, they may be formally adopted as a standard by the Internet Engineering Task Force (IETF). RFCs turn up a lot in the definition of LDAP and various other related protocols. Details of relevant ones, and URLs where you can find them, are in Appendix B.*

Anyway, LDAP v2 took the most commonly used features of DAP. Not only that, but it achieved a further simplification by divorcing itself from the X500 directory model, allowing LDAP servers to act as the directory agent, thus removing the complexity of X500 from the back end, while remaining backwards compatible with the X500 standard. It did this by firmly defining a client-server model, in which a client made a request to the directory server, and waited for a response. This model probably looks trivial these days – after all doesn't just about everything work that way? But it was a significant development a few years ago. The protocols for communication between the client and the server were designed in a way that allowed backwards compatibility with X500 directories, but the complexity was removed by dropping many of the less commonly used operations and aspects of the X500 protocol.

In the LDAP v2 model, a server had to respond to a client request with either a success or failure. There was no facility, for example, for the server to refer the client to another server. The operations defined were few in number, but included adequate support to allow browsing, searching, and modifying directory entries. More importantly, LDAP v2 did succeed in living up to its title of being Lightweight. It was sufficiently small to be able to be used on PCs.

Two important LDAP-compliant directories – that is to say directory services that satisfied all the specifications of LDAP - were written and became widely used. The first was the University of Michigan's LDAP directory implementation, which is downloadable from the University of Michigan web site, `http://www.umich.edu/~dirsvcs`. The second was Netscape's implementation, encapsulated by Netscape Directory Server, and downloadable from `http://www.netscape.com`. Both of these are in principle general directories, allowing any information to be stored and retrieved in a manner compatible with LDAP.

It's important to be aware of the distinction between the different aspects of the directory here. X500 defines the directory itself, DAP and LDAP define the operations that may be carried out in accessing it. For example, X500 defines that the directory should contain a schema that contains information about the structure of the directory. LDAP v2 defines that the client can send a request to modify a particular entry. LDAP v2 defines what information the client should pass with this request, and what information the server should pass back when it responds.

LDAP 3

Unfortunately, although the LDAP v2 standard did cause the idea of a directory to become commonly accepted, it also soon became apparent that the features included were too restrictive. LDAP v2 used ANSI rather than UNICODE strings, which restricted its ability to be internationalized. Support for security was inadequate, as was support for exposing the schema defined by X500. For this reason, a new version, LDAP v3 was defined in 1997, in RFC 2251.

LDAP v3 is a superset of LDAP v2, but is still a subset of the original DAP protocol. This new version addresses all these problems, as well as adding some other new functionality. LDAP 3 has become widely accepted, and is in fact now the version supported by both the Netscape and University of Michigan implementations. In addition, Microsoft has chosen to make Windows 2000's new Active Directory LDAP v3 compliant.

Although LDAP defines the protocol for how this happens, a standard has also emerged for both C and Java APIs that can be used to access the directories. The standard defines the method or function calls available, and several organizations have provided implementations of these standards – including the University of Michigan, Netscape, and Microsoft. All of these implementations may be used to access any LDAP directory.

On to ADSI

We've practically reached the point where ADSI enters the picture, which completes the historical introduction. We start Chapter 1 with an introduction to directories in the context of ADSI, and show exactly what ADSI is and how it fits in. I'll just remark here that the LDAP APIs are relatively low level ones: They consist of a large number of C-style function calls. Since the trend these days is to create COM interfaces, which both simplify client programming and allow VB and scripting languages to access the interfaces as easily as C++, APIs are moving out of vogue. ADSI is a set of COM interfaces designed to allow access to directories, and so is more suitable for high-level clients.

The other point about ADSI is it's not restricted to LDAP directories: Microsoft has supplied the ADSI LDAP provider – which essentially converts from LDAP to ADSI, and allows ADSI clients to easily access directories that are wrapped by the LDAP API, including Active Directory. But ADSI also allows other providers to be written to access other directories. The idea is that eventually ADSI will allow clients to access virtually any directory – including, but not restricted to, LDAP ones.

> It's important to be aware that while LDAP is a general, industry-wide, standard, ADSI is something that is Microsoft Specific, and is aimed specifically at Windows platforms.

A Word About the Languages: VB and C++

As I've remarked, it is possible to code up ADSI clients from any COM-aware language, and to allow for that I've tried to make sure that there are enough samples in all the different languages to give you an idea of how to perform common ADSI operations in VB and C++. However, there are some areas in which it is not possible to use some languages – for example, you cannot use VB to code up an ADSI provider at all easily. The approach in this book is to some extent based on using the appropriate language in each situation – which means that there is no attempt to divide the book up according to language. If one topic is best addressed in VB then I do so. If the next topic is best addressed in C++, then I'll swap languages. To give you a rough guide, the following table lists which languages are used in which chapter.

CHAPTER	ASP	VB	C++
Introduction	No code in these chapters		
1. Introduction to ADSI			
2. Simple ADSI Clients	Mixture of all languages. We're dealing with ADSI itself here rather than any application, so we need to present examples in all languages.		
3. Further Inside ADSI			
4. ADSI and Your Network	YES	YES	A little. These kinds of administrative tasks are often more suited to VB or scripts
5. Common Administrative Tasks	YES	YES	
6.ADSI and BackOffice: Exchange Server, IIS	YES	YES	

Table Continued on Following Page

CHAPTER	ASP	VB	C++
7. Searching	YES	YES	YES
8. Security	YES	YES	A little. Back to admin tasks here that are less suited to C++
9. ADSI Providers	NO – providers cannot be written in these languages	YES – also need ATL	
10. LDAP	NO VB code – requires C API functions. But general information about LDAP is still relevant to VB		YES
11.Advanced ADSI Topics	Extensions – the main subject here – cannot be written in Vb or scripting languages, but extension clients can. We do the extension in C++ and the test client in VB.		
12. Microsoft Management Console	NO – it will soon be possible to write snap-ins in VB, but at the time of writing, Microsoft have not yet released the required tools, so this chapter uses C++		YES – also need ATL
13.The Windows Installer	No. Although it is possible to write Windows Installer apps in VB and scripting languages, this is only a brief introduction to the topic and has space for only one sample – for which we happen to use C++.		YES
14. WMI and the CIM Repository	No code in this chapter.		

All the ASP code uses VB Script. I haven't put VBA in this table because it is so similar to VB Script, but there are a couple of VBA examples dotted through the book – just for variety.

Obviously you will want to concentrate on the samples in your own language. However, I would strongly urge you to at least *look* at the samples in other languages – the reason being that the way that the ADSI interfaces have been designed is with the requirements of all languages, from C++ to scripting languages, in mind. And if you really want to understand why the ADSI interfaces have been written the way they have, you need to appreciate the different ways that the different languages need to call them up.

You see, the two languages, VB and C++, have quite different approaches to how they use COM as clients. VB hides a lot of the low level COM processes from the developer, allowing COM objects to look not much different to ordinary variables when you're coding up. The cost of this is that there are sometimes some restrictions on how the COM objects should behave, which interfaces they should implement, and even in some cases, which methods should be implemented in order that the VB compiler can correctly hook up to the objects at compile time. (Or so the interpreter can do so at run time for the case of VB script). ADSI has been designed with C++, VB, and scripting clients in mind, and a lot of the interface design reflects this. In short, if you want to not just use ADSI, but really understand what it's doing and why it's been designed the way it has, then there's really no alternative but to examine how the interfaces look to VB and scripting clients, as well as to C++ clients.

Of course, this works the other way as well. If you're a VB programmer, then you'll be used to having pretty much everything to do with COM hidden under the surface, and all you ever have to worry about is calling `GetObject()` whenever you want anything. This is good enough when you're dealing with COM objects that only expose one interface each – in that case you easily get by in VBScript without even knowing what an interface is! But ADSI objects usually expose several interfaces – and you also start to find with ADSI that the similar combinations of interfaces are cropping up in different ADSI COM objects. So it is important to be aware of the distinction between object and interface. If you can try to follow some of the C++ samples, you'll start to see what is actually going on under the surface, and once again, you'll start to understand why bits of ADSI are designed the way they are. Either way the message is the same. If you really, *really*, want to understand what this exciting new technology is about, then it pays to be prepared to look at both VB and C++.

Summary

We've taken a brief tour of the principles of directories and seen how the need for an open standard eventually lead to the evolving of LDAP. We've also seen how Microsoft introduced ADSI to meet the more recent need for a higher level, COM-based API to access directories which could be used from clients written in any language. With that background, we are ready to start looking at ADSI itself and how it works – which we will do in the next couple of chapters, forming the first part of the book.

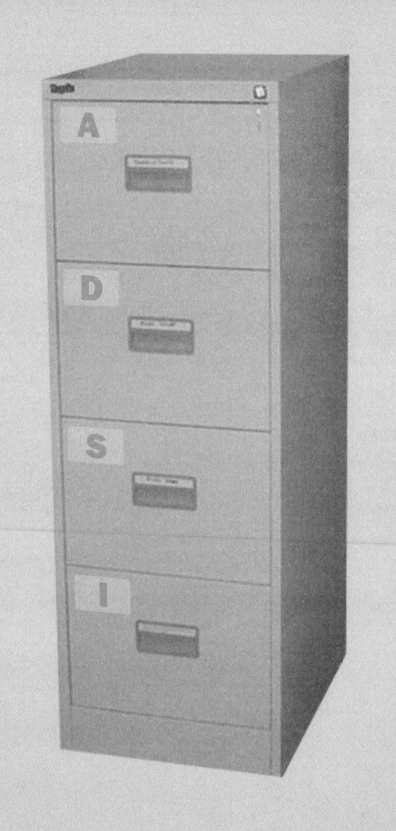

What On Earth Is ADSI?

This first chapter, strangely enough, introduces us to ADSI. We begin by looking at the kind of problem ADSI is designed to solve – how to unify directory access. From there, we use a simple ASP page to demonstrate how powerful ADSI is when it comes to letting us use the same code (or the same script or web page) to look at all sorts of different types of data. This leads us to a discussion of the concept and structure of directories. We move on to how ADSI itself is implemented, and take a look at the ADSI router and how to install ADSI. We finish with a quick tour of Active Directory, and of the tools Microsoft have provided that you can use to browse ADSI-compliant directories.

This chapter (almost) avoids actual coding like the plague – but expect to be introduced here to the concepts you need later. Examples of how to code up using ADSI wait until Chapter 2.

Areas we'll cover in this chapter include:

- ❑ What ADSI is
- ❑ What Directories are
- ❑ What Active Directory is

Unifying Directories – What's it All For Anyway?

We're going to begin by looking at the kind of problem ADSI has been designed to solve.

The StarRaiders Example

Let us suppose I've recently started up a new software business, and I've just launched my first product, *StarRaiders*. It's a software package that lets people store information about their favorite pop stars. It comes with a database with loads of data in it: you know, the things that are so essential to be able to quote at parties, like when Natalie Imbruglia's birthday is or what Mel B's three favorite foods are. The database can be customized – people can add their own data, like who their own all-time favorite stars are and how many of them they've actually met.

OK – lets come out with the word. My product is a **directory** of pop stars. So far, so good. It's got a cool user interface and a great directory at the back end. Only thing is, I know that some of my customers love programming, and they're probably not going to be content with my user interface – they're going to want to start coding up their own. In fact, once they've got their directory up and running they're probably going to want to do lots of things with it that had never occurred to me when I wrote the software – like hooking their directory up over the net and comparing directories to see who's met the most stars. So how do I satisfy these people? I do what so many software vendors have done before, and release an API with my product. The API lets client applications get at the back-end directory, browse it, and look up and modify entries. Now everyone's happy.

Across the other side of town, the new software company *PopSoft Plc* is also eyeing up the pop fan market. They've assembled a package that stores data about all the hit singles there have ever been since records began – highest chart position, weeks in the chart etc. (Exactly the sort of information that lets die-hard fans have arguments in the pub and in the newsgroups along the lines of: "Two Tribes was at Number One for nine weeks so that PROVES that Frankie Goes To Hollywood were better than Wham." – "Yeah but look how many more singles Wham had. FGTH were useless." – "How can you say that?" – *THUMP* – *KICK*.) Anyway, it's a great database, and it comes complete with a zappy user interface, etc. And of course *PopSoft Plc* has also understood the demand from programmers to be able to fiddle with the workings of their directory, so they too have released an API to let people write their own applications around it.

Now you may have noticed that these two products have very similar markets. The chances are that a lot of people will buy both packages, and you can bet that someone who wants to play with the API of *StarRaiders* is going to want to do the same with *PopSoft*'s directory. Of course, being nice, caring companies, we both realize that these customers are going to be a bit irritated if they have to learn to use two different APIs to do basically the same thing, so we agree to combine our forces and design one API, and hide any implementation differences between our two directories beneath it.

Anything else? Well we know these are the days of distributed computing and COM. We know that people use many different languages to code up clients, and COM is a pretty good standard at coping with this and letting applications talk to each other. So we decide that, rather than design a traditional low-level API, we'll make it a COM specification. We'll both expose our directories through the same COM interfaces. What's more, they'll mostly be automation interfaces, so people can use them through scripting languages as well as C++, Java and VB. Now that should make our customers really happy.

More to the point, we have pretty much described **ADSI** – the **Active Directory Service Interfaces**. ADSI was perhaps motivated by – shall we say – more enterprise-oriented aims than the software packages described above, but it's there to solve the same problem: how to unify access to different directories so that the same client software can, with little or no modification, look at any directory.

So What Else Can You Use A Directory For?

The short answer is pretty much anything. If you have data that you want to be openly available to multiple applications, then you might want to consider making that data available through a directory service. To give you an idea, some of the common directories you will encounter at the moment are:

- ❏ **The Exchange Directory** – this is the directory of mailboxes, recipients, etc. used by Exchange Server to manage a company's email.

- ❏ **The IIS Metabase** – the set of settings for Internet Information Server, the package you'll probably use if you want to host a website on a Windows platform.

- ❏ **The Site Server Membership and Personalization Directory** –this is the LDAP directory used by Site Server to ensure that individual visitors to your web site get web pages customized to their individual needs. It's also used by Microsoft NetMeeting to look up users for conference calls.

- ❏ **The WMI Repository** (formerly known as the **CIM repository**) – the database of information used to make it easy to manage and configure applications in Windows 2000.

- ❏ **Active Directory** – the directory of all network resources – computers, printers, security information, etc. – which is at the heart of Windows 2000, and which is used to manage domains.

- ❏ **Novell Directory Services** – which does a similar job for Novell networks.

- ❏ **Netscape Directory Server** – a general purpose directory service which can be used, for example, as a directory of company employees or of customers.

- ❏ **The openLDAP Directory Server** – which performs a similar task to Netscape Directory Server.

Although the emphasis in this list is on directories of information relevant to managing a network, that isn't the only purpose to which directories can be put – as shown by the *StarRaiders* example I started off with. Having said that, the problem of how to manage a network easily and cheaply is one of the problems that first motivated the development of directory technologies, so it's only natural that much of the available software is at present aimed at this area.

You may be wondering where relational databases, such as SQL Server and Oracle, fit into all this – we'll go into that later on in the chapter. Essentially, a directory can be seen as a specialist database, which is open (available to any application) and probably optimized for data which is read more often than it is written (though there are other differences as well, which we'll discuss later in the chapter). And with ADSI, you have the technology to read any one of many different directories (including all the ones listed above) using the same API calls. Not even just API calls, but calls to COM interfaces, which can be easily done *even* from ASP scripts. Get hold of any data and display it in a C++ program, an ActiveX Control, a VB app, or a web page. Get the idea of how useful that could be?

So what sorts of things might you write ADSI clients to do? Well, typical examples would include:

- ❏ Systematically monitoring failed login attempts for certain users in your organization

- ❏ Identifying all the computers in your organization that have a guest account enabled, and disabling those accounts

- ❏ Modifying settings on file shares

❑   Writing an NT service to monitor that certain other NT services are running OK, and taking some action to notify you if it detects any problems

❑   An application that allows users to query employee information from a corporate database

❑   An administrative tool that can be used to set the access permissions on the same employee database

As you can see from this list, ADSI has quite a wide variety of potential applications, ranging from simple 10-20 line scripts that you'd write to perform some one-off but repetitive administrative task, right up to complete sophisticated applications.

Unifying Directories on Windows

Before I go into details about the structure of ADSI, I want to show you a bit more about what unifying directories means in practice. The best way to do this is to show ADSI at work. I'm going to go through a few screenshots that demonstrate what ADSI can do for you – and if at the end of them you're not convinced that ADSI is an extremely powerful tool that is well worth learning, then I'll be very surprised.

Microsoft has written a couple of applications which can browse through the directories exposed through ADSI on your system. One of them is the **Active Directory Browser**, adsvw.exe, from which this screenshot is taken:

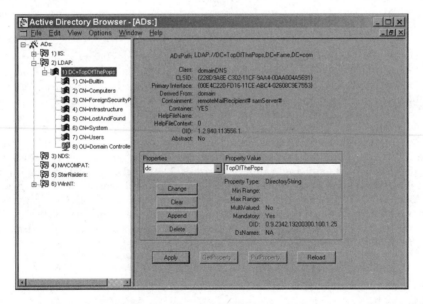

This screenshot contains a lot of information, and it's going to take us several chapters to get through it all. For the time being, the main point I want you to notice is the tree structure on the left side of the screen. Ignore the right hand side of the screenshot for now (if you're interested, it shows details of the selected entry on the left – which happens to be an entry that represents my local domain).

What we're looking at in the tree control on the left is the list of ADSI providers that happen to be on my main computer (which is a domain controller running Windows 2000 Server Beta 3). For the time being, think of a **provider** as a program that lets you hook up to a particular directory, so effectively, you're looking directly at the directories. ADSI has actually presented them in a merged form, so they look like they're all part of a super-directory called **ADs:**.

One of the powers of ADSI is the way that lots of different types of information can be accessed in the same manner – so the different bits of data can look like the same type to applications that want to get to them. The individual directories all appear in the tree as children of ADs:, and the entries within the directories appear at lower levels of the tree. I've opened up LDAP:, which is looking at Active Directory – Microsoft's directory of computers and resources in the domain. And I've selected the entry that corresponds to my domain itself, *TopOfThePops*.

The providers that appear on your computer depend on which operating system you've got installed and what options you specified when you installed it. On mine, you can see:

- ❑ **IIS:** – this allows access to the Internet Information Server metabase.

- ❑ **LDAP:** – on Windows 2000 machines, the default LDAP directory happens to be Active Directory, but more generally this could be any LDAP-compliant directory installed on your machine (for example, Netscape Directory Server)

- ❑ **NDS:** and **NWCompat:** – these allow you to read the Netware directories through ADSI (NDS: for NW4, NWCompat: for NW3).

- ❑ **StarRaiders:** And you thought I was making it all up about a pop star directory, didn't you! Actually, we're going to find out a lot more about StarRaiders: over the next couple of chapters, because it's the sample ADSI provider that we're going to write in Chapter 9.

- ❑ **WinNT:** This provider lets you get at information about computers and resources on your network. To some extent, you can think of it as a substitute for Active Directory for NT4-based networks, for which Active Directory is not available. However, it does expose some extra information that is not by default stored in Active Directory.

Apart from StarRaiders:, these providers all come with the standard installation of ADSI.

So that's one screenshot. I said I'd show you a few of them. The adsvw.exe screenshot above gives you a flavor of the tree structure of directories. But adsvw.exe isn't good at quickly showing you all the properties of any one object. To solve that, in Chapter 2 we're going to write two applications that will let you type in the pathname of an ADSI object and display all its properties. The applications do the same thing – except one is a dialog box written in VB, and the other is an Active Server Page, viewable through a web browser. In both cases, all you have to do is type in the path name (ADsPath) of the object you want to look at.

This is what the VB application looks like, with a pathname set to examine the DHCP service running on my computer.

And here's a web page, using the ASP application to look at the same object.

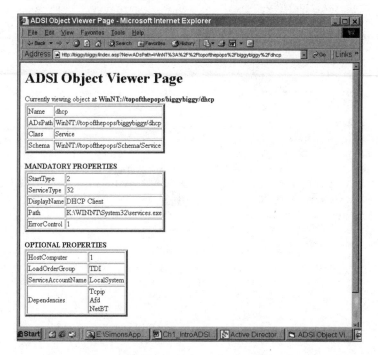

Here it is again, looking at some of the data I've put into StarRaiders:

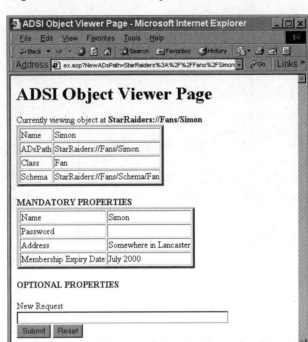

Or how about checking one of the print queues on your system:

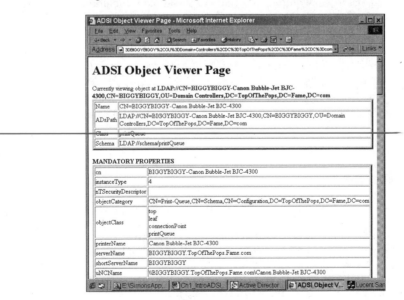

Or looking at one of the domain user accounts:

Get the idea? By typing in different strings in the text box marked **New Request** you could equally well use the same ASP page to view quite a lot of other information, including for example your IIS settings or stuff in your Exchange Directory. And all that for not very much code at all.

We will develop the code for this ASP page and the corresponding VB app in Chapter 2. You'll see that the code is pretty small in both cases – the kind of stuff you can easily write from scratch in less than an hour.

So that's what the results of using ADSI look like. We're now going to step into ADSI and see how it achieves this.

So What Is ADSI?

ADSI is designed as a set of COM interfaces (about 60 of them in fact, although for most purposes, you only need to use a small fraction of those). The idea is that if you write your own directory, you provide implementations of these interfaces that hook up to your directory. That way, true to the principles of COM, any client can get access to your directory without having any knowledge of the internal workings of it. All that the client (and for that matter the developer who writes the client) needs to know are the definitions of the interfaces – or as COM gurus like to talk about it – the contract that defines how the interfaces interact with clients.

The adsvw screenshot also reminds us that directories contain many items - or **directory objects**. The way ADSI works is that each item in the directory is represented by a separate COM object. The object will expose a number of ADSI standard interfaces – which ones it exposes depends to some extent on the type of directory object it represents (user, computer, etc.).

If you want to do something to a particular item in the directory, you need to create an instance of the COM object that represents that directory item, then start calling up methods or set properties on its interfaces. Internally, the COM object reads or modifies the corresponding entry in the directory itself.

Almost all of the ADSI interfaces are automation dual interfaces that are defined in a type library, adsvw.exe, so VB, J++ and C++ clients get the benefit of fast vtable binding, while scripting clients still get to use ADSI. The fact that clients in these languages cannot get to a couple of interfaces doesn't seriously affect the functionality they can access.

So far this gives us the kind of structure shown below:

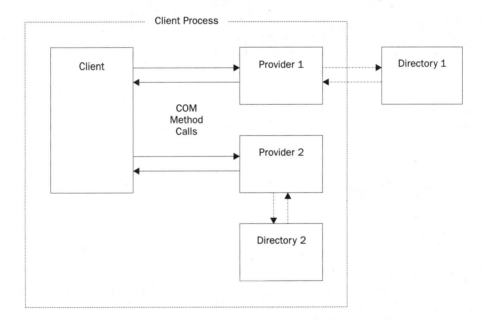

This is a diagram of the modules involved when a client accesses a directory using ADSI. Solid arrows indicate COM method calls, dot-dashed arrows indicate internal function calls within the provider implementations. This figure is a bit simplified – there are a couple of extra layers to go in that I don't want to talk about just yet – but it'll do for now. (If anyone's really nosey the full diagram is in the ADSI, OLE DB and Searching section later in this chapter).

What we see is a client talking to multiple directories via the ADSI COM layer. Note that ADSI is separate from the directory itself: it's a standard for how to access the directory, not for how to store information in the directory. The figure also introduces some new terminology. Usually in COM we talk about a client and a server. In ADSI, the server is often referred to as a **provider** – the same provider I mentioned earlier.

Actually, I should clarify this. The ADSI provider will usually sit in the middle. It acts as a COM server to the ADSI client application – the user interface – but it often also acts as a client to whichever application ultimately implements the directory. So you can think of your client and the ADSI provider sitting together as a combined client to the directory itself – which is why the documentation sometimes talks about ADSI as being a client-side set of interfaces. In some ways, you could also think of the ADSI provider as being the middle tier of an n-tier application.

As far as providers are concerned, we can further distinguish between **service providers** and **directory providers** (but note that you don't need to have both of them). A directory provider implements a directory and the ADSI interface around it. A service provider simply implements the ADSI layer, and internally hooks up to a pre-existing directory rather than actually implementing a directory.

> *By the way, **service** is one of quite a few terms that we're going to come across that have several meanings. We're not talking about formal NT services here – we simply mean a bit of software that does something useful.*

I've drawn a dashed box around the client process and included the providers in it, because ADSI providers are always in-process COM servers. Of course, there's nothing to stop the directory from residing in another process, on another machine, or even, for that matter, from being spread over several machines – the implementation behind the scenes within the provider is always up to whoever codes up that particular provider.

In the figure, provider 1 wraps a directory for which access is in a separate process, possibly on a separate machine, whereas provider 2 wraps a directory for which access can be entirely performed within the same dll. More formally, provider 1 is a service provider, while provider 2 is a directory provider.

More About Directories

We've now covered the basic ideas of what ADSI is and what problems it's designed to solve. Actually, we've come a long way vaguely going on about directories as if we know precisely what they are. That's fair enough, because it's a pretty intuitive concept – but even so, we need to be more precise.

We're going to need to understand a lot more about the typical internal structure of directories. And it's probably about time we took a detailed look at what sort of directories you're likely to encounter and what you would use them for. There's an awful lot of new terminology you need to know too, though most of it is reasonably self-explanatory.

So What Exactly Is A Directory

I've said a directory is an information store, and in the introductory chapter, I gave a telephone directory as the perfect example of a directory. Of course, you could easily argue that a database is an information store. So what's the difference?

Actually, you may notice I've been a little careless with interchanging the terms database and directory. To be honest that's deliberate. I may get a few attacks from the more theoretically minded for saying this, but there is in practice a fair bit of overlap between the ideas – they are both means of storing information. When you talk about a database, you'll probably think of a relational database: it arranges its data in lots of tables and you'd probably use a language like SQL to access the data in it. When we talk about directories, we think more of a hierarchical, tree structure.

Personally, I find the best way to think of a directory is as a specialist database, which tends to have the following characteristics:

- **Scalability**: it should perform efficiently when it's got 100 entries and one client accessing it, and still perform well when it's got 2 billion entries with a hundred thousand clients hungry to get at the data.

- **Security**: it should provide sufficient security to prevent unauthorized access to the data. That means being able to authenticate clients by requiring a user name and password, and then deciding which parts of the directory the user is allowed to access.

- **Replication**: it will be able to replicate itself, that is to say, store copies of itself on several machines. This is important both to allow efficient access to a large number of clients, and to make the directory reliable in the event of a hardware failure.

- **Infrequent updates**: it tends to be optimized around the expectation that data will be read a lot more often than it's written. Reading from the directory will typically be faster than writing to it.

- **Searching**: it should allow clients to search efficiently for items having particular characteristics. It should be able to handle reasonably complex search requests such as *find me all the users with names beginning with P who are administrators and who haven't logged on for at least a week*. Admittedly, relational databases are usually good at this as well – but this is an important characteristic of directories too.

- **Open** it will be accessible to any client application.

Set against that, there are a couple of characteristics of databases which you wouldn't expect to find in directories:

- Directories generally don't store very large objects. For example, the complete word document for this book isn't the kind of thing you'd expect to find in a directory. (On the other hand, you may find a *reference* to where you could access a given large object.)

- Directories aren't usually optimized to handle frequent updates.

- Directories don't usually incorporate transaction monitoring.

- Because directories are hierarchical, they aren't good at handling data where there are lots of complex relationships between the different data items. In directories, an item can contain (be a parent of) other items. In some cases there are facilities to form groups of items, or for items to link to other items, but that's generally as far as it goes. By contrast, a large relational database will typically contain a large number of links between tables, formed by tables having foreign keys.

Most of these items are really to do with the internal operation of a directory. They affect how efficiently the directory runs, but they don't really have any bearing on how to code up a client application that accesses the directory. We should be aware of these factors, but we won't really cover them in this book, which is primarily about ADSI – about how to access directories, not about directories themselves. Even if you're writing an ADSI provider, in many cases you'll keep the provider separate from the implementation of the directory. That's because, as we've discussed, the provider still consists of a set of client-side COM components.

The only items in these lists that we'll really be concerned with are searching, and the thorny issue of security – we'll deal with that in Chapter 8. Other than that, you should simply keep the above list in mind as a set of characteristics that are typical of most of the information stores we will be using ADSI to get at.

I'm guessing that you're probably a bit unsatisfied with this definition of a directory. It would be much neater if I could give you a one-line definition, but sadly things aren't that simple. If you really want one, then it's probably best to think of a directory as an open database that has a hierarchical structure. This isn't really a complete definition, but if you think of it that way, you won't go far wrong.

> By the way, although I've said that directories are hierarchical, there are a few directories that
> have a flat structure. However, even these can be considered to form a tree structure that happens
> to have only one level.

An Aside: A Bit Of Controversy

I don't really want to get bogged down any more in abstract questions about exactly what a directory is, but I do need to warn you about something. I'm afraid I will have to be honest here, and say that the definition I've given you of a directory isn't actually the only one you'll find. I've defined a directory by its internal characteristics. If you start reading around the Internet, you'll find a few sources in which a directory is stated as being a store or information about real objects (things such as computers and users).

You might want to contrast this with this definition from the University of Michigan's 'Introduction to Slapd and Slurpd', at the University of Michigan's web site. This definition is closer to the one I've used, and is also a widely quoted definition.

> **A directory is like a database, but tends to contain more descriptive, attribute-based information. The information in a directory is generally read much more often than it is written. As a consequence, directories don't usually implement the complicated transaction or roll-back schemes regular databases use for doing high-volume complex updates. Directory updates are typically simple all-or-nothing changes, if they are allowed at all. Directories are tuned to give quick-response to high-volume lookup or search operations. They may have the ability to replicate information widely in order to increase availability and reliability, while reducing response time. When directory information is replicated, temporary inconsistencies between the replicas may be OK, as long as they get in sync eventually.**

Although this looks confusing, in practice it doesn't make any real difference. Remember, storing network information about computers and resources was one of the main motivations for developing directory technologies. The result is that this is precisely the kind of information that directories are often used to store, and databases that are designed for that kind of information will normally have all the characteristics I've defined for a directory.

Having said that, I personally do feel quite strongly that it's better to define a directory by its internal characteristics, for two reasons:

❑ The sources that define a directory as a database that stores real objects have a problem: they generally never really give a definition of what exactly constitutes a *real object*. To my way of thinking, my bank account is as real as any computer, but it's generally accepted that directories are quite unsuited to storing details of bank accounts.

❑ There have been a number of directory servers on the market – notably Sun's NIS and Novell's NDS, but also including the Netscape and openLDAP general-purpose directory servers. These latter directories are designed to store pretty much whatever you want them to store, so it seems a bit perverse to me to end up in a situation where you can't technically call them directories if they happen to be being used to store the 'wrong' kind of information. Defining a directory by its internal characteristics avoids this problem.

This is a practical book: we don't want to worry too much about definitions. The bottom line is if you have some data, if there's an ADSI provider available to get at the data, and you find it convenient to work with the ADSI object model with its hierarchical data structure, then ADSI is the tool for you. If not, then you need to be looking at some other tool or language, such as OLE DB or SQL. But it's surprising just how much data ADSI *is* the best tool for.

A word about ADSI and Active Directory

Before we carry on, I just want to warn you about something that it's easy to get confused about: don't confuse ADSI and Active Directory.

> **ADSI is the standard set of COM interfaces that lets you access any directory for which a suitable ADSI provider is available.**
>
> **Active Directory is the new Directory in Windows 2000 that acts to control your Windows domains.**

To emphasize the difference, remember that ADSI can also be used to access the NDS directory for a Novell network, which can be seen as a direct competitor to Active Directory (although we won't be covering NDS in this book).

ADSI and Active Directory are quite closely linked, since ADSI is the standard recommended means of accessing Active Directory. Because of that, we're going to come across Active Directory quite a bit in this book – there's a section all about it later in this chapter for a start. However, they are still distinct technologies. Unfortunately, a number of authors have mixed the terms up in various books – and even Microsoft's own MSDN documentation often fails to make the distinction!

Directory Structure

Here's where we start looking at how the information is arranged in directories. Actually I should rephrase that –we're going to look at how it *seems* that information is arranged in directories, as exposed by ADSI.

You see, ADSI doesn't claim to be a standard for directories –it's a standard for *accessing* directories. It exposes a set of COM interfaces, and those COM interfaces make it *look* like a directory has a particular structure. Whether the directory actually has that structure internally is a matter for whoever codes up that directory, and it's something that the clients don't really have any business knowing. A directory might even internally have a relational structure (the Site Server 3.0 membership directory does so) but the ADSI clients will still see what appears to be a hierarchical directory. C++ and COM developers will recognize this idea as just another example of encapsulation.

So, the concepts I'm going to outline here represent how ADSI makes directories *look* like they are structured. If you understand this "pretend" structure, then you're half way to understanding how to write ADSI clients.

Having said that, ADSI does have a heritage stretching through LDAP and the old X500 standard, and what we're going to describe does look remarkably like an X500 directory.

Example: Structure of the StarRaiders Directory

We're going to use the StarRaiders directory as an example to illustrate what ADSI directories look like. Here's a diagram of a part of the directory where I've stored a couple of my favorite pop stars:

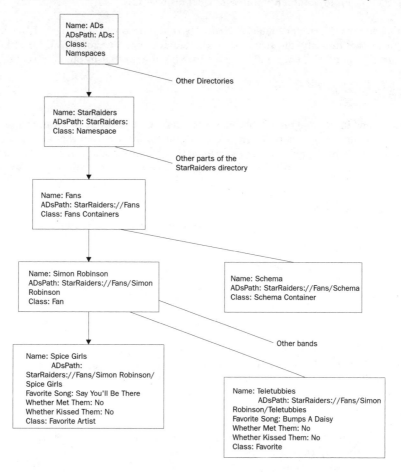

As you'd expect from the `adsvw` screenshot earlier, the very highest level object in the tree is ADs: – this isn't really part of the StarRaiders directory but is the container for all providers.

Let's get some new bits of terminology in here: ADs: is also known as the **Namespaces object**. The next object down, the one called StarRaiders: is (confusingly) a **Namespace object** (singular). That's the object that really forms the top of my directory. Both of these objects are **containers** because they are able to contain children. Objects that can't are called **leaves**. There is an analogy here with the Windows file system – containers looking like they are equivalent to folders, and leaves looking like files – but be careful here. It's not a very good analogy because containers in a directory can also contain data, whereas Windows folders can't (other than operational or security data such as the timestamps). Containers are not so much like folders as like files which can contain other files.

The structure from here on should be fairly intuitive. Under StarRaiders: is a container object called *Fans* – this just serves as the container in which the fans can put all the data they want to. Under it, amongst other records, is my own one, *Simon Robinson*. And under that are the two pop bands I've chosen to put in as my favorite bands. (NB. This might be a good moment to point out that you are here to learn ADSI, not to comment on my musical tastes – OK!).

There's another entry under *Fans*, called *Schema*. There are no direct data here. It's a special container that holds objects that describe the structure of the StarRaiders directory itself (or at least the portion of the directory that holds the fan's entries) – and we'll come to that in the next section.

Properties

Did you notice how, in the diagram of StarRaiders, there are some bits of information which every object has – like its name for a start. There are other bits of information that are only stored with certain objects. For example, both of my *Favorite Artist* objects have a property, *Whether Kissed Them*, which indicates whether I've – well I'm sure you won't need me to explain what. This property is absent from all the other objects.

In fact, when you think about it, all there really is to any object in the directory is a set of pieces of information. This brings up another concept – that of **properties** or **attributes**.

> **A property (or attribute) is one of the pieces of information attached to an object in the directory.**

So the `ADsPath` is a property, as is the Spice Girls' property, *Favorite Song*.

Note that each property actually has two bits of data: the name of the property (*Favorite Song*) and a value (*Say You'll Be There*). The name of the property is always a string. The value can be literally any type of data you like – for *Favorite Song* it's a string, for *Whether Met Them* it's a Boolean, but you can get a lot more imaginative than that.

If I decided to stick photos of my idols in this directory, there'd be a property (*Group Photo*, perhaps) for which the value type would be a bitmap. If I fancied actually putting the songs in the directory, so I could play them from my computer, then I guess there'd be a property, *Song Recording*, whose data type would be a `.wav` file. (Actually, in both these cases, it would probably be the file names of the `.bmp` and `.wav` files you'd store, because of the preference to keep small items in the directory, but you get the point.)

> **By the way, don't confuse the name of a property with the name of the object. The name of the object is the value of the property named** `Name` **The name of the object is sometimes referred to as the** relative distinguished name (RDN), **a term borrowed from the LDAP world.**

Oh – and do we call them properties or attributes? The terms are interchangeable. The ADSI documentation tends to use properties more often, while the Active Directory documentation prefers attributes. I'm going to stick mostly with properties, partly because I think the word sounds nicer, and partly because ADSI has rather tied my hands anyway, by naming several interfaces concerned with properties as `IADsPropertyXXX`.

36

PathNames: ADsPaths

One of the bits of information that every object has is the path name – the thing that we refer to as the **ADsPath**. The pathname is significant in that it should represent a unique means of identifying the object.

If I want to look at the record that describes the Spice Girls as being one of my favorite bands, it's no good asking the computer for the record named *Spice Girls*, because other fans registered on *StarRaiders* might have picked the Spice Girls as their favorite artists too. But if I supply the full path name, `StarRaiders://Fans/Simon Robinson/Spice Girls`, then we know exactly which object in the directory is required.

Well at least – that always works in most directories. There are one or two very rare cases in the WinNT ADSI provider where `ADsPaths` aren't unique. We'll come to how to deal with those cases (and for that matter, why they occur at all) in Chapter 3.

> *Perhaps I should also mention that in Active Directory, just to complicate things more, there are some other means of uniquely identifying objects besides the* `ADsPath` *– but again, we'll deal with that later*

Classes and Schemas

So, we've got some data in the directory. What we're missing though are some rules about what goes where. With our directory, it's perfectly sensible for the object *Simon Robinson* to have a property *Membership Expiry Date*, indicating when my subscription to *StarRaiders* needs to be renewed. It would be a bit silly for – say – the *Spice Girls* object to have that property. So somehow, the directory has to have some rules to stop me from doing something like that. And that leads us nicely on to the subject of **schemas**.

We need a way for the directory to store information about what properties are allowed to be stored with which objects. Well actually, we need more than that. For example, it's OK to say that artists can have photos, but we also need to say what data type a photo is. We don't want the directory to let us store – say – the number 27 as the value of the property *Photo*. Similarly we'd be a bit surprised if we asked the computer to look up how many number one singles the Teletubbies had had, and we got a cute little picture of Tinky-Winky back in response. So how can we handle this?

This is where the property called `Class` comes in. Take a look at the following figure:

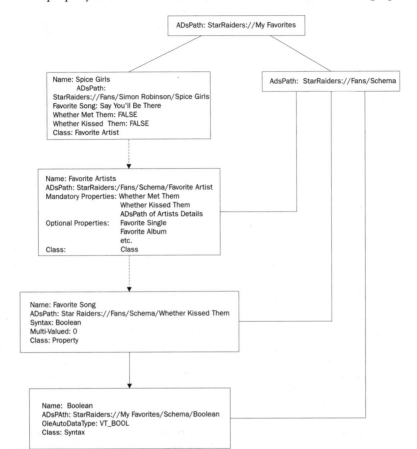

The figure shows a portion of the StarRaiders directory concerned with schema management. Solid lines show the position in the directory tree, dashed lines show the sequence of looking up entries to obtain schema information.

Notice that the value of `Class` is a string that describes the type of object: *Favorite Artist* for the objects *Spice Girls* and *Teletubbies*, *Namespace* for the namespace object, etc. (And no, don't argue –the Teletubbies have had a number one single in the UK, therefore they are pop stars. Period.) That is, the property `Class` tells us what type of object we are dealing with. So how does that help?

The computer sees that the object *Spice Girls* is of type Bands. So it goes and looks inside a special object in the directory known as the **schema container**. This is just the object named *Schema*, that was marked in the previous figure as being another child of *Fans*. This object has a number of children, and one of them is an object called *Favorite Artists*. This is the object that tells you about objects of class *Favorite Artists*, and it's known variously as a **class object**, **schema object**, or as a **class schema object**.

There's quite a lot of information in this object, but its key properties are two called **Mandatory Properties** and **Optional Properties**. These are pretty self-explanatory.

Mandatory Properties contains a list of the names of the properties which objects of type *Favorite Artists* must have. If you try to create an object that claims to be of class *Favorite Artists*, but it doesn't have a value for one of these properties, then the directory will refuse to create that object.

Optional Properties is a bit more flexible. It contains a list of names of properties that objects of class *Favorite Artists* are allowed to have, but they don't have to have values set for these properties.

That completes the information for *Favorite Artists*: no other properties are allowed for objects of that class. You could almost think of the lists *Mandatory Properties* and *Optional Properties* as guest lists for a party: if you're not on either of the two lists, then you don't get in. But even worse, if someone on the *Mandatory Properties* list doesn't show up, the whole party just gets cancelled. Now that is serious.

We're not all the way there yet. We know from the *Mandatory Properties* list that *Favorite Artists* must have a property called *Whether Kissed Them*. The directory needs a way of finding out what type of data is allowed to go there. Well, we stick with the `StarRaiders://Fans/Schema` container object, and look for another object there (in other words, another child of the schema container) called (surprise!) *Whether Kissed Them*. This object is known as a **property object**, and its role is to tell you about the type of data that can be stored in the property *Whether Kissed Them*.

The property object has several properties –the ones we're most interested in are *Syntax* and *Multi-Valued*. The value of *Syntax* says it's a Boolean, while the value of *Multi-Valued* says it isn't multi-valued. Multi-valued, by the way is ADSI parlance for saying that a property contains an array of data rather than just one data item. So the *Mandatory Properties* and *Optional Properties* properties of a class schema object are multi-valued, but the *Favorite Song* property isn't.

You might think that that's enough, but ADSI takes sorting out the syntax one step further. As far as the computer is concerned, a syntax name of Boolean is just an unintelligible lump of text – something that humans can understand easily, but the computer can't. The computer doesn't yet have a way of telling that the word Boolean means that we need a true/false value. So we go off again and look for an object called *Boolean*, still in the `StarRaiders://Fans/Schema` container. This object is a **syntax object**, and it contains just one property, called *OleAutoDataType*. This is an integer, which actually identifies the data type.

> *For anyone who wants programming details, it's actually the integer that represents the automation data type stored, and in this case will have the value 11, the value for* VT_BOOL, *which refers to a* VARIANT_BOOL *variable.*

Phew! This might sound a long way of doing it, but it leads to a very flexible architecture. It has the huge advantage that everything is stored as normal ADSI objects, so you access everything in the same way. The directory doesn't just store the data, it actually stores its own description of what it's allowed to contain and what type of data can be present. And this schema information can be accessed in exactly the same way as ordinary data. XML people will notice some similarity here to how XML works.

This architecture also makes it very easy to change the schema if you're not happy with what you can do with a directory. It's basically the same as modifying normal directory objects. For example, if you wanted to add a new type of class, say a special class to represent Blues bands, all you have to do is create a new class object in the container where the other class objects are, call it *Blues Bands*, give appropriate values to all its properties, and you're away! This process is known as **schema extension**.

A couple more new bits of terminology. The container where the class, property and syntax objects are stored is known as the **Schema Container**. The term **Schema** is used to denote the set of rules for what types of objects can contain what properties etc. You'll also hear the term **Content Rules** used to describe specifically the list of mandatory and optional properties.

While we're on the subject of terminology, you may have noticed that the terms class and property are starting to get a bit overused. A class in a directory is not the same as a C++ class or a COM class. A class in a directory has properties, but it doesn't have any methods: all it does is store data.

> *Incidentally, COM gurus might notice a strong similarity here between class objects in directories and COM interface definitions in type libraries. A directory class object stores information that tells you about what you can do with instances of that class. Similarly, a type library tells you what methods you can call up on a particular COM interface.*

As for property – well, a property in directories is simply a piece of information with a name and a value. It's not the same as an automation property (though, as we'll see in the next chapter, automation properties are often used to represent ADSI properties).

Finally, you may be wondering just how far having property objects to tell you about properties goes. Is there, for example, a property object in the schema container called Syntax, which tells you that the syntax property in property objects is a string? And if so, do you end up in an infinite loop?

Well the answer to that is no. There are some standard properties that are common to all directories, and which ADSI knows about automatically, without needing a property object. All the properties of class, property and schema objects come into this category, as do the Name and ADsPath of other objects. It's only really the data that's specific to a certain directory that needs to be dealt with by the schema. Similarly, you won't find a class object in the schema container called Class that describes class objects – ADSI already knows what a class object is.

Structure Rules

We've just covered how the directory imposes restrictions to stop silly types of information being stored with objects. We're now quickly going to move on to another aspect of maintaining good directory structure: making sure the objects themselves go into sensible places.

For example, in the StarRaiders directory, the *Favorite Artists* object, *Spice Girls*, is contained in an object of type *Fan*. This in turn is contained in an object of (originally named) type *Fans Container*. Presumably, we want to enforce this structure on the directory. We don't want the *Spice Girls* object to contain the *Teletubbies* object. To take an example from Active Directory, the computers should be contained within a domain, not the other way round! What we're really getting at here are rules about which class of object should be allowed to contain which other classes of object. Once again, this is handled in the schema.

How it happens is quite simple. Amongst the other properties of the class schema object are two called *Containment* and *Possible Superiors*. These store lists of which classes are allowed respectively to be children of and to be parents of instances of this class. Since these properties contain lists, they're going to be multi-valued properties. If the directory is about to move an object or create a new object, it just has to look at these properties in the relevant class schema objects to check it's not breaking any of the rules. These rules are known as **structure rules**.

ADsPaths Revisited

Finally before we move on from directory structure, we haven't said anything about the format of the `ADsPaths`. The rules are quite simple: if you want to connect to the namespace object in a provider, then the `ADsPath` is:

```
<ProviderName>:
```

If you want to connect to another object inside the directory, then the path name starts off with the name of the provider, and this bit must look like:

```
<ProviderName>://
```

Starting the pathname like that allows ADSI to determine what provider it needs to start up to get to the required object. However, after that initial part of the path name, everything beyond that is entirely up to the directory to decide – ADSI itself doesn't impose any rules (although obviously, each individual provider will have its own requirements for `ADsPath` syntaxes). For the StarRaiders directory, I've decided to stick with a URL-type format, and separate names with slashes right through:

```
StarRaiders://Fans/Schema/Favorite Artists
```

This format is also used by the WinNT provider, so there you tend to see names like:

```
WinNT://DomainName/ComputerName/UserName
```

LDAP directories generally use an alternative. Names are separated by commas, and every name is also prefixed by an attribute name, which indicates the type of object that exists at that level of the hierarchy. Active Directory is LDAP-based, so you would find that the Active Directory `ADsPath` of the user administrator, on the domain `TopOfThePops.Fame.com`, might be:

```
LDAP://CN=Administrator,CN=Users,DC=TopOfThePops,DC=Fame,DC=com
```

An oddity of this format is that, after the name of the provider, the pathname works *up* the directory rather than down it. The path name above gives you the administrator user account on my domain controller of my `TopOfThePops.Fame.com` domain.

> *By the way, before you start hunting round online for* `TopOfThePops.Fame.com`, *my network isn't actually connected to the Internet, so my domain name is one I've made up. It's not actually registered – well at least, not by me!*

Incidentally, the subject of pathnames in Active Directory is quite complex, since there are usually a number of alternative formats – this example isn't the only way of connecting to my administrators account. We'll cover Active Directory pathnames in Chapter 3.

You'll most likely find all the ADsPaths you meet are in a format closely related to one of these, but since there aren't any rules, it always pays to read the documentation for any new provider you use.

The provider name prefix is case sensitive – if you want to locate WinNT:, winnt: won't work. For the part of the ADsPath after the provider name, it's up to the provider concerned whether to make paths case sensitive. Both WinNT: and LDAP: are actually case-insensitive here, as is StarRaiders:.

There's no requirement for pathnames to be concatenated as you move down the directory hierarchy – in fact, we've already been using examples for which they are not. All providers are contained within the namespaces object, ADs:, but we've always started path names with, for example, LDAP://, never ADs://LDAP. Having said that, once you get inside a given directory, most providers will generally form names by concatenating pathnames, though that shouldn't be relied on. Besides, ADSI provides methods to navigate round the tree, without usually having to fiddle about with concatenating ADsPaths.

That pretty much completes our introduction to directory structure. We have only scraped the surface – there's a lot more to go. There's a mechanism for inheriting classes. There are alternative ways of identifying objects in some directories. There are a lot more properties in the class objects. And then there's the whole thorny issue of security. But between you and me I reckon we've had enough of directory theory for one chapter. We've covered enough to be able to get started doing ADSI programming, and we'll introduce other topics as we need them.

We've not met a single line of code yet, so let's get stuck into something closer to the actual programming.

The ADSI Router

We've established that ADSI is set of COM interfaces that can access any directory. We've loosely mentioned that if you want to get at an item in a directory, your client just creates a COM object. However there's a problem – let's think about this.

In C++ you get a COM object using something like:

```
HRESULT hRes;
IADs *pPutItHere;     // the interface, that is
hRes = CoCreateInstance(CLSID_TheObject, NULL, CLSCTX_INPROC_SERVER, IID_IADs,
         (void**)&pPutItHere);
```

Note that I've started filling in a couple of details about ADSI. IADs is a basic interface that is exposed by every directory entry, and is your usual starting point when you first get at an object.

The problem is there's nothing in this statement that shows where the object is. Say I've got my *StarRaiders* directory installed, and I want to look up some information about my mates (I wish!) the Spice Girls. How do I do it? There's nothing in the above code that links my object to the Spice Girls. I could go for the CLSID that identifies the type of object, but that's only really going to narrow it down to the directory, not the item within the directory. Besides, if I have to know specific CLSIDs for individual directories, that defeats the whole point of unifying directory access, doesn't it? In fact, the CLSIDs in ADSI are generally hidden from the client – all the client is expected to know is the interface IID.

That's the situation for C++. You VB people out there are probably wondering what all the fuss is about. After all, one of the standard ways of getting to a COM object in VB runs something like:

```
Dim objADs As IADs
Set objADs = GetObject("StarRaiders://Fans/Simon/Spice Girls")
```

No problem. In fact, VB people don't even need to know that they're looking for an IADs interface. They can happily code up:

```
Dim objADs As Object
Set objADs = GetObject("StarRaiders://Fans/Simon/Spice Girls")
```

In this last sample, by declaring the variable objADs as an Object, I'm not telling the compiler anything whatsoever about the nature of the COM object that's going to be placed in it. I'm basically giving the compiler a name, and asking it to get me the COM object that represents this name. I don't know what the object is, or what interface I want, but I do know it'll produce some code that manages it.

So what's gone wrong in C++? Well, VB's GetObject hides a huge amount of the functionality involved with tracking down an object given a string to identify it. Internally, COM defines an API function, MkParseDisplayName, an IParseDisplayName interface, and a number of different special types of object known as **Monikers** that expose the IMoniker interface. Between them, these items are charged with the responsibility of tracking down objects given a display name (that's COM parlance for the strings like StarRaiders://Fans/Simon/Spice Girls, or in more familiar computer territory, names like Excel.Application or C:\My Documents\My File – anything that might be passed to the VB GetObject function). And you VB guys never need to worry about all that – you don't know how lucky you are.

Let's be blunt: as topics in COM go, Monikers are *hard*. If you had to start using them every time you wanted to call up an ADSI object from C++, you can imagine how popular ADSI *wouldn't* be in the C++ community. So we need something else. Enter the ADSI router and the ADSI helper functions.

The **ADSI router** is what Microsoft has provided to resolve these kinds of issues. You can imagine it conceptually as a layer that is able to find out about the different providers available on your system, and in some cases, identify which provider you are interested in. The router provides a small API consisting of a number of **helper functions** that simplify some ADSI COM calls for C++ clients. Between them, these helper functions make binding to ADSI objects almost as simple from C++ as it is from VB.

One of the helper functions is `ADsGetObject()`. It does for C++ what `GetObject` does for VB: it hides all those nasty monikers, figures out which provider you want to call, hands the path name you've supplied to that provider and tells it to produce the correct COM object. Which all means that in C++ you can code up:

```
HRESULT hRes;
IADs *pPutItHere;
hRes = ADsGetObject(L"StarRaiders://Fans/Simon/Spice Girls", IID_IADs,
      (void**)&pPutItHere);
```

This isn't quite as nice as the VB command, but it does mean that you can use ADSI from C++ without being a real COM guru.

By the way, for the benefit of VB people, the `L` in front of the string makes sure the string is in the right format (UNICODE) for COM, the `hRes` is a 32-bit numeric value known as an `HRESULT` that can be used to check whether the call to `ADsGetObject` succeeded or not. You'll find this same `HRESULT` appearing in almost all COM method calls.

The `HRESULT` is used in VB, but in VB it's hidden by the development environment. The `HRESULT` is returned from COM method calls behind the scenes, and an error is raised if the `HRESULT` indicates a failure. `IID_IADs` is the GUID – that's a huge 128-bit integer, which uniquely identifies the `IADs` interface.

I don't assume you understand more advanced COM topics such as monikers. The only place we're going to need those is in Chapter 9, where we learn how to code up an ADSI provider, and you'll find a basic 'what-you-need-to-know' explanation of monikers and one or two other COM topics awaiting you there.

ADSI, OLE DB and Searching

We've now covered most of what we need to know about how ADSI works internally before we can start coding. However, there is one peculiarity of the ADSI COM interfaces that we've yet to look into.

I said earlier that all but three of the ADSI interfaces were automation interfaces, so you could talk to ADSI from any client written in any language. I also implied that the three remaining interfaces, which you can only get to from C++, aren't really that crucial, as you can't do much with them that you can't do from the automation interfaces just as well. I've got a confession to make – I lied.

You see, one of the non-automation interfaces is called `IDirectorySearch`, and that's the only interface that has any methods you can use to do searching. If you want to find all the users who've logged in since last Tuesday, or all the printers on the network that are currently either out of paper or not working because someone's left the printer door open, then `IDirectorySearch` is the interface for you (yes, you can do both of these using ADSI!)

So we've got a problem – at least, you guys who don't use C++ have a problem. `IDirectorySearch` is not dual, which means you can't use it from scripting languages. Not only that, but it's not described by any type library, which means you can't use it from VB clients either. So how can you do searching from a language that can't use vtables using a non-automation interface? This is where OLE DB comes in.

OLE DB is the main part of Microsoft's universal data access strategy, which has the ultimate aim of unifying access to data sources so that you only need to learn a single SDK in order to get to any data source. It replaces ODBC, which had a similar aim, but which was not based on COM and was more restricted in its functionality.

ADSI and OLE DB are actually quite similar concepts. OLE DB is a set of COM interfaces designed to unify access to some data source. It's been around longer than ADSI, and it's intended to be more of a general purpose SDK aimed at any data source, not specifically at directories (although it does have some bias towards relational databases). Just like ADSI, you can get providers for OLE DB, each provider wrapping a different data source. So if a client wants to talk to a data source, it calls up OLE DB, has the appropriate provider loaded, and then that provider handles communication with the data source.

As OLE DB is quite complex, Microsoft has come up with a smaller, lighter technology called ADO (ActiveX Data Objects). ADO basically sits on top of OLE DB, and exposes a simpler set of interfaces with more limited functionality, which clients can use to indirectly talk to OLE DB providers. What's more, the ADO interfaces are all dual ones (the straight OLE DB interfaces aren't). You gain simplicity, ease of use, and the ability to use the interfaces from VB and scripting languages, at the expense of an extra layer of processing. Alternatively, if you program in C++ and don't want the extra layer, ATL 3.0 includes some special wrapper classes that simplify using OLE DB, and hide the COM interface layer. MFC has some similar classes.

So that's OLE DB. But how does that help us? Well, here ADSI does something quite clever – it registers itself as an OLE DB provider. That's not an easy concept, so let's rephrase it to make it clearer.

When you install ADSI, you get all the Microsoft ADSI providers – the WinNT provider for ADSI, the LDAP provider for ADSI, etc. You also get the ADSI provider for OLE DB. In other words, a `dll` which is registered as an OLE DB provider, and which treats ADSI as its data source. Now we've got what we need. The OLE DB and ADO interfaces are automation interfaces, so they can be called from VB and scripting languages.

With all that, the sequence for searching from VB now runs as follows:

❑ The client calls up ADO, specifying the OLE DB ADSI provider as its data source

❑ The client passes a search command to ADO, which routes it through OLE DB to the ADSI OLE DB provider

❑ The OLE DB ADSI provider receives the search command, and responds by connecting to the appropriate ADSI directory and calling up a method in the `IDirectorySearch` interface

That's all shown in the following figure:

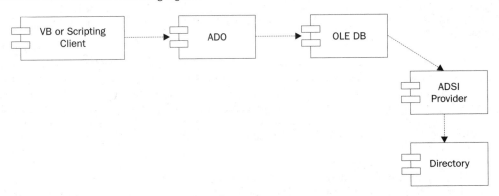

This will put an extra couple of wrapper layers in the sequence. It may sound complex, but as we'll see when we come to the chapter about searching, coding up a search request from VB using ADO really is simple – it takes no more than a few lines of code. Of course, by the time you've gone through all the COM layers, it's not that efficient to run – but hey, if speed and efficiency are really crucial to your particular application, then you wouldn't be using VB for it anyway, would you?

C++ clients, it should go without saying, can simply get an `IDirectorySearch` interface directly, by specifying `IID_IDirectorySearch` in a call to `ADsGetObject()`.Or, if they prefer, they can go through either OLE DB or ADO and OLE DB.

Remember, in our first diagram of how clients talk to a directory using ADSI, I said there were some layers missing. Well we've now covered all the remaining layers, so it's time to present the complete picture.

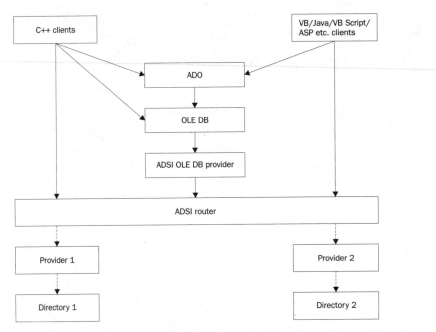

This figure shows all the possible ways that a client can use ADSI to connect to a directory. And after the preceding discussion it *ought* to be self-explanatory.

> *Solid arrows show COM method calls, dotted arrows show calls internal to the providers.*

Anyway, change of topic now. We've covered enough about how ADSI works. It's time to take a quick tour of its sister technology, Active Directory.

Introducing Active Directory

This is a book about ADSI, not about Active Directory. As far as we're concerned, Active Directory is simply another of the many directories you can access using ADSI. However, that said, it is going to be an extremely important directory in Windows 2000. ADSI has to some extent been designed as the interface for Active Directory (it even manages to include Active Directory in its name!), so we're not going to get very far without some mention of it. Well, to be honest, quite a lot of mention of it.

So what is Active Directory? Well let's start way back in the days when dinosaurs roamed the Earth and Bronze Age man was just emerging from his caves to discover the delights of Windows 3.1 (and I, incidentally, was blissfully helping to manage our group's network of HP workstations running – dare I say it – Unix). All the Windows 3.1 system configuration data was scattered around `config.sys` and those delightful `.ini` files. Then four years ago, Windows 95 emerged, closely followed by NT4, and we had the registry as a centralized data store for everything that was happening in your computer. Users, preferences, devices, COM classes, and – at least on NT – services. The registry was a huge improvement, but as always, computing has moved on. Two problems stand out.

Firstly, access to the registry is by means of low level API functions. And if I use a registry editor to look at it, I'm pretty much seeing the raw data – nice to play with but not exactly user friendly (if you're not convinced – just try using `Regedit` to navigate around under the HKEY_CLASSES_ROOT/CLSID key. Go on – I dare you!).

Secondly, the registry is computer-centric. You connect lots of computers in a domain, and each one has its own private little registry. And these days, that's not how networks really work. When I print my documents, I use a printer connected to the network. I don't particularly care which computer the printer is connected to: all I care about is that it's somewhere I can get to it. Similarly for a lot of services: if I want to do some administration work on our corporate DNS service (that's the service which maps Internet style names like www.wrox.com onto IP addresses), I'm not really bothered about what computer(s) DNS is running on – it's the service itself that I want to get to.

So we are really looking for something that has the same sort of information as you'd find in the registry, but which is based on the kinds of services and resources available on the network rather than on the individual computers (though they will figure as well). And something that you can access with a relatively high level set of interfaces. That's the Active Directory. It is a directory that covers computers, users, services, printers, and all the devices running from the domain.

> *Incidentally, it does have a low level interface too – it actually exposes itself to the outside world using LDAP, which means if your client uses ADSI to interact with Active Directory, it will use the ADSI LDAP provider.*

Now don't get me wrong – Active Directory is *not* a replacement for the registry. There is still a lot of information – including most of the stuff that's only relevant to the local machine – that is still only available in the registry. But for the information which is now stored in Active Directory (mostly stuff that is relevant to the domain as a whole) Active Directory provides a much more convenient way of getting at that information.

Active Directory has other benefits too. It is replicated: copies of the directory are made on all the domain controllers so access to the directory can be made from the most convenient machine (whereas NT4 had a primary domain controller and backup domain controllers, Windows 2000 simply has domain controllers). Active Directory uses a model in which differences between the data stored on different copies of Active Directory are tolerated for a short time, to allow for the replicas to be updated.

Security based on Kerberos Security is present, and managed on a fine level so that access can be controlled even to individual properties of items in the directory. Active Directory also introduces the idea of a **domain forest**. This is a group of domain trees which are separate (not part of the same tree structure), but which share configuration information. The system of distinguished names in Active Directory has been linked with the internet's DNS naming system, which is why I was able earlier to give examples of `ADsPath` names like:

```
LDAP://CN=Administrator,CN=Users,DC=TopOfThePops,DC=Fame,DC=com
```

In general, when using ADSI you will gain more functionality by using the LDAP provider and Active Directory to control resources on the network, rather than the WinNT provider. There is some overlap between the data made available through the LDAP provider, using Active Directory, and the information you can get to through the WinNT provider. Usually you will find that where there is overlap, the LDAP provider gives you a greater number of properties. This is because the WinNT provider is to some extent designed for backwards compatibility with NT4 machines.

The WinNT provider extracts its information directly from the registries of the various individual computers – and that means that the only stuff you can get to through WinNT is information that was available in NT4. Active Directory brings with it a huge new number of concepts (such as domain trees and forests) and properties (for example, much more descriptive information can be stored with user accounts). This information cannot be accessed using WinNT. On the other hand, the WinNT does give access to some stuff which is normally regarded as local to a machine, and therefore not by default stored in Active Directory – for example, local user accounts and NT Services.

It is possible to place this information in Active Directory, since Active Directory is, to some extent, designed as a general purpose directory as well as a directory of domain resources. However you would have to put the information there yourself – it's not there by default. You might want to copy that kind of data into Active Directory; for example, to provide an additional backup copy in the event of a system failure.

We'll look at Active Directory – and at the differences between Active Directory and the WinNT provider – in a lot more detail in later chapters. For this chapter, that's about it – we're just going to finish off now with a look at how you can get all these wonderful tools on your computer, and get ready to code up applications using them.

Installing ADSI

This depends a lot on what operating system you're running.

NT 4.0, Windows 95 and Windows 98

At the time of writing, the latest version of ADSI is ADSI 2.5. It is downloadable from Microsoft's web site, at `http://www.microsoft.com/adsi`. You'll need to download and install both ADSI itself and the ADSI SDK. If you download ADSI you'll get all the system files and `dlls` required to get ADSI working on your system, and to make the system providers available. The SDK includes the help files, a *huge* number of sample clients in C++, VB and J++, a sample ADSI provider, and all the relevant header files etc. you need to write your own code using ADSI. It also contains the `adsvw.exe` ADSI browser – from which one of the screenshots was taken earlier, and which you will definitely need in order to explore the various ADSI providers.

If you're using Visual C++, you do need to be aware that Visual Studio 6 shipped with ADSI 2.0. Quite a lot of additions were made between 2.0 and 2.5, as well as bug fixes, so do make sure that you download the latest version of ADSI, and set your paths in the Visual Studio to make sure the compiler picks up the newer versions of the ADSI headers. This book uses ADSI 2.5 throughout – and you'd be surprised how many of the samples won't work with ADSI 2.0.

ADSI itself is available in separate versions for NT (Intel and Alpha platforms), Windows 95, and Windows 98, but the SDK comes in one version for all operating systems.

If you're running Windows 95, you will need to install DCOM for Windows 95 before installing ADSI.

Windows 2000

If you are running Windows 2000 (currently the latest version is Beta 3), you won't need to install ADSI: it comes with Windows 2000. However, you will still want to download the SDK, just as for Windows NT, 95 and 98.

You should note as well that some of Windows 2000 tools for looking at ADSI objects are *not* installed automatically with Windows 2000, but come with the resource kit. At the time of writing, this is on the Windows 2000 Beta 3 CD – you need to separately run the `setup.exe` program in the `Support/Reskit` folder. Most of these tools are useful, though you can get by without them quite easily. It's worth pointing out, though, that the resource kit does include the `ADSIEDIT` browser, which I'll use in this book a bit – so if you want to try it out, you'll need to install it.

Appendix I runs through some of the more important samples that you get with the ADSI SDK

Writing ADSI Clients

If you're writing VB clients, you need to add the Active DS type library, `ActiveDS.h`, to the Project References. In addition, if you will be requesting searches through ADO, you should add the Microsoft ActiveX Data Object Library.

As usual, to write clients in scripting languages, you don't need to do anything special. Scripting languages use late binding, and so no particular knowledge of the interface is required by the script.

For C++, you'll need to #include the file ActiveDS.h in all source files that use ADSI. This is a general header file, which in turn #includes a large number of more specific headers. You will also need to link in the headers ActiveDS.h and ADsIID.h.

Tools to Browse ADSI Namespaces

I mentioned earlier that Microsoft had written a number of applications that you can use to browse ADSI directories. I'm going to use them fairly interchangeably throughout the book, as well as the ADsObjectViewer tool which we'll develop in Chapter 2 of this book, so we may as well get used to them now. They each have advantages and disadvantages that make each of them useful in different situations.

There are actually three main browsers floating around at the moment: the Active Directory VB Browser (dsbrowse), the Active Directory Browser (adsvw.exe) and the ADSIEDIT MMC snap-in. In addition, quite a few of the administrative tools in Windows 2000 will use ADSI to some extent, but since these are specialist tools rather than general ADSI browsers, we'll ignore them for the time being. Some of them are covered in Chapter 3.

dsbrowse

dsbrowse looks like this:

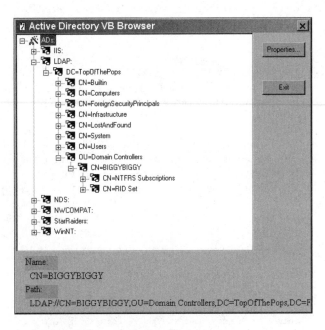

In this screenshot we're browsing through Active Directory.

Like both of the other browsers, it contains a tree control which you can expand to look at any part of any namespace. dsbrowse is somewhat unusual in being intended as a sample rather than as a real tool for everyday use. This has the advantage that the source code is available so you can see exactly what it's doing, or even change how it works – and the disadvantage that it's simply not as powerful as the other browsers. On the other hand, it excels for convenience when you just want to browse down the hierarchy – both ADSIEDIT and adsvw require you to select certain options every time you start up the application, whereas dsbrowse starts straight away.

If you want to look at the properties of an object in dsbrowse, you click on the Properties button, and you're given a separate dialog box to examine and modify properties.

Unfortunately, since dsbrowse is written in VB, it's slow – painfully slow if you're opening, say, a domain with a lot of computers in it. It also doesn't have much concept of class schema objects, and so gets confused if you try to look at their properties. And it has an odd bug – that if the Properties button is clicked over an object for which dsbrowse is unable to obtain any properties, the button gets disabled – and then doesn't get enabled again when you select a new object!

You can get dsbrowse with the ADSI SDK, which includes both the source and the executable files.

I'll occasionally present screenshots using dsbrowse just for the fun of it (and the variety).

adsvw

adsvw.exe, the Active Directory Browser, is not intended as a sample, so you don't get the source code for it (although the source code for a very early version of adsvw used to be available with ADSI 1.0). Its name is a bit of a misnomer, since it is a general ADSI browser, and is *not* Active-Directory specific.

It has a slightly checkered history, having been apparently intended as the browser to be released with Windows 2000. It in fact came as part of the operating system with NT5 Beta 2. However, Microsoft decided to replace it with an MMC snap-in, ADSIEDIT. As a result Windows 2000 beta 3 has emerged without Adsvw.exe – which is now shipped as part of the ADSI 2.5 SDK.

When you run adsvw.exe, you get a dialog asking whether you want to browse (ObjectViewer) or search (Query).

The difference is that browsing means opening up the tree structure to see what's inside, whereas searching means specifically looking for the objects that satisfy certain criteria (for example, all users with names beginning with S and accounts enabled). We'll cover searching in Chapter 7, so for now, we'll concentrate on the object viewer for browsing. Selecting this gives you another dialog asking where you want the root of your tree to be:

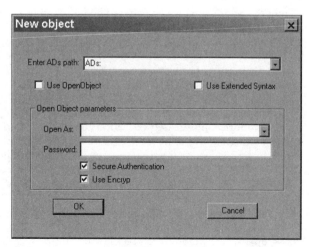

As you can see, you get a number of other options – including the optional ability to supply a password and username, if you think that the provider you're interested in will require it. If you don't want to supply a username and password, then you need to make sure the Use OpenObject check box is unchecked. If this checkbox is checked, then adsvw.exe will always attempt to bind by supplying user credentials.

The option to select the root of the tree (where it says Enter ADsPath) is a nice feature that allows you to confine your browsing to a particular provider, or even a particular subtree within a provider. Whatever ADsPath you type in will be the root of the tree control that adsvw creates, so you need only examine that node and nodes below it. You can't see anything above that node, but your view might be simplified if you know whereabouts in a directory you're interested in. For this example, I've entered ADs: so that I can look at all the ADSI providers installed on my computer:

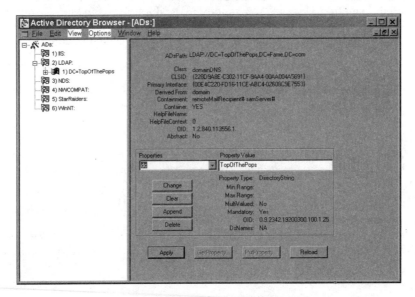

You get a window with two panes. The left pane is a tree control that you can use to select objects to look at, while the right pane lets you examine and change properties of your chosen object in detail. adsvw is quite sophisticated – for example, it can recognize the different COM interfaces a given object implements, and customize the right pane appropriately. dsbrowse won't do that. You can select a particular property to examine from the Properties drop down list box, and see the corresponding value displayed.

The four buttons below the Properties list box – Change, Clear, Append and Delete – allow you to perform more sophisticated operations on multi-valued properties, such as removing one of the values or appending some more values. Separate buttons – Apply and Reload – allow you to actually apply your changes to the directory, or discard your changes and load the original data back to the directory. We'll see in the next chapter how these functions actually correspond to certain method calls within the main ADSI IADS interface, and to how the ADSI property cache works.

adsvw.exe is a multiple-document interface app, which means you can open more windows just by choosing New from the main File menu. The new windows need not be related to any you already have open. New windows can be viewing completely different subtrees – you can even have a mixture of searching and browsing windows open, as shown in the next screenshot:

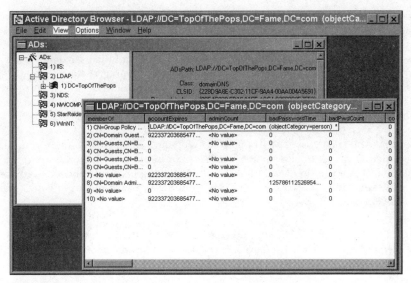

The front window here shows the result of a search for all user accounts. We'll cover how to do this in Chapter 7, which covers searching.

However, one problem `adsvw.exe` does have is that, because of the way properties are presented through a drop-down list box, it's not possible to see a complete list of all the properties and values of an object at once. `dsbrowse` is a bit friendlier here.

Having said that, `adsvw.exe` is still the most useful general browser available. At any rate, I'll be using `adsvw` quite a lot for screenshots in this book, because it's so convenient and sophisticated. I would strongly recommend you get a copy of it and stick it on your machine (probably as an icon on your desktop, because if you're serious about ADSI development, you'll be using it a *lot*). There are a couple of knowledge base articles that describe how to use `adsvw.exe`: Q186749 and Q188593.

ADSIEDIT

`ADSIEDIT` was originally being pushed as the replacement for `adsvw.exe`, although it does in fact serve a slightly different purpose. Like `adsvw.exe`, its name is also a misnomer. Where the so-called Active Directory Browser is really an ADSI browser, `ADSIEDIT` is actually specifically an Active Directory browser, not an ADSI one. (Can this go down as Microsoft's best howler of the year?)

So if `adsvw.exe` is so good, why the need for a third browser? Well partly, the answer has to do with the direction Microsoft is heading in for administration. You see, managing Active Directory is basically an administrative task. Some time ago, Microsoft made the decision that administrative tasks should be managed from a common user interface: Microsoft Management Console (MMC). And `adsvw`, good as it is, suffers from a politically incorrect disadvantage here: it's a standalone app, not an MMC snap-in.

The other reason why `ADSIEDIT` is needed is because of the problem that simply browsing sometimes won't uncover all parts of a directory tree. Active Directory suffers acutely from this problem. It's actually got three branches to the directory – the directory itself, the schema and the configuration. There's also a special object called the `rootDSE`, which gives general information about the directory. Browsing down the tree starting from ADs: or LDAP: will uncover only the main part of the directory: you need to know the `ADsPaths` of the objects at the root of the other parts of the tree to be able to see them.

`dsbrowse.exe` will only show you the main part of Active Directory – as will any tool that relies solely on browsing down starting with the ADSI router. Although strictly speaking, it is possible to view the other parts of the tree in Active Directory from `adsvw.exe` by typing in the appropriate `ADsPaths` as the root object, doing so requires some typing, and the user needs a fairly advanced understanding of LDAP directories in order to know how to do it. (We'll cover this area when we look at Active Directory and LDAP, in Chapters 3 and 10) It would be a lot easier here if we had a tool that has this more advanced knowledge of Active Directory hard coded into it, and so could locate all the branches of the directory automatically. That's where `ADSIEDIT` fits in.

I mentioned that `ADSIEDIT` is an MMC snap-in. We won't cover MMC snap-ins until Chapter 12. But for now, what we need to know is that being a snap-in means it comes as an `.msc` file rather than an `.exe` file. But if you run the `.msc` file by double-clicking on it in Windows Explorer, it'll start up just as if it's an executable. It'll actually be MMC running it, which means it won't run unless you have MMC installed.

Windows 2000 comes with MMC already installed as part of the operating system. It doesn't come by default with NT4, but it is possible to download it from Microsoft's web site – and much of Microsoft's software now relies on MMC, and installs it automatically if it's not there.

Let's look at what you see when you run `ADSIEDIT`.

When you run `ADSIEDIT` for the first time, you start off with, essentially, a blank screen:

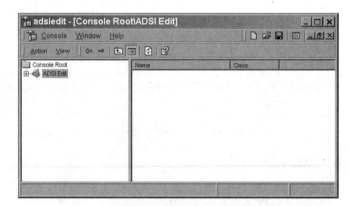

In order to actually see any COM objects, you need to right-click on the **ADSI Edit** item, and select **Connect To** from the context menu that comes up. This brings up a dialog box asking you to select an ADSI object to connect to:

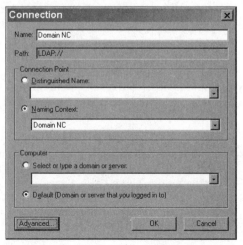

The screenshot shows the default options. The key choice is under the <u>N</u>aming Context drop-down list box. This gives you four choices for which part of Active Directory you want to connect to:

Name	Description
Domain NC	The actual directory information tree – the main part of Active Directory.
Configuration Container	The configuration data – deals with issues such as how Active Directory is replicated.
RootDSE	A special object called the rootDSE which contains information about how Active Directory is set up. The properties of this object include the root ADsPaths to get to the other three parts of Active Directory
Schema	The schema container.

Alternatively, you can choose to type in a distinguished name – and that really means an LDAP distinguished name, not an ADsPath, so we won't cover that yet. In a lot of cases, typing the ADsPath to an object in Active Directory, but without the initial LDAP://, will work. At any rate, that's really an option for advanced users, and it won't let you see any information you can't get to by making a selection from the drop-down list box instead.

The advanced button lets you supply additional authentication, or connect to a special part of Active Directory called the global catalogue. This is a copy of a portion of Active Directory, which contains only a limited number of key properties of the objects, allowing for faster searching.

The first time you use ADSIEDIT, I'd suggest you OK the default options. The interesting thing about ADSIEDIT is that it's possible to select the Connect To menu item several times, each time adding a new link to part of Active Directory. If you do this four times, to select all four of the options in the list box, this is what you'll end up seeing:

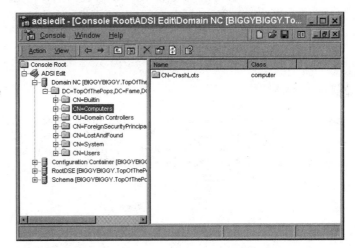

Here I've opened up the Domain NC node to look at the main containers inside it. It's currently showing the one extra computer I've got in my network besides the BiggyBiggy domain controller – a sweet little Pentium 133 named CrashLots.

Unfortunately ADSIEDIT isn't that friendly when it comes to viewing the properties of an object. You need to select the relevant object, right-click on it, and select **Properties**. This brings up a dialog box in which you can select the property you want to examine in another drop down list box:

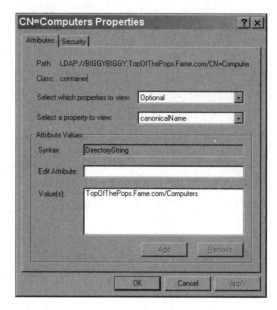

There's no facility to get an overview of all the properties of an object, and there's no facility to carry out searching. However, there is one useful feature. Remember how it took a fair bit of work to get ADSIEDIT initially set up to actually look at anything? Well now we've done that we can save the settings. Just exit from ADSIEDIT and you'll get a dialog asking if you want to save the settings. You can choose a filename – so you can end up with lots of versions of ADSIEDIT, all set up to examine different parts of Active Directory. This isn't something peculiar to ADSIEDIT – it's a common feature of MMC snap-ins.

Summary

We've covered a lot of ground very briefly in this chapter. You should now understand what a directory is and, qualitatively, what you would use ADSI for and how you would use it. Hopefully you've also made sure you've got ADSI installed on your machine – because I think it's about time we left the conceptual introductions and dived in to see how you actually start to write clients. That's the subject of the next chapter.

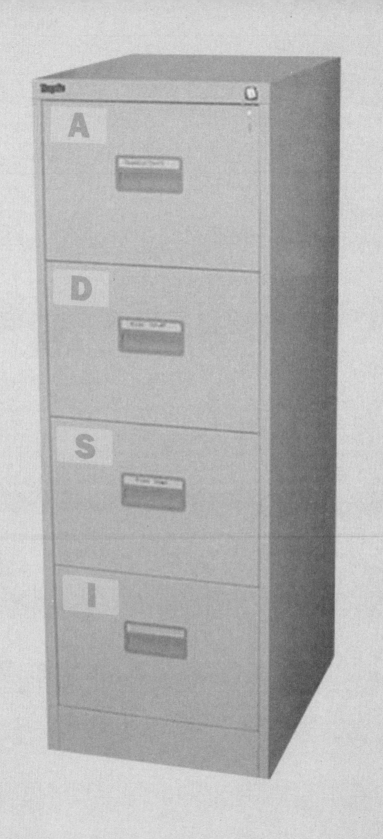

2

Simple ADSI Clients

At the end of this chapter you will hopefully

- ❑   Have a couple of useful web pages to help you examine objects in directories

- ❑   Know what the main ADSI interfaces are and what sort of objects you can manipulate with them

- ❑   Know how to use the two most important ADSI interfaces, `IADs` and `IADsContainer` (these two interfaces are sufficient for a lot of directory browsing)

- ❑   Be able to write simple ADSI clients in VBScript, VBA, VB and C++

- ❑   Have a good feeling for why some of the ADSI interfaces have been designed the way they have, and how they actually work.

Time to get your Developer Studios started up. In this chapter we're going to start programming with ADSI from both C++ and VB.

This is the first of two chapters that are designed to get you familiar with the theory behind the ADSI specifications and how ADSI works. And in the process you will meet many of the ADSI interfaces that you need to carry out most directory tasks. This means that by the end of chapter 3 you will know how to carry out the kinds of programming tasks in ADSI that are common to most directories – tasks like navigating through the directory and looking up schemas. We won't, however, cover much on security or searching – those are more specialist topics that are best left to their own chapters. And we'll be leaving provider-specific extensions to ADSI until Chapter 9.

However, apart from those areas, in the next two chapters we are going to tour through most of the interfaces defined by ADSI. That's going to be a lot of interfaces, and I suspect if you're a normal human being you'd be bored stiff with reading about different interfaces if you had to do all of them before you could see ADSI in action being applied to specific problems. Which is why there's two chapters here. This chapter starts off by presenting a couple of sample applications that will give you a feel for how to write ADSI clients. Then after we've got our hands dirty with these applications we'll have a quick overview of what interfaces are available to do what, then we'll step back into theory and carefully go over how the two most important interfaces, `IADs` and `IADsContainer` work. Chapter 3 is a bit more like a reference guide and runs you through all the other interfaces that we'll need (apart from the ones concerned with searching and security. As I've said these topics will be covered in separate chapters. There's also a bit of more advanced stuff that we'll leave till Chapter 12, on Advanced ADSI Topics).

Having said all that, although you will need to know how to use most of these interfaces in order to make full use of ADSI, there are a lot of tasks for which `IADs` and `IADsContainer` are adequate. So once you've got to the end of this chapter you will – if you're desparate to start applying your knowledge – be able to skip to Chapter 4, in which we start using ADSI to look around your network. You'll find a few references to interfaces you won't have covered, but you'll be able to get by – and Chapter 3 will be sitting there for you to refer back to. On the other hand, if you want to understand all the theory first then you can just carry on through the chapters in order.

Anyway, I bet you're keen to have a look at what a client that uses ADSI looks like in practice. So I'm going to start by developing the two object viewers that I used in the last chapter. I'll keep the explanations of the code fairly brief, as we'll go into more detail of how the interfaces work in the interface-by-interface guide later in the chapter.

In order to start coding, you should make sure you have the latest versions of both ADSI and the ADSI SDK installed, as described in the last chapter. Also, before we start coding, I want to quickly go over a couple of the common problems you might find. If you type in some code or download it from the Wrox web site and find it doesn't work as expected – check out the next section...

Getting Code To Work

The samples in this chapter, and the rest of the book, are downloadable from the Wrox web site, and should be ready to run, provided you have ADSI and all other relevant software installed. However, if you find that something that should work doesn't, you should check the following:

❏ **Hard coded pathnames**: Some of the names of ADSI objects are hard coded to my domain and machine name. Obviously you'll need to change them to your own domain and machine names.

❏ **Security Problems**. You will need to have administrator privileges on your computer and occasionally on your domain to run quite a few of the examples in this chapter. This generally follows common sense: if I'm doing something like reading the name of my computer, then you should be able to do that from any account. If an example actually does something like adding a new computer to the domain, then clearly the example won't work if you haven't got privileges to do that! So make sure you are logged in as an administrator. In Chapter 8, on Security, we'll explain how you can change your credentials in ADSI if you are logged in without suitable privileges and want to bind to a directory object as another user.

❏ **Not running Windows 2000**. If your domain is not being run by a Window 2000 domain controller, then the samples that use Active Directory won't work. You can however, still use the LDAP provider if you have an LDAP directory installed – examples of this would include Netscape Directory Server, Exchange Server, or Site Server Personalization and Membership services.

The VB Object Viewer

This project is called VB_ADsObjectViewer, and, like all the samples, is available for download from the Wrox web site, www.wrox.com. If you are typing this in yourself, remember that to access the ADSI interfaces, you need to check the Active DS type library in the project references.

Let's have a quick reminder of what the object viewer looks like when it's working:

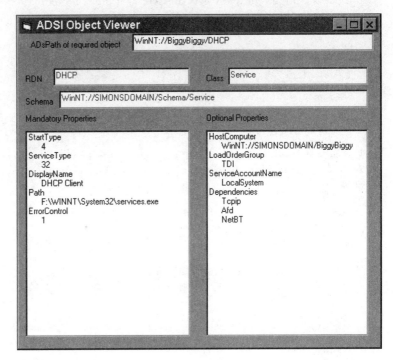

This is using the WinNT provider to look at the local DHCP service.

It's a VB application with a fair number of text boxes and list boxes on it. If you type in the ADsPath of the object you want in the text box at the top, the viewer will then display all the mandatory and optional properties, along with the name (relative distinguished name), class and schema ADsPath of the object in question.

Let's see the project setup. First, here are the names of the controls in the project.

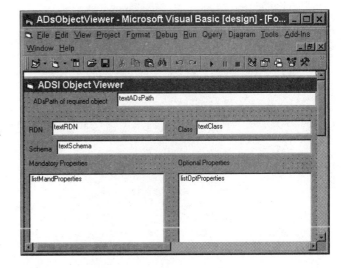

The text boxes are all disabled, except the `ADsPath` one.

Since the core of the code is the displaying of properties, this is all handled in a subroutine called `RefreshProperties`. This needs to be called whenever the user has just finished typing in something in the text box, `textADsPath`. How do we know that the user has finished typing? Well that'll happen if the return key gets pressed, or if the text box loses the input focus. This means we need to handle the events with this code:

```
Private Sub textADsPath_KeyUp(KeyCode As Integer, Shift As Integer)
    If KeyCode = 13 Then Call RefreshData
End Sub

Private Sub textADsPath_LostFocus()
    Call RefreshData
End Sub
```

These subs are both coded as events associated with the text box, `textADsPath`, because that's the only control in the dialog that hasn't been disabled – so it's the only one that can ever receive these events.

And as for `RefreshProperties` itself... Here's the code

```
Private Sub RefreshData()

' this subroutine displays the mandatory and optional properties
' of the object whose ADsPath has been typed in in the textbox
' called ADsPath

'first clear out the other boxes
listMandProperties.Clear
listOptProperties.Clear
textClass.Text = ""
textRDN.Text = ""
textSchema.Text = ""

' bind to the required ADSI object
On Error GoTo NoObject
Dim ADsObject As IADs
Set ADsObject = GetObject(textADsPath.Text)

' display some of the basic info about the object, as stored
' in the automation properties
On Error GoTo CantDisplayAutoProperties
textRDN.Text = ADsObject.Name
textClass.Text = ADsObject.Class
textSchema.Text = ADsObject.Schema

' display class information and
' bind to the class schema object that describes the required object
On Error GoTo NoSchema
Dim ClassObject As IADsClass
Set ClassObject = GetObject(ADsObject.Schema)
```

```
    ' display the mandatory properties
    On Error Resume Next
    For Each PropertyName In ClassObject.MandatoryProperties
        listMandProperties.AddItem PropertyName
        For Each PropertyValue In ADsObject.GetEx(PropertyName)
            listMandProperties.AddItem "        " & PropertyValue
        Next
    Next

    ' display the optional properties
    On Error Resume Next
    For Each PropertyName In ClassObject.OptionalProperties
        listOptProperties.AddItem PropertyName
        For Each PropertyValue In ADsObject.GetEx(PropertyName)
            listOptProperties.AddItem "        " & PropertyValue
        Next
    Next
    Exit Sub

NoObject:
    listMandProperties.AddItem "No such object"
    Exit Sub

CantDisplayAutoProperties:
    listMandProperties.AddItem "Error occurred retrieving automation properties"
    Exit Sub

NoSchema:
    listMandProperties.AddItem "Cannot bind to schema object"
    Exit Sub

End Sub
```

So what's going on in the code? Well, first of all there's some basic initialization. All the other controls may have data in them from a previous query – so we need to clear out the contents of all of them.

Then we need to bind to the object whose path has been typed in.

```
On Error GoTo NoObject
Dim ADsObject As IADs
Set ADsObject = GetObject(textADsPath.Text)
```

The `On Error` line simply skips the rest of the code and displays a suitable error message if we were unable to bind to the object (most likely, due to an invalid `ADsPath`). Notice that we've defined the object as of type `IADs` – `IADs` being the COM interface that lets us get to the ADSI properties.

Next we display a couple of bits of information about the object – its name (relative distinguished name), class and schema. Remember that the class says what type of object we are dealing with, while the schema gives the ADsPath of an object that describes all the properties that objects of this class can contain. These bits of information are all defined as automation properties exposed by IADs.

```
On Error GoTo CantDisplayAutoProperties
textRDN.Text = ADsObject.Name
textClass.Text = ADsObject.Class
textSchema.Text = ADsObject.Schema
```

We now want to display all the properties of our object – and we can check what properties are there to display by checking up the schema, as we described in the last chapter. So we first need to get the schema object. The interface this object exposes which gives us the information about the required properties is IADsClass.

```
On Error GoTo NoSchema
Dim ClassObject As IADsClass
Set ClassObject = GetObject(ADsObject.Schema)
```

Now we can actually display the properties. The list of properties exposed by our class is given by two automation properties of the IADsClass interface: MandatoryProperties and OptionalProperties. Each of these returns an array (for C++ people: a VARIANT containing a SAFEARRAY), which lists the names of all the properties. So we need to iterate through this array. For each name, we want to retrieve the value of that property from our object. The IADs method which does this is GetEx(), which returns an array containing all the values (some properties may have more than one value).

```
' display the mandatory properties
On Error Resume Next
For Each PropertyName In ClassObject.MandatoryProperties
    listMandProperties.AddItem PropertyName
    For Each PropertyValue In ADsObject.GetEx(PropertyName)
        listMandProperties.AddItem "        " & PropertyValue
    Next
Next
```

Notice that each property value may be of any automation data type. When we add the value to the list box, in the line:

```
listMandProperties.AddItem "        " & PropertyValue
```

the value will automatically be converted to text, if that's possible. If that's not possible (if the value is a binary value, for example another interface pointer) then VB will flag an error. That's the point of the On Error Resume Next statement – if any such errors occur, then we want the program to just carry on and display the next value.

That's the mandatory properties. The corresponding code for the optional properties is pretty similar:

```
On Error Resume Next
For Each PropertyName In ClassObject.OptionalProperties
    listOptProperties.AddItem PropertyName
    For Each PropertyValue In ADsObject.GetEx(PropertyName)
        listOptProperties.AddItem "       " & PropertyValue
    Next
Next
```

And, apart from the error handling stuff, that's the complete code!

By the way, this code obtains the information contained in the ADSI object by looking up the schema. This means that it will only work if a corresponding schema object is available. This is important because there are a few directory objects for which no corresponding schema object exists. One such object is an object in Active Directory known as the `RootDSE`, which contains useful information about the directory structure of Active Directory. (Although this is an isolated case – almost every other object in Active Directory does have a corresponding schema object). So although our code sample can tell us the values of the mandatory and optional properties for most objects exposed by all the ADSI providers, there are a couple of cases in which it won't work. In Chapter 3, we'll develop a similar application that uses a different technique to obtain all the properties of directory objects, without requiring the schema.

The Web Page Object Viewer

We're not going to need to go over this code in as much detail, as it's pretty much identical to the straight VB sample above. The only difference is because it's an ASP script to be viewed on a web page, the design of the user interface is a little different – with HTML tables instead of list boxes.

Here's a reminder of what the page looks like. The first time you bring the page up to view it, you won't have specified an `ADsPath` (unless you type it in the URL). This means that the page will attempt to bind to an object with a `NULL ADsPath` – and will, of course, fail, because there's no such object. So you'll see this:

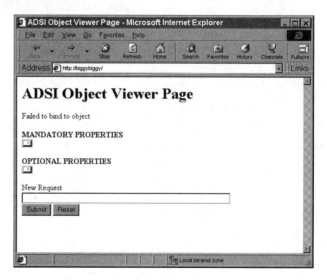

You can then type in the
`ADsPath` of the required
object in the text box
supplied, and submit the
information. This ASP page
works by `GET`ing rather
than `POST`ing the
information, so the
`ADsPath` will be appended
to the URL. You'll then see
something like this:

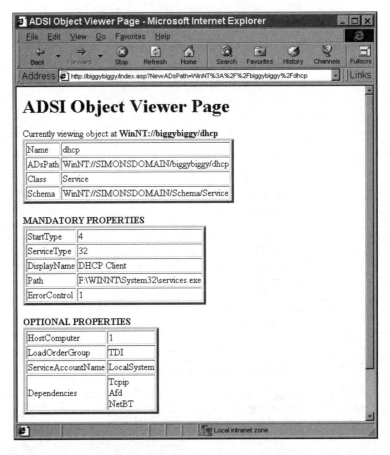

By the way, the form for submitting a new `ADsPath` is still there, at the bottom of the page – but the
page was too big to fit on the screen!

That's the page. Here's the code for it:

```
<%@ Language = VBScript %>
<html>
<head>
<title> ADSI Object Viewer Page </title>
</head>

<body>

<h1> ADSI Object Viewer Page </h1>

<%
on error resume next
Dim ADsObject
Set ADsObject = GetObject(Request.QueryString("NewADsPath"))
```

```
if not (Err.number = 0) then
    Response.Write "Failed to bind to object <strong>" & NewADsPath & "</strong>"
else
    Response.Write "Currently viewing object at <strong>" &
Request.QueryString("NewADsPath")& "</strong><br>"
end if
%>


<%
if (Err.number = 0) then
    Response.Write "<table border = 4>"
    Response.Write "<tr><td>Name </td><td>" & ADsObject.Name & "</td>"
    Response.Write "<tr><td>ADsPath </td><td> " & ADsObject.ADsPath & "</td>"
    Response.Write "<tr><td>Class </td><td> " & ADsObject.Class
    Response.Write "<tr><td>Schema </td><td> " & ADsObject.Schema
end if
%>


</table>
<p>
<strong> MANDATORY PROPERTIES </strong>
<table border = 4>

<%
    dim ClassObject
    set ClassObject = GetObject(ADsObject.Schema)
    ADsObject.GetInfo
    for each PropName in ClassObject.MandatoryProperties
        Response.Write "<tr><td>"
        response.write PropName
        Response.Write "</td><td>"
        dim PropValues
        PropValues = ADsObject.GetEx(PropName)
        for each Value in PropValues
            Response.Write Value
            response.write "<br>"
        next
        Response.Write "</td></tr>"
    next
%>


</table>
<p>
<strong> OPTIONAL PROPERTIES </strong>
<table border = 4>

<%
    ADsObject.GetInfo
    for each PropName in ClassObject.OptionalProperties
        Response.Write "<tr><td>"
        response.write PropName
        Response.Write "</td><td>"
        PropValues = ADsObject.GetEx(PropName)
```

67

```
        for each Value in PropValues
            Response.Write Value
            response.write "<br>"
        next
        Response.Write "</td></tr>"
    next

NextRequest:
%>
</table>

<p>
<form action = "index.asp" method = "get" id=form1 name=form1>
New Request<br>
<INPUT type="text" id=Request name=NewADsPath size = 60><br>
<INPUT type="submit" value="Submit" id=submit1 name=submit1>
<INPUT type="reset" value="Reset" id=reset1 name=reset1><br>
</form>

</body>
</html>
```

The actual ADSI object is obtained through these lines.

```
Dim ADsObject
Set ADsObject = GetObject(Request.QueryString("NewADsPath"))
if not (Err.number = 0) then
    Response.Write "Failed to bind to object <strong>" & NewADsPath & "</strong>"
else
    Response.Write "Currently viewing object at <strong>" &
Request.QueryString("NewADsPath")& "</strong><br>"
end if
```

The function `Request.QueryString("NewADsPath")` obtains the text that is supplied in the URL as being the `ADsPath`. In other words, if the URL is this:

```
http://biggybiggy/index.asp?NewADsPath=WinNT%3A%2F%2Fbiggybiggy%2Fdhcp
```

Then `Request.QueryString("NewADsPath")` returns the text after the `NewADsPath=` in the URL. The reason the URL contains the escape sequences %3A, %2F etc. is that the characters : and / have special meanings as separators in URLs and so cannot be inserted directly in the string. So the URL contains escape sequences that give the hexadecimal ASCII codes for these characters instead. The text is sent by the Submit button, which causes the text filled in in the text box to be appended to the URL:

```
<form action = "index.asp" method = "get" id=form1 name=form1>
New Request<br>
<INPUT type="text" id=Request name=NewADsPath size = 60><br>
<INPUT type="submit" value="Submit" id=submit1 name=submit1>
<INPUT type="reset" value="Reset" id=reset1 name=reset1><br>
</form>
```

In terms of the logic of the program code, the rest of the code is pretty much identical to the other example. Variables are no longer declared as `IADs` or `IADsClass` because VBScript uses late binding throughout. With late binding, the client does not talk directly to the required interface on the object, but rather always calls methods on the object's `IDispatch` interface that indirectly result in the intended methods getting called up internally by the `IDispatch` methods. Hence the client needs to hold only a pointer to an `IDispatch` interface – in VB this is exactly what a variable of type Object contains. In scripting languages it is not possible in any case to declare variables as being of a specific type, so object variables can only hold `IDispatch` pointers.

Also note that the error handling is different in the ASP page because VBScript doesn't have any equivalent of VB's `On Error Goto` statement – so for the web page we just plough through any errors regardless.

> *C++ Programmers might not be aware of ASP syntax. Basically anything written between the <% and %> is VB Script code, which must be interpreted and executed in order to generate plain HTML that can be returned to the browser. The main means of generating the HTML is by using the* `Response.Write` *statement, which causes whatever text or the value of whatever variable is passed to it as its parameter to be written to the HTML page that will be passed to the browser. If you need to brush up on your ASP, then a good reference is Beginning Active Server Pages 3.0 (ISBN 1-861003-3-82).*

So that's a quick demonstration of what you can do with ADSI. And it's given us two really useful tools that let us get a quick overview of all the data contained in any one ADSI object – something which the Microsoft ADSI browsers generally won't do. We're going to be making a lot of use of these tools later in the book when we investigate Active Directory and some of the other directories on your network.

Now we're going to start being a bit more thorough, and go through the more important ADSI interfaces to see what they can do for us. We'll do a quick tour of the interfaces before examining `IADs` and `IADsContainer` in detail – saving the other interfaces for chapter 3.

Quickie Tour of the Interfaces

Here's the inheritance tree of the ADSI interfaces.

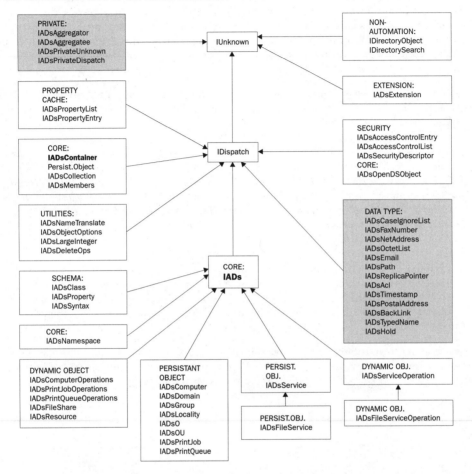

Although this looks complex, there are a lot of interfaces we'll be able to dispose of in a couple of paragraphs.

> *VB and VBScript developers might not have encountered the concept of a COM interface before. If you haven't, don't worry. As far as VB is concerned, an interface is really just a set of properties and methods, grouped together. Think of it as a convenient way of saying what methods and properties a COM object supports; instead of listing a vast number of methods and properties, you simply list a few interfaces.*

In the figure, I've put related interfaces together in the same boxes. You'll also notice that besides the interface names are written categories in capital letters. These are the categories into which Microsoft puts the interfaces for documentation purposes. The categories are useful for helping to understand what the interfaces do but they don't have any significance for the actual programming. In most cases Microsoft's categories and my boxes coincide though there are a couple of exceptions.

OK, The first thing to notice is I've highlighted the `IADs` and `IADsContainer` interfaces, as these are the two key interfaces that are essential if you want to do anything with ADSI. Remember we said that each directory object is represented by a COM object? Well `IADs` is the basic interface that must be exposed by every such COM object. It gives you access to basic information like the object's name and `ADsPath`. `IADsContainer` must be exposed by every object that can contain child objects. It implements methods to enumerate the children, obtain particular children by name, and move objects around the directory.

There are quite a large number of interfaces derived from `IADs`. Apart from the ones categorized as 'Schema', which deal with the object's class schema, these are all more specialised interfaces designed to represent particular types of object that you'll often find in directories, for example computers and users. Most of these interfaces do little more than add a few extra automation properties to the ones already exposed by `IADs`, though some of them have methods that instruct the object they represent to perform certain operations (like telling a computer to reboot!). Since these are fairly applied interfaces we'll for the most part deal with them as we come to need them in chapters 4 and 5.

Two sets of interfaces have been shaded in the figure to show that you probably don't really need to know them. Of these, the `DataType` interfaces are specific to Novell Directory Services (NDS). Apart from the usual `IDispatch` methods, they each simply contain a few extra automation properties that represent attributes specific to NDS data types. Since we're not dealing with NDS in this book, we won't talk about them again. The `Extension` interfaces are there to allow ADSI providers to expose provider-specific extensions to ADSI. We'll show how this is done in Chapter 9.

That all leaves us with a couple of small sets of interfaces that are important in most directories, and which, with the exception of some of the security interfaces, we will deal with in detail in this and the next chapter. Does that look a more manageable number of interfaces then?

Most of the ADSI interfaces are automation interfaces, with names like `IADsXXX`, (For **XXX** substitute the appropriate names). This means that those interfaces can be used by clients written in any COM-aware language, including scripting languages. The three non-automation interfaces that are designed for C++ clients are named `IDirectoryXXX`. Of these:

❑   `IDirectorySearch` is concerned with searching, which we will leave until Chapter 5.

❑   `IDirectorySchemaMgmt` is now obsolete and Microsoft no longer recommends its use. I've only mentioned it here for completeness – in case you come across it in any header files and wonder what it's doing there, undocumented. It was originally intended for schema-based functionality, but you should now use `IADsClass`, `IADsProperty` and `IADsSyntax` for these operations – we'll cover those interfaces in chapter 4.

❑   `IDirectoryObject` reproduces most of the functionality of `IADs` and `IADsContainer`, but with slightly improved performance. We'll cover how to use `IDirectoryObject` in chapter 3. I will mention though that since it does only support a subset of the usual ADSI operations, you may be better off relying completely on `IADs` and `IADsContainer` anyway.

The sample code in this chapter uses mixture of providers: WinNT, LDAP and StarRaiders. You will have WinNT, and LDAP is supplied with your installation of ADSI, and you can download the StarRaiders provider from the Wrox website. Because there's a lot to get through, I'm not really going to explain how the `ADsPath` pathnames in WinNT and LDAP are constructed – we'll cover that in greater depth in chapter 4 – for now I'll mostly ask you to accept that the `ADsPaths` we are using are correct.

If you happen to be running NT4 or Windows 95 or 98, then the examples in this and the following chapters which use the LDAP provider, giving Active Directory pathnames, that I've used as examples won't work your machine. If you want to try out those examples, just substitute a WinNT or StarRaiders pathname (you can use one from any of the WinNT or StarRaiders examples).

Anyway I reckon I've rattled on long enough. It's time for some real work...

Changing Your Windows 2000 Password

Well I always think there's no better way to learn how to write code than to start coding. First I want to write a little program that uses ADSI to change a local user password and account description. Simple enough? Here's the code...

Here it is in VB:

```vb
Private Sub Form_Load()

    ' get the directory object for my user account
    Dim user As IADsUser
    Set user = GetObject("WinNT://BiggyBiggy/Simon")

    ' display information about account and set the password
    List1.AddItem "User name: " & user.Name
    List1.AddItem "Description:   " & user.Description

    ' change the password and description
    user.SetPassword "Noo-Noo"
    user.Description = "I've just changed my description!"
    user.SetInfo

    ' make sure we have an up-to-date copy of the description and display it
    user.GetInfo
    List1.AddItem "Description has been changed to : " & user.Description

    ' free memory
    Set user = Nothing

End Sub
```

This bit of code produces this output.

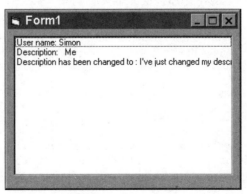

To build this program I created a new standard project in VB 6, and checked the Active DS type library in the references. I added a list box, called List1, to the form to display the results, and added the above code to the event procedure for the main form. Simple, huh!

And to prove this code works, here's what the Active Directory Users and Computers snap-in looked like after I'd run it.

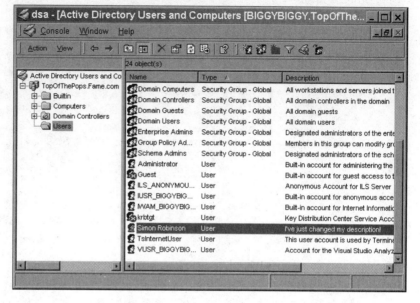

Obviously, you'll have to just believe the password really did change – since that's never displayed – but you can see the new description.

If you're not sure how to get to the User and Computer Manager SnapIn in Windows 2000, it's in the Start Menu – follow Program/Administrative Tools/Active Directory Users and Computers. If you're running NT4, you'll be using the old-style user manager dialog instead, which is also located in the start menu, under Programs/Administrative Tools/User Manager.

Changing Password and Description – C++ Code

It's about time we had a sample in C++, so here's the corresponding code to change my Windows 2000 password in C++, created as an empty console application.

```
#include <iostream.h>
#include <Windows.h>
#include "e:\ADSISDK\inc\ActiveDS.h"    // picks up the latest
// version of Active DS.h, not the one supplied with VC6

#include <atlbase.h>    // so I can use ATL smart pointers and CComBSTR

// check that COM error calls worked
#define ASH _ASSERT(SUCCEEDED(hr));
```

```
int main(argc, char* argv[])
{
   CComPtr<IADsUser> spUser;
   HRESULT hr;

   // initialize COM and bind to the user object
   CoInitialize(NULL);
   hr = ADsGetObject(L"WinNT://BiggyBiggy/Simon", IID_IADs, (void**)&spUser);
   ASH;

   // get the name and description
   CComBSTR bstrUserName;
   CComBSTR bstrDescription;
   hr = spUser->get_Name(&bstrUserName); ASH;
   hr = spUser->get_Description(&bstrDescription); ASH;

   // convert strings from unicode to ANSI so they can be printed
   USES_CONVERSION;
   LPSTR pszUserName = OLE2A(bstrUserName);
   LPSTR pszDescription = OLE2A(bstrDescription);

   // display the user name and description
   cout << "User Name is " << pszUserName << endl;
   cout << "User Description is " << pszDescription << endl;

   // change the password and description
   hr = spUser->SetPassword(L"Noo-Noo"); ASH;
   hr = spUser->put_Description(L"I\'ve just changed my description in C++ Now");
ASH;
   hr = spUser->SetInfo(); ASH;

   // make sure we have an up-to-date copy of the description
   hr = spUser->GetInfo(); ASH;
   hr = spUser->get_Description(&bstrDescription); ASH;
   LPSTR pszNewDescription = OLE2A(bstrDescription);

   // display new description
   cout << "User Description has now been changed to " << pszNewDescription <<
endl;
   return 1;
}
```

And here's the result:

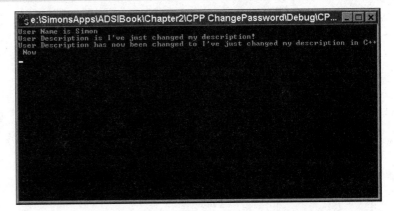

Now, let me explain what I'm going to do. You see – I've got a problem: I've aimed this book at C++ programmers *and* VB and VBScript programmers. I've done that for the very good reason that there are a lot of people wanting to use each of these languages to do ADSI stuff. There are good reasons for this. There are some tasks which involve ADSI that are better suited to C++ and other tasks that are best suited to VB. There will be parts of this book where one particular tool is far more suitable – and in that case I will only use the appropriate language (for example ADSI providers really have to be coded up in C++), but that leaves a lot of samples that might legitimately be in either language, depending on the sort of application you want to use it in. And to be honest I don't particularly fancy duplicating every bit of sample code in both languages, and I don't really think you want that either.

Anyway, the deal is this. You get the first couple of samples in C++ and either VB or VBScript, practically side by side. And I talk you through what's going on as far as ADSI is concerned, but I also compare how the code works in the two languages. That way you'll be able to see roughly what happens in whichever language is the one you don't normally use. After that I'll assume you're intelligent enough to be able to follow samples in either language, and that you'll be able to figure out how to turn samples back into your preferred language.

Explanation of the Change Password VB Code

OK – on to the analysis of the Change Password code. In VB, things could hardly be easier. We declare a variable as being an `IADsUser` interface (strictly a pointer to an `IADs` interface, but VB hides the pointer). `IADsUser` is derived from `IADs` and additionally has some properties and methods to manipulate user accounts. We display the RDN of the ADSI object, using the name automation property, and the account description. `Name` is an automation property exposed by `IADs` and `Description` is exposed by `IADsUser` – again an automation property. The password is not available or viewable as a property, but we can change it using an `IADsUser` method, `IADsUser::SetPassword`.

The interesting bit comes between displaying the description first time round and changing it:

```
user.SetPassword "Noo-Noo"
user.Description = "I've just changed my description!"
user.SetInfo

' make sure we have an up-to-date copy of the description and display it
user.GetInfo
List1.AddItem "Description has been changed to :" & user.Description
```

What we're doing here is changing the description to *I've just changed my description!* in the ADSI object. But ADSI caches data locally in order to save network calls. In order to actually update the description in the directory itself, we need to call the method, `IADs::SetInfo`. We then call `IADs::GetInfo`, which loads the data back from the directory – by doing this we are making sure that we do have an up-to-date copy of the data, so that what we display really does reflect what the directory now contains.

Explanation of the Change Password C++ Code

The C++ code has exactly the same sequence of actions as the VB code. The main differences are that because we're working at a somewhat lower level, we have to do more of the work ourselves when it comes to tasks like error handling and initializing resources. The following explanation is really aimed at VB people who might not be familiar with some of the C++ syntax.

Let's do the error handling first. Whereas in VB, COM calls will throw an exception if they fail, in C++, they return a value that needs to be checked manually to make sure there was no error. The standard way to do this – at least in sample code – is with the line

```
_ASSERT(SUCCEEDED(hr));
```

where `hr` is the variable that stores the return value from the COM method call. This statement will cause the program to stop executing and display a basic error message if `hr` contains a value indicating a failure. Because I'm going to need lines like that dotted around almost everywhere I've defined an abbreviation for it:

```
// check that COM error calls worked
#define ASH _ASSERT(SUCCEEDED(hr));
```

Now I can just put `ASH` wherever I need to check for an error. You'll see my little `ASH` statement in all the C++ samples in this book.

What else? `BSTR` is the variable type that is actually stored inside a `VARIANT` containing a string. `CComBSTR` can be thought of as a slightly more sophisticated version of it that handles memory cleanup automatically (just as VB does).

The `->` syntax in C++ is broadly equivalent to the `.` notation in VB. It'll tend to crop up where VB hides the fact that its handling pointers, but C++ is more open about the matter.

The automation properties in VB are treated as actual method calls in C++ – so where as VB has `Object.Property`, C++ has `pObject->get_Property()` and `pObject->put_Property`.

IADs Sample: Working Up A Directory Tree

We're going to try out one more sample before I go into a more theoretical discussion of the interfaces involved. The last one was to show you how you'd use ADSI to do something useful on your system. This next sample is aimed at showing you something of the internal structure of an ADSI directory. You remember the screenshot from the adsvw browser in Chapter 1? Well we're going to look at a bit of code that goes to the administrator user displayed in that screenshot, and then works progressively back up the directory information tree to the namespaces object, showing the names and classes of the objects it encounters en route.

This time I'm going to use ASP:

Working Up a Directory Tree: ASP Code

```
<%@ Language = VBScript %>
<html>
<head>
<title> ADSI Object Viewer Page </title>
</head>

<body>

<h1> ADSI Object Viewer Page </h1>

<%
    ' get the directory object for my user account
    Dim ads
    Set ads = GetObject("WinNT://BiggyBiggy/Simon")

    Dim parent
    parent = ads.parent
    Response.Write "ADsPath of Object is " & ads.ADsPath
    Response.Write "<br>Class of Object is " & ads.Class

    Do      ' loop through all parents
        Set ads = Nothing
        Set ads = GetObject(parent)
        Response.Write "<p>"
        Response.Write "ADsPath of Object is " & ads.ADsPath
       Response.Write "<br>   Class of Object is " & ads.Class
        parent = ads.Parent
    Loop Until parent = ""  'namespaces object has Parent = ""

    Set ads = Nothing
%>
</body>
</html>
```

This code simply obtains the IADs::Parent automation property, which gives the ADsPath of the parent object. It does this repeatedly, each time attempting to bind to the parent and displaying the ADsPath and Class of the object so obtained. Eventually it will reach the ADSI router, ADs:, which returns a NULL string for its parent – at that point the loop will exit.

Here are the results.

This page shows part of the tree structure exposed by WinNT provider – a user account is contained within a computer – which is contained within a domain. Above the domain is the WinNT namespace object, and above that the ADSI router – or namespaces object.

Working Up a Directory Tree: C++ Code

```
#include <iostream.h>
#include <Windows.h>
#include "e:\ADSISDK\inc\ActiveDS.h"    // picks up the latest
// version of Active DS.h, not the one supplied with VC6

#include <atlbase.h>    // so I can use ATL smart pointers and CComBSTR

// check that COM error calls worked
#define ASH _ASSERT(SUCCEEDED(hr));

void DisplayData(CComPtr<IADs> spADsObject);

main()
{
    CComPtr<IADs> spADsObject;
    HRESULT hr;

    // initialize COM and bind to the user object
    CoInitialize(NULL);
    hr = ADsGetObject(L"WinNT://BiggyBiggy/Simon", IID_IADs,
(void**)&spADsObject);
    ASH;

    CComBSTR bstrParent;
    do
    {
        DisplayData(spADsObject);
```

```
            hr = spADsObject->get_Parent(&bstrParent); ASH;
            spADsObject = NULL;
            if (bstrParent.Length() > 0)
                hr = ADsGetObject(bstrParent, IID_IADs, (void**)&spADsObject); ASH;

        }
    while (bstrParent.Length() > 0);

    return 1;
}


// actually displays the ADsPath and class of the supplied object
void DisplayData(CComPtr<IADs> spADsObject)
{
    HRESULT hr;

    // get the name and description
    CComBSTR bstrADsPath;
    CComBSTR bstrClass;
    hr = spADsObject->get_ADsPath(&bstrADsPath); ASH;
    hr = spADsObject->get_Class(&bstrClass); ASH;

    // convert strings from unicode to ANSI so they can be printed
    USES_CONVERSION;
    LPSTR pszADsPath = OLE2A(bstrADsPath);
    LPSTR pszClass = OLE2A(bstrClass);

    // display the user name and description
    cout << "ADsPath is " << pszADsPath << endl;
    cout << "Class is " << pszClass << endl;
    cout << endl;
}
```

In the C++ code I've separated out the code that actually displays the ADsPath and class of each object into a function, DisplayData().

This code produces

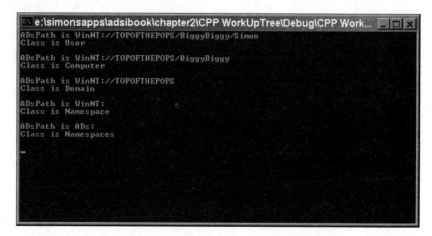

That's enough code for now: It's time for a bit of theory.

The Most Important Interface: IADs

There is some information that is basic to any object in a directory. For example, everything has a name, a class and an ADsPath. IADs is the interface that handles this kind of information. Every object in the directory must expose this interface, and a lot of the other ADSI interfaces are derived from it. You could almost think of it as ADSI's equivalent to IUnknown or IDispatch: In general in COM, if you want a particular object, but you don't know what interfaces it might usefully have, then in C++ you'd ask for IUnknown in your call to CoCreateInstance. In VB you'd declare a variable as type 'Object' which implicitly means that you're asking for the IDispatch interface. In ADSI if you don't yet know anything about the object you want, then you can safely ask for the IADs interface.

IADs Properties

Apart from the usual IUnknown and IDispatch stuff, IADs has 6 automation properties and 7 methods.

Name	R/W?	Type	Description
Name	R/O	BSTR	The name of the object
ADsPath	R/O	BSTR	The unique ADsPath of the object
Parent	R/O	BSTR	The ADsPath of the immediate parent of this object. Remember, you can't get ADsPath's by concatenating names with parent ADsPaths – so this does need to be stored as a separate parameter.
Class	R/O	BSTR	The name of the class of the object
Schema	R/O	BSTR	The ADsPath of the schema object that stores the information about this class.
GUID	R/O	BSTR	A unique GUID that can identify this object – it is only ever used by Active Directory

I'm using a format here that I'll use for all the tables of automation properties that I'll present for the interfaces. The second column shows whether the property is read/write (R/W) or read only (R/O). The IADs properties are all read only – you set them when the object in the directory is created then that's it. The third column shows the variable type. Strings are always BSTR. Later on we'll come across some that are arrays. The usual way of storing an array of type X in automation is as a VARIANT containing a SAFEARRAY of VARIANTs of type X. I'll usually abbreviate that to SAFEARRAY(X), eg. SAFEARRAY(BSTR).

IADs Methods

Name	Description
Get()	Gets the value of a named property
Put()	Sets the value of a named single-valued property
GetEx()	Gets the value of a named property
PutEx()	Sets the value of a named multivalued property
GetInfo()	Updates the cache
SetInfo()	Updates the directory
GetInfoEx()	Updates certain properties in the cache

And in case anyone particularly wants the full IDL definition, it is:

```
[
    uuid(FD8256D0-FD15-11CE-ABC4-02608C9E7553),
    dual
]
interface IADs : IDispatch {
    [id(0x00000002), propget] HRESULT Name([out, retval] BSTR* retval);
    [id(0x00000003), propget] HRESULT Class([out, retval] BSTR* retval);
    [id(0x00000004), propget] HRESULT GUID([out, retval] BSTR* retval);
    [id(0x00000005), propget] HRESULT ADsPath([out, retval] BSTR* retval);
    [id(0x00000006), propget] HRESULT Parent([out, retval] BSTR* retval);
    [id(0x00000007), propget] HRESULT Schema([out, retval] BSTR* retval);
    [id(0x00000008)] HRESULT GetInfo();
    [id(0x00000009)] HRESULT SetInfo();
    [id(0x0000000a)] HRESULT Get( [in] BSTR bstrName, [out, retval] VARIANT*
pvProp);
    [id(0x0000000b)] HRESULT Put( [in] BSTR bstrName, [in] VARIANT vProp);
    [id(0x0000000c)] HRESULT GetEx( [in] BSTR bstrName, [out, retval] VARIANT*
pvProp);
    [id(0x0000000d)] HRESULT PutEx( [in] long lnControlCode, [in] BSTR bstrName,
[in] VARIANT vProp);
    [id(0x0000000e)] HRESULT GetInfoEx( [in] VARIANT vProperties, [in] long
lnReserved);
};
```

This IDL snippet was reconstructed from OLEView, since Microsoft doesn't directly supply the IDL file itself.

Here's probably a good point to mention that you're going to find a lot of VARIANTs coming up in method parameter lists. Well what do you expect – these are automation interfaces. VB guys won't be bothered about the VARIANTs but C++ people who've spent a lot of time using custom COM interfaces you may not be so familiar with them. Well if you're a C++ guy and you don't quite feel comfortable with manipulating things like VARIANTs containing SAFEARRAYs of more VARIANTs, then have a flick through Appendix C sometime soon. (Like now?)

There are several new concepts here so let's go through them.

Automation vs Schema-Defined Properties

Let's look at the first two methods in IADs's method list above: Get() and Put(). Anyone who's really observant may be wondering why these methods exist when you can apparently get all the properties using get_Name(), get_ADsPath() etc. In fact, ADSI, confusingly, has two different ways of treating properties. Remember we said in the last chapter how the list of properties is defined in the schema? Well ADSI has some properties, like Name and ADsPath that are defined by the various interfaces as automation properties. These tend to be the ones that store data without which it'd be hard to use the relevant interfaces. You'll access these properties the same way you access all automation properties: by treating them as member variables in VB, and with the get_ and put_ methods in C++. Other properties are defined through the schemas – and these are the properties that will vary according to the class of object in the directory, even though objects may be expose the same interfaces. For example, the object's ADsPath is the sort of information that you need for any object – so it's exposed through an automation property, IADs::Name. On the other hand, in the StarRaiders provider, the *Favourite Artist* class has a property, *Whether Met*. This property only ever applies to objects of type *Favourite Artist* and so would be defined in the schema and not available as an automation property exposed by the IADs interface.

So the schema-based properties are often not explicitly defined by any of the ADSI interfaces, and need to be accessed using the Get() and Put() methods, for which you supply the name of the property as a BSTR parameter. I say often because we'll see in Chapters 4 through 6 that some schema-based properties are simultaneously exposed through some more specialist ADSI interfaces.

> *Actually it is debatable whether we are justified in using the term 'property' in the directory sense for the automation properties, as there's not a lot you can do with them. They are not referenced in the class schemas, so you can't dynamically find out about them at run time – you have to know their names at compile time. The IADsPropertyXXX interfaces which we'll encounter soon and which iterate through properties skip the automation ones, and it's not even guaranteed that you can search against them either. Some providers, such as WinNT, solve this by duplicating the interface-based properties in corresponding schema-based properties. But there is a lot of information contained in these properties, so I'll continue to treat them as properties, albeit somewhat special, restricted ones.*

The IADs methods Get(), GetEx(), Put(), and PutEx() do work very differently from the automation properties. Now admittedly, I need to be careful here because we are talking about COM, and one of the ideas of COM is that clients shouldn't need to know how a method is implemented. That's up to the server, and different ADSI providers are going to be implemented in different ways. But with that proviso, the principle of these methods is that they are very much based on the schema. They will typically work internally by checking up in the schema object – as obtained from the IADs::Schema automation property – to see what properties are available and what their datatypes are. This means that if there are any problems with accessing the schema object, then Get() and the others shouldn't strictly work at all. From what I've said about the typical structure of directories, you might think that shouldn't ever happen, since I've emphasized how important the schema is as a way of accessing information about the directory. But in fact the idea of incorporating the schema as a normal part of the directory only came into vogue recently and some older directories, such as LDAP version 2 directories, won't implement this. In those directories, IADs::Get() and similar functions will fail. However, since those directories are obsolete, you're unlikely to come across them much – we certainly won't be covering any in this book.

Later on in this chapter, we'll explain another interface, IADsPropertyList, which is able to obtain a named property, but bypasses the schema.

As for the `GetEx()` and `PutEx()` methods, let's compare `Put()` and `PutEx()` first. `Put()` is intended for a single-valued property, and `PutEx()` is intended for a multi-valued property. With `PutEx()` you are expected to supply a VARIANT containing a SAFEARRAY of VARIANTs containing the property values, and you also get to specify a flag that says what you want to do with the values you've supplied. With a single valued property, there's only one thing you can do: overwrite the existing value with the new value. With a multi-valued property, you may want to:

❑ Add the new values on to the list of values, leaving any existing values intact.

❑ Overwrite the existing values with the new values.

❑ Clear out all the values, leaving an empty property.

❑ Remove the specified values from the list of values, leaving any other values intact.

You specify these actions respectively by passing in the value `ADS_PROPERTY_APPEND`, `ADS_PROPERTY_UPDATE`, `ADS_PROPERTY_CLEAR` or `ADS_PROPERTY_REMOVE`. These four values form part of an enumeration known as `ADS_PROPERTY_OPERATION_ENUM`.

For example, in C++ you might use `Put()` and `PutEx()` in the following ways.

```
// set up VARIANT structures
VARIANT varSingleVal, varMultiVals;
varSingleVal.vt = VT_BSTR;
varSingleVal.bstrVal = SysAllocString(L"Picture Of You");
LPWSTR ppszHits[2] = {L"Picture Of You", L"Never Forget"};
ADsBuildVarArrayStr(ppszHits, 2, &varMultiVals);

IADs *pADs = NULL;
hRes = ADsGetObject(L"StarRaiders://Fans/Simon Robinson/Boyzone", IID_IADs,
    (void**)&pADs); ASH;
hRes = pADs->Put(L"Favourite Song", varSingleVal);
hRes = pADs->PutEx(ADS_PROPERTY_APPEND, L"Number 1 Hits", varMultiVals);

VariantClear(&varSingleVal);
VariantClear(&varMultiVals);
pADs->Release();
```

`ADsBuildVarArrayStr()` is a helper function that converts arrays of strings into the VARIANT form required by ADSI.

With `Get()` and `GetEx()` it's a bit more subtle. Originally, Microsoft sold `Get()` as being for single-valued properties and `GetEx()` for multivalued ones, but the two definitions seem to have merged and in fact you can use either method for any property, single- or multi-valued. If you use the methods for a multi-valued property, they both behave identically, returning a VARIANT containing a SAFEARRAY of VARIANTs that contains the actual values. The difference comes if you use them for a single-valued property. In that case `Get()` will simply return a VARIANT containing the value, but `GetEx()` will still return a VARIANT containing a SAFEARRAY of VARIANTs. In this case the SAFEARRAY will only contain one element. You should use whichever one is more convenient for whatever you happen to be doing.

This example should make things clearer. This is a VB program that illustrates use of Get and GetEx on the StarRaiders provider. It displays my Favourite Single of the Spice Girls – a single valued property using first IADs::Get() then IADs::GetEx()

```
Private Sub Form_Load()

    Dim oObject As IADs
    Set oObject = GetObject("StarRaiders://Fans/Simon/Spice Girls")

    'display a single valued property using Get()
    List1.AddItem "Favourite Single using IADs::Get: " & oObject.Get("Favourite
Single")
    List1.AddItem ""

    'display the same single-valued property using GetEx()
    List1.AddItem "Favourite Single using IADs::GetEx"
    For Each Value In oObject.GetEx("Favourite Single")
        List1.AddItem "   " & Value
    Next

    Set oObject = Nothing

End Sub
```

The point to note about this sample is that when using Get() the value is returned just as a single value. But when we use GetEx(), it is returned inside an array, so that even though there is only one value we still need to use a For Each loop to extract it.

Here's the output from this sample:

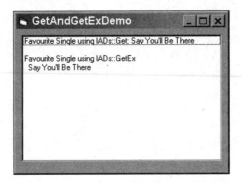

If the value is multivalued, then the data will be returned in an array irrespective of whether we use Get() or GetEx() to retrieve it – so we will need the For Each loop in either case. GetEx() is most useful if you don't know whether the value is going to be single or multi-valued.

By the way, we've been using a VB construct, which might throw C++ guys. The For Each loop is a way for VB to iterate through certain arrays. Instead of explicitly Counting from 0 (or what ever the start of the array is, since in VB arrays don't have to be zero indexed) up to the last element in the array, For Each handles the counting automatically. You can use it for SAFEARRAYs contained in VARIANTs, and in a few other situations that we'll meet soon.

If you write the same sample in C++ it becomes slightly more complex due to the need to manipulate the VARIANTs manually. The lines

```
'display a multi-valued property using Get()
    For Each Value In Band.Get("Members")
        List1.AddItem Value
    Next
```

will become

```
// Assume pBand is an IADs object
// and ListBox is a ListBox
VARIANT varArray, *pvarValues;
hRes = pBand->GetEx(L"Members", &varArray); ASH;
SAFEARRAY *psa = varArray.parray;
SafeArrayAccessData(psa, (void**)pvarValues);
for (unsigned i=0 ; i<psa->rgsabound->cElements ; i++)
    ListBox.AddString(pvarValues[i].bstrVal);
SafeArrayUnaccessData(psa);

VariantClear(&varArray);
pBand->Release();
```

The Property Cache - SetInfo, GetInfo and GetInfoEx

Now we come to the SetInfo(), GetInfo() and GetInfoEx() methods of IADs.

The way COM is defined you need a separate method call to get or set each automation property and the way the Get() and Put() methods are defined you need a separate method call for each schema-based property. Later on we're going to meet directory objects that have a lot of schema-defined properties. If your directory is actually stored on another computer so every call has to go over the network, and you want to retrieve lots or all of the properties, you can imagine how inefficient that's going to be. So ADSI implements what's called the *property cache*. All the schema-defined properties for an object are stored locally in a cache. The Get(), Put(), GetEx() and PutEx() methods read and write only to the cache, not the directory itself, and the GetInfo() and SetInfo() methods are available for transferring all the properties in a block to or from the cache, as illustrated in the figure.

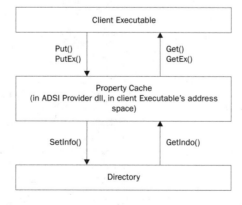

Since ADSI COM objects are all in-process, accessing the cache is very efficient. The only problem for you is you do have to watch how you use it. If you modify some properties in the cache, then inadvertantly call `GetInfo()` before you've called `SetInfo()` to write your changes to the directory, that'll overwrite the changes you've made.

The ADSI specification doesn't explicitly indicate whether the cache applies to the automation properties as well, so expect individual providers to behave differently in this regard.

You won't often need to call `GetInfo()` explicitly because that it is called implicitly for you whenever you try to get a property that isn't already stored in the cache, but you will want to call `SetInfo()` whenever you're ready to write your changes to the directory. In fact, if you look back through the samples I've presented so far, you'll notice I've almost never bothered to call `GetInfo()`.

`GetInfoEx()` is a more advanced version of `GetInfo()`, which lets you specify which properties you want to retrieve from the directory. It has three uses:

❑   You can use it to minimize network traffic if you know you only want certain properties.

❑   If you've got yourself into a situation where you want to update your cached values of certain properties because you suspect they've changed in the underlying directory, but you don't want to overwrite changes you've made in the cache to other properties, then you can use `GetInfoEx()` to update your values of just those properties.

❑   There are certain properties in some directories that are not retrieved by `GetInfo()`. These are properties that are regarded as of a sufficiently specialist nature that it's not worth retrieving them unless they are specifically requested by name. A good example of this is that Active Directory and other LDAP 3 directories maintain what are known as **operational attributes** or **constructive attributes**. These are special attributes that are maintained by the server for internal use, such as the date an object was last modified or who modified it. Mostly these attributes cannot be modified directly by the client. And for most purposes clients aren't going to be interested in them. But they are available through `GetInfoEx()` if a client specifically wants to examine their values.

Some Subtleties of Using the Property Cache

Using a property cache has great benefits for speed of access to data, but it does mean there are multiple copies of the data hanging around – at least one copy in the directory, and another copy sitting in the process space of every ADSI client that happens to be accessing that object. That brings up some subtle issues concerned with ensuring data is consistent between the property cache and the directory, which could catch you out if you're not careful.

The first point is that there is no intelligent monitoring of changes here. If you have several clients accessing the same directory object, then they will each have their own in-process property cache – and none of them will know about the existence of the other property caches. If you write your changes to the directory, then another client could theoretically overwrite your changes 0.1 seconds later without you knowing anything about it. There is no mechanism in ADSI to lock any part of directory to prevent other clients accessing it. You need to bear this in mind when writing clients. To make matters worse, there's also no callback mechanism in ADSI to request that a provider notifies you automatically when certain changes to the directory occur (though Microsoft are planning on adding this at some point in the future). If you hold on to an ADSI object for a long time, and there's a risk of other applications writing to the corresponding directory object, then its up to you to decide how out of date it's acceptable for your local cache to become, and to schedule calls to `GetInfo()` at appropriate intervals.

Secondly, it's important to be aware of what happens when `GetInfo()` is called. There's actually a difference between how it behaves when you call it explicitly and when it gets called implicitly.

Take a look at this code snippet, which I built very quickly. It's the usual VB code, base on a dialog box that contains a list control called List1. Three questions:

How do you think it'll behave, in particular, have I succeeded in updating my favourite single? Does it matter if I remove the call to `GetInfoEx`? How would you improve it?

```vb
Private Sub Form_Load()

    Dim OBand As IADs
    Set OBand = GetObject("StarRaiders://Fans/Simon Robinson/Spice Girls")

    ' change my favourite song - I can't make up my mind!
    OBand.GetInfoEx "Favourite Single"
    OBand.Put "Favourite Single", "Too Much"

    'display another property using Get()
    List1.AddItem "No Singles Bought" & _
        oBand.Get("No Of Singles Bought")
    OBand.SetInfo

    Set OBand = Nothing

End Sub
```

OK – answers:

1. Yes – I have succeeded in updating my favourite single. The point is at the line that calls `Band.Get` to get the property, *No Of Singles Bought*. You see, at this point, there is no value in the property cache for this property – the only one I've loaded into the cache is *Favourite Single* – which means ADSI will do an implicit call to `GetInfo()`. If I'd called `GetInfo()` explicitly here, then the contents of *Favourite Single* would get overwritten. However ADSI requires that the implementation of `GetInfo()` requires that *if* it has been called implicitly within the provider, then it won't override any values of properties that are already in the cache: it'll only update properties for which no value is loaded. (If you call `GetInfo()` explicitly, then it will overwrite all values already in the cache).

2. Technically, that call to `GetInfoEx()` isn't necessary. The call to `Put()` should place the value in the property cache even if that property has not been loaded. However, although that's what *should*, happen, personally I wouldn't rely on that. It's too subtle a point and I can easily imagine some provider writer implementing `Put()` the wrong way.

3. I'll leave you to do this one. It's not a hard problem. Just one comment to C++ programmers though: improving it does *not* mean you have to convert it to C++!

You can probably see from this that you do need to figure out what's happening to the property cache carefully sometimes. In general, if you're sensible about how you structure your programs and call `GetInfo()` and `SetInfo()` appropriately, and don't try to pull off tricks like using `Put()` or `PutEx()` to place values in uninitialized properties, you'll be OK.

One final point. You will often find that if there are any problems with modifying any property values, the problem only comes to light when you call `SetInfo()`. Providers do vary in how they implement this, but a lot of the time, if you try to set a value that is read-only, for which you don't have sufficient security rights to modify, or where the value you are trying to set it to is out of range or otherwise inappropriate, providers will quite often simply not check this when the call to `Put` is made. (Sensible really, because making the check might in some cases involve another call over the wire to the directory – which would defeat the whole point of having a property cache in the first place. In general when you call `Put()` or `PutEx()`, the provider only carries out those checks for which it doesn't need to call up the actual directory service.). So you *might* only get a fail when the call to `SetInfo()` is made. If you have any doubt whether the value you've put in the cache can be written to the directory then it might be worth calling `SetInfo()` to check. Or you could carry out some experiments to see how the particular provider you're working with behaves in that situation.

That's it for the `IADs` interface. I've covered `IADs` in a lot of detail because it's such an important interface, and besides, I want you to get a good feel for how the ADSI automation interfaces work. But don't expect the same treatment for the other interfaces. MSDN and the ADSI help files contain an exhaustive reference guide listing every parameter for every method and every property of every ADSI interface. There are a *lot* of interfaces and Microsoft's interface reference totalled 230 odd pages the last time I looked at it. This book is here to complement the MSDN documentation, not replace it, so from now on I'll explain what the interfaces we encounter are about, give you some examples, and trust you to look up MSDN for reference details.

Navigating Down the Tree: IADsContainer

We've covered the core information needed in every ADSI directory object, and we've learned how to move up the tree. That leaves an obvious question: how do you go the other way? Well, going down the tree is a bit more complex, since although an object has only one parent, it can have a lot of children. We need some more functionality, and you know what it means in COM when you want more functionality: you define another interface. `IADsContainer` is the one we want. It's the basic interface that exposes the functionality associated with finding out about the children of an object and getting hold of interface pointers for them. The `IADsContainer` interface will be exposed by every ADSI object that is capable of having children. In fact, the standard method of finding out whether an object can in principle contain children is by doing a `QueryInterface()` for `IADsContainer`, and seeing whether the call succeeded or not.

Browsing Sample: The W2K Service Lister

To illustrate the use of `IADsContainer`, this sample displays the names of all the Windows 2000 Services that are registered on a computer. We're going to look at Windows 2000 Services in more detail in Chapter 4, where we cover the kinds of objects you'll find on directories of computer networks. For the time being, just accept that a Service is a special process that doesn't necessarily need a logged in user to be present and to start it up. Services are started by the operating system, and they need to be registered so that Windows 2000 knows about them. Which also means we can find out about all the available services using ADSI.

In this book I'll refer to Windows 2000 Services, but you may be more used to hearing of NT Services. They are the same thing, but I've opted to refer to them as Windows 2000 Services because we are mostly using Windows 2000 in this book.

We're going to be using the ADSI WinNT provider (Now that name's really going to look funny when Windows 2000 is established and NT is just a distant memory, isn't it...). The way the WinNT directory is structured, Services are organised as children of the computer on which they are registered. We know the name of the computer, but we don't know the names of the services – that's what we want to find out – so we've got a clear need for a facility to enumerate children of a container – which is exactly what `IADsContainer` provides.

Here's what the web page that lists my services is going to look like:

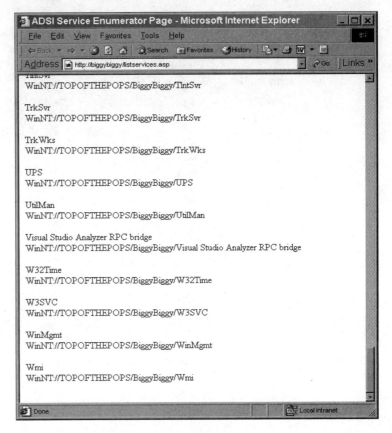

There's a *lot* of services that run on a Windows 2000 Server machine! From this screenshot you can start to see why Microsoft generally don't recommend installing Windows 2000 on an Intel 386 processor! Amongst the ones we can see here are W3SVC, the IIS World Wide Web service which responds to requests from browser, the UPS uninterruptible power supply service, and WMI – the Microsoft Windows Management Instrumentation Service, responsible for handling the common repository of application management information.

Anyway here's the script responsible for this page.

```
<%@ Language = VBScript %>
<html>
<head>
<title> ADSI Service Enumerator Page </title>
</head>

<body>

<h1> ADSI Service Enumerator Page </h1>

Windows 2000 Services on BiggyBiggy are:
<p>
<%

    Dim MyComputer
    Set MyComputer = GetObject("WinNT://BiggyBiggy")
    MyComputer.Filter = Array("Service")

    For Each service In MyComputer
        Response.Write service.Name & "<br>"
        Response.Write service.ADsPath & "<p>"
    Next

    Set MyComputer = Nothing



%>
</body>
</html>
```

As you can see, getting access to the children of a container in VB is pretty easy – just do a `For Each` loop on the container. The one new technique you should be aware of is the line:

```
    MyComputer.Filter = Array("Service")
```

This is just a way of restricting the results of the `For Each` loop. In WinNT a computer ADSI object contains other ADSI objects representing not just services, but user and group accounts, file services and file shares. We don't want any of these extra objects. We could retrieve them all anyway, and then only display the ones that had a class of *service*, but it's easier to set a filter from the start. When you attempt to enumerate the children of a container, the ADSI provider first checks to see if there are any values in the multivalued property `Filter` – and if there are, only returns objects of these classes.

The Service Lister: C++ Version

For C++, we're going to do something a little different. The first couple of samples were just straight C++ no-frills console applications, but I prefer something with a friendly looking user interface. Besides, I want to show you that you can use ADSI with MFC apps. So from now on for the rest of the book the C++ samples are wizard-generated MFC dialog applications unless I say otherwise.

I've done the following in all the subsequent C++ applications

I've made the applications UNICODE applications. (To do this, you change the entry point in Project|Settings|Link|Input to wWinMainCRTStartup, and add the symbol _UNICODE to the preprocessor definitions in Project|Settings|C++|Preprocessor). I've added a list box in the dialog to display the results, and attached a control member variable called m_ListBox to it. The result is an application that looks like this:

I've initialized COM in the application class InitInstance():

```
BOOL CListServicesApp::InitInstance()
{
    AfxEnableControlContainer();

    if (!AfxOleInit())
    {
        AfxMessageBox(L"Failed to initialize COM");
        return false;
    }
```

```
// etc.
```

I've added the #include <activeds.h> in the stdafx.h file, and also the #include <atlbase.h> so I can get access to the smart pointer and BSTR wrapper classes in ATL. (I can't always use CString because anything that is used in method calls has to be a BSTR – that's the type of string that COM – and incidently VB – use) As usual, on my machine, I've installed the latest version of the ADSI SDK (which at the time of writing is the ADSI 2.5 SDK) to the folder E:\ADSISDK.

```
#include <afxcmn.h>              // MFC support for Windows Common Controls
#endif // _AFX_NO_AFXCMN_SUPPORT

#include <atlbase.h>
#include "E:\adsisdk\inc\activeds.h"
```

I've linked to the libraries, `ActiveDS.lib` and `ADsIID.lib`:

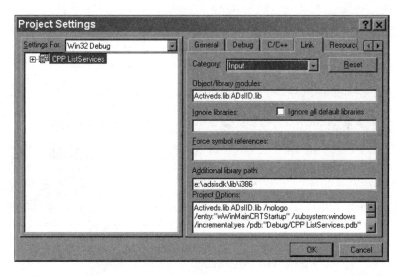

And finally, I've done all the ADSI stuff in the dialog class's `OnInitDialog()` function, so that the results are ready to display when the dialog starts up.

I won't repeat this in the future, as most of the future C++ samples will be this way – I'll just present what I've added to `OnInitDialog()`.

So on to the real bit of code I want to show you:

```cpp
BOOL CCPPListServicesDlg::OnInitDialog()
{
#define ASH ASSERT(SUCCEEDED(hr));

    CDialog::OnInitDialog();

    // get computer object
    HRESULT hr = S_OK;
    CComPtr<IADsContainer> spMyComputer;
    hr = ADsGetObject(L"WinNT://BiggyBiggy", IID_IADsContainer,
        (void**)&spMyComputer); ASH;

    // build VARIANT array for filter
    VARIANT varFilterList;
    LPWSTR szFilter = L"Service";
    hr = ADsBuildVarArrayStr(&szFilter, 1, &varFilterList); ASH;

    // set filter
    hr = spMyComputer->put_Filter(varFilterList);
    VariantClear(&varFilterList);

    // build enumerator
    IEnumVARIANT *pEnumerator;
    hr = ADsBuildEnumerator(spMyComputer, &pEnumerator); ASH;
```

```
      // enumerate services
      ULONG cElementsFetched;
      VARIANT varResult;
      VariantInit(&varResult);
      do
      {
          hr = ADsEnumerateNext(pEnumerator, 1, &varResult, &cElementsFetched); ASH;

          // if hr == S_FALSE then no more elements to display
          if (hr == S_OK)
          {
              CComPtr<IADs> spService;
              ASSERT(varResult.vt == VT_DISPATCH);
              hr = varResult.pdispVal->QueryInterface(IID_IADs, (void**)&spService);
ASH;

              CComBSTR bstrName;
              CComBSTR bstrADsPath;

              hr = spService->get_Name(&bstrName); ASH;
              hr = spService->get_ADsPath(&bstrADsPath); ASH;

              int i;
              // put the data in the list box
              i = m_listboxServices.AddString(CString(L"Name:          ") +
CString(bstrName));
              i = m_listboxServices.AddString(CString(L"ADsPath        ") +
CString(bstrADsPath));
              i = m_listboxServices.AddString(L"");


          }
      }
      while (hr != S_FALSE);

      ADsFreeEnumerator(pEnumerator);


      // rest of the wizard-generated OnInitDialog() continues...

      return TRUE;  // return TRUE  unless you set the focus to a control
  }
```

The relative lengths of those two samples must say something about the usefulness of the two languages when it comes to simple user interface apps! The VB sample took me a few minutes to write and worked first time. The C++ one was nearer half an hour by the time I'd set up all the libraries, debugged it and so on. But C++ programmers can look forward to later in the book when we start writing things like ADSI providers – which would be virtually impossible to write in VB.

Anyway, on my computer, this program produces the following output:

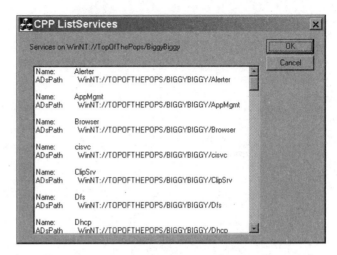

There's quite a lot of new information here. The C++ code shows up several new ADSI helper functions: `ADsBuildVarArrayStr()`, `ADsBuildEnumerator()`, `ADsEnumerateNext()` and `ADsFreeEnumerator()`. It's also worth noting that the existence of helper functions is a good indication that we're on to something that's easy to do in VB but takes a bit more code in C++. We can dispose of `ADsBuildVarArrayStr()` straight away. It's a useful utility that automates the tedium of building a `VARIANT` containing a `SAFEARRAY` of VARIANTs containing BSTRs – the preferred automation way of storing arrays of strings. It's covered in Appendix C. The other helper functions are a lot more interesting, and bring up the whole topic of **collections**. A collection can be thought of as a set of objects contained inside another object. They are relevant here because ADSI containers use collections for storing pointers to their children. We're going to look at this in some detail because collections come up a lot in ADSI. You *can* write code in either VB or C++ without understanding what's going on internally inside collections, but if you do understand them, you'll have a much better idea of why a lot of ADSI interfaces are designed the way they are, and C++ programmers may find debugging easier. So that's what we're going to cover now.

Inside Collections

First, lets have a refresher on what iterating through a collection looks like in VB.

If you have an array in VB (C++ people: remember that an array in VB actually means a C++ `SAFEARRAY`) the meaning of `For Each` is intuitively clear. It means something like *step through all the elements in this array*. It's a slightly easier alternative than a `For` loop, since it saves you having to know explicitly how many elements are in the array.

But what does it mean for a COM object? Remember that in the line

```
For Each service In MyComputer
```

`MyComputer` is an `IADsContainer` pointer, not an array.

Well, intuitively, the container object contains other objects – its children – and we know we need to iterate through them, so presumably `For Each` does just that. Of course though, that's the human way of thinking about it, and you can probably guess that's hiding a lot of COM functionality. So what's *really* going on?

For VB and scripting languages to be able to use the `For Each` loop on a COM interface, the interface must expose an automation property called _NewEnum, which is of type `IUnknown*`, but must be exposed by a COM component that also exposes the interface `IEnumVARIANT`. The `IEnumVARIANT` interface is a standard COM enumerator interface – it's got nothing particularly to do with ADSI (it's actually defined in `oaidl.idl`). Its purpose is to store a list of `VARIANT`s that contain some data of interest, and to supply these `VARIANT`s to the client. The methods it exposes allow the client to say 'Give me the next – say – 10 `VARIANT`s in the list.' 'Now give me the next 5' and so on. At each round, the client can decide how many new elements to retrieve – this means the client can decide what balance to draw between memory usage and network calls. If memory is at a premium, the client can ask for the `VARIANT`s one at a time, process each one and free the memory before asking for the next. On the other hand if network traffic must be minimized at all costs, then the client might ask for the `VARIANT`s in blocks of 10000. So that's the theory, how does it work in practice? Well, if we look at the definition of the `IEnumVARIANT` interface in the Interface Definition Language (IDL – that's the language used to define COM interfaces) it looks like this:

```
[
    object,
    uuid(00020404-0000-0000-C000-000000000046),
    pointer_default(unique)
]

interface IEnumVARIANT : IUnknown
{
    typedef [unique] IEnumVARIANT* LPENUMVARIANT;

    [local]
    HRESULT Next(
                [in] ULONG celt,
                [out, size_is(celt), length_is(*pCeltFetched)] VARIANT * rgVar,
                [out] ULONG * pCeltFetched
            );

    [call_as(Next)]
    HRESULT RemoteNext(
                [in] ULONG celt,
                [out, size_is(celt), length_is(*pCeltFetched)] VARIANT * rgVar,
                [out] ULONG * pCeltFetched
            );

    HRESULT Skip(
                [in] ULONG celt
            );

    HRESULT Reset(
            );

    HRESULT Clone(
                [out] IEnumVARIANT ** ppEnum
            );
}
```

The Next() method is the really useful one here: it's the one that returns the next few objects. Besides the array containing the VARIANTs, the method returns the number of objects actually returned (in pCeltFetched). This will be less than the number requested if the end of the list was reached, and the return value of the function also indicates this: S_FALSE if the method succeeded but did not return as many elements as requested, S_OK otherwise.

The other methods respectively skip a specified number of elements in the list, return to the start of the list and make a copy of the enumerator. I have to admit I personally have never used any of these other methods on any enumerator, and have never really seen that much purpose in them, but the methods are there in case you need them.

Notice that there is no method that returns the number of elements in the list. This is because Microsoft only supplies the interface definition. It's up to the individual COM server to decide how to implement it. Some servers may choose to generate the list of VARIANTs all at once when the enumerator is first instantiated, while others may generate the list incrementally as the data is requested by the client. If a server generates the list in this way, and the list is generated from data that is being updated as the client requests the elements, then the number of elements in the list may actually change between calls to Next(). Hence it's better for the server to simply indicate when all the elements have been fetched. You've probably guessed by now that in the case of IADsContainer, the list being returned is a list of the children. The definition of ADSI explicitly allows each provider to decide how to generate the list. So in this case, the size of the list could change if a provider generates it incrementally, and one client is adding or removing children to or from a container while another is enumerating the children of the same container.

So, getting back to the particular case of IADsContainer, we've established that VB's For Each loop internally hides functionality that requests a pointer to an IEnumVARIANT interface, then uses the Next() method of this interface to progressively obtain data about each child. What kind of data is stored in each VARIANT? The answer is that each VARIANT in the list holds an IUnknown pointer to the next child. VB internally does a QueryInterface() for IDispatch, then treats the child as a generalised COM object and uses the IDispatch methods to perform late-binding on the object and call the methods specified in the program. If you were going to do a lot of operations on each child, and were worried about the inefficiency involved in repeatedly performing late binding, you could in VB (but not VB script) replace

```
For Each Service In MyComputer
        List1.AddItem Service.Name
        List1.AddItem Service.ADsPath
```

with

```
Dim Service as IADsService
For Each child In MyComputer
    Set Service = child
        List1.AddItem Service.Name
        List1.AddItem Service.ADsPath
```

Well, I did say in the introduction to this book that VB programmers would learn a lot about what happens behind the scenes of their code...

By the way, in case anyone is wondering why I referred to `IEnumVARIANT` as a standard enumerator, it's because it isn't the only type of enumerator. In fact, it is possible to define an enumerator for any data type you want to. You simply define a new interface, giving it the name `IEnumMyDataType` and implement the corresponding `Next()`, `Skip()`, `Clone()`, and `Reset()` methods, replacing the `VARIANT` parameter in `Next()` and the `IEnumVARIANT` parameter in `Clone()` with the appropriate data type and interface type. (Strictly, you don't even *have* to use the same methods and method names, but it's a standard way of doing it, and other developers will have a harder time figuring out your code if you don't.)

Notice the leading underscore in the name of _NewEnum. That renders the property invisible to VB and scripting languages so that you can't refer to it explicitly. So code like:

```
Dim container As IADsContainer
    Set container = GetObject("StarRaiders:")
    Dim enumerator As Variant
    set enumerator = container._newenum
```

would fail. In fact this code won't even compile. But I stress that although you can't refer to enumerators explicitly, the VB compiler is able to internally generate code that recognizes _NewEnum and can internally grab and use the enumerator inside a `For Each` loop.

So after our little tour of the world of enumerators, let's have a look at what enumerating the children of a container would look like in C++ if we didn't have the ADSI helper functions available. This is the `ListServicesNoHelpers` sample, which lists services exactly as before – except that it avoids using ADSI helper functions to build `VARIANT`s or use the enumerator. It's still got `ADsGetObject()` there because getting into how `ADsGetObject()` works is complex and I don't want to go into that here. We'll cover the internal operation of `ADsGetObject()` in chapter 9, when we've got the necessary background about COM Monikers.

```cpp
BOOL CCPPListServicesNoHelpersDlg::OnInitDialog()
{
    CDialog::OnInitDialog();

#define ASH ASSERT(SUCCEEDED(hr));

    HRESULT hr = S_OK;
    CComPtr<IADsContainer> spMyComputer = NULL;
    hr = ADsGetObject(L"WinNT://TopOfThePops/BiggyBiggy", IID_IADsContainer,
        (void**)&spMyComputer); ASH;

    // create a VARIANT array to store the filter
    VARIANT varFilterList;
    VariantInit(&varFilterList);
    varFilterList.vt = VT_ARRAY | VT_VARIANT;
    SAFEARRAY *psa = SafeArrayCreateVector(VT_VARIANT, 0, 1);
    varFilterList.parray = psa;
    VARIANT *pSafeArrayData;
    SafeArrayAccessData(psa, (void**)&pSafeArrayData);
    pSafeArrayData[0].vt = VT_BSTR;
    pSafeArrayData[0].bstrVal = SysAllocString(L"Service");
    SafeArrayUnaccessData(psa);
```

```
    // set the filter
    hr = spMyComputer->put_Filter(varFilterList); ASH;
    VariantClear(&varFilterList);

    // get an enumerator
    CComQIPtr<IEnumVARIANT, &IID_IEnumVARIANT> spEnumerator;
    CComPtr<IUnknown> spEnumUnknown;
    hr = spMyComputer->get__NewEnum(&spEnumUnknown); ASH;
    spEnumerator = spEnumUnknown;

    ULONG cElementsFetched;
    VARIANT varResult;
    VariantInit(&varResult);
    do
    {
        hr = spEnumerator->Next(1, &varResult, &cElementsFetched); ASH;

        if (hr == S_OK)
        {
            CComPtr<IADs> spService;
            ASSERT(varResult.vt == VT_DISPATCH);
            hr = varResult.pdispVal->QueryInterface(IID_IADs, (void**)&spService);
ASH;

            CComBSTR bstrName;
            CComBSTR bstrADsPath;

            hr = spService->get_Name(&bstrName); ASH;
            hr = spService->get_ADsPath(&bstrADsPath); ASH;

            m_listboxServices.AddString(CString(L"Name:        ") +
CString(bstrName));
            m_listboxServices.AddString(CString(L"ADsPath      ") +
CString(bstrADsPath));
            m_listboxServices.AddString(L"");

        }
    }
    while (hr != S_FALSE);

// etc.
```

In terms of code size, the enumeration helper functions haven't actually saved us much. It's only
`ADsBuildVarArrayStr()` that we've had to replace by quite a large chunk of code – which is
explained in Appendix C. In one sense, using the helper functions has arguably cost us some clarity,
since by omitting them, I've been able to take advantage of ATL's `CComPtr` smart pointer class for
the enumerator – which I couldn't do in the previous sample because the destructor of `CComPtr<>`
would attempt to release an enumerator which had already been released by
`AdsFreeEnumerator()` – causing a crash.

Comparing the two code samples, we can now understand better the roles of the helper functions:
`AdsBuildEnumerator()` gets the enumerator object. `AdsEnumerateNext()` calls the `Next()`
method of the enumerator, while `AdsFreeEnumerator()` calls `Release()` on it. Internally you
could think of these functions as doing something like this:

For `AdsBuildEnumerator()`:

```
HRESULT WINAPI
ADsBuildEnumerator(
    IADsContainer *pADsContainer,
    IEnumVARIANT   **ppEnumVariant
    )
{
    HRESULT hRes;
    IUnknown *pEnumAsUnknown;

    hRes = pADsContainer->get__NewEnum(&pEnumAsUnknown);
    if (FAILED(hRes))
      return hRes;

    hRes = pEnumAsUnknown->QueryInterface(IID_IEnumVARIANT, (void**)ppEnumVariant);
    pEnumAsUnknown->Release();
    return hRes;
}
```

For `AdsFreeEnumerator()`:

```
HRESULT WINAPI
ADsFreeEnumerator(
    IEnumVARIANT *pEnumVariant
    )
{
    pEnumVariant->Release();
    return S_OK;
}
```

And for `AdsEnumerateNext()`:

```
HRESULT WINAPI
ADsEnumerateNext(
    IEnumVARIANT *pEnumVariant,
    ULONG        cElements,
    VARIANT FAR  *pvar,
    ULONG FAR    *pcElementsFetched
    )
{
    return pEnumVariant->Next(cElements, pvar, pcElementsFetched);
}
```

These snippets aren't necessarily the actual code used – the source code for the ADSI helpers isn't available – but they show what these helper functions are effectively doing.

By the way, that was one of the last samples you'll see in both languages. We've now covered all the major differences in how C++ and VB get COM objects. Unless there's something really important that I think you need to see in both languages, I'll assume you can follow both languages.

IADsContainer Properties

Before we leave the subject of container objects, for completeness, we'll give a full list of the properties and methods of `IADsContainer`.

Properties

Name	R/W?	Type	Description
_NewEnum	R/O	IUnknown*	Gets an enumerator object to allow access to children. You will not normally use this property directly.
Count	R/O	LONG	The number of children
Filter	R/W	ARRAY(BSTR)	Allows filtering of the type of children in the enumerator
Hints	R/W	ARRAY(BSTR)	Allows optimization of network traffic

Remember that `ARRAY(BSTR)` is my personal shorthand for `VARIANT` containing `SAFEARRAY` of `VARIANT`s containing `BSTR`. As far as VB is concerned, that's an array!

Of the properties we haven't yet covered, `Count` is pretty self-explanatory. `Hints` is used in much the same way as `Filter`. You set it to restrict the information returned from an attempt to enumerate the children of the object. But whereas `Filter` restricts the objects returned to be those of only a certain class, `Hints` restricts the properties that are automatically returned into the property cache for each object fetched. `Hints` is a `VARIANT` containing a `SAFEARRAY`, in which you place the names of the properties you want. If you don't specify anything, the provider completely fills the property cache on the objects it returns.

Methods

Name	Description
GetObject()	Gets a named child object
Create()	Creates a new object
Delete()	Deletes a child object
MoveHere()	Moves an object into this container
CopyHere()	Copies an object into this container

We're not going to look at any of the methods for the time being, as they are generally concerned with manipulating the child objects of the container – we'll cover that in the next chapter. `GetObject()` returns an `IDispatch` pointer on a single child object where you already know the name of the object – this method requires the name of the object (but not its full `ADsPath`) as a parameter. This contrasts with using the enumerator to obtain children when you don't know any of their names.

As a last exercise, you might like to try and modify the sample code by changing the `Filter`. Say you want to find out the names of the user accounts instead of the services...

```
<%@ Language = VBScript %>
<html>
<head>
<title> ADSI Service Enumerator Page </title>
</head>

<body>

<h1> ADSI Service Enumerator Page </h1>
(With filter changed to list users instead)

Windows 2000 Services on BiggyBiggy are:
<p>
<%

    Dim MyComputer
    Set MyComputer = GetObject("WinNT://BiggyBiggy")
    MyComputer.Filter = Array("user")

    For Each service In MyComputer
        Response.Write service.Name & "<br>"
        Response.Write service.ADsPath & "<p>"
    Next

    Set MyComputer = Nothing

%>
</body>
</html>
```

If I was concerned about readable programs I'd also change the variable name `service` to something more appropriate, but my main concern here is to show you how you can completely change the results of the enumeration by just changing one line of code. (I have however, added an extra line to the HTML so the web page gives some kind of correct indication of what it's listing)

This sample returns the following:

Summary

There's been a lot of theory in this chapter. But we have covered a lot of what we need to be able to use ADSI to browse around directories and modify the properties of the directory objects contained therein. Not only that but we've started to look at the background behind some of the ADSI interfaces – how and why they were designed the way they were.

We've taken a very quick look at all the interfaces available, written a couple of sample ADSI clients in VB, ASP and C++, and looked in detail at how the `IADs` and `IADsContainer` interfaces work – these are the two key ADSI interfaces that you will basically always be using in our ADSI travels.

If you think you've had enough theory for now then feel free to skip to Chapter 4 where we start applying it to seeing how we can use ADSI to look round your local network. If you do you will find a few references to material that is explained in chapter 3, but I think you'll still be able to understand what's going on – and you can always refer back.

Chapter 3 is going to continue the theory – we're going to finish our discussion from of schemas, begun in Chapter 1, and have a close look at some of the other ADSI interfaces.

We've also seen how short ADSI clients can be in terms of code size. Most of the VB samples here took me no more than 10 minutes to write and worked first time. (Admittedly the C++ samples took a bit longer and usually needed some debugging...). Once you've got the basic principles, ADSI is incredibly easy to use for carrying out simple queries on directories.

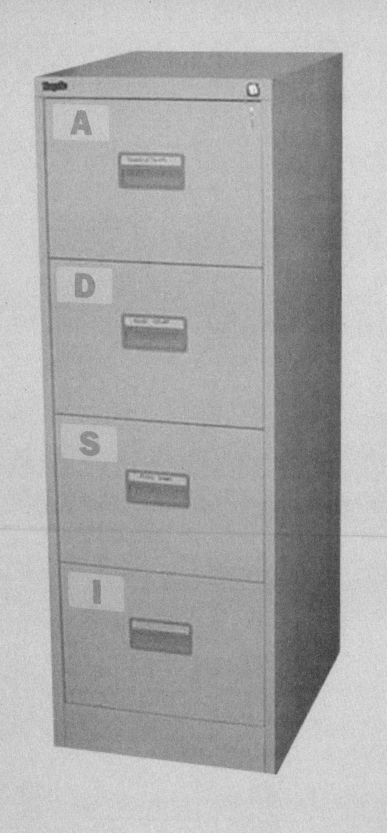

Further Inside ADSI

At the end of this chapter you will

- ❏ Have a couple of useful web pages to help you examine objects in directories

- ❏ Be familiar with the main ADSI interfaces and what sort of objects you can manipulate with them

- ❏ Be able to write simple ADSI clients in VBScript, VBA, VB and C++

- ❏ Have a good feeling for why some of the ADSI interfaces have been designed the way they have, and how they actually work.

- ❏ Have completely understood how directory schemas work (in other words, the stuff we missed out in the last chapter).

I'll be honest here. This is a pretty hard, theoretical chapter. The aim here is to show you not just how to code up ADSI clients but also what's really going on in ADSI under the hood. There's a lot of samples in here to show you how to do things, but there's also a lot of deep explanation of why things work the way they do. The aim of this chapter is really to help you understand how ADSI works. If you're not really interested in that – if all you want to do is to find out how to write a script to solve a particular problem, like listing all the user accounts on your machine, and you're quite happy to work from a sample that solves a similar problem, then you're probably better off skipping this chapter and heading for Chapter 4 or 5. In Chapter 4 I go over how to use Active Directory and the WinNT provider to access network resources, while Chapter 5 presents a large number of code samples for carrying out common administrative tasks. On the other hand, if you're keen to really understand what's happening inside your programs, then stick with this chapter, as you'll find out a lot here.

We're also going to finish the discussion of directory structure we started in Chapter 1, learning a bit more about how schemas work, and about uniquely identifying objects and classes.

In terms of structure, this chapter contains several different topics, which may appear to be unrelated, but which all add up to showing you how ADSI works. We start off by looking at how ADSI represents particular types of object using the **persistent object interfaces**. We move on from there to examine in more depth how the schema works and how you can get access to information about properties of directory objects – such as the data type used to store their values.

Different Types of Object: The Persistent Object Interfaces

We mentioned earlier that Microsoft have categorized the ADSI interfaces into groups for the purpose of documentation. The IADs and IADsContainer interfaces that we looked at in chapter 2 are considered Core interfaces for fairly obvious reasons: They are fundamental to the structure of any directory. We've also now briefly encountered the IADsUser interface, which is used to store information about a user account. Although we didn't use it in the ListServices samples, there is also an IADsService interface which exposes a couple of extra automation properties concerned with Windows 2000 (or Windows NT) Services. These are two of what are known as **Persistent Object interfaces**. Persistent Object interfaces form one of the largest interface categories, and are used to store information about particular kinds of objects that commonly occur in a directory of computer resources. As the interface hierarchy we looked at earlier shows, these interfaces are all derived from IADs, and in fact they don't add many more methods to the ones present in IADs. Their main characteristic is that they have a large number of extra automation properties that hold information typical of the object they represent. (although as we'll see in the next chapter, in may cases you can still access these properties using Get(), GetEx(), etc.)

And when I say a large number– these are the extra automation properties defined by IADsUser:

AccountDisabled	HomeDirectory	NamePrefix
AccountExpirationDate	HomePage	NameSuffix
BadLoginAddress	IsAccountLocked	OfficeLocations
BadLoginCount	Languages	OtherName
Department	LastFailedLogin	PasswordExpirationDate
Description	LastLogin	PasswordLastChanged
Division	LastLogoff	PasswordMinimumLength
EmailAddress	LastName	PasswordRequired
EmployeeID	LoginHours	Picture
FaxNumber	LoginScript	PostalAddresses
FirstName	LoginWorkstations	PostalCodes
FullName	Manager	Profile
GraceLoginsAllowed	MaxLogin	RequireUniquePassword
GraceLoginsRemaining	MaxStorage	

Most of these are strings with fairly obvious purposes. They include all the information needed to manage the user's account, and a number of extra fields to store other useful information, such as the telephone and fax numbers. A complete list of their meanings is given in Appendix C, which briefly explains all the properties and methods exposed by all the Windows-centric ADSI interfaces. IADsUser also defines a couple of methods to set the password, which isn't available as an automation property SetPassword() and ChangePassword(). We used SetPassword() in the last chapter.

Name	Description
SetPassword()	Sets the password. Requires administrator privileges.
ChangePassword()	Sets the password. Does not require administrative privileges, but the old password must be supplied as a parameter.

IADsService is a little more modest: it defines the following extra automation properties.

ComputerID	Model	Processor
Department	NetAddresses	ProcessorCount
Description	OperatingSystem	Role
Division	OperatingSystemVersion	Site
Location	Owner	StorageCapacity
MemorySize	PrimaryUser	

Most of this information relates not to the service itself, but to the computer the service is registered on: its location, which department it's in, it's role (whether it's a workstation, a server or a domain controller), and so on. If you want the full details of any of these properties, then it's all available in MSDN. The main point I want you to notice here is that this information is all of a *permanent* nature: it's the kind of stuff that doesn't change very often. What's missing from this list is things like whether the service is running at the moment. That's because the design of the ADSI interfaces distinguishes between persistent and temporary data, and defines separate interfaces for each. There is another interface, IADsServiceOperations, which handles events like starting, pausing or stopping a service and checking its current status. IADsServiceOperations is a member of a smaller group of ADSI interfaces known as **Dynamic Object Interfaces.**

So what other persistent object interfaces will you encounter? If you're looking at a directory of your computer network, you'll meet

- ❑ IADsComputer, which represents a computer.

- ❑ IADsDomain for your domain. Both WinNT and Active Directory are structured in such a way that all the computers in a domain, including the domain controllers, sit below the domain object in the directory hierarchy.

- ❑ IADsFileService, IADsFileShare, IADsPrintQueue and IADsPrintJob which represent the appropriate types of object on the domain.

We'll cover situations where you'd use these interfaces in more detail in Chapters 4 and 5.

Three persistent object interfaces that are sometimes useful in generic directories are `IADsLocality`, `IADsO` and `IADsOU`. Here the `O` stands for organization, and the `OU` stands for organizational unit. These interfaces originate in the traditional structure of some X500 directories and LDAP, in which it is expected that a directory might cover a number of locations, with a number of organizations in each one. Organizational unit might be the next item down the hierarchy, and may represent, say, a department in a company. You probably won't have much reason to use these interfaces since it's more useful to expose the properties they make available via the schema. They may come in useful if you're planning a large corporate directory. They expose automation properties to store such vital information as company addresses, phone numbers, and so on.

For completeness, I'll also mention here the other three persistent object interfaces `IADsGroup`, `IADsCollection` and `IADsMember`. These are useful for grouping together other ADSI objects that are located in different parts of the directory information tree (DIT) but which have certain features in common. These interfaces are quite useful across a wide range of circumstances and are covered later this chapter.

Enumerating All The Properties of an Object

So far much of the code we've demonstrated has involved displaying information where we already know the names of the properties we want. The only exception was the object viewer that we developed at the beginning of the last chapter, in which we didn't know the property names upfront, but we found out their names first by using the schema.

Another example of a browser that uses the schema to find out names of properties is the Active Directory browser. If we examine the right hand pane, we see a drop-down list box that allows you to select the property you want to examine or change.

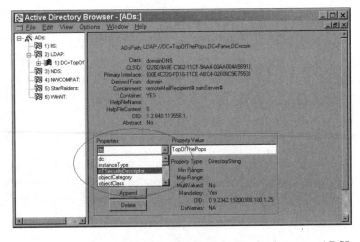

Now the Active Directory browser is a general-purpose ADSI browser, designed to look at any ADSI object – including ones implemented by providers that haven't even been written yet. Clearly, it can't have any hard-coded knowledge of the properties every object exposes to use to populate that list box. So it must be able to read properties dynamically at run time. How can it do this? Well the answer is in exactly the same way as we did in our object browser – by binding to the class schema object and finding out from it what the optional and mandatory properties are.

We're now going to go over this process in a bit more detail. This is because our object browser actually stopped halfway, and didn't get all the information you might usefully want. You see it retrieved the mandatory and optional properties and displayed them, but it didn't attempt to explicitly find out anything about the property types – their syntaxes. We just relied on the fact that when displaying values, VB and VBScript will automatically interpret data that's stored in a Variant and convert it into some text that can be displayed if at all possible, whether that data is a string or a numeric type. After we've done that we'll take a look at the property cache interfaces and see how they provide a way of letting us get to the data in an ADSI object's property cache directly, without going through the schema at all – and still without necessarily having to know the names of the properties.

We've actually already covered – from a non-programming point of view - all the material we need to use the schema to determine property syntax in Chapter 1, when we looked at schemas. We need to find the class schema object so we can get the list of mandatory and optional properties. Then, for each property we need to look up the syntax, and finally (assuming we want to display the property values), check the actual data type for that syntax.

To code this up we're going to need our old friend `IADsClass` as well as two new interfaces, `IADsProperty` and `IADsSyntax`. These three interfaces between them constitute all of interfaces categorized as Schema interfaces. In terms of new functionality, these interfaces all derive from `IADs` and expose a number of extra automation properties, in much the same way that `IADsUser` and `IADsService` do.

To recap the basic principles, here's a sample that displays the mandatory and optional properties of an object – for the demo I've picked the event log on my computer. For this example I've picked VB, and we'll only present the code in VB – no other languages.

```vb
Private Sub Form_Load()

    On Error Resume Next

    Dim oObject As IADs
    Set oObject = GetObject("WinNT://TOPOFTHEPOPS/BIGGYBIGGY/EventLog")

    List1.AddItem "Bound to object: " & oObject.ADsPath
    List1.AddItem oObject.Name & " is of class " & oObject.Class

    Dim oSchema As IADsClass
    Set oSchema = GetObject(oObject.Schema)

    List1.AddItem ""
    List1.AddItem "MANDATORY PROPERTIES FOR " & oObject.ADsPath
    Dim Values As Variant
    For Each property In oSchema.MandatoryProperties
        Values = oObject.GetEx(property)
        For Each Value In Values
            List1.AddItem property & ":       " & Value
        Next
    Next

    List1.AddItem ""
    List1.AddItem "OPTIONAL PROPERTIES FOR " & oObject.ADsPath
```

```
      For Each property In oSchema.OptionalProperties
          Values = oObject.GetEx(property)
          If (Error.Number = 0) Then
              For Each Value In Values
                  List1.AddItem property & ":      " & Value
              Next
          End If
      Next



      Set oObject = Nothing
      Set oSchema = Nothing

  End Sub
```

This sample produces the following output.

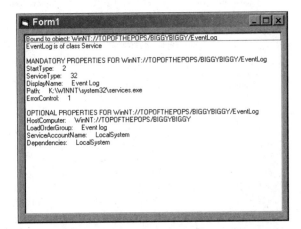

This code is fairly straightforward, and follows pretty much the same lines as our earlier VB object viewer from the last chapter. I've used the `IADs::Schema` automation property to locate the `ADsPath` of the schema, then grabbed the lists of mandatory and optional properties from the schema object, and used those lists to specify the names of the properties I request from the cache. Notice the error checking. In keeping with the spirit of only showing essential code, I've been very lax with the error checking – but I have specifically put a check round the bit of code that displays the optional properties.

```
      For Each property In oSchema.OptionalProperties
          Values = oObject.GetEx(property)
          If (Error.Number = 0) Then
              For Each Value In Values
                  List1.AddItem property & ":      " & Value
              Next
          End If
```

The reason for this that by definition an optional property might not be in the cache – it's optional! So there's quite a good chance that the `GetEx()` statement here will return an error due to the property not being present.

So far so good. Things get a bit more problematic if I decide to get more ambitious and print out not only the property values but also the syntax types, so I can see exactly what is being stored. Recall from Chapter 1 that this means that having got the class schema object, we need to find a property object that tells us what syntax this property is stored in, and finally a syntax object that tells us what automation data type is used to represent objects of this syntax. The syntax name is a string, while the automation data type is an integer. The property and syntax objects are contained in the same schema container as the class object.

To stop the code getting too long I've skipped the optional properties, and amended the previous sample to look for syntaxes as well. So the following code is the same as the previous sample, but displays only the mandatory properties, and also displays the syntaxes.

```
Option Explicit

Private Sub Form_Load()

    On Error Resume Next

    Dim oObject As IADs
    Set oObject = GetObject("WinNT://TOPOFTHEPOPS/BIGGYBIGGY/EventLog")

    List1.AddItem "Bound to object: " & oObject.ADsPath
    List1.AddItem oObject.Name & " is of class " & oObject.Class

    Dim oSchema As IADsClass
    Set oSchema = GetObject(oObject.Schema)

    Dim oSchemaContainer As IADsContainer
    Set oSchemaContainer = GetObject(oSchema.Parent)

    Dim oProperty As IADsProperty
    Dim oSyntax As IADsSyntax
    Dim strSchemaContainerPath As String
    strSchemaContainerPath = oSchemaContainer.ADsPath
    Dim strSyntax As String

    List1.AddItem ""
    List1.AddItem "MANDATORY PROPERTIES FOR " & oObject.ADsPath
    Dim varValues As Variant
    Dim strProperty As Variant
    For Each strProperty In oSchema.MandatoryProperties
        List1.AddItem ""

        'get property and syntax objects
        Set oProperty = oSchemaContainer.GetObject("Property", strProperty)
        strSyntax = oProperty.Syntax
        Set oSyntax = oSchemaContainer.GetObject("Syntax", strSyntax)

        varValues = oObject.GetEx(strProperty)
        List1.AddItem "property name: " & strProperty
        List1.AddItem "Syntax: " & strSyntax
        List1.AddItem "OleAutomation data type: " & oSyntax.OleAutoDataType
        Dim varValue As Variant
```

```
        For Each varValue In varValues
            List1.AddItem "          value: " & varValue
        Next

    Next

    Set oSchemaContainer = Nothing
    Set oProperty = Nothing
    Set oSyntax = Nothing
    Set oObject = Nothing
    Set oSchema = Nothing

End Sub
```

This code produces the following output

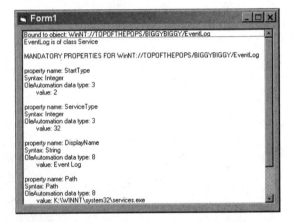

Let's step through the code. As before, getting the class object is easy because the `IADs::Schema` property gives us the `ADsPath` that we need to locate the class object. However, the `IADsClass::MandatoryProperties` automation property only tells us the name of each mandatory property, not the `ADsPath` of the corresponding property object. This means we can't instantiate the property object with a call to VB's `GetObject()` function since we don't know the `ADsPath` to pass to this function.

Our way out of this is to use the `IADsContainer::GetObject()` method. Note that despite having the same name, this `GetObject()` is an interface method, not the VB function. It performs a similar action - binds to an object, but it doesn't need the ADsPath. It specifically binds to a child of the container object against which it is called which means we only need to pass to it is the name of the object, as well as the class of the object which for some reason is required as well.

This means that the procedure we need to follow to get the property object from the schema object is:

1. Get the `ADsPath` of the parent of the schema object – the schema container

2. Get the name of the property object from the schema object

3. Use the schema container to bind to the object with this name.

Then we use the same procedure to obtain the syntax object – we can find the name of the syntax object from the `IADsProperty::Syntax` automation property.

The code looks like this.

```
Dim oSchemaContainer As IADsContainer
Set oSchemaContainer = GetObject(oSchema.Parent)

Dim oProperty As IADsProperty
Dim oSyntax As IADsSyntax
Dim strSchemaContainerPath As String
strSchemaContainerPath = oSchemaContainer.ADsPath
Dim strSyntax As String
```

```
List1.AddItem ""
List1.AddItem "MANDATORY PROPERTIES FOR " & oObject.ADsPath
Dim varValues As Variant
Dim strProperty As Variant
For Each strProperty In oSchema.MandatoryProperties
    List1.AddItem ""
```

```
    'get property and syntax objects
    Set oProperty = oSchemaContainer.GetObject("Property", strProperty)
    strSyntax = oProperty.Syntax
    Set oSyntax = oSchemaContainer.GetObject("Syntax", strSyntax)
```

This sounds a fairly complex process, but it leads to code that isn't too long – and fortunately displaying the contents of property and syntax objects isn't something that you're likely to need to do too often.

By the way, notice in the VB code that I haven't worried about what data type is contained in the properties as far as displaying it is concerned. That's once again because VB is quite comfortable figuring out for itself what type of data a VARIANT contains, and finding the most appropriate way to display it. C++ isn't as forgiving, and we'd need to explicitly convert the data to an appropriate type, usually a string, before displaying. The easiest way to do this is by calling the API function VariantChangeType() to convert the data into a VARIANT containing a BSTR, then display the bstrVal member.

We've achieved what we set out to do: we've got the names of all the schema-based properties and displayed them. That said, we've used a fairly clumsy method. Wouldn't it be nice if there were a couple of interfaces that let you iterate through all the properties without having to explicitly look up the schema? Well in fact there are – there are some interfaces which dispense with the schema and let you simply enumerate whatever happens to be in the ADSI COM component's property cache – and that's what we're going to look at next.

Looking Up Properties More Easily: The Property Cache Interfaces

We're going to look at using a couple of interfaces that let you get at all the properties in the property cache directly, even if you don't know what they are all called. The first one is `IADsPropertyList`. This acts like an enumerator, and has methods that let you iterate through the properties one at a time. The object you get back for each property is an interface pointer to a **Property Entry object**: That's a special object that exposes the interface `IADsPropertyEntry`. The `IADsPropertyEntry` interface gives you the name of the property, and a pointer to a **Property Value Object** – that is, an object that exposes the `IADsPropertyValue` and `IADsPropertyValue2` interfaces. Two interfaces because Microsoft decided to improve on the functionality of `IPropertyValue` – which in true COM style means creating a new interface while leaving the old one for backwards compatibility.

Don't confuse the property cache interfaces, `IADsPropertyList, IADsPropertyEntry` *and* `IADsPropertyValue`, *with the schema interface* `IADsProperty`. *They have completely different uses!*

Essentially, we're dealing with a couple of embedded structures here. Since before NT4 Service Pack 4, it wasn't possible to pass structures directly in dual interfaces, Microsoft have got round it by defining extra interfaces instead. It's a standard technique for passing structures around in automation.

The diagram should make it clearer what's going on.

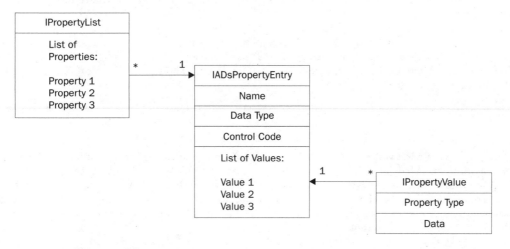

The property value consists of the data itself, along an integer that indicates the data type. This works in much the same way as a `VARIANT`, except that the set of data types available in `IPropertyValue` is different. Working upwards, we see from the diagram that the property entry contains the property name, along with the value, a control code and the data type. There's some duplication here, with the data type being stored twice. Presumably there's some 'historical' reason internal to Microsoft why it happened that way. (By the way, it isn't acceptable for different property values in the list to have different data types: they are all defined by the same property and syntax objects and so must have the same data type). The control code is one of the `ADS_PROPERTY_OPERATION_ENUM` constants that we encountered with the `IADs::PutEx()` method, and which indicate exactly how to perform changes on a multi-valued property.

That gives us enough information to have a stab at coding. Here's some VB code to enumerate all the properties for the same event viewer service. At this stage we're going to keep things simple by only displaying the property names, not their values. So we won't be using the `IADsPropertyValue` or `IADsPropertyValue2` interfaces. We're working on the basis of presenting a simple sample first so you can see roughly what's going on, then we'll go over the `IADsPropertyXXX` interfaces in more detail before we present our 'real' sample – a useful web page that uses the `IADsPropertyXXX` interfaces to list the properties of an object.

But first our VB sample.

```
Private Sub Form_Load()

    Dim oObject As IADs
    Set oObject = GetObject("WinNT://TOPOFTHEPOPS/BIGGYBIGGY/EventLog")
    oObject.GetInfo

    Dim oPropList As IADsPropertyList
    Set oPropList = oObject

    List1.AddItem "Bound to object at " & oObject.ADsPath
    List1.AddItem oObject.Name & " is of class " & oObject.Class
    List1.AddItem "No. of properties in the cache is " & oPropList.PropertyCount
    List1.AddItem ""
    List1.AddItem "Properties are: "

    Dim oPropEntry As IADsPropertyEntry
    Dim oPropValue As IADsPropertyValue2

    On Error Resume Next
    Set oPropEntry = oPropList.Next
    While (Err.Number = 0)
        List1.AddItem "    " & oPropEntry.Name
        Set oPropEntry = oPropList.Next
    Wend

    Set oObject = Nothing
    Set oPropList = Nothing
    Set oPropEntry = Nothing

End Sub
```

This produces the output:

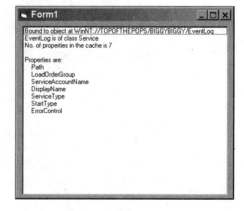

We should stress that this output lists the properties actually in the cache. Any optional properties for which no value is present will not be listed.

In this sample, we bind to the object as normal, but then additionally retrieve an IADsPropertyList interface on the object. We use the IADsPropertyList::PropertyCount property to show how many properties are in the cache.

```
Dim oObject As IADs
Set oObject = GetObject("WinNT://TOPOFTHEPOPS/BIGGYBIGGY/EventLog")
oObject.GetInfo

Dim oPropList As IADsPropertyList
Set oPropList = oObject

List1.AddItem "Bound to object at " & oObject.ADsPath
List1.AddItem oObject.Name & " is of class " & oObject.Class
List1.AddItem "No. of properties in the cache is " & oPropList.PropertyCount
```

Now we enumerate through the properties in the cache using the IADsPropertyList::Next() method. This method acts like an enumerator and we keep checking if there are more properties in the cache by checking the error object. (We'll explain why we've done it this way when we look at the property cache viewer web page). Each call to Next gives us another property entry object from which we can retrieve the name of the property

```
On Error Resume Next
Set oPropEntry = oPropList.Next
While (Err.Number = 0)
    List1.AddItem "    " & oPropEntry.Name
    Set oPropEntry = oPropList.Next
Wend
```

Notice the explicit call to IADs::GetInfo(). That is really needed here. These interfaces are called **Property Cache interfaces** for the very good reason that they only operate on the property cache. Unlike the IADs Get() and Set() methods, calling methods in IPropertyList will *not* cause an implicit call to GetInfo(). This can be easily demonstrated by the following code snippet:

```
Private Sub Form_Load()

    Dim oObject As IADs
    Set oObject = GetObject("WinNT://TOPOFTHEPOPS/BIGGYBIGGY/EventLog")

    Dim oPropList As IADsPropertyList
    Set oPropList = oObject

    List1.AddItem "Bound to object at " & oObject.ADsPath
    List1.AddItem oObject.Name & " is of class " & oObject.Class
    List1.AddItem ""
    List1.AddItem "No. of properties in the cache is " & oPropList.PropertyCount

    List1.AddItem "Properties are: "
```

```
        Dim oPropEntry As IADsPropertyEntry
        Dim oPropValue As IADsPropertyValue2

        On Error Resume Next
        Set oPropEntry = oPropList.Next
        While (Err.Number = 0)
            List1.AddItem "     " & oPropEntry.Name
            Set oPropEntry = oPropList.Next
        Wend

        oObject.GetInfo
        List1.AddItem ""
        List1.AddItem "After GetInfo, no. of properties in the cache is " &
    oPropList.PropertyCount

        Set oObject = Nothing
        Set oPropList = Nothing
        Set oPropEntry = Nothing

    End Sub
```

The way this sample works is similar to the previous sample but it attempts to display all the properties and does so *before* it calls `IADs::GetInfo()`. Having displayed the properties, it calls `GetInfo()` to check what effect this has on the property count.

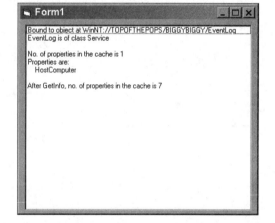

We've explained that `PropertyCount` is an `IPropertyList` automation property that tells you how many objects are in the cache. So you might expect that before you call `GetInfo()` the cache would be empty, so it would just return zero. Similarly, if you attempt to enumerate the properties before calling `GetInfo()` you'll just find an empty list. Our sample shows that this is almost true – in fact we had one property already in the cache before we called `GetInfo()` – the property, `HostComputer`. This reminds us that different providers do have their own idiosyncrasies. In this case, the `HostComputer` is a property that is really already known before we try to load the cache – since the WinNT provider clearly must know which server it had to contact before it bound to the event log object in the first place! Although the ADSI specifications don't require it, it's chosen to put this property in the cache automatically.

This all brings up an important point about the property cache interfaces:

> **The property cache interfaces only work on the properties that are actually already in the property cache. They will not cause other properties to be loaded from the directory. You'll also normally get an error if you attempt use `IADsPropertyList` to retrieve a property that's not in the cache.**

Now we've seen roughly how `IADsPropertyList` and `IADsPropertyEntry` work, we'll look at all the property cache interfaces in more detail.

Property Cache Interfaces - Summary

We're going to need to discuss the interfaces exposed by the property list objects in some detail, but first, here's a list of what the properties and methods actually are.

IADsPropertyList

This is the interface which is exposed by the ADSI directory object which lets you access those of its properties that are already loaded into the property cache.

Properties

Name	Read/Write?	Type	Description
PropertyCount	R/O	LONG	The number of properties in the cache

Methods

Name	Description
Next	Gets the next item in the list of properties
Skip	Skips a given number of items in the list
Reset	Returns to beginning of the list
Item	Gets a property. The property can be indexed by name or value.
GetPropertyItem	Gets a named property
PutPropertyItem	Sets a named property
ResetPropertyItem	Clears the value of a named property
PurgePropertyList	Clears all property values

There are several additional methods that may come in useful: it is possible to get a property by name if you know which one you want. Notice also that although in some ways this interface behaves as an enumerator, it can also treat the list as an array, accessing properties by index. If you use this feature, then bear in mind that there is no guarantee as to the order that properties will be stored in the list.

IADsPropertyEntry

This is the interface that is exposed by the property entry object which represents one property, and is returned by the `IADsPropertyList` methods.

Properties

Name	Read/Write?	Type	Description
Name	R/W	BSTR	The name of the property
ADsType	R/W	LONG	The data type
Control Code	R/W	LONG	Whether to append, update, clear or remove values from this property
Values	R/W	VAR array of VAR Dispatch	Interface pointers to the property value objects

The `Name` property of `IADsPropertyEntry` shouldn't be confused with the name property of `IADs`: Remember that `IADsPropertyEntry` isn't derived from `IADs`, and is never implemented by the same COM object. The `IADs::Name` property gives us the name of the ADSI object – in other words the name of the underlying directory object. On the other hand, the `IADsPropertyEntry::Name` property gives us the name of the *property*. This makes more sense if you remember that `IADsPropertyEntry` is exposed by special property entry objects, not by the objects that wrap the actual directory objects.

IADsPropertyValue2

This interface is used to access a single value of a property.

The difference between `IADsPropertyValue` and `IADsPropertyValue2` is that `IADsPropertyValue` exposes a set of properties to store different types of values, rather than having a method in which the data type is passed as a parameter. This means that the number of data types cannot be extended in `IADsPropertyValue`, whereas it can in the newer interface.

Also, `IADsPropertyValue` has an extra method, `Clear()` to clear the value of the property.

The interfaces have the same purpose and you can use whichever one you prefer.

`IADsPropertyValue2` does not expose any properties – only methods.

Methods

Name	Description
GetObjectProperty	Gets the actual data and data type
PutObjectProperty	Sets the actual data and data type

IADsPropertyValue

This interface is used to access a single value of a property. You can use either this interface or `IADsPropertyValue2`.

Methods

Name	Description
Clear	Clears the value

Properties

Apart from `ADsType`, which indicates which of the other properties are valid, the `IADsPropertyValue` properties correspond to the different data types that can be stored.

Name	Type	Access	Description
ADsType	LONG	R/W	Which other property contains valid data. Values are taken from the ADSTYPE enumeration
DNString	BSTR	R/W	Value as a distinguished name
CaseExactString	BSTR	R/W	Value as a case sensitive string
CaseIgnoreString	BSTR	R/W	Value as a case insensitive string
PrintableString	BSTR	R/W	Value as a string that contains only printable characters
NumericString	BSTR	R/W	Value as a string that contains a number
Boolean	LONG	R/W	Value as a Boolean
Integer	LONG	R/W	Value as an integer
OctetString	BSTR	R/W	Value as an octet string
SecurityDescriptor	IADsSecurity Descriptor*	R/W	Value as a security descriptor
LargeInteger	IDispatch*	R/W	Value as a large integer
UTCTime	DATE	R/W	Value as a time

By the way, if you're wondering, an Octet string is an ASCII string which may contain null characters. It is similar to a BSTR, the string type used by VB, except that it uses only one byte per character.

Comparing Property Cache Interfaces with IADs methods

OK – the code we've seen above gives us a flavour of how the property cache interfaces work. And I can't overemphasize that they do work completely differently from the IADs interfaces that retrieve data from the cache – even though in general terms they ultimately retrieve the same data. So let's go over the differences. (By the way, in this list, when I talk about the IADs methods, I mean `Get()`, `Put()`, `GetEx()` and `PutEx()` – not the methods that actually load the cache from the directory).

The **property cache interface** methods work directly with what's in the cache. They do not use the schema at all. On the other hand, IADs methods will normally check in the schema to find out about the properties that are being requested. As a result of this, the IADs methods will only work with properties that are actually defined in the schema. In some cases there is no schema object available – which means you have to work with `IADsPropertyList` instead.

`IADsPropertyList` allows you to enumerate through all the properties that happen to be in the cache, without necessarily knowing, their names. You can do this with the IADs methods – but only if you find out their names en route by looking them up in the schema. You can't tell from `IADsPropertyList` which are the mandatory and which are the optional properties.

If a property happens not to have been loaded into the cache, you will never be aware of its existence if you use `IADsPropertyList`. This is particularly significant for the LDAP provider, for which some attributes (the LDAP operational attributes) are not loaded into the cache with a call to `GetInfo()` – they have to be requested by name using `GetInfoEx()`. Because the property cache methods work without any direct knowledge of the schema, you have to be more explicit about what data type you want. They don't return the data using VARIANTs, but use the more refined `IADSPropertyValue` and `IADSPropertyValue2` interfaces. `IADsPropertyList` methods may work slightly faster since they don't need to access the schema but work off the cache directly.

From this list, you can see there's actually a lot of subtle differences between the IADs methods and the `IADsPropertyList` ones. However, in most cases you won't want to worry about it. Generally speaking, you will know what properties you want, or everything will be very clearly defined in the schema, and it'll be down to a matter of personal taste which interface you use. Personally I usually find IADs methods easier – especially if it's to get a particular property I already know the name of.

However, there are some instances in which it does matter. As I've hinted at a few times before, you will occasionally come across objects for which no schema object is available. This will never happen with the WinNT provider, but will occasionally happen with the LDAP provider – even if you only ever use LDAP 3 directories. There is a special object known as the **rootdse** (**root directory service entry**) which all LDAP version 3 directories have, which gives you important configuration information about the directory. We'll have a lot to say about this object in the next chapter – including the fact that it doesn't have a corresponding schema object.

> *The other time when you will have to work with the property cache interfaces is if you ever come across a legacy LDAP version 2 directory service. You'll be able to access such directories using the LDAP provider, but LDAP v2 does not require directories to expose a schema. Hence you will most likely find that none of the objects in LDAP v2 directories have corresponding class schema objects.*

Another factor that might sway you in favour of using `IADsPropertyList` with LDAP for the particular case of enumerating through all the properties is that objects in Active Directory generally have a very large number of optional properties, which are all defined in the schema. But only a few of them are likely to actually have any values in them. This means that using the schema to iterate through properties using the schema is going to be very inefficient and will return a huge number of blank properties, which will be skipped altogether by `IADsPropertyList`.

Broadly speaking, when you want to iterate through the properties, the message is that if you want to be absolutely certain you're retrieving all the properties defined in the schema, and you're not familiar with the implementation details of the provider you are accessing, then use the schema, not the property cache interfaces. On the other hand, if you want to get at properties not defined in the schema and you know what these properties are, the property cache interfaces may be a better bet.

ADSI Data Types

One of the differences you may have noticed between the property cache interfaces and the IADs interfaces is in the data types supported. IADs returns data types as `VARIANT`s, which means it'll assume property values are one of the standard automation data types. On the other hand, if you use the property cache interfaces, values are returned through the `IADSPropertyValue` interface, which defines its own set of data types – and these types are different from the automation types. There must be something funny going on here, since `IADs::Get()` and `IADsPropertyValue` are dealing with the same property values. Clearly, the same property value can't have two different data types!

In fact, there is a correspondence between the two types: Here's the list. This list isn't quite complete because I've removed the Netware-specific types from it.

ADSTYPE value	automation data type
ADSTYPE_DN_STRING	BSTR
ADSTYPE_CASE_EXACT_STRING	BSTR
ADSTYPE_CASE_IGNORE_STRING	BSTR
ADSTYPE_PRINTABLE_STRING	BSTR
ADSTYPE_NUMERIC_STRING	BSTR
ADSTYPE_BOOLEAN	LONG
ADSTYPE_INTEGER	LONG
ADSTYPE_OCTET_STRING	BSTR
ADSTYPE_UTC_TIME	DATE
ADSTYPE_LARGE_INTEGER	IDispatch
ADSTYPE_PROV_SPECIFIC	any
ADSTYPE_NT_SECURITY_DESCRIPTOR	IDispatch
ADSTYPE_INVALID	N/A

Let's explain what's going on here. The ADsType values are the actual data types that are recognised by ADSI. Each type has a very precise interpretation, which relates not just to the data type itself but to how it is used in operations. For example, when you're comparing two strings to see if they're the same, are you interested in case? Should 'say you'll be there' be regarded as the same value as 'SAY YOU'LL BE THERE' as a song title? Intuitively you'd say yes, so the appropriate data type here would be CASE_IGNORE_STRING.

However, once you've decided on the broad types you want to implement, you've also got to take the next stage of defining what variable type you're going to use to store the data. And since ADSI will be used with scripting clients, you haven't got much choice – you've got to use the automation data types. The only automation data type available for storing a string is the BSTR – it's the only string type that VB and VBScript understand. Which means that the ADSI data types CASE_IGNORE_STRING and CASE_EXACT_STRING have both got to be stored as a BSTR, even though ADSI regards them as different data types. The provider will deal with all this automatically.

And that's what the above table really is – a conversion table between ADSI data types and the automation data types used to actually store the values.

So how does this relate to the IADs methods and the property cache interface methods? Well, if you use the property cache, you're not using the schema. Which means that the interface methods have not got any information from the schema to help them interpret the data type. If you're using IADsValue to write a new value to the cache, you've got to make sure you specifically tell the object that implements IADsValue whether it's a CASE_EXACT_STRING or a CASE_IGNORE_STRING that you're giving it. On the other hand, if you're using IADs::Put(), you don't have to do it. Because IADs::Put() will look up in the schema to find out what type of data it's supposed to put in that property. So that's why IADs::Put() will accept a VARIANT for the value. You could even give it a VARIANT containing an integer, and IADs::Put() should be able to figure out that that particular property actually contains a CASE_IGNORE_STRING, and perform the appropriate conversion.

An ASP Property Cache Viewer

We've now covered all we need about the property cache interfaces. I mentioned at the beginning of the chapter that we would develop an object viewer that avoided using the schema. We need to do this for two reasons. Firstly, to really demonstrate how to use the property cache interfaces, and secondly because we are going to need it in the next chapter to examine the properties of the rootdse object in Active Directory – since this object doesn't have an associated schema object. I'm going to show you an ASP viewer, and then a C++ version, to make sure you are familiar with how to use these interfaces in either language.

Here's what the web page looks like. When you first start it up, you're not bound to any actual object so you get this:

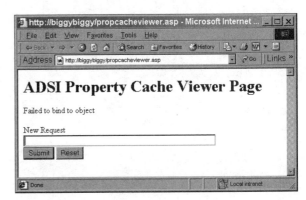

If you type in the ADsPath of the object you want to look at, the property cache viewer will bind to the object, call GetInfo on it to retrieve all the default properties, then use the property cache interface methods to examine the property cache. The results will look something like the screenshot below, which is using LDAP to look at the Active Directory domain object.

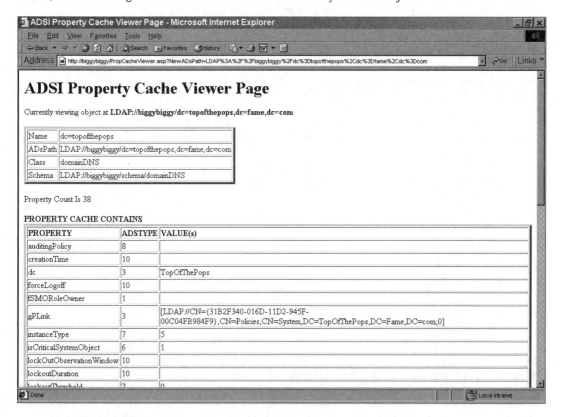

Let's have a look at the code that does this.

After the usual html headers, we attempt to bind to the requested object, and print out a failure message if we can't.

```
<%@ Language = VBScript %>
<html>
<head>
<title> ADSI Property Cache Viewer Page </title>
</head>

<body>

<h1> ADSI Property Cache Viewer Page </h1>

<%
' attempt to bind to the ADSI object and display message to say if succeeded
on error resume next
Dim ADsObject
```

```
    Set ADsObject = GetObject(Request.QueryString("NewADsPath"))
    if not (Err.number = 0) then
        Response.Write "Failed to bind to object <strong>" & NewADsPath & "</strong>"
    else
        Response.Write "Currently viewing object at <strong>" &
    Request.QueryString("NewADsPath")& "</strong><br>"
    end if
    response.write "<p>"
    %>


    Assuming we have successfully bound, we display the normal IADs automation
    properties

    <%
    ' display automation properties if we have bound to an object
    if (Err.number = 0) then
        Response.Write "<table border = 4>"
          Response.Write "<tr><td>Name </td><td>" & ADsObject.Name & "</td></tr>"
          Response.Write "<tr><td>ADsPath </td><td>    " & ADsObject.ADsPath &
    "</td></tr>"
          Response.Write "<tr><td>Class </td><td>    " & ADsObject.Class & "</td></tr>"
          Response.Write "<tr><td>Schema </td><td>    " & ADsObject.Schema &
    "</td></tr>"

        Response.Write "</table><p>"
```

This is where the `IADsPropertyList` interface comes in. After filling the property cache, we call `IADsPropertyList::PropertyCount` to find out how many values are in the cache, so we can write it out.

```
    ' fill the property cache and write out how many properties are in it
    ADsObject.GetInfo
    Response.Write "Property Count Is "
    Response.Write ADsObject.PropertyCount
```

And some fairly trivial code to set up the table we're going to display the properties in

```
    Response.Write "<p><strong> PROPERTY CACHE CONTAINS </strong>"
    Response.Write "<table border = 4>"
    Response.Write "<tr><td><strong>PROPERTY</strong></td>"
    Response.Write
    "<td><strong>ADSTYPE</strong></td><td><strong>VALUE(s)</strong></td></tr>"

    ' display the big table of all the properties
```

Here's the bit you might not expect. We're going to use the `IADsPropertyList::Next` method, which works like an enumerator. The first time you call it, it gets the first property in the list. Then each subsequent time you call it, it gets the next one. Seeing as we know how many properties are in the cache, it might seem sensible to use a `For Next` loop to retrieve them. But we're going to do some defensive programming here. You see, there are actually quite a few objects that implement `IADsPropertyList`, but which don't implement the `PropertyCount` property. Including that rootdse object which we're going to be very interested in in the next chapter. So we've got to code round the possibility that we actually don't know how many properties are there. The way I'm going to do that is by using a while loop which exits when a call to `IADsPropertyList::Next` returns an error – indicating that there are no more properties.

```
Err.Clear
Dim oPropEntry
Set oPropEntry = ADsObject.Next
While Err.Number = 0

    Response.Write "<tr><td>" & oPropEntry.Name
    Response.Write "</td><td>" & oPropEntry.ADsType & "</td><td>"
    Dim Values
```

We did it this way in the previous property cache sample, but without explanation.

Now we get to the logic of how we retrieve the values. `IADsPropertyList::Next` returns a property entry object, which implements `IADsPropertyEntry`. `IADsPropertyEntry` in turn exposes the automation property `Values`, which is a property value COM object – it exposes the interface `IADsPropertyValue`. (It also exposes the more up-to-date `IADsPropertyValue2`, but personally I find it easier to understand what's going on with `IADsPropertyValue`). `IADsPropertyValue` exposes lots of automation properties. The key one is `ADsType`, which tells you what the data type actually is. Depending on the value of this, we need to pick out the appropriate automation property that returns the data in the correct data type:

```
Values = oPropEntry.Values
Dim oValue
for each oValue in Values
    select case oValue.ADsType
    case 1
        Response.Write oValue.CaseDNString
    case 2
        Response.Write oValue.CaseExactString
    case 3
        Response.Write oValue.CaseIgnoreString
    case 4
        Response.Write oValue.PrintableString
    case 5
        Response.Write oValue.NumericString
    case 6
        Response.Write oValue.Boolean
    case 7
        Response.Write oValue.Integer
    end select
    response.write "<br>"
next
Response.Write "</td></tr>"
```

We've printed out the property value – so we can go ahead and get the next entry

```
' attempt to get the next entry - so the Error object is set to
' indicate whether we've succeeded
Err.Clear
set oPropEntry = ADsObject.Next
```

```
      Wend
  end if
  %>


  </table>
```

Finally we display the form that will allow the user to select the next item to be viewed.

```
<p>
<form action = "PropCacheViewer.asp" method = "get" id=form1 name=form1>
New Request<br>
<INPUT type="text" id=Request name=NewADsPath size = 60><br>
<INPUT type="submit" value="Submit" id=submit1 name=submit1>
<INPUT type="reset" value="Reset" id=reset1 name=reset1><br>
</form>

</body>
</html>
```

After all that, I bet you can see what I mean about IADs interfaces being easier to code up if you are able to avoid using the IADsPropertyList ones in your particular project.

C++ Property Cache Viewer

That would almost be all as far as the property cache interfaces are concerned, but since they do require some new techniques in programming, I ought to show you how it's done in C++. So here's the output from a similar C++ program, which basically does the same thing.

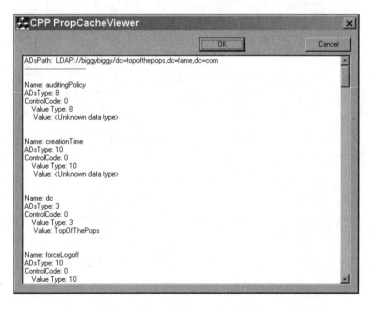

It's looking at the same object as our ASP page, though there are a couple of changes in how I've implemented it. Firstly, I've hard coded in the ADsPath of the object instead of letting the user input it. Allowing that kind of user interaction requires a fair bit more code in C++ and I don't want to get sidetracked too far into bits of code that aren't actually relevant to understanding ADSI.

I've also got the C++ code to display a bit more information. It gives us the control code automation property of IADsPropertyEntry. If I was actually setting data, I'd have to put a nonzero value in to indicate what kind of change needed to be made to the data – eg. updating or removing a value. Because I'm only retrieving values, I was curious to see what value got returned for the control code. (It turned out to be zero). I've also printed out the type as well as the value of each property. This lets us see what happened to some of the values that were blank in the ASP page. As it turns out it's because they are of property types that I hadn't allowed for in the code.

Anyway, on to the code. Firstly a useful utility function that we're going to need in it.

```
CString IntToString(int i)
{
    wchar_t pszText[30];
    _itow(i, pszText, 10);
    return CString(pszText);
}
```

CString does have a Format() member function that would do this, but it works less efficiently since it can take a wide variety of data types to convert to a CString, and so has to do some work to figure out what it has to do before it does the conversion.

Now the actual routine that displays the properties. First the normal stuff of binding to the object and getting and displaying its name and ADsPaths. On the way we also retrieve an IADsPropertyList pointer to it.

```
BOOL CCPPPropCacheViewerDlg::OnInitDialog()
{
    CDialog::OnInitDialog();


    CComPtr<IADs> spADs;
    CComQIPtr<IADsPropertyList, &IID_IADsPropertyList> spPropList;
    HRESULT hr;
    hr = ADsGetObject(L"LDAP://biggybiggy/dc=topofthepops,dc=fame,dc=com",
IID_IADs, (void**)&spADs);
    ASH;

    CComBSTR bstrName;
    hr = spADs->get_Name(&bstrName);
    m_listbox.AddString(CString(L"Name:   ") + bstrName);

    CComBSTR bstrADsPath;
    hr = spADs->get_ADsPath(&bstrADsPath);
    m_listbox.AddString(CString(L"ADsPath:   ") + bstrADsPath);

    m_listbox.AddString(L"--------------------------------");
    m_listbox.AddString(L"");

    spPropList = spADs;
```

Then, as in the ASP page, we fill the property cache and attempt to display the number of properties in it.

```
hr = spADs->GetInfo(); ASH;

long lPropCount;
hr = spPropList->get_PropertyCount(&lPropCount);
if (FAILED(hr))
{
    m_listbox.AddString(L"Failed to get Property Count");
}
```

On to the actual enumeration of properties. We do the same as in the ASP page – we keep calling `IADsPropertyList::Next()` until the return value indicates there are no more properties.

```
VARIANT varPropEntry;
VariantInit(&varPropEntry);
int i = 0;
hr = spPropList->Next(&varPropEntry); ASH;
while (hr == S_OK)
{
    i++;
```

In C++ we need to be more careful of data types. As far as ASP is concerned, `IADsPropertyList` returns a property entry object. But in reality it's a `VARIANT` that contains an `IDispatch` pointer to the object – we need to `QueryInterface()` this pointer for `IADsPropertyEntry`, then we can print out the automation properties in the list box.

```
CComQIPtr<IADsPropertyEntry, &IID_IADsPropertyEntry> spPropEntry;
spPropEntry = varPropEntry.pdispVal;
CComBSTR bstrPropName;
long lType;
long lControlCode;
hr = spPropEntry->get_Name(&bstrPropName); ASH;
m_listbox.AddString(CString(L"Name: ") + CString(bstrPropName));
hr = spPropEntry->get_ADsType(&lType); ASH;
m_listbox.AddString(CString(L"ADsType: ") + IntToString(lType));
hr = spPropEntry->get_ControlCode(&lControlCode); ASH;
m_listbox.AddString(CString(L"ControlCode: ") +
IntToString(lControlCode));
```

Now we can retrieve the values. This is also obtained as an automation property in `IADsPropertyEntry`. But whereas in ASP it was just a property value array, we need to code for the actual data type – a `VARIANT` containing a `SAFEARRAY`. The `SAFEARRAY` is an array of `VARIANT`s, each of which contains an `IDispatch` pointer to the property value object. We need to `QueryInterface` this interface pointer for `IADSPropertyValue`.

```
VARIANT varValues;
VariantInit(&varValues);
hr = spPropEntry->get_Values(&varValues); ASH;
if (varValues.vt == (VT_ARRAY | VT_VARIANT))
{
```

129

```
            SAFEARRAY *psa = varValues.parray;
            void *pvData;
            hr= SafeArrayAccessData(psa, &pvData); ASH;
            VARIANT *pvarData = (VARIANT*)pvData;
            for (unsigned j=0; j<psa->rgsabound->cElements ; j++, pvarData++)
            {
                ASSERT(pvarData->vt == VT_DISPATCH);
                CComQIPtr<IADsPropertyValue, &IID_IADsPropertyValue> spPropValue;
                spPropValue = pvarData->pdispVal;
```

Now we have the `IADSPropertyValue` pointer, we can display its contents. As for the ASP page, we need to check the `ADsType` automation property to find out what data type is held, then construct a big switch statement to retrieve the appropriate value.

```
                long iPropType;
                hr = spPropValue->get_ADsType(&iPropType); ASH;
                m_listbox.AddString(CString(L"    Value Type: ") +
IntToString(iPropType));
                CString csValue;
                CComBSTR bstrValue;
                long lValue;
                switch(iPropType)
                {
                case ADSTYPE_CASE_EXACT_STRING:
                    hr = spPropValue->get_CaseExactString(&bstrValue); ASH;
                    csValue = CString(bstrValue);
                    break;
                case ADSTYPE_CASE_IGNORE_STRING:
                    hr = spPropValue->get_CaseIgnoreString(&bstrValue); ASH;
                    csValue = CString(bstrValue);
                    break;
                case ADSTYPE_DN_STRING:
                    hr = spPropValue->get_DNString(&bstrValue); ASH;
                    csValue = CString(bstrValue);
                    break;
                case ADSTYPE_PRINTABLE_STRING:
                    hr = spPropValue->get_PrintableString(&bstrValue); ASH;
                    csValue = CString(bstrValue);
                    break;
                case ADSTYPE_NUMERIC_STRING:
                    hr = spPropValue->get_NumericString(&bstrValue); ASH;
                    csValue = CString(bstrValue);
                    break;
                case ADSTYPE_BOOLEAN:
                    hr = spPropValue->get_Boolean(&lValue); ASH;
                    csValue = IntToString(lValue);
                    break;
                case ADSTYPE_INTEGER:
                    hr = spPropValue->get_Integer(&lValue); ASH;
                    csValue = IntToString(lValue);
                    break;
                default:
                    csValue = L"<Unknown data type>";
                }
```

```
            m_listbox.AddString(CString(L"      Value: ") + csValue);
            m_listbox.AddString(L"");
        }
    }
```

We're done printing the values in that entry – all that's needed is to carry on enumerating through the property entry.

```
    VariantClear(&varPropEntry);


    hr = spPropList->Next(&varPropEntry);
    if (FAILED(hr))
    {
        m_listbox.AddString(L"No More Properties");
        break;
    }
    m_listbox.AddString(L"");

}
```

Enumerators and IADsPropertyList

If you're feeling particularly astute today, you might wonder about the `Next()`, `Skip()` and `Reset()` methods of `IADsPropertyList`. These look suspiciously like methods of the `IEnumXXX` interface – and they do do precisely the same job: Enumerating through a list. So given that I made such a fuss earlier on about how `IADsContainer` does things the proper COM way, letting you get a separate enumerator object which implements an `IEnumXXX` interface, you might wonder why `IADsPropertyList` doesn't do the same thing? Why have we suddenly departed from the accepted COM way of working?

The answer has got a lot to do with the fact that `IADsPropertyList` and `IADsContainer` will often be associated with the same object: After all, they are both interfaces exposed by the COM objects that represent the underlying directory objects. Any directory object that can contain other objects **and** can expose schema-defined properties will end up implementing `IADsContainer` and `IADsPropertyList`. And if `IADsPropertyList` did things the standard COM way, it would have to expose a property called _NewEnum, just like `IADsContainer`. Which would be potentially confusing.

If a client is using vtable binding, it would be confusing, though not disastrous, for both `IADsPropertyList` and `IADsContainer` to expose _NewEnum: Since vtable clients will be using a specific interface, it is theoretically possible for the ADSI provider to return a different enumerator according to which interface the method is getting called against. Unfortunately, we have to think about scripting clients too. And here's where the real problem comes in.

You see, scripting clients cannot call `QueryInterface()`, but must route every method call through the `IDispatch` interface. In the process of doing this, the information about which interface the method belongs to gets effectively hidden, so the client sees only the method name. If two interfaces both implement a property with the same name, the scripting client has no way of indicating which one it wants.

This is a deep topic which we'll cover in detail in Chapter 9, when we look at coding up providers. Related to it is a much bigger issue of how in general you can expose more than one interface simultaneously to scripting clients anyway. This is something that is difficult to do in COM, and ADSI Providers achieve this by a technique known as **DispID encoding**, which we'll discuss in detail in the next chapter. At any rate, we can see that it is important that two interfaces don't expose a property with the same name – which is why IADsProperty bypasses the usual COM technique for enumerators, and handles all the enumerating through the list itself.

More about Schemas: Inheriting Classes

We covered the basic mechanisms of schemas in Chapter 1. Since then we've used all the ADSI interfaces concerned with schemas: IADsClass, IADsProperty and IADsSyntax, and compared the advantages and disadvantages of using the schema compared to using the property cache directly to set and retrieve properties. We've come to the point where we really ought to take a closer look at what the ADSI schema interfaces can offer us. To start off with let's take a peek at the complete list of automation properties exposed by IADsClass:

IADsClass Properties

Name	R/W?	Type	Description
MandatoryProperties	R/W	Array(BSTR)	The mandatory properties
OptionalProperties	R/W	Array(BSTR)	The optional properties
Abstract	R/W	BOOL	Whether this class is abstract
Auxiliary	R/W	BOOL	Whether this class is auxiliary
Containment	R/W	Array(BSTR)	Classes that can be contained by instances of this class
DerivedFrom	R/W	Array(BSTR)	Structural and abstract classes this id derived from
AuxDerivedFrom	R/W	Array(BSTR)	Auxiliary classes this is derived from
PossibleSuperiors	R/W	Array(BSTR)	Classes that can contain instances of this class
NamingProperties	R/W	Array(BSTR)	Strings used to name this class
Container	R/W	BOOL	Whether instances of this class are containers
OID	R/W	BSTR	an object identifier that uniquely identifies this class
CLSID	R/W	BSTR	CLSID of the COM object that implements instances of this class

Name	R/W?	Type	Description
PrimaryInterface	R/O	BSTR	the IID of the main interface for instances of this class
HelpFileName	R/W	BSTR	name of a help file (optional)
HelpFileContext	R/W	BSTR	context of a help file (optional)

Most of these properties are marked as read/write, but some directories force the entire schema to be read-only. WinNT, and the Microsoft sample directory, for example, won't let you make any changes to the schema. Active Directory will, though our beloved StarRaiders provider has a read-only schema (I could have made it writeable, but then this book wouldn't have been published till next year. Coding up writeable schemas is *hard*.)

If you remember, we covered MandatoryProperties, OptionalProperties, and Containment in Chapter 1.

Container is a simple one – it just indicates whether objects of this class should expose IADsContainer so they can contain children. It's possible to use this property to test whether an given directory object is a container, though since if you want to do the test it probably means you want to use the IADsContainer interface if it's there, most of the time it's probably easier to just test for it by QueryInterface()ing for IADsContainer anyway.

PossibleSuperiors is concerned with structure rules. It lists the names of the classes of object that are allowed to contain classes of the object we are discussing.

What does that leave? Well, the HelpFileName and HelpFileContext are really provider specific and so we won't bother with them. NamingProperties is to do with the ADsPaths. It's intended for providers like Active Directory, which use LDAP format for ADsPaths , (LDAP://DC=TopOfThePops,DC=Fame,DC=com). NamingProperties lists the strings (like dc and cn) that are acceptable to refer to that object.

First we'll discuss the four properties concerned with inheriting classes: Abstract, Auxiliary, DerivedFrom and AuxDerivedFrom. In the section after, we'll move onto discussing OID, CLSID and PrimaryInterface

Abstract, Auxiliary, DerivedFrom and AuxDerivedFrom

So what do we mean by inheriting classes? Well pretty much the same thing as we mean by inheriting classes in C++ or in Java (sorry, fingers slipped, J++), or inheriting interfaces in COM. In C++, if class A derives from class B, then A gets all of B's member variables and functions as well as its own. It's the same with ADSI directory classes: if A inherits from B, then A gets all of B's mandatory and optional properties as well as its own ones.

If a class in C++ is abstract then it cannot be instantiated, but can be used as a base class for another class that can. ADSI has abstract classes too. If the Abstract property is set to true, then it is not possible to create any actual instances of directory objects of this class. But you can derive from abstract classes, so you can use them to specify a set of properties that form the basis of several other classes, but which aren't by themselves sufficient to make a class. Which classes a class is derived from is specified in the DerivedFrom property.

That leaves auxiliary classes. Originally in the X500 specification, the idea was that an object could be of a certain class, but could also specify auxiliary classes that contribute to it. This means that if a few objects of a certain class needed some additional data, those objects could be marked as having additional auxiliary classes, and so implement the required extra properties, without the memory overhead of all other instances of that structural class doing so.

That was the X500 way of doing it. In ADSI, the concept has mutated, because the list of auxiliary classes has become a property of the class object rather than the object instances themselves. You specify in the `IADsClass` property, `Auxiliary`, whether a class is auxiliary, and list in the `AuxDerivedFrom` property which auxiliary classes the class may be derived from. Auxiliary classes may only be derived from other auxiliary classes, never from structural classes, whereas abstract classes can be derived from instantiable classes. (A **structural class** is one that you can instantiate). Apart from that minor difference, the result of the ADSI way of doing things is that there really isn't a lot to choose between auxiliary and abstract classes. They are both classes that you can't instantiate, but which you can use to build other classes.

Having said that, there is a subtle difference in how you'd use them. Abstract classes should really be seen as base classes: use them for properties that form the basic building blocks for classes you really want to use. On the contrary, auxiliary classes should be where you'd group together some additional properties that you may want to use on some objects, but which aren't really fundamental to a class definition. To reinforce the point, it'd be pretty bad form to derive a structural class only from auxiliary classes – it really ought to be derived from at least one other structural or abstract class.

That probably all sounds a bit – well – abstract, so let's try and illustrate that with an example.

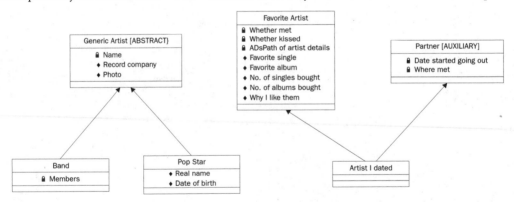

The diagram shows part of the schema from StarRaiders. There are two parts to the schema. *Solo Artist* and *Band* are the classes used to store useful information about bands, in the *Hit List* section of StarRaiders. However, they are both really types of an object, *Generic Artist*. So we've defined *Generic Artist* as an abstract class – there's no point in instantiating it, but *Band* and *Solo Artist* both derive from it.

On the other hand, in the *Fans* section of StarRaiders, Fans need to store information about their contacts with the stars. They'll usually do this through instances of the *Favourite Artist* class, which is good enough for most purposes. However, sometimes, they'll want to store stuff about Pop Stars that they used to go out with. This needs some extra information, such as when they started going out. This is an ideal case for an auxiliary class. Some extra information which isn't that useful on its own, but which can be added to other classes. So we define an auxiliary class, *Partner,* and derive the structural class Favourite Artist Partner from it and from Favourite Artist. This means that – reading from the schema in the figure *Favourite Artist Partner* has mandatory properties `Whether Met`, `Whether Kissed`, `ADsPath` of `Artist Details` and `Where Met`, and optional properties `Favourite Single`, `Favourite Album`, `No of Singles Bought`, `No of Albums` Bought and `Why I Like` Them.

Two other bits of terminology. If class A derives from B then B is a **superclass** of A, and A is a **subclass** of B.

Identifying Objects and Classes: OID

Both the `IADsClass` and `IADsProperty` interfaces expose a property called `OID`. This is a string that contains an **Object Identifier** (**OID**). Object identifiers are an attempt to uniquely identify directory object classes across all directories. However, whereas GUIDs uniquely identify objects by generating what can be thought of as random numbers, OIDs do so in a more structured way, which means that you can identify some information about the object from the OID.

The best way to understand how OIDs work is with an example. The Built-in Domain class in Active Directory is 1.2.840.113556.1.5.4. Where did this come from? Well, ISO are the root authority for OIDs. They issued the OID 1.2 to ANSI. This means that only ANSI are able to issue numbers starting with 1.2. ANSI decided that 1.2.840 would represent USA companies, and when Microsoft applied for an OID they got 1.2.840.113556. This number is now Microsoft's to control – Microsoft are free to add any other numbers on to the end of this to represent any classes or attributes which they decide to define. You'll always be able to tell from the initial 1.2.840.113556 that it's a Microsoft OID, and no one else should ever use an OID that starts the same way.

Microsoft chose to add 1 to this string for anything to do with Active Directory, then 5 for Active Directory classes. Finally 4 for the particular class, Builtin Domain, making 1.2.840.113556.1.5.4.

So what should you do if you want your own OID? Well obviously you can't just make one up – that would destroy the point of them being unique. You need to apply for one from a suitable authority. The easiest (and cheapest – it's free!) way is to apply for one under IANA's private enterprises branch. These are numbers that start with 1.3.6.1.4.1. You can apply for a number at the web site http://www.isi.edu/cgi-bin/iana/enterprise.pl. It takes about a week, and you get an extra number to stick on to the 1.3.6.1.4.1. Then it's up to you to decide on a suitable scheme for adding further numbers to define your individual classes and attributes. That's how I worked the OIDs for StarRaiders. I pestered my editors at Wrox to register for a private enterprises number. They got 1.3.6.1.4.1.4412. They then gave me the number 1 to add to that to indicate anything to do with this book, and I added another 1 to indicate StarRaiders. Then I just added numbers for the individual classes and properties, giving me things like...

❑ 1.3.6.1.4.1.4412.1.1.3.1 for the fans class

❑ 1.3.6.1.4.1.4412.1.1.2.6 for the Favourite Single property

❑ 1.3.6.1.4.1.4412.1.1.2.7 for the Favourite Album property

Any other ways of getting an OID? Well if you're a big company or a Government department you probably won't really want to get a little freebie number under the private enterprises namespace. You'll want a snappy, short, number, that says 'We're Important' rather than 1.3.6.1.4.1.whatever. In that case you can go to a higher authority like IANA or ANSI and get your number directly. You'll most likely have to pay for this – typically around $100. Appendix A lists a couple of URLs that are useful for finding out about OIDs and registering for one.

At the other end of the scale, Microsoft have figured out a way of generating OIDs automatically using GUIDs. This is for the really lazy. If you don't want to make the effort to register to get a number, the Windows 2000 Resource Kit includes a utility called oidgen, which will generate an OID for you by appending a randomly generated GUID to the OID 1.2.840.113556.1.4.7000. (an OID inside Microsoft's namespace). It's quick, but you have to put up with your objects having OIDs like 1.2.840.113556.1.5.7000.111.2014652.180672.30.178511.21908.1227698.1827075.1.
By the way, while we're on the subject, a couple of OID roots that you may come across:

- ❏ 0 - ITU-T assigned
- ❏ 1 - ISO assigned
- ❏ 2 - Joint ISO/ITU-T assigned
- ❏ 1.3.6.1 - the Internet OID
- ❏ 1.3.6.1.4.1 SMI network private enterprise codes – the ones I'm using for StarRaiders and part of the Internet OID namespace.

So comparing OIDs and GUIDs, you should be able to see that OIDs do take a little more work (unless you're using oidgen – which personally strikes me as cheating just a little...) but the result is something that is a bit more meaningful than GUIDs. On the other hand, because of the work involved, they are clearly generally only useful for identifying classes and properties – not instances of objects. Since you have to register manually for each OID root (unless you're using Microsoft's GUID-based fudge) it's clearly only possible to do that when you define the schema – not whenever an application automatically instantiates a class!

In ADSI, OIDs are stored with the class schema object. If the provider chooses to use GUIDs to identify classes as well, these are stored in the GUID property of the class instances. Incidentally, Active Directory also stores an unrelated guid, in the `objectGuid` property of each object, which does uniquely identify the instance as opposed to the class – and which we'll look at more in Chapter 5.

CLSID and Primary Interface Properties

Going back to the automation properties exposed by `IADsClass`, the final automation properties of the class object are the `CLSID` of the COM object that implements objects of this class, and the IID of the main interface. This will usually be `IADs`, though some classes will be represented by more specialist interfaces like `IADsUser`. Specifying an `IID` here doesn't imply that other interfaces are less valid - simply that this is the information that wraps the most functionality about the object. The CLSID will be provider-specific. Remember, the whole point of COM is that different objects can expose the same interfaces.

The CLSID and PrimaryInterface are optional – some providers will choose not to fill the values in, and clients shouldn't normally need to use them anyway. The PrimaryInterface may be useful if the client suspects a particular provider exposes a non-standard interface, but the CLSID shouldn't normally be used directly because connection to an ADSI object is via ADsGetObject() and the monikers, rather than by CoCreateInstance().

IADsClass exposes one extra method: Qualifiers() allows the client to gain any optional provider-specific information that an individual provider may choose to make available.

Properties and Syntaxes

We'll finish our discussion of ADSI schemas with a quick look at the property and syntax objects.

IADsProperty

Properties

IADsProperty exposes the following properties:

Name	R/W?	Type	Description
OID	R/W	BSTR	Another Object identifier
Syntax	R/W	BSTR	Name of the syntax object
MaxRange	R/W	LONG	Maximum value for the data value of this property
MinRange	R/W	LONG	Minimum value for the data value of this property
MultiValued	R/W	BOOL	Whether this property is multi-valued

As well as the same provider-specific Qualifiers() method exposed by IADsClass. These should be self-explanatory. The only proviso is that it is up to the provider how it interprets the minimum and maximum values for a particular data type. For an integer, they will normally be the limits of the allowed range. For a string, it would be more normal for them to indicate the length of the string, with 0 as the maximum value indicating that there is no limit to the length of the string.

Syntax

For a syntax object, you find only the one property

Name	R/W?	Type	Description
OleAutoDataType	R/W	LONG	The automation data type of this syntax

The same provisos apply to property and syntax objects as to class objects: although a property may be marked as R/W, some providers may choose to make the schema read only.

ADSI doesn't support all the automation data types. The ones that it does support are VT_BOOL, VT_BSTR, VT_CY (currency), VT_DATE, VT_EMPTY, VT_ERROR, VT_I2, VT_I4 (LONG), VT_R4, VT_R8 VT_I1 and VT_I1 | VT_ARRAY. This last data type needs special attention. If you want to store any binary data in a property, you should do so using the type VT_I1 | VT_ARRAY – in other words, a `VARIANT` containing a `SAFEARRAY` of UI1. This is the only time in which it is acceptable to put anything other than `VARIANT`s into a `SAFEARRAY` in ADSI If you do want to store binary data, remember to keep it small. Most directories are not optimized to handle large objects.

If an ADSI provider encounters an automation data type which isn't one of the ones recognized by ADSI, it will assume the type is VT_UI1 | VT_ARRAY instead.

In all this we haven't really said anything about schema extension. That's a big subject which Microsoft are really pushing for Active Directory. In terms of programming, however, there's not really anything to schema extension that we haven't already covered: Schema objects are normal directory objects, and you add new ones or change existing ones using the same ADSI method calls you'd use for any other object in the directory information tree. There are more restrictions, in the sense that even where a provider allows modifications to the schema in principle, there will probably be more security around the schema containers, and a well designed provider won't let you make changes to the schema that make the existing directory structure violate the schema. We'll cover schema extension in Active Directory in Chapter 4.

That was an awfully long bit of theory wasn't it? But you'll be pleased to know we have now completely covered ADSI schemas. Where the subject comes up again, it'll be in the context of particular providers. Anyway, I guess you're waiting to get back to some coding...

Grouping Directory Objects Together

There are times when the tree structure of directories just isn't enough. A good example is users and groups in Windows 2000. The idea of groups is that they are groups of users that have a similar status, and who should therefore share similar security privileges. For example, a college might want to group together students, and separately teachers – who'll have greater privileges.

So what's a sensible way of organising the users in a directory tree? Well, if all users are members of a group, then you might think of putting each user under his corresponding group in the directory tree. Unfortunately, there's two very good reasons why this won't work.

Modern directory structure emphasizes keeping similar types of object together. It's usually easier to administer a directory in which users are in all in a container called users and groups are in a container called *groups*. This is because in most organisations, people tend to move frequently between departments, so grouping them under any departments – or groups, since groups will often correspond to departments – will mean having to move them around the directory tree quite often.

Getting back to our college example above, in that example we forgot something very important: user accounts can belong to more than one group! Say in this college, a new Staff Student Consultative Committee gets formed. All the lucky committee members – both staff and students – need extra rights to be able to access various committee meetings. The easiest way to do this is to add the relevant people to a new group, imaginatively entitled Staff Student Consultative Committee Members – which will confer on them the appropriate access permissions.

The fact that users can be in more than one group has *really* knocked the nail in the head of the idea of containing users in corresponding group objects, since in any tree structure an object can only have one container. What we really need is a way that objects can refer to other objects elsewhere to indicate a group membership. That's where the IADsGroup interface comes in.

IADsGroup

We've got the concepts now – let's apply it to ADSI. We need two new interfaces, IADsGroup and IADsMembers. These are actually classed as Persistant Object interfaces because IADsGroup is intended partly to represent a special type of object. However, as persistant object interfaces go, these are unusual in that they primarily add extra functionality to the IADs interface rather than simply adding properties. The way they work is that IADsGroup contains an automation property called Members. This is a pointer to an IADsMembers interface, which contains methods to enumerate the members. IADsMembers contains the functionality required to be a VB Collection, so it works in the same way as IADsContainer: it exposes an automation property called _NewEnum, which lists the members as IDispatch pointers, as well as a property, Count, that says how many members there are.

To see how this works let's write a little VB application that lists the members of the administrators global group. Here it is.

```
Private Sub Form_Load()
' lists the members of a group. The group can be changed
' by changing the value of ADsPathGroup

Dim ADsPathGroup
ADsPathGroup = "WinNT://TopOfThePops/Administrators"

Dim oGroup
Set oGroup = GetObject(ADsPathGroup)
textGroup.Text = oGroup.Name

' list the members
For Each oUser In oGroup.Members
    listMembers.AddItem oUser.Name
    listMembers.AddItem "class: " & oUser.Class
    listMembers.AddItem ""
Next

Set oGroup = Nothing

End Sub
```

This produces this output.

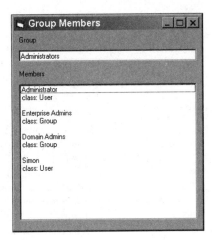

There's a couple of local groups in here as well as users. That's because we're listing the members of a *global* group and in Windows 2000 it is possible for local groups to be members of global groups. We'll cover this area more in the next chapter, but essentially a global group is a group for an entire domain whereas a local group is a group on one single machine.

By the way, although I've chosen to use the WinNT provider here, global groups are accessible through the LDAP provider using Active Directory as well. The code works equally well if I'd replace the line

```
ADsPathGroup = "WinNT://TopOfThePops/Administrators"
```

with

```
ADsPathGroup =
"LDAP://CN=Administrators,CN=Builtin,DC=TopOfThePops,DC=Fame,DC=com"
```

In terms of what's going on in the code, the interesting bit is this:

```
For Each oUser In oGroup.Members
    listMembers.AddItem oUser.Name
    listMembers.AddItem "class: " & oUser.Class
    listMembers.AddItem ""
Next
```

Notice the difference between this line and the way you would enumerate children of a container:

```
For Each oChild In oContainer
' etc.
```

The children of a container are obtained by enumerating the contents of the container. The members of a group are obtained by enumerating the contents of its members property – another COM object. We could equally well have written

```
' list the members
Dim oMembers
Set oMembers = oGroup.Members
For Each oUser In oMembers
' etc
```

This looks like we're doing exactly the same thing as enumerating children of a group – and to the VB client it is the same thing. But inside the provider it is different. A container object implements the _NewEnum property used to do the enumeration through the IADsContainer interface. A members object implements it through the IADsMembers interface. The difference would show up in C++ code when you do a QueryInterface, but is easy to hide in VB. (Though in VB you can show up the difference by explicitly declaring oMembers as IADsMembers).

The fact that IADsMembers and IADsContainer both allow enumeration means that it's not a good idea for a provider to ever implement any COM object which exposes both interfaces. This is precisely why the members object exists: by separating the enumeration of members into a separate COM object which is obtainable as a property on IADsGroup it means that there are no problems if a group object needs to act as a container to other objects as well, and hence also implement IADsContainer.

Summary of IADsGroup and IADsMembers

Let's do our quick round of listing the properties and methods exposed by IADsGroup and IADsMembers so we can see if there are any other goodies we can use...

First IADsMembers. There are no methods other than the property ones:

Name	R/W?	Type	Description
Count	R/O	LONG	The number of objects in the group that contains this members object
_NewEnum	R/O	IUnknown*	The actual enumerator
Filter	R/W	Array(BSTR)	Filter to restrict references returned by the enumerator

Not much unexpected here. The filter works the same way as the filter on a container, while the enumerator actually returns IUnknown pointers to the ADSI objects that wrap the members of the group.

Now for IADsGroup. First the property

Name	R/W?	Type	Description
Description	R/W	BSTR	A textual description of the group.

and the methods

Name	Description
Member()	Gets the IADsMembers interface of the members object
IsMember()	tests whether a given object is a member of the group
Add()	Adds an object to the group
Remove()	Removes an object from the group

Pretty essential methods when you think about it. There wouldn't be much point having groups if you couldn't add members to them!

IADsCollection

We've got one more interface to look at that can be useful for grouping data together: `IADsCollection`. `IADsCollection` works in pretty much the same way as `IADsGroup` and `IADsMembers`, except that one interface does all the work. It is intended for situations where you have a general collection of data, but you don't want to turn it into a formal group. The data might, for example, be temporary, such as a set of currently active print jobs.

We'll quickly list the property

Name	R/W?	Type	Description
_NewEnum	R/O	IUnknown*	The actual enumerator

and the methods

Name	Description
Add()	Adds an object to the collection
Remove()	Removes an object from the collection
GetObject()	Gets the ADSI object named, which is in the collection

No code samples yet, because `IADsCollection` isn't used in StarRaiders or in my WinNTdirectory, but be patient – something may come up later...

Moving, Copying, Creating and Deleting Directory Objects

One last topic – then we'll have covered all the automation ADSI functionality that we need for general use. Objects sometimes need to be moved. This is an area that often confuses developers new to ADSI because you'd intuitively expect that moving an object involves renaming it – but in reality, renaming an object is just another way of saying you're moving it. Besides, the automation property `Name` is a read-only property, so you can't move things that way. (If you ever have a free half hour you might enjoy scanning through the ADSI list server to see how many messages there are from puzzled developers who've just discovered that!) In fact, the way you move an ADSI object is to bind not to the object you want to move but to the container object immediately above it in the directory tree, and call an `IADsContainer` method called `MoveHere()`.

Moving Users Sample

Here's an example of renaming a domain user in Active Directory. One of my users, the delightful TeleTubby Laa-Laa, has after a whirlwind romance finally got married to Tinky Winky – so her user account needs to be renamed Mrs Tinky Winky.

I'm having a change of language here – I think we've had enough VB, ASP and C++ so for the moving/copying/deleting samples, so I'm going to use an Excel macro written in Visual Basic for Applications, VBA. You can find the code in the VBA `AddMoveDelete.xls` Excel worksheet in the samples at the Wrox website. Anyway, here's the code:

```
Sub RenameLaaLaa()
'
' Rename Laa-Laa Macro
' Macro recorded 30/05/1999 by Simon Robinson
'

    '
    Dim oUsers
    Set oUsers = GetObject("LDAP://cn=users, dc=TopOfThePops, dc=fame, dc = com")

    'bind to and print out info about LaaLaa
    Set oLaaLaa = oUsers.GetObject("User", "cn=LaaLaa")
    Range("A1").Select
    ActiveCell.FormulaR1C1 = "Name:"
    Range("B1").Select
    ActiveCell.FormulaR1C1 = oLaaLaa.Name
    Set oLaaLaa = Nothing

    oUsers.MoveHere "LDAP://cn=LaaLaa, cn=users, dc=TopOfThePops, dc=fame, dc =
com", "cn=Mrs TinkyWinky"

    Set oLaaLaa = oUsers.GetObject("User", "cn=Mrs TinkyWinky")
    Range("a3").Select
    ActiveCell.FormulaR1C1 = "Moving LaaLaa. Now..."
    Range("a4").Select
    ActiveCell.FormulaR1C1 = "Name:"
    Range("b4").Select
    ActiveCell.FormulaR1C1 = oLaaLaa.Name

    Set oUsers = Nothing

End Sub
```

And here's the output:

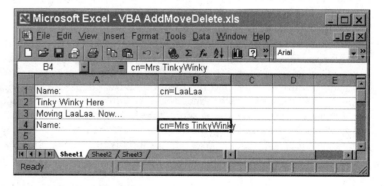

And just to prove it really did work – it's not just text written in an Excel worksheet, here's what my user manager for domains looked like afterwards.

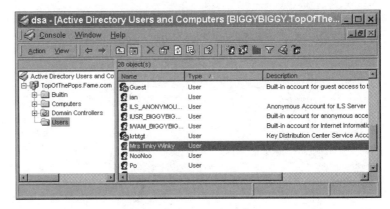

As far as the code itself is concerned, the interesting bit is the `MoveHere` line:

```
oUsers.MoveHere "LDAP://cn=LaaLaa, cn=users, dc=TopOfThePops, dc=fame, dc = com", "cn=Mrs TinkyWinky"
```

Notice that this line moves an object to be the child of the container it's called against. So whereas the full `ADsPath` is required for the old object name, only the relative DN is required for its new name.

This code by is also the first time I've used the `IADsContainer::GetObject()` method:

```
Set oLaaLaa = oUsers.GetObject("User", "cn=LaaLaa")
```

This is similar to the normal `GetObject()` function, but because it can only get a child of the container it's called against, only the relative DN, not the full `ADsPath` is required. The class name also has to be supplied because of some name ambiguity issues in the WinNT provider which we'll cover in Chapter 4.

About Moving and Copying

Renaming objects by calling a method in the container object might sound counter-intuitive at first, but it does make sense. For a start, if you rename an object, it's likely some data in the parent will have to change as a result. And good structured software architecture usually means having parent objects modifying their children rather than the other way around. More importantly, notice that in this sample code we actually specified the old `ADsPath` of the object to be moved, which would have given us the option of moving something in from another container if we'd wanted. There's a subtle point here: If the renaming was done by changing data in the object to be moved, then presumably, moving it to a different container would involve changing the `ADsPath`. If the client wanted to do this, it'd need to construct the new ADSI path for the object, which is potentially awkward because different providers have different formats for `ADsPaths`. You can see if you're not careful you're quickly going to end up knocking a little hole into the principle of unifying directory access. We've already got one hole in getting to property and syntax objects – we don't want another one! With the `MoveHere()` method that's not a problem. You use the *old* `ADsPath` of the object, which you will already know, and specify only the new *name*, not the new `ADsPath`. Directory unification survives another day, and everything is nicely object oriented. The only restriction on `MoveHere()` is that you can't move objects between providers. (Which makes sense as well, as there's no way to guarantee that different providers would understand the same object or class). And obviously, if you attempt an illegal move (like if there's already an object in the same container with the same name as your proposed new name) then `MoveHere()` will return an error code.

Copying works the same way as moving, with a method called `CopyHere()`. It has identical syntax and functionality to `MoveHere()`, except that it leaves the original object intact and makes a copy with the new name as a child of the container it's called on. Details are in MSDN.

Creating Objects

Creating objects is done using the `IADsContainer::Create()` method, which must be called on the parent of the new object to be created. Here's another Excel macro, which creates a new domain user, Noo-Noo (although I've chosen not to use the hyphen in the user name).

```
Sub CreateNooNoo()
'
' Create NooNoo Macro
' Macro recorded 30/05/1999 by Simon Robinson
'

' This Macro creates a user called NooNoo
' By the way, in case anyone is not yet sufficiently educated -
' NooNoo is the vacuum cleaner in Teletubbies. He's very sweet.
'
    Dim oUsers
    Set oUsers = GetObject("WinNT://TopOfThePops")


    Dim oNooNoo
    Set oNooNoo = oUsers.Create("User", "NooNoo")
    oNooNoo.Description = "First NooNoo created"
    oNooNoo.SetInfo



    Range("a1").Select
    ActiveCell.FormulaR1C1 = "Creating NooNoo"
    Range("a2").Select
    ActiveCell.FormulaR1C1 = "Name:"
    Range("b2").Select
    ActiveCell.FormulaR1C1 = oNooNoo.Name
    Range("a3").Select
    ActiveCell.FormulaR1C1 = "ADsPath:"
    Range("b3").Select
    ActiveCell.FormulaR1C1 = oNooNoo.ADsPath
    Range("a4").Select
    ActiveCell.FormulaR1C1 = "Schema:"
    Range("b4").Select
    ActiveCell.FormulaR1C1 = oNooNoo.Schema

    Set oUsers = Nothing
    Set oNooNoo = Nothing



End Sub
```

For a change this uses the WinNT provider instead of the LDAP provider. Both the WinNT provider and Active Directory are able to access domain users so it doesn't matter which one you use. But the ADsPaths are simpler in WinNT.

As before this code binds to the parent. In WinNT domain users are contained in the domain object directly rather than in a *Users* container object. We then call Create to actually create the user:

```
Dim oNooNoo
Set oNooNoo = oUsers.Create("User", "NooNoo")
```

Create returns an interface pointer to the new object. However, in order to complete the creation we need to call IADs::SetInfo on the new object.

```
oNooNoo.Description = "First NooNoo created"
oNooNoo.SetInfo
```

There's a good reason for this: IADsContainer::Create doesn't let us specify any information other than the name and class of the object. However some objects may have mandatory properties – and the directory service may not be able to actually create the object until these properties have been set. So ADSI doesn't actually create the object until SetInfo is called on it – thus giving us a chance to set any essential properties first. For WinNT users we're ok – the act of creating an object sets appropriate values for all appropriate properties implicitly, so we could just call SetInfo straight away. In the code above, I decided to set an optional property, the description, just for completeness, anyway.

Anyway, here's what that code produced. I got it to display out a couple of properties in the Excel worksheet to see what it came up with.

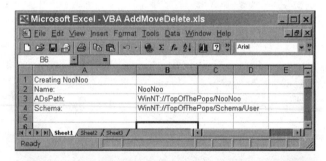

And in case you want the proof the code worked, here's the user manager for domains after I ran it:

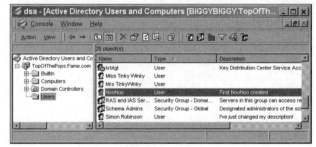

Deleting Objects

Deleting works pretty much the same way as creating objects – but using the `IADsContainer`
method `Delete()`. Since you're deleting the object, there's no interface pointer returned. The
deletion also works straight away – you don't have to call SetInfo to confirm the delete. (You couldn't
anyway – since you've just deleted the object, you don't have an interface pointer to call `SetInfo`
on!)

Here's the VBA script that removes our newly created NooNoo user.

```
Sub DeleteNooNoo()
'
' Create NooNoo Macro
' Macro recorded 30/05/1999 by Simon Robinson
'

' This Macro deletes the domain user NooNoo
'

    Dim oUsers
    Set oUsers = GetObject("WinNT://TopOfThePops")


    oUsers.Delete "User", "NooNoo"
    Range("a1").Select
    ActiveCell.FormulaR1C1 = "NooNoo deleted"

    Set oUsers = Nothing

End Sub
```

However, in the case of deleting users, there is an alternative way of doing it: from ADSI 2.5
onwards, a new interface has been provided that allows you to delete an object without going through
the parent. If an object implements the `IADsDeleteOps` interface, then you can just call
`IADsDeleteOps::Delete()` and tell the object to delete itself. Having an object implement this
interface is a bit like giving it a suicide pill that you can tell it to take any time. Personally, I don't like
it too much: It doesn't strike me as fitting in too well with my idea of structured programming and
parent-child relationships. For a start, doing it that way means that you've just deleted the directory
object, but paradoxically you must still be holding an interface pointer on the corresponding COM
object - which you need to `Release()`. You can see the potential for dodgy client code rising... On
the other hand, a good reason for using `IADsDeleteOps` with Active Directory is that the operation
is transacted. That is to say, it will either completely succeed or do nothing. There is no danger of
being left in a state where some of the children of the deleted node have been left but others have
been deleted due to some problem occurring partway through the operation – theLDAP provider's
implementation of `IADsDeleteOps::Delete()` will see to that.

On the other hand, one advantage of `IADsDeleteOps` is that if you call it on a container object, it'll
delete all the children automatically. For `IADsContainer::Delete`, you'll need to manually
recursively work up through all the children, progressively deleting them.

But anyway, the interface is there if you want it. The WinNT provider doesn't implement
`IADsDeleteOps`, but LDAP does. Details are in the MSDN documentation.

A Warning: Don't Confuse Directory Objects and Interface Pointers.

I've already mentioned the fact that if you do use `IADsDeleteOps::Delete`, you must be sure to release the interface pointer afterwards: something like (in C++)

```
IADsDeleteOps *pDeleteOps;
    hr = pObject->QueryInterface(IID_IADsDeleteOps, (void**) &pDeleteOps);

    if (SUCCEEDED(hr))
    {
        // delete the object and everything under it
        pOps->DeleteObject(0);
        pOps->Release();
        pObject->Release();
```

It's an easy point to miss because of the separation of the COM object and the directory object. The COM object acts to all intents and purposes to the client as if it *is* the directory object – but it is distinct, and deleting objects is one area in which this distinction crops up. If a directory object is released, then any interfaces pointers pointing to the corresponding COM object will still be around, and must be released separately (by calling `Release()` in C++ or using `Set object = Nothing` in VB). This applies whether the object was deleted using `IADsDeleteOps` or `IADsContainer::Delete()`.

ADSI doesn't specify what the results of calling any other methods on these dangling interface pointers are but the result's aren't likely to be what you want!

Fast Access to Directories for C++ Clients

The interfaces we've covered so far are comprehensive, but you've probably noticed several areas where some efficiency has been sacrificed for convenience or in order to make the interfaces automation compatible. Perhaps the most serious problem is that the need to call `SetInfo()` to update the directory means that all the properties are copied over the wire irrespective of how many were actually modified, although the effect of this can be reduced by careful use of `GetInfoEx()` so that unnecessary properties are not loaded into the cache in the first place.

It's also noticeable that there are a large number of interfaces. In some cases, for example `IPropertyValue` and `IPropertyEntry`, these interfaces are only really there in order to get round the difficulty of defining data structures for automation interfaces. Clients that use late binding aren't going to be affected at all by this, since `IDispatch` hides the existence of the different interfaces, but it can make coding a bit harder in C++.

The design of ADSI recognises that there will be a small number of clients for which performance is at a premium, and the `IDirectoryXXX` interfaces have been defined with these clients in mind. The main characteristics of these interfaces are

❑ A large amount of functionality is packed into relatively few interfaces and method calls

❑ Data does not need to be coerced into automation-compatible datatypes

❑ The property cache is by-passed: all data is read or written straight from the directory itself. As few or as many properties as are required may be passed in one method call

❑   This convenience does however come at a price. The main disadvantage is a loss of functionality.

The things you can do with `IDirectoryXXX` include

❑   Retrieving and modifying properties on directory objects.

❑   Looking up and modifying the schema and property definitions.

❑   Searching, with a wide range of options to limit the search.

The things you can't do include

❑   Browsing the children of any given object.

❑   Grouping objects together into groups or collections

❑   Accessing a small number of standard schema properties, including the class GUID and OID, if these are provided.

❑   Moving objects around the tree.

❑   Operations on computer network objects, such as setting a password or stopping a service.

❑   Accessing any of the automation properties, other than most of the ones exposed by `IADs` – unless these properties happen to be duplicated in the schema.

Some of these restrictions look quite fundamental – clearly your client doesn't have to be that sophisticated before it will find it needs functionality not available via the non-automation interfaces. The inability to browse children of an object at first sight looks crippling: how else can you navigate round a directory? But in fact it is possible to simulate the effect of browsing by carrying out a search with the appropriate parameters (restrict the search to children of a given object, and supply a search filter that will return every object – we'll see how to do this using the `IDirectorySearch` interface in Chapter 5). Having said that, this process isn't ideal: the search will only return the `ADsPaths` of the required objects, necessitating further over-the-wire calls to actually bind to the objects retrieved. (Whereas enumerating children from `IADsContainer` directly retrieves interface pointers to the objects).

A more serious restriction of using the `IDirectoryXXX` interfaces is the fact that not all providers implement them anyway. Of the system providers supplied by Microsoft, only the LDAP and NDS providers do implement them. This can cause a problem: Usually, if you want to use a particular interface, it tends to help matters if that interface is actually there. (At this point the astute reader might start to suspect that I'm not recommending use of the non-automation interfaces too highly. The astute reader would probably be correct. That's what being astute is all about isn't it?) These interfaces have their place, but personally I've usually found the disadvantages of using `IDirectoryObject` and `IDirectorySchemaMgmt` outweigh their usefulness. But we'll go over some examples, and I'll leave you to judge...

First we'll have a look at getting attributes. Notice I've changed terminology here. The non-automation interfaces refer to properties as attributes, so I'll follow suit. These examples all use the Active Directory because neither WinNT nor StarRaiders implement `IDirectoryXXX`.

Displaying Attributes using IDirectoryObject

This is the C++ `DisplayAttributes` sample, downloadable from the Wrox website. It hooks up to a particular object in LDAP – for convenience I've hard coded in the top of the Active Directory Information tree, and uses the `IDirectoryObject` interface to display all the object's properties. Here's what the output looks like:

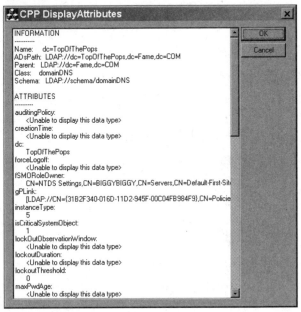

The top bit of the output, under **INFORMATION** is the stuff that corresponds to the standard `IADs` automation properties – with the exception of the Guid, which is not accessible through `IDirectoryObject`. It's labelled information that shows how that particular data is conceptually labelled in `IDirectoryObject` – it's retrieved through the method `IDirectoryObject::GetObjectInfo()`.

The second lot of data, under **ATTRIBUTES**, are the normal properties. These correspond to the properties which you would normally get through the `IADsPropertyList` interface.

And here's the code that does all that.

```
BOOL CCPPDisplayAttributesDlg::OnInitDialog()
{
    CDialog::OnInitDialog();


    CComPtr<IDirectoryObject> spADsObject;
    HRESULT hr;
    hr = ADsGetObject(L"LDAP://dc=TopOfThePops,dc=Fame,dc=COM",
IID_IDirectoryObject,
        (void**)&spADsObject); ASH;

    ADS_OBJECT_INFO *pObjInfo;
    hr = spADsObject->GetObjectInformation(&pObjInfo);

    m_listboxProperties.AddString(L"INFORMATION");
```

```
        m_listboxProperties.AddString(L"-----------");
        m_listboxProperties.AddString(CString(L"Name:      ") + CString(pObjInfo-
>pszRDN));
        m_listboxProperties.AddString(CString(L"ADsPath:   ") + CString(pObjInfo-
>pszObjectDN));
        m_listboxProperties.AddString(CString(L"Parent:    ") + CString(pObjInfo-
>pszParentDN));
        m_listboxProperties.AddString(CString(L"Class:     ") + CString(pObjInfo-
>pszClassName));
        m_listboxProperties.AddString(CString(L"Schema:    ") + CString(pObjInfo-
>pszSchemaDN));


        FreeADsMem(pObjInfo);

        ADS_ATTR_INFO    *pAttrInfo=NULL;
        DWORD    dwNFetched;


        m_listboxProperties.AddString(L"");
        m_listboxProperties.AddString(L"ATTRIBUTES");
        m_listboxProperties.AddString(L"----------");
        hr = spADsObject->GetObjectAttributes( NULL, 0xffffffff,  &pAttrInfo,
                                                      &dwNFetched); ASH;


        for(DWORD dw=0; dw < dwNFetched; dw++, pAttrInfo++ )
        {
            m_listboxProperties.AddString(CString(pAttrInfo->pszAttrName) + L":");
            for (DWORD i=0; i< pAttrInfo->dwNumValues ; i++)
            {
                ADSVALUE Value = (pAttrInfo->pADsValues)[i];
                switch (Value.dwType)
                {
                case ADSTYPE_DN_STRING:
                case ADSTYPE_CASE_EXACT_STRING:
                case ADSTYPE_CASE_IGNORE_STRING:
                case ADSTYPE_PRINTABLE_STRING:
                case ADSTYPE_NUMERIC_STRING:
                case ADSTYPE_OBJECT_CLASS:
                    m_listboxProperties.AddString(CString(L"      ") +
Value.DNString);
                    break;

                case ADSTYPE_BOOLEAN:
                case ADSTYPE_INTEGER:
                    // Boolean and integer are both DWORD in ADSI
                    wchar_t pszText[30];
                    _itow(Value.Boolean, pszText, 10);
                    m_listboxProperties.AddString(CString(L"      ") +
CString(pszText));
                    break;

                case ADSTYPE_PROV_SPECIFIC:
                    m_listboxProperties.AddString(L"      <Unable to display
prov-specific type>");
```

```
                              break;
                  default:
                         m_listboxProperties.AddString(L"         <Unable to display
this data type>");
                         break;
                  }


            }
       }
.
       FreeADsMem( pAttrInfo );

// rest of OnInitDialog()...
```

Not much there is there? Let's go through it.

Getting the Object Information

We start off by getting an interface pointer on the object – in this case `IDirectoryObject`, and as usual storing the result in a `CComPtr<>` smart pointer template. Then we call `IDirectoryObject::GetObjectInfo()` to get the standard `IADs` automation properties – in `IDirectoryObject` these are regarded as standard information. What's different here is that one method call retrieves everything, putting it all in an `ADS_OBJECT_INFO` structure specially designed for the purpose:

```
        ADS_OBJECT_INFO *pObjInfo;
        hr = spADsObject->GetObjectInformation(&pObjInfo);

// etc.
        m_listboxProperties.AddString(CString(L"Name:        ") + CString(pObjInfo-
>pszRDN));

// etc.
```

The `ADS_OBJECT_INFO` structure is defined as:

```
   typedef struct   _ads_object_info
       {
       LPWSTR pszRDN;
       LPWSTR pszObjectDN;
       LPWSTR pszParentDN;
       LPWSTR pszSchemaDN;
       LPWSTR pszClassName;
       } ADS_OBJECT_INFO;
```

As you can see, it includes all the `IADs` automation properties apart from Guid. By the way, one of the less fortunate aspects of ADSI that you'll have to get used to if you use these interfaces is the number of structure and enumeration definitions. And just to make things extra-challenging for you, there isn't any clear pattern in how these structures have been named.

As you'd expect for a COM [out] parameter, the memory to store the date is expected to be allocated by the server, and freed by the client. The interesting thing is how the memory has been freed:

```
        FreeADsMem(pObjInfo);
```

This uses an ADSI helper API function which we haven't encountered before – and it's important that this is the function used to free the `ADS_OBJECT_INFO` structure. The reason is that `IDirectoryObject` can potentially be implemented by any number of different providers. Since each provider has to allocate the memory, it is important that this is done in a consistent manner across all providers. The ADSI standard could have demanded that it be allocated using `CoTaskMemAlloc`, but instead the designers of ADSI opted to hide the details of memory allocation in two helper API functions, `AllocADsMem()` and `FreeADsMem()`. All providers must internally use `AllocADsMem()` to allocate memory for such structures as the `ADS_OBJECT_INFO` structures, then it's guaranteed that the client will always be able to free the memory using `FreeADsMem()`, supplying a pointer to the start of the memory to be freed.

Getting the Object Attributes

Next we use the `GetObjectAttributes()` method to obtain our chosen attributes. For this we require an array of `ADS_ATTR_INFO` structures. Each `ADS_ATTR_INFO` is used to store information about a single property, and contains an array of `ADSVALUE` structures. The role of `ADS_ATTR_INFO` is almost exactly equivalent to that of the interface `IPropertyEntry`, while `ADSVALUE` performs a similar role to `IPropertyValue`.

The `ADS_ATTR_INFO` structure is defined as

```
typedef struct  _ads_attr_info
    {
    LPWSTR pszAttrName;
    DWORD dwControlCode;
    ADSTYPE dwADsType;
    PADSVALUE pADsValues;
    DWORD dwNumValues;
    } ADS_ATTR_INFO;
```

While `ADSVALUE` is roughly defined as

```
typedef struct  _adsvalue
    {
    ADSTYPE dwType;
    union
        {
        ADS_DN_STRING DNString;
        ADS_CASE_EXACT_STRING CaseExactString;
        ADS_CASE_IGNORE_STRING CaseIgnoreString;
        ADS_PRINTABLE_STRING PrintableString;
        ADS_NUMERIC_STRING NumericString;
        ADS_BOOLEAN Boolean;
        ADS_INTEGER Integer;
        ADS_OCTET_STRING OctetString;
        ADS_UTC_TIME UTCTime;
        ADS_LARGE_INTEGER LargeInteger;
        ADS_OBJECT_CLASS ClassName;
        ADS_PROV_SPECIFIC ProviderSpecific;
// Extra NDS-specific types deleted out for clarity
        ADS_NT_SECURITY_DESCRIPTOR SecurityDescriptor;
        }  ;
    } ADSVALUE;
```

The resultant data structure is shown in the figure, which you might like to compare with our earlier data structure figure. The data types in the `ADSVALUE` structure are the same types as those supported by `IADSPropertyValue`. The structure and enumeration definitions can all be found in `IADs.h`.

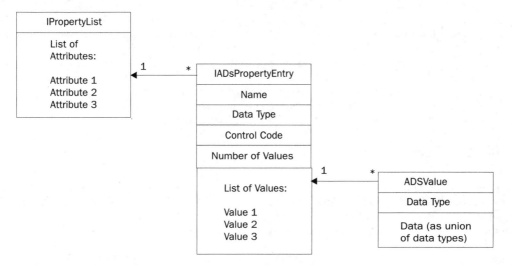

So that's the structures we're dealing with. How does that all work in the code? Well, first we use the method `IDirectoryObject::GetObjectAttributes()` to get all the data from the server.

```
    ADS_ATTR_INFO    *pAttrInfo=NULL;
    DWORD    dwNFetched;
// etc.
    hr = spADsObject->GetObjectAttributes( NULL, 0xffffffff,  &pAttrInfo,
&dwNFetched); ASH;
```

The last two parameters to `GetObjectAttributes()` are the [out] parameters that contain the data. `pAttrInfo` is the pointer to an array of `ADS_ATTR_INFO` structures – each one containing the value(s) of one attribute. `dwNFetched` tells us how many elements have been returned. As usual, the `ADS_ATTR_INFO` array will have been allocated internally in the provider using `AllocADsMem()` so we can use `FreeADsMem()` to free it up when we've finished.

The first two parameters to `GetObjectAttributes` are the ones that allow us to specify exactly what attributes we want. If we wanted to specify certain particular attributes, we'd send in an array of strings listing the names of them in the first parameter, and a DWORD saying how many strings are in the array in the second parameter. However in this case we just want all the attributes whatever they are, so we pass NULL in for the array, and –1 for the DWORD. What's that? –1 for a DWORD – as in an *unsigned* long? Don't you just love it when Microsoft do things like that! That explains the funny 0xffffffff in the parameter list above.

So getting the data was the easy part – now we've got to display it out:

```
for(DWORD dw=0; dw < dwNFetched; dw++, pAttrInfo++ )
{
        m_listboxProperties.AddString(CString(pAttrInfo->pszAttrName) + L":");
        for (DWORD i=0; i< pAttrInfo->dwNumValues ; i++)
        {
                ADSVALUE Value = (pAttrInfo->pADsValues)[i];
                switch (Value.dwType)
                {
                case ADSTYPE_DN_STRING:
                case ADSTYPE_CASE_EXACT_STRING:
                case ADSTYPE_CASE_IGNORE_STRING:
                case ADSTYPE_PRINTABLE_STRING:
                case ADSTYPE_NUMERIC_STRING:
                case ADSTYPE_OBJECT_CLASS:
                        m_listboxProperties.AddString(CString(L"        ") +
Value.DNString);
                        break;

                case ADSTYPE_BOOLEAN:
                case ADSTYPE_INTEGER:
// etc.
```

Now here's the bit that really puts me off using `IDirectoryObject`. Getting the name of the property is easy enough - that's just the `pszAttrName` field of the `ADS_ATTR_INFO` structure. Then the property values are stored as an array of `ADSVALUE` structures – the `ADS_ATTR_INFO` stores a pointer to the start of the array in the `pADsValues` member, and the number of values in the array in the `dwNumValues` field. But the `ADSVALUE` structure is a basically a *union*, with an extra member to say which member of the union contains valid data. Just like the `VARIANT` structure – except that here there are no nice API functions like `VARIANTChangeType()` to help us convert the contents of the `ADSVALUE` into a string to let us print it. We've got no choice but to make up a big switch statement to figure out what type of data is there and do the appropriate conversions.

I've cheated a bit in the above switch statement, partly by not bothering to deal with some of the less common data types, but covering them in a default statement instead:

```
        default:
                m_listboxProperties.AddString(L"        <Unable to display
this data type>");
```

and partly by grouping together data types which I happen to know are stored in different member variables, but the same variable type in the `ADSVALUE`.

Finally, when we've displayed out everything, we need to free the `ADS_ATTR_INFO` memory, using `FreeADsMem()` as normal:

```
FreeADsMem( pAttrInfo );
```

IDirectoryObject Summary

We haven't yet covered everything you can do with `IDirectoryObject`, but hopefully that's
enough to give you a flavour of how the interface works. It's also possible to:
Set attribute values, using the `SetObjectAttributes()` method. This works in pretty much the
same way as `GetObjectAttributes()` in terms of the data structures used, except that now
`ADS_ATTR_INFO` structure is an `[in]` parameter, and the client also has to fill in the fields to say
how the values should be changed (updated, added to, removed or cleared) – just as in
`IADs::PutEx()`.

Create and delete child objects using the `CreateDSObject()` and `DeleteDSObject()` methods.
`CreateDSObject` uses the same `ADS_ATTR_INFO` structure to specify the properties of the new
object.

I haven't provided samples for how to do these as it's well covered in MSDN. Besides I'm sure if
you're a C++ developer then you're intelligent enough to work it out. He he! Now having made that
provocative remark I'll just withdraw and let all you C++ and VB guys have a big fist-fight amongst
yourselves.

Methods

Anyway, to finish off before we move on to `IDirectorySchemaMgmt`, here's the summary of the
methods exposed by `IDirectoryObject`:

Name	Description
GetObjectInformation()	Gets basic information such as the name and `ADsPath`.
GetObjectAttributes()	Gets the values of the specified attributes
SetObjectAttributes()	Sets the values of the specified attributes
CreateDSObject()	Creates a new child of the current object
DeleteDSObject()	Deletes the specified child of the current object

ADSI Header Files and Libraries

We're going to take a short break from coding clients now, and take a quick look at what's going on
in the header files that C++ programmers include (VB guys can skip this section!). In fact the only
header file you really need to include is `ActiveDS.h` – and if you look in it you'll see why. All there
is in `ActiveDS.h` is:

```
//+-----------------------------------------------------------------------
//
//   Microsoft Windows
//   Copyright (C) Microsoft Corporation, 1996
//
//   File:        ads.h
//
```

```
//   Contents:    Master include file for Ole Ds
//
//   Notes:       All Ole Ds client applications must include this file. This
//                provides access to the primary Ole Ds interfaces, the error
//                codes, and function prototypes for the Ole Ds helper apis.
//
//--------------------------------------------------------------------------


//
// Interface definitions and well known GUIDS for Ole Ds
//

#include "iads.h"


//
// Helper function prototypes for Ole Ds
//

#include "adshlp.h"

//
// Error codes for Ole Ds - generated from ..\..\errmsg
//

#include "adserr.h"

//
// Globally accessible GUIDS
//

#include "adsiid.h"

//
// Status codes for ads objects
//

#include "adssts.h"


//
// Schema class names and other schema related definitions
//

#include "adsnms.h"


//
// Definitions in the OLE DB provider for ADSI
//

#include "adsdb.h"
```

So ActiveDS is a catch-all header that includes everything else. It is sufficiently well commented as to make it clear what is contained in the other headers. Don't be fooled by the references in the comments to 'Ole Ds', however, since the headers contain all the definitions needed for `IDirectoryXXX` as well as the automation interfaces. `IADs.h` by the way is the standard MIDL-generated header file.

If you're that bothered and some of your files only include certain ADSI features then you can speed up compilation times slightly by only #including the particular headers each of your source file uses. Personally I prefer to just `#include` ActiveDS in my precompiled header, `stdafx.h`, and then forget about it.

As for libraries – there's two you'll need. `ActiveDS.lib` and `ADsIID.lib`. `ADsIID.lib` contains the values of all the CLSIDs and IIDs you need for ADSI. If you forget to add it to the list of libraries your program links to then you'll get a link error like

```
ServiceDlg.obj : error LNK2001: unresolved external symbol _IID_IADs
```

for each ADSI GUID your client uses. Notice that the GUIDs are defined in the library file, in contrast to more recent ATL 3.0 practice for ATL-generated coclasses. New projects created with ATL 3.0 define the GUIDs in header files instead.

ActiveDS is needed to obtain the ADSI helper functions. Omitting that library will lead to complaints like

```
ServiceDlg.obj : error LNK2001: unresolved external symbol _ADsGetObject@12
```

Summary

We've taken in a lot this chapter. We've covered as much as we need of both the theory of directory structure and the ADSI interfaces needed to be able to navigate round and extract information from just about any ADSI directory. So far I've laid all the basics for you to be able to use ADSI. And I'd encourage you to play around. You've seen how short the VB samples are that I've shown you – most of them took me no more than 10 minutes to write and worked first time. (Admittedly the C++ samples took a bit longer and usually needed some debugging...). Once you've got the basic principles, ADSI is incredibly easy for carrying out simple queries on directories.

Now it's time to start applying that knowledge: to start seeing how ADSI can interact with the kinds of directories and related technologies you're likely to come into contact with. See you on the network...

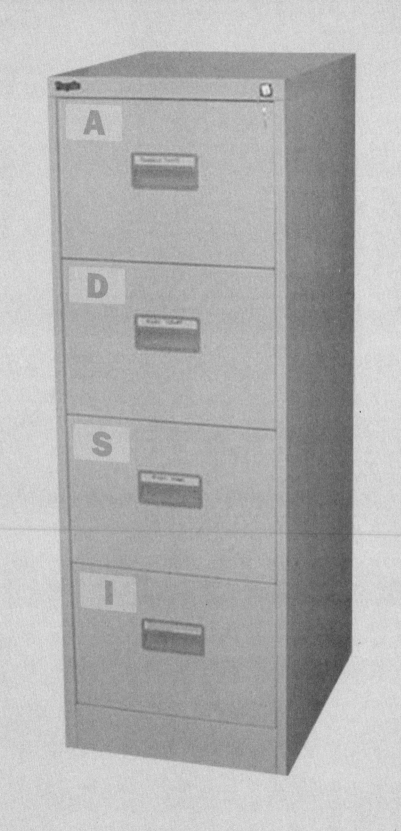

Section 2: Applying ADSI

Now we've got a firm grasp on ADSI itself (the Part 1 you never saw a lead in for!), have discussed its internals, and written ourselves a few handy tools to read and manipulate directories using ADSI, it's time to look at how to actually used our new found knowledge. Without a doubt this is the bulk of the book (after all, what's the point of a technology you can't do anything with?), so let's remind ourselves of the topics we're going to cover.

Chapter 4 - ADSI and Your Network

This chapter is about using ADSI to access resources on your network. You do this using either Active Directory or the ADSI WinNT provider. In this chapter, we'll look the overall directory structure that you'll see using either of these techniques – and the various peculiarities of these directories that you'll need to be aware of. We also study the basic background of how Windows domains work – with the emphasis on Windows 2000 and Active Directory.

Chapter 5 - Common Administrative Tasks with Active Directory and WinNT

Following on from Chapter 4 we'll apply our knowledge of ADSI to actually accessing network resources. We systematically go over the different objects on your network that you can access using ADSI: User, computer and group accounts, NT Services, File Shares and the File Service, and Print Queues and Print Jobs. For each one we run through common tasks you'll want to do with that type of object and show how to carry out those tasks using ADSI. We also provide the necessary background of how the objects themselves work.

Chapter 6 - ADSI and BackOffice: Exchange Server and IIS

We continue our application-centric approach by looking at two directories which are commonly accessed using ADSI: the Exchange Server Directory and the IIS Metabase. I don't assume you know anything about these BackOffice components, but briefly get you up to speed on what they can do, then show you how you can conveniently manage their respective directories using ADSI. We also briefly mention the other large Microsoft directory you can manage using ADSI: the Site Server Membership Directory.

Chapter 7 - Searching.

Searching in ADSI is a topic all its own, and not just because ADSI interfaces implement searching in a different way to almost all the rest of the ADSI functionality. Also, the way you'd do searching from C++ is completely different from the way you'd do it in VB and scripting languages. In C++ we'll use the ADSI interface `IDirectorySearch`. This interface is not directly available to VB and scripting languages, which instead use the ADO provider for ADSI. This chapter goes through both techniques, as well as showing how to use Microsoft's `adsvw.exe` browser tool to search from a user interface (as opposed to programmatically). ADSI's way of doing searches also owes a fair bit to its LDAP heritage – which means where necessary we'll go over some of the LDAP background, such as the workings of LDAP search filters.

Chapter 8 - Security

In this chapter we look at how an ADSI client can authenticate itself to a provider, and also how ADSI providers implement security – and the ADSI security interfaces that allow you to set and view who is allowed to do what to directory objects. This leads us naturally on to how Windows 2000 (and NT) implement security using Access control lists and Access control entries. In order to gain the necessary background, this means going into the basics of NT security. We finish with a look at the Kerberos security protocol used by Windows 2000.

Chapter 9 - ADSI Providers.

Up to now we've learned how to code up ADSI clients that use the services of providers that Microsoft and ISVs have written for us. This chapter covers the flip side of the coin: ADSI providers. We learn how to write ADSI providers using ATL by writing one: the StarRaiders provider, which allows access to a directory of Pop Stars, and which we use in some of the samples throughout this book.

To some extent, writing an ADSI provider with ATL is just writing a COM server with ATL – and I assume in this chapter you can already do that. The emphasis here is on picking out the aspects of coding ADSI providers which require more advanced knowledge of either COM/ATL or of the ADSI specifications So we'll cover areas such as Monikers, dispid-encoding, writing enumerators, and some of the subtleties of type libraries.

Theoretically, this is probably one of the hardest chapters – writing providers does require more in-depth knowledge of COM than writing clients – but by the end of the chapter you should have a pretty good grasp of how to write your own ADSI providers.

Chapter 10 - LDAP

This chapter dives behind the scenes. ADSI owes a lot of its design to its LDAP inheritance, and LDAP in turn owes a lot to its original X500 inheritance. Here we look in a bit more depth at the theory of LDAP, and at the how to use the LDAP C API. We also develop a sample project that you can use to browse Active Directory or other LDAP directories directly using the Microsoft LDAP API.

Chapter 11 - Advanced ADSI Topics.

At this point we've covered most of the ADSI topics, and we're going to wrap up our examination of ADSI with a lightening tour of the more advanced topics. We explore how you can use a provider to reverse engineer the calls a client makes, and so find out what some of Microsoft's clients expect providers to be able to do. We'll briefly discuss using connections carefully to improve performance of ADSI clients. But the bulk of the chapter is devoted to the subject of ADSI extensions – a topic that requires more advanced COM knowledge (of aggregation) than other areas of ADSI. Extensions are a powerful technique that allow you to add to the functionality of the providers available on your system, and we'll develop an extension that shows how to do this.

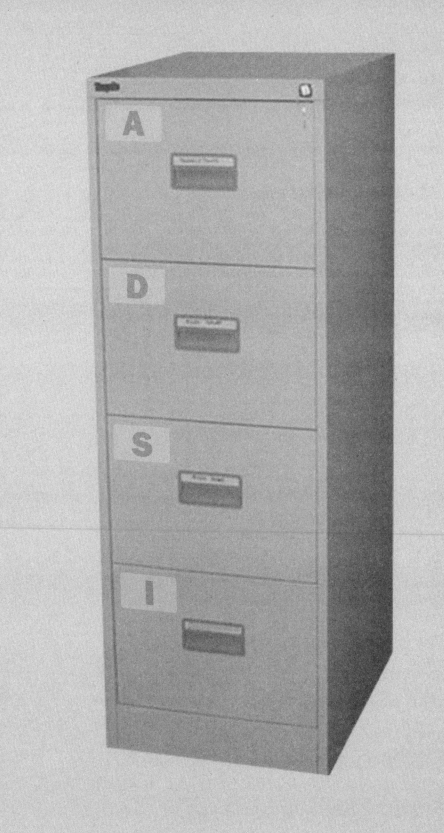

4

Your Computer Network and ADSI

This is the first of a couple of very applied chapters, in which you'll learn how to use ADSI to perform useful tasks on your network, on your web site or on other objects accessible through the various providers.

At the end of this chapter you should understand:

- ❑ Domains in Windows 2000
- ❑ Networks and the domain naming system
- ❑ The directory structure of Active Directory
- ❑ How Active Directory distinguished names work.
- ❑ The directory structure exposed by the WinNT provider

We're going to look at how you can use ADSI to access and manipulate your local network and domains. With the arrival of Windows 2000 this, to a large extent, means using Active Directory, so we're going to have to learn a lot about the structure of Active Directory on the way. ADSI has interfaces specially developed to control Windows 2000 (Windows NT) Services, file shares, print queues and print jobs, and we'll learn how to use those over the next couple of chapters. But we can't make full use of the ADSI interfaces unless we fully understand how the objects they are intended to access work, so we'll look at the underlying W2K objects themselves as well.

Before Windows 2000 was around, the only ADSI provider you could use to get to your local domain was the WinNT provider. Now that Windows 2000 and Active Directory are here, the LDAP provider, used to access Active Directory, can perform quite a few of the same tasks. The overlap isn't total – there are things you can do with the WinNT provider which you can't do with Active Directory, and other things you can do with the LDAP provider which you can't do with WinNT. Even where you can use either provider (for example, to manage global groups and users, and computer accounts), the apparent directory structure exposed by the two providers looks very different

The approach I'm going to take in this chapter is to browse through both WinNT and Active Directory – to get a feel for what the different directory trees look like and what you can do with the two providers. Then, in Chapter 4 I'll go through how to carry out some of the common administrative tasks that use these providers – like browsing through computers and users, and managing file shares and services – and show how you can do these tasks using ADSI with whichever provider is relevant. In general, you'll find that WinNT is much more restrictive in terms of its schema and the kinds of objects it can store. It is also essentially restricted to objects and tasks that were available in NT4, but it makes up for that by being a lot simpler to use. `ADsPaths` in particular tend to be easier in WinNT.

Of course, in order to do all this, we're going to have to learn a fair bit about Active Directory. Now seriously, Active Directory is a big, BIG, subject. I wouldn't be surprised if I walked into a bookshop in 6 months time and found whole books completely devoted to Active Directory (Now there's an idea for my next one. Wonder if anyone'll notice if I just cut and paste this chapter to put in a new book. I could even change a couple of the words somewhere...). We're only going to touch on some of the things you can do with Active Directory in this chapter – but I'd like to think I'll leave you familiar enough with the basics to be able to use ADSI to explore what Active Directory has to offer further.

Of course, exploring Active Directory is going to lead us into all sorts of concepts, like domains and groups etc, which are usually the province of your systems administrators. Ideally, your company's administrators handle all the management of your network, leaving you to concentrate on writing your apps. Hell – for months after I started my last job I had no idea what the domain structure round my own computer was. I didn't even understand what most of the networking options I had to set when I installed NT were for – I just copied down the settings from the scrappy bit of paper I had in my drawer. At that time I didn't need to understand any of that in order to write decent applications in NT4. But I don't want to risk losing you on those sorts of areas. So we're going to start off by going over the basics of domains and networking. From scratch. Let's go!

The Domain Concept in Windows

You can't get very far in Windows 2000 (or NT4) before you encounter **domains**. Even when you install Windows 2000, you'll get asked whether you want to join a domain or a workgroup. And when you log on, if you're using any company network, the chances are you authenticate yourself to a domain rather than just to the local machine.

We're not going to bother with workgroups in this book. They are, basically, a largely obsolete means of allowing computers to share resources as equal partners. If you have more than 2 or 3 machines in your company, they are a pain to administer. And besides, you can't actually do anything with them using ADSI. So we'll just concentrate on domains here.

> **The basic concept of a domain is pretty simple. It's best thought of as a security boundary.**

Instead of authenticating yourself to a single computer and using files and resources on that computer, you authenticate yourself to a group of computers known as a domain. Whenever you want to access any resources, your access permissions and rights are checked in the context of the domain instead of (and in a few cases as well as) the local computer. That means you can access any printers, fax machines or whatever that are connected to any machine in your domain and are registered with the domain – assuming you've been granted sufficient access permissions.

In Windows 2000, the domain is virtually synonymous with Active Directory. Active Directory is the directory of all information relevant to the domain – which computers are members of it, which users have accounts in the domain, what software has been installed in the domain, and what hardware is available.

Don't confuse Windows domains with Internet domains. They are not the same thing! An Internet domain isn't a security boundary – it's more of a convenient name with which to refer to the computers and web site of an organization. In this book, unless I say otherwise, I'm always talking about Windows domains.

Of course, any directory has to be stored somewhere. In the case of Active Directory, the computer(s) that store the directory are known as **domain controllers**. You can nominate any number of computers to be domain controllers for the same domain. Then, each will store a copy of the same directory. Active Directory has various sophisticated but efficient algorithms to ensure that if any updates are made to one copy of the directory, the changes will rapidly be replicated to other machines. There will be short period during which different copies of the directory will be out of sync, but Active Directory is designed to tolerate this and it's not going to cause any problems on your network. That said you do need to bear in mind when writing your applications that this short delay (typically a few minutes) may be present.

The really significant thing about Active Directory is, of course, that it meets open standards in how it is accessed. In particular, it is LDAP 3 compliant, which is why we can use the ADSI LDAP provider to manipulate it. This is in contrast to the situation in NT4, in which the database behind the domain was in a proprietary format, and was only accessible to a limited extent via Windows API functions. In the case of NT4, the domain database was also stored on one single machine – the primary domain controller. Other machines - backup domain controllers – could also store copies, but any modifications had to be sent through the primary domain controller.

Before we go on to see how domains work in practice, I'm going to run through the basic background material on some of the other characteristics of Windows 2000 domains.

Domain Trees and Forests

For small organizations, a single domain is all very well. But if you're a really huge company, with tens of thousands of employees in different departments and sites, you probably don't want one domain that big. In fact, you'll probably have a lot of different departments which need access to different resources. Your US sales department in Hawaii probably wouldn't have a lot of use for access to the laserjet printer in your research offices in Cannes. I mean – if you want a quick printout of that document you've just knocked together over lunch, it's easier if you don't have to make a 12 hour flight to pick up the bit of paper from the printer tray!

So your company is going to have different domains. The question then arises of how these domains are to be related. Well, we've been using tree-like directories for long enough now to realize (hopefully) that tree structures are quite a good model for organization – it makes sense to arrange your domains that way. Then, people who need access to resources across a lot of the company can go in a domain near the top of the tree, and people who only need to get at resources in one little office in a single department can go in a domain near the bottom of the tree, that contains resources and users in that office. Get the idea? That's how you get a domain tree. But there's a bit more to it than that. Take a look at the following diagram:

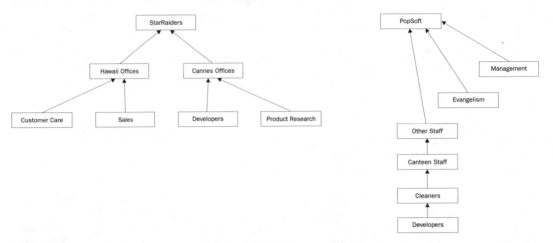

This figure shows a possible domain structure for the Windows 2000 domains on our network, following the recent merger of the highly successful multinational company, StarRaiders Inc., and the rather old-fashioned, hierarchical company, PopSoft.

The thing to notice is that there are two trees here – to use the correct terminology, we've actually got a **domain forest**. Why would we do that? Well, although we've merged, there are two pretty different organizations here, so there's no real need to have a single Windows 2000 domain that encompasses everything.

On the other hand, remember that Active Directory isn't just the thing that controls our W2K domains. It's a directory as well, which means you can store other things in it.

Suppose I added some more information concerning employees to the directory in the StarRaiders part of the domain, for which I needed to extend the directory schema. If I wanted to do the same thing in the PopSoft part of the domain, I'd need to make the same schema extensions. So it'd be nice – even though they are really different W2K domain trees – to be able to have them share a common schema. That's what a forest is.

> A domain forest is a set of independent domain trees which share schema and configuration data.

Trust Relationships

From what we've seen of domain trees and forests, it's clear that W2K domains can be built into quite a sophisticated hierarchy. It's not going to be long before we hit the problem of people in one domain needing to use resources somewhere in another, related domain. That's where trust relationships come in.

A domain – let's call it A because I'm in an imaginative mood today – can be set up to trust another domain, B?. This means that once domain B has authenticated a user, A will also accept that user as valid and authenticated.

> *The trust is one way. If A trusts B, B won't necessarily trust A. You'll still separately set B up to trust A. The correct terminology is that the trust relationship isn't **reflexive**. On the other hand, it is **transitive**. That means that if A trusts B and B trusts C, then A will automatically trust C. A is saying 'well since I trust you, I'll take it that if you trust anyone else, that's good enough for me'.*

It's important to remember that, due to the potential security risks, trust relationships don't apply to administrators.

W2K Domains and DNS Names

I mentioned earlier that you mustn't confuse W2K domains with Internet domains – in principle, they're completely unrelated. I'm going to backtrack on that a bit now. As far as naming your domains is concerned, Active Directory does allow you to select names that correspond to Internet DNS names.

How does this work? Well, say StarRaiders had got its own Internet web site, and had registered the domain name `StarRaiders.com`. (DNS names by the way aren't case-sensitive, but you might want to selectively put capitals in the names as a conventional way of writing your name to make it clearer). So that means anyone who wants to look at your web site will use the name `StarRaiders.com` – and most likely your emails will go to `whoever@starraiders.com`.

Now there's a nice StarRaiders Windows domain tree, used to share resources and implement security within the StarRaiders computer network. Even though this domain tree is quite unrelated to the registered DNS name, wouldn't it be convenient for people to remember if – say – the Windows domain at the top of the tree could be called `StarRaiders.com`, and domains further down could be called `Department.StarRaiders.com`, etc. Well that's exactly what you can do.

However, since Active Directory is LDAP 3 compliant, it needs its names to be in the form of LDAP distinguished names. So instead of StarRaiders.com, the root domain will be known as `DC=StarRaiders,DC=Com`. And if you're using ADSI to hook up to the domain object, the `ADsPath` you'll supply will probably be something like `LDAP://DC=StarRaiders,DC=com`. These names, like Internet DNS names, read from right to left down the tree. That is to say the object at the top of the tree (`.com` or `DC=com`) in this example is the one on the right. The `DC=` originates from the X500/LDAP way of naming objects, in which as well as the name you put a little prefix that gives some indication of the type of object. The DC prefix is specific to Active Directory and stands for Domain Component (although arguably it's not quite appropriate here since `com` is not a domain controller). You might intuitively expect that the prefix isn't really needed, but it is an essential part of the name in LDAP format and MUST be included.

Differences from NT4

All of the discussion above has been specific to Windows 2000. Just for the record, I ought to point out some features that are not available if your domain is still controlled by an NT4 primary domain controller.

Firstly, there is no concept of domain forests. The kind of structure I showed for the StarRaiders corporation would not be possible in NT4. All you can have in NT4 is lots of single domains, which might have trust relationships between them.

Secondly, in NT4 the trust relationships are not transitive. If A trusts B and B trusts C, than you'd still need to separately set up A to trust C. The security model used in NT4 was not considered sophisticated enough to allow transitive trust relationships without opening up possible security loopholes. But Windows 2000 uses the newer Kerberos security protocol, which I'll go over in Chapter 7, and which is regarded as sufficiently secure to allow transitive trust relationships.

And finally, since you can't have domain trees in NT4, it follows that you couldn't really use DNS names for domains. The only domain names in NT4 were NetBios names, which were nasty – a fairly restrictive character set, all uppercase and a maximum of 16 characters. In fact, when you create a new domain in Windows 2000, the Active Directory configuration wizard will still ask you to supply a NetBios name as well as the 'proper' domain name. That's so it has a name that NT4 clients can use to refer to the domain.

We've covered all we need of what domains are. Let's move on to see how to navigate domains in practice.

How Windows Explorer Sees Domains

You can see your domain structure fairly simply in the Windows Explorer. Bring up the Windows Explorer. You can either use the full Windows Explorer, or use the My Network Places icon on your desktop (in Windows NT4 and Windows 9x, this icon was called Network Neighborhood). Don't try and use the My Computer icon as that won't access the network. The screenshot shows the full Windows Explorer, with My Network Places expanded to look at some of the computers at the Wrox Offices:

I'm taking this screenshot from Andrew Tracey's Windows 2000 machine, by the way. If you're running NT4, there won't be a Directory node under Entire Network, and the icons won't look quite as pretty.

My Network Places has two branches under it: Computers Near Me and Entire Network. The difference between these two branches is that Computers Near Me is there to give you a quick view of all the computers in your local **domain** (or – if you're using one – workgroup). Domain here means your Windows domain – the set of all computers that are recognized by the same domain controllers. By contrast, Entire Network is more sophisticated, and it will give you a view of your **Network**. In most cases, this will be larger than the domain. Windows Explorer finds out what machines are on your network by performing network broadcasts and analysing the replies – so which computers you see under Entire Network depends on where your routers are configured to pass messages on to.

If we look further down the tree under Entire Network, we see that the Entire Network node itself is just a container to contain the different types of systems that you might have on your network (for example, Windows 2000, Novell). In our case, we are only running NT domains, so this item has only one child with anything in it – Microsoft Windows Network. Inside here are all the domains on your local network. If I expand the Microsoft Windows Network node out, you can actually see the Wrox domains here. The other difference between this node and Computers Near Me is that the domain is actually named at the appropriate node here. Andrew's domain is Wrox_UK.

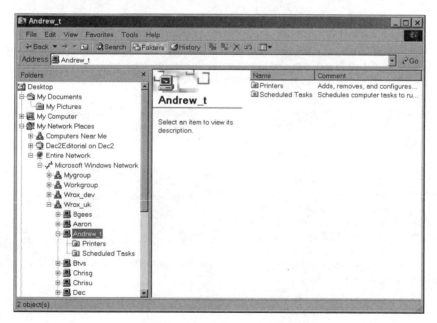

If you look in the Directory node, you'll find a mini directory browser for part of Active Directory.

It's a pretty restricted directory browser – in that it only lets you look at the subset of Active Directory concerned with users, groups and computer accounts. To a large extent it's read only, but it does have some elementary management capabilities.

This may all seem fairly trivial. What is slightly more interesting is that under the name of our computer, Andrew_t in both the **Computers Near Me** and **My Network Places** nodes, there aren't any of the normal folders or disk drives. That's because in going down either of these branches of the tree in Windows Explorer, we're taking a network view. We can only see the stuff on Andrew_t that has been exposed to the network. In other words, even though I'm sitting on Andrew_t, running Windows Explorer looking at this, I can only see the same objects that other computers would be able to see.

Folders are not exposed to the network by default – they have to be specifically set up to be exposed, which is done by a technique known as **sharing**. We're going to cover sharing in the next chapter. But for now, we can think of sharing as being a bit like creating a new folder, known as a file share, which directly maps on to the shared drive or folder. It is this file share that you see when you expand other computers in the network. Later on, we'll see how file shares can be manipulated using ADSI.

That's pretty much it for the theory of domains. We're just about ready to see what we can make of domains in ADSI, but first we need to go over another application that we can use to examine ADSI objects. You see, we're going to be interested, not just in the tree structure of WinNT and Active Directory, but in what interfaces the different objects expose. So we need a tool that will tell us about interfaces. We need a Quest for Interfaces...

The Quest for Interfaces Sample

The **Quest for Interfaces** is an extremely useful sample that is provided with the ADSI SDK. It's a little C++ MFC application that checks to see what interfaces are implemented by a given ADSI object, and allows you to examine the properties of certain interfaces in more detail.

> *If you want to try out the Quest for Interfaces, it's in the* `Samples` *folder of the ADSI 2.5 SDK, under* `Samples/General/ADQI`. *There's even an executable file, as well as all the source code already there.*

When you run it, it presents you with a dialog box. You need to type the `ADsPath` of the object you're interested in into the edit box at the top of the dialog. In this screenshot, I've gone for the DHCP service on my local machine. Incidentally, we're back to my own local computers for the screenshots instead of the Wrox network now.

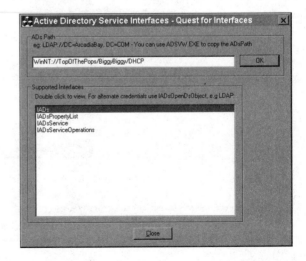

You can examine the properties exposed by selected interfaces by double-clicking on the name of the interface in the list box. For example, if I double-click on IADs in the screenshot above, this is what I get:

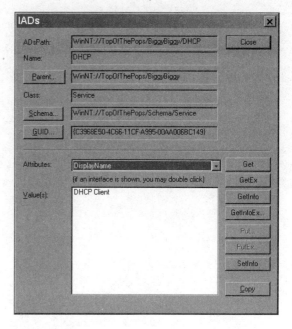

In order to display the DisplayName property in the above screenshot, I've also clicked on the **GetInfo** button to load the property cache, then selected **DisplayName** from the available properties in the **Attributes** drop-down list box.

But it gets even better. If I click on the <u>P</u>arent button, I get to look at the IADsContainer interface on the parent. This dialog lists all the children of the parent:

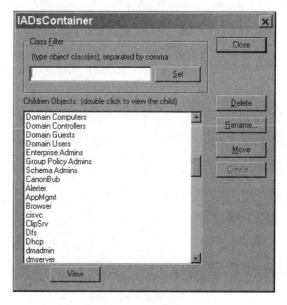

We're going to be using the Quest for Interfaces quite a bit in our exploration of the various directories on your system, starting with Active Directory and WinNT in this chapter.

Modifications to ADQI

However, there are a couple of problems with ADQI as supplied with the ADSI SDK: it's actually out of date, and doesn't tell you about all the interfaces now available in ADSI 2.5. For this reason, we're going to make a few modifications to it before we start using it.

The main way that the Quest for Interfaces works is by simply doing a repeat `QueryInterface` on the object for all the interfaces known to ADQI. This happens in this loop:

```
void CADQIDlg::EnumerateInterface()
{
    int xx=0;
    HRESULT hr;
    LPUNKNOWN pQI;

    m_cListIf.ResetContent();

    //////////////////////////////////////////////////////////////////
    // Query Interface all known ADSI Interfaces
    //////////////////////////////////////////////////////////////////
    while( !IsEqualIID( *adsiIfs[xx].pIID, IID_NULL ) )
    {
        hr = m_pUnk->QueryInterface( *adsiIfs[xx].pIID, (void**) &pQI );
        if ( SUCCEEDED(hr) )
        {
            m_cListIf.AddString( adsiIfs[xx].szIf );
            pQI->Release();
        }
        xx++;
    }
}
```

This loop basically goes through all the values in a global array `adsiIfs`. We don't need to go into too much detail here, but the values in the array are placed in it using a specially defined macro, `MAKEADSENTRY`. I've just added some more entries in the list:

```
ADSIIF  adsiIfs[] = {
    MAKEADSENTRY(IADs), DlgProcIADs,
    MAKEADSENTRY(IADsContainer), DlgProcIADsContainer,

// tons of interfaces removed for clarity....

    MAKEADSENTRY(IADsLargeInteger), DlgProcIADsLargeInteger,
    MAKEADSENTRY(IADsObjectOptions), NULL,
    MAKEADSENTRY(IADsPropertyValue2), NULL,

// these are the new interfaces I've added
    MAKEADSENTRY(IDirectorySchemaMgmt), NULL,
    MAKEADSENTRY(IADsDeleteOps), NULL,

//The following interfaces are CoCreateable, not living off on any object,
//so we comment this out, because QI won't return any of these interfaces
//   MAKEADSENTRY(IADsPathname), NULL,
//   MAKEADSENTRY(IADsNameTranslate),  NULL,
    MAKEADSENTRY(NULL), NULL
};
```

As usual, in order to make this compile, I've had to modify the project settings to ensure that the ADSI 2.5 headers are the ones that the compiler finds first.

While we're on the subject, we should also correct the following bug in the `DirectoryObject.cpp` file in the ADQI project:

```
//************This line has been changed for the ADSI book
//**********was (presumably in error)
// if ( nCount = 0 ) // can not find/convert the value
// now

    if ( nCount == 0 ) // can not find/convert the value
    {
        m_cValueList.AddString(_T(" > [No Value]"));
        continue;
    }
        else
    {
```

I don't think that needs any explanation, other than a reminder of how useful it is to set the Warning Level to 4 when you compile.

For copyright reasons the revised ADQI sample is not available on the Wrox website, but we recommend you make those changes before you use it.

We're now ready to go. And we'll start with a quick look at the object at the root of the **Directory Information Tree**(**DIT**) for Active Directory. (Recall that the DIT is the technical name for all of the part of the directory tree excluding schema and configuration information). This object shows the importance of two of the interfaces that were omitted from the original ADQI:

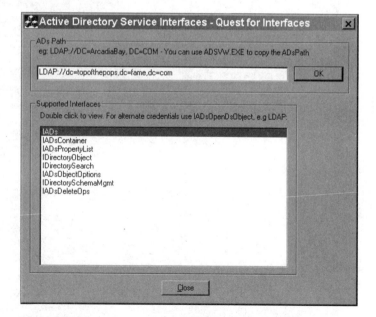

At last, we are now ready to have a look at the directory structures exposed through the WinNT and LDAP providers.

How the WinNT Provider Exposes Domains

Notice how careful I've been with the title here. As usual with ADSI, the WinNT provider does not itself store any directory. It simply exposes information it's obtained from elsewhere and puts that information in a suitable format. In doing so, it gives the information a certain tree-like structure. But this structure is only a characteristic of the presentation – something that will become obvious when we compare WinNT with Active Directory, and see exactly the same data exposed in a directory tree with a substantially different structure. What makes the WinNT provider unusual is that it does not get its information from any one identifiable directory – it gets it by scouring the local network and querying the respective computers on it for their user accounts, services, print queues etc. Then it gathers this information together and presents it as if it is a directory.

So let's have a look at what the domain looks like in WinNT. For this we'll use the `adsvw` Active Directory browser (and remember that its name is a misnomer: this tool is *not* specifically an Active Directory browser).

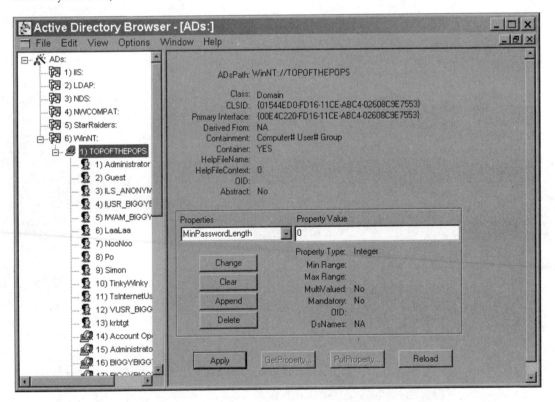

Under the WinNT: namespace are the domain objects – one for each domain on your local network, or in my case just the one domain. The WinNT provider has an NT4 inheritance. This means it only recognizes the NetBios name, which is why TOPOFTHEPOPS appears in capitals.

The number of children of my **TOPOFTHEPOPS** domain object is too large to fit on the screen, but it includes all the domain groups and users, as well as all the computers in the domain. Conveniently, the Active Directory Browser tells us this. In the right hand pane it has displayed some information obtained from the schema object which describes the selected object. That includes the `IADsClass` automation property **Containment**, which lists the classes that are allowed to be children of this class. They are **Computer**, **User** and **Group**. In fact, the schema as described here is not quite complete, as the schema container also appears as a child of the domain object.

Users and groups cannot have any children, but computer objects in WinNT can. The following screenshot is the same as the previous one, but scrolled down a bit more so we can see the computer objects. The **Schema** object is the schema container, and you can see some of the class schema objects inside it:

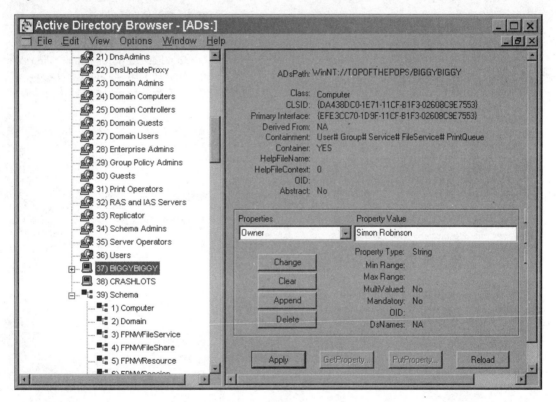

The most important point to notice is that in WinNT there is no distinction between domain controllers and ordinary member workstations. This screenshot of my local network shows that I have two computers with accounts registered in the domain: BiggyBiggy and Crashlots. BiggyBiggy is the domain controller, and Crashlots is a member workstation. But you can't tell this from the screenshot. In fact, unless a systems administrator manually sets a property to indicate whether a computer is a domain controller or not (the Role automation property exposed by `IADsComputer` – we'll discuss this more in the next chapter) there's no way to tell domain controllers and workstations apart using the WinNT provider. Both types of computers appear simply as computers.

A couple of other points to note while we're looking at this screenshot. The only reason CRASHLOTS hasn't appeared with a + sign next to it is I that haven't attempted to open that object. Remember – the Active Directory browser won't automatically show + signs on objects that contain other objects – you have to select the object first by clicking on it before the browser checks this. It's also worth bearing in mind that the WinNT provider gets the details of computer accounts from a domain controller – it won't actually try talking directly to any other computer in the domain unless you actually try to bind to the object that represents that computer or something contained in it. In the above screenshot, we've not attempted to open the CrashLots node, so WinNT won't yet have attempted to contact Crashlots directly – it doesn't need to yet. Something to bear in mind when you're thinking about performance.

> *Also, if you're wondering, the nice icons which represent each object's class, as well as the ordering of objects by class, is all done by* adsvw.exe *– they're not supplied by any ADSI provider.*

Once again, adsvw.exe has displayed the containment choices for the computer object. There's a bigger set here. Computers can contain users and groups – though in this case I should emphasize that these are the local computer user and group accounts. Also available are services, file services and print queues for that computer.

We've looked at the tree structure. We haven't yet said much about what interfaces the different objects expose, but it's actually pretty intuitive. User objects expose IADs and IADsUser. Services expose IADs and IADsContainer, etc. But to check round a bit, we can use the Quest for Interfaces. Here's what it turns up looking at the domain object:

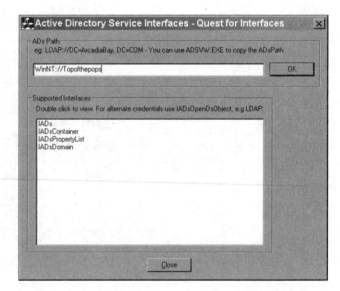

You'll probably find it a good idea to use ADQI.exe to hunt round WinNT, and see what it throws up. The main thing you will notice from it – as shown in the screenshot above – is that WinNT objects *do not* expose the IDirectoryXXX interfaces. So, even C++ clients will need to use the automation IADsXXX interfaces.

A more serious implication of this is that it's not possible to do searching in WinNT, because searching requires the IDirectorySearch interface. There is actually a good reason for this. Remember, WinNT is based around NT4, not Active Directory. And even on Windows 2000, the WinNT provider gathers together information about objects which is not stored in Active Directory, such as Windows 2000 Services. The underlying API calls used to get to these objects do not themselves support complex search queries as supported by IDirectorySearch – which would make it very difficult for the WinNT provider to do so.

Overall Structure of WinNT:

If you put all this together, this is the structure you get for the WinNT directory. It's not that complex a tree, although to some extent, the simplicity is at the cost of having containers which have lots of children:

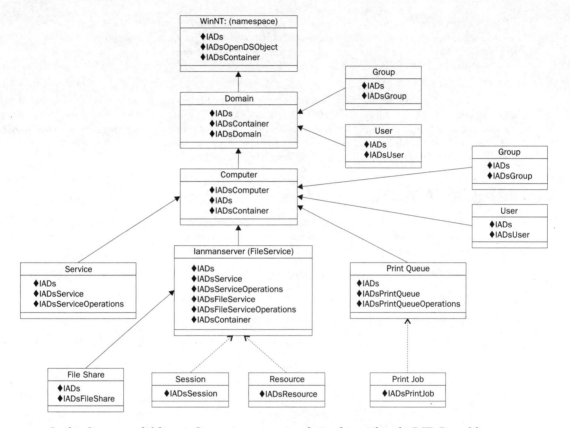

In this diagram, solid lines indicate a containment relationship within the DIT. Dotted lines indicate that a COM object is accessed as a property in another object, and does not form part of the directory tree. Containment relationships are all one-many, except that there is only one file service object per computer.

Besides the structure which is visible from the earlier `adsvw.exe` screenshots, there's some extra structure under the File Service and Print Queue objects. The file service object is a special Windows 2000 Service, known as the lanmanservice, which handles distributing file shares – that is folders which are made available to other computers on the network. Each File Share object represents an actual file share. The session and resource objects indicate sessions that are actually using the file shares. Because these are transient in nature, they are stored as properties of the file share object, rather than as separate directory objects.

Similarly, a print queue – which roughly corresponds to a particular printer attached to a computer – can have any number of print jobs currently pending. Print jobs are represented by separate ADSI objects, but these are accessed via a property of `IADsPrintQueue` rather than being part of the directory tree.

There are a couple of other points of interest in the WinNT directory structure. Firstly, notice that there is a schema container under every domain. Strictly speaking this is unnecessary, because the WinNT provider doesn't permit schema extensions, so the contents of every schema container will be identical. But the ADSI specification says that every top level node beneath the namespace object ought to have its own schema container, so that's what we find.

It's also interesting to notice the difference between the WinNT provider's view of the world and that of Windows Explorer. Windows Explorer is interested in which files and folders you have on a computer, whereas WinNT is more concerned with the administrative properties. For example, you can't use WinNT to start browsing round the folders.

Secondly, as I mentioned earlier, there is no special place in this hierarchy given to the primary and backup domain controllers. They are simply children of the domain, just like all the other computers. This is pretty much the same as in Windows Explorer. There, if you expand a domain, you simply see a list of computers, with nothing to tell you which is the primary domain controller, which are the backup domain controllers, and which are the user's workstations.

ADsPaths in WinNT:

`ADsPaths` in WinNT: are reasonably straightforward. The names of objects are separated by forward slashes (/) and objects in pathnames are always listed from the top of the domain tree. The initial WinNT is case sensitive, but the rest of the `ADsPath` is case-insensitive. Thus:

`WinNT://TopOfThePops/BiggyBiggy/Administrators`

or:

`WinNT://TOPOFTHEPOPS/BIGGYBIGGY/administrators`

will bind to the same object. However there are two complications in the `ADsPath`.

Firstly, it is possible to omit the name of the domain. If you do omit it, then the WinNT provider will assume you are talking about the local domain. So instead of `WinNT://TopOfThePops/BiggyBiggy/Administrators`, I could equally well attempt to bind to `WinNT://BiggyBiggy/Administrators` – with the same results.

Secondly, it is possible to add the class of the object required, with the class separated from the main part of the `ADsPath` by a comma. For example:

`WinNT://TopOfThePops/BiggyBiggy/Wendy,User.`

The reason for this option is in order to resolve ambiguous path names. The problem is that it is perfectly possible in Windows 2000 for a global user or group to have the same name as a computer. Since computers, global users and global groups are all exposed in WinNT as children of the domain object, this could potentially lead to two objects having the same `ADsPath`. This is the only case out of all the system ADSI providers in which an `ADsPath` could potentially not be unique. Appending the class name resolves this issue. For example, if you have a user called Wendy, who normally uses a computer called Wendy, you'd resolve the two corresponding WinNT objects using the `ADsPaths`

`WinNT://TopOfThePops/BiggyBiggy/Wendy,User`

and

`WinNT://TopOfThePops/BiggyBiggy/Wendy,Computer`

Properties of Objects in WinNT:

Before we finish off looking at the WinNT directory structure, there's one other area we need to cover – how WinNT exposes its properties. There's something quite remarkable about how it does this. Let's have a look at my domain controller – a computer object in WinNT – and see what our Object Viewer has to say about what mandatory and optional properties it has:

Hmm. That's nice. No mandatory properties at all, and just 6 optional properties. Clearly, WinNT doesn't believe in wasting memory storing too many properties! In fact none of these optional properties have any values assigned to them (somewhat surprisingly, given what these properties are).

But that's not the point I want to make. Since this is a computer object, it exposes the interface `IADsComputer`. `IADsComputer` is derived from `IADs`, but also exposes lots of extra automation properties. However, the documentation makes it clear that most of these properties are actually not implemented in the WinNT provider. Let's have a look at them:

PROPERTY	IMPLEMENTED IN WinNT
ComputerID	
Department	
Description	
Division	yes

Table Continued on Following Page

181

PROPERTY	IMPLEMENTED IN WinNT
Location	
MemorySize	
Model	
NetAddresses	
OperatingSystem	yes
OperatingSystemVersion	yes
Owner	yes
PrimaryUser	
Processor	yes
ProcessorCount	yes
Role	
Site	
StorageCapacity	

Do you notice something about these properties, comparing them with the web page? The ones that are implemented in WinNT are exactly the same as the properties that appear in the web page. The other properties will return E_NOTIMPL if you attempt to access them in the WinNT provider.

So does it surprise you that the two lists of properties are identical? Actually, it should because these are conceptually different properties.

> **The web page has given us a list of the properties that are defined in the schema, can be loaded into the property cache, and are therefore accessible using methods such as IADs::Get() and IADs::GetEx(). The table lists the automation properties implemented through IADsComputer. *In principle, there is no reason why these lists should match at all!***

The fact that they do shows that the WinNT provider has actually been carefully designed to expose properties simultaneously as schema and automation properties. It's not only IADsComputer that works like this. You'll find the same idea running through users, domains, and all the other types of objects that are exposed to clients by the WinNT provider.

This is useful because if you want to access a single property, code like this will work in VB:

```
oUser.Description = "This is Simon"
```

Of course, you could equally well write:

```
oUser.Put "Description", "This is Simon"
```

which means you're choosing to access Description through the property cache and the schema rather than as an automation property. In this case, I think most of you will agree that the first syntax is a lot easier.

On the other hand, because the same properties are exposed through the schema, it means that code like this will work in the same way on the same properties:

```
For Each Property in oClassObj.MandatoryProperties

    list1.AddItem oUser.Get(Property)

Next
```

A loop like that would never work for automation properties – you'd need to explicitly name each property you wanted to print.

I think that's quite a neat trick. It's something that you'll only really find in the WinNT provider. The LDAP provider relies a lot more exclusively on using the schema, which means you generally do have to use object.Get or object.Put, even on properties that you've named explicitly.

Anyway, we've now covered the entire WinNT domain structure. As you can see, it's not that complex. We're now going to have a look at the structure exposed by Active Directory.

Active Directory DIT Structure

Well, I said that Active Directory has a more complex structure than WinNT. If we want to get an overview of the structure, we've actually got two problems:

❑   Portions of the directory are not actually obtainable by straight browsing from the top level domain object – the one you'd probably think of as the root. In technical terms, Active Directory has more than one **naming context** (You can think of a naming context as being like a namespace).

❑   The structure is quite extensible – while it's true that there's a fairly standard structure that exists when you first install Active Directory, domain administrators are quite free to add several different types of object at various points in the structure. For example, although the domain users are all initially stored in the CN=Users container under the domain object, you could create new organizational unit objects and put extra users there – in order, perhaps, to give more of a structure to where your users are. The new objects can only be added as long as they are being added in places in the directory tree where those kinds of object are permitted by the schema – but since the Active Directory schema can be extended this isn't a real restriction in practice.

Despite those problems, we're going to start by browsing from the domain object. This will give us most of the information for the local domain, and the part of the data that's missing is really the schema and configuration naming contexts. So if we browse from here in the normal way, we will arguably pick up the entire structure of the 'real' DIT part of the directory. We're also going to look at the structure as it exists when you first install Active Directory with one single domain in the forest.

So here goes, using `adsvw.exe` again:

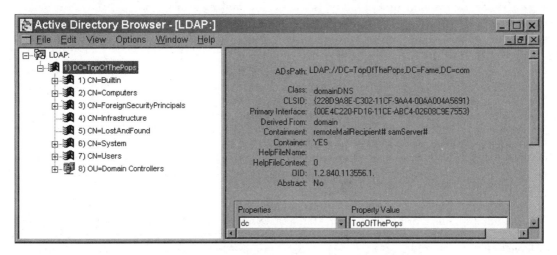

For this screenshot, I've asked to view the object **LDAP:** rather than **ADS:**, to avoid having all the other providers cluttering up the screen. I've also gone through and clicked on all the items in the tree view, to bring up the + signs that show which items are actually containers that have something else in them.

It shows that under **LDAP:**, the root of the tree is the domain object. If you had a Windows 2000 domain tree rather than a single domain, you'd actually see more of a tree structure stretching down here.

The schema information for the domain is somewhat revealing, since it tells us that the domain object is not of class domain, but of a derived class, **domainDNS**. It gets even more interesting if we use the Quest for Interfaces on this object:

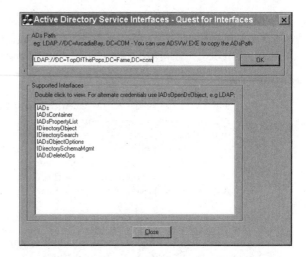

This is a very different set of interfaces from that exposed by the domain object in WinNT:. The basic `IADs`, `IADsContainer` and `IADsPropertyList` are there – as they will be on any object (or in the case of `IADsContainer`, any container). But `IADsDomain` is missing. This is something we're going to have to get used to in Active Directory: the persistent object interfaces, such as `IADsDomain` and `IADsComputer`, are not used as often as they are in WinNT. The LDAP provider tends not to expose properties of these types of object through extra interfaces that expose more automation properties – rather it goes through the schema instead.

This is fairly logical when you remember that the LDAP provider is not Active-Directory specific: it's there to handle any LDAP-compliant directory. That means it can't really have such an intimate knowledge of the objects it exposes to ADSI clients, so it also can't really know to expose additional interfaces that are dependent on certain types of object. It has to do the best it can with all the generic ADSI interfaces, and it actually does a pretty good job of it. We're seriously not going to notice the absence of interfaces like `IADsDomain` and `IADsComputer` that much. It does manage to expose a couple of extra interfaces on some objects: group objects do expose `IADsGroup`, print queues do expose `IADsPrintQueue` and `IADsPrintQueueOperations`, and – somewhat curiously – not only users but also computers expose `IADsUser`. (This is because `IADsUser` exposes methods to set a password. Active Directory computer accounts have passwords too, so having this interface is useful to allow computer account passwords to be set)

On the other hand, there are a whole new range of interfaces available to us. For a start, the `IDirectoryXXX` interfaces are there – `IDirectoryObject` and `IDirectorySearch`. This means we can do searches in Active Directory. We've also got `IADsDeleteOps`, allowing us to delete whole sub-trees in one go if we want. And there's a new interface which we haven't encountered yet: `IADsObjectOptions`. This allows us to set a couple of provider-specific flags – in the case of Active Directory, related to searching. If you use the Quest for Interfaces to check round Active Directory, you'll find pretty much all the objects expose this exact same set of interfaces – except of course that leaf objects won't expose `IADsContainer`.

Unfortunately for us, the `Containment` property listed on the right of the screen is now very incomplete, since it doesn't give all the classes that actually appear under the domain.

As for what's in these branches of the tree – we've got the following:

Name	Description
BuiltIn	Domain Groups
Computers	All the computers in the domain that aren't domain controllers
ForeignSecurityPrincipals	Security principals from external sources (security principals are objects that have a security identity, such as users or groups)
InfraStructure	Contains some settings used by the system
LostAndFound	This is for orphaned objects who are created on one domain controller just as their parents are deleted on another replica of Active Directory on another domain controller.
System	Stuff related to certain system services such as policies and RPC services
Users	Domain User Accounts
Domain Controllers	All the computers which are domain controllers

Let's check out the computers:

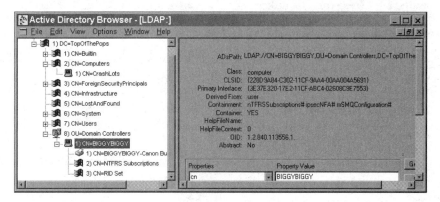

Voila, my complete domain! My domain controller, **BiggyBiggy**, and the workstation, **CrashLots**.

The main point I want you to see here is that the stuff inside the computers is actually quite limited. I can get to my printer and any other important hardware devices, but that's about it for things that are generally useful. The reason is that Active Directory is really a directory for your domain as a whole. It's not interested in stuff that's stored individually on particular PCs – like local user accounts and Windows 2000 Services. For that, you need to be looking at the WinNT provider.

Active Directory Roots

As we've mentioned, one of the problems with trying to do an exhaustive browse of Active Directory in its entirety is that there isn't one single node that can be seen as being at the top of the directory tree. In this section we're going to have a look at what all the different DIT roots are. As we'll discover, it's actually reasonably simple to obtain the information using the `rootdse` object.

> *Remember that in all the following pathnames, the initial* `LDAP://` *must be in upper case, but the remainder of the* `ADsPath` *is generally case-insensitive. I've used the abbreviation* `<DNS>` *to refer to your DNS name in distinguished name format – for example, on my computer this means* `dc=topofthepops,dc=fame,dc=com`.

Here's a complete list of all the objects you'd need to bind to and browse under to get the entire tree:

❑ `LDAP://rootdse` will allow you to bind to the RootDSE object, which contains information about Active Directory

❑ `LDAP://cn=schema,cn=configuration,<DNS>` gets you to the schema

❑ `LDAP://cn=configuration,<DNS>` gets you to the configuration

❑ `LDAP://<DNS>` gets you to the main part of the DIT

❑ `GC://<DNS>` gets you to the main part of the DIT for the global catalogue

❑ `GC://rootdse` gets you to the `RootDSE` again, but this time for the global catalogue.

These last two objects have an `ADsPath` that begins with GC: rather than LDAP:. This refers to something called the **global catalogue**, which is a copy of part of Active Directory, designed to allow more efficient searching. We'll cover the global catalogue later on.

The RootDSE

> The `RootDSE` object can in a real sense be thought of as *the* root. Bear in mind, though, that it is the root in the sense that it can be used to tell you what the `ADsPaths` of the nodes at the top of the various namespaces in Active Directory are. It is not, however a container: it does not contain any other objects.

The `RootDSE` is not specific to Active Directory – every LDAP 3 compliant directory should have one. It contains information about the directory as a whole. And something that's relevant to us is that it contains the `ADsPaths` of the roots of the remaining three directory branches.

One thing that the `rootDSE` doesn't have is any children – it really sits on its own as far as any tree is concerned. If you check `LDAP://rootdse` in the Quest for Interfaces program, you'll find it exposes only `IADs` and `IADsPropertyList`.

The next stage is to try to use one of the applications that we wrote in Chapter 2 to look at the properties of the `RootDSE`. In fact, if you try out one of the Object Viewer programs that uses the schema to identify mandatory and optional properties, you'll rapidly discover that it doesn't work. This is because the `RootDSE` doesn't have a corresponding class object. So we'll have to use one of our property cache viewers. Here's the result from our web page property cache viewer:

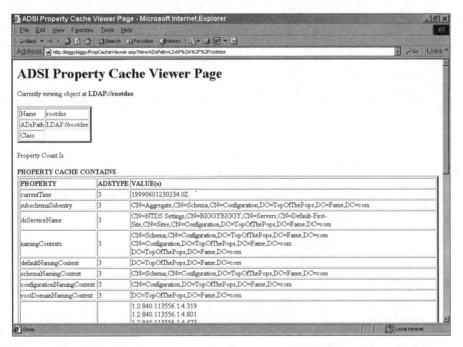

Notice in this screenshot that no value was returned for the Property Count. Unbelievably, the `RootDSE` – arguably the most important object in Active Directory – doesn't implement this property. So here's an example of where it's paid off that we coded up the script defensively, allowing for the possibility of having to work without knowing how many properties we had to display.

Anyway, since I believe this is such an important object, I'll also show you the screenshot scrolled down to see the rest of the properties:

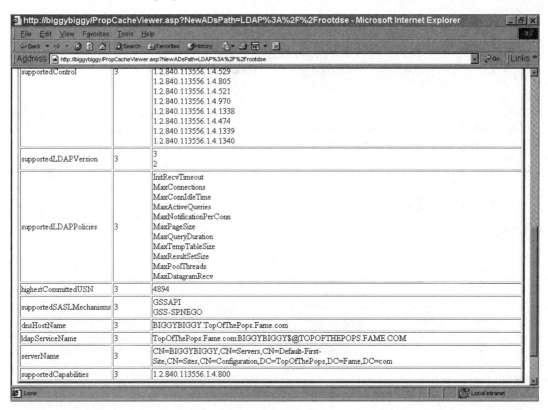

Interesting, huh? The ones that we are really interested in are namingContexts, defaultNamingContext, schemaNamingContext and configurationNamingContext. That's because these are the properties which tell you the ADsPaths you need to browse the rest of the directory. Recall that the three parts of Active Directory are called naming contexts.

❑   defaultNamingContext gives the local domain

❑   schemaNamingContext gives the schema container

❑   configurationNamingContext gives the configuration

❑   namingContexts is a multi-valued property which contains the ADsPaths of all of the three naming contexts

So if you want to browse through Active Directory in its entirety, namingContexts is the property you need to look at to figure out how to do it. Notice, however, that the rootDSE gives only the distinguished names. You need to prefix them with LDAP:// to get the ADsPath so you can bind to the objects.

The following table gives a quick summary of what the properties of the `rootdse` are for:

Property	Multivalued	Description
currentTime	no	Current time.
subschemaSubentry	no	Distinguished name of the subschema object.*
dsServiceName	no	The distinguished name of the NTDS settings object for this directory server.
namingContexts	yes	Distinguished names for all the roots (naming contexts) of the parts of the directory.
defaultNamingContext	no	Distinguished name for the local domain – the domain of which this server is a member.
schemaNamingContext	no	Distinguished name for the schema container.
configurationNamingContext	no	Distinguished name for the configuration container.
RootDomainNamingContext	no	Distinguished name for the first domain in the forest.
SupportedControl	yes	OIDs for any LDAP extension controls.*
SupportedLDAPVersion	yes	LDAP versions supported. Normally version 3.
HighestCommittedUSN	no	Highest USN used on this directory server.
SupportedSASLMechanisms	yes	Supported security mechanisms.
DnsHostName	no	DNS address for this directory server.
LdapServiceName	no	Service Principal Name
ServerName	no	Distinguished name for this directory server.

There are quite a few new concepts here. Where I've marked a * by an explanation, this means something that's part of the LDAP specification.

The property `HighestCommittedUSN` indicates a **user service number** (USN). USNs are used as part of the replication algorithm, in order to resolve conflicts between different replicas of the directory on different servers. In other words, the USNs are used to determine which copy of a part of the directory is the most up-to-date one and therefore should be used to overwrite another copy. They aren't going to concern us here, since as far as we are concerned they are an implementation detail of Active Directory – not something that we need to use.

The `LdapServiceName` – a Service Principal Name – is another property which we don't normally need to be bothered about. It's used in mutual authentication between servers.

The Active Directory Schema

You can find the `ADsPath` to the Active Directory schema using several techniques:

- ❑ Get it from the `schemaNamingContext` property in the rootdse

- ❑ Read it from the table of `ADsPaths` for naming contexts that we presented in the section, *Active Directory Roots.*

- ❑ If you only want the schema object for one object, use the `IADs::Schema` property to get it

I'm simply going to use the `ADSIEDIT` snap-in, with its inbuilt knowledge of the schema `ADsPath`. Here's what it shows:

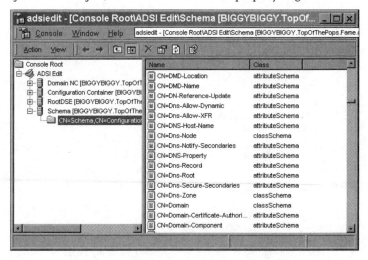

What we see here is the traditional schema container, with lots of schema elements in it.

> *By the way, the* `ADsPath` *of the schema container (the selected object) which is partly hidden is* `LDAP://CN=Schema, CN=Configuration, DC=TopOfThePops,DC=Fame,DC=com.`

A couple of disturbing things are apparent from this screenshot. Firstly, look at the size of that scrollbar on the right. The schema is massive! Microsoft have thrown everything they could think of into the Active Directory Schema, in the hope that it will be extensive enough that you don't need to extend it that often. In fact, there are 995 children of the schema container. Unfortunately, although Active Directory is supposedly an LDAP3 compliant directory, the schema also departs from the LDAP standard in some respects, for example the common name attribute is single-valued in Active Directory, but multi-valued in the LDAP standard.

Secondly, there's something funny about the classes of the schema objects. Normally in ADSI, you'd expect Class objects which expose `IADsClass`, as well as property and syntax objects. Instead of class and property objects we have classSchema and attributeSchema objects. And if I pick a `classSchema` object at random (dns-node) and run a Quest for Interfaces on it, look what I find:

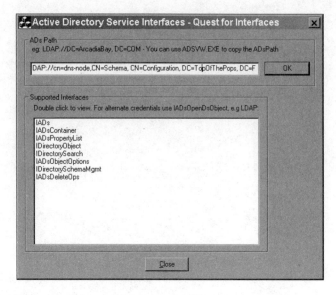

Remember that according to the normal ADSI way of doing things, we should expect to see `IADs` and `IADsClass`, possibly even `IADsPropertyList` and the `IDirectoryXXX` interfaces. So what's going on? Well bluntly, the schema for Active Directory – and for LDAP directories generally for that matter – doesn't follow the normal ADSI way of doing things.

The underlying principle is roughly the same – the classSchema object tells you what attributes the class can store, and the `attributeSchema` object tells you what data type is stored in that attribute. At this point we depart from the way ADSI works in principle because there's nothing corresponding to syntax objects. The reason is that the attribute objects each give an OID for the syntax. These OIDs and the corresponding data types are defined in the LDAP specification, so there's no need for extra objects in the directory to tell us what the various syntaxes mean.

However if the underlying principle is the same, the difference is in how the ADSI objects work. The usual ADSI way is for the Class and Property objects (as well as their syntax objects) to give the schema information as automation properties, by exposing the interfaces `IADsClass`, `IADsProperty` and `IADsSyntax`. Well, as we've seen, the LDAP provider doesn't do that. Instead, it entirely uses property cache properties, that must be retrieved using the `IADs` functions `Get()`, `GetEx()`, etc. I would say schema-defined properties, except for the fact that these are schema objects – there are no additional schema objects to define what they contain. You just have to know what properties to expect, or use the property cache interfaces to find out.

So we need to take a little look at what attributes are actually in the `classSchema` and `attributeSchema` objects.

The classSchema Objects

Here's a table of some of the attributes `classSchema` objects generally contain.

If you're wondering, I found out most of these by using our Property Cache Viewer web page. This list isn't exhaustive – it's just got the attributes that are most important.

191

Name	Multi-Valued	Corresponds To Which IADsClass Property	Description
systemMustContain	Yes	MandatoryProperties	Attributes that must be contained by objects of this class.
systemMayContain	Yes	OptionalProperties	Attributes that may be contained by objects of this class.
systemPossSuperiors	Yes	PossibleSuperiors	Which classes of object can contain objects of this class.
subClassOf	No	DerivedFrom	What this class is derived from.
rDNAttID	No	NamingProperties	Which attribute is used for the prefix in the relative distinguished name (eg. CN if objects of this class are known as CN=whatever).

The attributeSchema Objects

Remember that these are the objects that describe an attribute. Here's the corresponding (not exhaustive) table for these:

Name	Multi-Valued	Corresponds to which IADsProperty Property?	Description
isSingleValued	No	MultiValued (inverse of this property)	Whether the attribute is single valued.
attributeID	No	OID	The OID for this attribute.
attributeSyntax	No	Syntax	The OID of the *syntax* of this attribute. The OIDs are defined in the LDAP specification, hence there is no need for corresponding syntax objects.
rangeLower	No	MinRange	Minimum value.
rangeUpper	No	MaxRange	Maximum value.

Attributes of DIT Objects

In all this discussion, you may notice I've neglected any mention of what attributes are stored in most directory objects. The real objects that is – not the objects in the schema, but things like the actual users and computers. To be honest that's something I've been approaching with some trepidation. Here's why.

This is what our property cache viewer throws up if I look at my own user account object:

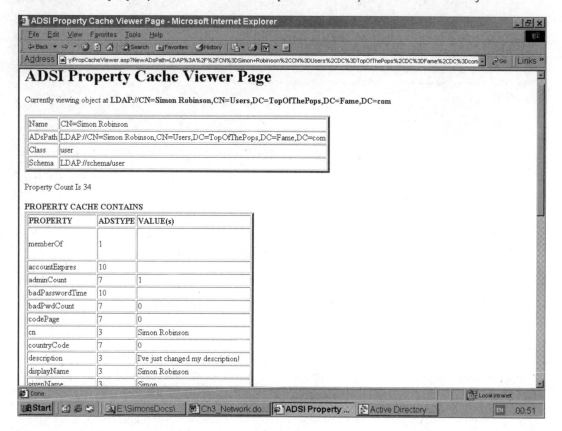

Now that itself doesn't look too bad, does it? According to this web page, I have 34 properties in the property cache, and most of the ones you can see look pretty self-explanatory: common name (cn), display name, description and so on.

But now look what happens if we try the same thing with the object viewer instead, to see what the mandatory and optional properties are:

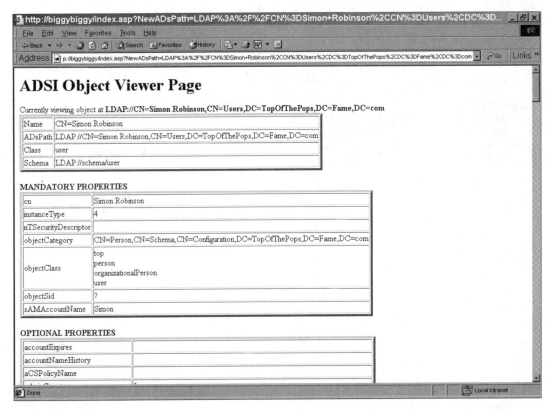

Not many mandatory properties. But look at the size of that scroll bar – there are a *lot* of optional properties.

That's the thing about LDAP – and where it really differs from WinNT. If you look at any object in WinNT, the only properties you'll find in the schema are for the most part those properties that are used by the operating system in NT4. In fact, they are almost exactly the ones that are defined by the extra persistent property interfaces like IADsUser. (Remember how we found that WinNT generally duplicates schema and automation properties). Well LDAP doesn't do that.

> **You'll find that LDAP generally relies on schema-based properties a lot more than WinNT does. The LDAP provider simply doesn't use automation properties that much.**

But what Active Directory does do is define an absolutely massive schema. Objects have huge numbers of optional properties. To see where most of these optional properties come from, we need to look no further than the values of the `objectClass` attribute. This attribute names not only the class of a directory object but also all the classes that it is derived from. `objectClass` works a bit like the `IADs` automation property, `class`. The difference is that where `IADs::Class` only tells you the class of this object, `objectClass` tells you the class of this object AND all the ones it's derived from. So our web page tells us that `user` is derived from `organizationalPerson`, which is derived from `person`, which is derived from `top`.

> **This is a basic principle of LDAP: all classes have to be derived ultimately from the class `top`.**

Well in Active Directory, `top` is a huge class. It has just four mandatory properties, `InstanceType`, `objectCategory`, `objectClass`, and `ntSecurityDescriptor`. (`instanceType` is used internally within Active Directory. `ntSecurity` should be obvious. We've just covered `objectClass`, and `objectCategory` is a single-valued version of `objectClass` which is useful in searching, and which we'll cover in Chapter 7.) This means that these four properties will be present in *every* active directory object.

But top has a lot of optional properties. The idea is that Active Directory should be flexible enough that you won't want to add to the schema. Remember, it may be in the first place a directory of network resources, but it is also there for you to add your own data to it, if you want to. By defining a large number of optional properties, it's more likely that any data you want to add will be covered by the properties already present, without your having to start defining new classes.

Having said that, you will still find a strong bias in the optional properties of `top` towards system data, and data useful to Active Directory. So the optional properties you'll find include things like when the USN was changed, and different versions of an object's path name.

Anyway, let's have a look at some of the most important properties. These are some of the generically useful properties you'll find on a lot of Active Directory objects. Again this list is nothing like exhaustive.

Name	Multi-Valued	Description
objectGUID	No	A unique GUID that identifies each object (that is, each instance of an object, not just each class). This GUID is generated when the object is first created.
nTSecurityDescriptor	No	IDispatch pointer to an object which implements IADsSecurityDescriptor and which gives information about who is authorized to access the object. We'll cover security descriptors in Chapter 8.

Table Continued on Following Page

Name	Multi-Valued	Description
objectClass	Yes	The class of this object. Note that this is multi-valued and contains all base classes, as well as the class of which this object is a member.
objectCategory	No	The category of this object. This is similar to objectClass but has one value, which indicates the broad type of object. It is generally recommended to use this value rather than objectClass when searching for particular types of object for performance reasons.
canonicalName	No	The ADsPath of the object in canonical form. Note that this property is not loaded into the cache by GetInfo, and must be individually requested.
distinguishedName	No	The DN of this object. Prefix it with LDAP:// to get the ADsPath.
cn	No	The common name – as close as you'll get to the name of the object. As we pointed out earlier, in LDAP this should be multi-valued, but Active Directory departs from the LDAP standard by making this property single-valued.

The Active Directory Configuration

We're not going to cover what's in the configuration container here, as it's generally stuff that you're only going to be interested in if you're involved with administering the configuration of Active Directory itself. By the configuration, I mean details of how the directory is replicated between servers, as well as topics like DNS name lookup.

The Global Catalogue

Likewise, we don't really need to cover the global catalogue much here. It is essentially a copy of Active Directory with only some attributes present. Which attributes are present for a given class of object is indicated by the property isMemberOfPartialAttributeSet of the corresponding attributeSchema. However, a couple of points are worth noting about the global catalogue.

❑ If Active Directory is installed, an ADSI client can bind to the namespace object, LDAP: enumerating children of this container, gets you into Active Directory . This is not the case for the global catalogue – binding to GC: and enumerating the children returns nothing. You must bind explicitly to an object inside the global catalogue.

❑ The rootdse, schema and configuration in the global catalogue work in pretty much the same way as for LDAP:

One reason why you might want to browse through the global catalogue is that the tree structure is more integrated – have a look at the ADsPaths for the configuration and schema in LDAP:

LDAP://cn=schema,cn=configuration,<DNS> gets you to the schema

LDAP://cn=configuration,<DNS> gets you to the configuration

Doesn't it seem suspicious that – from the `ADsPaths` – the configuration container looks like it ought to be a child of the main DNS root, and the schema container looks like it ought to be a child of the configuration container? Well, if you bind to the global catalogue, that's exactly what they are. Look:

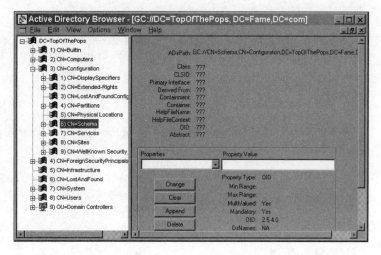

So if you do browse through the global catalogue, starting at the top of the default naming context, you can get to almost all the Active Directory objects – the only one you can't get to by browsing is the rootdse. This is not possible with Active Directory itself.

ADsPaths in Active Directory

We've now covered the internal directory structure of Active Directory. Apart from the large number of different parts of the tree, there are also quite a wide choice of ways that you can bind to it. So let's have a look at the different formats in which you can specify an `ADsPath` to connect to an object in the directory.

Serverless Binding

This is really the type of binding I've been using right up till now: you specify the prefix `LDAP`, followed by the distinguished name of the object in Active Directory:

```
LDAP://dc=TopOfThePops,dc=Fame,dc=com
```

It's quite simple in concept. It also hides the fact that Active Directory is actually replicated over a number of servers (domain controllers). This is significant, because any one of those domain controllers could theoretically respond to the request to bind to an object. By using serverless binding, you are choosing not to specify a server, which means you're leaving it up to the LDAP provider to choose the most appropriate server to get the information from.

> *Don't forget that the distinguished names (the parts of the* `ADsPaths` *after the LDAP prefix) are case-insensitive. Attempting to bind to*
>
> `LDAP://dc=TopOfThePops,dc=Fame,dc=com`
>
> *and to*
>
> `LDAP://DC=TOPOFTHEPOPS,DC=FAME,DC=COM`
>
> *will achieve the same results.*

197

Server Binding

This is pretty much the opposite of serverless binding – in this you actually specify the name of the domain controller you want to use when you bind to the object. Thus:

```
LDAP://BiggyBiggy/DC=TopOfThePops,DC=Fame,DC=com
```

This actually corresponds to the normal format of `ADsPaths` for the LDAP provider anyway. Recall from Chapter 1 that if binding to an object in any LDAP directory, not just Active Directory, one of the normal forms is:

```
LDAP://<ServerName:port >/<distinguished name of object>
```

In the case of Active Directory, you won't need to specify the port, since Active Directory defaults to the normal LDAP port of 389.

GUID Binding

The idea of GUID binding is that objects do occasionally get renamed: I might decide to change the name of a computer or a user account. This could be awkward for any software that subsequently attempts to bind to the object using its distinguished name. GUIDs get round this problem. Each object when created gets allocated a unique GUID, and this GUID will never change for as long as the object exists.

For example, my domain object, `LDAP://DC=TopOfThePops,DC=Fame,DC=com` has the GUID `f7ea2c7f9605d311887f0080c8d38c55`, so I could bind to it using the `ADsPath`:

```
LDAP://<GUID=f7ea2c7f9605d311887f0080c8d38c55>
```

There are two potential pitfalls to watch using this approach. Firstly, if you bind the object using its GUID, it will be the GUID that will be displayed for its distinguished name in browsers:

Secondly, when binding to the object using its GUID, the GUID needs to be in the format of a simple sequence of hex digits. Unfortunately, the GUID is accessed using the `objectGUID` attribute, which is present on every Active Directory object. However, the `objectGUID` attribute returns the GUID as an octet string, but in a different format:

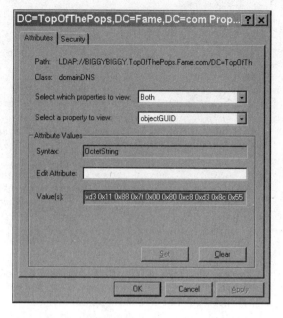

This means that you will have to convert the format by removing all spaces and all occurrences of 0x from the string before you can use it in a binding string.

SID Binding

The SID is the Windows 2000 security identifier.

Every Active Directory object has a unique SID, which is used internally by Windows 2000 for authorization purposes – and which we'll look at in Chapter 8. Binding to an object using its SID is similar to GUID-binding.

For example, my domain object has the SID `0104000000000005150000000b4b7cd22a837d66516c0ea32`, so I can bind to it by supplying the `ADsPath`

```
LDAP://<SID=0104000000000005150000000b4b7cd22a837d66516c0ea32>.
```

SID binding suffers from the same disadvantages as GUID binding: The SID is obtained from the `objectSID` attribute, but if I attempt to retrieve the `objectSID` attribute on my domain object, I get the octet string `0x01 0x04 0x00 0x00 0x00 0x00 0x00 0x05 0x15 0x00 0x00 0x00 0xb4 0xb7 0xcd 0x22 0xa8 0x37 0xd6 0x65 0x16 0xc0 0xea 0x32`. Clearly, after retrieving the SID, some text manipulation is necessary before it can be used!

Extending the Directory Structure of Active Directory

In the WinNT provider, the apparent directory structure exposed is fixed from the start. For example computers are always children of the domain object, and there's no way you can change that. That's not the case in Active Directory. It is quite easy to extend the directory structure.

Note I do say 'extend' rather than 'modify'. Obviously, the basic part of the structure that you're given at installation time is essential and shouldn't be removed! Also, be aware that I'm talking about extending the directory information tree here - as in adding new containers etc. I'm NOT discussing extending the schema (defining new classes of object and new attributes) – that will be covered in the next chapter.

How you extend the structure is entirely up to you – the schema is quite flexible when it comes to adding different types of object at different places in the tree. In this section, I'm just going to go over the most typical example of extending the structure: building a tree of domain users. There's nothing special about this particular example, it's just the one that I suspect domain administrators are most likely to want to do quite often.

If you want to check the ways in which it's possible to extend the structure, the easiest way is to use ADSIEDIT. This is because when you select the menu item to create a new object in ADSIEDIT, ADSIEDIT is intelligent enough to actually read the Active Directory schema, identify the different classes of object that you are allowed to add at that point in the tree, and present you with a list. `adsvw.exe` doesn't do that – it just presents you with a dialog box asking you to type in the name and class of the object you want to add – giving you no guidance as to which classes of object you are allowed to add at that location.

To create a new object in ADSIEDIT, just select the parent of the new object, right-click and select New | Object from the context menu. This brings up the dialog box with the list of possible `objectClasses`. Here's the list for new children of the domain object:

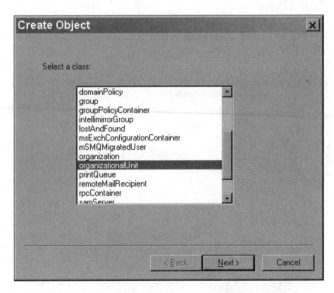

I've highlighted organizationalUnit because that's a good general purpose class for separating out sections of your company. If you click on Next >, you'll be prompted to enter the name of your object. You'll also get further dialogs asking you for the values of any mandatory properties that need to be supplied before the Active Directory Schema will allow the object to be created. In the case of organizational units, there are no further properties. For users you'll need to enter the `saMAccountName`.

ADSIEDIT isn't very good at refreshing itself when new objects are added or objects are moved. If you find that a newly created or moved object is listed in the tree control in ADSIEDIT, but produces an error message about the object not existing when you try to do anything to it, just exit and restart ADSIEDIT.

You could go ahead and use ADSIEDIT (or `adsvw.exe`) to add the users to your new organizational unit, but in this case, it's probably best not to do it that way. Those tools are very sophisticated, but in the end they are general-purpose ADSI browsers. When you add a user, you'll want to do things like sort out what groups the user belongs to and set a password, etc. It's easier to do that with a tool that is specifically concerned with users, and will give you a specialist user interface that concentrates on data specific to users.

So to actually add users, you're best off using the tool that Microsoft have provided for the purpose. In this case it's the Active Directory Users and Computers tool, which you'll find in the Start menu by following Programs | Administrative Tools | Active Directory Users and Computers.

Like most administrative tools in Windows 2000, it's an MMC snapin. It's also remarkably similar to an Active Directory browser, but it's designed to concentrate on users and computers. In this screenshot I'm using it to show off what I've actually done to my Active Directory:

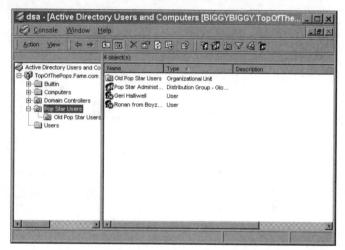

As you can see, besides the default Users container (which has all the users given to me by the system at installation, as well as the odd user I've added myself later on), I've now created a new organizational unit called Pop Star Users. That's there for the domain user accounts of all the pop stars who I just know are going to be flooding in to use my system once StarRaiders is really going!

I've also started to create a tree structure inside it, with another organizational unit for Old Pop Star Users – the ones from the sixties and seventies that I want to keep together. I've even started populating my organizational units. There's a new group, Pop Star Administrators, for those stars who hold especially trusted positions in StarRaiders, and a couple of user accounts. The red cross by them indicates that both accounts are currently disabled – that's because I made the mistake of using ADSIEDIT to create them, and ADSIEDIT just assumed default properties, including no password and (fortunately given that there is no password) account disabled.

And now you can hopefully get a sense of one of the reasons why you'd want to extend the Active Directory DIT like this. Suppose your domain is huge, with hundreds of domain users. It's a bit hard to administer them all if you've only got a flat structure, with all the users contained in the Users container. But if you can start to categorize the users in some way, and put them into different containers, the whole directory might become a bit easier to manage. You might want to do the same with groups and computer accounts as well.

Summary

We've now completed our tour of some of the main features of Active Directory and the WinNT provider. We've seen how when it comes to computer, and domain user and group accounts, we can use either the WinNT or LDAP providers to retrieve and set information, but that the two directory structures exposed are different. We're ready to see how to perform common administrative tasks on your network. We'll do this in the next chapter, going over how to manipulate computer, user and group accounts, Windows 2000 services, file shares and print queues.

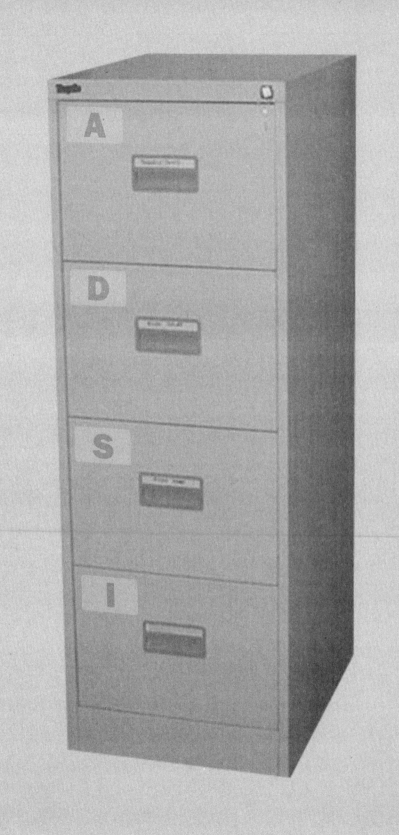

Common Administrative Tasks with Active Directory and WinNT

In the last chapter we had a look at both Active Directory and the WinNT provider. We went over the areas in which these two 'directories' (for want of a better term – Active Directory is a directory, WinNT is an ADSI provider) have quite a lot of overlap in the kind of information you can get or set with them, and at the areas where they differ (for example, WinNT gives you more access by default to local computer information).

In this chapter we're going to apply that knowledge by running through some of the administrative tasks that might need to be done on your network. Tasks like changing passwords and starting and stopping services. For each of these tasks we're going to discuss which provider (LDAP or WinNT) is likely to be the most appropriate one to use, and present sample code to carry out the task. Along the way we are going to encounter network objects such as services, file services and print queues. Since this book is aimed at developers rather than systems administrators, we won't assume you know anything about these objects so we'll introduce the principles behind them from scratch.

At the end of this chapter you will be introduced to, and understand how to manipulate, the following objects using ADSI:

- ❑ User and group accounts
- ❑ Windows 2000 (NT) Services
- ❑ File Shares, Sessions and Resources
- ❑ Print Queues and Print Jobs

Note that in this and future chapters we will refer to Windows 2000 Services. These are the same as Windows NT Services – so we could use either name. We've opted for Windows 2000 Services since we are mostly using Windows 2000, so we felt that the term NT Services could be confusing. But be aware that everything in this book about Windows 2000 Services applies equally to NT Services in NT4.

Users

As we've seen, local users can only be accessed using the WinNT provider, while global users can be accessed through either the WinNT or LDAP providers.

The IADsUser interface

Users expose the `IADsUser` interface in both WinNT and LDAP. Besides the normal `IADs` properties, `IADsUser` exposes the following automation properties (although they are not all actually implemented in both providers). I guess you might just possibly not want to memorize this list:

Name	In WinNT	In LDAP	Access	Data Type	Meaning
AccountDisabled	Yes	Yes	R/W	Boolean	Indicates if the account has been disabled
AccountExpirationDATE	Yes	Yes	R/W	Date	The account cannot be used after this date
BadLoginAddress			R/O	BSTR	This address is considered a possible intruder
BadLoginCount	Yes	Yes	R/O	Long	Number of failed logins since last reset
Department		Yes	R/W	BSTR	
Description	Yes	Yes	R/W	BSTR	
Division		Yes	R/W	BSTR	
EmailAddress		Yes	R/W	BSTR	

Name	In WinNT	In LDAP	Access	Data Type	Meaning
EmployeeID		Yes	R/W	BSTR	
FaxNumber		Yes	R/W	VARIANT	
FirstName		Yes	R/W	BSTR	
FullName	Yes	Yes	R/W	BSTR	
GraceLogins Allowed			R/W	LONG	Number of times user can log in after password has expired
GraceLogins Remaining			R/W	LONG	Number of grace logins left before account will be locked
HomeDirectory	Yes	Yes	R/W	BSTR	User's home directory
HomePage		Yes	R/W	BSTR	URL of user's home page
IsAccountLocked	Yes	Yes	R/W	Boolean	Indicates if account has been locked because of intruder detection
Languages		Yes	R/W	BSTR Array	
LastFailedLogin		Yes	R/O	DATE	Time of last failed network login
LastLogin	Yes	Yes	R/O	Date	Time of last network login
LastLogoff	Yes	Yes	R/O	Date	Time of last network logoff

Table Continued on Following Page

207

Name	In WinNT	In LDAP	Access	Data Type	Meaning
LastName		Yes	R/W	BSTR	
LoginHours	Yes	Yes	R/W	Variant	Times during which user is allowed to login
LoginScript	Yes	Yes	R/W	BSTR	Path of login script
LoginWorkstations	Yes	Yes	R/W	BSTR Array	Names of workstations user is allowed to login from
Manager		Yes	R/W	BSTR	
MaxLogins	Yes	Yes	R/W	Long	Maximum number of simultaneous logins
MaxStorage	Yes	Yes	R/W	Long	Maximum disk space allowed for this user
NamePrefix		Yes	R/W	BSTR	
NameSuffix		Yes	R/W	BSTR	
OfficeLocations		Yes	R/W	BSTR Array	
OtherName		Yes	R/W	BSTR	
PasswordExpirationDATE	Yes		R/W	Date	Date password will expire
PasswordLastChanged		Yes	R/O	DATE	Date password was last changed
PasswordMinimumLength	Yes		R/W	Long	Minimum length of password

Name	In WinNT	In LDAP	Access	Data Type	Meaning
PasswordRequired	Yes	Yes	R/W	Boolean	Whether password is required
Picture		Yes	R/W	VARIANT	
PostalAddresses		Yes	R/W	BSTR Array	
PostalCodes		Yes	R/W	BSTR Array	
Profile	Yes	Yes	R/W	BSTR	
RequireUnique Password			R/W	BOOLEAN	Indicates if any new password should be different from all known previous passwords
SeeAlso		Yes	R/W	VARIANT	
TelephoneHome		Yes	R/W	BSTR Array	
TelephoneMobile		Yes	R/W	BSTR Array	
TelephoneNumber		Yes	R/W	BSTR Array	
TelephonePager		Yes	R/W	BSTR Array	
Title		Yes	R/W	BSTR	

In this list I've only filled in the descriptions of those properties that have a specific effect on the account. The ones I've left blank are general descriptive properties in which you can put whatever value you want, but they are only intended for people to read – Windows itself will not use the values.

Note that all these properties are implemented both as automation properties and as schema-based properties, in both providers. However, in the case of LDAP, most of these properties have different names if you access them through the schema. Details of the names of the properties defined in the schema for users in Active Directory are in MSDN, in the classes part of the documentation for the Active Directory schema.

The above are the only automation properties available through the `IADsUser` interface. In the case of LDAP, there is the usual huge range of additional properties that are available through the schema only. For WinNT there are also a couple of extra schema-based properties. They are:

Name	Syntax	Description
HomeDirDrive	String	The user's home directory
ObjectSID	Octet String	The security ID of the user
Parameters	String	A string associated with the account which may be used by other applications
PrimaryGroupID	Integer	Primary group ID
UserFlags	Integer	Flags defined in the `ADS_USER_FLAG` enumeration that indicate things like whether the account is locked out, whether the user can change the password, etc.

Remember these properties can only be accessed through the property cache interfaces, or through `IADs::Get()`, *etc. These are not automation properties.*

UserFlags

Of these, the property `UserFlags` is the most interesting one, since it can be used to set a number of additional characteristics that define the user account. The property is an integer, and is constructed by performing a logical OR operation on the possible values. These possible values are:

Symbol	Value	Description
ADS_UF_SCRIPT	0x0001	A logon script will be executed
ADS_UF_ACCOUNTDISABLE	0x0002	Account is disabled
ADS_UF_HOMEDIR_REQUIRED	0x0003	Home directory required
ADS_UF_LOCKOUT	0x0010	Account is locked out
ADS_UF_PASSWD_NOTREQD	0x0020	No password required
ADS_UF_PASSWD_CANT_CHANGE	0x0040	User cannot change password
ADS_UF_ENCRYPTED_TEXT_PASSWORD_ALLOWED	0x0080	User can use encrypted password
ADS_UF_TEMP_DUPLICATE_ACCOUNT	0x0100	Other domains that trust this domain should not authenticate this account
ADS_UF_NORMAL_ACCOUNT	0x0200	Normal account (for trust relationships)
ADS_UF_INTERDOMAIN_TRUST_ACCOUNT	0x0800	*Permit to trust* account for a system domain that *trusts* other domains
ADS_UF_WORKSTATION_TRUST_ACCOUNT	0x1000	Account for a Windows NT® Workstation/Windows® 2000 Professional or Windows NT® Server/Windows® 2000 Server that is a member of this domain

Symbol	Value	Description
ADS_UF_SERVER_TRUST_ ACCOUNT	0x2000	Computer account for a system backup domain controller that is a member of this domain
ADS_UF_DONTEXPIREPASSWD	0x10000	Password never expires
ADS_UF_MNS_LOGON_ACCOUNT	0x20000	This is an MNS logon account
ADS_UF_SMARTCARD_REQUIRED	0x40000	User must use a smart card to logon
ADS_UF_TRUSTED_FOR_ DELEGATION	0x80000	This is a service account and is trusted for Kerberos delegation
ADS_UF_NOT_DELEGATED	0x100000	Security context will never be delegated to a service

The 0x in front of each number in the table indicates that the number is in hexadecimal form. In VB, the 0x should be replaced by h.

OK – that's all the theory we need. The following code samples show what this means in practice for how you perform various operations on users. The samples are all in VB or VBScript, because those are the languages in which you will normally want to perform these types of operations.

Listing all the Users on a Machine

This VB code will list all the users on a computer. For each user it also gives the description. If you run this code you will need to replace <ComputerName> by the name of your own computer

```
Private Sub Form_Load()

    ' get the computer object
    Dim oParent As IADs ' this is a computer object
    Dim oContainer As IADsContainer

    Set oParent = GetObject("WinNT://<ComputerName>")
    Set oContainer = oParent

    List1.AddItem "Computer name: " & oParent.Name
    List1.AddItem ""

    oContainer.Filter = Array("user")

    Dim oUser As IADsUser

    'list all the users
    For Each oUser In oContainer
      List1.AddItem "User name:    " & oUser.Name
      List1.AddItem "Description: " & oUser.Description
      List1.AddItem ""
    Next

    Set oUser = Nothing
    Set oParent = Nothing
    Set oContainer = Nothing

End Sub
```

Here are the results for my computer, BiggyBiggy:

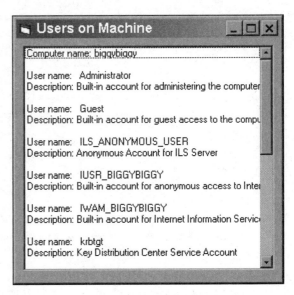

Note that I've specified the name of a computer in the ADsPath:

```
Set oComputer = GetObject("WinNT://biggybiggy")
```

Note that if the computer happens to be a domain controller, then the users listed will actually be the global domain users, since there is no distinction between local users on a domain controller and global users for the domain.

Listing Users in a Domain

The users in a domain can be listed using the WinNT provider with the same code as above, provided the computer name you give is actually the name of a domain controller

Alternatively you can bind to the domain object and enumerate the children of the domain that are of type user. To do this, you change the above code as follows.

```
Private Sub Form_Load()

    ' get the computer object
Dim oParent As IADs ' this is a domain object
Dim oContainer As IADsContainer

Set oParent = GetObject("WinNT://<DomainName>")
Set oContainer = oParent

List1.AddItem "Domain name: " & oParent.Name
List1.AddItem ""

oContainer.Filter = Array("user")

Dim oUser As IADsUser
```

```
    'list all the users
    For Each oUser In oContainer
       List1.AddItem "User name:    " & oUser.Name
       List1.AddItem "Description: " & oUser.Description
       List1.AddItem ""
    Next

    Set oUser = Nothing
    Set oParent = Nothing
    Set oContainer = Nothing

End Sub
```

Note that both ways of doing this will return the same results. In the apparent directory exposed by the WinNT provider, domain user objects are duplicated in the DIT as children of both the domain object and the computer objects that represent the domain controllers.

You can also list users using the LDAP provider. The resultant code is very similar to the previous sample, so only the significant changes have been shaded. Here's what it looks like for my own domain

```
    Private Sub Form_Load()

    ' get the computer object
    On Error Resume Next

    Dim oParent As IADs
    Dim oContainer As IADsContainer

    Set oParent = _
    GetObject("LDAP://cn=users,dc=topofthepops,dc=fame,dc=com")
    Set oContainer = oParent

    List1.AddItem "Computer name: " & oParent.Name
    List1.AddItem ""

    'etc.
```

Apart from the change in the ADsPath, note that the object which contains the users in Active Directory is NOT a computer or a domain object. It's simply a container for the users, so we've had to declare it as of type IADs. The two code samples for the WinNT provider would have worked if we'd declared oParent to be of type IADsComputer or IADsDomain respectively – this is not the case here.

However, note that this code will only find the users in the default Users container. If your domain administrators have been playing about with Active Directory, and have created other containers for users, then this code won't find them unless you change it to explicitly look in the other containers as well. This is in contrast to the WinNT provider, which has all the users in the same place so you can find all of them by enumerating the children of the domain object.

> *In Chapter 7 (on searching), we'll learn how to code up a client that searches the directory, and so will find users anywhere, without you having to know where they might be.*

Anyway, for comparison with
WinNT, this is the result:

Adding a User

The process to add a local or global user in either LDAP or WinNT is very simple. In WinNT, you
don't need to set any additional properties other than the user name, which you specify in the
IADsContainer::Create() method.

On the other hand, in LDAP, you will need to specify the saMAccount name, which is just the name
the user will log in as. That's because the name you specify as the user name in LDAP is intended as
the user's real name (actually the cn property), which isn't necessarily the same as the login name.

```
Private Sub Form_Load()

   ' get the computer object
   On Error Resume Next

   Dim oComputer As IADsContainer
   Set oComputer = GetObject("LDAP://cn=users,dc=topofthepops,dc=fame,dc=com")

   Dim oUser
   Set oUser = oComputer.Create("user", "Another Noo Noo")
   oUser.Put("saMAccountName", "AnotherNooNoo")
   oUser.SetPassword("Eh Oh")
   oUser.SetInfo

   Set oUser = Nothing
   Set oComputer = Nothing

End Sub
```

In this case, we've taken the extra step of setting the password on the user before saving it. You can create a user in both WinNT and LDAP without setting a password, but I hope that's something that you'll *never* do! We'll cover the different ways to set a user password next.

In the code above, if I wanted to use the WinNT provider, I'd just have to make sure I connected to my WinNT domain object, and also gave the actual account name as the user name.

Setting a User Password

There are two ways to set a user password. Both ways are exposed as `IADsUser` methods.

`IADsUser::ChangePassword` is intended to be used from the user account of the password to be changed. It requires that the old password be supplied as a parameter.

`IADsUser::SetPassword` does not require the old password to be supplied, but it can only be used if you have administrator privileges on the machine or domain on which you are changing someone's password.

The example of creating a user illustrated setting a password. The following example illustrates changing a password.

```
Private Sub Form_Load()

    Dim oNooNoo As IADsUser
    Set oNooNoo = GetObject("WinNT://biggybiggy/NooNoo")

' TubbyCustard is old password, GotFat is new one
    oNooNoo.ChangePassword "TubbyCustard", "GotFat"

    Set oNooNoo = Nothing

End Sub
```

Setting The User Flags

This VB sample shows how to modify the properties of a local user so that the user cannot change the password, using the WinNT provider.

We will use the `UserFlags` schema-defined property to do this. Since the value of this property is formed by combining bits that represent various flags, we will need to first read the value of the `UserFlags` so that we can add our new flag to the ones already set, and not overwrite the existing flags.

Looking back at the table of user flags that we presented earlier, the value that prevents the user from changing the password is `ADS_UF_PASSWD_CANT_CHANGE`, which has the value 40 in hex (64 in decimal). The account we'll modify is the NooNoo account again. Here's the code that does it.

```
Private Sub Form_Load()

    Dim oNooNoo As IADsUser
    Set oNooNoo = GetObject("WinNT://biggybiggy/NooNoo")
    List1.AddItem oNooNoo.ADsPath

    Dim iCurrentFlags As Integer
    iCurrentFlags = oNooNoo.Get("UserFlags")
    Dim iNewFlags As Integer
    iNewFlags = (iCurrentFlags Or ADS_UF_PASSWD_CANT_CHANGE)
```

```
        List1.AddItem "User Flags was " & Hex(iCurrentFlags)
        oNooNoo.Put "UserFlags", iNewFlags
        oNooNoo.SetInfo
        oNooNoo.GetInfo
        List1.AddItem "User Flags is now " & Hex(oNooNoo.Get("UserFlags"))

        Set oNooNoo = Nothing

    End Sub
```

Notice how after setting the flags we call `SetInfo` and `GetInfo` to ensure that both the directory and cache are up to date and synchronized, before displaying the new value of the user flags.

Here's the result of this code.

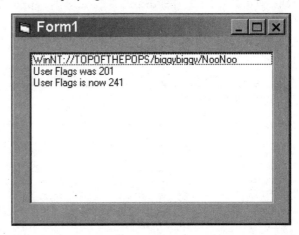

This clearly shows the value 0x40 being combined with the user flags. Reading back from the table of flags, the other flags that were already set were `ADS_UF_NORMAL_ACCOUNT`, indicating that this is a normal user account, and `ADS_UF_SCRIPT`, indicating that any logon script for this account will be executed.

Finding Out Who You Are

Now, I don't want you to start getting an identity crisis. I'm sure you all know who you are, even if I have my doubts sometimes. This section is here is because I've lost count of the times I've seen messages posted on listservers or newsgroups that basically say, 'Can someone please tell me how I find out who I am using ADSI?'

What they generally mean, of course, put a bit more precisely, is something like, 'How do I get the ADSI User object in WinNT or LDAP that corresponds to – well – to *me*?' Sometimes the question comes in more specific varieties: 'How do I find out my home directory?' or 'How do I find out my user profile using ADSI?'. But it always boils down to requiring information about yourself that you could get if only you had an interface pointer to your own ADSI user object that exposed `IADsUser`.

Well I can give you the answer in one line. Here it is:

You can't.

Well, perhaps I should qualify that a bit. You can't find out who you are using ADSI exclusively. There are various Windows API functions, etc. that will do the job instead. But what I really want to do here is explain why the question 'who am I?' isn't really a very sensible question anyway.

Let's think a bit about what you probably mean when you want your client to find out who you are. Let's make it very simple to start off with, and keep ADSI and ADSI providers out of the picture altogether. You want to write a simple application to display a dialog box that says 'I am Simon'.

That's actually do-able in C++. If you want to find out how, look up the Windows API function `GetUserName()`. It's a simple function and it returns a string that says who the user running the application is. Or does it? Let's have a look at how the MSDN documentation for it starts off:

> GetUserName: the GetUserName function retrieves the user name of the current thread. This is the name of the user currently logged onto the system...

The current thread? What's that? It's one of those terms that's probably more familiar to C++ people than to VB and scripting people. Think of the computer, trawling through memory, executing one assembly language instruction after another. Well that's a thread. A thread can be thought of as a sequence of instructions the computer is executing, corresponding to one task it is supposed to be doing. Usually the computer will appear to be doing quite a few things at the same time (letting you edit your document, printing something out, listening on the network for requests from other computers, etc.) Unless you have a multiprocessor machine, this appearance is an illusion. The computer actually performs one task (thread) for a short period of time, then the operating system cuts in and swaps over to another thread.

Anyway the point here is that you can think of a thread not only as a set of instructions, but also as an object with its own set of properties. Think of it as the object which is actually executing the code in your program. And since it's an object it has its own identity – it's user name, which you hope will correspond to your name.

VB programs normally have only one thread in them, but C++ programs can have more than one – and probably will do if the program is supposed to be doing more than one thing at the same time (like printing out a document, and simultaneously watching in case the user presses the cancel button). That's why I said that C++ people are more likely to be familiar with threads. So already the `GetUserID()` function isn't really returning who you are at all – it's returning who the thread is owned by.

Now that's for a simple dialog box. What happens when you bring COM into the picture? The client calls up a server, and let's say the server runs on a different machine, which the client doesn't even have a username on. Who are you now? Do you want the user ID of the thread the client is running on, or the (different) user ID of the thread the server is running on?

'But that won't affect ADSI', I hear you cry. 'ADSI providers are always in-process servers. They'll always run under the same user account as the client.' Well – that may be true enough at the client end, but what about the directory? The ADSI COM objects themselves may be in-process servers, but they have to talk to the directory service – which could easily be on a different machine. The thread that runs in the directory service to answer your queries almost certainly isn't owned by you.

Then of course there's impersonation, where a thread pretends to be another user for a short while, in order to perform a task on behalf of the other user. COM servers often impersonate their clients.

Have you had enough yet? I hope not, because it gets worse. What about your Active Server Pages? They run on the web server machine, and they don't run under the identity of the client. Unless the client has specifically authenticated to the web server (if you are not using anonymous web access), they won't even know what the client's user name is. The ASP scripts will normally run under the username of the Internet guest account, `IUSR_<ComputerName>`. Unless, of course, you've got site server personalization and membership installed and hooked up to your web site. In that case, the web server either authenticates the client as a personalized user account on the server machine, or as the account `IUSR<machine name>`, depending on whether Site Server is using NT authentication or membership directory authentication.

Well I could go on nagging you, but I'm sure you get the picture by now. ADSI is a great tool for administering users, but it's not really appropriate (or possible) to use ADSI to find out who you are. There are just too many unknown factors lurking around. If you are writing an ADSI client that needs to know who the current user is, then you need to find another way of doing it. But more importantly, you need to decide exactly what you want.

In most cases, it will be the username under which the client thread is running. If you're using C++, the `GetUserName()` API function will do you for this. It is also possible, though more difficult, to use the same API function in VB.

If you are writing an ASP script then your task is a bit harder. You cannot find out who the client is (as in the user name of the person running the web browser) unless the client has authenticated. If they have then you can do this:

```
<%
strUser = Request.ServerVariables ("LOGON_USER")
%>
```

If that's not quite the information you want, then you'll have to look carefully at the Request object to see if it can provide the information you require. You may be able to gain some information about the client from its IP address, also available through the Request object.

Groups

Groups implement `IADsGroup`. Like users, groups can be local to a machine or global to a domain. If you create a group on a computer which is a domain controller, it will generally be global. Active Directory only stores global groups. These are initially located in the BuiltIn container, which is under the domain object in the Directory Information Tree, but you can later on add other groups to other containers or organizational units that you might create.

The WinNT provider lets you access both types of group. Local groups in WinNT are situated under the computer on which they are defined, while global groups are children of the domain object, and of computers that happen to be domain controllers.

For both providers, local groups can only contain local users, but global groups can contain users or local groups.

Enumerating the Groups on a Computer

This needs to be done with the WinNT provider. The process is virtually identical to that of enumerating local users, except that you should set the filter on the container to `"group"`:

```
Private Sub Form_Load()

' get the computer object
  Dim oComputer As IADsComputer
  Dim oCompContainer As IADsContainer

  Set oComputer = GetObject("WinNT://biggybiggy")
  Set oCompContainer = oComputer

  List1.AddItem "Computer name: " & oComputer.Name
  List1.AddItem ""

  oComputer.Filter = Array("group")

  Dim oGroup As IADsGroup

' list all the Groups
  For Each oGroup In oComputer
    List1.AddItem "Group name:   " & oGroup.Name
    List1.AddItem "Description: " & oGroup.Description
    List1.AddItem ""
  Next

  Set oGroup = Nothing
  Set oComputer = Nothing
  Set oCompContainer = Nothing

End Sub
```

This sample results in this:

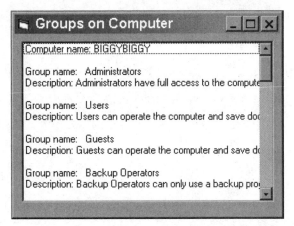

Note that if the computer happens to be a domain controller, the groups will actually be global groups, and will also be duplicated in WinNT as children of the domain object.

Enumerating the Groups in a Domain

This can be done with either the WinNT provider or the LDAP provider. However, as with users, if you use the LDAP provider, you will have the problem of possibly not knowing where all the groups might be stored.

We'll give the example here using LDAP, on the assumption that we know in advance that the only places where groups are located are in the BuiltIn container, and in the new Pop Star Users container that I created on BiggyBiggy. Just for a change, we'll also use a web page instead of plain VB.

```
<%@ Language = VBScript %>
<html>

<head>
<title> Groups in Domain </title>
</head>

<body>

<h1> Groups in Domain using LDAP Provider </h1>

This page lists the groups that are contained in
BuiltIn and in Pop Star Users, in the TopOfThePops.Fame.com domain

<%
dim arrContainers(2)
arrContainers(1) = "LDAP://OU=Pop Star Users,DC=TopOfThePops,DC=Fame,DC=com"
arrContainers(2) = "LDAP://CN=Builtin,DC=TopOfThePops,DC=Fame,DC=com"

dim oContainer
For i = 1 to 2
   set oContainer = GetObject(arrContainers(i))

   Response.Write "<p><strong>GROUPS CONTAINED IN " _
                  & oContainer.ADsPath & "</strong><p>"

   oContainer.Filter = Array("group")

   Dim oGroup
'  list all the Groups
   For Each oGroup In oContainer
      Response.Write "Group name:   " & oGroup.Name & "<br>"
      Response.Write "Description:   " & oGroup.Description & "<br>"
      Response.Write "<p>"
   Next

   Set oGroup = Nothing
   Set oCoontainers = Nothing

Next

%>

</body>
</html>
```

This ASP code looks like this in the browser:

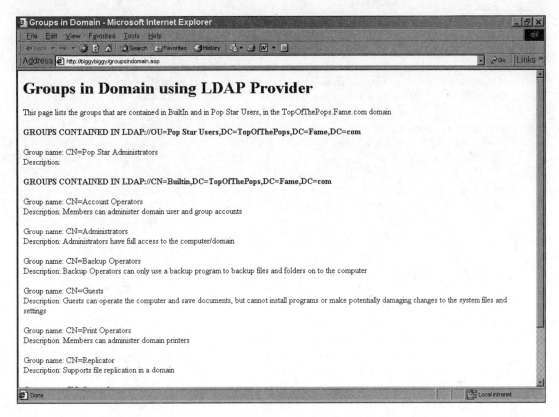

If we were using the WinNT provider, we would pick up all these groups just by looking in a single container: `WinNT://TopOfThePops`.

> *It's worth pointing out that sometimes administrators create local rather than global groups to manage the users. If you can't see the group you want to access in Active Directory, this is the most likely reason.*

Enumerating the Members of a Group

In VB and VBScript, this actually looks quite similar to the process of enumerating the children of any container. However, what's going on is slightly different. The members of a group aren't actually contained in the group object itself. Rather, the `IADsGroup` interface exposes a method, `Members`, which allows you to access another object: a members object. This object exposes the interface `IADsMembers`, which allows you to enumerate all the members in a `For Each` loop.

> *In C++ you'll use the `_NewEnum` property to obtain an enumerator – which is actually what is going on in VB under the surface.*

This means that the key statement you need to enumerate members of a group is

```
For Each oMember in oGroup.Members
```

The following ASP script lists out all the members of the Administrators group using the LDAP provider. Just out of interest, I've also used it to find out the class of each member in two different ways. Using the `IADs::Class` automation property, and using the multi-valued `objectClass` property in LDAP, which lists all the base classes contributing to a class as well.

```
<%@ Language = VBScript %>
<html>
<head>
<title> Members of Group </title>
</head>

<body>

<h1> Members of Group using LDAP Provider </h1>

<%
dim oGroup
set oGroup = GetObject("LDAP://CN=Administrators,CN=Builtin," & _
                       "DC=TopOfThePops,DC=Fame,DC=Com")

Response.Write "<p><strong>MEMBERS OF GROUP " & _
                oGroup.ADsPath & "</strong><p>"

Dim oMember

'list all the Members.
For Each oMember in oGroup.Members

    Response.Write "Member name:   " & oMember.Name & "<br>"
    Response.Write "Class:    " & oMember.Class & "<br>"

    For Each objectClass in oMember.Get("objectClass")
        Response.Write "objectClass: " & objectClass & "<br>"
    Next

    Response.Write "Description:   " & oMember.Description & "<br>"
    Response.Write "<p>"

Next

Set oGroup = Nothing
Set oMember = Nothing

%>

</body>
</html>
```

The output from this is quite interesting:

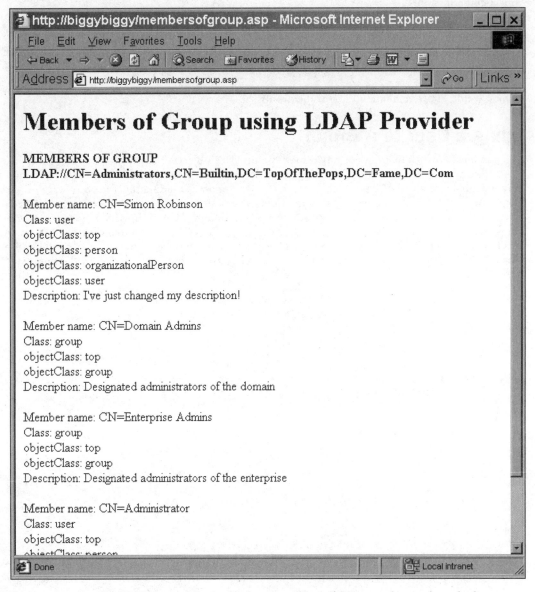

If I wanted to use the WinNT provider to do the same thing, I'd just need to replace the line:

```
set oGroup = GetObject("LDAP://CN=Administrators,CN=Builtin," & _
                    "DC=TopOfThePops,DC=Fame,DC=Com")
```

with:

```
set oGroup = GetObject("WinNT://TopOfThePops/Administrators")
```

But note that in this case, I would not now be able to obtain the objectClasses property, as that's not defined in WinNT.

By the way, if I wanted to go the other way, and find out what groups a particular user is a member of, I'd need to use the IADsUser::Groups method on the group. The key statement would be:

```
For Each oGroup in oUser.Groups
```

which would allow an enumeration of the groups.

Adding a User to a Group

To add a user (or for that matter, any other type of ADSI object) to a group, we need the IADsGroup::Add() method. The following VB sample uses one of the new users that I added to my machine at the end of the last chapter, in the section on Extending the Tree Structure of Active Directory. In that section I created a couple of new organizational units, *Pop Star Users* and *Old Pop Star Users*, to illustrate how you can split up users into different hierarchies. I'm going to use one of those users (Geri Halliwell, sAMAccountName: GeriH) here in order to demonstrate that having users in different organizational units in Active Directory has no effect on how you see those users in the WinNT provider – they still appear as children of either the domain or the local computer concerned.

In this sample I'm going to add GeriH to the administrators group. It also uses another IADsGroup method, IsMember, to check that the addition worked OK, before displaying a complete list of the members of that group.

```
Private Sub Form_Load()

' bind to the administrators group and add the new user
  Dim oGroup As IADsGroup
  Set oGroup = GetObject("WinNT://TopOfThePops/Administrators")

  oGroup.Add "WinNT://BiggyBiggy/GeriH"

' check the new user is now in the administrators group
  If oGroup.IsMember("WinNT://TopOfThePops/GeriH") Then
    List1.AddItem "Successfully added Geri to Administrators"
  Else
    List1.AddItem "Something went wrong"
  End If

  List1.AddItem ""
  List1.AddItem "MEMBERS OF ADMINISTRATORS NOW ARE:"

  For Each member In oGroup.Members
    List1.AddItem member.Name
  Next

  Set oGroup = Nothing

End Sub
```

Notice that this code works in WinNT, even though in Active Directory I had actually added GeriH to my Pop Star Users organizational unit, not to the default Users container. Also notice that at no point do I need to actually bind to the user object – all I need to do is supply its ADsPath to methods called on the group object. Though clearly, this code will raise an error if the user doesn't exist in the directory: The IADsGroup::Add() method will return an error if supplied with an ADsPath of an object that doesn't exist.

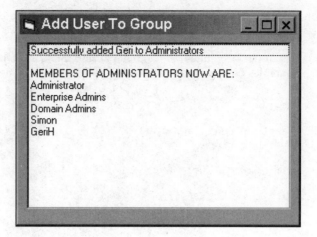

Removing a User from a Group

It is also possible to remove users from a group by calling `IADsGroup::Delete`, on supplying the `ADsPath` of the relevant user. Simply replace the line:

```
oGroup.Add "WinNT://BiggyBiggy/GeriH"
```

with:

```
oGroup.Remove "WinNT://BiggyBiggy/GeriH"
```

Computers

Manipulating Computers is quite similar to manipulating users – the only difference is that computers objects may be located at different points in the directory – eg. in the *Computers* of *Domain Controllers* containers in Active Directory. In this section, we show how to enumerate the computers, and how to add or remove a computer account. We also discuss the question of how to determine if a computer is a workstation or a domain controller.

Enumerating the Computers in a Domain

Once again, it is possible to do this using the WinNT or LDAP providers. In WinNT it's easy. You just bind to the domain object, set the filter to `Array("Computer")` and list all the children.

With LDAP it's slightly harder, because right from the start the computers are separated into two containers. The domain controllers are in the `Domain Controllers` container, and the other computers are in the `Computers` container, which means you have at least two containers you need to iterate over. And as usual, if it's not a new Active Directory installation, but one in which your systems administration people have been playing about with for a while, there's always the possibility that they'll have bunged computer accounts at other places in Active Directory. So your choice is really either to find out from them where all the containers that might contain computers actually are, or wait till Chapter 7 where we cover searching.

One other point you will need to be aware of is that if you bind to a computer object in WinNT, it'll expose the `IADsComputer` interface. If you use LDAP, it won't. It'll expose `IADsUser` instead.

Anyway here's the code sample for getting the computers using the WinNT provider. It's sufficiently similar to the previous samples that I've only highlighted the particularly interesting line.

```
Private Sub Form_Load()

  Dim oDomain As IADsContainer
  Dim oComputer As IADsComputer

  Set oDomain = GetObject("WinNT://TopOfThePops")

  oDomain.Filter = Array("computer")

  For Each oComputer In oDomain
    List1.AddItem oComputer.Name
  Next

  Set oComputer = Nothing
  Set oDomain = Nothing

End Sub
```

Enumerating the Computers More Quickly

If you have a large network, one problem you're likely to find is enumerating the computers runs very slowly. That probably won't happen in the above code, because it simply checks what computer accounts there are. This means you only need to check the directory on the domain controller. However, as soon as you start requesting any information, or attempting to bind to other objects – for which the WinNT provider actually has to talk to the computers concerned – your code will slow down.

You've probably noticed when running some of the samples, that even binding to one ADSI object in WinNT at computer level or lower in the directory tree can take a couple of seconds. Imagine if you're doing an enumeration that has to bind in turn to a couple of hundred computers. Your code could be held up for several minutes doing the binding.

This is not really a problem with ADSI – the problem is that network connections in general can be slow. One way to alleviate this is to make sure that your code is generating user output as it binds. In other words, don't attempt to bind to 50 computers *then* start displaying the results. Bind to the first one, then display any results to the user from that. Then bind to the next computer and so on. That won't solve the problem – your code will take just as long to execute as before – but it may make it less annoying to the user!

If that is not enough to solve the problem, then there is only one solution remaining – and it's one which will make C++ evangelists very happy, because the solution is to use multiple threads. This means that you will have to code in C++ – you won't normally be able to use VB or scripting languages, because these languages at present don't support the creation of extra threads. In C++ you simply need to create a number of threads, and have these threads work simultaneously in getting interface pointers to all the computer objects that you need. Since this code wouldn't demonstrate any new principles concerned with ADSI we won't give a sample for this.

Finding out if a Computer is a Workstation or a Domain Controller

This is probably a task for the LDAP provider. Assuming you're working with a reasonably clean install of Active Directory, the easiest way is to simply check whether the computer is contained in the `Domain Controllers` organizational unit or the `Computers` container.

The `IADsComputer` interface does have a property, role, which is intended to be used to indicate whether a computer is a workstation or a domain. However, this property is not populated automatically by the operating system. It is a read/write property and must be set manually. This means that it is possible to find out whether a computer is a workstation or a domain controller by looking at this property using the WinNT provider – but only if your system administrators have taken the trouble to set this property manually.

LDAP doesn't implement `IADsComputer`, but there is a similar schema-based property, `computerRole`. However, my tests seemed to indicate that this property again has to be set by the systems administrators rather than being set automatically.

Creating a Computer Account

Creating a computer account in either WinNT or LDAP is a simple matter of calling `IADsContainer::Create()` on the new object's parent. In WinNT, there is no need to set any properties, but in LDAP you will need to set the `sAMAccountName`. The following code adds a computer account named `CrashEvenMore` to my domain:

```
Private Sub Form_Load()

   Dim oDomain As IADsContainer
   Set oDomain = GetObject("WinNT://TopOfThePops")

   Dim oComputer As IADs
   Set oComputer = oDomain.Create("computer", "CrashEvenMore")

   oComputer.SetInfo

End Sub
```

Note that this only creates a computer account – it doesn't imply that the computer is actually there. If you are logged on to the workstation which you want to join the domain, then when you request to join the domain, you will normally be given the option to create a new computer account in the domain, or connect to an existing account.

Deleting a Computer Account

This is similar to creating a computer account, but you call `IADsContainer::Delete()` instead.

For example, to delete the new `CrashEvenMore` computer account that we've just created, you could do this:

```
Private Sub Form_Load()

   Dim oDomain As IADsContainer
   Set oDomain = GetObject("WinNT://TopOfThePops")
```

```
        Dim oComputer As IADs
        Set oComputer = oDomain.Delete("computer", "CrashEvenMore")

        oComputer.SetInfo

    End Sub
```

With the LDAP provider only, you can alternatively call `IADsDeleteOps::Delete()` on the computer object itself.

Windows 2000 Services

So what is a **Windows 2000 service**? Well the best way to understand it is to contrast it with a normal application.

> *A reminder. In NT4, there are NT services. These are the same thing as Windows 2000 services, so all of this section applies to equally to NT4 and NT services as well. We've opted for the more up-to-date name Windows 2000 Services because most of this book is concerned with Windows 2000.*

When you want to start an application, you'll do so most likely either by double-clicking on the executable file in Windows Explorer, or possibly by typing in the file name at the command prompt. If you want the application to start whenever you log in, you'll put a link to it in your startup folder. Since you're familiar with COM, you'll be aware of one other way of starting an application: if an executable houses COM objects, it may be started by a COM client calling `CoCreateInstance()`. And in general, a process may start another application, with a call to the API function `CreateProcess()`.

So far so good. Unfortunately, Windows 2000 (or Windows NT) needs more flexibility than that in how processes can be started. You see, Windows 2000 is doing a lot of other things while you're working – like monitoring network traffic, and controlling devices such as your monitor and CD drive. Even a COM server can only be launched because the COM Service Control Manager is already running and able to service the requests that come through `CoCreateInstance()` by locating objects.

Now, I don't know about you, but as I recall the last time I logged into Windows 2000, I didn't have to spend the first 5 minutes starting up device drivers and other essential processes. Strangely enough, they appeared to already be running. In fact, the processes that run the device drivers must have been running before I'd even logged in – if they weren't, then Windows 2000 wouldn't have been able to present me with a login dialog box. So by a process of logical deduction we've deduced that there are processes that aren't started by the user. Processes, indeed, that are already running before anyone has even logged on. These are the Windows 2000 services.

> **A Windows 2000 service is a special process that is started by the system, rather than by you.**

I should qualify that definition by saying that it is possible to start a service 'manually' – the user can request to the system that a service should be started – although ultimately it is still the system that starts up the process.

A service is housed in an executable file, just like an application. But there is one other difference between applications and services that you need to be aware of.

> **Each executable only contains one application (how can it have more – there's only one program entry point), but it is possible for more than one service to coexist in the same executable.**

This allows related services to share global data if required. The fact that Windows 2000 achieves this feat with only one entry point is something that I'll just ask you to accept. We don't have space here to go into the internal architecture of services.

> *If you want to know more about that side of things, check out Professional NT Services, by Kevin Miller (ISBN 1-861001-3-04), published by Wrox Press.*

Usually in software, the best way to understand something is to start using it and see what happens. So let's have a look at the services running on your machine. In Windows 2000, you actually need the Computer Management MMC snap-in tool to do this.

The Computer Management Tool

Click on the Start menu, and follow Programs | Administrative Tools | Computer Management. Once you've got the tool up, you'll need to open System Tools in the tree control, then select Services. You'll now be able to see a list of all the Windows 2000 services in the right hand pane of the snap-in. Like this:

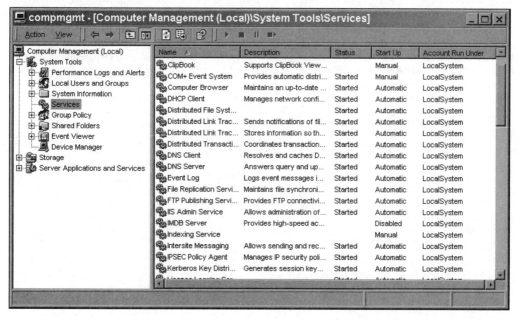

> *If you're running NT4, then you won't have this tool available. You'll need to run the services dialog box – which you can get by going to the control panel and clicking on Services.*

The computer management tool tells us that services have a Status – they can be started or not running. There are actually some other states they can be in – like paused or attempting to start, or stopping as well.

The tool also shows us how the service starts, in the Start Up column of the list view. Most of the services are Automatic, which means they'll start automatically when Windows 2000 boots up. If you've ever wondered what your blasted machine is doing during those infuriating minutes between Windows 2000 loading and you actually being able to log on, there's your answer!

Some Services are set to Manual startup. Now don't get me wrong – I said earlier that services are started by the system, they are not started by a user. And that's still true. A manual service still has to be started by the system – it just won't start up automatically at boot time. You have to tell the system you want the service started. We'll see how in a few minutes.

Services can also be disabled. In the previous screenshot, the IMDB service (which provides fast access to cached data) is Disabled – that means it cannot be started at the moment.

One other characteristic you'll notice is that most of the services are running under an account known as LocalSystem. This is a special user account intended only for services. It's not possible to log in with this user name. This account has practically unlimited privileges on the local computer – it even has some privileges that the Administrator doesn't have. But it has hardly any privileges to do anything on the network. Services are usually run under this account because they tend to be the kinds of processes that are doing important administration or maintenance to keep your computer running – so they need high privileges.

You can actually start, stop and pause services using the computer management tool. Try it – just click on the toolbar buttons that look like the play, pause and stop buttons on a tape player. (If you're running the NT4 Services applet, these are just normal Windows buttons).

If you click on a service to select it, some of these buttons may be grayed out, depending on what you can do with the service. For example, if you select Event Log, you'll find you cannot stop or pause it. The Event Log is the service that allows other applications to record events, errors or warnings in case you need to check the status of your system later. That's classed as an essential service, so it must always be running.

You can also look at the properties of a service, by right clicking on it and selecting **Properties** from the context menu. You'll get a dialog box like this:

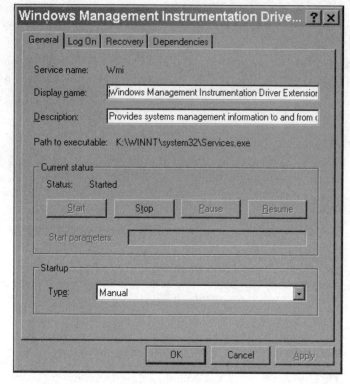

For this screenshot, I've selected one of the services that manage WMI, the means by which Windows 2000 stores management data for applications. (We'll be looking at WMI in more detail in Chapter 14.) This box lets you see where the executable that houses the service is, as well as allowing you to start or stop it, and select its start type.

> *Feel free to play, but unless you're certain you know what you're doing, make sure you restart any services that you stop or pause before you exit the Computer Management Tool. Also, don't change the start type of any service – or you might find your computer doesn't behave quite how you expect the next time you reboot!*

The Service Control Manager

I mentioned earlier that services could only be started by the system. In fact, services are controlled by a process known as the **Service Control Manager** (**SCM**)

When you change the status of any service using the Computer Management tool, what actually happens behind the scenes? The Computer Management snap-in communicates your request to the SCM, which in turn tells the service to carry out the requested action.

The SCM talks to the service by posting it messages, and there are 5 possible messages it can post: instructing the service to start, stop, pause, continue (after a pause), or notify the SCM of its current status.

> *In COM, it is common to talk about the COM Service Control Manager. This is not the same thing – the COM SCM is actually just a normal Windows 2000 Service, but it happens to be the one that controls the operation of COM. Don't get confused. In this book we are only concerned with the Windows 2000 SCM.*

ADSI and Services

As you've probably guessed, the reason we've covered services in so much detail is that services can be controlled using ADSI. Using the WinNT provider, it is possible to find out about the services on your computer, to obtain information about the status of each one, and also to start, stop, pause or continue services.

Services are implemented by WinNT as **Service objects**. These are ADSI objects that expose the interfaces IADsService and IADsServiceOperations.

IADsService is derived from IADs. It is classed informally as a persistent object interface, and – like most persistent object interfaces – it simply exposes some extra automation properties that convey information about the service.

IADsServiceOperations is a dynamic object interface. It is concerned more with the current state of a service than with its general (permanent) properties. This interface exposes one automation property – the service's current status – along with a number of methods to stop, start, pause or continue a service, as well as to set the password for the account under which the service is run. As you'll no doubt guess, you'll normally need administrator privileges to be able to use these methods.

Service objects are always children of the computer object corresponding to the computer on which the services are running.

Enumerating the Services on a Computer

We actually saw how to do this in Chapter 2, in the example that demonstrated how to list the children of a container.

Managing and Checking the Status of a Service

In this section, we'll demonstrate how to stop, start, pause and continue a service, as well as how to check the current status of a service, by developing a small VB application. Here's what the application looks like:

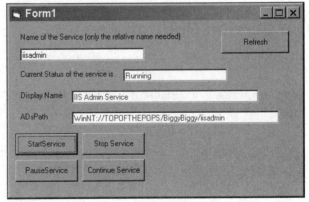

The idea is that you type the name of the service you want into the text box marked **Name of the Service**. By name here we mean the relative distinguished name that the ADSI service object in WinNT answers to (the `IADS::Name` property). The application then binds to the object and displays the service's current status, its display name and `ADsPath`. You can press the buttons to stop, start, pause or continue the service. There's also a **Refresh** button, which doesn't do anything to the service, but refreshes the display with the service's current status.

> *Note that this is a simple application. It doesn't make any attempt to detect what a service will and won't currently allow you to do to it and won't disable the buttons as appropriate. For example, if a service is running, it will not accept a request to start running. However the StartService button on this dialog is still active, and if you press it you will get an error message.*
>
> *You'll also get an error message if you try to stop a service that has other running services dependant on it. In both of these cases, the application does trap the error so that it won't crash the program.*

Anyway, let's have a look at the code. We need two global variables to store interface pointers to the service object we are currently bound to:

```
Dim oServiceOps As IADsServiceOperations
Dim oService As IADsService
```

There are going to be two big procedures in this application. `RefreshStatus()` actually does the job of displaying the current information about the services in the text boxes. `BindToNewObject()` attempts to bind to a new ADSI object that has just been typed in, and then calls `RefreshStatus()` to display the information for the new object. These are the procedures that actually do the guts of the work, but before we look at them, we'll check out what events cause them to be called.

Programming the Events

We need to bind to a new object when we detect that the user has typed a new name in the text box that requests it. This will be if the user presses *Enter* in that text box, or if the text box loses the input focus. That gives us this code:

```
Private Sub textName_KeyUp(KeyCode As Integer, Shift As Integer)

  If KeyCode = 13 Then
    Call BindToNewObject
  End If

End Sub
```

```
Private Sub textName_LostFocus()

  Call BindToNewObject

End Sub
```

`textName`, as you might guess, is the name of the text box.

If the user hits the **Refresh** button, then we need to refresh the data:

```
Private Sub buttonRefresh_Click()

  UpdateStatus

End Sub
```

Now here's where it gets more interesting. Suppose the user hits the **Stop Service** button. In this case we need to stop the service – which requires the `IADsServiceOperations::Stop` method. The code is pretty simple:

```
Private Sub buttonStop_Click()

  On Error GoTo failedstop

  oServiceOps.Stop
  Call UpdateStatus
  Exit Sub

failedstop:
    MsgBox "Error Occurred. Error Number: " & Err.Number & vbCrLf & _
           Err.Description

End Sub
```

So, to stop a service it's literally a one-line command with no parameters.

The error trap is there in case the service fails to stop for any reason. Then we need to display a message explaining why, but we don't want the whole program to bail out. This would happen, for example, if we attempted to stop a service that had other services dependant on it.

Starting, Pausing and Continuing a service works on pretty much the same principle:

```
Private Sub buttonStart_Click()

  On Error GoTo failedstart

  oServiceOps.Start
  Call UpdateStatus
  Exit Sub

failedstart:
    MsgBox "Error Occurred. Error Number: " & Err.Number & _
           vbCrLf & Err.Description

End Sub
```

```
Private Sub buttonPause_Click()

  On Error GoTo failedpause

  oServiceOps.Pause
  Call UpdateStatus
  Exit Sub

failedpause:
    MsgBox "Error Occurred. Error Number: " & Err.Number & _
           vbCrLf & Err.Description

End Sub
```

```
Private Sub buttonContinue_Click()

  On Error GoTo failedcontinue
```

```
        oServiceOps.Continue
        Call UpdateStatus
        Exit Sub

    failedcontinue:
        MsgBox "Error Occurred. Error Number: " & Err.Number & _
               vbCrLf & Err.Description

    End Sub
```

Binding to a New Object

Finally we get on to what happens when you actually need to bind to a new object. This only uses ADSI function calls that we've already covered.

```
    Private Sub BindToNewObject()

      On Error GoTo failedtobind

      Set oService = GetObject("WinNT://BiggyBiggy/" & textName.Text)
      Set oServiceOps = oService
      Call UpdateStatus
      Exit Sub

    failedtobind:
      MsgBox "Failed to bind to object WinNT://BiggyBiggy/" & textName.Text

    End Sub
```

Updating the Status

Printing out the status of a service is more interesting.

```
    Private Sub UpdateStatus()

      On Error Resume Next

    ' clear all the text boxes
      textDisplayName.Text = ""
      textADsPath.Text = ""
      textStatus.Text = ""

    ' fill in the properties of this service
      textDisplayName.Text = oService.DisplayName
      textADsPath.Text = oService.ADsPath

    ' get the status of the service
      Dim Status As Integer
      Status = oService.Status And 7

      Select Case Status
        Case 1
          textStatus.Text = "Stopped"
        Case 2
          textStatus.Text = "Attempting to Start"
        Case 3
          textStatus.Text = "Attempting to Stop"
        Case 4
          textStatus.Text = "Running"
```

```
      Case 5
        textStatus.Text = "Attempting to continue"
      Case 6
        textStatus.Text = "Attempting to pause"
      Case 7
        textStatus.Text = "Paused"
      Case 0
        textStatus.Text = "Error"
    End Select


  End Sub
```

So what's going on here? Well, printing out the `ADsPath` and display name is easy enough. We do those from the `IADsService` interface. The current status is more of a temporary value, and as such is handled from the `IADsServiceOperations` interface – in particular the automation property, status. This is an integer, whose value indicates the actual status.

Notice the line

```
    Status = oService.Status And 7
```

That's there because the `Status` property is another of these bitmasked numbers that often turn up. Only the last three bits of it indicate the actual current status. The ADSI documentation also indicates other values in more significant bits that relate to things like the start type of the service. The documentation doesn't make it clear whether any of these bits will actually be set when you retrieve the status, but I didn't want to take a chance, so I masked them out.

That just about wraps it up for Windows 2000 Services. Besides the functions I've illustrated, there's an `IADsServiceOperations::SetPassword` method to set the password you'd use to access a service, and a number of other automation properties on the `IADsService` interface. As usual, full details are in Appendix F.

File Shares

In this section, we'll look at what file shares are and how to manipulate them with ADSI.

How File Shares Work

File shares are how your computer makes its folders and files available to other computers. Recall that in the previous chapter, when we looked at how Windows Explorer views domains, we found that if you attempted to examine any computer – even your own computer – across the network, you couldn't actually see any of the drives, folders or files in it. That's because you have to specifically arrange for other computers to be able to see the relevant folders. This is done through a particular Windows 2000 Service, the **lanman** service.

You can see this service through the services MMC snap-in (or services applet in NT4), and you can start and stop it, just as you can any other service. It manages what are known as file shares.

> **A file share can be thought of as an instruction to expose a particular folder to the network, under a given name.**

The name through which it is exposed to the network doesn't have to be the name of the folder. If the computer receives a request from another computer on the network to browse folders or retrieve a specific file, the request is dealt with by the lanman service. This checks through the current file shares (and checks what permissions have been assigned to them) before deciding what, if any, data to return.

Setting up a File Share in Windows Explorer

The easiest way to set up a file share is through the Windows Explorer. For example, I have a folder on BiggyBiggy, E:\SimonsDocs, which is the folder where most of my documents, including this book, are stored. If I want to be able to see this folder from my other computer, CrashLots, then I'll need to set up a file share on it.

To do that I open Windows Explorer, and right-click on the folder E:\SimonsDocs to bring up the context menu. In the context menu, I'll select Sharing. That brings up this dialog:

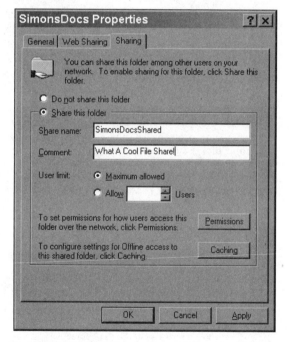

The default is not to share the folder. Click the Share this folder radio button, and type in the Share Name (this is the name the folder will appear under to other computers) and a Comment. You can also elect to limit the number of other users that are simultaneously allowed to use this folder across the network. Each connection from another user is known as a **session**.

Through the other buttons in this dialog, you can also set how the files are cached, and you can control – at a very crude level – who is allowed to access this folder over the network in what way:

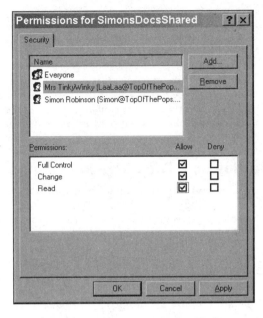

This dialog is interesting as it's a very crude example of an access control list, which we'll encounter more of in Chapter 9. You can specify permissions for any particular domain user or group. The possible permissions are read, write (change) and full control – which means the ability to read or change files, but also to modify security permissions and take ownership. Since the default when setting up a file share is to allow everyone full control, it pays to do a few seconds work on this particular dialog box.

ADSI, incidentally, along with Windows 2000, uses a similar system of access control lists to control security, but it has a finer gradation of permissions.

Once the share is set up, it is possible to see that in Windows Explorer, because a hand appears on the icon for that folder.

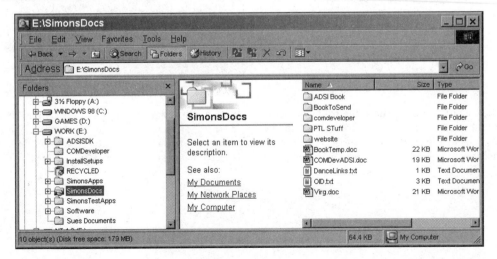

In this screenshot, the folder SimonsDocs has a hand by it in the tree view, indicating that this folder has been shared. And it's now possible to see this folder under My Network Places – this time under the shared name we selected in the file share dialog:

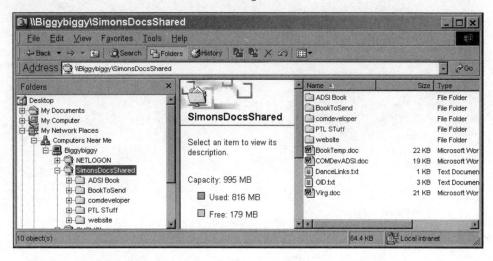

By the way the NETLOGON folder above SimonsDocsShared is itself a file share. It is set up automatically by the system when NT is installed, and is required for network logons.

It is also possible to create hidden file shares: you just make sure the shared name ends in the $ character, and the share will then be hidden from browsing. It is only possible for other machines to connect to the share by explicitly naming it and mapping a network drive to it. So, the share can only be used by people who have been told of its existence. Hidden shares are not viewable using ADSI either.

File Shares in ADSI

To access file shares, you need the WinNT provider. For a change, we're going to do this sample in C++. This code binds to the lanmanserver file service on my local computer and uses the IADsContainer interface on the service to enumerate the file shares. It then uses the IADsFileShare interface on each of the contained file shares to identify properties of the file share. Note that IADsFileShare is derived from IADs, which is why we are able to use this interface pointer to retrieve the automation property Name.

```cpp
CString IntToString(int i)
{
    wchar_t pszText[30];
    _itow(i, pszText, 10);
    return pszText;
}

//////////////////////////////////////////////////////////////////////////////
// CCPPListFileSharesDlg message handlers

BOOL CCPPListFileSharesDlg::OnInitDialog()
{
    CDialog::OnInitDialog();
```

```
    HRESULT hr;
    CComPtr<IADs> spADs;
    CComQIPtr<IADsFileShare, &IID_IADsFileShare> spADsFSrv;
    CComQIPtr<IADsContainer, &IID_IADsContainer> spCont;
    hr = ADsGetObject(L"WinNT://BiggyBiggy/lanmanserver", IID_IADs,
                      (void**)&spADs); ASH;
    spADsFSrv = spADs;
    spCont = spADs;

    CComBSTR bstrADsPath;
    hr = spADs->get_ADsPath(&bstrADsPath);
    m_listbox.AddString(CString("File Service ADsPath: ") + bstrADsPath);

    CComBSTR bstrName;
    hr = spADs->get_Name(&bstrName);
    m_listbox.AddString(CString(L"File Service Name:   ") + bstrName);
    m_listbox.AddString(L"");
    m_listbox.AddString(L"FILE SERVICES");

    IEnumVARIANT *pEnumerator;
    hr = ADsBuildEnumerator(spCont, &pEnumerator); ASH;
    DWORD dwFetched;
    VARIANT var;
    VariantInit(&var);
    hr = ADsEnumerateNext(pEnumerator, 1, &var, &dwFetched); ASH;
while (hr == S_OK)
    {
        m_listbox.AddString(L"");
        if(var.vt == VT_DISPATCH)
        {
            CComQIPtr<IADsFileShare, &IID_IADsFileShare> spFSh;
            spFSh = var.pdispVal;

            CComBSTR bstrName;
            hr = spFSh->get_Name(&bstrName); ASH;
            m_listbox.AddString(CString(L"Name:   ") + bstrName);

            CComBSTR bstrPath;
            hr = spFSh->get_Path(&bstrPath); ASH;
            m_listbox.AddString(CString(L"Path:   ") + bstrPath);

            CComBSTR bstrDescription;
            hr = spFSh->get_Description(&bstrDescription); ASH;
            m_listbox.AddString(CString(L"Description: ") + bstrDescription);

            CComBSTR bstrHostComputer;
            hr = spFSh->get_HostComputer(&bstrHostComputer); ASH;
            m_listbox.AddString(CString(L"Host Computer:  ") +
                                bstrHostComputer);

            long lCurrentUserCount;
            hr = spFSh->get_CurrentUserCount(&lCurrentUserCount); ASH;
            m_listbox.AddString(CString(L"Current User Count:  ") +
                                IntToString(lCurrentUserCount));
```

```
            long lMaxUserCount;
            hr = spFSh->get_MaxUserCount(&lMaxUserCount); ASH;
            m_listbox.AddString(CString(L"Max User Count:  ") +
                            IntToString(lMaxUserCount));
        }
        else
        {
            m_listbox.AddString(L"<Invalid Variant>");
        }

        VariantClear(&var);
        hr = ADsEnumerateNext(pEnumerator, 1, &var, &dwFetched); ASH;

    }
    ADsFreeEnumerator(pEnumerator);
    VariantClear(&var);
```

    ....

```
    }
```

The code should be pretty self-explanatory. Notice, though, that when I enumerate through the file shares, the enumerator as usual returns the results as VARIANTs containing IDispatch pointers. I explicitly check that the VARIANT is of this type:

```
    if(var.vt == VT_DISPATCH)
        {
            CComQIPtr<IADsFileShare, &IID_IADsFileShare> spFSh;
```

This is in marked contrast to all my other error checking, in which I'm content to do ASSERTs on the returned HRESULT. The reason I've taken the trouble to do it properly here is because I found that the enumerator inexplicably returned an empty variant: that is, one with the vt member set to VT_EMPTY at one point. This shouldn't happen, and may be connected with the fact that I am running this on a beta operating system. At any rate, it illustrates the point that you must be careful to trap errors appropriately when using ADSI.

Anyway, here are the results of the above code:

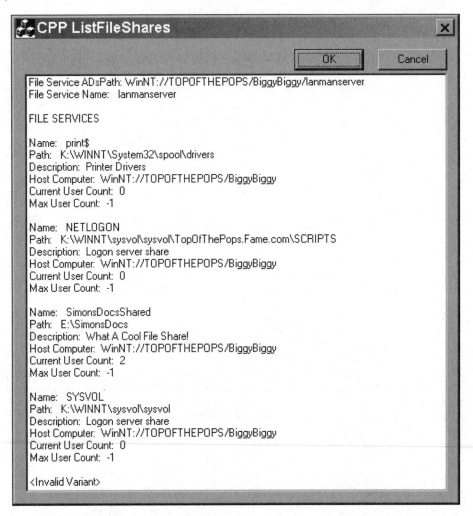

Notice the <Invalid Variant> text on the last line of the screenshot, which corresponds to the NULL Variant that I mentioned occasionally gets returned from the enumeration. Apart from the share that I added, the one named SimonsDocsShared, these are all system file shares that are created for every disk partition. Notice that SimonsDocsShared has a current user count of 2. That's because I carefully opened two Windows Explorer windows and navigated down the tree into the file share under My Network Places in both of them.

Note that at the time of writing, there seems to be a bug in the Active Directory Browser, which means it is unable to list file shares contained in a file service: the file service appears as if it contains no children. Not only that, but it appears as being of class service rather than file service.

Sessions and Resources

If you actually connect to a file share from the network you will open up a **session** and possibly a **resource**. A session can best be thought of as the actual connection from the remote machine.

> An ADSI session exposes the `IADsSession` interface. This implements such properties as the computer and user that have accessed the file share, as well as how long the connection has been up for. A resource object describes the actual object that is being accessed by the remote session, for example, which actual folder has been accessed.

Sessions and resources are much more ephemeral than the file shares themselves. A file share, once set up on your system, will stay there until you decide to remove it – typically months or years later. On the other hand, session and resource objects are only present while the file share is being used – this might be a little as a few seconds. Because of this, sessions and resources are generally deemed inappropriate for inclusion in the directory tree itself. In fact, in terms of interface categories, `IADsFileShare` and `IADsResource` are categorized as dynamic object interfaces rather than persistent object interfaces.

In order to access a session or resource, you need to go through the file service. The file service exposes the interface `IADsFileServiceOperations`, which is derived from `IADsServiceOperations`, and implements two additional methods:

Name	Description
Session	Returns an `IADsCollection` interface which can be used to obtain an enumerator for the session objects.
Resource	Returns an `IADsCollection` interface which can be used to obtain an enumerator for the resource objects.

Both of these methods work in the same way. For the session object, you'll call `IADsFileServiceOperations::Session`, which will return an `IADsCollection` interface pointer (presumably on a separate COM object, though this is immaterial to us).

Recall that the `IADsCollection` interface is intended to enable enumeration over a VB-style collection of objects, and tends to be used where the objects are of a transitory nature. It exposes the `_NewEnum` method, which returns a standard enumerator. The enumerator implements `IEnumVARIANT` and so is able to return `VARIANT`s. The `VARIANT`s contain `IDispatch` pointers to the session objects. You need to `QueryInterface()` these objects for the `IADsSession` interface, at which point you're away.

That probably sounds a very indirect way of doing it, but it does make sense if you think about it. It isn't really possible to obtain the session objects (or the resource objects) in any more direct way. The interfaces have to be designed like this, because the ADSI file service object already exposes an enumerator through its `IADsContainer` interface (to allow enumeration of the file shares). So the enumerators to get the session and resource objects have to be obtained from separate COM objects.

We're going to see how this works in a moment, when we write the C++ code to enumerate and display the properties of the session and resource objects currently in use on my computer. But first, to get a feel for what the sessions and resources actually are, let's look at what the sample produces:

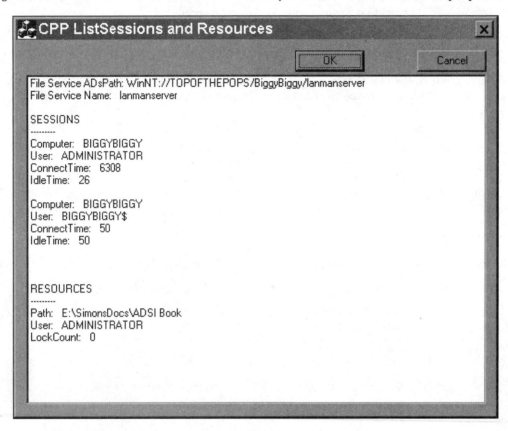

These results were obtained at a time when I still had two Windows Explorer windows open with the tree view used to navigate down through the file share.

The session objects tell me:

❑   The user name under which the Explorer windows were running

❑   Which computer they were running on (notice that I still get active resources even though I'm actually running the Explorer windows on the same computer as the file share is on)

❑   How long I've been using the sessions and how long they've been idle for (both in minutes)

The resource object tells me what folder I'm actually looking at. As it happens, both Explorer windows are being used to browse into the same folder – the one that's got this book in it! Because of that there is only one resource currently in use.

C++ Sample to Display Sessions and Resources

The code starts off as normal. We bind to the file service object and display a bit of information about it, just to make sure we've got our bearings:

```
/////////////////////////////////////////////////////////////////////////
// CCPPListSessionsDlg message handlers

BOOL CCPPListSessionsDlg::OnInitDialog()
{
    CDialog::OnInitDialog();

    // bind to the file service object and display its name
    HRESULT hr;
    CComQIPtr<IADsFileService, &IID_IADsFileService> spADsFSrv;
    CComQIPtr<IADsFileServiceOperations, &IID_IADsFileService> spADsFSrvOps;
    hr = ADsGetObject(L"WinNT://BiggyBiggy/lanmanserver",
        IID_IADsFileServiceOperations, (void**)&spADsFSrvOps); ASH;
    spADsFSrv = spADsFSrvOps;

    CComBSTR bstrADsPath;
    hr = spADsFSrv->get_ADsPath(&bstrADsPath);
    m_listbox.AddString(CString("File Service ADsPath: ") + bstrADsPath);

    CComBSTR bstrName;
    hr = spADsFSrv->get_Name(&bstrName);
    m_listbox.AddString(CString(L"File Service Name:    ") + bstrName);
    m_listbox.AddString(L"");
    m_listbox.AddString(L"SESSIONS");
    m_listbox.AddString(L"---------");
```

Now we actually obtain the collection object for the sessions. The collection object is obtained as an IADsCollection interface pointer. We then use this to get the enumerator. Since the _NewEnum property returns an IUnknown pointer, we need to QueryInterface for IEnumVARIANT:

```
    // get the collection object which will enumerate the sessions
    CComPtr<IADsCollection> spSessions;
    hr = spADsFSrvOps->Sessions(&spSessions); ASH;

    // get the enumerator
    CComPtr<IUnknown> spEnumUnknown;
    CComQIPtr<IEnumVARIANT, &IID_IEnumVARIANT> spEnumerator;
    hr = spSessions->get__NewEnum(&spEnumUnknown); ASH;
    spEnumerator = spEnumUnknown;
```

Now we've got the enumerator, we can use it to enumerate over all the session objects, displaying the main automation properties for each one:

```
    // enumerate over the sessions -
    // for each one print out the automation properties

    VARIANT var;
    VariantInit(&var);
    DWORD dwFetched;
    hr = spEnumerator->Next(1, &var, &dwFetched); ASH;
```

```
while (hr == S_OK)
{
    ASSERT(var.vt == VT_DISPATCH);
    CComQIPtr<IADsSession, &IID_IADsSession> spSession;
    spSession = var.pdispVal;

    CComBSTR bstrComputer;
    hr = spSession->get_Computer(&bstrComputer); ASH;
    m_listbox.AddString(CString(L"Computer:    ") + bstrComputer);
    CComBSTR bstrUser;
    hr = spSession->get_User(&bstrUser); ASH;
    m_listbox.AddString(CString(L"User:    ") + bstrUser);

    long lConnectTime;
    hr = spSession->get_ConnectTime(&lConnectTime); ASH;
    m_listbox.AddString(CString(L"ConnectTime:    ") +
                        IntToString(lConnectTime));

    long lIdleTime;
    hr = spSession->get_IdleTime(&lIdleTime); ASH;
    m_listbox.AddString(CString(L"IdleTime:    ") +
                        IntToString(lIdleTime));

    m_listbox.AddString(L"");

    VariantClear(&var);
    hr = spEnumerator->Next(1, &var, &dwFetched); ASH;
}
```

Finally we can repeat the whole process for the resources:

```
// now get the collection object that will allow us to enumerate
//the resources
CComPtr<IADsCollection> spResources;
hr = spADsFSrvOps->Resources(&spResources); ASH;
m_listbox.AddString(L"");
m_listbox.AddString(L"");
m_listbox.AddString(L"RESOURCES");
m_listbox.AddString(L"---------");

// get the enumerator for the resources
spEnumUnknown = NULL;
spEnumerator = spEnumUnknown;
hr = spResources->get__NewEnum(&spEnumUnknown); ASH;
spEnumerator = spEnumUnknown;

// and enumerate over the resources
VariantClear(&var);
hr = spEnumerator->Next(1, &var, &dwFetched); ASH;

while (hr == S_OK)
{
    ASSERT(var.vt == VT_DISPATCH);
    CComQIPtr<IADsResource, &IID_IADsResource> spResource;
    spResource = var.pdispVal;
```

```
        CComBSTR bstrPath;
        hr = spResource->get_Path(&bstrPath); ASH;
        m_listbox.AddString(CString(L"Path:    ") + bstrPath);

        CComBSTR bstrUser;
        hr = spResource->get_User(&bstrUser); ASH;
        m_listbox.AddString(CString(L"User:    ") + bstrUser);

        long lLockCount;
        hr = spResource->get_LockCount(&lLockCount); ASH;
        m_listbox.AddString(CString(L"LockCount:    ") +
                             IntToString(lLockCount));

        m_listbox.AddString(L"");

        VariantClear(&var);
        hr = spEnumerator->Next(1, &var, &dwFetched); ASH;
    }

}
```

VB Sample: Listing Sessions and Resources

We're going to finish off with one of those samples that should make C++ guys so jealous that we'll definitely be able to start a language war. Here's the VB equivalent of the C++ sample to list sessions and resources:

```
Private Sub Form_Load()

  Dim oFileService As IADsFileService
  Dim oFileServiceOps As IADsFileServiceOperations

  Set oFileService = GetObject("WinNT://BiggyBiggy/lanmanserver")
  Set oFileServiceOps = oFileService

  List1.AddItem "File Service: " & oFileService.Name

  List1.AddItem "SESSIONS"
  List1.AddItem "--------"

  Dim oSession As IADsSession
  For Each oSession In oFileServiceOps.Sessions
    List1.AddItem "Computer: " & oSession.Computer
    List1.AddItem "User: " & oSession.User
    List1.AddItem "Connect Time: " & oSession.ConnectTime
    List1.AddItem "Idle Time: " & oSession.IdleTime
    List1.AddItem ""
  Next

  List1.AddItem "RESOURCES"
  List1.AddItem "---------"

  Dim oResource As IADsResource
  For Each oResource In oFileServiceOps.Resources
    List1.AddItem "Path: " & oResource.Path
    List1.AddItem "User: " & oResource.User
    List1.AddItem "Lock Count: " & oResource.LockCount
    List1.AddItem ""
  Next
```

```
    Set oResource = Nothing
    Set oSession = Nothing
    Set oFileService = Nothing
    Set oFileServiceOps = Nothing

    End Sub
```

So why is it so simple in VB? VB has actually done an extremely good job here of hiding the very indirect path that we need to get to the session and resource objects. It's actually hidden all the details down into one line (or two if you count the variable declaration):

```
    Dim oSession As IADsSession
    For Each oSession In oFileServiceOps.Sessions
```

`IADsFileServiceOps.Sessions` returns the `IADsCollection` interface. When VB encounters the `For Each … In` statement, it knows to use automation to obtain the `_NewEnum` property of the collection object. It automatically `QueryInterface()`s the enumerator returned for `IEnumVARIANT`, and also knows to extract the `IDispatch` interface pointer from inside the `VARIANT`. Because we've explicitly declared `oSession As IADsSession`, VB will `QueryInterface()` the `IDispatch` pointers for this interface. (If we hadn't done so, VB would use late binding on this object).

The result is an impressively short piece of code. No screenshot for this by the way, as it would virtually identical to the screenshot for the C++ sample.

Print Queues and Print Jobs

Print queues shouldn't need much explanation, as they are fairly intuitive.

> **The print queue is responsible for sending print jobs to the printer as the printer becomes available.**

Roughly speaking, a print queue is associated with a particular printer, though there are exceptions. For example, you may want to run multiple printers off the same print queue if that queue is to be used very heavily. You would still keep the one queue servicing those printers if you didn't want the end users to see the distinction between the printers.

As far as ADSI is concerned, print queues are implemented as ADSI **PrintQueue objects**. These objects expose the `IADsPrintQueue` and `IADsPrintQueueOperations` interfaces. `IADsPrintQueue` exposes properties which control how the print queue operates, for example whether a banner page is printed, and what the default job priority is. `IADsPrintQueueOperations` is concerned more with the current state of the print queue rather than with its general properties. It exposes methods to pause, purge or restart the print queue, as well as to get to the print jobs. There is also a property to get the current status of the print queue.

The PrintQueue objects are children of the Computer objects.

Enumerating Print Queues

This sample is an ASP script that demonstrates the IADsPrintQueue properties. It enumerates all the print queues on my computer (although there's only one of them – for my Canon bubble jet printer). It also lists all the IADsPrintQueue automation properties. Here's the script, which shouldn't need any explanation:

```
<%@ Language = VBScript %>
<html>
<head>
<title> ADSI Service Enumerator Page </title>
</head>

<body>

<h1> ADSI Print Queue Enumerator Page </h1>

Print Queues on BiggyBiggy are:
<p>
<%
    on error resume next

    Dim MyComputer
    Set MyComputer = GetObject("WinNT://BiggyBiggy")
    MyComputer.Filter = Array("PrintQueue")

    For Each oPrintQueue In MyComputer
        Response.Write "Name: " & oPrintQueue.Name & "<br>"
        Response.Write "ADsPath: " & oPrintQueue.ADsPath & "<br>"
        Response.Write "BannerPage: " & oPrintQueue.BannerPage & "<br>"
        Response.Write "DataType: " & oPrintQueue.DataType & "<br>"
Response.Write "DefaultJobPriority: " & _
                        oPrintQueue.DefaultJobPriority & "<br>"
        Response.Write "Description: " & oPrintQueue.Description & "<br>"
        Response.Write "HostComputer: " & oPrintQueue.HostComputer & "<br>"
        Response.Write "Location: " & oPrintQueue.Location & "<br>"
        Response.Write "Model: " & oPrintQueue.Model & "<br>"
        Response.Write "PrintDevices: " & oPrintQueue.PrintDevices & "<br>"
        Response.Write "PrinterPath: " & oPrintQueue.PrinterPath & "<br>"
        Response.Write "PrintProcessor: " & oPrintQueue.PrintProcessor & _
                        "<br>"
        Response.Write "Priority: " & oPrintQueue.Priority & "<br>"
        Response.Write "StartTime: " & oPrintQueue.StartTime & "<br>"
        Response.Write "UntilTime: " & oPrintQueue.UntilTime & "<br>"
        Response.Write "<p>"
    Next

    Set MyComputer = Nothing

%>
</body>
</html>
```

And here's what the web page looks like:

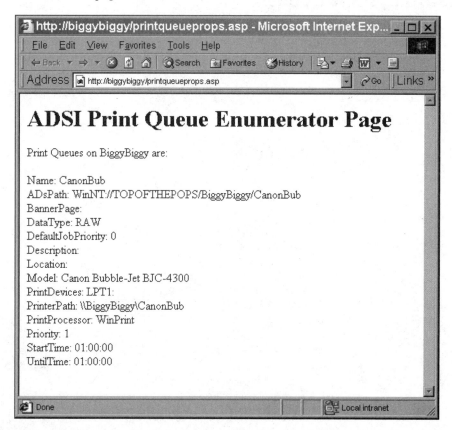

Notice that the banner page is blank – this means that there is no banner page set for my printer. `Description` *is blank because this property happens not to be implemented in my install of the WinNT provider.*

A full table of the properties exposed by `IADsPrintQueue` is given in Appendix D.

Print Jobs

Print queues don't exist in isolation. They tend to have print jobs submitted to them.

> **A print job is a single request to print something (for example a document or part of a document)**

So how do you get at the print jobs?

Actually it works in pretty much the same way as for sessions and resources:
IADsPrintQueueOperations exposes a method, PrintJobs, which returns an
IADsCollection interface pointer. The enumerator obtained from this collection object gives you
print job objects – that is objects which expose IADsPrintJob and IADsPrintJobOperations.

The reason for doing it this way should be familiar by now: print jobs are temporary in nature, so
they shouldn't really be included in the directory tree. As for the two interfaces exposed by the print
job object, they play roles that you can probably predict. IADsPrintJobs exposes properties that
are characteristic of the print job as a whole. I would say permanent properties, if it wasn't that print
jobs had such a temporary nature anyway. IADsPrintJobOperations exposes methods to pause
or resume a print job. This interface has properties that will change as the print job progresses, for
example the status of the print job, and how many pages have actually been printed.

> *In quite a nice feature, you will find that the Active Directory Browser* adsvw.exe *is able to*
> *apparently open the print queue objects in the directory tree and list print jobs, just as if they are*
> *contained within the print queue objects. Don't be fooled by this. The print jobs aren't children of*
> *the print queue object.* adsvw.exe *is intelligent enough to recognize a print queue object and*
> *access the print jobs using the* IADsPrintQueueOperations::PrintJobs *method.*

This ASP page lists the print jobs currently on my bubble jet print queue, and prints out a selection of
IADsPrintJob and IADsPrintJobOperations properties for each job.

```
<%@ Language = VBScript %>
<html>
<head>
<title> ADSI Print Job Enumerator Page </title>
</head>

<body>

<h1> ADSI Print Job Enumerator Page </h1>
<%
    on error resume next

    Dim oPrintQueue
    Set oPrintQueue = GetObject("WinNT://BiggyBiggy/CanonBub")

    Response.Write "<strong>Print Queue: " & oPrintQueue.Name & "</strong>"
    Response.Write "<p>"

    Response.Write "Print Jobs are:<p>"

    For Each oPrintJob In oPrintQueue.PrintJobs

        ' These are IADsPrintJob properties
        Response.Write "Description: " & oPrintJob.Description & "<br>"
        Response.Write "User: " & oPrintJob.User & "<br>"
        Response.Write "Size: " & oPrintJob.Size & " bytes<br>"
        Response.Write "TotalPages: " & oPrintjob.TotalPages & "<br>"
        Response.Write "TimeSubmitted: " & oPrintJob.TimeSubmitted & "<br>"

        ' These are IADsPrintJobOperations properties
        Response.Write "PagesPrinted: " & oPrintJob.PagesPrinted & "<br>"
        Response.Write "Status: " & oPrintJob.Status & "<br>"
        Response.Write "<p>"
```

```
    Next

    Set MyComputer = Nothing
%>
</body>
</html>
```

The complete set of properties for print jobs is as usual listed in Appendix D.

Here's the web page:

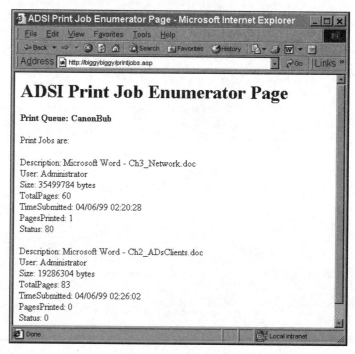

This page shows I'm currently attempting to print two chapters of this book. The properties should be fairly self-explanatory, apart from the status, which is a numeric code. The meanings of the codes are:

SYMBOL	Hex Value
ADS_JOB_PAUSED	0x00000001
ADS_JOB_ERROR	0x00000002
ADS_JOB_DELETING	0x00000004
ADS_JOB_PRINTING	0x00000010
ADS_JOB_OFFLINE	0x00000020
ADS_JOB_PAPEROUT	0x00000040
ADS_JOB_PRINTED	0x00000080
ADS_JOB_DELETED	0x00000100

The second job in my print queue in the screenshot, Ch2_ADSClients.doc, has a status of zero. This means nothing's really happening to it – it's just waiting for its turn to be printed. The first job, Ch3_Network.doc, (the last chapter!) has a value of 80. You might be tempted to read from the above table that this means it has just been printed (ADS_JOB_PRINTED) – but that would be wrong! The web page prints the status as a decimal value, whereas they are listed in this table as hex values.

> *The reason for listing them in hexadecimal is that the values can be combined with a bitwise OR operator.*

So to determine what the decimal value of 80 means, you have to write it in hexadecimal (or binary), and see what bits are set. 80 base 10 is actually 50 in hexadecimal, or hex 40 plus hex 10. So the job is currently printing, but it's got stuck because the printer is out of paper. (Actually that was deliberate – I only put two sheets in. You don't think I'd really want to waste 60-odd sheets of paper printing out a chapter that isn't yet quite finished do you, just to get a screenshot!)

By the way, it's worth pointing out that, if you want to get the status of a print queue, that is also obtained by an integer composed of bit-wise values. You need the IADsPrintQueueOperations::Status property, which has a range of values representing print queue paused, pending a job deletion, or door open, etc. The full list is in Appendix D.

Operations on Print Queues and Print Jobs

The operations you can carry out on queues and jobs using ADSI are actually fairly limited. For a start, you can't use ADSI to create or delete individual print jobs. You can use ADSI to delete all the print jobs in one go, using IADsPrintQueueOperations::Purge(), and you can pause and resume either the print queue or an individual job in it. The methods that do this are pretty obvious and listed in Appendix D, so you don't get a code sample!

Active Directory Schema Extension

We finish this chapter with a quick look at **schema extension** in Active Directory. This really means Active Directory only, because the WinNT provider doesn't permit any modifications to its schema.

> **In general, schema extension can be thought of as the process of making changes to the schema of a directory in order to allow the storage of different types of object.**

For the case of Active Directory, schema extension is actually a very appropriate term, because Active Directory only ever permits additions to its schema. That is, you can add new classObject and propertyObject objects to the schema container, but once you've added them, you can never remove them again. That's because of the potential problems it could cause if any objects of that type were in the directory. (Or even worse, objects of that type are in the directory, but in a different replica from the copy on which you're making the changes, so the problem only comes to light later on). It is, however, possible to disable classes and attributes, which means that it's no longer permitted to make any new instances of the corresponding objects. If you find that you've made lots of schema extensions and you want to tidy up your Active Directory installation by removing the ones that you no longer use, the only way to do this is currently by reinstalling Active Directory.

Schema extension is in many ways no different from making any other changes to the directory. You simply use `IADsContainer::Create()` in the normal way, but on the schema container to create the appropriate schema objects. However, there are a couple of conditions you have to satisfy before you can do this:

❑ It's not sufficient to be a domain administrator. You have to be authenticated to Active Directory as a **schema administrator**. `Schema administrators` is a new Windows 2000 group, created specifically for the purpose of enabling schema modifications. By default the administrator is not a member of this group – no one is. So you need to create a new user account, add this account to the `schema administrators` group, and log in as that user. For security reasons, I'd suggest you do create a new account rather than making the user, `administrator`, a `schema administrator` as well.

❑ Schema extensions are by default disabled. You need to enable them by setting a key in the registry.

❑ If there are several domain controllers in your forest, then only one of them at any one time is allowed to accept extensions to the schema. This is because of the difficulty of resolving the situation if a couple of extensions were simultaneously made on more than one replica of Active Directory. It is possible to change which computer is allowed to accept schema extensions by changing an attribute in Active Directory.

There are also some restrictions on the changes that can be made to the schema anyway. There's not really space to go into it here, but full details are in the MSDN documentation under the Active Directory section.

Summary

In this chapter we've examined how to perform common administrative tasks involving the WinNT provider and the LDAP provider using Active Directory. In particular we've looked at manipulating:

❑ User and Group Accounts

❑ Windows 2000 (Windows NT) Services

❑ The File Service and File Shares

❑ Print Jobs and Print Queues.

We haven't yet looked at the administrative tasks involving the Exchange Directory or IIS – those will be covered in later chapters, starting in the next chapter, when we examine how to use ADSI with Microsoft Exchange Server.

6

ADSI and BackOffice: Exchange Server, IIS, Site Server

In the last couple of chapters, we've looked at how ADSI can be used to manage your network – carrying out such administrative tasks as managing user, group and computer accounts, print queues and starting and stopping NT/Windows 2000 Services. For this we used both the WinNT provider, and the LDAP provider, hooked up to Active Directory. The significant new thing about what we were looking at was that ADSI makes it easy to carry out these administrative tasks from VB and scripting languages – before the arrival of ADSI such tasks were previously largely the province of C++.

In this chapter we're going to leave the WinNT provider behind, although we'll still be using the LDAP provider a fair bit, but this time hooked up to some different directories. We're going to have a look at two directories that have different purposes, but which are related to the extent that they have all traditionally been viewed as part of Microsoft BackOffice. In this chapter we'll have a look at how to use ADSI to manage

❑   Internet Information Server using the IIS Metabase, using the IIS provider.

❑   The Exchange Directory of Microsoft Exchange Server, using the LDAP provider.

We'll also briefly mention the Site Server Membership directory, which can also be accessed using the ADSI LDAP provider.

Once again I'm not going to assume any familiarity with any of the back-end directories we will be dealing with, so I'll spend a bit of time going over the purpose of each, as well as how to access them using ADSI.

I'm also not going to give you many code samples in this chapter. In the last couple of chapters we've covered numerous samples to do almost every conceivable operation you might want to do using ADSI: add directory objects, look at their properties, move objects, modify properties, and so on. The principles of how to do these don't really change when you go from one ADSI provider to another. You still use – say – `IADs::GetEx()` or `IADsContainer::MoveHere()` in exactly the same way, so if I presented many more code samples I'd simply be repeating earlier samples but with different `ADsPaths`. And I'm sure you didn't buy this book just to see lots of repeats! What this chapter does instead is looks at the two new directories – the IIS metabase and Exchange Server, and point out the idiosyncrasies of each, where the ADSI providers behaves slightly differently from how you would have expected from your experience with Active Directory and the WinNT provider. We can do this most easily by using the various ADSI browsing tools that we've encountered such as `adsvw.exe`. Once we've done that I'll assume you're intelligent enough to figure out how to substitute the appropriate `AdsPaths` and class names into the earlier code samples so they'll work against the IIS metabase and the Exchange Directory.

We are going to see some interesting differences. Most notably, in this chapter we are going to have our first encounter with another ADSI provider: the IIS provider. We are going to find that the IIS provider implements some new interfaces that we haven't yet met (and for which I will supply a couple of code samples).

For Exchange Server, we are talking about using the LDAP provider – the same ADSI provider that we used to access Active Directory, so some of what we've learned about accessing Active Directory in the last two chapters will apply to the Exchange Directory too. However we will have to get used to a new directory structure, and we'll also find some inconsistencies between the names of classes and objects as seen through ADSI and as seen through the Exchange administrator program, which we need to resolve.

As usual for the code that we do present we'll mostly use VB, since we are still showing how to write ADSI clients. For quick user interfaces that make some queries against the directories, VB and VBScript are arguably the 'best' languages, in the sense of letting you write programs quickly – and in terms of allowing you to write web pages that can perform simple administrative tasks from over the web. There is some C++ code, but we won't use any ASP since the VB samples generally translate very easily into VBScript.

With that, let's proceed...

Internet Information Server

In this section we'll start off by looking at what IIS is, at its architecture, and what its capabilities are. Naturally, this will lead us to consider some of the configuration and management options that need to be set for IIS, after which we'll go on to look at the IIS ADSI provider and see how we can use the provider to manage IIS.

What Is IIS?

We'll start with the basics. Internet Information Server (IIS) is the Microsoft package that presents active web sites to browsers. Let's say you want to host a web site on your computer. You'll create files that store the actual pages – most likely a mixture of HTML and ASP files, perhaps with some GIF and JPEG files for images. Your computer will then receive requests from other computers on the network for these pages – the requests generally having been issued by Internet browsers such as Internet Explorer and Netscape Communicator. How is your computer going to respond to these requests? Well, you need some software that listens out on the appropriate port(s) for the requests, then for each one maps the URL on to the appropriate file on your system, does any processing of the file (eg. interpreting ASP scripts into plain HTML) as well as determining whether the browser does have appropriate permissions to view the file, and blocking transfer if it doesn't. This may involve authenticating the browser, by some mechanism such as using NT challenge/response authentication or reading a cookie. That's where Internet Information Server comes in. It's a suite of applications that handles all this, as well as handling ftp requests for files and some other related services. Listening for HTTP requests from browsers is handled specifically by an NT/Windows 2000 Service, the World Wide Web service. (Using ADSI, with the WinNT provider, this appears as the ADSI object named W3SVC).

IIS isn't the only web server designed to handle all the above tasks – there are others. Most notably, Apache Web Server is a popular choice. But IIS is the standard offering from Microsoft in this field. You will obviously have been using it extensively if you program Active Server Pages, since IIS is currently the only web server that can handle ASP (apart from its smaller sister, Microsoft's Personal Web Server, which is designed to run on Windows 9x and NT4.0 Workstation, not really intended for a commercial Internet site, and some products such as the ChilliSoft Unix ASP port).

IIS Versions

This section will throughout use IIS version 5, which comes as part of the operating system with Windows 2000 Server and Windows 2000 Advanced Server. The code has not been tested on IIS 4, but we don't have any reason to believe that it won't work with IIS 4. There have been a number of new features, including many new configuration options introduced with IIS 5, as well as a small number of management properties removed and a couple of changes in the default behavior – these are documented in the MSDN documentation for IIS. However these changes generally affect only more advanced settings, whereas in this chapter we have space only to go over some elementary administrative tasks.

What IIS Can Do

The best way to see exactly what IIS does is to look at its administration tool. The administration tool is something called the Internet Service Manager. This sounds like a good fancy name, but in reality all it is (yet) another MMC snap-in. Well, strictly, it's an MMC console file, of the sort we discuss in Chapter 12. Here it is:

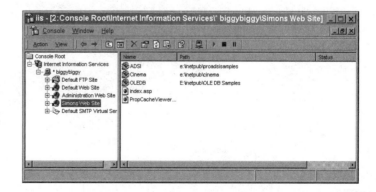

The console has the IIS snap-in loaded in this screenshot. You'll sometimes see it combined with the Microsoft Transaction Server (MTS) administration snap-in. The reason for this is that, as of version 4, IIS is actually written as an MTS application. Since MTS is beyond the scope of this book, we're ignoring that aspect of it here. What we're interested in here is understanding some of the configuration options for IIS – so that we can go on to see how to manipulate them using ADSI. So here we'll concentrate on the IIS snap-in.

> *There is another administrative tool, known as the HTML Internet Service Manager, which can perform many of the same tasks but from an ASP web page. We won't be using the HTML Internet Service Manager, though it's interesting to note that the current version of it is written using the same ADSI interfaces that we will be using later on! If you need more sample code, the HTML Internet Service Manager is a good source.*

The screenshot gives us quite a fair idea of the capabilities of IIS. If we work down the tree on the left, starting from *Internet Information Services*, we first come to the name of the computer on which IIS is running. Below this we see the main facilities that are provided. IIS hosts an FTP site named *Default FTP Site*, which answers ftp requests, and a *Default SMTP Virtual Server*, which handles mail-related SMTP requests. We're going to largely ignore those in this chapter and concentrate on the World Wide Web service, which handles HTTP requests for web pages. The screenshot shows three web sites – the *Default Web Site* and the *Administration Web Site*, which are supplied by default when you install IIS, and *Simons Web Site*, which I added later on.

> *Note that, depending on the options that you selected when you installed IIS, some of these nodes may be absent in your installation.*

This gives us our first indication of both the power of IIS and the kinds of things you might want to use ADSI to manage: For a start IIS can host more than one web site at the same time. That means we'll need some way of setting up the different sites.

Let's have a closer look at *Simons Web Site*. This is in fact the site that supplied all the web browser screenshots in this book. In this screenshot I've opened up *Simons Web Site* to see what's in it.

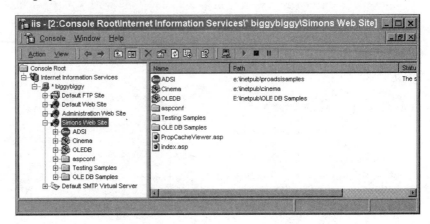

Under Simons Web Site are a number of folders and other objects. This snap-in actually works very much like Windows Explorer. Windows Explorer displays folders in both the tree and list views and files only in its list view, just as in this screenshot of Windows Explorer looking at my E:\inetpub folder.

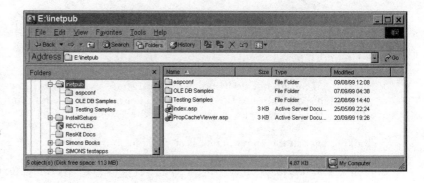

The Internet Services Manager screenshot is following the same principle – those items in it with the folder icon are real folders, while PropCacheViewer.asp and index.asp are real files – and they all appear in both screenshots. So what's going on? Well what's happening is that each web site is mapped to a particular folder on your hard drive. When I created the web site called *Simons Web Site* I mapped it to a folder I created called E:\inetpub, which means that Internet Services Manager can see all the files and subfolders of that folder.

So what happens if a browser request comes in with the URL http://BiggyBiggy/PropCacheViewer.asp, asking to run the ADSI property cache viewer ASP page that we developed in Chapter 3? Well, by default the request comes in on port 80 – that's the standard port of HTTP protocol requests. As it happens I've set up IIS so that *Simons Web Site* is the only web site that answers to port 80 – so that's where the request will get sent. IIS looks in the directory that this site has been mapped to for the file PropCacheViewer.asp, finds it, and assuming all the security credentials are in order (they will be because I've got anonymous access enabled for all the files in that web site) the asp file will get processed and returned as HTML. If a browser request comes in with the URL http://BiggyBiggy, then index.asp will be returned because I have this file set up to be the default file to be returned if no file was explicitly named.

Similarly if a browser request indicates subfolders, such as http://BiggyBiggy/aspconf/asptest.htm, then on this site the file e:\inetpub\aspconf\asptest.htm will be returned (you'll have to trust me that that file really does exist on my computer). IIS is quite happy to navigate around your folders in its search for pages.

That's covered most of the Internet Service Manager screenshot, but what about those other items in the tree with the new icons – ADSI, Cinema and OLE DB. What are they? Well, to answer that, we need to notice one of the main limitations of the model we've just described. You see, I've just said that a browser can request any file or subfolder of the home directory, and this will be returned. The URL must contain the pathname, exactly as it appears in the file system from the folder to which the web site was mapped to downwards. That's a bit restrictive on two counts. The most obvious one is that you might not *want* to put all your files in one place. You might have your own reasons why it's convenient to you to keep some of your html files in a different folder, or on a different drive. You might even want to keep them on a different computer for load balancing purposes. The other, related but less obvious reason, is that if you keep all your files named exactly as they are seen by a web browser, you might be making it that little bit easier for a hacker who's broken in to navigate around your hard drive. If the hacker knows the structure of your web site, he'll automatically know something about the folder structure in part of your drive.

That's where **virtual directories** come in. A virtual directory can be thought of as a mapping. Say a request comes in for `http://biggybiggy/cinema/index.htm`. IIS will see that there it has a virtual directory set up called cinema, so it will look to see which folder cinema is mapped to. On my computer it happens to be `E:\Simons Books\Beg Comp ASP\CinemaSamples`. So IIS will attempt to return the file `E:\Simons Books\Beg Comp ASP\CinemaSamples\index.htm`. Virtual directories do not exist an any physical sense in the file system – they are nothing more than configuration settings inside IIS – but using them means you can keep the files you want to be made available to web browsers anywhere on your file system.

So looking back at the above screenshot, Cinema and OLEDB are virtual directories. ADSI is also a virtual directory, but one that I'm no longer using. It's giving an error because I've actually removed the folder that it is mapped to, but I haven't yet got round to removing the virtual directory.

So that tells us something of the structure of IIS. One other point to note is that if you select the web site in Internet Service Manager, you get a *huge* tabbed dialog box inviting you to set all manner of properties for the web site.

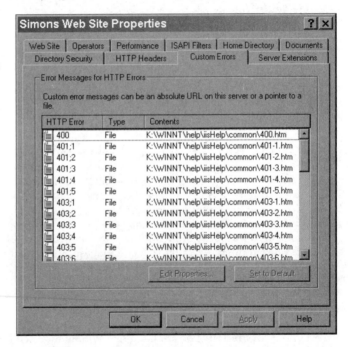

This screenshot shows the tab that lets you select which folder the web site is mapped to. The other tabs allow you to configure various options, such as

- ❑ The IP address and TCP port the web site answers to

- ❑ How many simultaneous connections are allowed and what expected load the site should be optimized for

- ❑ What default files should be available where browsers don't specify a file name in the URL

- ❑ Whether any ISAPI filters should be enabled

- ❑ HTML files that can be returned to the browser in the event of errors being generated

- ❑ What authentication is required

- ❑ What clients are allowed to do with files (read, execute, run scripts, etc.)

We're not going to go over all of these options – this isn't after all a book about IIS! Besides, if you are that interested you probably won't find it too hard to open the Internet Services Manager and play around to find out for yourself exactly what's there. The reason I've listed some of these properties is to give you a flavor of how many different properties need to be set on a site – and the reason I want you to be aware of them is because these properties are exactly the kind of thing that the ADSI IIS provider is there for.

IIS Metabase Architecture

Before we look at what the ADSI IIS provider can show you of IIS, I want to take a quick run through something of the structure of the directory that controls all the IIS settings.

You'll notice that the Internet Service Manager – in common with most MMC snap-ins – presents a lot of the configuration data as if there's a treelike structure to it. At the top is the computer that IIS is running on. Beneath that are the various web and ftp, etc. sites. Beneath each web site are the folders and virtual directories. And so on. At each stage, we have objects on which many properties can be set. In other words, we appear to have a typical directory tree structure!

From IIS Version 4 onwards, this directory was stored in a single binary file known as the **metabase**. Prior to version 4, it was all in the registry, but according to the MSDN documentation, storing this treelike set of data in the metabase gives higher performance than the registry. (Unfortunately, the MSDN documentation didn't get as far as explaining why, if that's really true, Microsoft haven't simply ported the entire Windows registry into the IIS metabase in order to take advantage of this improved performance!).

The IIS metabase is stored in binary format in a file – by default `metabase.bin` though it is possible to change the file name. So the IIS ADSI provider can be considered to be a provider that simply accesses this file.

The metabase has a similar structure to the registry, in that it contains a number of keys, each of which can have one or more values, as well as child keys. However there is one important difference. Take a look at this screenshot of the properties of *Simons Web Site*, looking in particular at the **Custom Errors** tab, which lets you specify the files to be returned when errors occur.

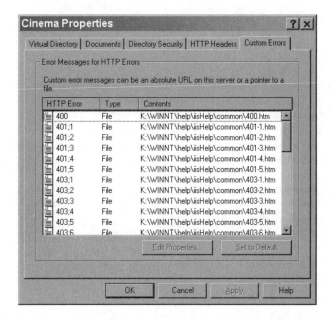

Now look at one of the tabs of the properties of the Cinema virtual directories

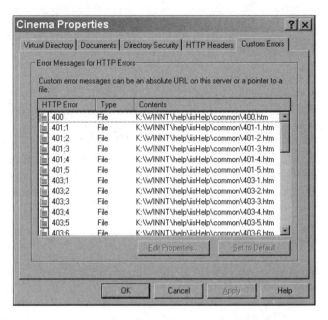

Notice the similarity? The Cinema virtual directory is a child of *Simons Web Site*, but it has some of the same properties. The reason is that the metabase has been designed to allow properties to be inherited down the tree. If you set a property on an object anywhere in the directory tree that forms the metabase, all the children will inherit this property. If you want to override that for some children, then you can set that property again for those particular children – assuming it's a property that makes sense in the context of a child. (eg. it wouldn't make sense to change the port and IP address for a virtual directory – that kind of information must apply to the entire web site as a whole).

So having seen that the metabase has a tree structure, let's take a look at its typical structure (again, the details will vary somewhat depending on what parts of IIS you actually have installed). The figure doesn't show all the objects in the tree, but it shows a good cross section of the important ones.

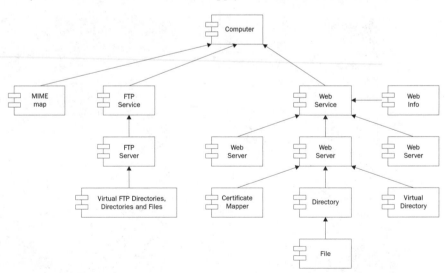

The diagram shows us that a computer object is at the top of the tree– the computer that IIS is running on. Beneath the computer is the web service, the object that is associated with the W3SVC NT service that answers HTTP requests from browsers. Beneath the web service lie all the different web servers – one server for each web site. And beneath each web server lays the usual mix of directories (windows file system folders), virtual directories, and files. Also lurking around the tree as one of the other children of the computer object is the FTP service, which contains a similar structure to the web service, but which is responsible for handling ftp requests from ftp clients. A MIME map is responsible for figuring out how to process different type of files – MIME is the Internet's equivalent of the file extensions that Windows uses to determine file types. A Web info object is responsible for some configuration properties and a certificate mapper is used to handle client certificates supplied by web browsers.

IIS and ADSI

We've now seen what IIS is capable of and (hopefully) got a good feel for some of the administrative settings you would want to manage. The Internet Services Manager is the tool you would use if you want to use a user interface to configure IIS, or to examine how it it's set up, what web sites are available, etc. The IIS ADSI provider is the main tool you will probably use if you want to do the same thing programmatically. There are other lower level APIs which are available to C++, but we will concentrate on the IIS ADSI provider here, since it is the easiest API to use, and is the only one that is available to VB and scripting languages.

By the way, the IIS provider is supplied with IIS and will be installed when you install IIS, assuming you have ADSI installed.

If you are running an early version of ADSI you may encounter a bug in the ADSI IIS provider. The bug will cause the provider to crash if you attempt to call `IADs::Get()` *on the IIS computer object. Since* `adsvw.exe` *calls this method automatically as it explores an object, this bug will cause* `adsvw.exe` *to crash if you use it to browse around IIS. The sample VB browser,* `dsbrowse`, *is fine since it doesn't call* `IADs::Get()` *unless you explicitly attempt to examine properties of an object. This bug is reported to have been fixed in the latest version of ADSI.*

Directory Structure Exposed by the IIS Provider

To get some idea of the structure exposed through the IIS provider, let's have a look at a screenshot of `dsbrowse` looking into the IIS directory tree.

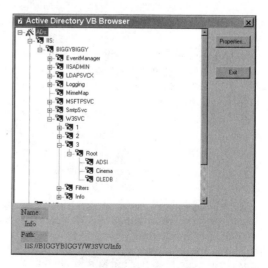

In this screenshot I've browsed down through the web service into *Simons Web Site*. The screenshot shows that the directory structure exposed by the IIS provider quite closely matches the actual structure of the metabase. The most important difference is that the IIS provider labels the web sites numerically – so in this screenshot the nodes under W3SVC are named '1', '2' and '3', rather than having been given their more human readable names of 'Default Web Site', 'Administration Web Site' and 'Simons Web Site' that the Internet Services Manager uses. This does mean that when using ADSI you will need to take care that you are accessing the correct web site!

If you compare this screenshot with the previous diagram of the structure of the IIS metabase, you'll see that the IIS provider doesn't really do any significant translation with the tree structure. The directory hierarchy that you see through ADSI matches pretty closely the actual structure of the metabase.

Properties Exposed by IIS Objects

We'll start off with a look at the object that represents *Simons Web Site*. We'll use the VB version of the object viewer that we developed in Chapter 2 here.

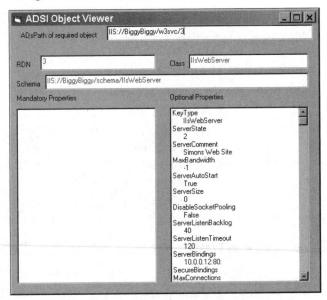

We can see from this that there are no mandatory properties, but a large number of optional properties. We won't go through all the optional properties here but some of the more important ones are:

❑ ServerComment – this is the name of the web site, as displayed in the Internet Services Manager.

❑ KeyType – an indication of the class of the object. This is the same as the IADs::Class property – but is accessed through the schema.

❑ AnonymousUserName – the name of the user account to be used for anonymous binding.

The remaining properties roughly correspond to all the options available in the Internet Services Manager Properties tabbed dialog – and they have reasonably self-explanatory property names. You'll also need to be aware that many of these properties are available on all objects exposed by the IIS provider going right down the directory tree. This is in accordance with the way that metabase properties can be inherited and defined at any point down the hierarchy.

Interfaces Exposed by the IIS Provider

The first thing I want to do is look at a typical IIS ADSI object – I'll pick the web service, and use the Quest for Interfaces on it. The `ADsPath` of the web service in IIS is `IIS://<ComputerName>/W3SVC`. Here's what the Quest for Interfaces found.

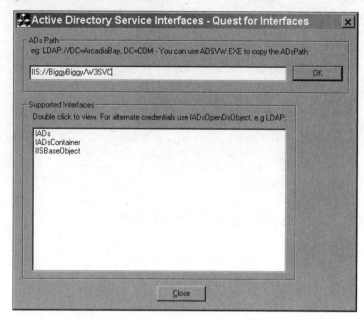

If you're paying attention you'll immediately notice three things.

Firstly, this object does not expose `IDirectoryObject` or `IDirectorySearch`. So the IIS provider apparently doesn't support searching, and it doesn't support the fast interfaces designed for C++. All clients, even C++ ones, will have to use the `IADsXXX` automation interfaces.

Secondly, this object doesn't expose `IADsPropertyList`. So the property cache interfaces are missing from the IIS provider too. If you want to get at any properties, you *have* to use `IADs::Get()` or `IADs::GetEx()` and go through the schema.

Thirdly, there's a new interface sitting there – `IISBaseObject`. That's an interface that we haven't encountered before. It contains a couple of methods that give you more information about a property and whether and how that property is inheritable. It's also an interface that you won't find listed in the ADSI MSDN documentation because it is IIS-specific. (Actually at the present time, you won't find it listed in the IIS MSDN documentation either – the IIS documentation is aimed specifically at ASP clients who call methods through `IDispatch` and therefore don't need to know which interfaces expose the methods they are calling. If you're using ASP all you need to know is how to use the methods exposed by the objects, and the fact that the methods might actually have been exposed through different interfaces is of no interest. Result – the documentation says little or nothing about most of the interfaces. I tracked `IISBaseObject` down by trawling through the type libraries and C++ header files, but that's another story.)

This is something we're going to have to get used to. As far as ADSI is concerned, the IIS provider is a bit of a renegade provider. It doesn't implement several of the interfaces that ADSI providers supposedly really ought to implement. And the directory objects exposed by the IIS provider also implement a number of other interfaces that are not defined by ADSI. `IISBaseObject` can be thought of as the main one since it is exposed by *all* IIS ADSI objects with the exception of the namespace object. There are a number of other interfaces exposed by specific IIS ADSI objects. The only one of these that we will examine in detail is `IISBaseObject`. Details of the other interfaces are in MSDN.

I guess it's about time I admitted that last screenshot wasn't taken using the plain Quest for Interfaces application, as we left it in Chapter 3. It was taken using Quest for Interfaces, but I made a couple more changes to it so it could pick up all those extra IIS-specific interfaces. I'll go over the technical details of the changes later in the chapter – for now, just accept that we're using a version of `ADQI.exe` which knows about all the interfaces exposed by the IIS provider as well as the standard ADSI interfaces.

The IISBaseObject Interface

This interface defines two methods:

GetDataPaths	Finds `ADsPaths` of IIS objects at which a property is defined
GetPropertyAttribObj	Returns an object that describes the attributes of the specified property

To understand what these methods do, it's necessary to understand that in the IIS metabase, properties themselves can have certain characteristics. We've already indicated that properties can be inherited – so one of the characteristics of a property is whether that property can be inherited. Other attributes include whether a property has actually been inherited and whether it is volatile. (A volatile property is subject to frequent changes in its value and so should not be cached).

Across most directory services we use the terms *property* and *attribute* interchangeably. That's not the case for IIS. Here, the term *property* is reserved for the actual properties of a directory object, while the term *attribute* specifically means a characteristic of a property. In other words, in the IIS metabase, properties can have attributes.
That should explain the purpose of the `GetPropertyAttribObj()` method: it enables you to find out the attributes of a given property.

`GetDataPaths()` is specifically concerned with inheritance. An inheritable property will cascade down the metabase directory tree until another object is reached at which the value of this property is explicitly set (to something else). Thereupon, if the new value is set to be inheritable (via one of its attributes), the new value will cascade down the subtree. If the new value is not marked as inheritable, the property will not be copied further down the tree.

This process is good for saving you from having to explicitly set properties on child objects in the tree, and also very flexible. Unfortunately, it also means that it can be very hard to tell precisely what the effect of setting a property on an object high up the tree will be. What other objects will receive this new value? That depends on where else the property has been explicitly defined. The `GetDataPaths()` method is designed to help solve this problem: It returns an array of strings that contains the `ADsPaths` of all the child objects (below the object against which the method is called) in the tree on which the specified property has been explicitly set.

IIS Coding

We've now had a chance to look at the sorts of things available through the IIS provider. We're ready to do a couple of small code samples.

Adding a Virtual Directory

Adding a virtual directory is relatively easy, using the `IADs::Create()` method. This VB code creates another virtual directory in Simon's web site, *Samples*, which gives access to my folder `E:\Samples`.

```
Private Sub Form_Load()

Dim oServer As IADsContainer
Set oServer = GetObject("IIS://BiggyBiggy/W3SVC/3/Root")

Dim oVirtDir As IADs
Set oVirtDir = oServerCont.Create("IISWebVirtualDir", "Samples")
oVirtDir.Put "Path", "e:/Samples"
oVirtDir.SetInfo

Set oServer = Nothing
Set oVirtDir = Nothing
End Sub
```

When creating the object I've set the property, *Path*, which for a virtual directory indicates the path in the file system that the virtual directory has been mapped to.

The interesting thing is that this sample clearly shows how properties are automatically inherited down the tree in the IIS metabase. Notice that I've explicitly set just one property on this object, as well as implicitly setting a couple of properties such as the name, ADsPath and class. But if I look at the new object using our VB object viewer, this is the result:

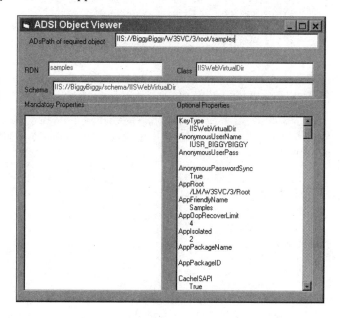

Several other properties have been set. In fact our new virtual directory has inherited almost all the relevant properties from its parent object.

Examining the Property Paths

In this VB sample we show how to use the `IISBaseObject::GetDataPaths` method to retrieve the `ADsPaths` of an object at which a property is defined. We'll do so for my site, *Simons Web Site*, and we'll start off with the `KeyType` property.

We start off by defining a couple of constants that we'll need, then bind to the object and display its `ADsPath` and Class.

```
Private Sub Form_Load()

Const IIS_ANY_PROPERTY = 0
Const IIS_INHERITABLE_ONLY = 1
Const MD_ERROR_DATA_NOT_FOUND = &H800CC801

Dim objWebServer As IISBaseObject
Dim objWebServerADs As IADs
Dim objPathList
Dim varPropName As Variant
varPropName = "KeyType"

'Bind to the object
Set objWebServer = GetObject("IIS://BiggyBiggy/W3SVC/3")
Set objWebServerADs = objWebServer

List1.AddItem "Bound to object " & objWebServerADs.ADsPath
List1.AddItem "Class: " & objWebServerADs.Class
List1.AddItem ""
List1.AddItem "Examining property: " & varPropName
List1.AddItem ""
```

Now we actually call the `GetDataPaths` object. This returns a path list component – which contains the names of the paths, which can be enumerated in a `For Each` loop. We pass the `GetDataPaths()` method the name of the property we are interested in and a flag – one of the constants we've defined. This flag can take one of two values `IIS_INHERITABLE_ONLY` or `IIS_ANY_PROPERTY`. In the latter case, the method will always return the `ADsPaths`. In the former case, it will only do so if the property is inheritable – otherwise it will return the error `MD_ERROR_DATA_NOT_FOUND`. That explains the constants we defined at the beginning of the sample! This sample looks only for inheritable properties, so we check the error object to examine whether an error occurred before we attempt to display the results.

```
'Display the paths where the property varPropName is explicitly defined
On Error Resume Next
objPathList = objWebServer.GetDataPaths(varPropName, IIS_INHERITABLE_ONLY)
If Err.Number = 0 Then
    List1.AddItem "Property is defined at these objects:"
    List1.AddItem ""
    For Each Path In objPathList
        List1.AddItem Path
    Next
```

```
ElseIf Err.Number = MD_ERROR_DATA_NOT_FOUND Then
    List1.AddItem "Property is not inheritable."
Else
    List1.AddItem "Error " & Err.Number & " " & Err.Description
End If

End Sub
```

Running this code produces this output:

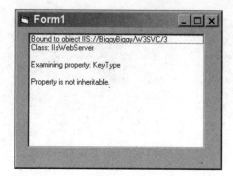

Which tells us that the `KeyType` property is not inheritable – unsurprisingly since this property gives the class of each object. A good example of an inheritable property that is inheritable but by default explicitly defined in virtual directories is `AccessExecute`, which indicates whether web browsers have access to run executables in a given web site or directory. So to examine this property we change the property name in this sample as follows:

```
Dim varPropName As Variant
varPropName = "AccessExecute"
```

Running the code now produces this output.

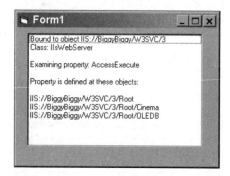

Which lists those objects which explicitly specify the `AccessExecute` property.

ADQI Changes

In this section I'll quickly summarize the changes I made to the Quest for Interfaces sample.

As in chapter 3, the changes centered on the interface entries, where I added the following to the file `ADQIdlg.cpp`.

```
// these are the new interfaces I've added
   MAKEADSENTRY(IDirectorySchemaMgmt), NULL,
//   MAKEADSENTRY(IADsAggregator), NULL,
//   MAKEADSENTRY(IADsAggregatee), NULL,
   MAKEADSENTRY(IADsDeleteOps), NULL,
   MAKEADSENTRY(IADsAccessControlList), NULL,

   // these are the interfaces for IIS
   MAKEADSENTRY(IISBaseObject), NULL,
   MAKEADSENTRY(IISMimeType),NULL,
   MAKEADSENTRY(IISIPSecurity),NULL,
   MAKEADSENTRY(IISSchemaObject),NULL,
   MAKEADSENTRY(IISPropertyAttribute),NULL,
   MAKEADSENTRY(IISDsCrMap),NULL,
   MAKEADSENTRY(IISApp),NULL,
   MAKEADSENTRY(IISApp2),NULL,
   MAKEADSENTRY(IISComputer),NULL,
```

Since we're using some more interfaces, we need the header file in which they are defined. The header file turns out to be `iiis.h`, which is supplied with Visual Studio 6. We also need the values of the GUIDs, so I added these lines near the top of the `ADQIDlg.cpp` file.

```
#include "adslargeinteger.h"
#include "security.h"
#include "iisguids.h"
#include "iiis.h"
```

> *Be careful of these names. Interface names generally start with an I. For the IIS interfaces, Microsoft have simply taken advantage of the I's already in the IIS acronym, so the interfaces have names like* `IISBaseObject` *instead of the more logical (but harder to read)* `IIISBaseObject`. *Oddly, though, an extra I has found its way into the file name* `iiis.h`.

`iiis.h` is a standard MIDL-generated header so it gives us the interface definitions, but we need the values of the IIDs for the interfaces as well. Unfortunately a long search of my computer and the platform SDK failed to reveal any such file. Somewhere along the line, Microsoft didn't anticipate that people would want to be manipulating the IIS admin objects from any language other than VB and VBScript! So I created a header file by cutting and pasting the IIDs from the type library viewed using `oleview`. The header file is called `iisguids.h`, and can be downloaded from the Wrox web site along with the rest of the samples for this chapter. This is how it starts off.

```
#ifndef _INCLUDED_IISGUIDS_H_
#define _INCLUDED_IISGUIDS_H_

const IID IID_IISBaseObject =
    {0x4B42E390,0x0E96,0x11D1,{0x9C,0x3F,0x00,0xA0,0xC9,0x22,0xE7,0x03}};

const IID IID_IISMimeType =
    {0x9036B027, 0xA780, 0x11D0, {0x9B, 0x3D, 0x00, 0x80, 0xC7, 0x10, 0xEF, 0x95}};
```

I'm sure you don't need to see the rest of the file. All it consists of is a list of GUIDs!

If you want to use the extra IIS provider interfaces from C++, then you may find it easiest to download this file from the Wrox web site and #include it in your own programs.

Exchange Server

Exchange Server is the package responsible for handling email. Well, strictly speaking, it's responsible for handling messages, but most of the time that just means email. It receives incoming emails and holds them ready for viewing. It works very much on a client-server principle in that it is there in order to hold the emails. Actual viewing of the emails requires another application with a user interface, which is able to use an API to query the server for the emails. Typical clients would be Outlook Express, Outlook or Outlook Web Access – but there is nothing to stop anyone from using the Exchange APIs to write other user interfaces. These client programs are what most users will ultimately regard as their email programs.

Similarly, if a user wants to send mail, it will be sent first from the mail client program to Exchange Server. If the mail is destined for another user served by the same Exchange Server installation, then Exchange Server will simply hold on to the message until a mail client requests the email on behalf of the recipient. If the mail needs to be sent across the network or the Internet to reach its intended recipient(s) then Exchange Server will do so as soon as it is able to.

Exchange Server is highly optimized for scalability. It is able to be distributed across several servers, and will replicate the information stored between servers.

Exchange Server contains two stores that hold information:

❑ The **Directory** holds information concerning the mailboxes, distribution lists, servers and system configuration.

❑ The **Information Store** holds the actual mailboxes and mail messages themselves.

It is not possible to access the information store using ADSI – the recommended API to use to get to the information store is **collaborative data objects** (**CDO**) – which like ADSI is a set of COM components that expose dual interfaces and so can be called up by any COM-aware language including scripting languages.

On the other hand, the directory in Exchange Server 5.5 is an LDAP v3 compliant directory. This means it is possible to access it using the ADSI LDAP provider. It is also possible to get some limited read access to it via CDO, but in general ADSI is the recommended tool to access the directory, and CDO for the information store.

So full access to all the information made available through Exchange Server really requires the use of ADSI – to perform some of the administrative tasks using the directory – and CDO, to actually manipulate the mailboxes and send mail. We are not going to cover CDO here, but will concentrate on using ADSI to explore the exchange directory.

> *If you do want to use CDO to access the information store as well, you might want to check out Professional ADSI CDO Programming with ASP (ISBN 1-861001-90-8) by Todd Mondor and Mikael Friedlitz, which shows how to combine ADSI and CDO to use Exchange Server.*

Exchange Server and Active Directory

Before we carry on, I need to make one important point about versions. At the time of writing the current version of Exchange Server is 5.5. This was written for NT4, and although it will work on Windows 2000 (all the screenshots and samples in this chapter were taken using Windows 2000 beta 3) it has not been made compatible with Active Directory. This is important because both the Exchange Directory and Active Directory are LDAP directories – and a machine can only host one LDAP directory that uses a given port. I've resolved this issue in this chapter by showing you how to change the port used by the Exchange Directory so it doesn't clash with Active Directory. However, that's a temporary fix. Microsoft have promised to release a new version of Exchange Server soon, and it currently appears that when this happens the Exchange directory will actually be merged into Active Directory.

This all means that while the general principles of how we use the Exchange directory using ADSI are unlikely to change – so most of this chapter will still be relevant, you may find that there are some differences when the next version of Exchange Server is released – particularly with regard to the `ADsPaths` you use to bind to objects. You should therefore use this chapter in conjunction with the latest MSDN documentation to check what features have changed when you upgrade to the next version of Exchange Server.

Exchange Server Architecture

We can look at the architecture of Exchange Server by using its administration tool.

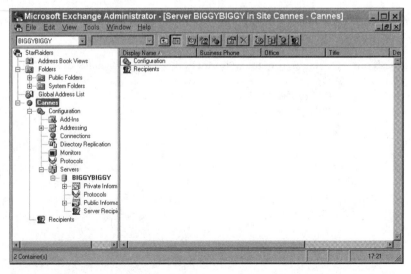

This screenshot shows the Exchange server setup on my computer. There are quite a few levels in the tree, as you can see. At the top level is the **Organization** – in this case StarRaiders. This really is the company or organization that Exchange is running on behalf of. And here I do mean the entire company – if you have offices in several countries, then they will all be contained within the organization – as far as Exchange Server is concerned.

Progressing down the tree, the next level is the **Site**. In this screenshot, I've selected the site, Cannes. A site is the set of all machines which are interconnected by fast, high-capacity, network connections – and in many cases this will mean all your offices that are in one location and so connected by a local area network or a wide area network. When you install Exchange Server on a computer, you will be asked whether you want to create a new site or join an existing site. The significance of the site is that information will be replicated very frequently between the various Exchange Servers installations that claim to belong to the same site – Exchange Server assumes it can do this because computers on one site are supposed to have high bandwidth connections between them.

Carrying on down the tree, we meet a node called *Servers*, under which is my domain controller, BiggyBiggy. A server is just that. It's a computer on which Exchange Server has been installed. I happen to have put my installation of Exchange Server on my domain controller because I don't have that many computers, but in general it's recommended not to use domain controllers for your exchange servers, but to use machines running NT4 Server or Windows 2000 Server that are set up as ordinary members of the domain – simply because running Exchange Server and running a server as a domain controller both put a lot of load on your machine.

The Recipients

There's clearly a lot of different types of object in the Exchange Directory, and clearly we don't have enough space to explain the entire directory in this half-chapter, so we're going to home in on the objects that your Exchange Installation is all about: the recipients.

Recipients are what the name suggests – they are objects that are able to receive messages. Notice that I say objects, since recipients are not necessarily people. In fact Exchange recognizes five types of recipient:

Mailboxes

A mailbox is what corresponds to a person in your organization who can receive mail. It's a box that mail can be sent to and end up in – which means of course that the mailbox is not stored in the directory at all – it's stored in the Information Store, with all the messages it contains. What is stored in the directory is a reference to the fact that this mailbox exists – along with configuration data for it, such as its email address, display name, and which NT account owns this mailbox. (In other words, the NT account of the person who owns the mailbox).

Custom recipients

Like a mailbox, a custom recipient corresponds to a person who can receive mail. The difference is that a custom recipient is someone outside the organization – which means he doesn't have a corresponding mailbox in the Information Store. In fact, all a custom recipient is really, is an alias that maps a given display name (Simon) to an email address (`simon@StarRaiders.com`). The reason for creating custom recipients is that they can appear in the global address list – so people in the organization can email them without needing to look up their address – because Exchange Server can then do that part for them.

Distribution Lists

A distribution list is just a set of names of recipients. It makes it convenient to email a group of people, since you can just send an email to the distribution list, and Exchange Server will see to it that the email gets forwarded to everyone in the list. An organization will typically have distribution lists such as *All staff* and *All staff based at this site*, or *All staff working on this project* and so on.

Public Folders

Much the same as mailboxes, except that a public folder is a mailbox in the Information Store which can be accessed by a group of people, instead of just the individual who owns the mailbox.

Mailbox Agents

These aren't something that we need to be concerned with here. They correspond to actual processes – NT services for example – which are able to receive messages.

Having seen what the types of recipient are, let's have a look at where they are stored in the directory. By default they're under the object known as `Recipients`, which appears under the name of the site. The object named `Recipients` is known as a **recipients container**. Although each site gets one recipients container by default when you install Exchange Server, it is possible to create more containers, though this isn't generally recommended. This next screenshot shows the recipients container for StarRaiders' Cannes site, showing the recipients I've created in it.

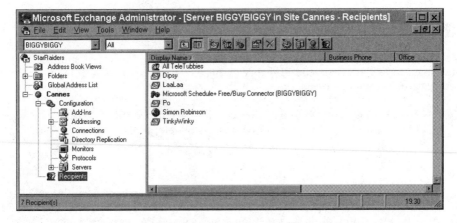

In this screenshot, Simon Robinson is a custom recipient – as shown by the globe icon indicating the outside world, while TinkyWinky, Dipsy, LaaLaa and Po are mailboxes. All TeleTubbies is a distribution list that contains all the Teletubbies, so I can email them all at the same time, shown by the group icon, while Microsoft Schedule+ is a mailbox agent and is the only recipient that was supplied automatically when Exchange Server was installed.

The main point here, however, is not really the existence of all these types of recipient. It's rather that there's a lot of scope here for writing some client applications that can automate the process of creating recipients. You see I had to create every one of those recipients by hand, using the wizards available in the Exchange admin tool. I didn't mind doing that too much for the six recipients shown here– but if it was several hundred?

As an example, the mailboxes are created by clicking on the File menu, then New Mailbox. This brings up this tabbed dialog box:

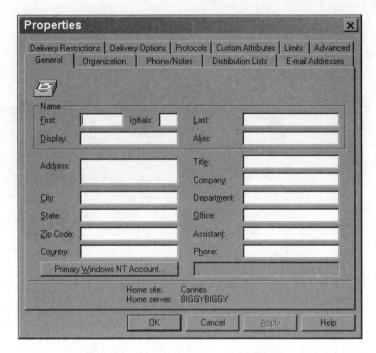

There's a lot of information to fill in there! Most of it is optional, and I left most of it blank because I was only creating sample mailboxes. But in a real organization you probably will need a lot of it filled in.

To its credit, the wizard can offer to create an NT account corresponding to the new mailbox, if you click on the Primary Windows NT Account... button:

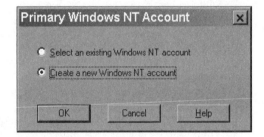

But the account will get created with no password, and if you need to add the new account to certain groups or set up particular permissions, then you'll have to do that manually afterwards. *Some* of this might be automated with the next release of Exchange Server, when the Exchange Directory gets linked in with Active Directory, but even so you can see that if you're in a situation where, for example, someone new is joining the company and needs to be set up with a new NT account and mailbox etc. there are a lot of tasks to be done, where having a script that automates them can save a lot of time. The Exchange Server sample, which we will present later in the chapter, shows how to set up a new mailbox and an associated NT account at the same time, and can be used as a basis for more sophisticated applications that automate the process of creating mailboxes.

We've now covered as much as we need of the structure of Exchange and the Exchange Directory – we're nearly ready to see where ADSI can fit into the picture. But first, recall that the Exchange Directory is an LDAP directory. For Exchange Server, we need to make sure that the LDAP service is configured correctly for us to be able to use it.

Setting up LDAP

Before you attempt to access the Exchange Directory using ADSI you will need to ensure that the Exchange LDAP service is configured correctly. To do this, you will need to open the Exchange admin tool and locate the *Protocols* node under the site configuration.

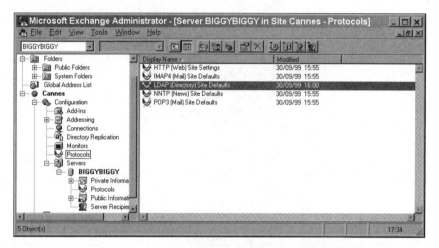

If you select this node in the tree view, a number of different protocols will appear in the right hand pane. Double click on the **LDAP Site Defaults** to bring up a tabbed dialog box that lets us specify the configuration settings for LDAP. The first tab is the **General** tab. You should obviously make sure that the protocol is enabled. Also, if you have your machine set up on Windows 2000, it's a good idea to change the port number. This is important if you are running Exchange on a member workstation and essential if you are running it on a domain controller.

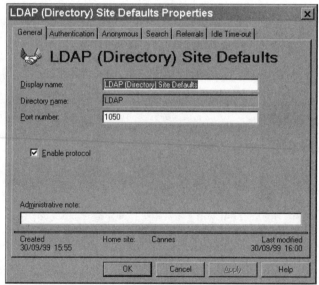

The reason is that when Exchange Server is installed, it will have defaulted to port 389, since that is the port that LDAP uses by default. Unfortunately, in Windows 2000, Active Directory already answers to that port! And in Exchange Server 5.5, the directory has not yet been integrated with Active Directory – it's a completely separate directory, so we need to make sure that the Exchange Directory listens out for LDAP requests on a different port. Here I've chosen port 1050.

Most of the other tabs are self-explanatory. The one other tab that I want to discuss is the Search tab:

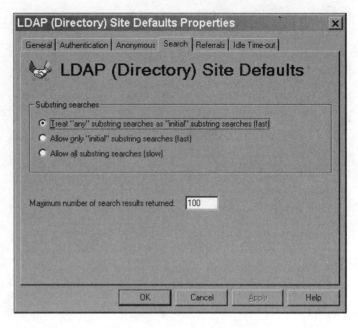

We haven't yet covered searching – we will do so in Chapter 7. However, when we do searches using ADSI, we are asking the directory to return all the objects that match a certain criterion, such as 'all recipients whose names begin with A'. You will normally expect a directory to return all suitable objects, no matter how many there are. However, Exchange has an option to restrict the number of results returned in any one query – and by default this is set to 100. When this number of results has been returned in response to a search request, the Exchange Directory will simply assume it's satisfied the request, and not return any more results. We'll leave it at 100 for now, but you should be aware that if you use ADSI to carry out searches against the Exchange directory, you should ensure this field is set to a high enough value to be able to respond correctly to all your searches.

Exchange LDAP Directory Structure.

We'll use `adsvw.exe` to explore the directory. Since I've selected a different port from the default LDAP port, I cannot simply browse down through the LDAP namespace object. If I try to list the children of LDAP:, I'll simply get my local Active Directory installation. To avoid this, I need to give the pathname of the node at the top of the directory explicitly. For the Exchange directory, this has the distinguished name `o=<Organization>`. Since my organization name is StarRaiders, the root of the main part of the Exchange directory has the distinguished name `o=StarRaiders`. The LDAP provider requires me to prefix this with `LDAP://`, and since I'm not using the default port I also have to specify the server name and port number, so the `ADsPath` I need to bind to this object is

```
LDAP://BiggyBiggy:1050/o=StarRaiders
```

Note that as usual for the LDAP provider, the initial `LDAP:` is case sensitive and must be capitalized, but the following text is case insensitive.

If we attempt to bind to the object with this `ADsPath` using `adsvw.exe`, and expand out the tree a little, this is the result:

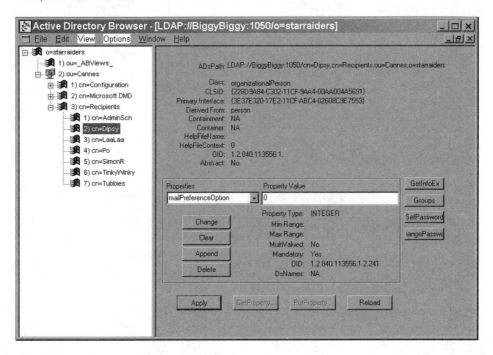

I'm looking at my StarRaiders Exchange installation, and have selected one of the new mailboxes I added, the one belonging to that delightful TeleTubby, Dipsy.

To some extent the directory structure exposed through LDAP and ADSI mirrors that exposed through the Exchange admin tool – not surprisingly since we are to some extent just looking at the same directory through a slightly different view. We still see the basic organizational structure with the organization at the top. Now we're dealing with LDAP distinguished names, so the top-level object is called `o=starraiders`, rather than the simple StarRaiders as seen in the Exchange admin tool.

We'll leave the `ou=_ABViews_` node – that just contains some information about the address books and is beyond the scope of this chapter. Instead we'll concentrate on the node that represents the site, `ou=Cannes`. Below this lie three containers:

❑ `cn=Configuration` contains some more configuration data

❑ `cn=MicrosoftDMD` contains the schema of the directory

❑ `cn=Recipients` contains the recipients (although not the mailbox agents), as we can see in the screenshot

What this means is that the structure of the Exchange Directory, as viewed through ADSI, typically looks like this:

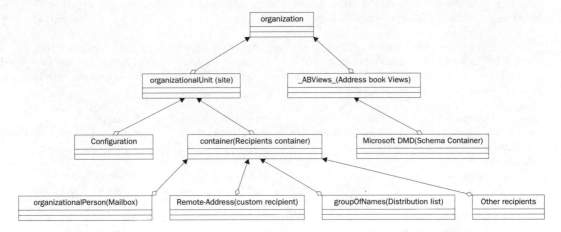

Names in LDAP vs Exchange

One potentially confusing area is that the names of the objects and the classes of object you see when using ADSI or LDAP are not the same as the name as the names used by the Exchange Admin tool. For example, the last screenshot shows that Po is viewed by LDAP as an `organizationalPerson`, *not* as a mailbox. And you may have been surprised that most of the class names in the above diagram of the Exchange directory structure didn't match the names of the objects we'd been talking about.

The table summarizes the different names used for the main classes. Note that the names are *not* case sensitive, though I've written the LDAP names with their customary case.

Exchange name	LDAP name
Organization	organization
Site	organizationalUnit
Recipients Container	container
Mailbox	organizationalPerson
Custom Recipient	Remote-Address
Distribution List	groupOfNames
Mailbox Agent	Mailbox-Agent

This difference doesn't just extend to class names. Names of instances of objects can be different when you view the object using LDAP, against viewing the object through the Exchange admin tool. For example, the distribution list that I added is referred to as All Teletubbies in the earlier screenshot of the Exchange admin tool, but as cn=Tubbies in the adsvw.exe screenshot.

The reason for this difference is to do with the fact that, although the Exchange Directory is accessible using LDAP, its internal structure is not based on LDAP. The Exchange Directory existed in earlier versions of Exchange Server, before it was decided that making it compatible with the LDAP protocol would be a good idea.

Now LDAP has its own schema. For example, you may have noticed that the class organizationalUnit exists in both the Exchange Directory (viewed through ADSI) and Active Directory. That's not just a coincidence. That's happened because organizationalUnit is a standard class defined by the LDAP protocol. organization and organizationalPerson fall into that category too. Unfortunately, the result of the Exchange Directory having evolved independently of LDAP is that the Exchange Directory's schema is incompatible with the LDAP schema. So it was necessary to map some of the names in Exchange Directory onto LDAP-compliant names when the directory was accessed using the LDAP service. When we use ADSI, we go through the LDAP provider and the Exchange LDAP service, so we see the LDAP-mapped names and class names, whereas the Exchange admin tool simply accesses the internal directory directly. You can think of the situation like this:

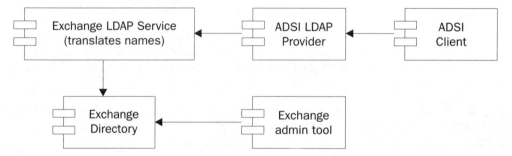

The upshot of this is that when writing ADSI clients that use the Exchange Directory, you will need to make sure that you use the LDAP-ified names, not the names you see in the Exchange admin tool. That's easy enough for the class names I've mentioned, since I've just given you a table to tell you what names to use! But clearly, you need a more general way of finding out the correct LDAP names. That's the subject of the next section.

Mapping Exchange Names to LDAP Names

The principle that the Exchange directory uses here is quite simple. Each object in the Exchange Directory has a property called the Alias. It is the value of the Alias that is used for the name of the corresponding instance when viewed through LDAP. For the names of classes themselves it's slightly different. Each class in the Exchange Directory has an attribute called Description. This attribute contains the LDAP-ified name of the class.

For example, in the above screenshots, the alias of the Distribution List, *All Teletubbies* is Tubbies, resulting in the LDAP name `cn=Tubbies`. While on the other hand, the Description property of the class schema object that describes the Mailbox class is `organizationalPerson`, so LDAP will see this class as being an `organizationalPerson`.

For the name of an instance of an object, we can see this by double clicking on the object in the Exchange admin tool:

In fact this is essentially the same dialog box that I had to fill in when I first created the distribution list.

For classes of object, it's a little harder to get to the information since the Exchange admin tool doesn't normally let you get to the schema. That's because the admin tool itself normally processes the data in the directory in order to hide some of the configuration stuff, which if modified directly, could irreparably damage your installation of Exchange Server. To get round this you need to do what's known as running the admin tool in raw mode. That means running the executable file and passing it the parameter `/r`. You can't do this from the Start menu; from which you'd normally run the admin tool (unless you define a new shortcut which includes the `/r` parameter). Instead the easiest way is to start the executable file from the command prompt. The file concerned is called `admin.exe`, and if you installed Exchange Server to drive `X:`, and accepted the default installation folders then its pathname will be `X:\exchsrvr\bin\admin.exe`. That means to start the admin tool in raw mode you need to go to the command prompt and type

```
X:\exchsrvr\bin\admin.exe /r
```

Once you've started the tool, go to the View menu and click on Raw Directory. The admin tool will now be directly looking at the entire directory, and you will be able to see the schema.

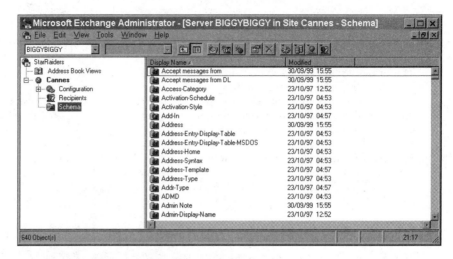

In fact what you're seeing is exactly the view that you see through ADSI, except using the raw Exchange Directory names instead of the corresponding LDAP names.

If we double click on any of the class or attribute objects in the schema, we can view its description property. For example, selecting the Mailbox class schema object gives us this:

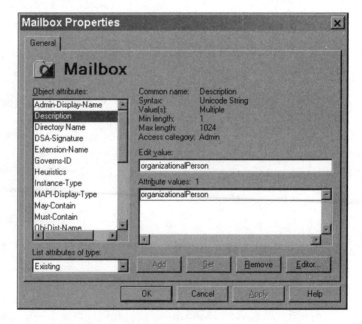

Doing this tells us what name we should use for this class in ADSI.

> **This is probably a good time to remind you of the dangers of using the Exchange admin tool in raw mode. If used carelessly, you can trash your Exchange installation. In general, unless you're certain you know what you're doing, don't attempt to change anything in the directory when you're using raw mode!**

Adding a Mailbox

This sample shows how to add a mailbox, including creating the associated Windows user account.

Unfortunately it is not possible to do this without bringing in some security stuff that we haven't yet covered, since we discuss security in chapter 8. The security material comes in two places. Firstly, when we associate the Exchange mailbox with a user account, we actually identify the Windows account using a security identifier (SID) for the account, rather than using the account's username. And secondly, we do need to set some security access permissions on the mailbox so that the user does have access rights to read his email. The Exchange admin tool handles both of these automatically, but we need to do this explicitly with ADSI.

Because we haven't really covered how ADSI implements security yet in this book, we'll just give brief explanations of the relevant parts of the sample – enough to give you an idea of what's going on without going too much into how the relevant COM components work.

The sample is fairly long so we'll break it up. There are broadly three things we need to do:

❑ Create the new user account

❑ Create the mailbox

❑ Set the permissions on the mailbox

The sample is in VB, and has the details of the new user hardcoded in – I'm going to add a mailbox for the old rocker, Alice Cooper. First up, we set up some information that we need.

```
Private Sub Form_Load()

' set up the details of the new user

strUserName = "alicec"
strPassword = "COMDude"
strFirstName = "Alice"
strLastName = "Cooper"


' set up other info needed for the mailbox
strDisplayName = strFirstName & " " & strLastName
strSMTPAddr = strUserName & "@microsoft.com"
strMTA = "cn=Microsoft
MTA,cn=BiggyBiggy,cn=Servers,cn=Configuration,ou=Cannes,o=StarRaiders"
strMDB = "cn=Microsoft Private
MDB,cn=BiggyBiggy,cn=Servers,cn=Configuration,ou=Cannes,o=StarRaiders"
```

Most of that should be fairly self-explanatory. `strSMTPAddr` is the actual mail address of the new account – which we figure out from the user name. The two strings you won't be familiar with are two LDAP distinguished names, `strMTA` and `strMDB`. These respectively specify the message transfer agent (a component of Exchange Server) and the home server, and are the `ADsPaths` of objects in the configuration container for the Cannes site in the Exchange Directory. The objects with these `ADsPaths` already exist by default in the directory, but we will need to set properties on the new mailbox to refer to them.

Now we carry out our first real operation – creating an NT (or Windows 2000) account. This just uses the standard techniques we learned from the last chapter.

```
' create the associated NT or W2K account
Set objDomain = GetObject("WinNT://TopOfThePops")
Set objUser = objDomain.Create("user", strUserName)
objUser.SetInfo
objUser.SetPassword strPassword
```

Next up, it's time to create the mailbox. We do this by binding to its parent object in the directory, and using the `IADsContainer::CreateObject()` method. We also set the display name of the mailbox and a couple of extra properties that are necessary for the mailbox to work correctly.

```
' bind to the recipients container
strRecipCont = "LDAP://BiggyBiggy:1050/cn=Recipients,OU=Cannes,O=StarRaiders"
Set objCont = GetObject(strRecipCont)

' create the mailbox
Set objMailBox = objCont.Create("organizationalPerson", "cn=" & strUserName)
objMailBox.Put "mailPreferenceOption", 0
objMailBox.Put "givenName", strFirstName
objMailBox.Put "sn", strLastName
objMailBox.Put "cn", strDisplayName
objMailBox.Put "uid", strUserName
objMailBox.Put "Home-MTA", strMTA
objMailBox.Put "Home-MDB", strMDB
objMailBox.Put "mail", strSMTPAddr
objMailBox.Put "MAPI-Recipient", True
objMailBox.Put "rfc822Mailbox", strSMTPAddr
```

We haven't yet called `SetInfo()` on the mailbox object because we haven't yet finished setting all its properties. There's one more property, called `Assoc-NT-Account`. And here's the bit of the code where we'll have to jump forward a bit and refer you to chapter 8 for more details. Essentially, the way that Windows identifies your account is not using your username, it's by using a data structure known as the SecurityID (SID). So we need to extract the security ID – and the easiest way to do that is by using a COM component known as the ADsSID component. This is not part of ADSI itself, but forms part of the ADSI resource kit, which you get as part of the ADSI 2.5 SDK.

We need to create an `ADsSID` component, set it to point to the appropriate user by supplying the `ADsPath`, and then retrieve the user back again as a security ID. We use two methods, `GetAs` and `SetAs` exposed by this object, which take as a parameter an integer that defines the format in which we are identifying the user account. So we first define a couple of constants that indicate the required format. Then we retrieve the SID and store it in the mailbox. The whole code looks like this.

```
' declare a couple of security related constants
Const ADS_SID_HEXSTRING = 1
Const ADS_SID_WINNT_PATH = 5

' associate the Mailbox with the user account
Dim sid As New ADsSID
sid.SetAs ADS_SID_WINNT_PATH, "WinNT://TopOfThePops/" & strUserName & ",user"
sidHex = sid.GetAs(ADS_SID_HEXSTRING)
objMailBox.Put "Assoc-NT-Account", sidHex
```

Now we are ready to actually tell the Exchange directory to create our new mailbox.

```
' write the changes to the Exchange Directory
objMailBox.SetInfo
```

Finally we need to set the access permissions so the user can – amongst other things – send and receive mail. We are using another component from the ADSI resource kit here, the `ADsSecurity` component, along with three more ADSI interfaces related to security, `IADsSecurityDescriptor`, `IADsAccessControlList` and `IADsAccessControlEntry`. We won't explain this code here, but you will learn how these ADSI interfaces work in chapter 8.

```
Const ADS_RIGHT_EXCH_MODIFY_USER_ATT = &H2
Const ADS_RIGHT_EXCH_MAIL_SEND_AS = &H8
Const ADS_RIGHT_EXCH_MAIL_RECEIVE_AS = &H10

' make sure the user has permission to send and receive mail
' and modify his attributes
Dim sec As New ADsSecurity
Dim sd As IADsSecurityDescriptor
Dim dacl As IADsAccessControlList
Dim ace As New AccessControlEntry

Set sd = sec.GetSecurityDescriptor(objMailBox.ADsPath)
Set dacl = sd.DiscretionaryAcl
ace.Trustee = domain & "\" & strUserName
ace.AccessMask = ADS_RIGHT_EXCH_MODIFY_USER_ATT Or ADS_RIGHT_EXCH_MAIL_SEND_AS Or
ADS_RIGHT_EXCH_MAIL_RECEIVE_AS
ace.AceType = ADS_ACETYPE_ACCESS_ALLOWED
dacl.AddAce ace
sd.DiscretionaryAcl = dacl
sec.SetSecurityDescriptor sd

End Sub
```

And that's it. The new mailbox has been created.

We've presented the example of creating a mailbox in full because – as you can see – it brings together quite a number of concepts and does require some knowledge of the peculiarities of the Exchange Directories. We will, however, leave the Exchange Server examples there.

Site Server

Site Server is a series of tools and components that can be used to enhance the functionality of Internet Information Server. We mention it here because it features (yet) another directory which can be accessed using ADSI: the Site Server Membership Directory. This directory forms part of the Site Server Membership and Personalization functionality, by which visitors to your web site can be automatically identified, and customized web pages presented to them. The Site Server Membership Directory is the directory which stores details of the accounts of web site visitors. It also includes – currently as a subdirectory – the Internet Locator Server (ILS) directory, which is a memory-based directory intended to store details of people currently logged on and available for chats or conferencing. The ILS directory is the directory used by Microsoft NetMeeting to identify people it is currently possible to chat to.

Site Server Membership is an LDAP directory, which means that you can access it using the LDAP provider, just as for Exchange Server and Active Directory. And just as for Exchange Server, it will be incorporated into Active Directory when Site Server 4 is released – which at the time of writing is promised reasonably soon. At present (current version of Site Server is Site Server 3.0) the membership directory is an independent directory service.

Since it's not at present clear what form the Membership Directory will take when it's integrated into Active Directory, we've chosen not to cover it in detail in this book. If you do want more information for about the Membership Directory in Site Server 3.0, you might want to have a look at *Site Server 3.0 Personalization and Membership* by *Robert Howard (ISBN 1-861001-9-40)*.

Summary

In this chapter we've taken a close look at The Exchange Server Directory and IIS Metabase with a view to examining what we can do with these directories using ADSI. We've concentrated on the particular idiosyncrasies of these directories – the areas where you need to be aware that these directories behave differently from other directories or providers you'd use from ADSI clients – since to do more would be largely to repeat material that we've covered in chapters 4 and 5. I can't emphasize enough that once you've got past the odd peculiarities of each directory, working with any one directory using ADSI involves using exactly the same techniques as working with any other directory. That's where the power of ADSI lies – and that's what unifying directory access means in practice.

On the IIS side, we've seen that the IIS metabase implements a number of other interfaces besides the standard ADSI ones. And we've examined one of these interfaces in more detail, `IISBaseObject` – since this is the only interface that is exposed by all IIS ADSI objects, and we've seen that its purpose is to allow access to some of the additional features that properties have in IIS, which they don't have in most other directories - ie. you can control their characteristics. Other IIS interfaces play specific roles related to particular classes of object – for example the IIS computer object implements methods to back up and restore the IIS metabase (the IIS metabase applies to the computer as a whole).

For Exchange Server we've examined the directory structure and focused on the fact that, due to the Exchange Directory's non-LDAP background, care has to be taken in the choice of the names of classes and instances of objects, as the names that LDAP – and hence the ADSI LDAP provider – uses are not the same names that the Exchange directory uses internally and which you will see if you use the Exchange admin tool to examine or configure Exchange Server.

We've now nearly completed our tour of some of the various providers you can access using ADSI, and will move on to discuss more about ADSI itself in the next couple of chapters – starting with how to perform searches in the next chapter. In that chapter we will also, incidentally, examine one more directory service that we have not yet covered: Netscape Directory Server, another LDAP directory.

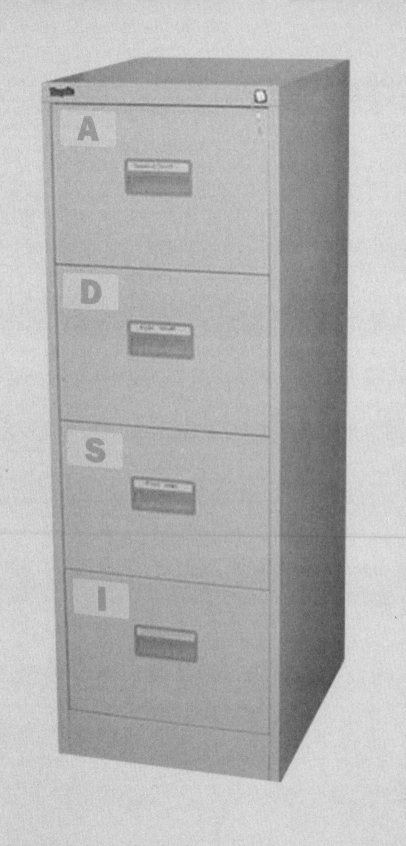

7

Searching

In this chapter you will learn:

- ❑ How to do directory searches using `adsvw.exe`
- ❑ How to use LDAP search filters
- ❑ How to write VB and scripting clients which use ADO to search ADSI-compliant directories
- ❑ How to write C++ clients that use `IDirectorySearch` to search a directory
- ❑ What the relationship between ADSI, OLE DB and ADO is

And, coincidentally (even though it hasn't got much to do with searching):

- ❑ About Netscape Directory Server – another LDAP directory you can access with ADSI

Searching is one of the most important operations you can perform on a directory.

I've kept searching in a separate chapter because it is a fairly large topic in ADSI. Not only that, but the way that ADSI handles searching is also quite different to the way it handles most of its other functionality. There are two reasons for this.

Firstly, the interface used to carry out searching, `IDirectorySearch`, is a custom rather than a dual interface. This means that it cannot be used by scripting clients, who must use the ADO ADSI provider to do searching. Secondly, even for C++ clients using `IDirectorySearch`, the way the results are returned is quite different from the way most of the other ADSI interfaces work. Instead of seeing a directory tree structure, we have to get used to working with rows and columns of data – something you'd usually associate with relational databases, not hierarchical directories.

In this chapter we're going to start off by looking at how searching works using the Active Directory Browser, `adsvw.exe`. `adsvw.exe` gives us a ready-made user interface that will let us experiment with the possibilities and allow us to see the power of searching, without having to go into any programming details. Once we've done that, we can have a look at how searching is actually done from a programming point of view.

We'll work through the different ways of searching in order of increasing complexity, which means ADO first, then `IDirectorySearch`, and finishing with a brief discussion of the possibilities of using OLE DB. On the way, we'll learn about how LDAP search filters work, and what sorts of search preferences ADSI lets you specify.

Introducing Netscape Directory Server

Before we start a search, we need a decent directory to search against. Of the ADSI providers available, only the LDAP provider supports searching. This would normally imply we'd have to use either Active Directory or one of the two LDAP directories we investigated in the last chapter: the Exchange or Site Server directories.

Unfortunately, I'm not a huge multinational company. As I'm sure you've noticed, I've only got two computers – *BiggyBiggy*, and my Pentium 133, *CrashLots* – which means I haven't actually got much data in any of those directories. Sure, the tree structures are all there, but my system's not exactly brimming with thousands of users. If we're really going to do some clever searching and see how search filters work, we ideally need a directory that's got a decent amount of data in it.

I haven't yet introduced you to the other big LDAP directory that's in common use: **Netscape Directory Server**. This is an LDAP 3 directory that doesn't actually have a specific purpose. Unlike the Exchange Directory, which is there specifically as a directory for Exchange Server, Netscape Directory Server is a general-purpose LDAP directory service – you can use it to store whatever data you want in it. It's also highly regarded in the industry as a reliable, scaleable directory service.

Installing Netscape Directory Server

It is possible to download a free 60-day evaluation version from Netscape's download site, `http://www.iplanet.com/downloads/index.html`. It also comes with a very nice sample database, which you can use to populate your directory from the start – the kind of database that we're going to have fun doing searches against.

If you want to install the Netscape directory to try out the samples in this chapter, you should make sure you select the custom install option. Type in the name airius.com for the directory root, and choose the option to populate the directory with the sample database.

In addition, if you are installing to Windows 2000, make sure you choose a different port number from the default LDAP port of 389, because Active Directory uses this port. I don't know what exactly would happen with another LDAP directory service competing with Active Directory to accept requests on port 389, but I'm sure it wouldn't be pleasant. The same principle applies if you are running NT4 but have any other LDAP directory service running on port 389. I've chosen to use port 390 for the directory service and 391 for the administration service (The administration service is something particular to Netscape Directory Server. There is no equivalent in Active Directory, which uses one port.). This means I have to explicitly specify the port in all `ADsPaths` when I wish to use Netscape Directory Server.

Strictly, when claiming other ports for your own use on machines on a network, you should use ports with numbers above 1000, but since I know exactly what's running on my machine, I know that ports 390 and 391 are free.

More information about Netscape Directory Server can be found in Mark Wilcox's Implementing LDAP (ISBN: 1-861002-21-1), also published by Wrox.

Exploring Netscape Directory Server

So let's have a look at the Netscape sample directory. Here's the view from the Active Directory Browser:

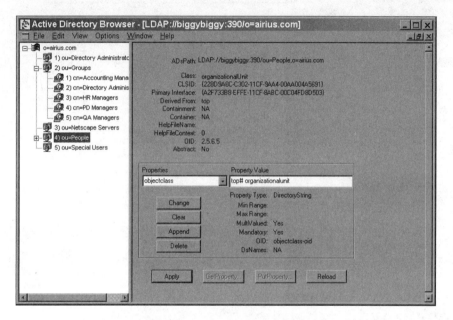

What we see is a fairly intuitive directory of people in a company. Below the root of the naming context, `o=airius.com`, are five organizational units. Only two have any data in them: Groups has a small number of companies in it, whereas People has the details of about 150 employees.

If you do want to explore the sample database, take a look at the `rootdse` object. From that, you'll learn that there are two naming contexts: `o=airius.com` which contains the actual directory, and `o=NetscapeRoot`, which contains configuration information.

What makes this sample directory particularly suitable for demonstrating searching is that it also has a fairly simple schema. Directory objects usually have a manageable number of properties. For example, this is what we get if we use our property cache viewer to look at one of the people in the directory:

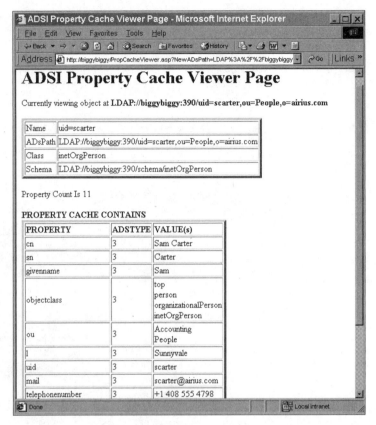

That said, you'll notice there are a number of other optional properties for which no value has been supplied.

Searching with adsvw.exe

We're now ready to start searching – and we're going to start off by using the Active Directory browser, adsvw.exe. adsvw.exe is quite a good tool to use here because its user interface for searching is a relatively low-level one, in the sense that the choices you are asked to make tend to correspond quite directly with the underlying features of ADSI: there's little attempt to map them onto a more friendly interface. (And besides, there's the minor matter that Microsoft haven't actually released any other general browser tools that support searching.)

To start a search, open the Active Directory browser as normal, but in the first dialog box, select Query instead of ObjectViewer.

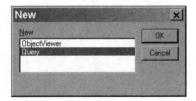

You'll then be presented with a large dialog box asking you to type in your query:

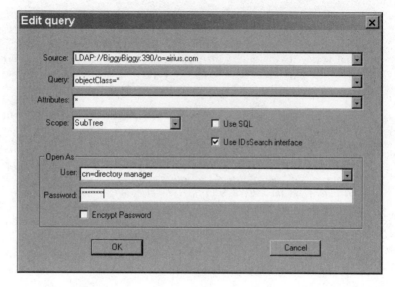

You need to be careful what you enter in this dialog – and unfortunately there's no documentation to help you.

Let's start off with **Source**. This is the `ADsPath` of the ADSI object which is actually used for the search. It's the object which `adsvw` will bind to internally and ask to perform the search. What we need to be aware of is that ADSI objects only ever search down the directory tree – they don't start querying their parents during searches.

How far down the tree they go is determined by what you choose in the drop-down list box marked **Scope**. The options here are **Base**, **OneLevel** and **Subtree**. If you choose **Base**, you will get results back *only* for the `Source` object. **OneLevel** will mean the search will cover all of the immediate children of the source object (excluding the source object itself). If you choose **Subtree**, the search will recurse right down the directory tree from the source object (this time, including the source object).

You might wonder what the point of having **Base** object as an option is – all this will do is retrieve the properties of the `Source` object, which you can do using the `IADs` interface anyway. The reason really comes from the ADSI's LDAP heritage. As we'll find out in Chapter 10, LDAP doesn't have a separate concept of browsing a directory or of viewing an object's properties. The only way you can look at an object in LDAP is by doing a search. So a base object search is the way that you'll normally examine the properties of a single object in LDAP. There is an extra benefit in that – since LDAP search filters can be quite complicated, it's possible to use a base level search to easily find out if a given object satisfies a fairly complex set of conditions.

Anyway, back to our dialog box. The edit box marked Query is possibly the most crucial one. This is the one in which you get the chance to say what you're looking for. If you want to find all the people whose surnames begin with S, and who have a 6 but not an 8 in their phone number, then this is the box that you write that query in. We'll cover how to write search queries later in this chapter. For the time being, I'm going to request all the objects in the directory. Just take my word for it that the way you ask for everything is by specifying objectClass=*.

Query is where you specify what objects you want to find. The Attributes box is where you specify what attributes (properties) you want to examine in those objects. Again, I'm going to ask for everything here – and to do that all I need to type in is *.

> *Requiring an * here is actually a feature of* adsvw.exe, *NOT a part of ADSI. When you actually make the method call in ADSI, you specify* all properties *by passing in a* NULL *parameter. However* adsvw.exe *wants an * here. In my experience, if you do the intuitive thing and leave this field blank,* adsvw.exe *has an unfortunate tendency to crash.*

That's actually completed our search request. The Use SQL check box indicates whether we've used SQL rather than an LDAP search filter for our request – we haven't, so leave this blank.

The Use IDsSearch interface checkbox indicates whether or not we want to go through the ADO provider to do our search. In fact, that doesn't affect the results, so we'll ignore it. Since this option doesn't ever seem to make a difference, I assume that it's there for testing purposes.

The remaining boxes are concerned with authentication. I've chosen to authenticate myself as the directory manager for the directory – that's a user who has practically unlimited privileges – though for the default install of Netscape Directory Server, it doesn't really matter. If you leave the user name and password blank, adsvw.exe won't try to authenticate to the directory, so you'll end up with default access permissions. For Netscape Directory Server that means guest privileges. For Microsoft's directories, that means whatever access permissions are associated with the Windows 2000 account you're logged in as. What you shouldn't do is carelessly leave the user name filled in (adsvw.exe normally tries to be clever by sticking in the username you last used to authenticate there), but not type a password. In that case, adsvw.exe will try to authenticate with that username and no password – which will almost inevitably lead to an authentication failure.

The option to encrypt the password should be self-explanatory. We'll discuss ADSI's various encryption options in the next chapter.

Phew! That's the first dialog box out of the way. To recap, I've used it to ask for all the entries in the entire directory to be returned, and for all properties on all entries to be returned as well.

When we click on OK, the search does not take place immediately: I'm afraid we get presented with another dialog box:

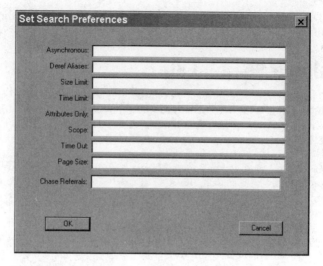

This one asks us to select various preferences on exactly how the search is to be carried out: for example, whether it should be done synchronously or asynchronously. Most of these options will not affect the results of the search, but they may affect system performance – so in most cases you probably won't bother filling in any values here. For the time being, we're going to leave all these boxes blank.

When we've made all our choices and click OK, we'll actually be presented with the results of the search. Here it is:

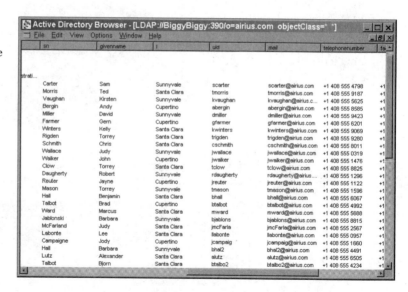

adsvw.exe has presented the results to us in a listview – and they have the form of a table. Each row in the listview corresponds to a row that is returned to us as a search result – and as we can see there is a one-to-one mapping between a row and an object in the directory. Each column in the listview is a column returned as part of the search result. The column name is the name of an attribute, and the column data is the value (or values) of that attribute.

There are quite a few columns returned, and I've scrolled the screen horizontally to find the interesting ones. Almost all of the entries in the sample directory are people.

Using a Search Filter

The previous example has hopefully given you a flavor of how easy it is to do searches. The dialog boxes took a lot of explanation, but once you're familiar with them, carrying out a complex search with `adsvw.exe` isn't much more than a few mouse clicks and filling in a couple of edit boxes – a few seconds work.

However, what we've done so far isn't really much of a search. Asking for *all* objects might technically be a search, but it's not really in the spirit of the meaning of the word! Normally, we'd imagine search means something like, say, give me all the technicians in a particular department. So we need to do something about our **search filter**.

We probably also want to narrow down our results a bit, in terms of what properties we want. So I'm going to try a narrower search. I'm going to ask for all the people with surnames beginning with S. And the properties I'm interested in are their user ID, their common name (the LDAP equivalent of the ADSI name), their surname, and `ADsPath`. So here's what my query now looks like:

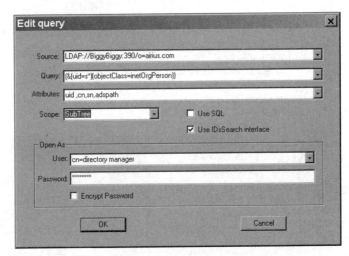

Even without going into the details of how search filters work, you can probably see that I've asked for everything for which the uid attribute begins with s, and the `objectClass` includes the value inetOrgPerson (I say *includes* because `objectClass` is a multivalued property).

Here are the search results:

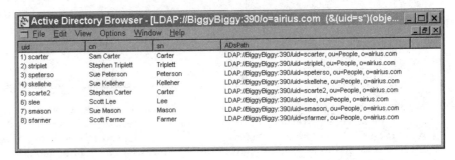

Let's look at one more example to illustrate searching before we start to look at it in a bit more depth. This time, I'm going to try a search on Active Directory instead of the Netscape directory server. I'm going to look for all the users on the system. Recall that this is something that's difficult to do on Active Directory by the usual ADSI interfaces, because users are potentially spread across multiple containers across the directory. Anyway, here's my query:

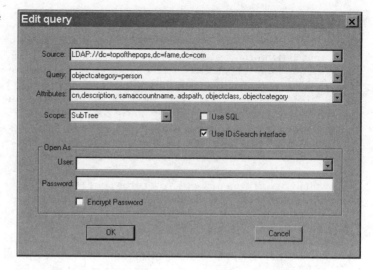

And here are the search results:

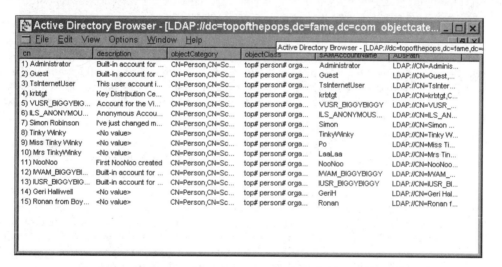

Notice that the search has picked up all the users in the default Users container, as well as the new ones that I added to my new Pop Star Users organizational unit, in Chapter 3.

Hopefully that should have given you some idea of the power of searching using ADSI. We're almost ready to go behind the scenes a bit more and look at how searching works, and how to actually write clients that request searching. But first, there are a few more things about searching that you can deduce from looking at the results from our adsvw.exe searches.

About the Search Results

One of the most important consequences of the table format in which results are returned is that there is no special significance attached to the name or the ADsPath of an object. Indeed, in the above results, there is no column that directly indicates the object's name, as in the IADs::Name property. The closest is the column, cn, which in this case does happen to be the object's relative distinguished name. There is a column, ADsPath (not in the scrolled area of the screenshot), but there's nothing special about this column – it's simply one of the columns that can be requested, just like any other column. There's nothing in the ADSI specifications that says this column has to be returned. And – other than ADsPath - there are also no columns that really correspond to the IADs automation values. Searching for the most part returns schema-defined properties.

Incidentally, we've seen that each row corresponds to one ADSI object. The ADsPath is what uniquely identifies each object, so it's possible that if the ADsPath is not returned as one of the results, and if two objects in the directory have identical values for each of the requested properties, then duplicate rows may be returned.

The other thing you might notice is that all the columns are printed out as strings. That's actually not a part of ADSI: it's adsvw converting whatever ADSI data types it finds into strings to print out. However, the point here is that the only things you'll get back are property values. The one thing you never get back from a search is an interface pointer to the object.

Compare this with browsing using the IADsContainer methods. There what you get back are interface pointers to the objects, whereas when you do a search, you get a list of the properties and property values instead. If you want to actually do anything to the object, you'll have to make sure you do a search that specifies the ADsPath as one of the properties to be returned, then use the ADsPath to bind to the object. This might seem a long way of doing it, but there are good reasons for it:

❑   Remember that the searching is done through IDirectorySearch, which is to some extent intended to interface to OLE DB or ADO. Neither OLE DB nor ADO know anything about ADSI, so neither of these SDKs would know what to do with an IADs interface pointer anyway!

❑   Search queries can return a *lot* of data. The Netscape sample directory only has about 150 objects in it. But what if you're doing a search on a big corporate directory with millions of entries – and the search returns hundreds of thousands of results. There is an overhead associated with creating a COM object and binding to it. Not much overhead, but it could add up in a big search. For this reason, it makes more sense not to actually attempt to bind to all the objects. Better to wait to see if the client actually decides after the search that it wants to bind to some of them.

❑   This is possibly the most crucial reason. The searching mechanism in the LDAP provider is really only a very thin wrapper over the underlying LDAP search mechanism. And LDAP itself knows nothing about ADSI or COM objects. If the search was to return interface pointers, then the LDAP provider would have to sort out getting the COM objects etc. after it had obtained the search results – which all adds to the overhead.

What this does mean though, is that if you think you might want to bind to objects that you've searched for, you will need to make sure that you ask for the ADsPath with the search results. That's a significant point, because the ADsPath isn't really a property cache property, so it probably won't be returned in a search unless you specifically ask for it. In fact – and this is one area where adsvw.exe is quite useful – whatever you put in for the attributes requested, adsvw.exe will always query for the ADsPath as well – just to make sure it gets returned.

LDAP Search Filters

In this section, we're going to look at how search filters actually work. You might wonder why the title is LDAP Search Filters – surely we're using ADSI, which can access any directory.

Well that's true. And in principle, when you use ADSI to perform a search, the string that you use to specify your query is simply handed over to the directory service to process. So, the format you use to write your filter should depend on the provider you're using. However, the only ADSI provider commonly available that supports searching (apart from the Netware one which we're not covering here) is the LDAP one. So effectively, the only search filters you are going to be using at the moment are LDAP ones.

Besides, LDAP is a widely used standard. The search filters defined by LDAP are powerful, so I wouldn't be surprised if other vendors who write ADSI providers that support searching choose to recognize LDAP filters anyway.

Filters and Conditions

So let's look at how LDAP filters work by reminding ourselves of the filters we used in our earlier samples:

- ❑ `(objectClass=*)` to retrieve anything
- ❑ `(objectCategory=person)` to retrieve all users
- ❑ `(&(uid=s*)(objectClass=inetOrgPerson))` to retrieve people with user ids beginning with s.

Actually, I've modified these filters slightly by putting brackets round them. These brackets should strictly be there, but `adsvw.exe` seems to be able to process requests without them. Most likely, `adsvw.exe` is adding these brackets before it passes your request to the ADSI interfaces.

What we can see from these is that:

> A filter consists of one or more conditions. A condition is a statement that a particular attribute must have a certain value.

The condition will have brackets round it, like:

```
(objectCategory=person)
```

Equals (`=`) isn't the only condition. LDAP also recognizes less than or equal (`<=`) and greater than or equal (`>=`). So you can have things like this:

```
(revision >= 3)
```

You can also use an operator that means similar to – the symbol is ~=. What similar to means is up to the directory service to determine.

> *Note that LDAP search filters do not recognize > (greater than) or < (less than). This can be quite a restriction – the normal way to get round it is to rephrase your request using >= and <=. For example, instead of asking for all objects whose value for some integer attribute is greater than 3, ask for all the ones that are greater than or equal to 4.*

Wildcards are acceptable in strings. So you can have things like (uid=s*) to mean all uids that begin with s, or (cn=*hen*) to mean all common names with hen somewhere in them. Or of course, (objectClass=*) to mean an objectClass of anything whatsoever.

The conditions are joined together by logical operators. Notice, however, that we use something that mathematicians know as Polish notation or sometimes prefix notation here (the Lisp programming language uses a similar convention). The operator precedes the conditions. The possible operators are & (AND), | (OR) and ! (NOT). AND and OR may connect any number of conditions, whereas NOT must act only on one condition.

From this, some more examples of valid search filters are:

```
(&(objectClass=*)(uid=d*e)(ou=sales))
```

This returns all objects with any object class, a user id that starts with d and ends in e, and an organizational unit of sales.

```
(!(givenname=*n*))
```

This returns all objects which do not have an n in their given name (similar to common name).

And let's go for a really complex one:

```
( & ( | (givenname=g*) (! (objectcategory=person)) (description=*noo*) ) (version>= 2) )
```

This one's probably going to take a bit of thought. The trick is to work from the innermost brackets outwards. What this filter will actually request is all the objects that have a version greater than or equal to 2, and also satisfy at least one of these conditions: either the given name begins with g, or the objectcategory is not a person, or the description contains the string noo somewhere in it.

Clearly, if you're dedicated enough, filters can get really sophisticated! There is no theoretical limit to how complex they are allowed to get.

Points to Note

There are a few other points worth making.

Firstly, the brackets can be nested to any level of depth. There is no limit.

Secondly, about spaces. You shouldn't really arbitrarily insert spaces into search filters. I did it in the examples I've just quoted to make it easy for you to read them. However, if you're actually using those filters in a query, don't put spaces in, as they're likely to be interpreted as part of the string you want to match. Having said that, we are dealing with the real world here, and nothing is ever perfect. In practice, I found that Netscape Directory Server ignores whitespace in search filters, but Active Directory has trouble with them. In the earlier example, in which I tried to use `adsvw.exe` to do a search in Active Directory, I was very careful not to put any spaces in the search filter.

Thirdly, about special characters. There are some characters which have a special meaning in the search filters. Not many, but noticeable ones are the brackets, `(` and `)`. The NULL character is awkward as well, since it might theoretically occur inside a binary value or some strings, and it might be something you want to compare against. However, a NULL character is liable to be interpreted as marking the end of the search filter string! To avoid this, LDAP has defined an escaping mechanism. Any character may be represented by a backslash followed by its UTF-8 value, written in hexadecimal. So for * you'd write \2a, for NULL you'd write \00, and so on.

> *If you haven't encountered UTF-8, it's a way of representing strings. It is a Unicode way of representation, but not the Unicode that C++ and COM programmers will have encountered, in which every character is represented by two bytes. In UTF-8, characters are represented by a variable number of bytes according to the nature of the character. But assuming you live in a country that uses the Latin alphabet, all the characters you're likely to encounter have single-byte UTF-8 representations that are the same as the ASCII values. We'll cover UTF-8 in more detail in Chapter 8. For high level coding, you don't need to worry about it because all conversions between character sets are handled by the underlying LDAP APIs.*

Fourthly, about quotes. LDAP version 3 search filters do not use quotes around strings. If there are any special characters required in the strings, then use the escape mechanism we've just described.

Fifthly, about case sensitivity. That's really up to the provider. For LDAP, attribute names are case-insensitive. `Objectclass` is the same as `objectClass`, although the latter is technically the correct way of writing it. Attribute values are another matter – that really depends on the data type. ADSI recognizes several types of strings, including `ADS_CASE_EXACT_STRING` and `ADS_CASE_IGNORE_STRING`, and these data types often reflect underlying LDAP data types. Doing searches is one instance in which it is important which of the ADSI string types is the real data type used in an attribute. In practice, `ADS_CASE_IGNORE_STRING` is the type most commonly used.

That's covered the main points of LDAP search filters. There is one extra thing you can do with them: it's possible to specify custom ways of making comparisons between objects. This would be appropriate, for example, for comparing phone numbers. Presumably you'd like (017773) 335233 to be regarded as the same as 017773-335233. Unfortunately, defining custom comparisons requires a more advanced knowledge of LDAP and LDAP OIDs so we can't really go into it here. We'll cover that side of search filters in Chapter 10.

Before we leave search filters entirely, I just want to comment a bit more on our earlier `adsvw.exe` examples.

In the first search, I specified a filter of `(objectClass=*)` and indicated that it would return everything. How does that work? Well, this is actually the standard way of asking for all objects in the search scope. Strictly speaking, this filter means everything that has any string whatsoever in the attribute, `objectClass`, which means all objects for which the attribute `objectClass` is present will be returned. But the LDAP specifications require that *all* objects in the directory have this attribute. So this filter will return all objects.

You also might notice that in my second Active Directory search, I used the subfilter `(objectCategory=person)` instead of `(objectClass=person)` to specify I wanted objects of class person. This is something that is Active Directory specific. `(objectClass=person)` would have worked, but it would have picked up all objects that have the objectClass `person` anywhere in their hierarchy of object classes – remember, `objectClass` is a multi-valued property, which contains the actual `objectClass` of the object, and also anything it's derived from. Since in Active Directory, `computers` are derived from `persons`, specifying `(objectClass=person)` would actually have picked up all the computers too! `objectCategory` is a property defined in Active Directory which indicates the general type of object, and Microsoft recommend that where possible you use the `objectCategory` attribute rather than `objectClass` to restrict search results by class of object. Doing so will improve the speed of your search as well.

Searching using ADO

We've got to the point now where we have enough background to start some real coding.

Searching is one area where there is virtually no overlap between coding techniques in the different languages you can use to write clients: VB and scripting languages *must* use ADO, but C++ clients will almost never do so. In C++, you're most likely to use the ADSI `IDirectorySearch` interface directly. Alternatively, if you want access to some more advanced OLE DB features, you will use OLE DB. Theoretically you could use ADO, but there is very little reason to do so, since ADO indirectly calls OLE DB anyway, giving you a performance hit. The only circumstance I can think of in which you'd use ADO from a C++ client is if your developers are skilled mostly in ADO, so using it saves on training time.

We're going to cover VB and VBScript first, so we'll use Active Data Objects (ADO) to do the searches.

Here's a simple VB app that looks for all the users in my Active Directory install. As usual, I simply display everything in a list box.

```
Option Explicit

Private Sub Form_Load()

  On Error Resume Next

  Dim oConnection As New Connection
  Dim oRecordset As New Recordset

  oConnection.Provider = "ADsDSOObject"
  oConnection.Open "Active Directory Provider"

  Dim strCommand
  strCommand = "<LDAP://dc=TopOfThePops,dc=Fame,dc=com>;" & _
               "(objectCategory=person);sAMAccountName,Description;subtree"
  Set oRecordset = oConnection.Execute(strCommand)
```

```
   While Not oRecordset.EOF
     List1.AddItem oRecordset.Fields(0).Value
     oRecordset.MoveNext
   Wend


End Sub
```

I've used ADO COM objects, which means in order to compile and run this code you need to have checked one of the Microsoft ActiveX Data Object libraries in your project references. (There are several there, but if you choose the latest version you have you'll be OK. At the time of writing the latest one is 2.5, which is contained in the file `msado15.dll`*)*

Did you notice that I haven't actually created a single ADSI object here? Let's check out what's going on.

I start off by creating the ADO objects I'm going to need. A **Connection** is a COM object that handles connecting up to a data source and sending it a command. A **Recordset** is a set of records (I think Microsoft was showing a rare streak of user-friendliness when they named the ADO objects). A record is all the data that's been returned for one object. When we do a search, we'll (hopefully) return data for lots of directory objects, so we need a set of records to hold the information.

Anyway, we have the Connection object. We need to tell it what data source to connect to – and since we ultimately want an ADSI provider, the one we need is the ADSI OLE DB provider:

```
oConnection.Provider = "ADsDSOObject"
oConnection.Open "Active Directory Provider"
```

Yes it is the ADSI provider we want – nothing specifically to do with Active Directory.

Once we've hooked up to the data source, we want to send it a command. The command we want to send it is to hook up to the object `LDAP://dc=TopOfThePops,dc=Fame,dc=com` and do a subtree search for all the users – we'll identify them with the filter `(objectCategory=person)` – returning the `sAMAccountName` for each of them:

```
Dim strCommand
strCommand = "<LDAP://dc=TopOfThePops,dc=Fame,dc=com>;" & _
             "(objectCategory=person);sAMAccountName,Description;subtree"
Set oRecordset = oConnection.Execute(strCommand)
```

From what I've said, you should be able to figure out how the syntax of commands accepted by the ADSI provider for OLE DB works.

Once we've got the command, we just need to iterate through the records. We've only asked for one field in each, the `sAMAccountName`. So for each record in the Recordset, we just print out the first field:

```
While Not oRecordset.EOF
  List1.AddItem oRecordset.Fields(0).Value
  oRecordset.MoveNext
Wend
```

*A **field** is one attribute that has been returned. You can think of the records as corresponding to the rows and the fields as corresponding to the columns in the* `adsvw.exe` *search results.*

So that's the code. And just to prove it works:

About ADO and OLE DB and ADSI

Now you've got a flavor of how searching can work, let's recap what's going on here. The following figure illustrates the relationships between OLE DB, ADO and ADSI for some typical data sources:

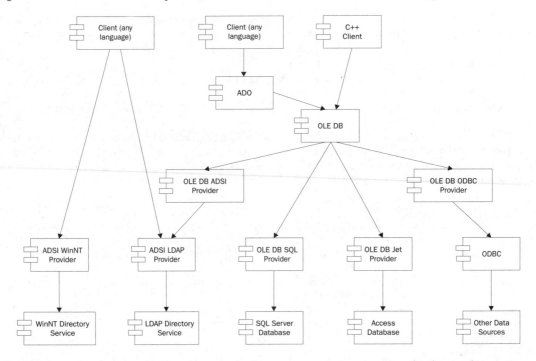

This diagram shows the main routes by which clients can connect to various databases, directories and other sources of data. The clients are at the top of the diagram, the data sources are at the bottom, and in the middle are some of the different components that help the clients talk to the data sources.

The game here is how can a client access some source of data. The data might be in a relational database, like SQL Server, Oracle, or Microsoft Access. It might be in a simpler form – an Excel spreadsheet or a simple text file. Or it might be an LDAP directory or some other directory service. The point is that although I've only mentioned a few of the places where data might be stored, that's already an embarrassingly large number of sources, each with its own unique API. If you're writing clients that use data from these different sources, you'd probably quite like it if you didn't have to learn a separate API for each one. That was the whole point of ADSI, remember, and to some extent of LDAP too. But ADSI is specifically for directories. The set of interfaces defined for ADSI are tailored specifically to work with hierarchical data structures. You'd struggle to find a good design of directory service that works well with the ADSI interfaces and can access a Microsoft word document!

So in the bigger picture we're talking something that can be used to access *any* data source – something that does the same as ADSI, but is more general. At the moment, that something is OLE DB. In fact, OLE DB is at the heart of Microsoft's Universal Data Access strategy – Microsoft's aim to have just one programming tool that will let you get at data from virtually anywhere. The idea is that ultimately OLE DB will be that tool.

OLEDB

OLE DB is a set of COM interfaces. It's quite a large set – about 60 – implemented by a number of different types of object. In many ways, the concept is the same as for ADSI: there are lots of OLE DB providers lurking around. Each one hosts COM objects which implement the same OLE DB interfaces, but each one hooks up to a separate data source. For example, if I look on my system I've got these providers:

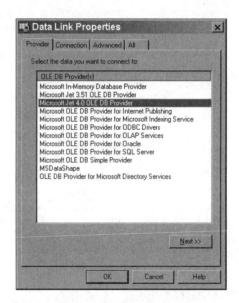

That's a fair selection. The Jet provider is the one that hooks up to Access databases.

ODBC is now on the way to being obsolete, although it will likely still be in use in legacy code for some years yet. It was the forerunner of OLE DB, and it provides a common way of getting at relational databases. When OLE DB was introduced there were already a fair number of different ODBC providers around, so it made sense to have a provider that translated from ODBC to OLE DB, in order that OLE DB could access the services of all these providers for free.

You can also get to SQL Server and Oracle, amongst other sources. At the bottom is the OLE DB provider for Microsoft Directory Services – the OLE DB ADSI provider. This one will treat any ADSI provider as a data source, so you can ultimately get to whatever directory the ADSI provider is servicing. You can think of this provider as a package that translates from ADSI to OLE DB.

By the way, for our purposes you don't need to do anything with the above dialog box. But in case you're wondering how to bring it up anyway, there are several ways to do it. I find the easiest is to create a blank text file, and rename it with the .udl extension. Then double-click on the file. A udl file contains information about the setup for an OLE DB data source, so if you open it you get this dialog, asking you about properties of different sources.

Since the OLE DB interfaces need to cope with a more general category of data sources, it's important that they're designed in a way that doesn't really make any assumptions about how the data in the source is arranged. That means the interfaces are a lot more generic than the ADSI ones. How you work with them is conceptually quite different. In ADSI, we're used to binding to an object in the directory, then doing things to it like asking for or modifying properties, or enumerating its children. In OLE DB there is no concept of binding. Rather, you create an instance of the OLE DB provider itself, and use it to send a command to the data source. You may get back some data from the command. If so, it'll be in the form of a recordset – a set of records each containing lots of fields – in other words a table of data. The command may also include an instruction to modify some data.

Generally OLE DB works very well, and largely does provide a means of universal data access. There are some differences between providers that you need to be aware of. Partly, this takes the form of some providers not implementing all the functionality offered by OLE DB – so a client has to be prepared to accept that some interfaces or methods just might not be implemented. Also, differences arise in the precise format that the different providers will accept commands in. As far as possible, this has been minimized by having most providers understand SQL – but even here there are slightly different dialects. Incidentally, it's possible to use a form of SQL with the OLE DB ADSI provider, as an alternative to the semi-LDAP format we used in the above example.

If you haven't encountered SQL before, it stands for Structured Query Language. It's a very high-level language that can be used to access relational databases. We'll have a very brief introduction to SQL later in the chapter.

Well, for a section whose title includes ADO, we've come an awful long way without mentioning ADO. Where ADO fits in is as a client of OLE DB. You see, OLE DB is complex. 60 COM interfaces are a lot for anyone to learn, so we really need a simpler way of getting to the services offered by OLE DB. There's also the problem that the OLE DB interfaces are not dual ones, so they cannot be accessed from scripting languages. ADO solves both of these problems. It's a set of COM objects which expose a very simple set of dual COM interfaces, and implements them by calling up the corresponding functionality in OLE DB.

The ADO Objects and Interfaces

There are 7 ActiveX Data Object (ADO) objects:

❑ **Connection**: responsible for maintaining the connection to the data source, and setting some of the properties of the connection. It's also able to send commands to the data source.

❑ **Command**: to some extent this duplicates the functionality of the Connection. The emphasis here though is on more flexibility in how the Command object sends commands to the data source.

❑ **Recordset**: receives data back from the data source as a set of records. Implements methods to navigate through and examine the records. Could be considered as a view of a table of data.

- ❏ **Parameter**: stores parameters that might be sent with commands.
- ❏ **Property**: an object that holds information about the capabilities of the data source.
- ❏ **Field**: a single data item within a record. Think of it as a single cell in a table of data.
- ❏ **Error**: provides detailed information about any errors that occurred.

However, the only ones we're going to be concerned with are the Connection, Recordset and Field objects. Unfortunately, we don't have the space here to go into the aspects of ADO that we don't need in order to hook up to the ADSI providers.

> *I should point out that the OLE DB ADSI provider is read-only. You cannot yet (ADSI 2.5) use it to modify objects in directories, though this ability has been promised for a future version of ADSI. This means that, at the moment, the only use we will have for ADO is for searching.*

So let's go through the process that we need to carry out searching.

The ADO Searching Process

First, we create a Connection object, and tell it to hook up to the ADSI provider. In VB we'll normally do it like this:

```
Dim oConnection As New Connection
oConnection.Provider = "ADsDSOObject"
oConnection.Open "Active Directory Provider","UserName","Password"
```

In VB script, we can't declare the types of variables, so the corresponding code is more likely to be something like:

```
Dim oConnection
Set oConnection = CreateObject("ADODB.Connection")
oConnection.Provider = "ADsDSOObject"
oConnection.Open "Active Directory Provider","UserName","Password"
```

Notice that if we need to supply a user name and password in order to authenticate to the directory, we must do so here. If we don't need to authenticate, then we just omit those parameters – as I did in the earlier example. What ADSI does with those parameters will be covered in the next chapter, on security.

Alternatively, you may if you wish create a separate command object to use to submit the command. In VBScript, that would look like this:

```
Dim oConnection
Set oConnection = Server.CreateObject("ADODB.Connection")
Dim oCommand
Set oCommand = Server.CreateObject("ADODB.Command")

oConnection.Provider = "ADsDSOObject"
oConnection.Open "Active Directory Provider"
Set oCommand.ActiveConnection = oConnection
```

If we have any preferences as to how we want to carry out the search, we can set those using the `Properties` property on the Command object.

We then create the text of the command to do the search. The command will specify the base object of the search, the scope, the search filter, and the list of attributes to be returned. There are two syntaxes for the command – an LDAP-based syntax and an SQL-based syntax – and the OLE DB ADSI provider will accept either of these. We'll discuss the differences between these syntaxes later.

When we actually execute the command, this will return a `Recordset object`. Note that at this point, if we've asked for the `ADsPath` to be one of the fields returned, we might want to use this to bind to the ADSI objects in the usual way. We'd need to do this if we actually wanted to modify any objects. This is the only point at which we would actually be directly using ADSI.

Finally, we step through the records and fields in the Recordset. And once we've finished we can clean up memory etc.

That's literally it!

There are still two bits that we haven't fully explained: what the syntax for the commands is and what the search preferences you can select are. I'm going to deal with the command syntaxes next. Then we'll go through a bit of sample ASP code – a web page that you can use to perform searches on an ADSI object. I'll leave the detailed explanation of the search preferences until after the ASP sample, since these apply to C++ clients as well as VB and scripting clients.

Command Syntaxes

There are two syntaxes you can use for the command you send to the ADSI data source: one very loosely based on LDAP, and one based on SQL. Although Microsoft refer to them as LDAP and SQL syntaxes, the LDAP syntax actually bears very little relation to anything actually in the LDAP specifications, other than the fact that it uses an LDAP search filter buried inside it.

The LDAP Command Syntax

The LDAP syntax has the format `<SearchBase>;Filter;Attributes;scope`. In other words, the four parts of the command are separated by semi-colons. The `SearchBase` should be the `ADsPath` of the search base, enclosed by angled brackets. The `Filter` should be the LDAP search filter, and the `Attributes` list, should consist of the names of attributes separated by commas. The scope should be one of the strings `base`, `onelevel` or `subtree`.

For example, the following is a valid command. It will find all the people with an h in their user ids in the Netscape sample directory on my computer, returning their `uid`s and `ADsPaths`.

```
<LDAP://BiggyBiggy:390/o=airius.com>;(&(objectClass=inetorgPerson)(uid=*h*));
uid,ADsPath;subtree
```

The SQL Command Syntax

The SQL syntax uses the same components, but puts them together in a more readable manner. It's based on the SQL `SELECT` statement – which is why it's loosely referred to as the SQL syntax. The `SELECT` statement is the standard way of returning a query in SQL. (In relational databases, a query performs pretty much the same role as a search in a directory.)

To understand the SELECT statement, you need to remember that relational databases store their data in a series of tables. Each row of a table can be thought of very roughly as corresponding to one object – though the correspondence isn't exact. Relational databases don't really recognize the concept of an object. What we would think of as an object in a directory might actually be spread across several tables in a relational database.

Also, a requirement of relational databases is that each field should only contain one value, and fields may not be repeated in the same row. So if an object contains a multi-valued property, then it'll need to be stored across several rows in a table to accommodate all the values.

Anyway, the SELECT statement in SQL, in one of its simplest forms (there are other options that aren't relevant here) looks like this:

```
SELECT <Properties> FROM <Table> WHERE <Condition>
```

This identifies one of the Tables in the database, and it returns all those rows that satisfy the Condition. For those rows, the columns corresponding to the listed Properties should be returned. By the way, the angled brackets don't appear in the command, I've just used them to indicate that you fill in what your requirements actually are.

This has a pretty easy correspondence with our search requests. We just have to replace the parameters in the SELECT statement by this:

```
SELECT <List of Properties> FROM <SearchBase> WHERE <Condition>
```

The List of properties is – as in the LDAP syntax – just a comma-separated list. You can also use * to denote everything. The search base is just the ADsPath: again unchanged from the LDAP syntax, except that here it should be enclosed in single quotes. The Condition is more interesting, since this really uses SQL syntax rather than LDAP search filter syntax. That means the logical operators, AND, OR and NOT are written as the English words, and occur between the items they are joining rather than at the beginning. Wildcards are still allowed, but all attribute values (even wildcards) must be in single quotes.

All this means that the LDAP example we saw above would be written in the SQL dialect as:

```
SELECT uid, ADsPath FROM 'LDAP://BiggyBiggy:390/o=airius.com' WHERE
objectClass='inetorgPerson' AND uid='*h*'
```

Get the idea? It all looks a bit more user-friendly. And the advantage of using SQL is that it brings us nearer to the idea of universal data access, since the command strings used for ADSI are closer to those used for other data sources, for which SQL is common. The only disadvantage is that it's not possible to set the search scope with the SQL dialect. If you're using SQL, you will need to set the search scope via the preferences instead. In particular, search preferences are set using the Properties collection of the command object. We'll see how this is done in the sample ASP search page that we'll look at next.

The ASP Search Page

We're going to illustrate searching using ADO by developing an ASP script that allows users to search a directory. Here's what the page looks like when you first start it – you are presented with some text boxes and radio buttons allowing you to select your search parameters and some preferences:

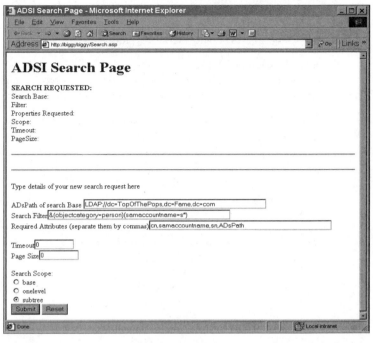

The page allows you to type in your search base, filter and required attributes, as well as to select the scope. These are the essential items. In addition, you're allowed to enter values for the timeout and page size (the default value, zero, actually indicates unlimited). These values are unlikely to have much effect unless you're performing a huge search, but they've been included here for – shall we say – demonstration purposes.

Once you enter your options, as I've done above, and click on submit, the search is performed. In this case, I've asked for all users in Active Directory with account names beginning with S. It turns out I'm the only one – well I did say I only had a small network...

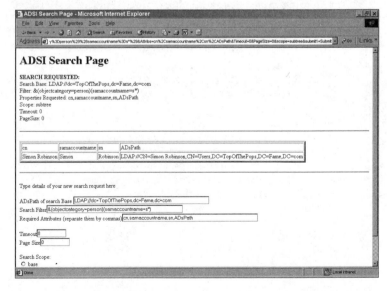

As usual for all samples in this book, you can download the script for this page from the Wrox web site, `www.wrox.com` .

The page tries to be reasonably intelligent in terms of remembering the search options you last typed in, though it's not very forgiving of any errors in the format in the search filter or required attributes. The only check it makes is that none of the required fields are blank. Otherwise, it just hands over what you've typed in to the Directory Service. So you do need to be careful, particularly with the filter, since things like mismatched brackets don't go down too well with Active Directory.

Anyway, let's go over the code for the page. It starts off with the normal headers:

```
<%@ Language = VBScript %>
<html>
<head>
<title> ADSI Search Page </title>
</head>

<body>

<h1> ADSI Search Page </h1>

<%
on error resume next
```

Then we declare some variables to hold the strings that the user has entered. These strings all come from straight text boxes, apart from `strScope`, which will store one of the strings `base`, `onelevel` or `subtree`, depending on which radio button the user pressed. We also display the details of the search we are about to perform:

```
Dim strSearchBase
strSearchBase = Request.QueryString("SearchBase")
Dim strFilter
strFilter = Request.QueryString("Filter")
Dim strAttribs
strAttribs = Request.QueryString("Attribs")
Dim strScope
strScope = Request.QueryString("scope")
Dim strTimeout
strTimeout = Request.QueryString("Timeout")
Dim strPageSize
strPageSize = Request.QueryString("PageSize")

Response.Write "<strong>SEARCH REQUESTED:</strong><br>"
Response.Write "Search Base: " & strSearchBase & "<br>"
Response.Write "Filter: " & strFilter & "<br>"
Response.Write "Properties Requested: " & strAttribs & "<br>"
Response.Write "Scope: " & strScope & "<br>"
Response.Write "Timeout: " & strTimeout & "<br>"
Response.Write "PageSize: " & strPageSize & "<p><hr><p>"
```

Now we check that the user has actually entered something for the search base, filter, and attribute list. If so, we can go ahead and create the OLE DB command and connection objects, and set up the connection. Just for variety, we're going to do this one a bit differently from the earlier sample, in that we'll use the command object rather than the connection object to actually send the command:

```
if (len(strSearchBase) > 0 and len(strFilter)>0 and len(strAttribs) > 0) then
    Dim oConnection
    Set oConnection = Server.CreateObject("ADODB.Connection")
    Dim oCommand
    Set oCommand = Server.CreateObject("ADODB.Command")

    oConnection.Provider = "ADsDSOObject"
    oConnection.Open "Active Directory Provider"
    set oCommand.ActiveConnection = oConnection

    response.write "<p><p><p>"
```

The command is fairly easy to set up – we just concatenate the values we got from the URL. Notice that we're careful to add brackets round the search filter, just in case the user has forgotten them. If the user had remembered the brackets then we'll just get two nested lots of brackets like ((...)) which will still be understood by the directory, and so won't do any harm:

```
oCommand.CommandText = "<" & strSearchBase & ">;(" _
                    & strFilter & ");" & strAttribs & ";" & strScope
```

We take our chance to set the preferences, and finally execute the command:

```
'   set preferences
    oCommand.Properties("Timeout") = strTimeout
    oCommand.Properties("PageSize") = strPageSize

    Dim oRecordset
    Set oRecordset = oCommand.Execute(strCommand)
```

Now's where it gets interesting. We need to find out what fields actually got returned, so we can print their names at the top of the table of results. The way we do this is to use the fact that the `Fields` property of the Recordset object is actually a normal collection of fields – so we can just iterate through them in a `For Each` loop. One of the properties exposed by the `Field` object is `Name`:

```
Response.Write "<table border = 4><tr>"
if (Not oRecordset.EOF) then
    For Each oField in oRecordset.Fields
        Response.Write "<td>"
        Response.Write oField.Name
        Response.Write "</td>"
    next
end if
Response.Write "</tr>"
```

And then we can use the `Value` property of the fields objects to print the actual values.

```
      While Not oRecordset.EOF
           Response.Write "<tr>"

           For Each oField in oRecordset.Fields
               Response.Write "<td>"
               Response.Write oField.Value
               Response.Write "</td>"
           next

           Response.Write "</tr>"
           oRecordset.MoveNext
      Wend
      Response.Write "</tr></table>"

end if
```

The rest of the page is really concerned with setting up the form for the user to submit the next search query:

```
Response.Write "<p><hr><p>"
Response.Write "<form action = Search.asp method = get id=form1 name=form1>"
Response.Write "Type details of your new search request here<p>"

Response.Write "ADsPath of search Base "
Response.Write "<INPUT type=text value=" & strSearchBase & _
               " id=SearchBase name=SearchBase size = 60><br>"

Response.Write "Search Filter"
Response.Write "<INPUT type=text value=" & strFilter & _
               " id=Filter name=Filter size = 60><br>"

Response.Write "Required Attributes (separate them by commas)"
Response.Write "<INPUT type=text value=" & strAttribs & _
               " id=Attribs name=Attribs size = 60><br>"

Response.Write "<br>Timeout"
Response.Write "<INPUT type=text value=0 id=Timeout name=Timeout size = 10><br>"

Response.Write "Page Size"
Response.Write "<INPUT type=text value=0 id=PageSize name=PageSize size = 10><br>"
Response.Write "<br>Search Scope: <br>"
%>

<INPUT type=radio value=base name=scope id=scope> base<br>
<INPUT type=radio value=onelevel name=scope id=scope> onelevel<br>
<INPUT type=radio checked value=subtree name=scope id=scope> subtree<br>

<INPUT type="submit" value="Submit" id=submit1 name=submit1>
<INPUT type="reset" value="Reset" id=reset1 name=reset1><br>
</form>

</body>
</html>
```

Search Preferences

I've hinted a few times at the existence of a number of search preferences you can select. There was that whole dialog box in `adsvw.exe` asking for the values of them. And the last ASP script offered the chance to select a timeout value and page size. In this section, we'll go over what the actual options are.

The search preferences are distinct from the main options, partly through the fact that they generally only affect the performance of the search, not the actual results obtained (though there are a couple of exceptions to this), and partly because they are set separately from the main command. In ADO, you set the preferences by setting values of the `Properties` property on the command object, as illustrated by the previous ASP sample:

```
oCommand.Properties("Timeout") = strTimeout
oCommand.Properties("PageSize") = strPageSize
```

C++ clients that use `IDirectorySearch` will set them in a dedicated method, `IDirectorySearch::SetSearchPreferences`. This is demonstrated in the C++ sample we'll develop later.

The search preferences are as follows.

Asynchronous Search

The default is a **synchronous search**, which means that the directory service first grabs all the search results, and then returns them to the client. The client thread will block until the results are returned. It is possible to break the results up a bit by using the page size options described below – in which case results are returned at the end of each page. The important point, though, with a synchronous search, is that no results are returned to the client until a large number of results (either a page or everything) have been found by the server.

In an **asynchronous search**, by contrast, results are sent back as they are gathered. This means network traffic happens a bit more evenly. Each time the client asks for the next record, it only has to wait until the next one record has been identified and sent back.

> In a synchronous search, when the client asks for the next result, the calling thread will block until a set of results are ready. In an asynchronous search, the client thread will block only until the next result is ready.

Note that this is completely different from how you would normally expect a method call in COM to work if you want it to happen asynchronously. In COM, method calls are synchronous. If you want to work asynchronously, you will normally arrange for the server to call back the client, possibly using connection points – the result is more complex code. This is not the case for asynchronous searches using ADSI. If you request an asynchronous search, the only change in your client code will be an extra line to set the relevant search preference. The different way in which asynchronous searches work is largely hidden within the provider.

Chasing Referrals

A **referral** occurs if the server identifies that it doesn't know all the properties on one of the objects that needs to be returned, but needs to query another server for the information. This is a time consuming operation, which you might not always want the server to do. It is possible to specify under what conditions the server should actually contact other servers.

The options are described by an ADS_CHASE_REFERRALS_ENUM enumeration, which is listed in Appendix F.

Dereference Aliases

An **alias** is different from a referral in that it doesn't involve going across servers. It is simply an ADSI object that acts as an alias for another object elsewhere in the directory. This preference allows the client to specify under what circumstances aliases should be dereferenced in order to track down objects.

Since we are not going across servers here, performance is not likely to be an issue. It's more a case of the client deciding whether it is in principle going to be interested in results that were returned through aliases.

The options are described by an ADS_DEREFENUM enumeration, listed in Appendix F.

Size Limit

It is possible to specify a size limit – in other words a maximum number of objects that should be returned. This might be done if the client just wants to see a small sample of a large number of results.

It's also very useful when used in conjunction with the option to sort results. Say you have a directory of cars, and you want to know what the 10 most powerful ones are. You can do this by asking for the results to be sorted in decreasing order of power, and adding a size limit of 10. But do note that you only get these 10 results: you can't pick up the rest of the returned values later

The default behavior is no size limit.

Time Limit

This works in much the same way as size limit, except that here you are instructing the server to spend no more than a certain period of time on the operation. You might do this if you're worried that the server has other more important things to be getting on with, and you don't want it to spend too much time on your query. When the time limit is reached, the server will return whatever results it happens to have and then regard your query as completed – so you won't get any more results.

The default is no time limit.

Time Out

This is subtly different from the time limit, in that the emphasis is on how long the client is prepared to wait for the data. When the time limit is reached, the (in-process) ADSI provider will simply return the execute search method call, and notify the directory service that the search request is to be abandoned, irrespective of whether the results have arrived.

The default is no time out.

Sort

The client can request that results should be sorted by the value of any one property, in either ascending or descending order. The default is no sort.

Caching Results

To understand how this preference works, recall that the ADSI provider actually sits in the process space of the ADSI client, and itself acts as a client across the network to the directory service. If this option is switched on, then the provider will itself store copies of the results. This allows the client to move forwards or backwards through the results when examining them, but takes up more memory.

If the results are not cached, the provider frees the memory for each row as soon as the client has moved on to the next row – which means the client cannot subsequently move back through the results. The default is to cache the results.

Return Attributes Only

This option is switched off by default, and should be set if the client is only interested in seeing what attributes are available, not what their values are. With this option switched on, the directory service will only return attribute names, not values. Clearly, this means the performance of the search will be enhanced.

Page Size

The client can specify a page size (number of records). This means that after the specified number of records have been found, the directory service will return those records en bloc (as a page) rather than waiting for all the remaining results to be found first. Specifying a page size can therefore speed up the flow of results. It also reduces memory requirements in the server. By default it is switched off.

Paged Time Limit

This works exactly the same way as a page size. It specifies how long the directory service should spend before returning all the results it has so far as a page, and then carrying on the search. By default it is switched off.

One last point before we leave the subject of search preferences. Technically, the scope is also a preference which should set as a search preference. This is actually slightly awkward, as if you are using the LDAP syntax in an ADO command, you can also specify it in the command. Not only that, but if you are using adsvw.exe to carry out a search, you are asked to select a scope twice – in the dialog box asking for your search options, and again in the second dialog that asks for your preferences. (To see this, check out the screenshots from adsvw.exe again.) When I tried it out, I found that if you only specify a scope in one of the places, that choice will be respected – but I couldn't find any obvious pattern for what happens if you make different selections in both places. My advice is to make sure you only specify the search scope once.

> By the way, if you are filling the adsvw.exe dialog box that asks for your preferences, it's expecting the numerical values of the preferences, as listed in the ADSI enumerations in Appendix F in this book and in the MSDN documentation. It doesn't want any strings in the edit boxes!

C++ Clients: Searching Using IDirectorySearch

In this section, we're going to work through an example to show how C++ clients can use `IDirectorySearch` to perform a complex search query.

`IDirectorySearch` returns results in conceptually the same way as the ADO Recordset object does. You get a set of rows and columns – and it's basically up to you to step through them using `IDirectorySearch` methods.

We'll approach this in three parts. Firstly, I'll list the `IDirectorySearch` methods, so you get an idea of what you can do with them. Then I'll talk you through the typical sequence of events that conducting a search involves, and also go through some of the C structures you're going to need to use. Finally, we'll get to the actual sample, and go through that.

IDirectorySearch Methods.

Here's the complete set of methods implemented by `IDirectorySearch`. Note that there are no properties, because it's not an automation interface.

Method	Description
ExecuteSearch	Actually carries out a search. It does not return all the results, but it returns a handle – a variable of type ADS_SEARCH_RESULT – which can be used to obtain all the results.
SetSearchPreferences	Allows the client to specify the preferences for how the search is to be carried out. This pretty much exactly corresponds to the options adsvw presents you in the second search dialog box.
GetFirstRow	Gets the first row, allowing the client to iterate through the rows of a search result.
GetNextRow	Iterates to the next row.
GetPrevRow	Returns to the previous row. Some providers won't implement this.
GetColumnNames	Once you're at a certain row, this returns the names of all the columns available for that row.
GetNextColumn	Gets the actual data (the property value) contained in the next column.
AbandonSearch	Abandons a search that was started asynchronously.
CloseSearchHandle	Instructs the provider that no more methods will be called to fetch data from the specified search, and all associated memory and resources can be freed.
FreeColumn	Instructs the provider to free any memory it allocated in a call to GetColumn.

How To Execute a Search

There are quite a few new concepts in the preceding table, and to see how they are used in practice, we'll go through the typical sequence of operations the client goes through in order to conduct a search.

- ❑ The client will bind to the ADSI object at the top of the subtree covered by the search, and `QueryInterface()` for its `IDirectorySearch` interface. It will then call the `SetSearchPreferences()` method, to indicate any preferences for how the search is to be carried out. The preferences are specified by an array of `ADS_SEARCH_PREFERENCE` structures.

- ❑ The client will call `ExecuteSearch()` to have the provider actually carry out the search. The in call to this method is where the client tells the provider about the search filter and the list of requested attributes. The client gets a search handle back from this method, which it must save. This search handle is passed in all subsequent calls in order to identify the particular search referred to. Note that the client can have multiple searches being conducted simultaneously, simply by calling `ExecuteSearch()` more than once. That's fine, because each search has a different search handle.

- ❑ The client will call `GetFirstRow()` to indicate that it is ready to go through all the data for the first row (directory object) retrieved.

- ❑ The client will recursively call `GetNextColumnName()` to retrieve the names of all the columns available. Strictly, this only returns the column names for this row.

- ❑ The client will call `GetColumn()`, passing in the name of a column in order to retrieve the actual property values for this column. The client will probably use a `for` loop to iterate through all the names returned from `GetColumnNames()`. Note that the call to `GetColumn()` returns a provider-allocated data structure containing the column information. The client should call the `FreeColumn` method to free the memory when it's finished with the column.

- ❑ The client will call `GetNextRow()` to indicate that it is ready to retrieve results for the next row. It then repeats steps 4-6 until a call to `GetNextRow()` returns S_ADS_NOMORE_ROWS instead of S_OK.

- ❑ The client calls `CloseSearchHandle()` to indicate that it has finished with the results of a search.

We haven't quite covered all the methods here. `AbandonSearch` would be used if the client wants to abandon an asynchronous search – more about this later. `GetPrevRow` would be used if the client wants to start doing more sophisticated processing/moving around the search results.

We've almost covered enough to be able to go through the actual code. We just need to have a closer look at the two main structures that we're going to be using: ADS_SEARCHPREF_INFO and ADS_SEARCH_COLUMN.

The ADS_SEARCHPREF_INFO Structure

This is defined as follows

```
typedef struct ADS_SEARCHPREF_INFO
{
    ADS_SEARCHPREF  dwSearchPref;
    ADSVALUE        vValue;
    ADS_STATUS      dwStatus;
} ADS_SEARCHPREF_INFO, *PADS_SEARCHPREF_INFO, *LPADS_SEARCHPREF_INFO;
```

It's there to supply information about any of your search preferences. You can express which search preference you want to specify by putting the appropriate value in dwSearchPref – the value is chosen from an ADS_SEARCHPREF enumeration. The actual value goes in the vValue member.

The reason an ADSVALUE structure is used here is that different search preferences require different data types to specify them. For example, the timeout requires an integer, whereas the field to sort by is a string. Recall from Chapter 2 that the ADSVALUE structure contains a field that indicates what data type is stored, along with a union of member variables that correspond to the different data types – in much the same way as a VARIANT.

The final member of ADS_SEARCHPREF_INFO, dwStatus, is not filled in by the client. It's filled in by the provider when you call IDirectorySearch::SetSearchPreferences() to indicate whether your preference was accepted or whether there was a problem. The value you'd like to get back is ADS_STATUS_S_OK. If you get ADS_STATUS_INVALID_SEARCHPREF or ADS_STATUS_INVALID_SEARCHPREFVALUE you back then you passed in some dodgy data.

This means that the code to fill in a SEARCHPREF structure would typically look like this for an integer value.

```
ADS_SEARCHPREF_INFO Prefs[1];
Prefs[0].dwSearchPref = ADS_SEARCHPREF_TIME_LIMIT;
Prefs[0].dwStatus = ADS_STATUS_S_OK;    // just for the sake of putting
                                        // something here.
                                        // the provider will overwrite it anyway.
Prefs[0].vValue.dwType = ADSTYPE_INTEGER;
Prefs[0].vValue.Integer = iWhateverTimeLimitYouWant;
```

Get the idea? You just fill the ADSVALUE structure in the normal way. The complete set of possible values for the ADS_SEARCHPREF enumeration are in Appendix F, along with the data types you need to use for the corresponding search preference values.

The ADS_SEARCH_COLUMN Structure

This structure is returned from a call to `IDirectorySearch::GetColumn()`. It contains complete information about the column – which basically means the name of the column (the name of the property the column corresponds to) and all the values stored with that property. With the values, we need an integer to indicate their data type, as well as how many of them there are.

> *Notice that there is a conceptual difference here from a conventional cell in a table. In a relational database, each field in a table holds only one value. An* ADS_SEARCH_COLUMN *is in many ways analogous to a cell in a table, in that it stores the value of one property. However, it can actually store multiple values – which is presumably why Microsoft has named it a column.*

Here's how the `ADS_SEARCH_COLUMN` is defined:

```
typedef struct ADS_SEARCH_COLUMN
{
    LPWSTR     pszAttrName;
    ADSTYPE    dwADsType;
    PADSVALUE  pADsValues;
    DWORD      dwNumValues;
    HANDLE     hReserved;
} ADS_SEARCH_COLUMN, *PADS_SEARCH_COLUMN;
```

Most of this should be fairly self-explanatory. `pszAttrName` contains the name of the property, and `dwADsType` is its value, taken from the ADsType enumeration. `pADsValues` is the pointer to the start of an array of ADSVALUE structures (so if you want to access the i'th value, it will be given by `pADsValues[i]`) and `dwNumValues` tells you how big the array is. Don't touch `hReserved` – that's for internal use by the providers.

So getting values out of the `ADS_SEARCH_COLUMN` structure involves the usual process of looking up the type of an ADSVALUE then extracting the relevant field. How the memory for the structure should be allocated and deallocated is a lot less clear. You call `IDirectorySearch::GetColumn()` to obtain one of these structures – that effectively makes it appear like an [out] parameter, so you might expect the memory for it to be allocated by the provider. And that's even what the documentation for `GetColumn()` currently seems to imply. But – unusually for a COM method call – that's *not* what happens. In fact, you can see this if you check out the definition of `GetColumn`:

```
HRESULT GetColumn(
  ADS_SEARCH_HANDLE hSearchHandle,
  LPWSTR szColumnName,
  PADS_SEARCH_COLUMN pSearchColumn
);
```

Now `PADS_SEARCH_COLUMN` is `typedef`ed as `ADS_SEARCH_COLUMN*S`, so what you pass in is a pointer to a search column. If it was the method that was going to allocate the memory, you'd need to pass in a pointer to a pointer to a search column.

What actually happens is that the client allocates the memory for the structure, and the provider fills in all the fields in it. However, the `ADS_SEARCH_COLUMN` structure does contain an embedded pointer to an ADSVALUE array – and the provider has to allocate the memory for this.

Since the provider has allocated some embedded memory, it could be awkward for the client to free it. So ADSI provides another method, `IDirectorySearch::FreeColumn()` to deal with this. You pass in a pointer to the search column, and the provider hunts through it and frees the memory associated with any embedded pointers that it allocated. Then it's up to the client to free the `ADS_SEARCHPREF_INFO` structure itself.

This is all quite an unusual way of doing it, but it does work very nicely. We'll see how this works in practice in the sample code, coming up next.

The C++ Sample Search Program

The sample we're going to go through performs a search, and lets you effectively scroll through the results one at a time. Here's what the application looks like when it's running:

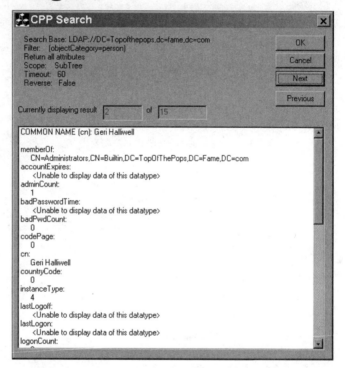

As usual, I write everything into a list box in order to try to keep the non-ADSI side of the coding as simple as possible. In order to keep things simple, I've also hard coded in the actual search parameters – the base, scope and filter etc. – although these constants are kept together in one part of the program so you can change them easily.

When you start the application, it gets the search results and displays the first row (object) in the list box. You can then move around the results using the Next and Previous buttons – although at present in the LDAP provider, it only seems to be possible to move forward because `IDirectorySearch::GetPrevRow()` appears to not be implemented.

An extra feature is that the results are sorted by the common name – the same attribute that is listed at the top of the list box for ease of reading. Doing this is perhaps a bit risky, since you can't absolutely guarantee the presence of a `cn` attribute, but it is almost always present.

Oh – and the search I've hard coded in? As usual, it's a request for all the users in my Active Directory install, by doing a subtree search from my domain object. I've requested all attributes to be returned, and specified a timeout of one minute – besides asking for the data to be sorted.

As always, this sample can be downloaded from the Wrox web site.

Variable Definitons

So let's go through the code. To start with – it's implemented in the dialog class of a dialog-based MFC App, so we need some member variable definitions.

By the way, if you're wondering, the reason why my class names have got two Cs in front is because I named the project CPP Search, and MFC added an extra C.

```
class CCPPSearchDlg : public CDialog
{
// Construction
public:
    CCPPSearchDlg(CWnd* pParent = NULL);        // standard constructor

// Dialog Data
    //{{AFX_DATA(CCPPSearchDlg)
    enum { IDD = IDD_CPPSEARCH_DIALOG };
    CButton        m_buttonPrevious;
    CEdit          m_editICurrentResult;
    CEdit          m_editNResults;
    CButton        m_buttonNext;
    CStatic        m_StaticText;
    CListBox       m_listbox;
    //}}AFX_DATA

// standard MFC stuff deleted for clarity

// extra functions for ADSI searching
public:
    void DisplayCurrentRow();

//extra variables for ADSI searching
private:
    ADS_SEARCH_HANDLE m_hSearch;
    int m_iNRows;
    int m_iScope;
    CStringArray m_csarrColumnNames;
    CComPtr<IDirectorySearch> m_spSearchBase;
    int m_iCurrentRow;

};
```

In terms of variables, I've got controls for all of the controls in the dialog – even including the static text that displays the search parameters. Then there are variables to store (in the same order as in the code above) the search handle, the number of rows returned, the search scope, the names of the columns returned, a pointer to the ADSI object we use to perform the search, and the 1-based index of the row we are currently looking at. There's also a function that actually does the job of displaying the current row in the list box.

Apart from the `DisplayCurrentRow()` function, the guts of the code are all at the end of the `OnInitDialog()` function.

The OnInitDialog Function

We start off by declaring the variables to store the search parameters. These are only used locally within the `OnInitDialog()` function so don't need to be member variables. While we're at it, we also disable the **Next** and **Previous** buttons, because they can't be used unless we discover that we do actually have some search results.

```
        // start of directory searching stuff added for ADSI sample
        HRESULT hr;

//*************to change the search details: Modify these
// these are the search parameters - hard coded in

        CComBSTR bstrSearchBase = L"LDAP://DC=Topofthepops,dc=fame,dc=com";
        m_iScope = ADS_SCOPE_SUBTREE;
        CComBSTR bstrFilter = L"(objectCategory=person)";
        int iTimeOut = 60;                          //only wait a minute for results
        unsigned char iReverse = false;             //don't reverse sort order

//*********************************************

        // disable next and prev buttons till we know we have some results
        m_buttonNext.EnableWindow(false);
        m_buttonPrevious.EnableWindow(false);
```

The next lines are fairly mundane – they're just concerned with making sure the static text control actually is displaying the details of our search. No actual ADSI stuff yet:

```
        // display details of the search
        CString csText;
        csText = CString(L"Search Base: ") + CString(bstrSearchBase) +
                 CString(L"\nFilter:     ") + CString(bstrFilter) +
                 CString(L"\nReturn all attributes");

        switch (m_iScope)
        {
            case ADS_SCOPE_BASE:
                csText += L"\nScope:     Base";
                break;
            case ADS_SCOPE_ONELEVEL:
                csText += L"\nScope:     OneLevel";
                break;
            case ADS_SCOPE_SUBTREE:
                sText += L"\nScope:     SubTree";
                break;
            default:
                ASSERT(false);
        }
        csText += CString(L"\nTimeout:    ") + IntToString(iTimeOut);
        csText += CString(L"\nReverse:    ") + (iReverse ? L"True" : L"False");
        m_StaticText.SetWindowText(csText);
```

Here's where ADSI comes in. We bind to the ADSI object as normal. Then we set our search preferences – to timeout after a minute and to request the results sorted:

```
//bind to the object
CComQIPtr<IADs, &IID_IADs> spADsBase;
hr = ADsGetObject(bstrSearchBase, IID_IDirectorySearch,
    (void**)&m_spSearchBase); ASH;
spADsBase = m_spSearchBase;

// set the search preferences
ADS_SEARCHPREF_INFO Prefs[3];
Prefs[0].dwSearchPref = ADS_SEARCHPREF_TIMEOUT;
Prefs[0].dwStatus = ADS_STATUS_S_OK;
Prefs[0].vValue.dwType = ADSTYPE_INTEGER;
Prefs[0].vValue.Integer = iTimeOut;

ADS_SORTKEY SortKey;
SortKey.pszAttrType = L"cn";
SortKey.pszReserved = NULL;
SortKey.fReverseorder = iReverse;

Prefs[1].dwSearchPref = ADS_SEARCHPREF_SORT_ON;
Prefs[1].dwStatus = ADS_STATUS_S_OK;
Prefs[1].vValue.dwType = ADSTYPE_PROV_SPECIFIC;
Prefs[1].vValue.ProviderSpecific.dwLength = sizeof(ADS_SORTKEY);
Prefs[1].vValue.ProviderSpecific.lpValue = (LPBYTE) &SortKey;

Prefs[2].dwSearchPref = ADS_SEARCHPREF_SEARCH_SCOPE;
Prefs[2].dwStatus = ADS_STATUS_S_OK;
Prefs[2].vValue.dwType = ADSTYPE_INTEGER;
Prefs[2].vValue.Integer = m_iScope;


m_spSearchBase->SetSearchPreference(Prefs, 2);
ASSERT(Prefs[0].dwStatus == ADS_STATUS_S_OK);
ASSERT(Prefs[1].dwStatus == ADS_STATUS_S_OK);
ASSERT(Prefs[2].dwStatus == ADS_STATUS_S_OK);
```

This code shows that how the search preference is set depends to some extent on what preference we are dealing with. If we're setting a preference that can be described by an integer, we just need to put the integer in the ADSVALUE structure. A sorting preference is more complex, since we need to specify both the attribute we are sorting against and which direction the sort is in. ADSI uses another structure – an ADS_SORTKEY structure – for that.

We are now ready to perform the search:

```
// perform the search. We are asking for all attributes to be returned
hr = m_spSearchBase->ExecuteSearch(bstrFilter, NULL, 0xffffffff, &m_hSearch);
    ASH;
```

`IDirectorySearch::ExecuteSearch()` requires four parameters. The first is the filter. The second is an array of strings that indicate which attributes we're interested in. We're asking for all of them, so we pass NULL in here. And we pass –1 to the following parameter, which tells the provider how many strings are in the array. The final parameter is a pointer to the search handle – a variable of type `ADS_SEARCH_HANDLE` – the value of which will be supplied by the provider and needs to be stored by the client.

In order to be user-friendly, our application displays how many results we have returned. There's actually no method in `IDirectorySearch` which recovers this information automatically – so we just have to get our hands dirty and actually count them!

```
// count how many rows we've got
hr = m_spSearchBase->GetFirstRow(m_hSearch); ASH;
while (hr == S_OK)
{
    ++m_iNRows;
    hr = m_spSearchBase->GetNextRow(m_hSearch);
}
```

`GetNextRow` will return `S_ADS_NOMORE_ROWS` when it hits the last row. The next couple of lines are being friendly to the users – and we also enable the **Next** button when we know it's worth enabling it:

```
m_editNResults.SetWindowText(IntToString(m_iNRows));
if (m_iNRows == 0)
{
    m_listbox.AddString(L"No results were returned.");
    return true;
}

if (m_iNRows > 1)
    m_buttonNext.EnableWindow();
```

The next stage is to get the names of the columns. Now in general, you would need to do this step for each row. Since a search may return many different classes of object, each row is potentially going to have a different set of column names (for example, if your search returns users and computers, then the rows that contain results for computer objects will have columns corresponding to extra attributes not present for users). This leads to user interface problems – like how to present the data – which we'll skirt around by assuming that, since this program is hard coded to only ask for users, all rows will have the same set of columns. Hence, for this sample, we will only retrieve the column names once, for the first row, and we will assume that all other rows have the same column names. In this case this approach does work:

```
// get names of columns
hr = m_spSearchBase->GetFirstRow(m_hSearch); ASH;
LPWSTR pszColName;
hr=m_spSearchBase->GetNextColumnName(m_hSearch, &pszColName ); ASH;

while(hr != S_ADS_NOMORE_COLUMNS )
{
    m_csarrColumnNames.Add(pszColName);
    FreeADsMem( pszColName );
    hr=m_spSearchBase->GetNextColumnName(m_hSearch, &pszColName ); ASH;
}
```

We're at the first row – since we called `GetFirstRow()` earlier – so we can go ahead and display it in the list box:

```
    // we can start displaying the results now
    m_iCurrentRow = 1;
    DisplayCurrentRow();

    return TRUE;        // return TRUE unless you set the focus to a control
}
```

And that's the end of the `OnInitDialog` function.

Moving to the Next and Previous Row

Before we go through how `DisplayCurrentRow` actually iterates through the columns, I just want to go over what happens when we press the **Next** and **Previous** buttons.

```
void CCPPSearchDlg::OnNext()
{
    // TODO: Add your control notification handler code here

    HRESULT hr;
    hr = m_spSearchBase->GetNextRow(m_hSearch); ASH;
    m_buttonPrevious.EnableWindow();

    if (m_iCurrentRow == m_iNRows-1)
    {
        m_buttonNext.EnableWindow(false);
    };

    ++m_iCurrentRow;
    DisplayCurrentRow();
}

void CCPPSearchDlg::OnPrevious()
{
    // TODO: Add your control notification handler code here
    HRESULT hr;
    hr = m_spSearchBase->GetPreviousRow(m_hSearch);

    if (FAILED(hr))
    {
        m_buttonPrevious.EnableWindow(false);
        return;
    }

    m_buttonNext.EnableWindow();

    if (m_iCurrentRow == 2)
    {
        m_buttonPrevious.EnableWindow(false);
    };

    --m_iCurrentRow;
    DisplayCurrentRow();
}
```

These just really increment or decrement the row by calling the `GetNextRow` or `GetPreviousRow` methods of `IDirectorySearch`. The only extra bit of logic is that I've allowed for the possibility of `GetPreviousRow` not being implemented – the **Previous** button is disabled if that turns out to be the case.

The DisplayCurrentRow Function

Just one thing left now – to actually display out all the columns in a row:

```
void CCPPSearchDlg::DisplayCurrentRow()
{
    CString csText;
    ADS_SEARCH_COLUMN Column;
    HRESULT hr;

    m_listbox.ResetContent();

    m_editICurrentResult.SetWindowText(IntToString(m_iCurrentRow));
```

Before we actually display all of the columns, it'd be nice to display some sort of header, to make it easy for the user to see what record we're actually looking at. That means we need to select an attribute to look at – and in this case we can't simply go for the `IADs::Name` property, because we don't have any interface pointers to the objects returned. The property I've gone for is common name (cn) – it's a very standard attribute on LDAP directories, so there are not likely to be many cases where this attribute isn't present. If by any chance it isn't, then we'll just go without the header.

We get the value of the column name by calling `IDirectorySearch::GetColumn()`. This method assumes we've already navigated to the appropriate row, and takes a string that gives the name of the column. To simplify coding, I'm making the additional assumption that common name is a `case-ignore-string` (it is in Active Directory).

Notice the subsequent call to `ADsFreeColumn`. That frees up the memory for the `ADSVALUE` structure embedded in the `Column` variable, but leaves `Column` (a local variable) intact for the next call to `IDirectorySearch::GetColumn()`:

```
    // display some sort of header if we can
    hr = m_spSearchBase->GetColumn(m_hSearch, L"cn", &Column);
    if (SUCCEEDED (hr))
    {
        ASSERT(Column.dwADsType == ADSTYPE_CASE_IGNORE_STRING);
        csText = CString(L"COMMON NAME (cn): ") +
                Column.pADsValues[0].CaseIgnoreString;
        hr = m_spSearchBase->FreeColumn(&Column);
        m_listbox.AddString(csText);
        m_listbox.AddString(L"");
    }
```

We're now all set to iterate through the columns. That's fairly easy – the awkward bit is coping with the variety of data types that you might find in an ADSVALUE. In this code I haven't been that thorough – I've only picked out the main data types:

```
for (int i=0; i<m_csarrColumnNames.GetSize() ; i++)
{
    csText = m_csarrColumnNames[i];

    // need to convert CString to LPWSTR
    LPWSTR pszColName = new wchar_t[csText.GetLength()+1];
    wcscpy(pszColName, csText);
    hr = m_spSearchBase->GetColumn(m_hSearch, pszColName, &Column);
    delete [] pszColName;

    if (hr == S_OK)
    {

        m_listbox.AddString(csText + L":");
        unsigned k;

        switch (Column.dwADsType)
        {
        case ADSTYPE_CASE_EXACT_STRING:
        case ADSTYPE_CASE_IGNORE_STRING:
        case ADSTYPE_DN_STRING:
        case ADSTYPE_NUMERIC_STRING:

            for (k=0; k<Column.dwNumValues ; k++)
            {
                csText = CString(L"    ") +
                         Column.pADsValues[k].CaseIgnoreString;
            }
            break;

        case ADSTYPE_INTEGER:
            csText += L":    ";
            for (k=0; k<Column.dwNumValues ; k++)
            {
                csText = CString(L"    ") +
                         IntToString(Column.pADsValues[k].Integer);
            }
            break;
        default:
            csText = L"    <Unable to display data of this datatype>";
            break;
        }

        m_listbox.AddString(csText);
        hr = m_spSearchBase->FreeColumn(&Column);
    }
}
}
```

Using OLE DB with C++

Apart from directly calling up the `IDirectorySearch` methods, it is possible to do searching in C++ by going through the ADSI OLE DB provider. This works in much the same way as for VB and scripting clients that use ADO – except that the additional level of indirection of using ADO to talk to the OLE DB objects is not needed, as C++ can directly use the OLE DB interfaces.

Using OLE DB will inevitably result in a slight performance hit compared to using `IDirectorySearch` directly, however C++ clients may wish to do this in order to take advantage of OLE DB's ability to merge data from different sources. This would allow, say, objects in other databases such as SQL Server or Access to be updated directly from data in an ADSI-compliant directory. Alternatively, a search can be conducted across several ADSI directories, or across an ADSI directory and another database.

> *We don't have space here to go into programming with OLE DB, as it's a more complex subject than programming with ADO, but Wrox do publish another book, Visual C++ 6 Database Programming Tutorial by Wendy Sarrett, which covers that subject. Yeah, I know – trying to get as much money out of you as possible. There's also a C++ sample, `adsqry`, in the ADSI SDK, which demonstrates using OLE DB to carry out searching.*

If you do think about using OLE DB, the easiest way will be to use ATL's OLE DB consumer template classes, which hides many of the details of OLE DB in boilerplate code generated by the wizards.

Efficient Searching in Active Directory

So far we've covered the basics of how to actually do a search. For small systems, like mine, you're probably not going to be that bothered about the efficiency of the search. But for large networks, in which there is a lot of information in Active Directory, designing a search for efficiency is going to be a lot more important. These guidelines will help performance when searching against Active Directory, although many of the general principles will apply to other directories too.

❑ Some of the attributes in Active Directory are indexed. This means that Active Directory maintains ordered indexes for these attributes, which allow it to quickly locate where objects that have given values for these attributes are located. The result is that the system will be able to look up those attributes a lot more efficiently. So your search will run faster if it includes at least one indexed attribute in the filter. You can check which attributes are indexed by looking up the relevant `attributeClass` object in the schema. This object will have an attribute, `searchFlags`, which specifies how this attribute behaves when searched against. The least significant bit of this attribute indicates whether the attribute is indexed (1 for indexed, 0 for not indexed). Incidentally, if you change this value to 1, an index will automatically be built on a background thread in a domain controller, and this index will – as with all other data stored in Active Directory – quickly be replicated across the domain controllers.

❑ If you are searching for a particular kind of object, use `objectCategory` instead of `objectClass`. There are several reasons for this. Firstly, `objectCategory` is indexed, whereas `objectClass` is not. Secondly, `objectClass` is a multi-valued property, which itself makes searches against it less efficient. `objectCategory` is single-valued. But also, searching against `objectClass` can cause unexpected results, since such a search will pick up all objects that have the specified class anywhere in their hierarchy. For example, as I mentioned earlier, a search of `objectClass=person` will pick up computers as well as people.

❑ If you are looking for text, try to avoid looking for text in the middle or at the end of a string. `cn=si*` will yield better performance than `cn =*on`.

❑ Try to have one fairly restrictive condition on an indexed attribute in your filter. This is because Active Directory is quite sophisticated at examining the indexed attributes in the search filter, and picking the condition that is likely to yield the smallest set of results to search against first.

❑ Try to use the global catalogue for subtree searches that will cover more than one server. This saves Active Directory from having to chase referrals.

❑ If you are expecting a large number of results, then use paging to reduce the memory requirements on the server and even out the network calls, so that data is sent gradually rather than in one large chunk.

❑ This should be fairly obvious, but don't ask for more results than you need. At the same time, try to get all the properties in one single search.

Summary

This chapter completes our discussion of how searching works in Active Directory. We've seen how to use `adsvw.exe` as a ready-made user interface for searching, how to write LDAP search filters and how search preferences can be specified.

We've also discussed the different ways that searching is implemented in the different programming languages. First we used ADO to write VB and scripting clients for directory searches. Then we saw how it's done in C++ code, using `IDirectorySearch`.

In the next chapter, we'll tackle the subject of security.

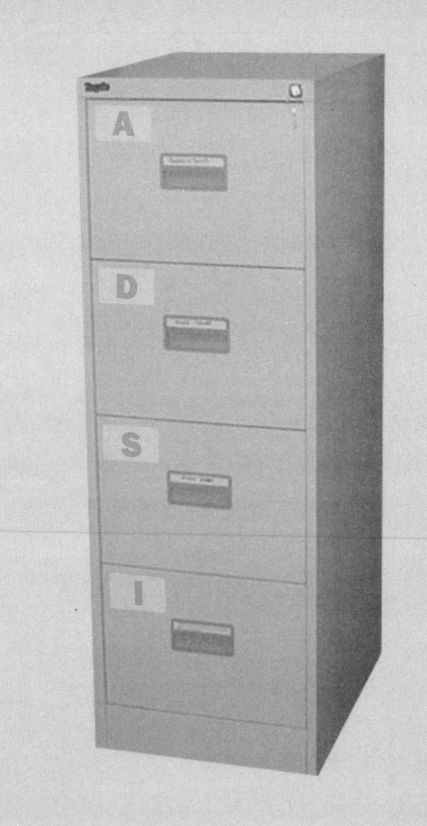

8
Security

In this chapter you will learn

- ❑ How to authenticate yourself to a directory service using ADSI
- ❑ How the ADSI security interfaces work
- ❑ How to write a web page that lets you look at the security settings on an ADSI object
- ❑ What Security Descriptors and access control lists and entries are and how to manipulate them for Active Directory objects using ADSI
- ❑ How ADSI security is related to the underlying Windows 2000 security
- ❑ How to set up auditing
- ❑ About encryption
- ❑ What Kerberos is and how it works

But only, of course, if you've got sufficient access rights to learn all this.

OK – I know we all think security is a boring issue. When I started this book, I couldn't wait to write the StarRaiders provider. I loved creating my little database of pop stars. I enjoyed writing the chapters about ADSI clients as well – it was great writing that little Active Server page to view any ADSI object, but I realized that sooner or later my editors at Wrox were going to start wondering where Chapter 8 was...

It's not as if it's undocumented – I actually find Microsoft's MSDN documentation on security quite readable. It's not as if I don't have a bookshelf full of other books with good chapters on security that I could refer to if I got stuck. It's just that – well be honest – when you've got all these exciting pop stars around, those Windows 2000 (or Windows NT) services that you can start and stop, and you can play with web pages that let you look at just about anything just by typing in a different ADsPath – would you honestly rather be fiddling with access control entries and security descriptors? Do you enjoy programming where the sign that your code doesn't work is an Access Violation message, and the sign that it works is that it comes up with an Access Denied Error message instead? I know I don't.

But we do need to understand how ADSI providers can implement security. Security coding may not be much fun, but it's even less fun repairing your database after some idiot with nothing better to do has hacked into it, replaced all the references to your company president with *Mr. SmartyPants*, and then moved all your *Dear Cuddleplum* emails from your girlfriend to the public mail folder...

In this chapter I'm going to try and make security look a bit fun – I'm going to do that by writing a neat little VB dialog that gives you an even neater user interface that examines all the security settings for a given ADSI object. The dialog uses most of the ADSI security functionality. In the process we'll get to compare up how ADSI implements security with how NT does it. We'll have a look at how to arrange for events to be audited using ADSI. Finally we'll have a more theoretical bit where we examine how security works under the covers in Windows, before moving on to some basic encryption theory. We'll finish with an overview of the Kerberos security protocols used in Windows 2000. But first we need to learn how to authenticate to an ADSI provider.

Authentication in ADSI

So far in everything we've done, we've just gone in and used the ADSI object we want. We've not actually specified any credentials. If we don't specify credentials, ADSI assumes what are known as *default* credentials. What this means depends on the provider or directory you are accessing. In general, all the providers that are supplied by Microsoft and related to your network will use the credentials associated with the user account you are logged in as when you make the call to obtain the object. More precisely, they'll assume the credentials of the thread that made the call to ADSI. This makes sense really. If you use the WinNT provider to – for example – stop a service, then ultimately the IADsServiceOperations::Stop call which you will use is actually using Windows API functions to carry this out. Those API functions will work to the account you are logged in as! The same principles apply to Active Directory – when you use ADSI to manipulate Active Directory you'll get the privileges associated with the account you're running under. That's why in Chapter 2 I strongly advised you to be logged in as a user with administrator privileges in order to try out the samples. Doing so will largely have enabled you to do pretty much anything in all the C++ and VB samples. It won't have helped much with the ASP samples, since ASP code will run by default under the IUSR_<machine-name> account, which basically has guest privileges only. (Assuming, that is, that you haven't changed the default account anonymous users run under and that you are not using Basic Authentication or NT Challenge/Response in your ASP pages).

Netscape Directory Server is a different example as far as security is concerned. There is not necessarily any direct relation between the user credentials that are valid in Netscape Directory server and those valid in Windows – simply because Netscape Directory Server is not intended to be related to Windows user accounts. It might not have even been installed on Windows. So if you don't authenticate to Netscape Directory Server somehow, then all you will get is guest access to the directory. There is no attempt to use any Windows accounts. Luckily for us in the last chapter, guest access to the Netscape sample database by default means that you get to see everything.

Similarly the StarRaiders provider that we develop in the next chapter is unrelated to Windows accounts. The StarRaiders provider will let you see very little if you don't specifically authenticate to it.

So how do you authenticate. Well we're going to present a C++ example first. Because, unusually for ADSI, authenticating is easier in C++ than it is in VB. As usual, code for both the C++ and ASP samples can be downloaded from the Wrox web site, as can all the code presented in this chapter.

Authenticating: C++ Example

Here's what our program is going to look like. It's a useful little tool that lets you specify all the bind parameters to attempt to authenticate to any ADSI object. After I'd written it, I found it quite handy for experimenting with what works and what doesn't. Basically, you type in the ADsPath of the object you want to look at, the user name and password that you want to use for your authentication, and a flag, which we'll leave at zero for now. When you hit the Bind Now button, the program attempts to bind to the object using the credentials you've specified, and tells you the results in the list box at the bottom.

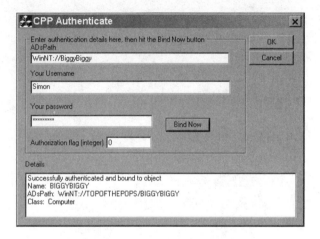

In this screenshot I've specified the username Simon for the WinNT provider. Because the WinNT provider simply uses Windows accounts, what I'm actually doing is saying that I want to bind to this object as if I were the user, Simon. Since Simon actually has administrator privileges on my machine, that means I'll get administrator privileges to this object (and incidentally, to all subsequent objects I bind to until I change my credentials – ADSI providers remember and cache credentials you supplied to ADsOpenObject). Note that I now get these privileges even if I was logged in to Windows with an account that didn't have many privileges. For the Microsoft providers take their security credentials from the Windows NT credentials, what's happening is the ADSI provider is impersonating the new user on your behalf. Of course, it goes the other way too. If I'm logged in to Windows as an Administrator and try to authenticate to an ADSI object giving the credentials of an account that doesn't have administrator privileges, then I'll be restricted in what I can do using ADSI because the ADSI WinNT objects I bind to will behave as if I'm logged in with the account that I have bound to them as.

Let's have a look at the code that does all this. Actually, despite all the different controls in the dialog box, it's not all that complex. Because all the action happens when you hit the Bind Now button, the only place that needs any significant coding beyond what the MFC Wizard gives us is in the message handler that gets called when Bind Now is clicked. We also need to note the control variables for the controls – m_listboxResults, m_editADsPath, m_editUserName, m_editPassword and m_editFlags. I'll leave you to figure out which variable corresponds to which control. Think of it as an exercise. For added incentive, I've asked Wrox if we can give away a $2 million prize to whoever works it out first. Think our money's fairly safe there…

```
void CCPPAuthenticateDlg::OnButtonbindnow()
{

    // get the stuff entered in the edit boxes
    CString csADsPath, csUserName, csPassword, csFlags;
    m_editADsPath.GetWindowText(csADsPath);
    m_editUserName.GetWindowText(csUserName);
    m_editPassword.GetWindowText(csPassword);
    m_editFlags.GetWindowText(csFlags);

    // get flags as integer
    DWORD dwFlags = unsigned(_wtoi(csFlags));

    //ADsOpenObject won't accept CStrings because no conversion from CString to
LPWSTR
    // - so convert:
    CComBSTR bstrADsPath = csADsPath;
    CComBSTR bstrUserName = csUserName;
    CComBSTR bstrPassword = csPassword;

    CComPtr<IADs> spADs;
    HRESULT hr;
    hr = ADsOpenObject(bstrADsPath, bstrUserName, bstrPassword, dwFlags, IID_IADs,
        (void**)&spADs);
    m_listboxResults.ResetContent();
    if (SUCCEEDED(hr))
    {
        m_listboxResults.AddString(L"Successfully authenticated and bound to
object");
        CComBSTR bstrName, bstrADsPath, bstrClass;
        hr = spADs->get_Name(&bstrName); ASH;
        m_listboxResults.AddString(CString(L"Name: ") + bstrName);
        hr = spADs->get_ADsPath(&bstrADsPath); ASH;
        m_listboxResults.AddString(CString(L"ADsPath: ") + bstrADsPath);
        hr = spADs->get_Class(&bstrClass); ASH;
        m_listboxResults.AddString(CString(L"Class: ") + bstrClass);
    }
    else
    {
        m_listboxResults.AddString(L"Failed to bind to object");
    }

}
```

So what's going on? Well, most of this code is really standard MFC stuff to retrieve the data from the edit boxes and stick any results in the list box. The only really new line is this one:

```
hr = ADsOpenObject(bstrADsPath, bstrUserName, bstrPassword, dwFlags, IID_IADs,
    (void**)&spADs);
```

Put simply, we have another of those API functions that are there to make life easier for C++ people. Instead of `ADsGetObject` we have to call a similar function, `ADsOpenObject()`. `ADsOpenObject` works in pretty much the same way as `ADsGetObject()`. You supply the `ADsPath` of the object you want, along with the IID of the required interface and a memory location to put the interface pointer in. The difference is there's a couple of extra parameters: the user name and password, which should be self-explanatory, and an extra number. This is partially provider specific, and indicates various options to go with the authentication, such as whether you want to use SSL encoding (whether your password should be encoded for transmission across the network). As I mentioned earlier, we'll leave that number at zero for now.

Simple, huh? So in C++ you only need to change one line to actually authenticate to an ADSI object. The line:

```
hr = ADsGetObject(bstrADsPath, IID_IADs, (void**)&spADs);
```

which you would use if you weren't authenticating, becomes:

```
hr = ADsOpenObject(bstrADsPath, bstrUserName, bstrPassword, dwFlags, IID_IADs,
    (void**)&spADs);
```

Now let's see the hoops you have to go through to do the same thing in VB and VB Script.

Authenticating: ASP Example

Here's a web page that lets you authenticate to an object

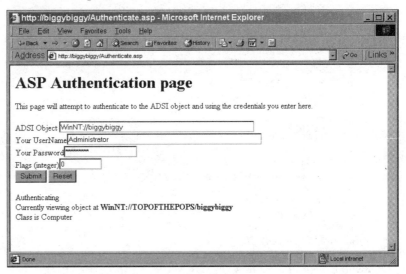

This web page works in pretty much the same way as the C++ example. You fill in the name of the ADSI object along with your user name, password and flags, hit the Submit button and hey presto – there's the details of the object. The only difference is I've made the web page a little bit more sophisticated in that it notices if the user name is blank. If it is, it doesn't even try to authenticate – it just uses `GetObject` as normal. Authenticating supplying a blank user name and password has the same effect as `GetObject` – the provider assumes default credentials.

Anyway, the web page produced by this code is this. It's a bit more complex than the C++ code so I've broken it up a bit with comments about what's going on.

```
<%@ Language = VBScript %>
<html>
<head>
<title> ASP Authentication Page </title>
</head>

<body>
```

We start off with the form that lets the user choose which object to authenticate to. We also declare and set variables that hold the values that were in the text boxes when the user last hit the submit button. We will use these later on to do the authentication, and to rewrite those values back into the text boxes – just to be that little extra user-friendly.

```
<h1> ASP Authentication page </h1>

<%
on error resume next

Dim strADsPath
strADsPath = Request.Form("ADsPath")
Dim strUserName
strUserName = Request.Form("UserName")
Dim strPassword
strPassword = Request.Form("Password")
Dim iFlags
iFlags = Request.Form("Flags")
%>

This page will attempt to authenticate to the ADSI object and using the
credentials you enter here.<br>
<form action = "Authenticate.asp" method = "post" id=form1 name=form1>
ADSI Object <INPUT type="text" id=ADsPath name=ADsPath size = 60 value =
<% Response.Write strADsPath %> ><br>
Your UserName<INPUT type="text" id=UserName name=UserName size = 60 value =
<% Response.Write strUserName%> ><br>
Your Password<INPUT type="password" id=Password name=Password size = 20 value =
<% Response.Write strPassword%> ><br>
Flags (integer)<INPUT type="text" id=Flags name=Flags size = 10 value = 0><br>
<INPUT type="submit" value="Submit" id=submit1 name=submit1>
<INPUT type="reset" value="Reset" id=reset1 name=reset1><br>
</form>
```

Now the next bit of code is where it gets interesting. We check whether there is anything entered for the ADsPath. If there isn't (and there won't be the first time the user brings up this page), then we don't want to do anything. If there is some text for the ADsPath, then we check whether there is anything for the user name. If there isn't, then we can just call GetObject() and be done with it – you get the default (in ASP, probably low-privilege) sign on. If there is a user name there, we then get down to the business of authenticating. I don't want to break this code up too much so I'll explain how the actual authentication works at the end of the code.

```
<%
if (not strADsPath= "") then

    ' bind to the ADSI object. If user has supplied a username, then
    ' authenticate too
    Dim oADsObject

    if (strUserName = "") then
        response.write "Not Authenticating<br>"
        Set oADsObject = GetObject(strADsPath)
    else
        response.write "Authenticating<br>"
        Dim strADsNamespace
        Dim oADsNamespace
        strADsNamespace = left(strADsPath, instr(strADsPath, ":"))
        set oADsNamespace = GetObject(strADsNamespace)

        Set oADsObject = oADsNamespace.OpenDSObject(strADsPath, strUserName,
strPassword, 0)
    end if
```

The binding has now been attempted. All that remains is to display some information about whether it did actually work.

```
    ' we've only managed to bind if err.number = 0
    if not (Err.number = 0) then
        Response.Write "Failed to bind to object <strong>" & strADsPath &
"</strong><br>"
        Response.write "Error number is " & err.number & "<br>"
        response.write err.description & "<p>"
    else
        Response.Write "Currently viewing object at <strong>" & oADsObject.ADsPath &
"</strong><br>"
        Response.Write "Class is " & oADsObject.Class & "<br>"
    end if
    response.write "<p>"

end if
%>

<p>

</body>
</html>
```

OK. That's the page. The key lines that attempt to authenticate are these ones:

```
    Dim strADsNamespace
    Dim oADsNamespace
    strADsNamespace = left(strADsPath, instr(strADsPath, ":"))
    set oADsNamespace = GetObject(strADsNamespace)

    Set oADsObject = oADsNamespace.OpenDSObject(strADsPath, strUserName,
strPassword, 0)
```

So the authentication happens in two stages. First we have to locate and bind to the appropriate namespace object. Then we use a method on the namespace object to actually authenticate to the object we want. Binding to the namespace object takes a bit of string manipulation – basically we've got to grab the bit of the `ADsPath` up as far as the first colon (:) – that bit will be the `ADsPath` of the namespace (eg. the namespace object corresponding to WinNT://BiggyBiggy is WinNT:)

What's going on here results from the fact that in VB the normal way to get a COM object is to use the `GetObject()` API function. This is a standard COM function – not a specifically ADSI one. And it comes in only one variety. There is no `GetObject()` equivalent of `ADsOpenObject()` that can take a user name and password. We're stuck with a simple `GetObject()` for the very good reason that the underlying COM methods that are internally called by `GetObject()` can't take a user name and password. So that's why we have to be a bit more devious.

What actually happens is that all ADSI namespace objects expose an extra interface: `IADsOpenDSObject`. This interface exposes one method, `OpenDSObject()`. This method is the one that's analogous to the `ADsOpenObject()` API function used by C++ people. It takes a user name, a password, the same integer that indicates options like the kind of encryption you want, and, of course, the `ADsPath` of the object you want. However, it *only* works for objects exposed by that provider. It's no good hooking up to – say – the LDAP namespace object, and using its `OpenDSObject()` method to bind you to an object in the WinNT directory – it won't work because the LDAP namespace object only knows how to bind to ADSI objects exposed through the LDAP provider. Each namespace object only knows how to authenticate you to other objects inside its own provider because the other ADSI objects do not expose any COM methods allowing you to authenticate. The namespace object is the only one that exposes `IADsOpenDSObject`. The process of authentication to other objects is provider-specific and therefore something that uses code internal to the provider, and which is therefore only available to other objects within the same provider to use.

What this means is that if you're given an `ADsPath` and want to authenticate to it supplying a user name and password, you've got to get the appropriate namespace object first. Which means you need to do that string manipulation to find out what the `ADsPath` of the namespace object is from the `ADsPath` of the required object. If you want to bind to – say `LDAP://DC=TopOfThePops,DC=Fame,DC=Com` supplying credentials then you'll have to bind to `LDAP:` first and call `OpenDSObject()` on the LDAP namespace object. On the other hand, if you want to bind to WinNT://BiggyBiggy/Administrator supplying credentials then you'll have to bind to WinNT: first in order to supply the credentials.

Of course, all this getting the namespace object is actually happening in the C++ code as well – it's just taken care of automatically by the `ADsOpenObject()` function. This is quite an unusual case of reversal of roles of C++ and VB. Usually you expect VB/VB Script to hide all the programming details, which get exposed if you're programming in C++. In this case, it's our ASP script which shows you what's actually going on under the scenes when you authenticate to an ADSI object, while C++ buries it all inside an API function call, saving the C++ programmers the burden of having to understand how it actually works. I don't know why, but somehow I find that extremely satisfying.

You may be wondering just why it is that you can only get to the appropriate provider from a namespace object. After all, that messing around with strings doesn't exactly make for nice code. Wouldn't it have been so much easier to be able to create a universal ADSI COM object that you could use to bind to anything? The problem is that it's not that simple. Thing is, ADSI objects are COM objects, and COM objects don't inherently have that kind of security built in. Don't get me wrong, COM isn't lax on security – there's a lot of work in COM and DCOM on security, with a number of interfaces devoted to the topic. It's just that COM security is devoted to figuring out whether you're allowed to use an object, not to finding out who you are. There's no standard interface to request a user name and password. What this means for ADSI is if you look under the hood, you'll find there's no standard way for an ADSI object to be authenticated. For example, in the LDAP provider, the actual authentication will be done by calling up some LDAP API functions that bind to an object using a user name and password. In StarRaiders, the user credentials are stored in a cache in the provider, and checked, because the provider has a hard coded knowledge of which groups of users can access which bits of the directory. In WinNT it'll be totally different again.

What that all means is that the method that actually handles the authenticating is going to have to have the knowledge of how authentication works in that provider. But no one has any way of knowing what other providers are going to turn up in the future. (I'm sure the designers of ADSI never anticipated the StarRaiders provider!) Which means each namespace object is only going to know how to authenticate users to objects within its own provider. So ASP and VB guys are stuck with string manipulations. C++ is able to implement all this under the hood because in C++ it's easy to call Windows API functions – and ADSI has supplied an API function for this purpose, namely `ADsOpenObject()`. In principle you could call this function from VB, but calling API functions from VB is more difficult. To achieve the same result in VB and VBScript of hiding all this functionality, you would really need a COM component that was able to do this. In principle there is no reason why you could not write such a component, but it happens that Microsoft have not done so.

UserNames

I'll have to admit that the screenshots I showed in the authentication examples were a rather cunning example of my carefully choosing the data I put into the samples to make things unusually simple. You see I've glibly talked about user names and passwords without giving you much information about how you know what user name and password to type in. I've hinted that the accounts you could authenticate as are the same as the Windows accounts. Which is true for the WinNT provider, and also for the LDAP provider when you talk to Active Directory or Exchange Server. It's also true for the LDAP provider talking to the Site Server membership directory *if* the membership directory is set up to use NT authentication (not if it's set up to use membership authentication). Naturally enough, I know I've got a user name, Simon, on my main computer, BiggyBiggy – so I just typed in that user name and the corresponding password to authenticate to an object in WinNT. It worked! And that is how you give your usernames for the WinNT provider.

Now in principle, according to Microsoft, the same thing ought to work in Active Directory. You should be able to authenticate yourself using the name you would normally use to log on. In practice I was unable to do so on my machine when I tried it. However, in Active Directory, the situation for user names isn't quite so simple – there's something else we need to know.

The missing link is that it's a general principle with LDAP directories that the directories usually expect you to authenticate *as if you are an object in the directory*. LDAP directory objects (or at least – the ones that represent people) are able to double up as both directory objects and objects that can log in. Active Directory is an LDAP directory – it has to comply with both the strict definitions and the broad spirit of LDAP. Which means when it comes to authenticating, Active Directory is expecting you to supply credentials in which you tell it you *are* one of the objects (one of the users) stored in Active Directory. You might be wondering what the problem is there, since all the domain user accounts are stored in Active Directory. But the problem is that Active Directory recognizes objects from their distinguished names. If I want to log in as *Administrator*, there is no object in Active Directory with the distinguished name *Administrator*. But there is an object (at least on my machine) with a distinguished name,

`cn=Administrator,cn=Users,dc=TopOfThePops,dc=fame,dc=com`. And I guess that's the one we want. Let's look at it:

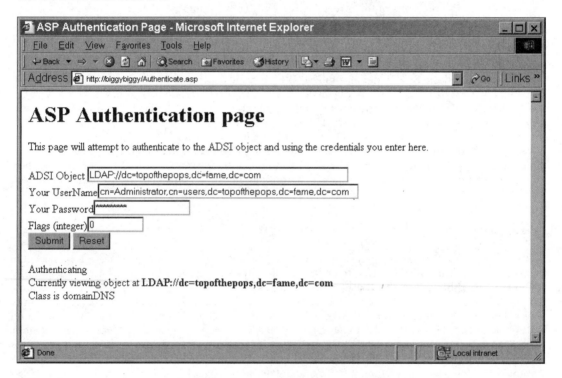

This rather torturous route is the 'proper' way to authenticate yourself to Active Directory.

I said 'distinguished name' for a reason – it really is the distinguished name of the user you need, not the `ADsPath`. You don't need to bother with the initial `LDAP://` (in fact if you do the authentication will fail). This is a manifestation of the fact that really the LDAP provider simply serves as a wrapper around LDAP directories. And – let's face it – LDAP directories aren't very interested in ADSI. In fact an LDAP directory will typically know nothing about even the existence of ADSI, and so will be interested only in distinguished names, not in `ADsPaths`. In fact, when you supply the `ADsPath` of the LDAP object you want to bind to using `GetObject()`, etc., the LDAP provider will strip off the leading `LDAP://` before handing what's left to the relevant LDAP API functions. That initial `LDAP://` is only there for the benefit of ADSI.

Note that Active Directory might not be able to recognize your distinguished name if you put any spaces in it. You are best advised to type in your distinguished name without any extraneous whitespace.

Of course, even with the `LDAP://` stripped off, the distinguished name of the object that represents me in active directory is rather long. I don't really want to have to type `cn=Administrator,cn=Users,dc=TopOfThePops,dc=fame,dc=com` every time I want to use a script to do something in Active Directory. There's also another problem. Remember users don't have to sit in the same place in the Active Directory tree. There's nothing to stop a domain administrator from creating a new organizational unit in Active Directory for some users, and moving any account there for ease of administration. Moving an account to a different container has absolutely no effect on the account. The fact that my account has been moved within the Active Directory Tree is something that I shouldn't even have to know about to use my account. But it does mean that my old distinguished name will no longer be valid – so I'd now need to supply a different `dn` if I wanted to authenticate to a script or C++ program that uses Active Directory. That's distinctly user-unfriendly! Quite apart from the fact that you probably don't want end users who know nothing about LDAP to have to remember a complex LDAP distinguished name. Or rather, you might not have any qualms about wanting your users to use `dns`, but they probably will!

So even though distinguished names are technically the correct way to go about binding, we really need something a bit friendlier. Fortunately, in addition to distinguished names, Active Directory will also recognize the following formats of name when you are trying to authenticate:

User Principal Name

This name is your username in the format that is generally used for email addresses – in other words `<username>@location`. So in my case, I have a DNS name of TopOfThePops.Fame.com, so I might have a user principal name of `Simon@TopOfThePops.fame.com`, or it might be `Simon@fame.com`. There's no particular requirement for the part of the user principal name that follows the @ sign to correspond to your domain name, since there's actually nothing magic about the user principal name – it's just an attribute on the user object in Active Directory, which you can set to whatever value you want – within reason anyway. Generally, I found if you set the `userPrincipalName` attribute to something that's not in the spirit of the idea of UPNs – something like `simonATHello` – then you won't be able to authenticate using it. Generally, although it's not required, you will want to set the user principal name to something related to your domain name, just to make life easier for your users.

The advantage of the user principal name is – apart from being simpler and easier to remember as you can set it to be the same as a user's email address – it won't change if you move the user within the directory tree.

Downlevel Logon

This is a name in the format `DomainName\UserName`. The domain name in question is NOT necessarily part of your Internet domain name – it's actually the NetBIOS domain name recognized by NT4 machines. When you set up Active Directory, you are asked for this name as part of the installation process – it needs to be supplied so that NT4 machines can join the domain because NT4 won't recognize the DNS name. Even if you know you won't be running any NT4 machines on your network, you still have to supply this name – just in case! I have a DNS name of `TopOfThePops.fame.com` and a NetBIOS name of `TOPOFTHEPOPS`. So my downlevel logon name is `TopOfThePops\Simon`. (The NetBIOS name is case-insensitve, though it always appears in capitals when the computer displays it. In general, you'll make life easy for yourself if you choose a NetBIOS name that's similar to the DNS name, though you don't have to do that.)

Which has taken us back full circle. According to Microsoft, you should be able to simply use your User Name, without the domain name – which is the name you would use to authenticate to the WinNT provider, but I found in practice this doesn't work. So authenticating simply as 'Administrator' or 'Simon' should be possible. One of the reasons I took you all round the houses showing you the other ways of authenticating is that I wanted to emphasize that this is only implemented to make things easier for users. The real method of authentication uses distinguished names.

> *I also should remark again that I have not found I'm able to authenticate using my downlevel logon name in my own machine. This may be due to the newness of Windows 2000 and the fact that I am still using beta software.*

Authentication Flags

In this section we'll take a quick look at the final parameter in the calls to `IADsOpenDSObject::OpenDSObject()` and `ADsOpenObject()`, the one I've referred to up till now as the flag and left at zero.

This value is taken from an enumeration list called `ADS_AUTHENTICATION_ENUM`. It's another of those values that is formed by combining bits – so you use a logical OR operator to combine whichever of the flags you want. The aim is to specify any of a number of different preferences you might opt for when authenticating. Because different providers may support different options, this is really a provider-specific flag, so you'll need to check the documentation for whichever provider you happen to be using. Also, different providers may default to different settings if you don't specify any flags. Having said that, a full list of the flags defined by Microsoft for use with the system providers is given in Appendix F, but to give you a flavor of the kinds of options we are talking about some of the main flags are detailed here:

ADS_SECURE_AUTHENTICATION (value =1)

This flag requests that authentication will be done using secure authentication – which if you are using only Windows 2000 computers, means using Kerberos. If you are logging in using an NT4 workstation, the NT LAN Manager will be used instead, since NT4 doesn't support Kerberos. We'll explain how Kerberos works later in this chapter.

ADS_USE_ENCRYPTION (value = 2)

This forces ADSI to encrypt the data exchanged across the network. With Active Directory this will mean using SSL.

ADS_READONLY_SERVER (value = 4)

This is an option for the WinNT provider. Because in WinNT domains, there is only one domain controller, the primary domain controller, which actually stores the master copy of the NT directory, you must always go to the primary domain controller if you intend to write any data. This flag indicates that you only intend to read data, which means it's fine to connect to a backup domain controller instead – this may be faster. This flag is redundant for Windows 2000 domain controllers, but if your network is an NT4 network, failure to specify this flag will force the WinNT provider to talk only to your primary domain controller – just in case you will need write access. If lots of ADSI clients are doing this there is the risk of a bottleneck.

A full list of the options for Microsoft providers is in Appendix F.

Displaying Security Information: The ADsHackerView

Everything we've covered up till now is about **authenticating**. That is – telling the system who you are. But when we're dealing with security, that's only part of the story. Once we've established who you are, the operating system (at least for Active Directory and WinNT – for other directories it'll be the directory or some other agent) has to decide what you are allowed to do. In Windows 2000 and NT4, that kind of security is built right into the operating system. When you attempt to do anything – be it open a file, look in a folder, run a program, or attempt to access an object in Active Directory – literally anything at all, the first thing that Windows does is ask whether you are allowed to do it. It will check up, and only if you are allowed to carry out the operation you wish to do will you be permitted to proceed. And it doesn't even end there. Whether or not you have been permitted to carry out your action, Windows (again NT4 and W2K – none of this section applies to Windows 9x) will perform a further check to see if this action should be audited – in other words whether a record should be made of your attempt to access this object or perform this action – so that systems administrators can later check what's going on. Now don't get too paranoid – this doesn't generally mean that the systems administrators are able to check up on every single file you've accessed. By default, auditing is disabled when you first install Windows – otherwise you'd rapidly either (depending on the maximum size of your event log) fill up your event log or run out of disk space from all the audits for a start! Audits are really intended to allow administrators to watch for potential attempts to hack into or otherwise abuse the system. For example, a couple of thousand logs of a failed attempt to log in as the administrator is a pretty certain indication that someone is trying to crack the administrator's password – and appropriate action needs to be taken.

Well that's a taster of what happens anyway – we're going to explore all that in a lot more detail. But first we're going to get our hands dirty again, by writing a VB application that displays all the security settings on an object in Active Directory. This is the application which I hope will convince you security can be fun, since it allows you to see *everything* at a glance – something that none of the available Microsoft tools will do. It is a dialog – a very large dialog as you can see from the screenshot coming up. You type in the `ADsPath` of the object in which you're interested in the text box at the top of the dialog, and then the list boxes display all the security data for that object. I've dubbed it the Hacker Viewer application – and here it is in action:

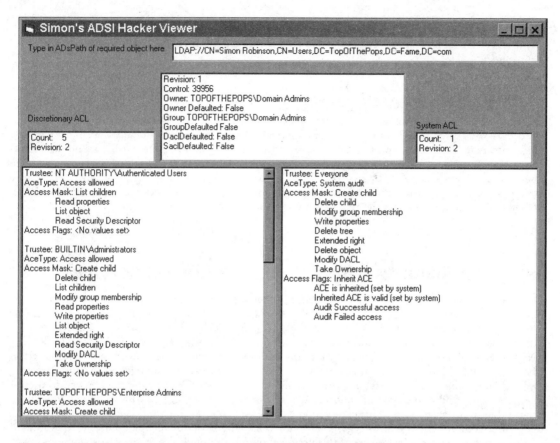

I've set it to look at my own user account, and you can see from the size of that scroll bar that there's a lot of stuff associated with my account that governs access permissions. Remember that apart from the ADsPath in the top text box, none of the information displayed in this dialog is to do with attributes of the object itself – everything is about the access rights to it.

Since there's a lot to take in here, the approach I'm going to take is this. We'll start off with a quick summary of what some of the information that my Hacker Viewer has come up with – to give you a broad feel for what is there and how it's organized. Then we'll go through the code that actually uses ADSI to get to all this information. We'll follow up with more samples to let you modify the security data and set up auditing. Then we'll start a more theoretical section, and go through all the various rights and permissions in NT and Windows 2000 in more detail.

So before we go through the code, let's take a look at what the information there actually means.

Security Descriptors and Access Control Lists – an Introduction

The Security Descriptor

Let's start off with the list box in the middle near the top of the dialog. This is the one that gives information about the object's security descriptor. The security descriptor is the entry point for information about an object's security settings. Every object in Active Directory has one, as does every file or folder on your hard drive.

> *Actually I should amend that. Every file or folder has a security descriptor, provided your drive is formatted as NTFS. If it is formatted as any variation of FAT, then it won't have, because the FAT file system has no ability to store security information. Almost none of the rest of this chapter does not apply if you are running Windows 9x.*

The security descriptor is basically there to say who owns the object. Think of the owner as the person responsible for the object. More significantly, the owner can usually do anything with the object, irrespective of what the security settings say. The security descriptor's got a few extra bits of information that tell you a bit about how the owner got determined in the first place – for a freshly installed copy of Active Directory most entries will have defaulted to being owned by the Domain Admins group. So for our screenshot the two fields we're interested in here are the Owner (TOPOFTHEPOPS\Domain Admins) and the Group the owner belongs to (strangely enough, also TOPOFTHEPOPS\Domain Admins)

The Access Control Lists and Entries

The final two types of object we need to consider are the **access control lists** (**ACLs**) and **access control entries** (**ACEs**). The ACE is really where the action happens. Each ACE is an object that gives one instruction about someone being able or not able to do something. An ACL is simply a list of ACEs, which is inserted into the security descriptor.

In our VB Hacker Viewer application, notice how the dialog splits symmetrically into two halves. The left of the screen concerns the **discretionary access control list** (**DACL**). This is the list which says who is and isn't allowed to do what to an object. The right of the screen is devoted to the **system access control list**. This list is identical to the discretionary ACL in structure, but the access control entries here give instructions about what actions should be audited.

The list box near the top left of the Hacker Viewer application gives some information that applies to the ACL as a whole, including the count of how many ACEs are in the list. In this case there are 12. The big list box below it indicates what is stored in the ACEs themselves. Similarly, on the right of the dialog, the small list box at the top tells you about the system ACL as a whole, and the big list box below it tells you about each of the ACEs in it – in this case just one.

The ACEs are where the action really happens. Take a look at the big ACE list box on the bottom left of the screenshot. The first ACE starts by saying that the Trustee is NT AUTHORITY\Authenticated Users. The **trustee** is the user or group to which this ACE applies. We've got the new term *trustee* here because saying 'users or groups' all the time can get a bit awkward. If the trustee is a user, then the permissions outlined apply just to that user. In this case, it's the built-in group Authenticated Users, which means that this ACE applies to all users in that group. The next line gives the access type – in this case it's Access Allowed, which means that this ACE is going to tell us that all authenticated users are allowed to do something with my account. Other possibilities here are access denied and system audit. The system audit value will only occur in a system ACE, the other values will occur only in a discretionary ACE.

Next we come to the Access Mask. What's this? Well, we've established that the authenticated users are allowed to do something. The access mask tells us what they are going to be allowed to do. In this case, it's not long. It basically tells us that members of this group are allowed to read the entry, including the security descriptor (notice that reading security information is considered a separate permission from reading the object itself), and list its children, if any. No write permissions are present, so members of Authenticated Users cannot modify this object, unless they also belong to another group that does have the appropriate permissions in a later ACE in the list.

If we move down to the next ACE in the list, we see that administrators have a much longer list of things they can do to this object. They have extensive permissions to read or modify the object, and can also take ownership of it. A big list – not surprisingly because administrators are a powerful group of people! Most of the items in the list should be self-explanatory. They can read or modify any of the attributes on this object. They can create child objects (assuming this object is of a class that can be a container), and list who those children are. They can modify the DACL – in other words the very DACL that we're looking at right now. Again, this is separate from the permission to write properties because the DACL is not really regarded as an attribute of the object.

For many purposes, those three bits of information – the trustee, the ACE type and the Access mask, suffice to completely define the ACE. There are a number of other properties that can be important, though. The field, **Access Flags**, which you can also see in the screenshot, indicates other options. Partly this is to do with what happens when you create a child of this object – should the child inherit the access control list of its parent automatically? Partly these flags are to do with auditing – if we're dealing with a system ACL, do we want to generate audits for a successful action or a failed action (or both)? For the discretionary ACLs in this list, none of the access flags have been set. However, if you look in the right hand list box, which gives this object's one system ACL, you'll see this flag has been set, with quite a few values. The values here indicate that audits must be generated for both successful and failed operations that come within the list specified in the access mask. There is also a value to indicate that this ACE has actually been placed here because it was inherited from the parent of this object in Active Directory, rather than being placed here. In fact, in Active Directory, all objects have the same system ACE, which instructs most operations to be audited. This ACE was originally set by default in the top-level domain object, and marked to be inherited by all children – so that this ACE propagates throughout Active Directory.

Although you can manually set a flag to indicate that an ACE is inheritable, it is the system which always sets the (different) flag that indicates if an object has been inherited as well as the remaining flag, which indicates that the inheritance proceeded OK and a valid ACE was created. The reason for these flags is that it is possible to set one of the bits in the access flag to indicate that inheritance should only proceed to one level of descendancy in the directory tree. So in that case the system needs to know whether this ACE has been inherited so it knows whether to continue the inheritance if further children of this object are created.

That screenshot has showed us most of the information you can get from a security descriptor and the ACLs and ACEs. But there are a couple of other settings to notice, for which we need to check out another object in Active Directory. Here's another screenshot of the Hacker Viewer app, this time set to examine the root domain object in Active Directory:

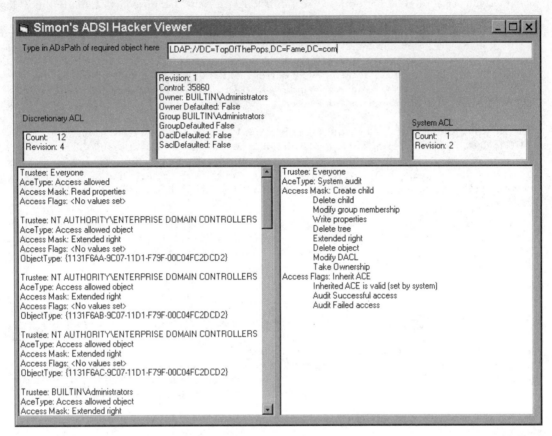

Here, on the right you can see the same system auditing access control entry – the one that is to be inherited down the directory tree. However, the interesting bit is across in the discretionary ACL. Most of the ACEs have a new AceType – **Access allowed object**. This is the same as **Access allowed**, but indicates that the ACE does not apply to the entire Active Directory entry. To match this, you'll see an extra property, **Object Type**, which is a GUID. The reason for this field is that sometimes you don't want an access control entry to apply to a whole object. You might want a permission to apply only to one attribute in the object. For example, you probably want to give normal users access to modify their telephone number, and possibly their description, but you wouldn't want them to be able to modify their `sAMAccountName`! If a GUID is specified here, then it'll be the GUID of an `attributeClass` object in the Active Directory schema – and it will indicate that this ACE only applies to that attribute. (Remember that *all* objects in Active Directory have GUIDs associated with them).

How the ACLs and ACEs are Used

How the security information is used is pretty simple actually. When you attempt to do something to an object, the system reads through the discretionary access control list in order to try to determine whether you are allowed to perform that action. It looks at each ACE in sequence, until it finds one which gives it the answer. If it gets to the end of the DACL without finding an ACE that tells it whether you are allowed to perform the action, it assumes that you are NOT allowed to do what you want to do. Security is important in Windows NT so we don't take chances. Notice that this system means it is important what order the ACEs are placed in the list. If two ACEs in the list give conflicting instructions, then it is the one that comes first in the list which will control whether the user can perform the action: As soon as Windows discovers one ACE which gives it a definite answer about whether the action should be allowed or denied, it stops reading further ACEs.

Similarly, if auditing is enabled for this type of action, Windows will then read through the system ACL to determine whether the attempted action matches any in the list that should be audited. If it finds an ACE that covers this action, it will write an appropriate entry in the event log (we'll cover how to use the Event Log later in the chapter). Otherwise, if it gets to the end of the system ACL without finding a relevant ACE, it assumes the action should NOT be audited. (No point wasting memory!)

Note that in future in this book, we're going use the terms security objects/information/data to refer to any of the security descriptor, access control lists and access control entries together, and the information contained in them. Listing all three types of object is a bit too much of a mouthful!

ACLs, ACEs, Security Descriptors and ADSI

You may have noticed a subtle shift in the last section. I started this chapter by talking about security in ADSI providers, and somewhere along the line we seem to have ended up talking about NT security. That's not a coincidence. We're talking about the LDAP provider – and in particular we've focused on Active Directory. Since Active Directory is *the* directory that defines all the domain security permissions in Windows 2000, ADSI security (in the context of Active Directory) and NT Technology security really are the same thing.

What's made it convenient for us is that ADSI has actually defined COM objects and interfaces that very closely mirror the underlying objects used in NT security. Let's be more specific. You'll have figured from the previous discussion that NT security uses three types of object: Security descriptors, access control lists and access control entries. Well, ADSI defines and implements three different COM objects: Security Descriptor objects, which expose `IADsSecurityDescriptor`, Access Control List objects which expose `IADsAccessControlList`, and Access Control Entry objects which expose `IADsControlEntry`. When you use ADSI, you are actually talking to, for example, a security descriptor COM object. That security descriptor object wraps a real NT security descriptor. It's exactly the same principle as with other ADSI objects. Recall how an object that exposes `IADS` is actually a COM object that wraps – and pretends to be – the underlying directory object. For objects in the directory, the distinction between the COM object and the underlying directory object is apparent because we occasionally need to call `GetInfo` or `SetInfo` in order to copy modifications between the property cache and the actual directory object. You can't do that on the security objects because the security objects are not technically directory objects – as we're going to see when we go over the code for the Hacker Viewer app, they are attached to directory objects and available as an attribute of the corresponding object. Hence they do not expose the `IADS` interface. However, you do still need to call `SetInfo` on the directory object to which the security objects are attached.

Coding the VB Hacker Viewer App

We're now going to look at how this security stuff is implemented, so it's time to go through the code that produced the Hacker Viewer application. There's quite a bit to it so I'm going to break it down with explanations throughout. At the end of the code we'll have a recap on how the ADSI security interfaces work.

There are quite a few controls in the Hacker Viewer dialog, so here's what they are all called.

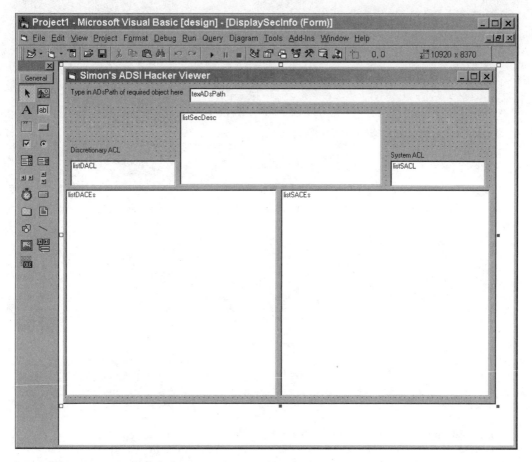

There's only one control that actually allows the user to enter data: The `texADsPath` text box. So all the action really happens when we detect that the user has typed something into this box. So here are the event handlers.

```
Private Sub texADsPath_KeyUp(KeyCode As Integer, Shift As Integer)

If KeyCode = 13 Then
   BindToNewObject
End If

End Sub
```

```
Private Sub texADsPath_LostFocus()

BindToNewObject

End Sub
```

OK. So that tells us that the interesting stuff is going to happen in a sub called `BindToNewObject`. Here it is.

```
Private Sub BindToNewObject()

listSecDesc.Clear
listDACL.Clear
listSACL.Clear
listDACEs.Clear
listSACEs.Clear

On Error Resume Next
Err.Clear
Set oADsObject = GetObject(texADsPath.Text)
If Not (Err.Number = 0) Then
  listSecDesc.AddItem "Failed to bind to this object"
  Exit Sub
End If

' make sure we can read the system ACL
Dim oADsObjectOptions As IADsObjectOptions
Set oADsObjectOptions = oADsObject
oADsObjectOptions.SetOption ADS_OPTION_SECURITY_MASK, 15

RefreshData

End Sub
```

Obviously the real action happens in a sub called `RefreshData`. All `BindToNewObject` does is attempts to bind to the object we've specified. If the bind is unsuccessful, we just print an error message – otherwise we can go in and actually look at the security data.

There is something new here though – we've declared a local variable of type `IADsObjectOptions` and used it to set an option. The `IADsObjectOptions` interface is one we haven't encountered before. I don't want to get sidetracked too much here so I'm going to save a detailed explanation for later on when we write our sample to modify the auditing information. For now, just accept that we have to call the `IADsObjectOptions:SetOption` method with the parameters as in the code above before we can access at the system ACL.

By the way, the variable `oADsObject` is our one global variable – and is defined to be of type `IADS`:

```
Option Explicit
Dim oADsObject As IADs
```

Anyway, on to `RefreshData`. Here's where I *really* start splitting the code up. We start by declaring some more variables.

```
Private Sub RefreshData()

On Error Resume Next
Dim oSecDesc As SecurityDescriptor
Dim oDACL As AccessControlList
Dim oSACL As AccessControlList
Dim oACE As AccessControlEntry
```

Now at last we can see how we get hold of the security descriptor. I've hinted that the security objects are not objects in the directory tree. In fact, if an object has a security descriptor, that security descriptor may still be stored in the directory, but it will be obtainable as a property on the object with which it is associated rather than as a separate object. In other words, in ADSI, security descriptors are properties rather than objects. In Active Directory, the relevant property is `nTSecurityDescriptor`, although other directories may have different names for the property that stores the security descriptor. I don't think I'm exaggerating when I say the following couple of lines of code are the key to the whole business of displaying security information.

```
Err.Clear
Set oSecDesc = oADsObject.Get("nTSecurityDescriptor")
If (Err.Number > 0 Or oSecDesc Is Nothing) Then
  listSecDesc.AddItem "Failed to obtain a security descriptor for this object"
  Exit Sub
End If
```

Notice I've been careful with my error checking. If the `nTSecurityDescriptor` property is defined in the schema, but this object doesn't happen to have one, then it is conceivable that our call to `IADS::Get` could return an empty object without actually raising an error. To avoid causing problems later on in the code, I make sure I check for this.

Now I have the security descriptor, I can actually display all its properties in the security descriptor list box. No surprises here – the information is all available as COM automation properties exposed by the `IADsSecurityDescriptor` interface. After we've displayed them, we do some more declarations of variables and attempt to get the discretionary access control list. This is also exposed as an automation property on `IADsSecurityDescriptor`:

```
listSecDesc.AddItem "Revision: " & oSecDesc.Revision
listSecDesc.AddItem "Control: " & oSecDesc.Control
listSecDesc.AddItem "Owner: " & oSecDesc.Owner
listSecDesc.AddItem "Owner Defaulted: " & oSecDesc.OwnerDefaulted
listSecDesc.AddItem "Group " & oSecDesc.Group
listSecDesc.AddItem "GroupDefaulted " & oSecDesc.GroupDefaulted
listSecDesc.AddItem "DaclDefaulted: " & oSecDesc.DaclDefaulted
listSecDesc.AddItem "SaclDefaulted: " & oSecDesc.SaclDefaulted

Err.Clear

' some declarations we're going to need
```

```
Dim strRights(20) As String
Dim iNRights As Integer
Dim i As Integer
Dim strACEFlags(20) As String
Dim iNACEFlags As Integer

Set oDACL = oSecDesc.DiscretionaryAcl
If (Err.Number > 0 Or oDACL Is Nothing) Then
  listDACEs.AddItem "Failed to obtain a descretionary acl for this object"
Else
  listDACL.AddItem "Count:  " & oDACL.AceCount
  listDACL.AddItem "Revision: " & oDACL.AclRevision
```

Right. We've got the discretionary access control list. We've displayed the properties associated with
the list as a whole. Access control entries next. You probably won't be surprised to learn that they are
exposed by having the access control list as a collection, with the access control entries inside it.
Which means there's a `For Each` loop coming up.

```
For Each oACE In DACL
listDACEs.AddItem "Trustee: " & oACE.Trustee
listDACEs.AddItem "AceType: " & AccessType(oACE.AceType)

' display access mask
Call AccessMask(oACE.AccessMask, iNRights, strRights)
listDACEs.AddItem "Access Mask: " & strRights(0)
For i = 1 To iNRights - 1
   listDACEs.AddItem "         " & strRights(i)
Next

  ' display access flags
Call AccessFlags(oACE.ACEFlags, iNACEFlags, strACEFlags)
listDACEs.AddItem "Access Flags: " & strACEFlags(0)
For i = 1 To iNACEFlags - 1
   listDACEs.AddItem "         " & strACEFlags(i)
Next

' show if any object GUIDs are present
If (oACE.Flags And 2) Then
listDACEs.AddItem "InheritedObjectType: " & oACE.InheritedObjectType
End If
If (oACE.Flags And 1) Then
   listDACEs.AddItem "ObjectType: " & oACE.ObjectType
End If
listDACEs.AddItem ""
  Next
End If
```

And that is it, as far as the discretionary access control list is concerned. The stuff inside the `For
Each` loop looks quite complex. The reason is I've tried to make the Hacker Viewer app fairly user-
friendly in how it presents its information. In theory, everything is simply exposed as automation
properties by `IADsAccessControlEntry`. Unfortunately, a lot of the information is numeric – and
rather than simply saying this property is – say – 3, the Hacker Viewer actually interprets it to say
what the 3 means. So if we quickly run through the properties:

`Trustee` is pretty simple – a string that we can just print out. The access type is an integer, but I've defined a function, `AccessType`, which converts this number to more meaningful text. We'll see the source code for this and the other conversion functions soon.

The mask and access flags are more complex. Both of these are numbers formed by doing a bit-wise combination of bits to indicate a series of flags. So the procedures that convert these integers to strings need to each give us an array of strings, each of which requires another `For` loop to display.

Finally we get to two strings – `ObjectType` and `InheritedObjectType`. We discussed `ObjectType` earlier – it is a GUID that indicates if this ACE only actually applies to one attribute rather than the entire object. If the ACE applies to the entire object then this GUID will be blank. If the ACE applies only to one property, then this GUID will equal the objectGUID of the property. (In Active Directory, all properties as well as all objects are identified by GUIDs, - the GUID that identifies a property is obtainable as an attribute in the relevant property object).
`InheritedObjectType` is a similar GUID, but tells us if this ACE can only be inherited by one particular class of child objects. A further automation property, Flags (not to be confused with the property, `ACEFlags`) indicates whether either of these GUIDs are present and contains valid data. Hence I've checked the value of Flags before printing either of these GUIDs.

We need to check out the conversion functions, but first, we'll finish off the `RefreshData` procedure – which is still running! We need to do exactly the same processing for the system ACL that we did for the discretionary ACL:

```
Err.Clear
Set oSACL = oSecDesc.SystemAcl
If (Err.Number > 0 Or oSACL Is Nothing) Then
  listSACEs.AddItem "Failed to obtain a system ACL for this object"
Else
  listSACL.AddItem "Count:   " & oSACL.AceCount
  listSACL.AddItem "Revision: " & oSACL.AclRevision
  For Each oACE In oSACL
    listSACEs.AddItem "Trustee: " & oACE.Trustee
    listSACEs.AddItem "AceType: " & AccessType(oACE.AceType)

    ' display access mask
    Call AccessMask(oACE.AccessMask, iNRights, strRights)
    listSACEs.AddItem "Access Mask: " & strRights(0)
    For i = 1 To iNRights - 1
      listSACEs.AddItem "        " & strRights(i)
    Next

    ' display access flags
    Call AccessFlags(oACE.ACEFlags, iNACEFlags, strACEFlags)
    listSACEs.AddItem "Access Flags: " & strACEFlags(0)
    For i = 1 To iNACEFlags - 1
      listSACEs.AddItem "        " & strACEFlags(i)
    Next

    ' show if any object GUIDs are present
    If (oACE.Flags And 2) Then
    listSACEs.AddItem "InheritedObjectType: " & oACE.InheritedObjectType
    End If
```

```
      If (oACE.Flags And 1) Then
        listSACEs.AddItem "ObjectType: " & oACE.ObjectType
      End If
      listSACEs.AddItem ""
  Next
End If

End Sub
```

And that is the end of our work. We've just got those conversion functions to look at now. Firstly, the `AceType`. Basically a simple switch statement:

```
Private Function AccessType(iType As Integer) As String

AccessType = "<Invalid value>"
Select Case iType
Case 0
  AccessType = "Access allowed"
Case 1
  AccessType = "Access denied"
Case 2
  AccessType = "System audit"
Case 5
  AccessType = "Access allowed object"
Case 6
  AccessType = "Access denied object"
Case 7
  AccessType = "System audit object"
End Select

End Function
```

That tells you what all the possible values are for the `AceType`. Fuller details, along with similar details for the `ACEFlags`, `AceMask` and `Flags` are – as usual – in Appendix F.

The `AceMask` is a bit more complex since we need to do a bit-wise comparison. We don't know how many bits of the flag are actually going to be set, so to keep the code simple, I've arbitrarily sized the array to hold the strings at 20. That'll easily be big enough. There's a lot of flags in the mask, but not *that* many!

```
Private Sub AccessMask(iMask, iNRights As Integer, strRights() As String)

If (UBound(strRights) < 20 Or LBound(strRights) > 0) Then
  Err.Raise "Sub AccessMask was passed an array with invalid bounds"
End If

iNRights = 0

If (iMask And &H1) Then
    strRights(iNRights) = "Create child"
    iNRights = iNRights + 1
End If
If (iMask And &H2) Then
```

```
        strRights(iNRights) = "Delete child"
        iNRights = iNRights + 1
End If
If (iMask And &H4) Then
        strRights(iNRights) = "List children"
        iNRights = iNRights + 1
End If
If (iMask And &H8) Then
        strRights(iNRights) = "Modify group membership"
        iNRights = iNRights + 1
End If
If (iMask And &H10) Then
        strRights(iNRights) = "Read properties"
        iNRights = iNRights + 1
End If
If (iMask And &H20) Then
        strRights(iNRights) = "Write properties"
        iNRights = iNRights + 1
End If
If (iMask And &H40) Then
        strRights(iNRights) = "Delete tree"
        iNRights = iNRights + 1
End If
If (iMask And &H80) Then
        strRights(iNRights) = "List object"
        iNRights = iNRights + 1
End If
If (iMask And &H100) Then
        strRights(iNRights) = "Extended right"
        iNRights = iNRights + 1
End If

If (iMask And &H10000) Then
    strRights(iNRights) = "Delete object"
    iNRights = iNRights + 1
End If
If (iMask And &H20000) Then
    strRights(iNRights) = "Read Security Descriptor"
    iNRights = iNRights + 1
End If
If (iMask And &H40000) Then
    strRights(iNRights) = "Modify DACL"
    iNRights = iNRights + 1
End If
If (iMask And &H80000) Then
    strRights(iNRights) = "Take Ownership"
    iNRights = iNRights + 1
End If
If (iMask And &H100000) Then
    strRights(iNRights) = "Synchronize"
    iNRights = iNRights + 1
End If
If (iMask And &H1000000) Then
    strRights(iNRights) = "Read and write SACL"
    iNRights = iNRights + 1
End If
```

```
If (iMask And &H80000000) Then
   strRights(iNRights) = "Generic Read"
   iNRights = iNRights + 1
End If
If (iMask And &H40000000) Then
   strRights(iNRights) = "Generic Write"
   iNRights = iNRights + 1
End If
If (iMask And &H20000000) Then
   strRights(iNRights) = "Generic Execute"
   iNRights = iNRights + 1
End If
If (iMask And &H10000000) Then
   strRights(iNRights) = "Generic All"
   iNRights = iNRights + 1
End If

' make sure there is something in the list to display
If (iNRights = 0) Then
   iNRights = 1
   strRights(0) = "<No values set>"
End If

End Sub
```

If you're not clear what the meanings of all those different permissions are, that's detailed in the Appendix. For now, I just want to remark on a couple of things: there are a lot of flags because Microsoft have allowed for a very fine degree of control over what you can do with an object. It's a bit different from my old days back when I worked with Unix systems and the permissions we could set were read/write/execute! Hopefully most of the flags are self-explanatory. Notice that Microsoft have separated out permission to read/modify the object itself from permission to read/write its security information, and to list any children it might have. If you don't have permission to see an object, then any function which would return that object will behave as if the object simply isn't there. A couple of specific permissions that are worth commenting on:

Take Ownership. I think this is one of the cleverest permissions around. It makes sure that systems administrators can legitimately check up what's happening in the system, without completely violating your privacy. Let's say you are an administrator and you suspect someone on your system has copied some confidential data about your organization, which they shouldn't have access to. You can't verify this because they've set the permissions on their relevant files to deny everyone else read access (even system administrators). (I know I've swapped from Active Directory to file system here, but don't worry – the same permissions still apply). So what you as a system administrator can do is take ownership of the files, then read them. This may seem like it means the administrators can do whatever they want. However, there's a big disincentive for them not to abuse this power. You see, there's no equivalent permission, *give ownership*. In principle, if you have the appropriate permissions, you can take ownership of a file but you can never renounce ownership by 'giving' a file to someone else. Once the system administrators own a file, they're stuck with it. They can't give it back to the person they've taken it from – that person has to take it back themselves (which they will only be able to do if they too have the Take Ownership permission on that object). So if you take ownership in order to look at a file, the evidence is there that you've done so.

Synchronize. This probably won't be of interest to VB or scripting programmers who write single threaded programs. However, C++ people who write multithreaded programs often have to have threads wait for objects or events. You can only do so if you have permission to synchronize with the object or event you are waiting for.

Generic Read/Write/Execute. These are convenient flags that combine some of the more specific read/write/execute permissions.

Finally, the access flags.

```
Private Sub AccessFlags(iACEFlags, iNACEFlags As Integer, strACEFlags() As String)

If (UBound(strACEFlags) < 20 Or LBound(strACEFlags) > 0) Then
   Err.Raise "Sub AccessFlags was passed an array with invalid bounds"
End If


iNACEFlags = 0

If (iAceFlags And &H2) Then
    strAceFlags(iNAceFlags) = "Inherit ACE"
    iNAceFlags = iNAceFlags + 1
End If
If (iAceFlags And &H4) Then
    strAceFlags(iNAceFlags) = "Don't propagate Inherit ACE"
    iNAceFlags = iNAceFlags + 1
End If
If (iAceFlags And &H8) Then
    strAceFlags(iNAceFlags) = "Inherit only ACE"
    iNAceFlags = iNAceFlags + 1
End If
If (iAceFlags And &H10) Then
    strAceFlags(iNAceFlags) = "ACE is inherited (set by system)"
    iNAceFlags = iNAceFlags + 1
End If
If (iAceFlags And &H20) Then
    strAceFlags(iNAceFlags) = "Inherited ACE is valid (set by system)"
    iNAceFlags = iNAceFlags + 1
End If
If (iAceFlags And &H40) Then
    strAceFlags(iNAceFlags) = "Audit Successful access"
    iNAceFlags = iNAceFlags + 1
End If
If (iAceFlags And &H80) Then
    strAceFlags(iNAceFlags) = "Audit Failed access"
    iNAceFlags = iNAceFlags + 1
End If

' make sure there is something in the list to display
If (iNACEFlags = 0) Then
  iNACEFlags = 1
  strACEFlags(0) = "<No values set>"
End If

End Sub
```

The `ACEFlags` are slightly more interesting, as they break up into three broadly distinct groups. The first three bits indicate whether this access control entry should be automatically copied to any child objects. The possibilities are

❑ Children to inherit this ACE

❑ Children to inherit this ACE but only to one level of depth

❑ Children to inherit the ACE, but this is the only thing the ACE is there for: it shouldn't be applied to this object.

(There's also a 4th option – don't inherit anything – in other words, don't set any of these bits!).

The next two bits are set by the system to indicate if this ACE has been set up as a result of it having been inherited.

The final bits relate to something completely different, which attempts to access this object should be audited – successful attempts in which permission was granted, failed attempts in which permission was denied, or both. Clearly, there's no point setting these bits except in a system ACE.

The Architecture of Security Objects

The Hacker Viewer app was a long bit of code – and I'm not going to apologize because there was a lot of security information we had to get through. That's hopefully given you a flavor of how to read security information from an ADSI object in Active Directory. To make sure things are clear, we'll do a quick recap on how the different ADSI COM objects related to security fit together. Here's the diagram.

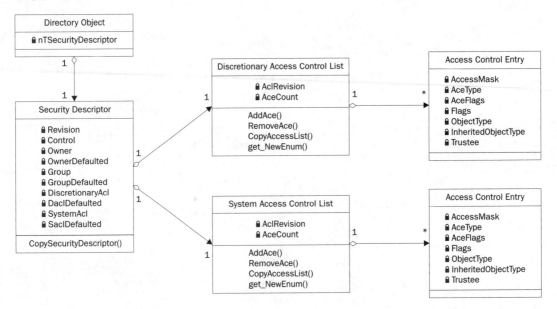

In this diagram, all the objects marked are real COM objects. I've shown all the properties and methods exposed by the security objects. (Although for clarity I've omitted the `IUnknown` and `IDispatch` methods). Strictly, `_NewEnum` in the access control lists should be classed as a property rather than a method but I've marked it as a method since that's usually how it's used. It's the property that lets you get at the collection of access control entries, and as usual is hidden to VB and scripting clients.

The main point I want you to pick up on is that the security objects do NOT form part of the directory tree. That's why we had to write a separate application to look at them – those useful property cache viewers and ADSI object viewer pages that we developed in Chapter 2 and 3 can tell us that there is a property present called `nTSecurityDescriptor`, but they can't look into it to see what's there because they are designed to look at the properties of directory objects.

The fact that these objects do not form part of the directory tree goes hand in hand with a couple of other observations. Let's have a look at the code for that Hacker Viewer app again – in particular the bit where I declare the variables to hold the security objects.

```
Dim oSecDesc As SecurityDescriptor
Dim oDACL As AccessControlList
Dim oSACL As AccessControlList
Dim oACE As AccessControlEntry
```

Notice something funny about it? Why didn't I just write:

```
Dim oSecDesc As IADsSecurityDescriptor
Dim oDACL As IADsAccessControlList
Dim oSACL As IADsAccessControlList
Dim oACE As IADsAccessControlEntry
```

I used the names of the objects rather than the names of the interfaces. In fact, for these particular objects, either set of declarations would have worked quite happily in the code.

The key to understanding why lies in the fact that the security objects are not provider-specific. Let's contrast that with other ADSI objects which represent real objects in the directories. There is no such thing as, for example, a generic ADSI Container COM object, because objects in the directory are provider-specific, the individual providers implement them. If you bind to a container using the LDAP provider, you are binding to a totally different type of COM object from if, say, you bind to a container object using the WinNT provider. It just happens that both COM objects expose the same interfaces, including `IDispatch`, `IUnknown`, `IADS` and `IADsContainer`. For that reason, for the provider-specific objects, you must specify the name of the interface (`IADsContainer`) not the name of the object in VB and C++ code when you bind to an ADSI container object. Ditto for any other ADSI object in the DIT. Indeed, for most directory objects, details of the COM object type are not even placed in the registry so it's not possible for a client application to specify the name of the type of COM object – it just has to ask for an object with the specified `ADsPath`. (The exceptions are the namespace object, and an object known as the provider object – we'll look at the provider object in the next chapter).

However, security objects are different. They are not directory objects. And their implementation is completely provider-independent. For that reason, the COM objects themselves are defined and implemented by the ADSI runtime – and defined in the ActiveDS type library. In fact, you can see this if you look use the OLEView COM object

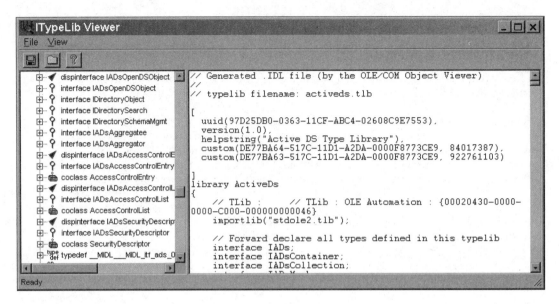

This shows the various interfaces and objects defined in the ActiveDS type library. Lots of the interfaces are there – IADsOpenDSObject, IDirectoryObject, IADsAccessControlEntry, etc., including a few we haven't encountered yet (IADsAggregator, used in provider specific extensions) or which are intended for internal use within ADSI only (like IDirectorySchemaMgmt). The interfaces are the ones marked by lollipops.

There are also a few objects (coclasses) there too, marked by the blue cubes. All the security objects are shown in the screenshot.

So there actually is such a thing as a generic security descriptor COM object. It exposes IADsSecurityDescriptor, which is its **default interface**. This means that in VB it's possible to declare an object as of type SecurityDescriptor, and VB will actually know to look for the IADsSecurityDescriptor interface. Ditto for the ACL and ACE objects. That's why declaring either the object or the interface will work in VB. The two approaches are completely equivalent.

> *Declaring an object as an object rather than an interface is of course only possible in VB. In C++, you must always use only the interface, while in VBScript, the whole discussion is irrelevant since you can't declare the object as anything – you have to rely on late binding and the IDispatch interface to track down the correct methods on the object.*

By the way, if you're not sure how to reproduce this screenshot – type oleview at the command prompt. In the tree that comes up in the left pane, locate **Type Libraries** then under that, **Active DS Type Library** and double click on it.

> *It's crucially important to appreciate that the security objects really are separate objects – not normal ADSI objects. You probably won't be able to browse or search for them anywhere in the directory. And they won't implement IADs – there wouldn't be any point when they don't exist at any point in the directory tree. The only way you can gain access to the security objects is through the nTSecurityDescriptor property of the corresponding ADSI object.*

A complete list of the methods and properties exposed by `IADsSecurityDescriptor`, `IADsAccessControlList` and `IADsAccessControlEntry` is given in Appendix F.

Well, if it looks like I've made a really big deal about the security objects not really being directory objects, there is a good reason for it. Up until now we've merely tried to read the security objects. When you're just reading them, the fact that they are generic COM objects rather than provider specific has little effect on your code. The only noticeable effect is the one we've just discussed – that you can use the object names rather than the interface names when you declare the variables in VB.

That's not the case if you actually want to modify the security information for an object. That's the subject of the next code sample, and we'll see there that the fact that we're dealing with non-provider-specific security objects is actually quite significant when we set about modifying them.

Modifying Security Information: Web Page Sample

I'm going to start off with a bit of code that – from everything I've told you so far – you might have expected to be able to use to change security information with.

I don't want to change anything too drastic, so I'm going to modify a reasonably unimportant user account on my system – Geri Halliwell's account – the account I added at the end of Chapter 4. I'm going to set all the access control entries in the discretionary access control list to be inheritable. That means setting the `ACEFlag` in each ACE to 2. Usually for setting a particular flag in a value which contains lots of flags bit-wise-ORed together, as the `ACEFlags` are, setting a flag would involve reading the value, then performing a bit-wise OR operation of the old value with the new flag and writing the result back. In this case, I'm not interested in the other flags in the `ACEFlags` value. The `ACEFlags` include a couple of flags to do with auditing – and I'm going to assume here I don't want any auditing – and a few other flags that are set if the ACEs in the ACL have already been inherited. But I want Geri's ACEs to look like they are original ACEs from which inheritance may take place afresh. So I don't want any of these flags set either. For these reasons I'm OK just writing a straight 2 into the `ACEFlags` value.

Here's the code. Notice, by the way, that I've taken the trouble to authenticate myself as the Administrator. I need to do that because changing security permissions on someone's account needs high privileges – and the web page will normally run under the Internet guest account.

```
<%@ Language = VBScript %>
<html>
<head>
<title> Modifying ACEs </title>
</head>

<body>

<h1> Modifying ACEs </h1>
```

This page sets all the Access Control entries in Geri Halliwell's user account to be inheritable.

```
<table border = 4>
<tr> <td> Trustee </td><td>Old ACEFlag </td> <td> New ACEFlag </td> </tr>
<%
```

```
Dim oADs
Dim oSecDesc
Dim oACL
Dim oACE


Set oADsNamespace = GetObject("LDAP:")

Set oADs = oADsNamespace.OpenDSObject("LDAP://CN=Geri Halliwell,OU=Pop Star
Users,DC=TopOfThePops,DC=Fame,DC=com", _
       "Administrator@Fame.com", "MyPassword", 0)
Set oSecDesc = oADs.Get("ntSecurityDescriptor")Set oSecDesc =
oADs.Get("ntSecurityDescriptor")

Set oACL = oSecDesc.DiscretionaryAcl
For Each oACE In oACL
  Response.Write "<tr><td>" & oACE.Trustee & "</td>"
  Response.Write "<td>" & oACE.ACEFlags & "</td>"
  oACE.ACEFlags = 2
  Response.Write "<td>" & oACE.ACEFlags & "</td></tr>"
Next

oADs.SetInfo
%>
</table>

<p>

</body>
</html>
```

This code works on the principle that if the flags are exposed as automation properties, we should simply change the values of these properties and call SetInfo to write the changes to the directory. In fact so confident am I that this will work that I haven't even bothered adding any error handling. I've been a bit cheeky in that I haven't called SetInfo then GetInfo again before writing out the 'new' results, which I strictly should do. I haven't done so because I don't want to get sidetracked into showing lots of extra code that stores arrays of data to put in the table in what's supposed to be a simple page that changes some flags. I do, however, call SetInfo at the end of the script to (hopefully) write my changes to the directory. My check on whether the changes worked will be to refresh the page.

So let's look at the results.

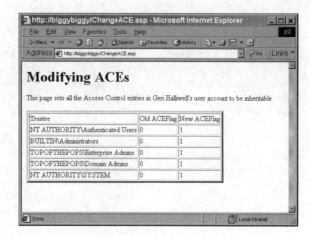

So far so good. Don't you think that's an ace page? Unfortunately when I ran the script again by refreshing the page, I got exactly the same results. In other words, despite calling SetInfo, our changes hadn't actually gone past the property cache to the actual directory. So what's gone wrong?

I'll start by telling you the solution, and then we'll discuss what the problem with the above code is. The solution is to insert an extra line before we call SetInfo, as follows:

```
oADs.Put "ntSecurityDescriptor", oSecDesc
oADs.SetInfo
```

The reason why we need to do this has to do with the security objects not being normal objects in the directory tree. Let's recall that an ADSI object that actually wraps a directory object will maintain a property cache that mirrors the contents of the directory. Calling SetInfo will write any changes to the directory.

But since the access control list and entry are not properties of the directory object, they are not stored in the cache. In fact, they cannot be. You see I made a big issue of the fact that the security objects are implemented by the COM runtime – not by the individual providers. That means that the implementations of the security objects cannot include any knowledge about any individual provider. The ADSI security descriptor, access control list, and access control entry objects *must* simply be COM objects that store a few properties without being aware of any relationship to any outside objects (such as the *real* Windows 2000 security descriptors etc.) You could even argue that I was misleading you a bit when I said earlier that the security COM objects were wrappers around the real NT objects – they're not, they're just isolated sets of properties. They have no way of writing themselves to the actual directory. This is the cost of having generic pre-written COM components.

So what links them to the directory? That's where the ADSI directory object comes in. The object that exposes IADS is provider-specific, and really does know how to write data to the directory when SetInfo is called. It is this object that knows that if any change is made to the security descriptor – as described in the case of Active Directory by the nTSecurityDescriptor attribute – then it will need to read through the security descriptor and access control lists etc. and replicate the information in them to the directory. But without the line that sets the security descriptor the directory has no way of knowing that the security descriptor has been changed. (Strictly speaking, we haven't changed the security descriptor; we've only changed other objects it refers to).

```
oADs.Put "ntSecurityDescriptor", oSecDesc
```

By adding this line, we are fooling the ADSI object into thinking that a new security descriptor has been placed in the cache, when actually it's just the same (possibly modified) security descriptor sitting there. Hence the directory object now believes that when `SetInfo` is called, the security descriptor will be one of the properties that need to be updated. (Luckily for us, the LDAP provider isn't intelligent enough to notice that we're actually putting the same security descriptor back again!).

The same principle actually applies to the property entry and property value items. Recall that these COM objects do not wrap up any object in the directory tree. Like the security objects, they are implemented by the COM runtime and are not provider-specific. The difference is that for these property cache objects, there is no temptation to think you can modify them by simply setting properties on the property list and property entry objects because there are well defined methods in `IPropertyList` that are there in order to apply changes made in property entries and values to the property cache.

Security Information in other Directories

All the discussion up till now has focused on Active Directory. In fact, of the Microsoft-supplied providers, both of the previous two samples of reading and writing security information will *only* work with Active Directory. The Hacker View app will also, as it happens, work with the StarRaiders provider because I've written StarRaiders in a way that allows clients to view its security information with security descriptors etc., although in StarRaiders they are read-only. More on that in Chapter 9.

Not all directories exposed by ADSI providers expose their security information. This doesn't mean they don't implement security. It simply means that the settings that govern the permissions for different people to access different objects are not made visible to ADSI clients.

The WinNT provider falls into this category. When it comes to deciding who is allowed to do what to particular objects in the directory, WinNT implements exactly the same security as Active Directory does on the same objects. This must be the case because both the WinNT and Active Directory take their security from the underlying NT technology. However, the WinNT provider doesn't expose any security information to clients to view or modify. There are simply no properties corresponding to `nTSecurityDescriptor` in WinNT, so if you want to access security descriptors etc. then you will need to use Active Directory, not WinNT.

The Microsoft 5.5 Exchange Directory – also accessed through the LDAP provider – does implement the security objects, so in principle our samples should be able to work with the exchange directory. However our sample code won't work with the Exchange directory because of a technical detail. The property on each directory ADSI object which let's you get at the security descriptor isn't called `nTSecurityDescriptor` in Exchange: It's called `NT-Security-Descriptor`. Apart from that everything works the same way as for Active Directory.

Now if you're anything like me, you're probably thinking that is rather frustrating (to put it mildly). The unfortunate fact is that there is no standard for what attribute name the security descriptor should have, so we are going to have to cope with differences between providers. At the moment it's not clear whether this difference will be resolved when the next version of Exchange Server – the one that should be compatible with Active Directory – is released. Until then, if we want our Hacker Viewer client – or any similar ADSI client – to be able to look at security information in different directories, including Active Directory and the Exchange Directory, we're going to potentially have to do some workarounds.

One way you might think of is to go by which provider we are using – which basically means extracting the namespace from the `ADsPath` of the object we are looking at, and using that to work out how to get to the security descriptor. Unfortunately this approach won't work because Active Directory and the Exchange Directory are both accessed through the same LDAP provider. If we are given an LDAP `ADsPath`, there is no way of deducing from the `ADsPath` whether it is the `ADsPath` to an object in Active Directory, the Exchange Directory, the Site Server Membership Directory, or any other LDAP directory. That basically leaves us with the option of trying out all the different attribute names we know about which could possibly lead us to the security descriptor – and seeing if any of them work! That's clearly not a particularly neat solution.

Before we see what the solution to this problem is, there is another point I want to mention here. We know that objects in directories aren't the only things that have security descriptors attached to them to enable security permissions to be set. Files and folders on NTFS file systems do, as do registry keys. The access control lists on these are the same NT access control lists that we see in Active Directory – so they are going to be implemented in exactly the same way. Wouldn't it be nice if we could use ADSI to access any of this security information? Well Microsoft have come to the rescue here. They've released a resource kit with ADSI 2.5, which contains objects designed to let you do things that are difficult or impossible to do with ADSI itself, but which are sufficiently related to ADSI that it would be useful to be able to do them. That's the subject of our next section.

The ADSI 2.5 Resource Kit.

The ADSI 2.5 Resource Kit consists of a set of COM components to perform extra tasks that are difficult to do with the main ADSI interfaces and runtime. They aren't all related to security, but since here is a good place to introduce them, they are

- ❑ `ADsFactory`
  Lets you create ADSI objects in client-side scripts running web browsers.

- ❑ `ADsSecurity` and `ADsSID`
  Lets you access security descriptors and security ID s in Active Directory or Exchange Server. Also works for registry keys and files.

- ❑ `ADsRas` (WinNT ADSI Extension) for RAS Permission
  Lets you set RAS permissions.

- ❑ `ADsVersion`
  Lets you check what version of ADSI you are running.

- ❑ `ADsError`
  Makes it easier for you to display ADSI extended error messages.

If you use any resource kit components, it is important to be aware that they are unsupported. Microsoft recommends you treat them as samples. However, they are quite useful, and we're going to use the `ADsSecurity` object here to extend the capabilities of our Hacker Viewer. We'll also use it as a demonstration of how to register all the other resource kit components.

The ADsSecurity object

The `ADsSecurity` object allows us to get or set a security descriptor or SID (security ID – we'll cover what these are later in the chapter). The full list of methods it implements is

Name	Description
GetSecurityDescriptor	gets a security descriptor
SetSecurityDescriptor	sets a security descriptor
GetSID	gets a security ID
GetSecurityDescriptorAs	gets a security descriptor in alternative formats

These functions all take as a parameter the path name of the object you want the security descriptor or SID for. Note I've been careful to say pathname here, not `ADsPath`. This is because the names accepted by the `ADsSecurityObject` methods are:

❑ The `ADsPath` of an Active Directory object

❑ The `ADsPath` of an object in the Exchange Directory

❑ The pathname of a file or folder, in the form `file://[\\ServerName/]Path`

❑ The pathname of a registry key, in the form `RGY://[ServerName/]Path`

Apart from that, I shouldn't need to explain what the methods do should I! The difference between `GetSecurityDescriptor` and `GetSecurityDescriptorAs` is that `GetSecurityDescriptor` returns an ADSI SecurityDescriptor COM object that exposes `IADsSecurityDescriptor`. `GetSecurityDescriptorAs` allows you to select other formats that are closer to the format in which the descriptor is actually stored, including as a hex string, as a simple array of bytes, and – on Windows 2000 – as a string that represents the contents of the descriptor in a security descriptor language. However, here we're going to stick to COM objects. Easier to get at the ACEs that way!

Modifying the Hacker Viewer to use the ADsSecurity object

The first step is to register the `ADsSecurity` object. Because it is not technically part of ADSI, it needs to be installed separately. It is supplied with the SDK, and you can install it by running `regsvr32` on the dll `adssecurity.dll`, which you'll find in the resourcekit folder of the ADSI 2.5 SDK. In other words – since I installed the SDK to `E:\ADSISDK`, I type at the command prompt:

```
regsvr32 E:\adisdk\resourcekit\adssecurity.dll
```

You'll find this folder contains dlls for all the resource kit objects – you'll need to run `regsvr32` separately to register any others you want to use.

If you are running VB, you will need to add a reference to the appropriate type library in your project. For the `ADsSecurity` object, it's the ADsSecurity 2.5 type library. If you're working in C++, you can either `#import` the type library, or `#include` the C++ headers. You'll find these in the ResourceKit/SDK folder of the ADSI SDK. The relevant GUIDs you need are `CLSID_ADsSecurity` and `IID_IADsSecurity`, for the interface `IADsSecurity`.

Since the security object accesses the security descriptor directly from the pathname, this means that we no longer need to separately bind to the ADSI directory object in our Hacker View app. There is a downside to this, in that we are no longer able to call `IADsObjectOptions::SetObjectOption()` on our object to enable us to read the system ACL. If we are using the `ADsSecurity` object there's unfortunately no way round this. If you know that you will need to use the system ACL then you'll have to access the `nTSecurityDescriptor` property in Active Directory manually rather than using the `ADsSecurity` object.

This means we can get rid of our `oADsObject` global variable that was used to perform this bind, and we can simplify our `BindToNewObject` procedure. Recall that this procedure is there to bind to the ADSI object, and – if that succeeded – call `RefreshData` to actually get the information. Now this procedure simply reads:

```
Private Sub BindToNewObject()

listSecDesc.Clear
listDACL.Clear
listSACL.Clear
listDACEs.Clear
listSACEs.Clear

RefreshData


End Sub
```

The only other change is to the start of the procedure to refresh the data, for which we now need to create an `ADsSecurity` object and use it to get the security descriptor:

```
Private Sub RefreshData()

On Error Resume Next
Dim oSecDesc As SecurityDescriptor
Dim oDACL As IADsAccessControlList
Dim oSACL As IADsAccessControlList
Dim oACE As AccessControlEntry
Dim oADsSec As New ADsSecurity

Err.Clear
Set oSecDesc = oADsSec.GetSecurityDescriptor(texADsPath.Text)
If (Err.Number > 0 Or oSecDesc Is Nothing) Then
  listSecDesc.AddItem "Failed to obtain a security descriptor for this object"
  Exit Sub
End If
```

Notice we have directly created a new security object rather than attempting to bind to one. In C++ the equivalent code would read:

```
hr = CoCreateInstance(CLSID_ADsSecurity, NULL, CLSCTX_INPROC_SERVER,
IID_IADsSecurity, (void**)&spADsSec);
```

The results of making these changes can be seen here. Our new revised Hacker View app can still see Active Directory objects, but it can also now be used to view registry entries, or – as shown in the screenshot – folders.

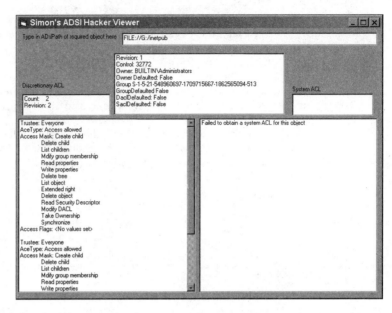

Note, however, that viewing and modifying security information is as far as you can get with ADSI and the ADSI resource kit. You cannot, for example, start browsing or adding folders. You need the Windows Scripting Host to do that. If you need to go down that road, you might want to consult the Wrox book, *Windows Script Host Programmer's Reference by Dino Esposito* (ISBN 1-861002-65-3).

Modifying Security Information with the ADSI Browsers

Up until now I've shied away from using the standard Microsoft-supplied ADSI Browsers to view or modify any security information. The reason was that I wanted to give you a good idea of the architecture of the security objects. And I wanted to give you a feel for seeing how security descriptors and so on work, by showing you an application that put all the information on the screen at once. The standard Microsoft ADSI browsers don't really do that – so I just took the chance to write our own one instead!

But having said that, `adsvw.exe` and the `ADSIEDIT` snap-in are reasonably convenient for viewing and modifying security information on ADSI objects, without having to do any coding. And this chapter wouldn't be complete without a brief explanation of how to do that. So here goes.

ADSVW.EXE

In `adsvw.exe`, you can get to view the security information by selecting the `nTSecurityDescriptor` property of an object in Active Directory thus:

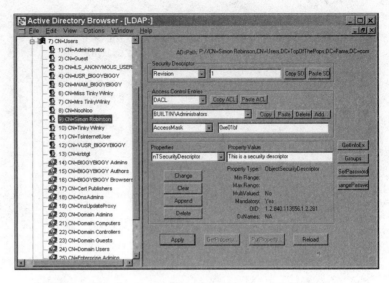

`adsvw.exe` is able to see that it is looking at an Active Directory security descriptor attribute, and hence modifies its user interface in the right hand pane to let you modify security descriptor settings. A drop down list box in the **Access Control Entries** area of the pane appears to let you select either the discretionary or system access control list – but don't be fooled. You can't use the present version of `adsvw.exe` to look at or modify the system ACL. If you try selecting the system ACL the other list boxes will go blank, and so you won't be able to look at the ACL

The next drop down list box lets you select (by trustee) the ACE to examine, and the final list box gives you access to the properties of the ACE. It's not a brilliant user interface when it comes to giving you a quick overview of the security information, since it only lets you look at one property of one access control entry at a time, and the bit-wise flags, such as the access mask, are only displayed in hexadecimal numerical format. There are also a couple of properties that you cannot see (such as the revision level of the ACLs and whether they are defaulted). But it is convenient for letting you check a specific property. Modifying an ACL or ACE is also easy, using any of the buttons supplied for that purpose.

ADSIEDIT

To view security properties in ADSIEDIT, you have to locate the object you want to examine in the tree view, right click on it and select Properties to bring up the properties property sheet. Click on the Security tab and you'll see the list of Access Control Entries, with some of the permissions for the selected entry.

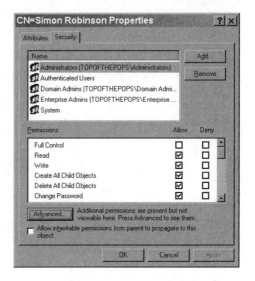

This screenshot is taken from ADSIEDIT examining my own user account. In fact this dialog box is almost identical to the one you get for file security if you right click on a file or folder in Windows Explorer , select Properties then select the Security tab of the property sheet that pops up. It's not surprising since the two dialog boxes are doing basically the same thing to different objects. The Advanced button allows you to see information for the system ACL – and with ADSIEDIT you really can get to the auditing information. As with `adsvw.exe` you can add or remove objects. ADSIEDIT has a smaller range of properties that you can examine, but it does have the advantage of breaking the access mask into the individual permissions, which you can check or uncheck – as in the screenshot.

Auditing

So far, although I've indicated that the system access control lists used for auditing work in exactly the same way as the discretionary access control lists used to determine permissions, our discussion has focused entirely on the discretionary ACLs. In the next couple of sections we're going to turn our attention to the system ACLs, and show how to arrange for objects in Active Directory to be audited. We will cover how to do this both by using the Active Directory management tools supplied for this purpose, and by using ADSI to do the same thing programmatically.

But before we can do any of this, we need to enable auditing.

Enabling Auditing: Group Policies

By default, all auditing is disabled on a Windows 2000(or NT4) computer, and in a Windows 2000 (or NT4) domain. This is sensible because auditing can quickly take up a lot of file space, as well as having a negative performance effect, so it really should only be enabled when it is really needed. The way to enable auditing is using the **group policy editor**. We haven't yet encountered this tool – or for that matter **group policies**. A group policy is a set of settings that indicate how computers in a domain should work. It applies in particular to many aspects of security – such as how often users should be forced to change their passwords and how long locked out accounts should stay locked out for. It also covers areas like hardware devices – some of the settings for print queues etc. The idea is that by setting a group policy, there is no need to configure computers individually – a computer can simply be assigned to a certain policy, in much the same way that user accounts are assigned to groups. The main difference is that a computer can only be assigned to one group policy, whereas users can be assigned to as many groups as desired.

As you'll have guessed from this discussion, it is the group policy that controls whether auditing is enabled.

For a computer in a domain, there are two levels of policy to consider. Firstly, there is a local group policy for that computer. This is not stored in Active Directory, since Active Directory is only interested in domain settings. Then there is the domain group policy to which the computer has been assigned. The domain group policy always takes priority. If a particular setting has not been configured in the domain group policy, then Windows will check the local group policy; otherwise the domain group policy applies.

Within Active Directory, group policies are stored under the Policies container in the System container, as shown on the left of this `adsvw.exe` screenshot

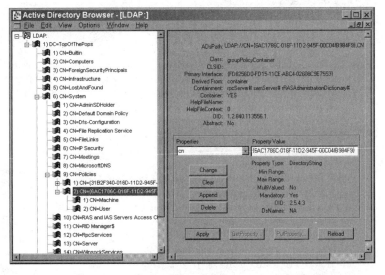

The entries under the Policies container are all group policies. The two that are supplied when you install Active Directory are the **default domain policy** and the **default domain controllers policy,** but you can create other policies if you want. The difference is that the default domain controllers policy applies to domain controllers (unless you specifically assign a domain controller to another group policy), whereas the default domain policy applies to everything else. The one I've selected is the default domain controllers policy – though I guess I might just forgive you if you don't think that's obvious from its distinguished name! These GUIDs get everywhere... If you're interested you can look at it quite easily by using the property cache viewer web page we developed in Chapter 2 to look at it, and here's a screenshot of what you should see:

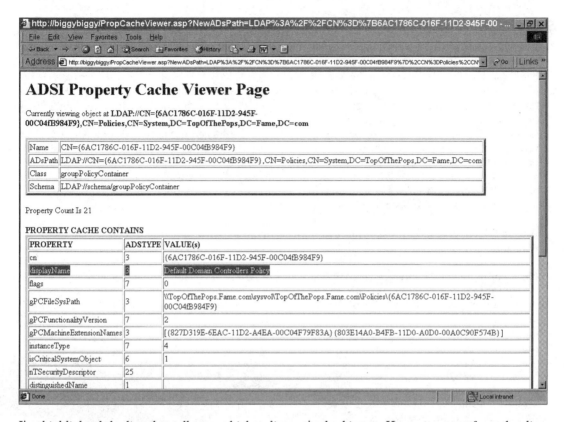

I've highlighted the line that tells you which policy we're looking at. However, apart from that line there's not that much in the properties that is that meaningful at first glance – in fact, at present it's not possible to use Active Directory to modify the group policies programmatically, though Microsoft have promised that such a facility will be added in the future. So for the time being we're stuck with Microsoft's group policy editor tool.

The Group Policy Editor

The Group Policy Editor isn't one of the administrative tools that Microsoft have made very easy to access, since it's not considered the kind of tool most people – even most administrators – are going to need that often. As usual in Windows 2000, it's an MMC snap-in, but in this case it's not one that you can get to from the Start Menu. This means you're going to have to run MMC from the command prompt and add the snap-in manually. So at the command prompt type MMC. When the blank console appears, click on the Console menu, and then select Add/Remove Snap-in. You'll get an Add Snap-In property sheet.

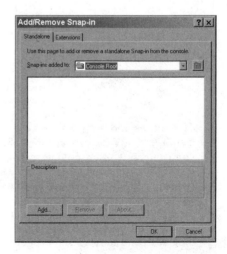

Leave the Standalone tab up, and click on Add. This gives you a dialog in which you can actually select the snap-in you want to add. Locate the Group Policy snap-in, and click on Add.

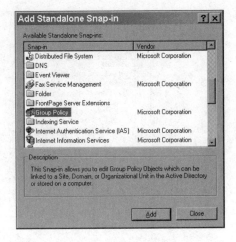

For most snap-ins, this would be enough and you would now be able to go back through the various Close and OK buttons to get back to the console – now with the Group Policy editor in place. However, for Group Policy, this isn't enough. Recall that there are a number of different group policies available, ranging from the one for the local computer to any of the ones stored in Active Directory. You might even want to use the group policy editor to manage group policy on another computer. So the next stage here is a little wizard that asks you what group policy you want to manage and configures the group policy editor appropriately. The default is your local computer group policy, but you can browse around for other policies. Here I've looked for the domain policies

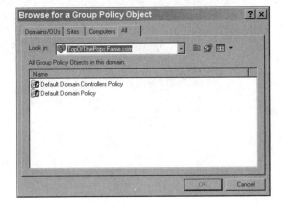

Having selected an appropriate policy you can return to the MMC console. If you think you'll want to play with group policies again it might be worth your while saving the console – either to the desktop or to the Start Menu so you can get to it again without having to manually add the group policy editor to a blank console.

Anyway, here's a snap-in to help me manage my audits which I prepared earlier. I've taken the liberty of adding three different instances of the Group Policy Editor to it, to manage policy on my local computer (in this case, my BiggyBiggy domain controller), and also the default domain and default domain controllers policies.

In these snap-ins, the audit policy is under Computer Configuration/Windows Settings/Security Settings. Before we actually set the audit policy settings, we need to enable auditing in the security options (select the appropriate item in the right hand pane, right click on it and select Properties to change a setting). In this case I've just enabled the Audit Access to Internal System Objects.

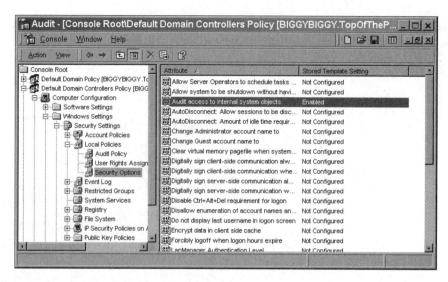

Having done that, I proceed to actually set the audit policy:

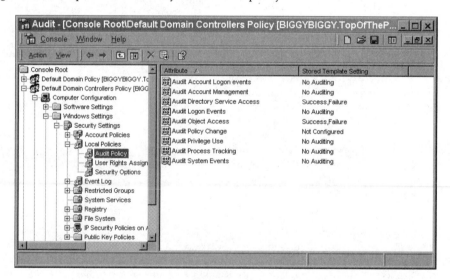

As this screenshot shows, there are a number of different types of event that might be audited. I've enabled Directory Service Access – which means accessing active directory objects, and Object Access – which will allow auditing of access to folders and files. In both cases, I've enabled auditing for successful and failed attempts to perform operations.

That, actually, is it. We have now set auditing for domain controllers in my domain. I've picked that group policy because it happens that I'm going to be working on my domain controller. If I'd wanted to enable auditing on a member workstation, I would have gone for the default domain policy instead.

I've spent a while going through this process because it's not obvious (or particularly well documented), but in practice once you know what to do it's not much more than a few mouse clicks to set up auditing.

One more screenshot. This is just to demonstrate what I was saying about the local group policy being overridden by a domain one if possible. If, in the same console, I look at the audit settings for the local group policy I find this:

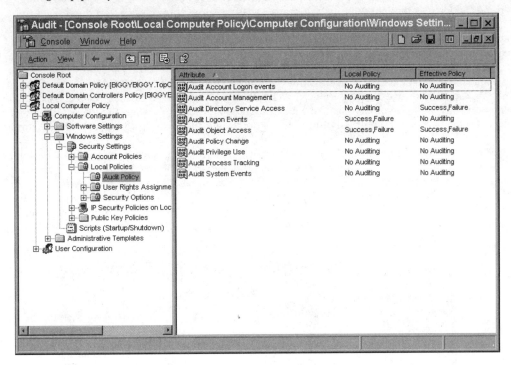

In this screenshot, I've actually made a couple of changes to the local auditing policy – but in both cases I've been overridden by the domain policy, which appears as the Effective Policy.

If you are running NT4, you won't have a group policy editor. But you'll actually find editing policies is easier than in Windows 2000. Just open the user manager or the user manager for domains in the Administrative Tools menu, and select the Policies menu option. This will give you access to all of the options just discussed (apart, of course, from the ones that aren't applicable to NT4).

We have now enabled auditing. Now there are two requirements before access to a particular object is audited. The relevant type of auditing should be enabled in the Group Policy, but also, appropriate access control entries should be set in the system ACL for the object in question. As it happens for Active Directory, this is taken care of for us already. Recall from the Hacker Viewer screenshots that all Active Directory objects already have an auditing system ACL inherited from the domain object, and which instructs auditing for both failed and successful attempts to access the object by anyone, and for a wide range of actions. This means that – if we don't care what Active Directory object is audited – we can move straight on to looking at the auditing results without having to do any extra ADSI programming. For this we need the event viewer.

The Event Viewer

We've mentioned the **event log** a couple of times without really going into any detail of what it is. It's actually an NT Service. You'll find it in the Services snap-in as the Event Log Service, or in the WinNT provider in ADSI as the object named `Eventlog`. It's considered a service that is essential to the running of Windows, so you won't be able to stop or pause it. It consists of a number of logs, to which *events* may be written. An event in this context is not a VB event – it's simply anything that happens which it is thought administrators may wish to know about. Since you don't want to be bothered with something like a dialog box every time something occurs which meets this description, details of the event are quietly written to the event log in the background, for administrators to inspect later on if they wish.

It is possible to set a maximum size for the event log in order to prevent it filling up your hard disk. (In fact, a maximum size is set by default). When the log has reached this size, it will by default stop logging events, though you can instead set it so that each new event when the log is full will simply overwrite the earliest event already in the log, so that only the most up-to-date events are stored.

There's a fairly sophisticated API around the event log, allowing applications to read and write events in the log, but the easiest way to view it is using a tool called the **Event Viewer**. On Windows 2000, the event viewer comes in two flavors – as an MMC snap-in which you can load by starting an empty MMC console and adding the Event Viewer snap-in, or as an executable, `eventvwr.exe`, which you can either run from the command prompt, or which is also available on the Start menu, under Programs | Administrative Tools. On Windows 2000, `eventvwr.exe` is designed to look to some extent like an MMC snap-in:

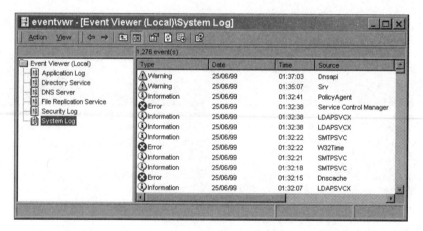

On NT4, you can also type `event vwr` *to run an event viewer, although the user interface is different and has only one pane.*

The screenshot shows that the event log has a number of sections, designed to hold different types of events. Within each section, there are also different categories of events: Information/Warning/Error/System Audit. Events generated by Windows itself are written to the system log, whereas if your application needs to generate events it will generally write them to the Application log. System audits are written to the security log, and there are certain services that have their own logs: Active Directory itself, as well as the DNS Server and File Replication Services. To check up on the events we've caused to be audited for Active Directory, we need to look at the Security Log:

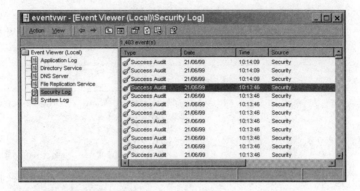

We can find out more information about an event by double clicking on it in the Event log, although for system audits the additional information isn't that great.

Back to ADSI: The IADsObjectOptions Interface

There's not really any point giving an example of how to manipulate the system ACL using ADSI since it's pretty much identical to the discretionary ACL for which we've already gone through a couple of examples.. The only difference is that before accessing the system ACL it is necessary to call the IADsObjectOptions::SetOption() method. Since we haven't gone over what this ADSI interface does yet, we'll do so here.

The point of the IADsObjectOptions interface is that there are some features of ADSI objects – particularly objects in Active Directory, though the principles apply to other providers too – which are not commonly used. It therefore doesn't make sense to have these features enabled, taking up space in the property cache and possibly giving a performance hit, when they will most likely never be used. IADsObjectOptions allows us to specify whether we do actually want an option to be enabled. It implements two methods, GetOption() and SetOption(), which respectively let you check what options have been set, and set new options.

We've seen the SetOption method at work in the Hacker Viewer app. To recap, it went:

```
' make sure we can read the system ACL
Dim oADsObjectOptions As IADsObjectOptions
Set oADsObjectOptions = oADsObject
oADsObjectOptions.SetOption ADS_OPTION_SECURITY_MASK, 15
```

SetOption and GetOption both take two parameters: an integer to specify the option in which we are interested, and a VARIANT that stores the value of the option. Since this example is in VB, it is possible to use a more specific data type for the value – in this case the number 15, and it will be automatically converted to a VARIANT for us.

The options we can set are defined in an `ADS_OPTION_ENUM` enumeration. The one we're interested in this chapter is `ADS_OPTION_SECURITY_MASK`. For this option, the value is an integer that is combined as a bit-wise mask from the following values:

Symbol	Value	Meaning
ADS_SECURITY_INFO_OWNER	1	Allows reading/writing to security information concerned with the owner of the object
ADS_SECURITY_INFO_GROUP	2	Allows reading/writing to security information concerned with the group of the object
ADS_SECURITY_INFO_DACL	4	Allows reading/writing to security information concerned with the discretionary ACL
ADS_SECURITY_INFO_SACL	8	Allows reading/writing to security information concerned with the system ACL

If these flags are not set, you will not be able to access the relevant information in the security descriptor and access control lists for the object. So by setting this option to 15, we are making sure we can get to all the security information. It's not however necessary to do this unless you specifically want to get to the system ACL because by default if you do not explicitly set this option, it will have a value of 7.

The remaining options which you can set are concerned with searching, and will need to be set if you wish to specify in a search that either names of servers are to be returned, referrals are to be set or a page size will be set. Full details are in Appendix F.

Modifying System ACLs Using ADSIEDIT

I've already mentioned that we cannot get to the system ACL using `adsvw.exe`. It's hard to be certain but I'd hazard a good guess the reason is that internally, `adsvw.exe` doesn't enable the appropriate object options.

However, it is quite simple to set up auditing for any given object using ADSIEDIT or `adsvw.exe` – just bring up the security dialog and select the advanced options, then Auditing, and create a new Access Control Entry. We're going to have a go programmatically. And since we haven't had a VBA example for a while, I'm going to code it up in an Excel macro.

Permissions and Privileges

So far, we've implicitly covered authentication (telling the system who you are) and one aspect of authorization (where the system decides what you are allowed to do).

There are actually two aspects of authorization, and so far we've only covered one of them. The questions to be asked when you want to perform an action are: Do you have the **privilege** to do the type of action you want to do? And do you then have **permission** to access the particular object? Note I've chosen my words carefully there, as privilege and permission are specific technical terms with different meanings.

A privilege (often called a **right**) is something like 'Perform Backup Operations' or 'Access the Computer from the Network'. It is associated with a user or a group.

A permission is something like 'Read' or 'Write'. It differs from a privilege in that it is associated with an object like a file, rather than just with a user account. It's permissions that are checked against access control lists – this never happens with privileges. When I say objects – we are usually talking about files or folders, but there are other objects to which permissions can apply. For example, kernel objects such as mutexes or semaphores. The general term for an object that has its own security descriptor and access control lists is a **securable object**. Privileges are not associated with any particular object. The privilege to Perform Backup Operations doesn't apply to any one file – if you have this privilege, then you have the right to backup anything on the whole computer.

Auditing can be applied to permissions or privileges, depending on what you choose to audit. If you look back at the screenshot from the Group Policy Editor above, in which the items you could audit were listed, you'll see a number of options that are clearly associated with permissions – like the two we've been using, *Audit Object Access* and *Audit Directory Service Access*, as well as one that is explicitly to do with privileges, *Audit Privilege Use*, which will audit actions taken by the trustee that require use of that trustee's privileges.

Before we take a look at the privileges available in more detail, there's just one more term I want to introduce you to, which we're going to need before we delve much deeper into NT security. We've encountered **trustee** as the generic term for a user or group that an access control entry applies to. More generically, any entity, be it user, group, or process, which attempts any operation requiring security access, is termed a **security principal**. There. Bet you never thought of yourself as a security principal before.

Anyway, time to run through the privileges available on Windows 2000. This is the list of available privileges. Note that most of these privileges also apply to NT4 as well.

Privilege	Description
Act as Part of the Operating System	This privilege effectively gives the process virtually unlimited rights on the local machine. It can authenticate as any user and request additional accesses be put in its access token. It is generally not recommended that this privilege be given to any account other than the LocalSystem account, under which many systems processes run and which has this privilege by default.
Add Workstations to a Domain	This privilege allows a process to add a computer to a domain.
Back Up Files and Directories	This is required for backing up your file system. This privilege allows the process to read files and traverse down the folder hierarchy, irrespective of whether the individual files and folders grant the process permission to read them.
Bypass Traverse Checking	This privilege means that the user can locate a file or folder even if folders higher in the folder hierarchy do not give permission to examine their contents. In other words, the user may not be able to list the files in a folder, but he can pass through that folder in order to locate a specific file.

Table Continued on Following Page

Privilege	Description
Change the System Time	This privilege grants the right to set the time for the computer's internal clock.
Create a Token Object	Allows the process to create a token in order to get access to local resources. This privilege is by default given to the LocalSystem account, and it is recommended that it should not be given to any other accounts.
Create Permanent Shared Objects	Allows creation of shared objects.
Create a pagefile	This privilege allows the computer to set the size of the page file used to store data that has been temporarily swapped out of memory.
Debug programs	Grants the right to attach a debugger to any other process.
Enable trusted for delegation on user and computer accounts	Gives the right to set the Trusted for Delegation flag on a user or computer object – this flag gives processes running as that user to access resources on other machines.
Force shutdown of a remote system	Grants the right to shut down a computer from across the network
Generate security audits	Grants the right to generate auditing entries in the security log
Increase quotas	Allows a process to modify the processor quotas assigned to other processes.
Increase scheduling priority	Grants the right to increase the execution priority of any other process provided you have write access to that process
Load and unload device drivers	Allows a process to install Plug and Play device drivers. Note that this does not apply to non Plug and Play drivers, which can only be installed by administrators.
Lock pages in memory	This privilege is obsolete in Windows 2000.
Manage auditing and security log	Allows a process to modify the options for auditing individual resources, and to view and clear the security log in which audits are recorded.
Modify firmware environment values	Grants the right to modify system environment variables
Profile a single process	Allows use of performance monitoring tools to monitor non-system processes.
Profile system performance	As for Profile a Single Process, but grants the right to use performance monitoring tools to monitor system processes

Privilege	Description
Replace a process-level token	Grants the right to replace the default access token associated with a sub-process
Restore files and directories	Needed in order to restore backed up files and folders. Grants rights to write files even if the files have not given the relevant permissions to this process
Shut down the system	Gives the right to shut down the system.
Take ownership of files or other objects	Gives the right to take ownership of any object in the system
Undock a laptop	Allows undocking of laptops

If you want to edit the rights, or just see who's got what rights, the Group Policy is the place to look.

On NT4 you may be used to editing rights under the Policy menu of the user manager. However, you won't find the rights under the equivalent Windows 2000 tool, the Users and Computers snap-in. In Windows 2000 you will have to load up the Group Policy Snap-in.

The User Rights Assignment is located next to the Auditing Policy, under Computer Configuration/Windows Settings/Local Policy. The screenshot is of the local policy on BIGGYBIGGY, and once again, the local policy is in many cases overridden by the domain controllers policy.

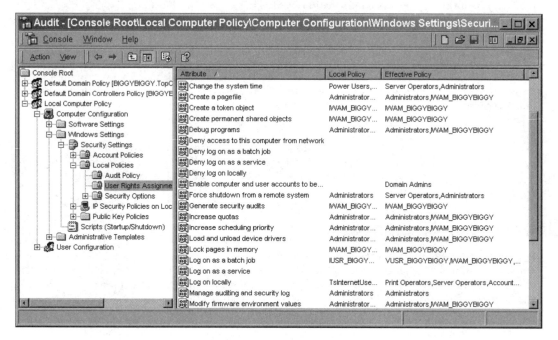

How Windows Checks Your Rights: Security IDs and Access Tokens.

We've now pretty well finished seeing how to modify security permissions using ADSI. The last part of this chapter gets a bit more theoretical, and we're going to have a brief look at what is going on behind the scenes when Windows authenticates you and authorizes you to do whatever you want to do. We'll cover the access tokens that are used to tell Windows what you can do, before going on to look at data encryption and Kerberos security.

One of the attributes that user accounts have in both Active Directory and the WinNT provider is the **security ID**, or **SID**. This is also retrievable as a method `GetSecurityID` on the `ADsSecurity` resource kit object. The SID is actually the real account name of a user or group. Think of it in much the same way that you'd think of GUIDs used for naming things (although the format is different from a GUID. A SID is not a 128-bit number. Just as the 'real' name for `IUnknown` isn't really `IUnknown` but 00000000-0000-0000-C000-000000000046, and the 'real' names of all Active Directory objects are their GUID attributes – because these never change and duplicate GUIDs should never be generated, so the real name of my user account isn't Simon at all, it's some string that forms the SID and identifies my account.

SIDs are the reason why it is never possible to copy an account. When a new user account is created, Windows will generate a new unique SID for it. Although you can read the SID, it is never possible to modify it, or copy it to another account. You might create another account called Simon (perhaps on another machine in the domain, or another domain, if you wanted to move the account), and try to allocate it to exactly the same groups, and generally give it all the same settings as the original account, but it will still be a different account because it will have a different SID. That's why I'm not really giving away any sensitive information by sticking my SID in this book.

When you log in, Windows will use your SID to generate an **Access Token** for you. An access token is the object that will be actually used to determine whether you should be allowed to do every operation you attempt while you are logged on. It contains your SID, along with data concerning all the groups you are a member of and all the privileges you have by virtue of being a member of those groups. Every time you start up a process or thread, the process gets this access token. If a process temporarily needs to impersonate someone else, it will do so by grabbing a copy of their access token.

We're going to move on now and have a look in more detail at what actually happens to your password when you type it in to your computer. That's going to lead us naturally onto the whole process of making sure that data you send over the network isn't read or tampered with by unauthorized users, and to encryption.

Introduction to Encryption

Encryption is really related to the age-old problem of trying to prove that you are the person you say you are. In an ideal world, this wouldn't be necessary. If everyone were honest, you would just have to say who you are and that would be enough. (That's not such an abstract point as it sounds. Until a few years ago, security on many Unix systems worked just like that: a process would declare the name of the user it was running on behalf of, and that would be it).

So, for example, you might say something like 'I am Caesar, We attack the Gauls tomorrow' (Well actually if you were Caesar you'd probably say something more like *Caesar sum. Cras Galli oppugnemus,* but let's not get too pedantic). And because everyone was honest, the person you were talking to would automatically be able to trust you, and start making the arrangements for the attack as instructed. This method of enforcing security usually fails because there are lots of people who aren't as nice or honest as that. So the idea of a password evolved. Some arrangement would evolve by which Caesar and the general he was talking to would both have been made aware of the password, and Caesar could say, 'I am Caesar. Salad. See, I really am Caesar. I can give you your orders.'

This is a bit better, but the problem with this approach is that Caesar has to actually utter the password. Who could be listening behind that pillar? (In computer terms, on the network). Well whoever it is now knows the password and can use it in future to pretend to be Caesar and give out lots of false orders to the generals. In the process of proving that he knows the password, Caesar has given other people a chance to learn it. What we really need is a way that our little dictator can prove he knows the password without actually having to give away the password itself.

The way we do that is to use the password to encrypt some data. The simplest technique would involve replacing each letter of the alphabet with another letter of the alphabet. One way might be to – say – shift each letter forward by n places in the alphabet (with z wrapping back round to a), where n is a number known to recipient and sender. What happens is this. Caesar encrypts a simple message. For the sake of argument, the message might be (or might include) the current date and time. The person he's talking to then decrypts the message using the known algorithm. If the result of decrypting the message is (roughly) the current date and time, then the General knows that he's talking to someone who knows the password – so he can be pretty sure it's Caesar. If decrypting the message leads to garbage, then you know that the message wasn't encrypted properly in the first place, and you can safely lock the sender up in the dungeons as an imposter.

But what about someone behind the pillar listening? Can't they just copy down the encrypted message and still send that whenever they want to pretend they are Caesar? Well, in principle, yes, but I've covered that by suggesting that the message should include the current date and time. If an eavesdropper did try to copy and reuse the message the fact that it is now has the wrong date and time will alert the receiver to the problem.

Now that's a pretty simple encryption scheme. It wouldn't take long for an eavesdropper to copy it down, and then figure out what the password is by trial and error – you just keep attempting to decrypt the encoded message with different passwords until you find one that doesn't lead to garbage. For this scheme, you wouldn't even need a Pentium 500! But my scheme does illustrate a couple of points. Notice that there are two aspects to the encryption algorithm – the nature of the algorithm itself (shift each letter forward by n places in the alphabet), and the actual number n that is fed into the algorithm. For such a simple encryption scheme, you'd probably want to keep both aspects a secret. But suppose for the sake of argument, it is publicly known that Caesar likes an encryption scheme where letters are shifted by so many places. Then the private bit of the code is that the number of places currently happens to be 4. No one is supposed to know that apart from Caesar and a few trusted generals. This number now serves the role of a password.

Applying this to NT

So far you have a way of authenticating yourself. You know the password and that proves who you are. To recap; by using the password to encrypt some data, you've managed to demonstrate that you know the password – but you've managed to do it without actually communicating the password. And that is a real improvement. We now need to flesh this scheme out in terms of modern technology and actual computer networks. The modern analogy of Caesar talking to his general is you logging in to your workstation and needing to authenticate yourself to the domain controller. In general we assume that the process of you typing in the password to your workstation is safe. The dangerous point is when the password – or the encrypted data – actually leaves your workstation and travels across the network to a domain controller. That's where someone might have a network eavesdropping program running – and that's the equivalent of Caesar talking to his general, not knowing who is hiding behind the door.

In my example, I tried encrypting the date to make sure that the encrypted data would be useless if reused by a third party. NT uses a more sophisticated mechanism to solve this problem, known as **the challenge-response** mechanism. What happens is your workstation indicates to the domain controller that it needs to authenticate as you. The domain controller, which stores an encrypted form of your password, then asks the workstation a question about the password. The question will take the form of 'perform some mathematical operation on the encrypted form of your password and tell me the result.' The precise details of the operation – the challenge – vary randomly every time you authenticate, so it is not possible for an eavesdropper to get any useful information by listening to the answer your workstation gives the domain controller.

There are still some problems lurking around with our scheme. For a start, the person you're speaking to has to know the password – somehow you have to have communicated it to them in the first place. But we do now have the basic principles on which we can start to build a security system. However, there is one key point I want you to notice. I've presented the encryption scheme entirely as a way of proving who you are, but it actually happens to solve another problem at the same time – that of ensuring that confidential data cannot be read by unauthorized people. All you have to do is use your password to encrypt the actual confidential data, and you're away. Only someone who knows the password can read the data.

Making the Password and Encryption Scheme More Complex

Of course, a number as a password is pretty limiting. We're accustomed to using long character strings (or even better – alphanumeric strings) as passwords. So let's give Caesar a better encryption scheme. He's taken on a new encryption advisor to improve security against those dastardly Gauls. The new advisor has got enough sense to find a password worthy of a ruthless dictator, and has picked *Thunderbolt*. How could we use this in an encryption scheme? Well, one way would be to number each letter of Thunderbolt by its position in the alphabet, and write out the numbers as a sequence: 20, 8,21,14,4,5,18,2,15,12,20. Now let's say our message is Help! Gauls Have Found the Password! We shift the H forwards by 20 characters, making B, (we wrap around the Z), the e of help forwards by 8 characters, making m, and so on. When we've used up all the letters in Thunderbolt, we go back to the T again. This will turn our message into (putting everything into lowercase)

bmgd kfmnh tupm acysv vwq juankswv

That's a bit harder to decrypt without the password – even if you know the general principles of the algorithm. (Though still not too hard for a specialist with a computer).

However, modern encryption algorithms are far more sophisticated. They take up a lot of computational work – enough so that you wouldn't even want to start encrypting a message if you didn't have a computer to do the encrypting for you. And complex enough so that I've got no intention of actually going through a real encryption algorithm here! Incidentally the actual encryption algorithms are not a secret. They are complex enough that it doesn't matter that much if someone knows in principle how the algorithms work because you still can't get anywhere without knowing the password too.

> *Because it's so hard to decrypt messages without a password, one of the main techniques of trying to illicitly steal passwords or decrypt data is by guessing passwords. A hacker will simply take an encrypted message that he's got by eavesdropping on a message and work through a dictionary, trying out one word after another to decrypt the data. Every incorrect guess will produce garbage when fed into the decryption algorithm. As soon as a guess yields valid data, the hacker has the password – and your network is in trouble. Working through an English dictionary doesn't take that long. That's why it's so important to choose passwords that aren't in any dictionary – eg. by combining letters and numbers – and why so many organizations now enforce this requirement through the Group Policy.*

There are a couple of other differences worth noting. With our primitive algorithm, there was a one-to-one mapping of each letter of the original text with each letter of the encrypted message. That's important because it means that if you want to add some text to the original message, the new version of the encrypted message still starts exactly the same way. For example, if I want to change the message to *Help! Gauls Have Found the Password and are on the March!*, then the new encrypted message reads.

bmgd kfmnh tupm acysv vwq juankswv ccp ulm jb xmw ypdwb

which for the first part of the message reads exactly as our earlier encrypted message.

That in principle would make it easy for a hacker to modify bits of the message even without knowing how to decrypt it. For example, he could remove a few letters from it. The result might be a message that reads a bit funny in one bit, but you might assume that was a mistake by the sender. So this form of encryption offers very little protection against tampering with the message.

Modern encryption messages are more sophisticated than that. There's no such one-to-one mapping of characters. One character of the encrypted message may have been computed by combining quite a large number of characters of the original. Perhaps even every character of the original. This makes the encrypted message a lot more tamper-proof. If someone took the message en route, and modified even just a couple of bytes in it, the result would probably be that the entire message, when decrypted using the correct password, would look like garbage. That makes it quite easy to tell that someone who didn't know the password has fiddled with the message.

However, behind all this lie two things that haven't changed from early algorithms. There is always an algorithm, which is publicly known, and the password (or key), which is known only to, trusted people.

By the way, this discussion has focused on something called symmetric encryption – which means that the same password is used for encrypting and decrypting. If you've heard of public key encryption – which involves using different passwords to encrypt and decrypt data, and you're screaming *what about public encryption?* at the book, then don't worry, I'll come to that soon.

First we're going to have a look at how Windows 2000 applies all the encryption stuff, using the Kerberos version 5 protocol.

Kerberos

Designing encryption algorithms is only one part of protecting your system. The algorithms work at quite a low level, and at a higher level, we still need a scheme that tells us when to apply the encryption and with what passwords. You see, just having a password that is known by both parties involved in a conversation and encrypting it is fine if your entire network *only* consists of those two parties. The trouble is most networks are a lot more complex than that.

When you log on to a workstation in a domain, you authenticate yourself to the domain controller. Unfortunately that's not the only time that your workstation needs to authenticate on your behalf. During your log in session, you're probably going to use the services of various file shares and other network resources. And really, every time you do so, you need to be able to prove who you are. Not only that, but the resource you are using needs to be able to prove who it is so you know you're not passing confidential data to an imposter. If we don't try to design some intelligent protocols around this we're going to end up with every workstation in the entire domain needing to store (or at least store encrypted versions of) every password relevant to the domain. That's clearly not satisfactory.

In Windows NT 4, this was all handled by the NT LAN Manager (NTLM)– which basically solved everything by referring all the requests back to a domain controller for verification. Under Windows 2000, that's all changed, and the protocol used to sort out security is an industry-standard recognized protocol, known as **Kerberos Version 5**. Windows 2000 domain controllers will only use NTLM if they are talking to NT 4 workstations on the network.

Kerberos is a name you've probably heard bandied about as one of the big new things in Windows 2000. Explanations of what it actually is and how it works are less common, so I'm going to do a quick run through now of what happens in a domain that is running Kerberos 5.

What Kerberos is There For

Kerberos is a security system designed to work on networked computers. It's not a proprietary system – it's an industry standard. The original version of Kerberos was developed at the Massachusetts Institute of Technology (and originally for Unix networks) in the late 1980s. The current version, 5, is defined in Request for Comments 1510. Requests for Comments (RFCs) are one means by which standards for use on the Internet are suggested – they are described in Appendix B.

Kerberos is basically there to deal with the following problem:

How can a user, logged into one computer, securely obtain the services of a server (eg. a server application, or a printer or other network resource) located somewhere else in the network?

This is pretty much identical to the purpose of Windows domains: to allow users to access network resources. By *securely* we mean that users and servers should be able to authenticate themselves to each other without having to pass sensitive data – like passwords – over the network where intruders might be able to examine them.

Kerberos assumes that we are dealing with a network of computers in which the weak spots, security-wise, are the actual connections between the computers. We assume that as soon as any data travels from one computer to another, all the data is susceptible to attack or eavesdropping en route. Within a computer the data is presumed to be relatively safe. When I say relatively, I don't mean that you want to leave passwords lying around in files: I mean that attacks from the 'enemy' are going to take place by listening on the network. There's no danger of – say – someone physically coming into the room, tying you up and taking over your workstation.

Actually, that might sound a bit far fetched, but something similar can happen. I remember in my days at university, one of the worst security problems was students simply forgetting to log themselves out, and walking out of the room, leaving their terminal open for someone else to come in and take over their session. Kerberos won't protect you against that sort of stupidity – there's not much that can!

One other restriction of Kerberos – it assumes that your users are sensible about their choice of passwords. No computer security system can really guard against an intruder who has already discovered your password. If your password is something like 'Picard' or 'Hello', and a hacker grabs a packet of data encrypted using your password off the network, it won't take him long to use a program that works through the English dictionary trying to use every word to decrypt your password to find what it is. If your password is something like 'SimonX921Hi', the hacker's probably going to have a lot less luck with his password-cracking program.

The Players in Kerberos

Kerberos is a very centralized protocol. It relies on the domain controller(s) knowing all the passwords, and it works in such a way that no other computer needs to know any password, apart from each server needing to know the password required to access any network resource which it hosts. In other words, it will allow a client and a server to authenticate to each other securely, without either of them knowing the other's password. That's quite a remarkable feat – and Kerberos achieves this by a cunning combination of encrypting various related messages using different passwords and sending them out together. It takes a fair effort to understand how it does this, but I think the end result is rather neat.

Let's introduce the main players. They are shown in the following diagram. In the diagram, the client is the workstation that needs something done on behalf of a certain security principal. For example, say the client is the computer you're logged in on and you intend to use a network resource. In fact, in this discussion I'm not really going to distinguish between the client and the user (the person logged in to the client). The server is the machine that hosts the resource that needs to be accessed. In the diagram, the double-headed arrows indicate which players talk to each other at some stage. Notice that there is no direct communication between the server and the domain controller – everything happens through the client.

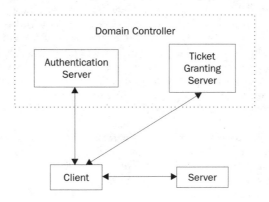

So we have the client and the server – they are obvious. But we also have two other players. The **Authentication Server** and the **Ticket Granting Server**. These are the big central processes that handle the authentication. Logically, it's best for us to treat them as completely separate objects, but actually in Windows 2000 they will be running on a domain controller. In fact, they are implemented within the same process, the Key Distribution Center (KDC) service. This is quite common in Kerberos generally (eg. on Unix), not just on Windows 2000. Although we have one physical process, it is performing two separate tasks in Kerberos, which is why it's convenient to think in terms of two separate logical servers at work.

Just to prove that this really is relevant to Windows, it's quite easy to see the Kerberos key distribution center running on Windows 2000 domain controllers. It's a standard NT Service, so you can check it out with the Services Snap-in.

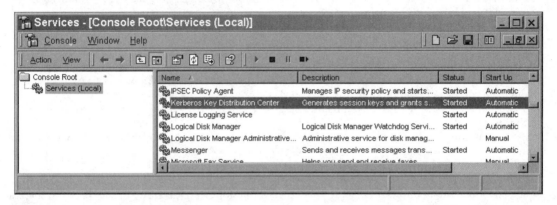

There it is – you'll find it on any Windows 2000 Domain Controller – the Kerberos Key Distribution Center – the service that is ultimately responsible for the security on your domain.

Sending Messages over the Network

Now let's think about this. The idea of authenticating yourself is that you tell the server something that only you know. What's the thing that only you know – yep, it's the password. You tell the server that you know the password by encrypting some data. The server decrypts it successfully, and that proves it was you who sent it – because no one else knew the password so no one else could have encrypted it. OK? Well as we've already pointed out, this is actually not OK. What if an eavesdropper picked up the message? The eavesdropper might not be able to decrypt it, but they could still send the same message again. Suppose the encrypted message was an authentication request to use a printer. An eavesdropper who's not supposed to use that printer could just keep resending the encrypted message whenever he wanted to use the printer – and the printer server would think it's that's successfully authenticated you.

Earlier we got round this problem by sending a timestamp that would quickly get out of date. The way Kerberos gets round this problem is quite similar. Each request is accompanied by an **authenticator**. We'll come to how the authenticator is generated in a moment – but the point is that the authenticator can only be used once. If an eavesdropper manages to copy the message, it'll do him no good because the authenticator is useless from the moment the server accepted the original client request. If the client wants to reuse the same server later, it'll have to generate a different authenticator – and that can only be done with knowledge of the client's password. Since the password is never transmitted across the network, the hacker can't easily find it out.

That's some of the principles out of the way. We are now ready to go through what actually happens.

The user logs into a workstation. The first stage is to authenticate. This is where the authentication server (AS) – running on the domain controller – comes in. Basically, the user types in his password, and the workstation sends the username to the AS, which checks the password (on Windows 2000, using the challenge-response mechanism). What the client gets back in response is known as a **ticket granting ticket** (**TGT**). Don't stop reading now; the terminology doesn't get any worse than that, I promise you.

I'll explain. The TGT can be thought of as a temporary substitute for the user's password. You see we're going to be doing a lot of using-the-password-to-encrypt-data. Like every time we want to use a new network resource. This would mean the client's workstation is going to need to have the user's password on hand quite a lot. There's two ways to achieve this. You can ask the user to type in his password again every time we need to authenticate him. Or the workstation can cache the password for as long as the user is logged in. Neither of these is very palatable. I know I said Kerberos assumes the computers themselves are relatively secure – but that only means relative to the network connections. You still don't really want passwords lurking around in memory for a hacker to steal. Even the domain controllers don't actually store the passwords – they store one-way encrypted versions of the passwords. You can get to the encryption from the password, but you can't get the password back from the encrypted version.

So that would leave us with having to ask for the password every time we need to authenticate. Imagine the user is in Windows Explorer, looking round the network. Clicks on one of the computers to see the shared folders inside. Instantly a dialog pops up. *Password, please?* User types it in. No, wrong computer, the file we want must be on that computer. Click in Windows Explorer. Dialog pops up instantly. *Can you enter your password?* Ah. Got the right computer. There's that document. Just right click on it to print it out. Select *Print.* And hey – what do we see. Yep, you got it, a dialog box asking the user for his password so that the workstation can authenticate you to the print server. I'd hazard a guess that if we tried implementing that security system, our popularity would swiftly decline amongst our users.

See the problem? We've got to cache something, and if caching the password is too much of a security loophole, we'll have to find something else we can use instead. That's the ticket granting ticket. The ticket granting ticket – as we'll see, acts like a password for all future authentications, but with one difference: it expires, typically in about 8 hours. And if we suspect it has been copied, we can expire it early and ask the authentication server for another one. The ticket granting ticket contains a **session key** – and that session key is what the client uses to encrypt data from now on.

There's an extra benefit of using the ticket granting ticket as well. Since it's only ever used by the computers, and never actually typed in by any people, it's OK for it to be a nice long stream of random numbers. The sort of password that is very hard to crack.

It might not look like it yet, but it's now starting to come together.

The client requests a ticket granting ticket from the AS. Now here's the clever bit. The ticket granting ticket basically contains the user name of the person who wants to use the service, along with their IP address and some other useful information. It also includes the session key. It is encoded using the password from the **ticket granting server** (**TGS**). This means that the ticket granting server is the only entity that will be able to decrypt it. Separately, the AS encrypts the session key with the *client's* password. The whole lot gets sent back in a bundle to the client. The client can decrypt the session key – that effectively is now its password, which it can use to encrypt data, for the next 8 hours (precise time depending on the Kerberos policy settings for that domain).

So the client has a password – the session key. Now let's say you want to access a network resource. You need to authenticate yourself to that resource. Perhaps it's a file share. So you need to get a **ticket** from the ticket granting server, which will prove to the file server who you are. So in order to do that, you need to convince the ticket granting server of who you are. You do this by sending it the ticket granting ticket that you got from the authentication server. Remember that you've got an encrypted copy of it, which you can't do anything with, except pass on to the TGS. So the TGS gets the ticket, decrypts it, finds it contains your user name and IP address – and hey presto – it knows you are the real you, and it can issue you with a ticket. (Recall that all network packets will come with the IP address of the sender in plain text form, so the server knows who to reply to. So the TGS will be able to check that the ticket granting ticket decodes to the correct IP address).

Brilliant! Well, actually, not quite. Remember, anyone else might have copied the encrypted TGT, and it's very easy to change the IP address on a computer, so the fact that the packet has your IP address doesn't really count for anything. The hacker can just change his IP address to match yours. So, as far as the TGS is concerned, just receiving a correctly encrypted TGT doesn't prove it came from you. What have we forgotten? Oh yes – the authenticator. The client has to send an authenticator with the TGT. So what is the authenticator? Well the client needs to prove who it is by proving that it knows something that no one else could know. The thing that only the client knows would have been its password – which we have replaced by the session key. So the client has to prove it knows the session key – and it does that by using the session key to encrypt some data. What it encrypts is the current time. So it sends that along with the TGT. Our earlier Julius Caesar example wasn't as far out after all!

The TGS decrypts the TGT. From this it is able to obtain the client's identity and the session key. The fact that decrypting the TGT didn't leave it with garbage proves that this is a valid TGT issued by the AS. Now it uses the session key to decrypt the authenticator. The fact that doing this doesn't lead to garbage proves that the authenticator was created by someone else with access to the session key – which basically means the client. *Now* the ticket granting server can be certain it is dealing with a valid request, not an impersonation of a request. It's ready to send the client the ticket. But before it does so, it does one other thing. It stores the details of the authenticator in a cache. If any request comes in over the next few minutes, which contains the same authenticator, the TGS will be able to see that this authenticator has already been used, and therefore is invalid. Remember, authenticators must only be used once. The authenticator will expire in a few minutes anyway, so it doesn't have to be stored in the cache of used authenticators for long.

So far so good. We are ready to give the client a ticket to authenticate himself to the server. In fact, you're going to recognize quite a lot of this process because it's essentially the same procedure as the authentication server just used.

The TGS creates a new session key. We'll call it session key 2. This is going to be the password that the client must use when talking to that particular server. The TGS will create a ticket, consisting of the session key, and the client's name and IP address, as well as other useful information like the expiry date (this will be the same as the expiry date on the TGT). The TGS then encrypts this using the *Server's* password. (Remember that the TGT is running on a domain controller – so it does have access to all the passwords in the domain). This means that the client (or any eavesdroppers) will be able to do nothing with the ticket – other than pass it on to the server for decrypting. The TGS separately encrypts the same session key 2 using the client's password. This means that the client will be able to at least extract the session key. The whole bundle gets sent back to the client.

Now we're almost in business. The client is able to send a message to the server, effectively saying, 'here I am. I want to use your services.' What the client does is that it sends the encrypted ticket to the server. The server will be able to decrypt the ticket – and the fact that doing so doesn't lead to garbage proves that this ticket was issued by the ticket granting server. It doesn't yet prove that the ticket hasn't been copied and isn't actually being sent by an eavesdropper acting on behalf of the client. The proof of that comes because the client sends an authenticator with the ticket. The authenticator consists of the timestamp, and information about the client, encoded using the session key 2. The server now knows this session key 2 because it decrypted it from the ticket. It can use it in turn to decrypt the authenticator. It'll check in its cache that this authenticator isn't being reused, store it in the cache to prevent reuse, and it can now be satisfied that this request came from the client.

Notice that the server will store the recently used authenticators for a few minutes. It'll need to know its own password, but it doesn't need to store anything else. If the client later wants to make more requests to the same server, it will simply resend the ticket, along with a new authenticator. So the client does need to store all the tickets along with the session key – but since these will expire within a matter of hours, this is less dangerous than storing the user's own password. The client also needs to store its ticket granting ticket and the original session key supplied with it. These will be needed if it needs to contact a new server – in which case it must first talk to the ticket granting server to ask for a ticket valid for that server.

We're almost done. We just need to close a couple more potential loopholes.

Firstly, everything is about the client authenticating itself to the server. However security works both ways. We want to protect our servers from imposters pretending to be clients. But we also want to protect our clients from imposters pretending to be servers. Think of all the confidential data you could obtain if you could write a program that pretended to be a certain print server, responding to authentication requests and then allowing clients to send you lots of confidential information to print. So how can the server prove it is the correct server? The answer comes down to those authenticators again. After the server has decrypted the authenticator, it adds a bit more information to it (usually its own name) and re-encrypts it using the session key 2. It then sends it back to the client. No imposter would be able to do this because any imposter would be unable to decrypt the ticket to obtain the session key 2 in the first place – you can only do that if you know the server's password. Once the client receives the correctly encrypted and modified authenticator back from the server, the client can be sure it's dealing with the real server. And you can start to send those embarrassing *Dear CuddlePlum* letters from your girlfriend across for printing, without fear that they're actually being sent to a journalist who's managed to set a server up to pretend to be your printer...

That's probably all quite a lot for you to take in, but the following diagram shows the broad sequence of events. In the diagram, the text alongside the arrows shows what data is being passed in what sequence. The text in capitals says what the data actually is; the text in lowercase says whose password or which key has been used to encrypt the data. In following this remember that the ticket granting ticket includes session key 1, and the ticket includes session key 2. Also remember that the communication with the authentication server (nos. 1 and 2 in the diagram) only takes place once, when the user first logs in. Communication with the ticket granting server (nos. 3 and 4) occurs whenever the client wants to talk to a new server which it has not yet authenticated to. Communication with the server (nos. 5 and 6) occurs whenever the client wants to make a new request to any server.

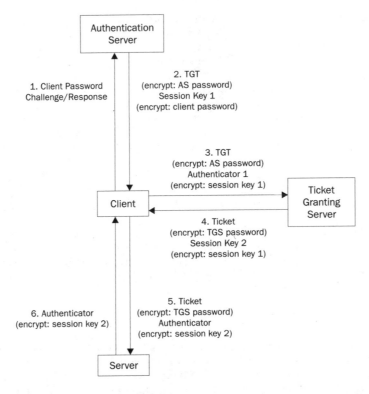

Applying Kerberos to Windows 2000

So far most of what we've described is applicable to Kerberos in general. The main Windows-specific part of the explanation above is that I've repeatedly referred to domains, which is a Windows concept. More generally, Kerberos uses **realms**, which are equivalent to Windows domains. If we get a bit more Windows 2000-specific, now, the account that Kerberos runs over is the krbtgt account, which you'll find gets installed automatically with Windows 2000 Server and Windows 2000 Advanced Server. You won't be able to log in with this account. It's there entirely to run the Kerberos security system. The krbtgt password is randomly generated, and is changed frequently.

The Kerberos settings – things like how long a ticket granting ticket is valid for – are grouped under the name Kerberos Policy, and you won't be surprised to find that they are part of the group policy, and can be examined or modified using our familiar Group Policy Editor:

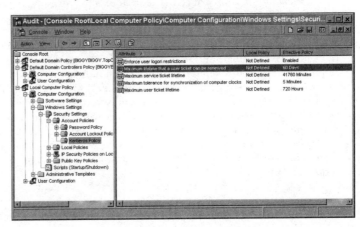

Once again, there is a local policy – not configured, and an effective policy governed by the domain. The settings in this screenshot are very lax – you'd probably want much more restrictive times in a real commercial and online network. The ticket lifetimes tell you how long a ticket and a TGT are valid for – you'd normally want this to be somewhere in the region of 8 hours. The lifetime for synchronization of computer clocks is the 5 minutes grace allowed before an authenticator will expire, even if it hasn't been used. The maximum lifetime that a ticket can be renewed gives a period within which tickets (and TGTs), if expired, can be renewed by request to the TGS. Beyond this period, there is no alternative but to request a new TGT from the authentication server.

Public Key Encryption

This is the last area we are going to look at before we end our discussion of security issues. It's not something that you're ever likely to have to deal with directly as an ADSI programmer, since it's hidden behind the scenes even more so than Kerberos. But it's a term you're likely to hear referred to a fair amount, so we may as well take a quick look at what it involves.

Public Key encryption can really be seen as a way of getting round the one problem that still exists in all the encryption schemes we've so far talked about: The fact that in the end a password (or key) has to be known by both the person encrypting and the person decrypting a message. Which means that somewhere along the line the password itself is going to be transmitted at least once. This is a problem. In Kerberos, there are a whole series of extra protocols that have been developed to make this aspect of the system secure (see RFC 1964).

In public key encryption, the idea is that the encryption algorithm has been carefully designed so that the password used to decrypt the data is different from the one used to encrypt it. In other words, the password actually comes as a pair of passwords. But there's one additional requirement. You carefully plan out your algorithm and the first password. You then apply some mathematics to the first password to figure out what the second password is. It's easy, given the first password, to work out the second one. However, if you were only told the second password, there is no known way to use it to figure out the first password. It's something that's sometimes known in the mathematics/coding theory world as a **trapdoor function**; it's simple to work it out one way, but impossible to do the reverse. Well, perhaps, not impossible, but it would take even the fastest computers millions of years to do it.

You're going to have to take it on trust that all this is possible. It is. There are encryption algorithms in existence such that data encrypted with one password must be decrypted with another password, which is reached by applying a trapdoor function to the first password. (You can also do it the other way round, encrypt with the trapdoor-calculated password and decrypt with the second password). It takes some serious mathematics to do it, so it's not the sort of thing you'll do lightly – and the encryption algorithms themselves will put a fairly big performance hit on your computer. But it is possible.

So how does this help us? Well, what we do is generate a password and keep it to ourselves This will be known as the **private key** because we are literally not going to tell *anyone* what it is. We then apply our trapdoor function to generate the second password, which will be known as the **public key**. This we will freely publish to anyone who wants it. We don't care how many hackers we tell what it is because it won't do them any good.

Then when we want to prove who we are, we encrypt a message using our private key. Anyone can decrypt the message – so we haven't hidden the contents of it. But we have proved that that message could only have been sent by us. No one else could because we haven't told anyone else our private key. And the fact that everyone knows the public key doesn't make any difference because it's impossible to work out what the private key is from that.

So that authenticates us beyond – well beyond – any doubt at all really. Having been authenticated – and having similarly authenticated the other party, we then might want to send some confidential data across the network. That's quite easy to do as well. We just reverse the roles of public and private keys. We know the public key of the person we want to send the information to – everyone knows that. So we encrypt our sensitive data using their public key. This says nothing about who sent the data, but it does mean that no one except the intended recipient will be able to decrypt the data because you need his private key to do that.

That all works extremely well, apart from being computationally intensive. In fact, the Kerberos protocol, as defined in RFC 1510, doesn't use public key encryption. It uses **symmetric key encryption**, which is just the fancy term for what we've been talking about for most of this chapter: an encryption scheme in which the same key is used to encrypt and decrypt data. However, Windows 2000 extends Kerberos to support public key encryption. It can be enabled – as usual – via the group policy, and you can find it in the group policy editor under Computer Configuration/Windows Settings/Security Settings.

Summary

In this chapter we've had an overview that covers how security is implemented in Windows 2000 and the implications this has for ADSI providers. Other than how to authenticate yourself to a provider, for which a standard interface IADsOpenDSObject is available, security is something that is provider-specific, so we can't really give any details that apply to all providers, but we've seen how Active Directory exposes the security descriptors and access control lists that are used by Windows 2000 to control access to the objects, while the WinNT provider simply does not make this information available – a restriction on the capabilities of WinNT.

We've also run through some of the underlying principles behind NT/Windows 2000 security and the Kerberos protocol, which are important to understand in order to make the best use of the security facilities available in Active Directory.

Security is an area that is traditionally somewhat neglected by programmers, but when writing ADSI clients it is important to understand how providers implement security in order that you can gain access to the directory objects you need. Similarly, when writing providers, it is important to ensure that security is implemented in a way that makes it easy for clients to authenticate to carry out their required tasks, while not compromising the security of your directory. Access control lists, following the model used by Windows 2000/NT are one good way of achieving this.

We've completed our tour of security. In the next chapter we're going to look at how to write an ADSI provider.

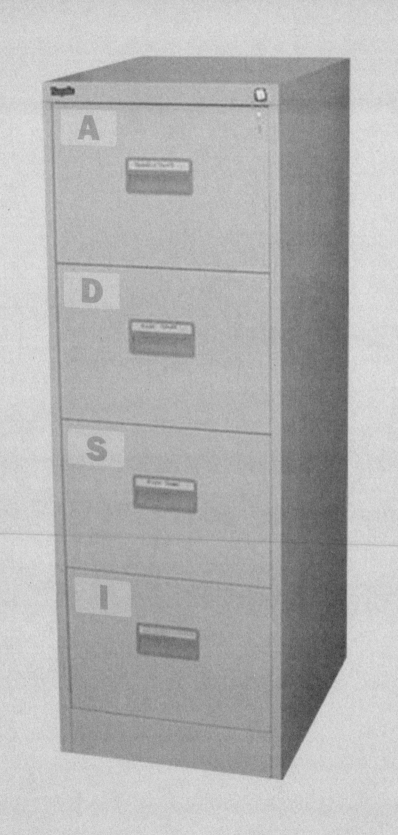

9

Writing a Provider

In this chapter you will learn how to write a provider using ATL 3.0, including

- ❑ Architectural considerations when planning your provider
- ❑ How to register your provider so the ADSI router recognizes it
- ❑ Implementing `IParseDisplayName` to provide a way for clients to bind to objects in your provider
- ❑ Implementing enumerators
- ❑ What your provider must implement and what can be left out

In this chapter we're going to learn about developing ADSI providers – by writing the StarRaiders provider. In the process we'll learn about registering a provider and implementing the ADSI interfaces. We'll dive under the covers of the `ADsGetObject()` API function and understand how COM monikers are used to hook up to an object in a directory. We'll take a peek at some of the factors you'll need to consider when deciding how to architect your provider. We'll also cover the suggested standards for what functionality a provider must implement, and what things could be left out.

This Chapter is for Everyone

I'm guessing that there are a lot more people writing ADSI clients than there are writing providers. After all, the whole idea of an ADSI provider is that it can be used by lots of different clients. So if there weren't a lot more client applications than providers around, that would kind of suggest that the providers that do exist weren't very useful!

If you are someone who's only really interested in using ADSI as a client, then you may be tempted to skip this chapter entirely. Even so I'd urge you to think twice before flicking to Chapter 10. For a start, throughout this book I'm trying to emphasize the reasons for why things are designed the way they are, trying to get under the hood of the ADSI interfaces. And this is just as important for providers. If you have some grasp of the issues that face provider writers, that can only help your understanding of how to use the ADSI interfaces when coding clients. Besides, some of the information in this chapter is more directly relevant to ADSI clients as well, particularly the discussion of compulsory and optional features for providers to implement. If you've got this far with the book you'll already know that every ADSI provider is unique. Each one has its own idiosyncrasies, which means you've always got to watch for unexpected failed method calls. Well this isn't totally random: Microsoft does provide some guidelines for what clients really ought to implement, and if you understand those guidelines you'll have a better idea of what to expect from new providers. Besides, if all that isn't incentive enough, you know how much fun it is to pick on the biggest, most successful, company in any industry, don't you. Well later on in the chapter I shall give you the chance to have a laugh at Microsoft's expense. There! You must read this chapter now, to find out why!

So the message is – even if you don't want to look through the code in detail, it'll still be worth your while skimming through the text.

Why ATL?

The coding in this chapter is entirely done in C++ using ATL. To see why, let's take a peek at some of the other options available.

Let's dispose of VB first. Yes, VB is great for writing ADSI clients. I can tell you, when I used to write my C++ COM clients in my former daytime job, and I was mucking around debugging my SAFEARRAYs and enumerators, I'd grow green with jealously at you VB guys and your nice simple For Each loops. And it's true that you can write COM servers as well as clients in VB. But you will not want to code up an ADSI provider in VB. Full stop. The main reason is that ADSI providers must have the threading model *both*. The current version of VB (VB6) is only able to produce components that are single-threaded or apartment-threaded. The ADSI specifications require this for performance reasons. An ADSI provider is designed to be the main access point to a directory service, so in general it should be expected that it will be used by a wide variety of clients with different performance requirements. In order to satisfy this the provider will need to meet the expectations of the client that requires the highest performance and scaleability – which really means coding the provider in C++ and using the both-threaded model.

It's also worth pointing out that an ADSI provider is not a simple COM component – rather it contains a large number of components that interact. As such, an ADSI provider is going to be a relatively complex application anyway. VB excels at allowing developers to produce simple applications quickly and easily. But for something as complex as an ADSI provider, the advantage of simpler and more maintainable code is more likely to lie with languages such as C++, since C++ code can take advantage of C++ features such as inheritance and templates – designed to simplify complex code.

I should point out this discussion above isn't quite correct since it omits other languages such as Visual J++ and Delphi. Both of these languages are COM-aware and support multiple threads, and so could be used to code up ADSI providers. However, these languages do not give you the benefits of ATL. Also, we are trying to stay Microsoft-specific in this book, and it is questionable whether J++ will give the same performance as C++, so we will stick with C++ here.

So having established that we will be coding in C++, we've got the usual three options for writing COM servers: doing all the COM code from scratch, using ATL or using MFC. The need for the free threading model pretty much eliminates MFC from the start, even before we consider things like code size. That narrows our options down to two.

The present version of ATL, ATL 3.0, isn't totally geared up to ADSI. If you opt for ATL, you'll find a couple of areas where you need to work round or actually modify the behaviour of the wizard-generated code in order to comply with the ADSI standards. Even with the snappy new wizards that come with ATL 3.0 there's a lot we need for ADSI that the wizards simply can't cope with. And I know of at least one company that rejected ATL and chose to code a provider in raw C++ because of these problems.

Nevertheless, unless you've got special reasons why your project should be in raw C++ (maybe you've already got some boiler plate code already written, or you have exceptional performance requirements), I'd generally recommend you use ATL. The effort involved in getting round the default ATL behaviour is a lot less than the effort in coding up class factories and `IUnknown` implementations yourself.

That aside, I had two extra reasons for choosing ATL for the StarRaiders provider:

❑ The Microsoft sample provider is coded in raw C++, so if that's how you want to do your provider, you've already got a sample to look at. At present there's no similar publically available sample that uses ATL.

❑ If I code the provider in raw C++ I'll have to do a lot of basic work writing class factories etc. That might be useful in a book about COM, but this is a book about ADSI. If I code in ATL then adapt the ATL code, the modifications I'll be making to the ATL code are directly relevant to understanding how ADSI providers work.

So in this chapter we're going to go through the process of writing a provider in ATL. I referred just now to a couple of problems with ATL and ADSI. We will cover these as they arise, but in short the main one is to do with ATL's implementation of `IDispatch`. As we saw in Chapter 2, ADSI requires that scripting clients are able to see any of the ADSI interfaces implemented by an object. Unfortunately, ATL's implementation of `IDispatch` will only expose the methods of any one selected interface. This behaviour could potentially cripple scripting clients, and will need to be overridden.

ADSI Requirements for Providers

Before we start coding, I'd better quickly go over Microsoft's guidelines for providers. If you remember back to Chapter 2, where I presented the inheritance tree of the ADSI interfaces, you may recall there are a lot of ADSI interfaces. Last time I counted I made it 58, but each new version of ADSI brings out a few more, and then I may have missed a couple... If you had to implement all of those, writing an ADSI provider would be a horrendous task. Fortunately, you rarely need to implement all the interfaces. For a start, there are all the NDS-specific ones that you won't need unless you are doing a provider related to Netware. On a similar note, many of the persistant data and dynamic data interfaces, such as `IADsService` and `IADsComputer` may not be relevant to your directory. It is highly unlikely, for example, that a directory of opening hours of local shops would contain any objects that would need to implement the `IADsFileShare` interface!

On a different level, there are actually some interfaces that providers never need to implement. `IADsNamespaces` is one obvious one here. This interface will be covered in Chapter 10 and allows you to set default ADSI objects that you can bind to – but this interface is intended to be exposed only by the ADSI router, not by any objects in any provider – so you may use this interface as a client, but you will never need to implement it. But there are also other interfaces which are exposed through the providers but which don't actually need directory-specific implementations because for various reasons they don't interact directly with the underlying directory. These are generally the interfaces that are exposed not by the COM object that represents a directory object, but by other COM objects accessed as properties. In this list go all the security interfaces, as well as two of the property cache interfaces, `IADsPropertyEntry` and `IADsPropertyValue`. Most of the NDS-specific interfaces also fall into this category, as do the utility interfaces, `IADsNameTranslate` and `IADsLargeInteger`. Don't get me wrong: your provider may need to use these interfaces. It's just that Microsoft has already coded up the corresponding COM objects. And since these objects and interfaces are perfectly general, your provider can simply call `CoCreateInstance()` to get at Microsoft's implementation. Microsoft does try to reduce your workload when it can!

You can see the complete list of objects that are pre-coded by Microsoft by having a look at the ActiveDS type library in OLEView:

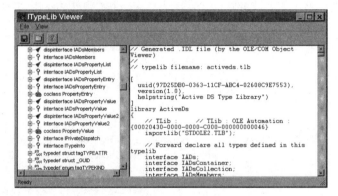

For example, in the screenshot you can see the `Property Entry` object and the `Property Value` object mixed up with all the interfaces. (The COM objects are the ones with the blue icon that looks like a transparent cube with the familiar `IUnknown` lollipop popping out the top). The complete list of pre-coded ADSI objects implemented by the COM runtime is:

OBJECT	INTERFACES (excluding `IUnknown`)
PropertyEntry	IDispatch
	IADsPropertyEntry
PropertyValue	IDispatch
	IADsPropertyValue
SecurityDescriptor	IDispatch
	IADsSecurityDescriptor
AccessControlList	IDispatch
	IADsAccessControlEntry

OBJECT	INTERFACES (excluding `IUnknown`)
AccessControlEntry	IDispatch
	IADsAccessControlEntry
AccessControlList	IDispatch
	IADsAccessControlList

There is also one interface that is not an ADSI interface, but which you'll need to implement for every ADSI provider: `IParseDisplayName`. The COM runtime itself is able to use the `ADsPaths` passed to `ADsGetObject()` and to VB's `GetObject()` to figure out which provider is required, but then it's up to your provider to cough up the appropriate COM object. To allow the router to talk to your provider to achieve this, you will need to expose a special provider object which implements this standard COM interface.

That should give you an idea of some of the issues involved. To make things more consistent, Microsoft has produced guidelines on what functionality you should implement. The guidelines are divided into two sections: **Core Requirements**, which every provider must implement if it is to be considered a true ADSI provider, and **Optional Requirements**, which are strongly recommended, but which you don't *have* to implement if you don't want to. Roughly speaking, the optional requirements are for security and searching, and the core requirements cover everything else that is common to all directories. Options that are only relevant to some directories, such as `IADsFileShare`, don't appear on either list. For these interfaces, it is up to the individual provider to decide what it's appropriate to implement.

In more detail the requirements are:

CORE FEATURES

- ❑ All directory objects should expose the `IADs` and, where appropriate, the `IADsContainer` interfaces.

- ❑ The namespace object must implement `IADsOpenDSObject`, to allow clients to supply authentication credentials.

- ❑ There should be a provider object (this could be the namespace object itself) that implements `IParseDisplayName` to resolve `ADsPaths` within that namespace.

- ❑ All directory objects must expose `IADsPropertyList`, allowing properties to be manipulated via the property cache interfaces.

- ❑ All directory objects must expose `IDirectoryObject`, to allow fast access for C++ clients.

- ❑ There should be schema containers that contain all required class, property and syntax objects. There are no formal requirements for where the schema containers should go, other than that, as a minimum there should be one container for each node just below the namespace object.

- ❑ Enumeration support via `IEnumVARIANT` should be implemented where your provider uses collections (for example all container objects will allow access to their children via collections). As should the `IADsMembers` and `IADsCollection` interfaces if your provider uses groups or collections.

- ❑ It isn't necessary for all properties in an interface to be implemented, but those that aren't should return `E_ADS_PROPERTY_NOT_SUPPORTED`.

Optional Features

The optional, but recommended, functionality includes

- ❑ IDirectorySearch to allow searching.
- ❑ The security interfaces, IADsSecurityDescriptor, IADsAccessControlList, and IADsAccessControlEntry. Strictly, you do not need to implement these interfaces since Microsoft has already implemented security objects, but it is recommended that you make these objects available.

Now is where the fun starts, and where you get to have that laugh at Microsoft that I promised you. Remember those core interfaces? Remember that all providers *must* implement them? Now have you ever tried a bit of code like:

```
IDirectoryObject *pDirObj;
hRes = ADsGetObject(L"WinNT:", IID_IDirectoryObject, (void**)&pDirObj);
```

Well if you have tried that on any object in the WinNT provider, you'll have got E_NOTIMPL back. Now which company was it that developed the WinNT provider? Oh dear, my mind's gone totally blank.

Perhaps I'm being unfair to rub it in like that, but the lines I've just quoted are almost exactly the first bit of ADSI code I ever wrote. That was back in June 1998, when my boss just told me to start learning ADSI. It was in the days of the early ADSI 2.0 beta documentation, which didn't mention the fact that WinNT didn't implement IDirectoryObject. I spent *ages* trying to figure out what I was doing wrong!

Anyway, to be fair to Microsoft, the restrictions on what is implemented in each of the system providers is now documented. Generally, the stuff that's not implemented comprises various automation properties on the persistant object interfaces, as well as security, searching, and the IDirectoryXXX interfaces in WinNT. My favourite oddity is in the sample provider, which has schema containers located at Sample://Toronto/Schema, and Sample://Seattle/Schema. If you supply these ADsPaths directly, you will be able to connect to these objects, but if you try to browse the children of Sample://Toronto and Sample://Seattle, you won't see the schema containers. I mention this because it's quite an interesting oddity in that it's not really how you'd expect the provider to behave, but strictly speaking it doesn't break any ADSI rules. There's no requirement in ADSI for the entire directory tree to be visible to browsers – in fact in some situations you'd expect it not to be, for example where some parts of the tree are hidden to users who don't have the appropriate security privileges.

I should also add that my StarRaiders provider doesn't implement IDirectoryObject *either*

A Word of Warning

Before we start writing StarRaiders, a word of warning about the code – there's a lot of it. As I said, writing an ADSI provider isn't a trivial task. This means how I approach presenting the code in this chapter is going to be a bit different from all the samples we've looked up to now for ADSI clients. So far, I've generally displayed all the code that I've written, so even if you don't fancy downloading it from the Wrox press web site, you can still follow it easily. It's not practical to do that for the StarRaiders provider because there is so much code. It would be pointless as well since a lot of the code in the provider is repeated (different ADSI objects in the StarRaiders directory that do nearly the same thing, but in situations where inheritance would be difficult to use). So for the rest of this chapter you're only going to see the bits of code that are relevant to the point I'm explaining. If you want to see how it all fits together in the provider you'll have to download the sample.

Another related point is that if you do download the code you may find in places it's different from what I've presented in this chapter. Don't worry – you're not being cheated. It's just that in the code snippets displayed in this chapter I've sometimes removed bits that aren't relevant to the explanation at hand.

StarRaiders Comes At Last...

I'm not sure if I've mentioned it yet but I *really* like Jonathan Pinnock's book, *Professional DCOM Application Development (Wrox Press, ISBN: 1-861001-31-2)*. That book starts off with a great introduction to how easy COM programming is these days: he tries to time an egg by how long it takes to create a simple COM server using ATL – a matter of minutes. Well I don't need to do that, since my method of timing an egg involves throwing it in the saucepan then going away and leaving it for 10 minutes or so, by which time I know it's definitely cooked. But even so I loved Jonathan's idea of timing yourself going through a wizard to show how easy it is, and since my philosophy is 'What use is a great idea if you can't copy it?', I'm gonna do some timing of my own. I'm going to show you how quickly you can set up the framework for an ADSI provider.

In fact, it's a very special day for me today. You see you've got used to seeing my fabulous StarRaiders provider, but I haven't yet: Today's the day when coding up StarRaiders is due to start. So confident am I that I can get it all set up in – say – under an hour – that I'm even putting myself at a big disadvantage: I've got to keep stopping to cut and paste the screenshots into Word 2000 as I work through the wizards. Of course we won't get the full directory working in that time, but the top-level namespaces object will be there, and it'll be registered as an ADSI provider.

I'm going to be implementing StarRaiders using C++ 6/ATL 3.0. If anyone is still using C++ version 5, with ATL 2.1, then you can still implement an ADSI provider. In that case you won't be able to use the Implement Interface Wizard, so for the steps where I've done that, you'll need to actually use OleView to look at the relevant interfaces in the ActiveDS type library, and manually cut, paste and edit the interface definitions into your C++ files, as well as derive your C++ classes from the appropriate interface classes. You can also omit the step of #defineing _ATL_NO_UUIDOF. If you're doing it that way, I'd strongly suggest you *don't* try timing yourself.

Before I go through the steps in detail, I'll just summarize what the steps actually are:

1. Create an ATL in-process server project

2. Create a Namespace Component using the wizards, and use the Implement Interface Wizard to have this component expose IADs, IADsPropertyList, IADsContainer and IADsOpenDSObject (also IDirectoryObject and IDirectorySearch if you are supporting these interfaces)

3. Ensure the latest version of the Microsoft-supplied header `ActiveDS.h` is included, and the libraries `ActiveDS.lib` and `ADsIID.lib` are referenced. (Don't `#import` the type library)

4. Make sure the symbol `LIBID_ActiveDS` is defined (it has the value {0x97D25DB0, 0x0363, 0x11CF,{0xAB, 0xC4, 0x02, 0x60,0x8C, 0x9E, 0x75, 0x53}})

5. Ensure that the symbol `_ATL_NO_UUIDOF` is defined

6. Add a registry script to register the component as an ADSI provider. Modify the `DllRegisterServer()` and `DllUnregisterServer()` functions to run this script.

7. Implement the stub `IADs` Name, `ADsPath` and Class property methods

Later on you will also need to

8. Implement the Provider Object

We're now ready to go through those in more detail.

Creating the Provider

So it's now 3.50 pm on Saturday, 19th June 1999. Sit back in your seats as you prepare to enjoy the experience of a lifetime. Because the biggest, the best, the most fabulous directory ever created in the history of mankind is about to be created. I give you...

3.50 PM Create ATL In-Process Server Project

Start the developer studio. Choose **File|New Workspace**, and choose an ATL project with the name StarRaiders.

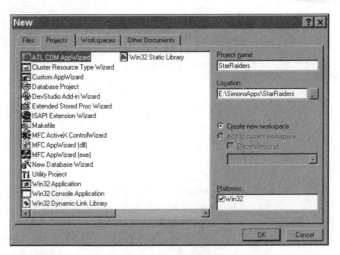

3.51 PM

Select a DLL project. For performance reasons the ADSI specifications stipulate that providers should be in-process. We're going to select the Support <u>M</u>FC option because I like using the MFC CString and collection classes, but that's not essential. If you're concerned about code size or you happen to particularly dislike MFC you can easily use the standard template library classes instead.

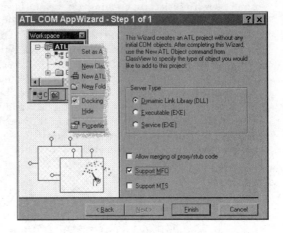

3.52 PM Create Namespace Component

Add a new COM object using the wizard, selecting **Simple Object**. This will be the StarRaiders Namespace object so give it the name StarRaidersNamespace.

and

As the screenshots show, we have left most of the other names with the default values, except that I changed the interface name to IDontNeedThis. We only need standard ADSI interfaces, but the object wizard insists on creating a new interface for us, so we'll put up with having it there for now. The only other change we'll make is to the Prog ID name. The wizard suggests `StarRaiders.StarRaidersNamespace`. This is in accordance with the usual ATL technique of using a project name to indicate roughly the type of object. The default value will work, but I've got two reasons for changing it to just `StarRaidersNamespace`. One is that this is the convention used for the ADSI system providers, and I don't want to depart from ADSI convention here. The other is that later on we're going to create a provider object, and I will *have* to give that object the ProgID StarRaiders, otherwise I'll muck up COM's ability to locate the object using StarRaiders `ADsPaths`. The StarRaiders namespace object and the StarRaiders provider object are the only two COM objects that will be registered, and it makes sense to keep them together in the ProgID part of the registry, so I'll give the namespace object a similar name.

3.54 PM

In the properties tab, make sure the interface is a dual, both-threaded interface that does not support aggregation.

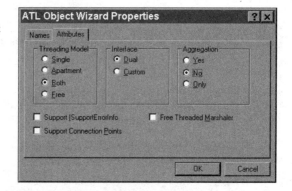

There's no harm in allowing the namespace object to support aggregation, but there's no point in doing so either – since that's not how you would use an ADSI provider.

3.55 PM

Build the project by pressing *F7*. That shouldn't be necessary at the moment, but if you don't, the next stage of adding interfaces sometimes produces a mysterious Failed to Add Interfaces error, presumably due to some bug in the wizard.

Once the build has finished, right click on the name in class view and select Add Interface. You'll be offered a list box with the project's new type library in it. That's no good to us – we want the Active DS type library, so click on Browse Type Libraries, to bring up the full list. Select the Active DS type library.

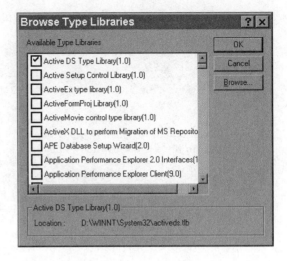

3.58 PM

You'll now get a screen asking which interfaces to add. Check the following interfaces: IADs, IADsContainer, IADsOpenDSObject and IADsPropertyList. Incidentally, if you were going to implement `IDirectoryObject` and `IDirectorySearch`, you'd want to check those here too.

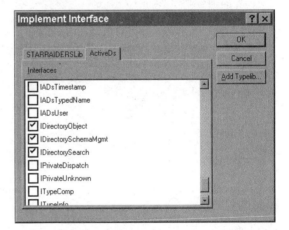

3.59 PM Ensure the Appropriate Headers and Libraries are Referenced

That's as far as the wizard will take us. We've now got to start coding. We've got make a few modifications to the wizard-generated files for three reasons. Firstly, the code as it stands isn't quite right, and will actually fail to compile! Secondly, although all the COM registry entries are created when the project is built, we've still got to deal with the ADSI registry entries. And thirdly, when the ADSI router hunts round to see what providers are on the system, it doesn't just look in the registry. It actually instantiates the namespace object and calls up a couple of methods on it – and if it encounters the wizard-generated stub functions that return `E_NOTIMPL`, it's not going to be too happy. In fact, it'll conclude there's a problem with the StarRaiders provider, and simply refuse to have anything to do with it...

411

Our first job is to look in the `StarRaiders.h` file, and find the line that imports the ActiveDS type library.

```
#include "resource.h"        // main symbols
#import "D:\WINNT\System32\activeds.tlb" raw_interfaces_only, raw_native_types,
no_namespace, named_guids
```

This line will cause the C++ compiler to create a C header file called `ActiveDS.tlh`, using the data in the type library. Unfortunately the type library includes a couple of definitions that have already been defined in the standard windows header file, and this will cause compilation errors. To be honest I don't like the results of `#import`ing type libraries anyway. You get a lot of extra code to do things like letting you access COM properties VB style, which some people like, but which I think complicates your code and gives you another set of language features to learn. Besides, in this case Microsoft has already written a standard ADSI header file for us. That file contains definitions of not just the interfaces but also other essentials such as the ADSI API helper functions, which you won't get in the type library. That file is what we really need here. So we'll comment out the offending line.

```
#include "resource.h"        // main symbols
// #import "D:\WINNT\System32\activeds.tlb" raw_interfaces_only, raw_native_types,
no_namespace, named_guids
```

And we'll `#include` the ADSI header file instead. I'm going to do this in the precompiled header, because most of our C++ files will need it. A good place is after the `#include`s that fetch the ATL headers, in `stdafx.h`:

```
#include <atlbase.h>
//You may derive a class from CComModule and use it if you want to override
//something, but do not change the name of _Module
extern CComModule _Module;
#include <atlcom.h>
#include <e:\adsisdk\inc\activeds.h>
```

Notice that I've taken the trouble to specify the correct path to include the ADSI 2.5 headers, not the ADSI 2.0 headers supplied with Visual Studio.

4.01 PM Define the ActiveDS LibID

Now let's attack the `CStarRaidersNamespace` class definition. Look at the long list of base classes, including the `IDispatchImpl` template classes – one for each ADSI dual interface:

```
//////////////////////////////////////////////////////////////////////////////
// CStarRaidersNamespace
class ATL_NO_VTABLE CStarRaidersNamespace :
    public CComObjectRootEx<CComMultiThreadModel>,
    public CComCoClass<CStarRaidersNamespace, &CLSID_StarRaidersNamespace>,
    public IDispatchImpl<IDontNeedThis, &IID_IDontNeedThis, &LIBID_STARRAIDERSLib>,
    public IDispatchImpl<IADs, &IID_IADs, &LIBID_ActiveDs>,
    public IDispatchImpl<IADsContainer, &IID_IADsContainer, &LIBID_ActiveDs>,
    public IDispatchImpl<IADsPropertyList, &IID_IADsPropertyList, &LIBID_ActiveDs>,
    public IDispatchImpl<IADsOpenDSObject, &IID_IADsOpenDSObject, &LIBID_ActiveDs>
{
```

These won't link because of the reference to the address of the variable `LIBID_ActiveDs`. This variable is declared as a const extern GUID in `ADsiid.h`, which is implicitly `#include`d by `ActiveDS.h`. It is supposed to be the GUID of the type library, and is needed to allow `IDispatch` to do its work. Unfortunately our code doesn't have an actual definition for `LIBID_ActiveDs` anywhere. (OK – I know – I lost it when I removed the `#import` statement). Our solution is messy, but it's quick and it works: we put the definition back in manually.

To do this we need to know the value of the GUID. The easiest way to get it is to use OLEView. So click on **Tools | OleView** to bring up the tool. Inside the left hand pane of OleView, expand the **Type Libraries** node, then the **Active DS Type** node. The right hand pane gives us the value. It's the one that starts 97D25…

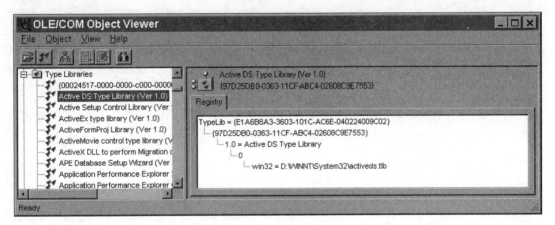

If you like, spend a couple of seconds cursing the programmer who wrote this bit of oleview, and didn't add any code to let you cut and paste the GUID from this screen through the clipboard. (Actually you can cut and paste from the regedit, but even that won't help you much since the value is presented in registry format and we need it in C++ format). Then add this code near the beginning of the `StarRaiders.cpp` file in your project (it's as good a place as any!). Check the GUID carefully for typos!

```
#include "StarRaiders_i.c"
#include "StarRaidersNamespace.h"
const GUID LIBID_ActiveDs  = {0x97D25DB0, 0x0363, 0x11CF, {0xAB, 0xC4, 0x02, 0x60,
0x8C, 0x9E, 0x75, 0x53}};
```

By the way, it doesn't really matter what file we put the definition in as long as it's there somewhere. I just picked `StarRaiders.cpp` because it is the main project file. The one thing you mustn't do is try to add the definition in what might look the most obvious place – the same place as all the other GUID definitions, in `StarRaiders_i.c`, because that file will get overwritten the next time the project's IDL file gets compiled…

One other point while we're looking at `StarRaiders.h`. You might notice that `CStarRaidersNamespace` is still derived from `IDontNeedThis`:

```
class ATL_NO_VTABLE CStarRaidersNamespace :
    public CComObjectRootEx<CComMultiThreadModel>,
    public CComCoClass<CStarRaidersNamespace, &CLSID_StarRaidersNamespace>,
    public IDispatchImpl<IDontNeedThis, &IID_IDontNeedThis, &LIBID_STARRAIDERSLib>,
```

At some point we ought to remove this line, and all references to `IDontNeedThis`, but I'm leaving it in for now because I want to use it to illustrate something to do with type libraries later on. When we do delete all references to this interface, we'll want to remove it from the IDL file as well. By the way, if you've compiled (and therefore registered) your provider while `IDontNeedThis` or a similar unwanted interface was still defined, don't forget to run `Regsvr32 -u` on the compiled dll to remove the `IDontNeedThis` registry entries before you start removing it from files!

Anyway, back to writing StarRaiders...

4.04 PM

Next, we need to make sure we have the right libraries in the project. Select Project|Settings|Link|Input and add the libraries `ActiveDS.lib` and `ADsIID.lib`. Make sure when you do this that you've selected All Configurations in the list box.

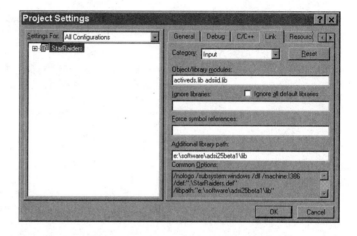

Depending where you've put the ADSI libraries and headers you may need to modify the search path for the libraries. Remember this is especially important because Visual Studio 6 currently comes with out of date versions of these libraries. Make sure the order of the search paths stops the compiler from finding the Visual Studio versions first. You can do this either by (i) explicitly giving the path name of each library to be included, (ii) modifying the search path under the Tools|Options|Directory dialog, or (iii) specifying additional paths in the Input section of the Link tab of the Project | Settings dialog. As you can see from the screenshot, I've used the third method.

4.18 PM Define _ATL_NO_UUIDOF

We're getting there. Another change to the project settings now. Go to Project|Settings|C/C++|Preprocessor, and add the symbol _ATL_NO_UUIDOF to the preprocessor symbols. This is necessary to prevent compilation errors because we are getting the ADSI GUID's from the library, `ADsiid.h`, and ATL 3.0 normally expects to find them in header files.

4.19 PM Add Registry Script

The next step is to sort out the registry. ATL will create self-registering code that can register all your COM objects for you, but we also need to register the fact that our dll is an ADSI provider. We could do it manually. If we did it that way, the required entry would be under the `HKLM/Software/Microsoft/ADs/Providers` key. This key contains all the ADSI providers. Each provider needs a subkey whose name is the name of the provider, and whose default value is the ProgID of the namespace object. In other words, in our case, we need to create a key `HKLM/Software/Microsoft/ADs/Providers/StarRaiders` with default value `StarRaidersNamespace`. The screenshot shows what this looks like in Regedit.

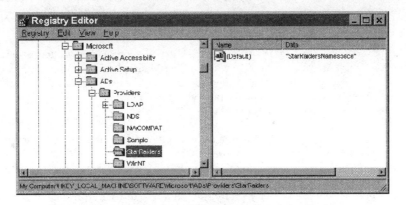

To get our provider to self-register itself as an ADSI provider, we'll create a new registry script. Open up a text editor – any one of Wordpad, Notepad or Word will do nicely, and type in the following code.

```
HKLM
{
    NoRemove SOFTWARE
    {
        NoRemove Microsoft
        {
            NoRemove ADs
            {
                NoRemove Providers
                {
                    ForceRemove StarRaiders = s 'StarRaidersNamespace'
                    {
                    }
                }
            }
        }
    }
}
```

If you haven't seen registry scripts before, they are fairly simple.

Roughly speaking, the registry script lists one or more registry keys, with instructions on what should be done with each key. The curly braces are used each time you step one level into the registry, and the usual abbreviations HKCR, HKLM, etc. are used for the registry hives. So for the script above, if you ignore the keywords NoRemove and ForceRemove for a moment, you can see that we are navigating down to the key HKLM/SOFTWARE/Microsoft/ADs/Providers/StarRaiders. Everything after the = indicates the default value that should be placed in that key. If you want to add other named values, use the syntax

```
val <Name> = <Value>
```

The s indicates that the value type is a single string, and the single quote marks force the registrar to take everything, including spaces, within the quote marks as one unit. Otherwise, it would assume a space indicates a new key word.

The general rule for a key listed in a registry script is that the key will be added during installation (assuming the key is not already present, in which case it'll simply be left untouched), and removed during uninstallation. If any values are supplied for any keys, these will be set during installation. In our StarRaiders script, the only value we've specified is for the StarRaiders key itself. We don't care about the values of any of the other keys above it.

This would be fine as it stands, except for one little problem. We don't really want to remove HKLM/SOFTWARE when we uninstall StarRaiders, since we'd probably still like to be able to reboot our computer again sometime – which might prove difficult with a sizeable part of the local machine registry hive deleted! Which is why the NoRemove keywords are liberally dotted through the script. These indicate the specified registry key should be left alone during uninstalls. Registry scripts are very useful, but you need to be careful you don't accidently wipe out half your registry with them! The other keyword, ForceRemove, has a different function. In the above example, it is applied to the StarRaiders key itself. This indicates that if the key already exists when an installation is attempted, then it should be removed completely, then rewritten with the values specified. This ensures we clear out any extra unwanted values that might have been stored in the StarRaiders key from previous installations.

So our StarRaiders registry script will cause the StarRaiders key to be added under HKLM/SOFTWARE/Microsoft/ADs/Providers when we install StarRaiders. This key will contain the default value, StarRaidersNamespace. If we uninstall StarRaiders, then this key will be removed, but all the keys above it will be left untouched.

To get our script into the StarRaiders project, first save the file as a text file in the same directory as the project, and giving it the name StarRaiders.rgs. Note that, although the format of the file is plain text, it doesn't have a .txt extension. (Be careful of this point. Some text editors, including WordPad, will simply refuse to accept that you don't want a .txt extension on a text file, and stick one on the end of the .rgs extension – which you'll then have to remove manually).

If we'd created an ATL executable or service, then AppWizard would have already created a registry script called projectname.rgs, which contains registration information for the executable. This isn't necessary for a dll, so AppWizard doesn't create any registry scripts. The only scripts you'll get automatically from the wizards for a dll are the ones created by the object wizard for your COM objects. Which leaves projectname.rgs as a rather convenient unused name for our script.

4.25 PM

We need to get the registry script we've just created into our project as a resource. Registry scripts are not a standard resource type recognised by the developer studio, but the ATL appwizard has created a custom resource type, 'REGISTRY', for us. The easiest way to include our new script is to go to the resource pane of the project workspace, and right-click over any of the items to bring up the context menu. Choose Import Resource and type the file name StarRaiders.rgs into the dialog box.

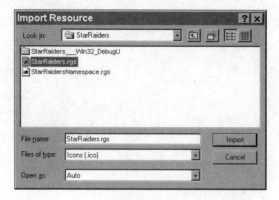

When you click on Import, you will be presented with a new dialog, asking you to confirm the custom resource type. Select "REGISTRY".

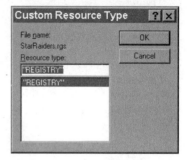

That completes the process. You should now be able to see the resource in the project. As a last point, you'll probably want a better name for the resource ID than the default "IDR_RESOURCE1". I've changed the ID to IDR_STARRAIDERS – you can do this by right clicking on the resource in the project workspace to bring up the Properties dialog, then modifying the ID.

4.26 PM

To make sure our script is processed, we need to add code in the dllRegisterServer and dllUnregisterServer functions. These functions are the exported functions that are called up by RegSvr32 when you use it to register or deregister a dll server, and must be implemented by any in-process COM server. Locate these functions in the file StarRaiders.cpp, and add the following code.

```
/////////////////////////////////////////////////////////////////////////////
// DllRegisterServer - Adds entries to the system registry

STDAPI DllRegisterServer(void)
{
    // add the extra code to register StarRaiders as an ADSI provider
    HRESULT hRes = _Module.UpdateRegistryFromResourceD(IDR_STARRAIDERS, true);
    _ASSERTE(hRes == S_OK);
```

```
    // registers object, typelib and all interfaces in typelib
    return _Module.RegisterServer(TRUE);
}


//////////////////////////////////////////////////////////////////////////
// DllUnregisterServer - Removes entries from the system registry

STDAPI DllUnregisterServer(void)
{
    // add the extra code to register StarRaiders as an ADSI provider
    HRESULT hRes = _Module.UpdateRegistryFromResourceD(IDR_STARRAIDERS, false);
    _ASSERTE(hRes == S_OK);

    return _Module.UnregisterServer(TRUE);
}
```

The line

```
    return _Module.RegisterServer(TRUE);
```

is the one that registers all the COM classes, by the way. It runs every registry script that has been mentioned in a DECLARE_REGISTRY_RESOURCE_ID macro. How the registry scripts get processed is something we don't need to worry about. Suffice to say that internally, ATL creates a COM object that exposes the IRegistrar interface and calls methods on that that read through the registry scripts.

By the way, our registry script assumes that ADSI has actually been installed on the computer. If you're writing a commercial-grade provider, you'll probably want an installation routine that checks for things like that. We'll cover installing Windows 2000 applications later in the book. One other point to bear in mind is that I've designed the StarRaiders dll as a self-registering dll because that's the easiest way to get it up and running and at the same time show you what registry entries are actually needed. If you're writing a commercial package these days, Microsoft recommends that you use the Windows Installer instead to write all your registry entries. We'll cover how to use the Windows Installer in Chapter 13.

4.27 PM

You may be relieved to know we have almost finished. Well at least, we've done most of what is strictly necessary. The next and final step is more a personal preference of mine (though with good reasons). Let's look at those stub interface methods. The Implement Interface Wizard has bunged them in the *header* file, presumably to follow ATL's philosophy of inlining everything to speed execution time. Strictly, you could leave them there, but I don't like it. For one, it'll slow compilation times because every time you change any methods, you'll have to recompile every file that includes that header. Secondly, this is an ADSI provider – a dll, so it's going to be running on client machines. There's no telling how low spec these machines will be, so I'd be concerned about executable file page sizes if too many functions are inlined. But most seriously, if you leave the implementations of *all* the methods in the headers in every class you create, you can bet the project will quickly become uncompileable due to circular dependencies of header files on each other. For all those reasons I prefer to keep my function definitions strictly in implementation files during development. Then when I've written the code, if I'm really that concerned about execution speed I can browse through it to see if any functions are suitable for inlining.

So after that little lecture, let's copy and paste the methods en bloc from
`StarRaidersNamespace.h` into `StarRaidersNamespce.cpp`. There's a bit of hand-coding
here, to separate the definitions from the implementations, as these are combined in the wizard-
generated code. You'll need to change all the `STDMETHOD` macros in the .cpp file to
`STDMETHODIMP` ones, and remove the function bodies from the header file. And since the wizard has
given us something like 30 methods, I'm not going to show you all the code, but after you've finished,
your header should look something like this:

```
      COM_INTERFACE_ENTRY(IADsOpenDSObject)
END_COM_MAP()
```

```
public:
// IADs
   STDMETHOD(get_Name)(BSTR * retval);
   STDMETHOD(get_Class)(BSTR * retval);
   STDMETHOD(get_GUID)(BSTR * retval);
   STDMETHOD(get_ADsPath)(BSTR * retval);
   STDMETHOD(get_Parent)(BSTR * retval);
   STDMETHOD(get_Schema)(BSTR * retval);
   STDMETHOD(GetInfo)();
   STDMETHOD(SetInfo)();
   STDMETHOD(Get)(BSTR bstrName, VARIANT * pvProp);
   STDMETHOD(Put)(BSTR bstrName, VARIANT vProp);
   STDMETHOD(GetEx)(BSTR bstrName, VARIANT * pvProp);
   STDMETHOD(PutEx)(LONG lnControlCode, BSTR bstrName, VARIANT vProp);
   STDMETHOD(GetInfoEx)(VARIANT vProperties, LONG lnReserved);
// IADsContainer
   STDMETHOD(get_Count)(LONG * retval);
   STDMETHOD(get_NewEnum)(IUnknown * * retval);
// etc. remaining definitions removed for clarity
```

4.32 PM Implement IADs Methods

Now we can hunt out a couple of stub functions and replace them by real implementations. Find the
`IADs` `get_` methods amongst them all (wow – did the wizard really give us that many methods to
implement?), and change the code to

```
// StarRaidersNamespace.cpp : Implementation of CStarRaidersNamespace
#include "stdafx.h"
#include "StarRaiders.h"
#include "StarRaidersNamespace.h"


///////////////////////////////////////////////////////////////////////////
// CStarRaidersNamespace

// IADs
STDMETHODIMP CStarRaidersNamespace :: get_Name(BSTR * retval)
{
   if (retval == NULL)
      return E_POINTER;
```

```
        *retval = SysAllocString(_T("StarRaiders:"));
        return S_OK;
}
STDMETHODIMP CStarRaidersNamespace :: get_Class(BSTR * retval)
{
    if (retval == NULL)
        return E_POINTER;

    *retval = SysAllocString(_T("Namespace"));
    return S_OK;
}
STDMETHODIMP CStarRaidersNamespace :: get_GUID(BSTR * retval)
{
    if (retval == NULL)
        return E_POINTER;

    *retval = SysAllocString(_T(""));
    return S_OK;
}
STDMETHODIMP CStarRaidersNamespace :: get_ADsPath(BSTR * retval)
{
    if (retval == NULL)
        return E_POINTER;

    *retval = SysAllocString(_T("StarRaiders:"));
    return S_OK;
}
STDMETHODIMP CStarRaidersNamespace :: get_Parent(BSTR * retval)
{
    if (retval == NULL)
        return E_POINTER;

    *retval = SysAllocString(_T("ADs:"));
    return S_OK;
}
STDMETHODIMP CStarRaidersNamespace :: get_Schema(BSTR * retval)
{
    if (retval == NULL)
        return E_POINTER;

    return E_NOTIMPL;
}
```

By the way, I'm quite impressed by the wizard here –it actually checks the parameter lists for the methods and adds code to check for NULL pointers.

I've hard-coded the strings into the source code. My justification is that this is the sample code for a book. You'll probably want to do something slightly more flexible, like use a string table perhaps.

That – literally – constitutes the complete implementations of the IADs methods. All the get_ methods simply return the appropriate text. In StarRaiders we are not going to support class GUIDs so we return a blank string for the get_Guid method. Also, I haven't changed the wizard-generated code for get_Schema, because we aren't implementing a class schema object for the namespace class. (There's nothing in ADSI that says you can't do that, but it's not something that's commonly done, and generally I wouldn't recommend it. A class schema object implies you are going to put some schema-defined properties in the namespace object, but I'd be more inclined to view the namespace object as the point of access to the directory, rather than as something that is there to store properties in its own right). Similarly, I haven't modified any of the remaining IADs methods: Get(), Put(), GetEx(), PutEx(), GetInfo(), SetInfo() and GetInforEx(). There's no need for any implementations, because these methods implement the property cache and our namespace object doesn't have any modifiable properties to go in the property cache!

We have finished implementing the entire IADs interface on our namespace object. We haven't done the other interfaces yet, but we'll come to them.

There's something else that is an absolute must, but which a lot of programmers forget. Before we build the project, click on the **Tools** option on the main menu. Select **Options**, and pick the very last tab of the options property sheet that pops up – the one marked **Format**. This lets you choose the colours for when you edit your source and header files. For the category, **All Windows**, select red for comments, lime green for strings, and yellow for keywords and operators. This colour combination will make your project much more robust.

4.36 PM

Finally I've also selected the Unicode debug configuration, so we're now ready to compile the project.

Time for the final test. Have we just successfully built the StarRaiders provider? Let's see. Bring up the Active Directory browser (or if you're running NT4 and don't have adsvw, bring up dsbrowse. For the sake of being different I'll use dsbrowse.exe here.), and open the Namespaces object, ADs: Let's take a look…

One more point. I've presented what strikes me as the easiest way to set up a provider in ATL. It's not the only way to do it. The most obvious alternative option is to import the type library instead of `#include`ing `ActiveDS.h`. If you do this, you are to some extent on your own as the type library doesn't contain all the definitions that are picked up by `ActiveDS.h` – for example, the helper functions which are declared in `adshlp.h` (and implicitly included by `ActiveDS.h`) aren't there. You'll need to do some experimenting to find out what you do and don't need, depending on what features your provider implements. I'd see that as one good reason for using `ActiveDS.h` instead. Incidently, things weren't always that easy. The wizard to add interfaces from type libraries only arrived with Visual C++ 6 and ATL 3.0. Before that there was a lot of messing about with copying ADSI function definitions from `IADs.h` and figuring out what to do with IDL files. The first time I had to write a provider was a few months ago. I can't remember if we were still on VC++ 5 or whether VC++ 6 had just arrived but we hadn't yet discovered the power of its new wizards. At any rate I didn't have the benefit of this book, of the new ADSI 2.5 beta documentation – or of any documentation whatsoever on how to do a provider in ATL for that matter. It took me a couple of weeks to figure out and implement a complicated procedure involving lots of typing in of ADSI methods, recreating the ADSI IDL file, and generating a new type library. So count yourselves lucky!

Provider Architecture

I hope that's whetted your appetite for provider writing. Unfortunately it would be stretching the truth a bit to consider what we've done as implementing a provider. All we've got so far is a namespace object that the ADSI router can identify, but which doesn't contain any other ADSI objects. We've got a lot more work to do to get the stuff inside the directory sorted out. In a few minutes (or pages) I'm going to give you an architectural run-down of the StarRaiders provider, but first I want to step back a minute and look at the issues you'll face in general when deciding on your provider design.

The most important point to make is this:

> **In most cases an ADSI provider will be a service provider, not a directory provider.**

The reason is quite simple: ADSI providers are dlls, and hence reside on the same machine as the client. (Remember, a directory provider implements the directory as well as the interface, a service provider doesn't).

Think about it. The most obvious ADSI provider that is a directory provider is the Microsoft sample provider. It implements the directory in the registry. In fact, if you've installed the Sample, you can actually read the directory directly, under the `HKLM/Software/Microsoft/ADs/Sample` key. But this means that the directory is local to the machine you are running the sample on. If you hook up to the same Microsoft Sample Provider on a different machine, you'll actually be looking at a different directory, stored in the new machine's registry. This behaviour may be fine in a few cases, but in most cases will be unacceptable. After all, isn't the whole point of having a directory to make it available for people to use? The two system providers we use in this book are certainly service providers. The LDAP provider simply hooks up to the LDAP interface that another directory service has exposed, while the WinNT provider runs off to the local network domain controllers and uses information in their registries and API calls to construct the directory it exposes to clients.

So the usual structure will be something like as shown in the figure. The directory will be located on a central server, and the ADSI providers will connect to it over the network.

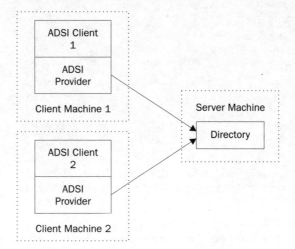

If the client base is large, or reliability is essential, the directory may be replicated over several servers. At any rate it will be separate from the providers. Again, if the client base is large, it will probably be appropriate to code up the directory as an NT service.

As for communications? Well, you've got all the standard options available. DCOM, RPC, etc. Which you choose depends on the precise nature of your problem. These days, for most situations DCOM is probably as easy a choice as any. (Especially since the ADSI provider already uses COM anyway!). The other advantage of using DCOM here is that if required you can use Microsoft Transaction Server (MTS) to implement transactions and improve scaleability. This means that providers will simultaneously act both as in-process COM servers and as clients to remote servers. Well they say this is the age of distributed computing!

One other point I would like to make is that I'm assuming that the directory exists as a centralised directory. This isn't necessarily true. We've just demonstrated that the WinNT provider does not really access a central directory, but ultimately gleans its information from the registries of computers on the network. If your directory is of this nature, then you've probably got a choice between the following two architectures:

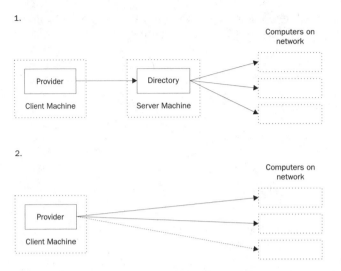

In the first architecture, the ADSI provider directly runs round the system, gathering the information it needs in response to a query. The alternative, shown underneath, uses the provider to connect to a central server directory, which periodically updates and stores the information. Of these, the first example has the advantage of being easier to code up, but may give poor performance as it searches round your network to answer each query. If many clients are running, this may also give rise to a lot of network traffic. The alternative, using a central server directory, will give you a more complex architecture to code up. On the other hand, response times should be faster and network traffic may be reduced as each query from the client simply involves one request to the server, which hopefully has already cached the information. (Though this is not necessarily true. Network traffic might actually be greater if the server is gathering and refreshing a lot of information in case any clients ask for it, but no clients do so!). You would also need to consider the implications of the central server having information that is slightly out of date.

It should be obvious from this discussion that the architecture of a provider and the corresponding directory service is not a trivial problem. A large number of factors concerning client load, the need for up to date information, and the kind of network traffic generated by directory queries, needs to be balanced. Anyway, since this book is about ADSI, not about how to write directory services, I'll leave the subject there.

OK – so let's have a look how I've chosen to put all this into practice in StarRaiders.

StarRaiders Architecture

The previous discussion was for a real commercial ADSI provider. For StarRaiders, my aim was to get up a reasonable working provider that illustrates the main points about implementing the ADSI interfaces. Because of that, I've not followed all of what I've just recommended. In particular, StarRaiders uses an access database as its back-end database and doesn't make any attempt to use any form of data remoting – which means it is a highly machine-specific provider.

I've called the central registry based StarRaiders database the *StarBase*, and if you download and install StarRaiders, you'll find the database with some sample data in it in the file StarBase.mdb. Internally, StarRaiders accesses it using ATL's OLE DB consumer template classes, which are beyond the scope of this book, although they are covered in Wendy Sarret's *Visual C++ 6 Database Programming*, available from Wrox, ISBN 1-861002-41-6.

We're going to move on to look at the code I've added to the basic Namespace object we've got so far, to actually expose the entire StarRaiders directory. I've mentioned that we won't be presenting the whole code. ADSI providers are big projects, and there's a lot of behind the scenes work going on inside StarRaiders. What I'm going to do for the rest of this chapter is pick out and talk about the bits you need to know to understand key issues in coding a provider, and the bits that illustrate potential traps and pitfalls that may make your provider misbehave if you're not careful.

Anyway, before we begin, let's check out the actual directory structure exposed by the StarRaiders provider. Here it is:

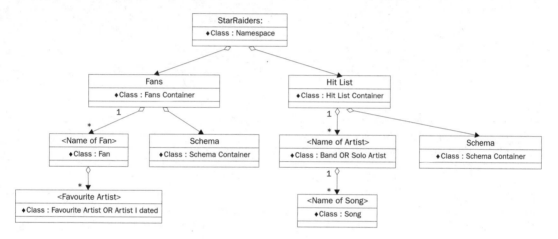

The figure shows the directory information tree for StarRaiders – with the exception that the individual objects in the schema containers are not shown (These are the class, property and syntax objects relevant to that subtree). Where relationships between classes are marked 1...*, many children may be contained by one parent. Each object is marked in the diagram with its name and its class.

The following diagram lists the properties exposed by each class. It includes abstract and auxiliary classes which can never be actually instantiated in the StarRaiders provider. Recall that to find all the properties for a class, you need to check the ones exposed by that class, as well as the ones exposed by any abstract and auxiliary classes from which it is derived.

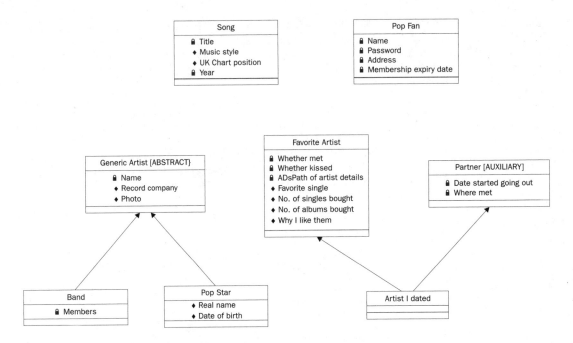

You'll notice that fans are able to store some incredibly useful information in the objects in the Fans subtree of StarRaiders. For example whether you've kissed your favourite artist. This kind of stuff is useful to artists too. As you can probably imagine, the job of being a pop star involves kissing quite a few people, and it's quite easy to forget who you've actually kissed. So having such information in a central database can save a lot of struggling to remember.

So – a quick overview of the main C++ classes in StarRaiders. Firstly, the ones that represent the COM objects. Since I'm using ATL, these are all implemented as templates of the form CComObject<CMyClass>.

Class	Function
CComObject<CStarRaidersNamespace>	The top level namespace object
CComObject<CStarRaidersProvider>	The object that implements IParseDisplayName, allowing direct access to other objects
CComObject<CStarRaidersContainer WithCache>	Implements the objects that are containers and have properties defined in the schema – that is Fans, Bands and Solo Artists.
CComObject<CStarRaidersLeaf>	Implements the leaf objects: Songs, Favorite Artists and Artists Dated.

Class	Function
CComObject<CStarRaidersClass>	Implements class schema objects in the schema containers
CComObject<CStarRaidersProperty>	Implements property objects in the schema containers
CComObject<CStarRaidersSyntax>	Implements syntax objects in the schema containers
CComObject<CStarRaidersFans Container>	Implements fans container
CComObject<CStarRaidersHitList Container>	Implements hit list container
CComObject<CStarRaidersFanSchema Container>	Implements schema container for fans schema
CComObject<CStarRaidersHitListSchema Container>	Implements schema container for hit list schema

There are quite a few different classes here, but almost all the code is common across the classes. The only places where the different classes need different code is in enumerating children and returning standard information like `ADsPaths`. Here the C++ classes that implement more than one different ADSI class use C-style switch statements to figure out what to do based on the ADSI class, stored as a member variable. I haven't used inheritance here to implement similar functionality because I figured the class hierarchy imposed by ATL is already complex enough without me adding to it! For the same reasons of not wanting to make the code too complex in ways not related to ADSI, I've chosen not to define my own templates to achieve the same effect.

That's quite a long list, but these C++ classes for the most part don't do that much. They handle the `IADs` methods like `get_Name`, `get_ADsPath`, etc. And they enumerate children and are able to create COM instances for their children, but that's about it. All the stuff related to the property caches is handled by a separate class, `CPropertyCache`. An instance of this class is contained as a member variable in each of the C++ classes which have property caches – that is `CStarRaidersLeaf` and `CStarRaidersContainerWithCache`. In general, the property cache methods exposed by ADSI objects – that is to say the `IADs` and `IADsPropertyList` methods (but not the `IADs` automation properties) simply defer to the corresponding function in the `CPropertyCache` – like this:

```
STDMETHODIMP CStarRaidersLeaf :: Put(BSTR bstrName, VARIANT vProp)
{
   AssertValid();
   return m_pCache->Put(bstrName, vProp);
}
```

Similarly, all communication with the StarBase is handled by another class, `CStarBaseConnection`. An instance of this class is associated with every ADSI COM object (apart from ones like the `namespace` object and the `schema` objects, which don't actually need the back-end database for anything).

We're going to be covering the `CPropertyCache` class quite a bit, since it illustrates quite a few general principles concerning the property cache. On the other hand, we won't really be talking about `CStarBaseConnection` much, since communication with the back-end database is very provider-specific. We just need to be aware that it's got functions that let you grab the relevant data from the registry.

There are also a few utility functions, which I've defined in files `Utilities.cpp` and `Utilities.h`. These are generally concerned with manipulating Variants. Some of these functions are covered in Appendix C. The most important ones are:

Name	Description
`ConvertVariantType()`	Changes a Variant from one type to another. This is more sophisticated than the `VariantChangeType()` API function, since it allows for the source or destination Variant to contain a `SAFEARRAY`.
`GetToGetExFormat()`	Converts a value stored in the format used by the `IADs::Get()` method to the format used by `GetEx()`
`GetExToGetFormat()`	The reverse of `GetToGetExFormat()`

As far as the COM objects themselves are concerned, there's not that much to them apart from implementing the interface methods. I have however added one extra method to most of the classes that implement COM objects:

Name	Description
`ADsInitialize()`	Initializes the object with whatever data is required to ensure that the C++ instance is connected to the correct directory object, and with the correct security credentials.

Defining an initialization function for COM objects might look dangerous since we've no guarantee that clients will use it. However, we are safe here. The only objects that are externally createable for an ADSI provider are the namespace and provider objects. All other objects can only be created by calling methods on other objects above them in the directory tree. Hence we can always ensure that `ADsInitialize()` is called on an object when it is created. The namespace and provider objects have no need for this function and don't implement it.

ATL Class Structure

If you're new to ATL, and you're confused by these `CComObject<>`s lurking around, a word of explanation. ATL works by providing some standard classes that implement all the boilerplate code that most COM objects need. Stuff like `QueryInterface()` and `AddRef()`, as well as class factories. MFC does the same thing – but with MFC you get given a class right at the bottom of the inheritance tree that you can customize. In other words you write a class that's derived from the standard MFC classes. ATL doesn't do that. With an ATL COM object, your class fits in the middle of the inheritance tree, and one of the standard ATL classes (or rather, templates), derives from your class. This means if you look at the inheritance tree of a C++ class that implements a COM object, using ATL, you see something like this:

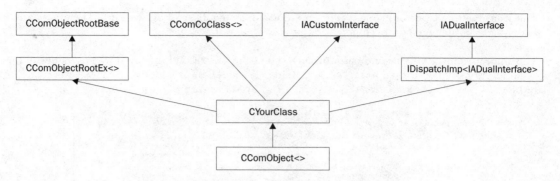

The figure shows the most common structure. There are alternative templates for some of the classes in the inheritance tree, that may occur – for example CComObjectRootEx<> is sometimes used in place of CComObjectRoot<>.

CYourClass is the class that you customize – the one that you actually put the implementations of the COM interface methods in. CComObject<CYourClass> is the actual COM object, and is the thing that must actually be instantiated. CYourClass is in fact an abstract class – if you try a declaration in an ATL project like

```
CYourClass variableName;
```

you'll get a compiler error complaining about pure virtual functions defined but not implemented.

CComObjectRoot and CComObjectRootEx, by the way, implement IUnknown. ComCoClass deals with the class factory, and IDispatchImpl<> deals with the IDispatch methods. The other classes, the ones with names beginning with I are the abstract classes in the header files produced by the IDL compiler. CComObject<> actually overrides and provides implementations for some of the IUnknown stuff.

Security

The StarRaiders security model is quite simple. There are three categories of users:

- ❑ **Administrator**. These have authenticated using the administrator user name and password, stored in the StarBase.

- ❑ **Customers**. These have authenticated using the username and password of a particular fan.

- ❑ **Guests**. These have not been authenticated.

There is no connection between StarRaiders authentication and Windows accounts.

It is possible to set three levels of security:

- ❑ **None**. Access to read and write any part of the directory is open to everyone.

- ❑ **Read Only**. The administrator has full read/write access, but every one else has only read access.

- ❑ **Secure**. The administrator has full read/write access. Customers have read access to the schema and hit list and read/write access to their own data. Guests have only read access – and then only to the schema and hit list. They cannot view any customers' records.

The secure setting is the only one you'd want to use once the directory is working. The others are really there for debugging/development purposes.

The administrator username and password, as well as the security setting are stored as values in the same registry key that is used to register StarRaiders as an ADSI provider: HKLM/Software/Microsoft/ADs/Providers/StarRaiders:

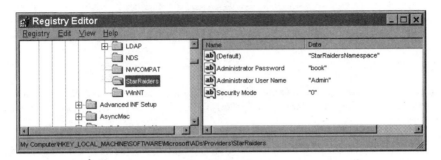

These settings are not part of the directory, and not accessible through ADSI. Mostly because in Chapter 12, when we cover MMC, we're going to develop a StarRaiders management snap-in, and I want some settings outside the directory that we can manage!

Security is not going to be a major part of our coding effort. The CStarBaseConnection class handles it in a very simple way. This class stores the user name and password by which the client is authenticated to this object. If the client does not have write access to the object, the function that writes properties will fail. If the client has no access to certain children of the object, then these children will be skipped when the StarBaseConnection enumerates over those children. This means that the COM classes will not even see that these children exist, making it impossible for any ADSI client to see them or bind to them. Once again, this is possible because all the COM objects below the Namespace are not externally createable.

Believe it or not, we've now got enough theory to start coding properly. We'll soon have to take two more theory breaks to cover how to override ATL's IDispatch implementation and how COM uses Monikers to bind to an object, but we'll come to those in good time. For now – let's play Pop Stars!

Coding Non-Externally-Createable ADSI Objects.

In this section we'll go through how to make sure the COM objects within your provider are correctly hidden from your registry.

One key point to understand about the ADSI COM objects (other than the namespace and provider object), is that clients should not be able to access these objects directly through CoCreateInstance(). You get an ADSI object either through browsing the directory, or through calling ADsGetObject(). Browsing through a directory means the object is created through calls to methods on its container, while ADsGetObject() means you obtain the object indirectly through a moniker (we'll cover monikers later in the chapter). This means that clients should be handed interface pointers on these COM objects, but shouldn't be able to find out about the objects directly. So there shouldn't be any registry entries for these objects, and they won't need class factories either.

For those objects that aren't created externally, it's often easier to type in the class definitions rather than using the wizard to create the object. You don't need any of the stuff in the IDL file that Object Wizard gives you, nor the registry script. All you need is the class definition and implementation, just like any non-ATL C++ class.

I'm going to use as an example the CStarRaidersLeaf abstract class, which implements objects right at the bottom of the tree.

Since all the COM objects implement some of the same interfaces as the Namespace object we'll create the CStarRaidersLeaf class by cutting and pasting. Create new files called StarRaidersLeaf.h and StarRaidersLeaf.cpp, cut and paste the entire contents of StarRaidersNamespace.h and StarRaidersNamespace.cpp into these files, and then do global substitutions of 'Leaf' for 'Namespace'. Now go to the StarRaidersLeaf.h file and remove all the method calls for IADsOpenDSObject and IADsContainer, and make sure that CStarRaidersLeaf is not derived from IDispatchImpl<IADsOpenDSObject>, or IDispatchImpl<IADsContainer>. You'll also need to remove the line DECLARE_REGISTRY_RESOURCE_ID, and the #include "resource.h" line. Both of these are near the top of the file. Also, remove the line that causes CStarRaidersLeaf to be derived from CComCoClass<>: we don't need class factory support. Finally, since the Leaf class also needs to implement IADsPropertyList, use the Implement Interface Wizard to add this interface. This means your CStarRaidersLeaf definition should look like:

```
#ifndef _ADSIBOOK_INCLUDED_STARRAIDERSLEAF_H_
#define _ADSIBOOK_INCLUDED_STARRAIDERSLEAF_H_

class CStarRaidersLeaf :
    public CComObjectRootEx<CComMultiThreadModel>,
    public IDispatchImpl<IADs, &IID_IADs, &LIBID_ActiveDs>,
    public IDispatchImpl<IADsPropertyList, &IID_IADsPropertyList, &LIBID_ActiveDs>,
{
    CStarRaidersLeaf()
    {
    }

DECLARE_NOT_AGGREGATABLE(CStarRaidersLeaf)

DECLARE_PROTECT_FINAL_CONSTRUCT()

BEGIN_COM_MAP(CStarRaidersLeaf)
    COM_INTERFACE_ENTRY2(IDispatch, IADs)
    COM_INTERFACE_ENTRY(IADs)
    COM_INTERFACE_ENTRY(IADsPropertyList)
END_COM_MAP()
```

If you were typing in a non-externally createable class, this code would be all you'd have to type.

If you do choose to use the wizard to create a class that isn't createable through CoCreateInstance, then you'll have to work through the wizard in the normal way, but manually remove:

❑   All references to your object in the IDL file

- ❑ The reference to your class in the object map (in the `ProjectName.cpp` file, in the block of MACROs that starts `BEGIN_OBJECT_MAP`).

- ❑ The `DECLARE_REGISTRY_RESOURCE_ID` line in your class's definition

- ❑ The line in your class's definition that derives your class from `CComCoClass<>`.

- ❑ The registry script for your class. You'll want to actually delete the `.rgs` file as well as delete the resource from your project.

The class, property and syntax objects may be added in the same way. In these cases, you will again need to remove all references to the `IADsContainer` interface from the C++ classes if you simply cut and paste the code from `CStarRaidersNamespace`. And you will need to respectively implement the interfaces `IADsClass`, `IADsProperty` and `IADsSyntax`.

We're doing a fair bit of hand coding here, and we are also subsequently running the ATL Implement Interface wizard on our customised code. It's possible that the Wizard might occasionally get confused by your non-wizard-generated code and refuse to work. To some extent you can minimise this risk by trying to use the wizard as early on as possible if you know you are going to need it. And if all else fails, you can create a new COM object (or even a new ATL project), use the wizard to get the code you want there, then cut and paste it into your provider. Luckily, when I tried it, I found that the Implement Interface wizard will work on classes that I've edited or typed in by hand, but it's worth checking what the wizard places in the COM MAP as it's not too intelligent about it. For example:

`IADsPropertyList`, `IADsClass`, `IADsProperty` and `IADsSyntax` are all derived from `IADs`, and this means that the entries:

```
COM_INTERFACE_ENTRY2(IDispatch, IADs)
COM_INTERFACE_ENTRY(IADs)
COM_INTERFACE_ENTRY(IADsClass)
```

will need to be changed to, for example:

```
COM_INTERFACE_ENTRY2(IDispatch, IADsClass)
COM_INTERFACE_ENTRY2(IADs, IADsClass)
COM_INTERFACE_ENTRY(IADsClass)
```

The Implement Interface wizard won't do this for you! This isn't a problem for `IADsContainer`, which is derived from `IDispatch` not `IADs`.

By the way, `IADsClass` defines a *lot* of methods (about 30), so be prepared for a lot of mundane typing and editing.

That's the basic COM objects inside the directory out of the way. But to get to any of them, we need to be able to browse through the directory. And that means that every container object must implement its associated enumerator object, which is the topic of the next section.

Collections: Enumerating Children of Containers.

Allowing clients to enumerate through the children of container objects means implementing the `IADsContainer::get_NewEnum` method. For this, you will need to create a COM object that implements `IEnumVARIANT` and initialize it with `IDispatch` pointers to all the child ADSI objects. Writing enumerators from scratch is actually relatively simple – if you're familiar with the `IEnumXXX` interfaces, then it should only take a couple of hours. However, if you're feeling lazy, then ATL provides template classes that will implement the enumerator for you. Unfortunately, if you look in MSDN to find out how to use them, you'll have a hard time of it, because these classes are almost completely undocumented. So we'll go through the process for an ADSI provider here. There's also a problem with one of the ATL helper classes which we'll have to work around, but we'll come to that in a bit. To start off, we'll go through the process of generating an enumerator using ATL throughout.

Creating a wrapper class requires only a couple of lines of code. First up, to simplify things, a useful `typdef`:

```
//  typedef for an enumerator class, CStarRaidersEnumerator, that uses ATL
// templates to implement IEnumVARIANT
typedef CComEnum<IEnumVARIANT, &IID_IEnumVARIANT, VARIANT,
    _Copy<VARIANT> > CStarRaidersEnumerator;
```

Because enumerators crop up quite often, I've put this line in the precompiled header in StarRaiders, `stdafx.h`.

You can now create the enumerator with something like:

```
CComObject<CStarRaidersEnumerator> *pEnum;
CComObject<CStarRaidersEnumerator> :: CreateInstance(&pEnum);
```

And initialize it with:

```
VARIANT *pVariants;
int iNItems;
// pVariants points to start of the array of VARIANTs in the enumeration list
// iNtems is the number of VARIANTs
hRes = pEnum->Init(pVariants, pVariants + iNItems, NULL, AtlFlagCopy);
pEnum->AddRef();
```

Apart from a slight problem that I'll explain in a minute, that's literally all you need!

So what's going on here then? Well, `CComEnum` is a template class that implements a generic enumerator. The template takes four parameters. The first two are the interface to be implemented and its IID. The third parameter is the data type that is to be enumerated over, and the fourth is a small class that implements functions to create, copy, and delete instances of this object. This class is necessary because in principle we could be enumerating over any arbitrary structure that you've dreamed up, and the enumerator must be able to correctly perform these basic operations on your structure. If you were implementing an enumerator for one of your own data types, then you'd need to write this class yourself, but since `VARIANT`s are fairly standard, ATL has already implemented a class for them, called `_Copy<VARIANT>`.

Since you want your enumerator to be a proper COM object, you wrap it up in a CComObject to provide all the IUnknown etc. stuff. Finally, you call the Init() function (actually implemented by another ATL template class, CComEnumImpl<>) to initialize your enumerator with the required VARIANTs. There are several flags that determine precisely how this is done, but the easiest to use for our purposes is AtlFlagCopy, which ensures that the enumerator takes a copy of the data, allowing you to subsequently delete the original data passed to the enumerator without worrying about corrupting the enumerator. For VARIANTs, ATL's _Copy<VARIANT> template will perform a deep copy. This means that if the VARIANT contains any pointers, the memory pointed to will be copied rather than just the pointer. It also means that if any pointers to interfaces need to be 'copied' then these pointers will be copied, but _Copy<VARIANT> will also automatically call AddRef() on them. As for the other parameters to Init, the third parameter should be left as NULL if you are using the AtlFlagCopy flag. The first two parameters point to the memory locations of the start and end (actually one byte past the end) of the data to be enumerated over. Since CComEnumImpl<> is a template class, the compiler knows the data type being pointed to, so it's safe to use expressions like pVariants + iNItems for the second parameter. According to the rules of pointer arithmetic, this expression will in fact be correctly evaluated to pVariants + iNItems*sizeof(VARIANT).

Finally that call to AddRef() is there because CComObject<>::CreateInstance() creates an object with a reference count of 0. We need to bump it up, either by calling AddRef(), or by QI()ing for an interface, before our enumerator will behave correctly as a COM object.

Now, on to that problem I mentioned. The trouble occurs in the _Copy<VARIANT> class that we need to carry out copy operations. If we dive into the ATL header files to look for its definition we find this:

```
template<>
class _Copy<VARIANT>
{
public:
    static HRESULT copy(VARIANT* p1, VARIANT* p2) {return VariantCopy(p1, p2);}
    static void init(VARIANT* p) {p->vt = VT_EMPTY;}
    static void destroy(VARIANT* p) {VariantClear(p);}
};
```

The problem with this is that the copy method of _Copy<VARIANT> simply calls the API function VariantCopy(). VariantCopy() will copy a variant correctly but only if the address to which the copy is made (p1 in the above code) already contains a valid VARIANT. VariantCopy() will fail if an attempt is made to copy to uninitialized memory. The problem with this is that this is the method which will be used to copy the VARIANT to the rgvars parameter of IEnumVARIANT::Next(). But if we look at the definition of IEnumVARIANT::Next(), we find

```
[local]
    HRESULT Next(
                [in] ULONG celt,
                [out, size_is(celt), length_is(*pCeltFetched)] VARIANT * rgVar,
                [out] ULONG * pCeltFetched
            );
```

In other words, rgvar is an [out] parameter with array dimensions specified by size_is(). According to the rules of COM the client will be expecting to have to allocate the memory, but not to have to initialize it. (Indeed, if ADSI providers weren't in-process servers, then initializing it would actually be a waste of time because the marshaller wouldn't bother transmitting the initialized values to the server anyway!). Realistically, your provider will have to expect that some ADSI clients will attempt to pass uninitialized memory in, which would be forwarded on to:

```
_Copy<VARIANT>::copy().
```

To make sure that our enumerator will work with any client, we need to supply our own class to replace _Copy<VARIANT>. The following code, replacing the earlier typedef for CStarRaidersEnumerator, will do the trick.

```
class _CopyCorrect
{
public:
    static HRESULT copy(VARIANT* p1, VARIANT* p2) {VariantInit(p1); return
VariantCopy(p1, p2);}
    static void init(VARIANT* p) {p->vt = VT_EMPTY;}
    static void destroy(VARIANT* p) {VariantClear(p);}
};


typedef CComEnum<IEnumVARIANT, &IID_IEnumVARIANT, VARIANT,
        _CopyCorrect > CStarRaidersEnumerator;
```

The only change here from ATL's class is that I've added a call to VariantInit() to ensure that any memory is initialised.

That is really all we need to know about enumerators in order to implement an ADSI provider. If you want more details about enumerators in ATL, there are good sections on this in both *Professional ATL COM Programming* by Richard Grimes (ISBN 1-861001-40-1), and *Beginning ATL 3 COM Programming*, by Grimes, Reilly, Stockton, Templeman and Watson(ISBN 1-861001-20-7), both published by Wrox. For now, let's see how we can put all this into practice in StarRaiders.

Enumerating Children of Containers

Enumerators need to be created when a request is made to a container to enumerate its children. This request will come via a call to the IADsContainer::get_NewEnum() property method. So let's see how this is implemented. For our example we'll take the Fans container object, which has as its children the fans schema container, along with all the objects representing the individual fans. Here's the code for CStarRaidersFansContainer::get_NewEnum().

We start off by getting a list of the children. This is done by requesting the list from the backend directory. We do this using a specially defined function, CStarBaseConnection::GetChildNames() which sticks the list of the names of the children in a CStringArray. The flag passed to this method indicates that we want all children rather than those of any one class. For StarRaiders, the StarBase only contains the 'real' data for fans, not the schema information, so we need to add one to the number of children to allow for the schema container.

By the way, note that this is the point at which security in StarRaiders is implemented: any children to which we do not have read access rights will simply not be returned by the call to `GetChildNames()`.

```
STDMETHODIMP CStarRaidersFansContainer :: get_NewEnum(IUnknown * * retval)
{
    if (retval == NULL)
        return E_POINTER;

    // get list of fans
    CStringArray csarrFans;
    m_pStarBaseConnection->GetChildNames(csarrFans, FLAG_ENUM_ALL);
    const int iNFans = csarrFans.GetSize();
    const int iNChildren = iNFans + 1;
```

Now we initialize the array of VARIANTs to be copied into the enumerator. Remember that an enumerator actually needs to return VARIANTs containing the IDispatch pointers to the COM objects. Having created the VARIANT array and the enumerator, we can go on to create the COM objects representing the children. The fan objects are represented by standard ATL COM objects based on the CStarRaidersContainerWithCache class. Notice that after each object is created, we immediately initialize it with a call to our ADsInitialize() function, which will bind the COM object to the appropriate directory object, and pass on the correct security credentials.

```
    // create the variant array that will be used to initialize the enumerator
    VARIANT *pVariants = new VARIANT[iNChildren];
    for (int i=0 ; i<iNChildren; i++)
        VariantInit(&(pVariants[i]));

    // create the enumerator
    CComObject<CStarRaidersEnumerator> *pEnum;
    CComObject<CStarRaidersEnumerator> :: CreateInstance(&pEnum);

    // create the child ADSI objects
    HRESULT hr;
    IDispatch *pDispatch;

    // the fans
    for (i=0 ; i<iNFans ; i++)
    {
        CComObject<CStarRaidersContainerWithCache> *pFan;
        hr = CComObject<CStarRaidersContainerWithCache>::CreateInstance(&pFan); ASH;
        pFan->ADsInitialize(csarrFans[i], L"Fans", m_pStarBaseConnection-
>GetUserName(),
            m_pStarBaseConnection->GetPassword(), FLAG_CLASS_FAN);
        hr = pFan->QueryInterface(IID_IDispatch, (void**)&pDispatch); ASH;
        pVariants[i].vt = VT_DISPATCH;
        pVariants[i].pdispVal = pDispatch;
    }

    // the schema container
    CComObject<CStarRaidersFanSchemaContainer> *pFanSchemaContainer;
    hr =
```

```
CComObject<CStarRaidersFanSchemaContainer>::CreateInstance(&pFanSchemaContainer);
ASH;
    hr = pFanSchemaContainer->QueryInterface(IID_IDispatch, (void**)&pDispatch);
ASH;
    pVariants[iNFans].vt = VT_DISPATCH;
    pVariants[iNFans].pdispVal = pDispatch;
```

There's no need to explicitly initialize the schema container, as there is only one fans schema container in the whole directory! Finally, we can initialize the enumerator by passing in our array of VARIANTs in to it.

```
    //initialize the enumerator and return it.
    hr = pEnum->Init(pVariants, pVariants + iNChildren, NULL, AtlFlagCopy); ASH;
    pEnum->AddRef();
    *retval = pEnum->GetUnknown();


    return hr;
}
```

We now have enough code in the provider to start browsing through the directory. To prove that it works, here's what it looks like from adsvw.exe

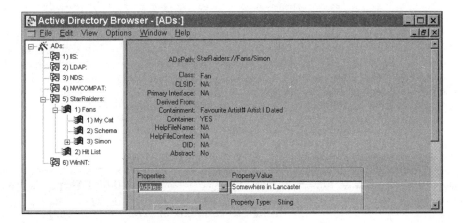

Creating Multiple Instances of Objects

The code above unquestioningly creates new COM objects whenever a client attempts to enumerate through a container. There's no code in there to check whether the appropriate COM objects are already up and running, and if so, to simply hook up to them instead. This is not only simpler but is the correct behavior. Although it's not documented, the strong advice I've had from Microsoft is that in this ADSI, providers should create new COM objects. The only difference it makes to the client is that there are two separate property caches, each of which won't know anything about the existence of the other. This is potentially a dangerous situation to be in, so if you're coding ADSI clients it's probably worthwhile taking care to try to avoid requesting multiple interface pointers for the same Directory Object.

The reason I say it's a dangerous situation is because of this scenario.

Let us say we have separately obtained interface pointers to two objects with the same `ADsPath`, stored in `strPath`:

```
Set oObj1 = GetObject(strPath)
Set oObj2 = GetObject(strPath)

oObj1.Description = "Nice Description"
strDesc = oObj2.Description
oObj2.SetInfo
```

Do you see the problem? We've set the description on `oObj1`, which means that the property `Description` in `oObj1`'s property cache has been updated. Then we work with the property cache of `oObj2`. But because this is a different property cache, it does not have the updated description in it. `strDesc` will be set to the old value of the description, while the new description will not be written to the directory service with the call to `SetInfo`.

So the message is that if you independently retrieve different interface pointers that represent the same directory object, then those interface pointers will be pointing to different COM objects, and so you must be aware that you are dealing with separate property caches.

From the above, you might expect that it would be better for the client if the provider checked if it already has an interface pointer for a certain directory object when asked for another one, so it could simply return the same object if appropriate. However, you should still not do this, simply because that is not how Microsoft have decided that providers should behave, and for consistency it is important that your provider should behave the same way as other providers. One other reason for keeping to separate COM objects is that a client may bind multiple times to the same directory object, but give different security credentials each time – that would be hard to resolve if all bindings connected to the same COM object.

Working with the Property Cache

To a large extent, what you do with the property cache is a matter for your own internal architecture. The reason for putting in a section on it here is because in some ways the ADSI specifications for how the property cache works aren't entirely intuitive. Which means this is an area that, if you're not careful, you can easily end up with a provider that you think behaves correctly but in fact doesn't. So let's review what you should be doing in the `IADs` methods.

`GetInfo()`, `SetInfo()` and `GetInfoEx()` are conceptually reasonably simple. Your implementations of these methods will need to copy the data from the property cache to the directory, or vice versa. Depending on how much error and schema checking you've put into your `Put()` and `PutEx()` methods, you may need to check that your data is valid. It's fairly normal to do some schema checking in the `Put()` and `PutEx()` methods but leave any questions of security or whether you have the right to modify the data to be checked by `SetInfo()`.

If during a call to SetInfo(), the provider is unable to write some properties to the directory, then it should still attempt to write all the remaining ones that it can, and return a partial success code, for example S_ADS_ERRORSOCCURRED. Remember, it's ultimately the responsibility of the directory service to decide whether or not to accept a change. The fact that SetInfo() can return this success code reminds us that when writing clients you should always check for a success or failure of a method call by using the SUCCEEDED and FAILED macros. For the case of SetInfo() the client may then subsequently wish to check whether a SUCCEEDED result is S_OK or S_ADS_ERRORSOCCURRED.

For GetInfo(), the main point to watch is that GetInfo() called explicitly should be ruthless: any stuff already in the cache will need to be overwritten. If there is some data that's more up to date than data in the directory, then tough! If GetInfo() has been called implicitly, it should be more forgiving, and not attempt to load values that are already present in the cache. I've handled this in StarRaiders by having a separate function, GetInfoInternal(), which is the one actually called if GetInfo() needs to be called implicitly. GetInfoInternal() will not overwrite any values that are not blank. My actual implementation of the COM GetInfo() method simply clears out the property cache then calls GetInfoInternal().

Get() is a more interesting case. The ADSI specifications require that Get() should retrieve the value of the property if it is in the cache, and call GetInfo() if it isn't. However, it is also important that Get() does correctly handle things via the schema. The ADSI specifications require that correct implementation of Get() involves using the schema: Get() should not return any properties that are not explicitly defined in the schema, even if they happen to be present in the cache. The IADsPropertyList methods can use the cache directly, but the IADs methods should make sure they are referring to the schema.

This means that your implementation of Get() should normally involve the following steps:

1. Look for the specified property in the schema. If it's not there, then return an error.

2. Look for the specified property in the cache. If it's there, then return with its value.

3. If we couldn't find the property in the cache, then implicitly call GetInfo() (in the case of StarRaiders, implemented as GetInfoInternal()).

4. Now look for the property in the cache. If it's there, then return it, otherwise return a fail code, most probably E_ADS_PROPERTY_NOT_FOUND.

This isn't the only way of doing it, but you will need to implement Get() in a way that gives the same results as this algorithm.

GetEx(), obviously, should behave exactly like Get(), apart from always returning single-valued properties in a SAFEARRAY.

Put() and PutEx() should normally always succeed if the property you are trying to Put() is defined in the schema. If the property is not in the cache, then a new value should be written to the cache. Bear in mind that if the ADS_PROPERTY_CLEAR flag is passed to PutEx(), then this should actually remove the property from the cache, not merely set it to an empty value. If there are problems with the value supplied, for example it is an invalid value for that particular property, or the client does not have access to write to that property, then it is legitimate for Put() or PutEx() to still succeed, but for the error to be detected when the call to SetInfo() is made. This relieves the provider of some of the burden of performing some error checking which the central server may be better placed to carry out. On the other hand, it's equally OK for Put() and PutEx() to carry out any checks that can be done without referring to the directory service, and return an error if these checks indicate the requested change should not be allowed. So clients need to be aware that a failure may be returned on either method call.

Moving on to the IADsPropertyList methods: there shouldn't be any problems with these. The main point to watch out for is that IADsPropertyList::getPropertyCount() should return the number of properties actually in the cache at that time. This may be less than the number of properties set for the corresponding directory object, and will be zero if the cache hasn't been initialised yet. Also, be aware that the IADsPropertyList methods shouldn't waste any time looking at the schema. They are designed to work directly with the cache.

It probably occurs to you that a lot of the behaviour I've just described isn't entirely user-friendly or intuitive, but it is how ADSI has been defined. You may choose to do something slightly different with your own provider. And if you did, you wouldn't be the first to depart from the ADSI specifications. (For example, my own tests seem to suggest that in ADSI 2.5, calling GetInfoEx() in the WinNT provider appears to update the whole cache, not just the requested property!). But if you do so then be aware that you are departing from the standard, so your provider will be behaving in a way that clients may not be expecting.

So let's see how I've implemented these principles in StarRaiders. The relevant code is entirely in the CPropertyCache class, since this class deals with property caches in a generic fashion.

Implementing the Property Cache in StarRaiders

StarRaiders doesn't have any of the problems that plague providers like the LDAP provider – with some objects having property cache but no schema etc., or operational attributes not being loaded by default. Everything here is neat and clear-cut: if you call GetInfo() then *all* properties defined in the schema are loaded. When writing your own providers, you'll make life a lot simpler for your clients if you follow this principle too!

Because things are simple in StarRaiders, I've been able to organise the schema by storing a couple of arrays of PROPERTY_VALUE structures. A PROPERTY_VALUE is a structure I've defined which stores all the information there is to know about a property:

```
struct PROPERTY_VALUE
{
    PROPERTY_VALUE() :pszName(NULL), vtOuter(0), vtInner(0), pvarValue(0) {};
    ~PROPERTY_VALUE() {delete pvarValue;};
    LPCWSTR pszName;
    VARTYPE vtOuter;
    VARTYPE vtInner;
```

```
    int iADsType;
    bool bIsMandatory;
    CComVariant *pvarValue;
};
```

Apart from a useful constructor and destructor, we have the name of the property, two VARTYPEs that indicate the normal way it is stored in a VARIANT, its ADSTYPE (ADSTYPE_CASE_IGNORE_STRING, etc.) for the benefit of the IPropertyList methods, a boolean to indicate if this is a mandatory property, and a pointer to the actual value, stored in a VARIANT (OK, ATL's derived CComVariant class). There are two arrays of these structures permanently available, one for the mandatory properties, and one for the optional properties:

```
private:
// other member variables of CPropertyCache removed for clarity
    int m_iNMandProps;
    int m_iNOptProps;

    PROPERTY_VALUE *m_arrMandProps;
    PROPERTY_VALUE *m_arrOptProps;

    int m_iEnumPos;    // for IPropertyCount::Next() to figure out where we are
    CRITICAL_SECTION cs;
};
```

If a value happens not to be in the cache, then this will be indicated by the pvarValue member of the corresponding PROPERTY_VALUE structure being NULL. These arrays are set up in the constructor of the CPropertyCache.

The VARTYPEs indicate the format in which the value should be returned in a call to Get(). The StarRaiders property cache also makes sure that values are stored internally in this same format. There are two of them because a multi-values property will have two VARIANTs – the main one, and the inner ones contained in the SAFEARRAY. So, for example, for a single valued BSTR, we'd have vtOuter=VT_BSTR, vtInner=0 because Get() will return a single valued BSTR as a VARIANT containing a BSTR. On the other hand, a multi-valued BSTR would have vtOuter=(VT_VARIANT | VT_ARRAY), vtInner = VT_BSTR, because Get() will return such a value as an array of VARIANTs, each of these VARIANTs in the array containing a BSTR. Get the idea?

This means we can have a relatively simple implementation of Get():

```
HRESULT CPropertyCache :: Get(BSTR bstrName, VARIANT * pvProp)
{
    ASSERT_VALID(this);

    if (pvProp == NULL)
        return E_POINTER;

    PROPERTY_VALUE *pValue = GetPropValueFromName(bstrName);
    if (pValue == NULL)
        return E_ADS_PROPERTY_NOT_FOUND;
```

```
    // if the value isn't in the cache, we need to do a GetInfo()
    if (pValue->pvarValue == NULL)
       GetInfoInternal();

    // if value still isn't in the cache, then it's just not there!
    if (pValue->pvarValue == NULL)
       return E_ADS_PROPERTY_NOT_FOUND;

    VariantInit(pvProp);
    VariantCopy(pvProp, pValue->pvarValue);

    ASSERT_VALID(this);
    return S_OK;
}
```

Clear? The only bit of that we haven't covered in the above discussion is my helper function, GetPropValueFromName(), which takes the property name and tracks down the corresponding PROPERTY_VALUE structure.

GetEx() can now be even simpler:

```
HRESULT CPropertyCache :: GetEx(BSTR bstrName, VARIANT * pvProp)
{
    CComVariant varValue;
    HRESULT hr;
    hr = Get(bstrName, &varValue);
    if (FAILED(hr))
       return hr;
    hr = GetToGetExFormat(*pvProp, varValue);

    return hr;
}
```

Here we're using one of the Variant conversion utility functions, GetToGetExFormat(), that we develop in Appendix C.

Implementing IADs::Put() is relatively simple as well – the only complication is that we need to allow for the possibility that the value might have been supplied in the wrong format inside the VARIANT – so we need to make sure it's in the right format using the ConvertVariantType() utility which we also develop in Appendix C.

```
HRESULT CPropertyCache :: Put(BSTR bstrName, VARIANT vProp)
{
    ASSERT_VALID(this);

    PROPERTY_VALUE *pValue = GetPropValueFromName(bstrName);
    if (pValue == NULL)
       return E_ADS_PROPERTY_NOT_FOUND;

    HRESULT hr;
    CComVariant *pvarNewValue = new CComVariant;
```

```
    hr = ConvertVariantType(*pvarNewValue, vProp, pValue->vtOuter, pValue-
>vtInner);
    if (FAILED(hr))
        return hr;

    delete pValue->pvarValue;
    pValue->pvarValue = pvarNewValue;
    return S_OK;
}
```

Implementing IADsPropertyList methods

Implementing these methods is different from the IADs methods because IADsPropertyList has very particular requirements for how it expects values to be returned. Instead of a VARIANT containing the value directly, we need a VARIANT containing an IDispatch pointer to a property entry object. In turn, this object should contain IDispatch interface pointers to property value objects. The property entry and property value objects are implemented by the COM runtime – so this is the only part of the StarRaiders provider where we want to call up external COM objects using CoCreateInstance.

We'll take as an example the IPropertyList::Item() method. This method is called to obtain an item specified by either its index or its name – supplied in a VARIANT:

```
HRESULT CPropertyCache :: Item(VARIANT varIndex, VARIANT * pVariant)
{
    if (pVariant == NULL)
        return E_POINTER;

    PROPERTY_VALUE *pPropValue = GetPropValueFromVariant(varIndex);
    GetPropertyAsEntry(pPropValue, pVariant);
    return S_OK;
}
```

This function itself is fairly simple: it calls a function, GetPropValueFromVariant(), which tracks down which PROPERTY_VALUE structure in the property cache holds the required property value. The process of returning the property value(s) in the appropriate format is handed to another function, GetPropertyAsEntry(). The reason for this is that there are a couple of other IPropertyList methods (Next() and GetPropertyItem()) which also need to use the same functionality to retrieve values – so it makes sense to have all methods call a common function to actually do the work.

Let's have a look at GetPropertyAsEntry(). It's fairly complex, partly as there are a fair number of automation properties on IPropertyEntry to set, and partly because we have to cope with the possibility of our property being single or multi-valued.

```
void CPropertyCache :: GetPropertyAsEntry(const PROPERTY_VALUE *pPropValue,
VARIANT *pvarProp)
{
    HRESULT hr;
    CComVariant *pvarAsADs = pPropValue->pvarValue; // this contains the value we
want,
```

```
    // but in IADs::Get() format.
    ASSERT(pvarAsADs != NULL);

    // first construct the property values (the property value objects not the
    // PROPERTY_VALUE structures, that is...

    // find out how many property values there are
    int iNVals = 1;
    if (pvarAsADs->vt == (VT_VARIANT | VT_ARRAY))
        iNVals = pvarAsADs->parray->rgsabound->cElements;
```

Now we've got the number of values, we need to prepare a VARIANT that will contain a SAFEARRAY of IDispatch pointers to the property value objects (technically a SAFEARRAY of VARIANTs containing IDispatch pointers.) This variant will become the Values automation property of the property entry. The VARIANTs containing IDispatch pointers to the property values are created by another member function, CreatePropValueObject(), which we'll look at in a moment.

```
    // prepare the VARIANT to take the property values
    CComVariant *pvarNewValues = new CComVariant;
    pvarNewValues->vt = (VT_ARRAY | VT_VARIANT);
    SAFEARRAY *psa;
    SAFEARRAYBOUND rgsabound[1];
    rgsabound[0].cElements = 1;
    rgsabound[0].lLbound = 0;
    psa = SafeArrayCreate(VT_VARIANT, 1, rgsabound);ASSERT(psa != NULL);

    // stick the property values in the SAFEARRAY
    if (pvarAsADs->vt == (VT_VARIANT | VT_ARRAY))
    {
        VARIANT *pvarOld;
        for (long i=0; i<iNVals ; i++)
        {
            hr = SafeArrayGetElement(pvarAsADs->parray, &i, (void**)&pvarOld); ASH;
            hr = SafeArrayPutElement(psa, &i,
                CreatePropValueObject(pvarOld, pPropValue->iADsType));
            ASH;
        }
    }
    else
    {
        long index = 1;
        hr = SafeArrayPutElement(psa, &index,
            CreatePropValueObject(pvarAsADs, pPropValue->iADsType));
        ASH;
    }
    pvarNewValues->parray = psa;
```

Now we have the VARIANT of values, we can create the property entry object. The final stage is to put the property entry object in the variant to be returned.

```
    // Create a propertyEntry object
    CComPtr<IADsPropertyEntry> spEntry;
```

```
        CComQIPtr<IDispatch, &IID_IDispatch> spDispatch;
        hr = CoCreateInstance(CLSID_PropertyEntry,
                        NULL, CLSCTX_INPROC_SERVER,
                        IID_IADsPropertyEntry,
                        (void**)&spEntry);
        hr = spEntry->put_Name(const_cast<LPWSTR>(pPropValue->pszName));
        hr = spEntry->put_ControlCode(0);
        hr = spEntry->put_ADsType(pPropValue->iADsType);
        hr = spEntry->put_Values(*pvarNewValues);

        // put the property entry in the VARIANT to be returned
        spDispatch = spEntry;
        pvarProp->vt = VT_DISPATCH;
        pvarProp->pdispVal = spDispatch;
    }
```

Finally, we'll check out the `CreatePropValueObject()` function which creates a
`PropertyEntry` COM object and puts the property value in it. There's no alternative here but to
use a big switch statement to cover all the different value types, but it's not too huge here because
StarRaiders only actually uses three of the ADSI data types – the case ignore string, the integer and
the boolean.

```
CComVariant *CPropertyCache :: CreatePropValueObject(
            const VARIANT *pvarValueAsADs, int iADsType)
{
    HRESULT hr;
    CComPtr<IADsPropertyValue> spVal;
    hr = CoCreateInstance(CLSID_PropertyValue, NULL,
                    CLSCTX_INPROC_SERVER,
                    IID_IADsPropertyValue,
                    (void**)&spVal);
    hr = spVal->put_ADsType(iADsType);
    switch (iADsType)
    {
    case ADSTYPE_CASE_IGNORE_STRING:
        ASSERT(pvarValueAsADs->vt == VT_BSTR);
        hr = spVal->put_CaseIgnoreString(pvarValueAsADs->bstrVal); ASH;
    case ADSTYPE_INTEGER:
        ASSERT(pvarValueAsADs->vt == VT_I4);
        hr = spVal->put_Integer(pvarValueAsADs->lVal); ASH;
    case ADSTYPE_BOOLEAN:
        ASSERT(pvarValueAsADs->vt == VT_I1);
        hr = spVal->put_Boolean(pvarValueAsADs->iVal); ASH;
    default:
        ASSERT(false);
    }
    CComVariant *pvarNewVal = new CComVariant;
    CComQIPtr<IDispatch> spDispatch = spVal;
    ASSERT(spDispatch != NULL);
    *pvarNewVal = spDispatch;
    return pvarNewVal;
}
```

Opening Providers to Scripting Clients

We mentioned in Chapter 2 that ADSI is fully accessible to scripting clients: these clients should always have access to methods from every ADSI interface on an object. We've also mentioned earlier in this chapter that this doesn't happen with the default ATL `IDispatch` implementation. Clearly we need to do something to override ATL.

So let's remind ourselves what actually happens when different types of clients attempt to execute a method on an object.

C++ clients use vtable binding: they obtain a pointer to the appropriate interface on an object either by specifying that interface in a call to `CoGetClassObject()`, or by performing a `QueryInterface()` call on another interface. The `CoGetClassObject()` call may be wrapped inside `CoCreateInstance()` or `CoCreateInstanceEx()`. Once the client has the interface pointer, the method can be called directly, using the `vtable`. The process should be very familiar because these calls explicitly appear in C++ code.

```
IADs *pNamespace;
HRESULT hRes;
hRes = CoCreateInstance(CLSID_StarRaidersNamespace, NULL, CLSCTX_INPROC_SERVER,
    IID_IADsNamespace, (void**)&pNamespace);
```

By the way, this code is here as an example. You wouldn't normally obtain an instance of a namespace object, or any other ADSI object in this way – you'd normally use `ADsGetObject()`. `CoCreateInstance()` is used where you explicitly know the CLSID of the object. But it'll do as an example for our discussion.

VB clients will use exactly the same process provided that the object variable is explicitly typed to the appropriate interface in the source code, and the method name is recognised. The only differences are that the `QueryInterface()` call is hidden by VB, and that the interface must be defined in a type library: VB uses the universal marshaller to perform marshalling using a type library, and cannot use standard or custom marshalling. However, where the object is explicitly typed VB can still use vtable binding.

If the object variable is explicitly typed, but the interface is a dispinterface and not available through the vtable, then VB will use `DispID` binding. This is less efficient than vtable binding, and involves the compiler actually calling up the `IDispatch` interface on the object, *while it is compiling*. The compiler will specifically call `IDispatch::GetIDsOfNames` to obtain the dispatch ID of the requested interface, and the IDs of the parameters passed to it. The VB compiler will then generate code to call `IDispatch::Invoke()`, passing it the IDs it has obtained.

You'll sometimes hear the term **early binding** used to indicate either vtable or `DispID` binding.

VB Scripting clients are more restricted. They cannot explicitly call QueryInterface(): the interpreters wouldn't be able to make any sense of the interface pointer returned because the only data type these languages know about is the VARIANT. And the only interface these clients know about is IDispatch (that is, a VARIANT of type VT_DISPATCH). At run time, these languages will internally call the IDispatch::GetIDsOfNames() method, passing it the name of the method or property that is required, and getting back an integer known as a DISPID which identifies the method. The clients will then call IDispatch::Invoke(), passing in the DISPID along with any parameters. The procedure is identical to that used in early binding, except that the call to IDispatch::GetIDsOfNames() occurs at run time rather than compile time. Late binding is also used in VB if a variable is declared as simply being of type 'Object' rather than having the required interface explicitly declared in the source code.

The process involved in late binding can be understood from the equivalent C++ code. This code snippet (not part of StarRaiders) binds using late binding to call the IADs::GetInfo() on a StarRaiders namespace object.

```
IDispatch *pNamespace;
HRESULT hRes;
hRes = CoCreateInstance(CLSID_StarRaidersNamespace, NULL, CLSCTX_INPROC_SERVER,
    IID_IDispatch, (void**)&pNamespace);

DISPID DispID;
OLECHAR *pszMethod = L"GetInfo";

hRes = pNamespace->GetIDsOfNames(
    IID_NULL,                // reserved parameter
    &pszMethod,              // name of the method we want to call
    1,                       // how many methods we are asking about
    LOCALE_SYSTEM_DEFAULT,   // what language we've supplied name in
    &DispID                  // the dispatch ID we want back
    );

unsigned uErrorParam;
DISPPARAMS DispParams = {NULL, NULL, 0, 0};;

hRes = pNamespace->Invoke(
    DispID,                  // the method we are calling
    IID_NULL,                // reserved parameter
    LOCALE_SYSTEM_DEFAULT,   // the language we are using
    DISPATCH_METHOD,         // says we are calling a method, not a property
    &DispParams,             // the parameter
    NULL,                    // variable to receive result
    NULL,                    // variable to receive exception info
    &uErrorParam             // more info about any errors
    );
```

Usually, IDispatch::GetIDsOfNames() will work internally by examining the type library to obtain the DispIDs. You can start to see the amount of processing involved for this code – and this is for the GetInfo() method which takes no parameters, and returns no result. If we'd been calling a method that had parameters, we'd have had to fill the DISPPARAMS structure, DispParams, with data about the parameters. And we'd have had to pass the address of a VARIANT instead of NULL in as the 6th parameter to Invoke, to accept the result. And we've been lazy here and not bothered about exception information – VB isn't as lazy and would normally pass in the address of an EXCEPINFO structure here.

To see what scripting clients expect from our provider, let's write a small test program – and for a change I'll use VBA rather than VBScript – that uses the WinNT provider. I've done this one as a quick Excel macro:

```
Sub TestADs()
'
' TestADs Macro
' Macro recorded 11/5/98 by Simon Robinson
'
    ' get a domain object and examine a couple of properties on it
    Dim Object
    Set Object = GetObject("WinNT://NT1")

    ' Set the filter to something so it isn't blank in the test
    Object.Filter = "Computer"

    ' IADs property
    Range("a1").Select
    ActiveCell.FormulaR1C1 = Object.Class

    ' IADsContainer property
    Range("a2").Select
    ActiveCell.FormulaR1C1 = Object.Filter

    Set Object = Nothing
End Sub
```

The important point to notice about this code is that it makes use of properties that are exposed by two different interfaces: IADs::Class and IADsContainer::Filter. The fact that it is using multiple interfaces is hidden by the fact that the COM object is represented by an untyped variable. So actually both method calls are invoked using IDispatch. Which means that for this COM object, IDispatch must be implemented in such a way that it is able to identify the correct method to call, even when the method may be exposed by any one of a number of interfaces. This is putting us beyond what ATL will do for us, since the implementation of IDispatch that ATL supplies can only invoke methods on one interface.

Here's the result of running this code:

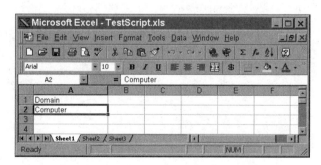

Now take a look at the definition of the property `IADs::Class`, as taken directly from the ADSI type library using oleview:

```
interface IADs : IDispatch {
        [id(0x00000002), propget]
        HRESULT Name([out, retval] BSTR* retval);
        [id(0x00000003), propget]
        HRESULT Class([out, retval] BSTR* retval);
        [id(0x00000004), propget]
```

Now look at the definition of `IADsContainer::Filter`

```
interface IADsContainer : IDispatch {
        [id(0x00000002), propget]
        HRESULT Count([out, retval] long* retval);
        [id(0xfffffffc), propget, restricted]
        HRESULT _NewEnum([out, retval] IUnknown** retval);
        [id(0x00000003), propget]
        HRESULT Filter([out, retval] VARIANT* pVar);
        [id(0x00000003), propput]
        HRESULT Filter([in] VARIANT pVar);
```

See anything funny? Yep, they've both got the same `DispID`. So, even if we allow for Microsoft's implementation of `IDispatch` on the WinNT domain object being able to supply the `DispID` of any method on any of interfaces an object implements, our VBA code still shouldn't work. The call to `Invoke`, supplying a `DispID` of 3, should either invoke `Class`, or `Filter`. Not both of them. Hmmm. This needs further investigation.

What I'm going to do is a quickie bit of C++ code to call `GetIDsOfNames()` and see what dispatch IDs I get back. By the way, I have to do this in C++ because `GetIDsOfNames()` is marked as 'restricted' in IDL, and so can't be called directly in VB.

So here's the code. As usual it's in the `OnInitDialog` function in an MFC dialog app.

```
BOOL CTestWinNTDlg::OnInitDialog()
{

// MFC stuff deleted  for clarity

    // find out the DispIDs of some the class and filter properties
    // for a domain object in WinNT.

    // declare relevant variables
    IDispatch *pWinNTObject;
    HRESULT hRes;
    OLECHAR *ADsPath = L"ADs:";
    DISPID DispIDClass, DispIDFilter;
    OLECHAR *ClassName = L"Class";
    OLECHAR *FilterName = L"Filter";
```

```
    // bind to the object
    hRes = ADsGetObject(ADsPath, IID_IADs, (void**)&pWinNTObject);
    ASSERT(SUCCEEDED(hRes));

    // get the two dispatch IDs
    hRes = pWinNTObject->GetIDsOfNames(
        IID_NULL,                // reserved parameter
        &ClassName,              // name of the property
        1,                       // how many methods we are asking about
        LOCALE_SYSTEM_DEFAULT,   // what language we've supplied name in
        &DispIDClass             // the dispatch ID we want back
        );
    ASSERT(SUCCEEDED(hRes));

    hRes = pWinNTObject->GetIDsOfNames(
        IID_NULL,                // reserved parameter
        &FilterName,             // name of the property
        1,                       // how many methods we are asking about
        LOCALE_SYSTEM_DEFAULT,   // what language we've supplied name in
        &DispIDFilter            // the dispatch ID we want back
        );
    ASSERT(SUCCEEDED(hRes));

    // convert to string and display in message box
    OLECHAR pszClassID[10], pszFilterID[10];
    _itow(DispIDClass, pszClassID, 16);
    _itow(DispIDFilter, pszFilterID, 16);
    CString Text = CString(L"Class DispID is ") + pszClassID +
        CString(L"\nFilter DispID is ") + pszFilterID;
    AfxMessageBox(Text);

    return TRUE;  // return TRUE  unless you set the focus to a control
}
```

And here's the result:

As you can see, `GetIDsOfNames` doesn't bring up the correct `DispIDs`. When called to request the `DispID` of Class (an `IADs` property), it brings up 3, as expected, but when asked to supply the `DispID` of the `IADsContainer::Filter` property it produces the wrong value.

If you check out the lines:

```
    _itow(DispIDClass, pszClassID, 16);
    _itow(DispIDFilter, pszFilterID, 16);
```

in the above code you'll see that I've arranged for these two `DispIDs` to be displayed in base 16. This means we can see exactly which bits of the `DispIDs` have been set. So the output from this code tells us that the 'wrong' value for the `DispID` of the filter has an extra high order bit set. It is 0x10003 instead of 0x00003

So that's how the WinNT provider is pulling it off. It's setting an extra bit to mark which interface the method comes from. Clearly, the implementation of `Invoke()` is able to test for this bit, and hence see which method is actually required. Incidentally, it's the principle of setting this bit that is important, not which bit is set. If you try the same code on different objects in WinNT, you'll find that, for example, the `DispID` returned for `IADsContainer::Filter` is different for different objects because different marker bits are set.

At least that tells us what we need to do in principle. In fact the technique is not unique to ADSI providers: it's the well-known technique of **DispID-encoding**. It involves exactly what we've just seen. Typically some bit in the high order part of the `DispID` will be set to indicate the interface that the required method belongs to. This method still relies on the original method names passed to `GetIDsOfNames` being unique, but that isn't a problem for us. There is some collision between names in some of the specialised persistant object methods but since these interfaces refer to specialised objects, we shouldn't ever encounter any object that implements more than one of the affected interfaces. Certainly of the common interfaces (`IADs`, `IADsContainer`, `IADsGroup`, `IADsClass` etc.) there should be no problems.

The main problem with `DispID` encoding is that some of the bits in the `DispID` must be reserved for the interface flags. These bits therefore cannot be used to identify methods. If we were free to choose all the `DispID`s, this would not be a problem, since we could simply choose `DispID`s that avoid the selected bits. Unfortunately, with ADSI the `DispID`s are all chosen by Microsoft. Strictly speaking, even if we check through the entire ADSI type library to make sure we do not cause any other collisions with our choice of interface bits, we cannot guarantee that collisions won't arise with a future release of ADSI in which more interfaces are defined. However I'm going to allocate the entire upper 16 bits of the `DispID` for interface flags. Why am I so confident? Well firstly because the WinNT provider uses some of these bits in this way. I have a reasonable amount of confidence that Microsoft isn't intending to break their own system provider, so these bits should be safe. Secondly, methods tend to be numbered in order from 1 upwards anyway, and you don't get many interfaces with more than 65535 methods! In fact come to think of it I don't think I've ever seen a single interface that big.

That's the theory bit almost out of the way. We're almost ready to go into the practice of how to implement `DispID` encoding. But before we do that it's just occurred to me that it might be an idea to make sure we understand what ATL normally does, before we start mucking about with it. Let's have a look at the wizard-generated definition of our `CStarRaidersNamespace` class:

```
class ATL_NO_VTABLE CStarRaidersNamespace :
    public CComObjectRootEx<CComMultiThreadModel>,
    public CComCoClass<CStarRaidersNamespace, &CLSID_StarRaidersNamespace>,
    public IDispatchImpl<IDontNeedThis, &IID_IDontNeedThis, &LIBID_STARRAIDERSLib>,
    public IDispatchImpl<IADs, &IID_IADs, &LIBID_ActiveDs>,
    public IDispatchImpl<IADsContainer, &IID_IADsContainer, &LIBID_ActiveDs>,
    public IDispatchImpl<IADsPropertyList, &IID_IADsPropertyList, &LIBID_ActiveDs>,
    public IDirectoryObject,
    public IDirectorySchemaMgmt,
    public IDirectorySearch
{
```

To take IADs as an example, the IDispatch interface for IADs is implemented by deriving CStarRaidersNamespace from another template class, IDispatchImpl<IADs>. IDispatchImpl<> is derived from the first class in its parameter list – in this case IADs, so it defines all the IADs methods, and also implements the IDispatch methods. Each IDispatchImpl<> contains a static member of the class (wait for this one) CComTypeInfoHolder. It is this class that (invisibly to you, the developer) actually grabs the type information. To do this, it needs to know which type library to look in, and which interface to look for. Which is why the relevant GUIDs are supplied as additional parameters to the IDispatchImpl<> template definition. Hang on, did I just say 'which interface to look for'? I believe I did. That's why ATL's dispatch implementation will only give you the methods from one interface. Because internally, CComTypeInfoHolder will accept an interface IID that you've given it, and simply look up that interface. Which interface you use is selected by you when you code up your class by which entries you put in the COM map. Let's have a look at the COM map as it currently stands.

```
BEGIN_COM_MAP(CStarRaidersNamespace)
    COM_INTERFACE_ENTRY(IDontNeedThis)
    COM_INTERFACE_ENTRY2(IDispatch, IDontNeedThis)
    COM_INTERFACE_ENTRY(IADs)
    COM_INTERFACE_ENTRY(IADsContainer)
    COM_INTERFACE_ENTRY(IADsPropertyList)
    COM_INTERFACE_ENTRY(IDirectoryObject)
    COM_INTERFACE_ENTRY(IDirectorySchemaMgmt)
    COM_INTERFACE_ENTRY(IDirectorySearch)
END_COM_MAP()
```

The key is that COM_INTERFACE_ENTRY2 macro. At present it's telling us that if the class ever receives a QueryInterface() for IDispatch, it should actually return a pointer to the IDispatchImpl<IDontNeedThis> class. Which means that the only interfaces scripting languages can ever 'see' is IDontNeedThis. I could change that COM_INTERFACE_ENTRY2 macro to point to another, more useful, C++ class, say IDispatchImpl<IADs>, then scripting languages could see the new interface, but that doesn't solve our problem: IDispatch still gives you only one interface.

So what can we do about it? Well we know we need to put in some code to modify the dispatch IDs returned from IDispatch::GetIDsOfNames(). To do that our code will need to know about the interfaces implemented by each object. This really gives us two alternatives:

❑ We can write specific code to override GetIDsOfNames() and Invoke() for each CoClass that we implement.

❑ We can use the information in the type library to automate the process.

Of these, the second option is in principle the most attractive from the point of view of code maintenance, especially as there is a class written and available on the web that will do exactly that. But there are some problems specific to ADSI providers, which mean you have to be very careful with this approach. I'm going to explain this option so I can show you what the potential pitfalls are, then we'll go on to see how to code up the first option, of manually writing code for each coclass, which is what is actually done in StarRaiders.

Replacing CComTypeInfoHolder

Now doesn't that sound fun? Digging into ATL and replacing an obscure internal class that most ATL developers have probably never even heard of. But it does make some sense. The key here is the remark I made about CComTypeInfoHolder looking up an interface in the type library. The type library doesn't just store interfaces – it also tells you about CoClasses and what interfaces each one implements. Suppose we had a type info holder, say CComTypeInfoHolderEx, which instead of taking the interface IID, took the class CLSID and looked up all the interfaces exposed by that CoClass until it found the method you were asking for. What if, in the process, it automatically performed DispID-encoding – in other words, added the interface flags to say which interface it was looking at? And what if it could check these flags to invoke the appropriate method when Invoke() was called? That would solve our problem nicely. The great thing is, such an interface exists. Here's how you use it.

First, put this line in your stdafx.h:

```
#include "bxcomext.h"
```

Now, change the definition of the class that implements the ADSI interfaces to, for example:

```
class ATL_NO_VTABLE CStarRaidersNamespace :
    public CComObjectRootEx<CComMultiThreadModel>,
    public CComCoClass<CStarRaidersNamespace, &CLSID_StarRaidersNamespace>,
    public IDispatchImplEx<IADs, &CLSID_ADs, &IID_IADs, &LIBID_ActiveDS>,
// etc.
```

That (apart from obtaining the header file bxcomext.h) is literally all you have to do! If it's not clear, the changes in the class definition are that all the references to IDispatchImpl<> have been changed to IDispatchImplEx<> and a new parameter, the CLSID of the object, has been added to the template parameter list.

OK. I suppose you want to know what's going on here. IDispatchImplEx<> is an extended dispatch interface that contains an instance of a CComTypeInfoHolderEx<>. It's defined in the file, bxcomext.h (There's no .cpp file as all functions are inline), and as you can see it takes an additional template parameter, the CLSID of the coclass to look up. These classes have been written by Kjell Tangen, and given the inevitable prominence of complex templates in the classes, I'm impressed by his programming skills. The files are publicly available in separate versions for ATL 2.1 and ATL 3.0, and can be downloaded from Chris Sells' web site http://www.sellsbrothers.com.

Well if it's so easy, what's the problem? The most obvious one is that these are freebie C++ files, written by a private individual and available for download. As such they carry no warranties. We don't think they contain bugs, but these are use-at-your-own-risk files. You may not want to use software on that basis.

The second reason for not doing things this way is a lot more subtle, but potentially more serious. You see, I mentioned about CComTypeInfoHolderEx looking up the CLSID in the type library. That would be fine if you could be sure of having a type library that exactly described your objects, but the StarRaiders provider doesn't have one!

You see, we used the Implement Interface wizard to generate our header files. The implement interface wizard imports an existing type library into your code, it doesn't create a new one. Let's look at the description of our namespaces object in the library section of our IDL file:

```
library STARRAIDERSLib
{
    importlib("stdole32.tlb");
    importlib("stdole2.tlb");

    [
        uuid(4ADB9052-9047-11D2-80B9-0000E8DC2D45),
        helpstring("StarRaiders Namespace Class")
    ]
    coclass StarRaidersNamespace
    {
        [default] interface IDontNeedThis;
    };
```

This will have created a StarRaiders type library for us. It describes the StarRaidersNamespace object, and tells us that it implements one interface, namely IDontNeedThis! Note that none of the ADSI interfaces are mentioned in this snippet or anywhere in our IDL file – so they won't be described by the StarRaiders type library. They are all defined in ActiveDS.tlb, which, being the generic ADSI type library, not only doesn't have any mention of the StarRaidersNamespace object, but also defines *all* the ADSI interfaces, only a small number of which will normally actually be implemented by any given ADSI COM object. The CComTypeInfoHolderEx class is going to have a lot of trouble looking up interfaces here!

So if you do want to use the IDispatchImplEx<> technique to implement an ADSI provider, you'll need to make sure you do create a type library that correctly defines your objects. It's not that hard to do this. You'll simply need to make some manual changes to your IDL file. For example, to make sure the StarRaidersNamespace class is defined, I'd make these changes:

```
library STARRAIDERSLib
{
    importlib("stdole32.tlb");
    importlib("stdole2.tlb");
    importlib("ActiveDS.tlb")

    [
        uuid(4ADB9052-9047-11D2-80B9-0000E8DC2D45),
        helpstring("StarRaiders Namespace Class")
    ]
    coclass StarRaidersNamespace
    {
        [default] interface IADs;
        interface IADsContainer;
// etc.
    };
```

With this change, using type library information to carry out `DispID` encoding will work. However, it does bring up another issue which it is important to be aware of. Whenever you register a type library COM adds entries in the registry, under the `HKCR/Interface` key, for the interfaces described in the type library. If any interfaces are already described by another type library, then the existing interface entries will be overwritten. So if you write your own type library for an ADSI provider, then on registering it, COM will overwrite the interface registry keys, so that those interfaces which your provider uses will always be marshalled through your type library, rather than the standard ADSI one. This will happen whichever ADSI provider is being called up. Provided that you have described the interfaces correctly in your type library, there shouldn't be any problems, *yet*. But if your provider is uninstalled at a later date, and your type library is unregistered, then those interface entries will be removed unless your uninstaller takes specific action to prevent this. The result is you will break other ADSI providers.

So now we've looked at how a type library based technique might work, I'll show you the alternative technique we're actually going to use in StarRaiders.

Overriding the IDispatchImpl<> Methods

The title says it all really. And if you're an experienced C++ developer this should have been obvious from the start. If you don't like the way a function behaves, then override it. Here's how I did it in StarRaiders.

First add some definitions we're going to need to `stdafx.h`. These are the bits we're going to use in the mask for each interface. I've also put in some `typedef`s to make the code simpler when we refer to the different `IDispatchImpl<>` templates, which we're going to do rather a lot.

```
const DISPID INTERFACE_MASK = 0xffff0000;
const DISPID DISPID_MASK = 0x0000ffff;

const DISPID DISPMASK_IADs             = 0x00010000;
const DISPID DISPMASK_IADsContainer    = 0x00020000;
const DISPID DISPMASK_IADsClass        = 0x00040000;
const DISPID DISPMASK_IADsProperty     = 0x00080000;
const DISPID DISPMASK_IADsSyntax       = 0x00100000;
const DISPID DISPMASK_IADsPropertyList = 0x00200000;
const DISPID DISPMASK_IADsOpenDSObject = 0x00400000;

extern const GUID LIBID_ActiveDs;

typedef IDispatchImpl<IADs, &IID_IADs, &LIBID_ActiveDs> IDispatch_IADs;
typedef IDispatchImpl<IADsContainer, &IID_IADsContainer, &LIBID_ActiveDs>
IDispatch_IADsContainer;
typedef IDispatchImpl<IADsPropertyList, &IID_IADsPropertyList, &LIBID_ActiveDs>
IDispatch_IADsPropertyList;
typedef IDispatchImpl<IADsClass, &IID_IADsClass, &LIBID_ActiveDs>
IDispatch_IADsClass;
typedef IDispatchImpl<IADsProperty, &IID_IADsProperty, &LIBID_ActiveDs>
IDispatch_IADsProperty;
typedef IDispatchImpl<IADsSyntax, &IID_IADsSyntax, &LIBID_ActiveDs>
IDispatch_IADsSyntax;
typedef IDispatchImpl<IADsOpenDSObject, &IID_IADsOpenDSObject, &LIBID_ActiveDs>
IDispatch_IADsOpenDSObject;
```

I've defined a bit to use in the mask for every dual interface that is going to be implemented in StarRaiders. Obviously there's no need to do the same for the `IDirectoryXXX` interfaces as these cannot be accessed through `IDispatch` anyway.

Now we add the function definitions to the `CStarRaidersNamespace` definition:

```
class ATL_NO_VTABLE CStarRaidersNamespace :
// etc. list of derived classes deleted for clarity
{
public:
    CStarRaidersNamespace()
    {
    }

    STDMETHOD(GetIDsOfNames)(REFIID riid, LPOLESTR* rgszNames, UINT cNames,
        LCID lcid, DISPID* rgdispid);
    STDMETHOD(Invoke)(DISPID dispidMember, REFIID riid,
        LCID lcid, WORD wFlags, DISPPARAMS* pdispparams, VARIANT* pvarResult,
        EXCEPINFO* pexcepinfo, UINT* puArgErr);
```

I've literally got these definitions by cutting and pasting from the corresponding definitions in `atlcom.h`.

Now add the implementation in `StarRaidersNamespace.cpp`:

```
// StarRaidersNamespace.cpp : Implementation of CStarRaidersNamespace
#include "stdafx.h"
#include "StarRaiders.h"
#include "StarRaidersNamespace.h"
#include "StarRaidersContainer.h"
#include "Utilities.h"

/////////////////////////////////////////////////////////////////////////////
// CStarRaidersNamespace

// IDispatch overrides
STDMETHODIMP CStarRaidersNamespace :: GetIDsOfNames(REFIID riid, LPOLESTR*
rgszNames, UINT cNames,
    LCID lcid, DISPID* rgdispid)
{
    // overrides GetIDsOfNames to add the mask bit which indicates which
    // interface we are referring to
    HRESULT hRes;

    hRes = IDispatch_IADsContainer::GetIDsOfNames(riid, rgszNames, cNames, lcid,
rgdispid);
    if (SUCCEEDED(hRes) && rgdispid[0] == DISPID_NEWENUM)
        return hRes;
    else if (SUCCEEDED(hRes))
    {
        rgdispid[0] |= DISPMASK_IADsContainer;
        return hRes;
    }
```

```
    hRes = IDispatch_IADs::GetIDsOfNames(riid, rgszNames, cNames, lcid, rgdispid);
    if (SUCCEEDED(hRes))
    {
        rgdispid[0] |= DISPMASK_IADs;
        return hRes;
    }

    hRes = IDispatch_IADsPropertyList::GetIDsOfNames(riid, rgszNames, cNames, lcid,
rgdispid);
    if (SUCCEEDED(hRes))
    {
        rgdispid[0] |= DISPMASK_IADsPropertyList;
        return hRes;
    }

    hRes = IDispatch_IADsOpenDSObject::GetIDsOfNames(riid, rgszNames, cNames, lcid,
rgdispid);
    if (SUCCEEDED(hRes))
    {
        rgdispid[0] |= DISPMASK_IADsOpenDSObject;
        return hRes;
    }

    return DISP_E_UNKNOWNNAME;
}

STDMETHODIMP CStarRaidersNamespace :: Invoke(DISPID dispidMember, REFIID riid,
    LCID lcid, WORD wFlags, DISPPARAMS* pdispparams, VARIANT* pvarResult,
    EXCEPINFO* pexcepinfo, UINT* puArgErr)
{
    // overrides Invoke() to check which mask bit has been set and
    // call the appropriate interface version of invoke.

    // Check for __NewEnum as a special case
    if (dispidMember == DISPID_NEWENUM)
        return IDispatch_IADsContainer :: Invoke(dispidMember, riid,
            lcid, wFlags, pdispparams, pvarResult, pexcepinfo, puArgErr);

    DWORD dwInterface = dispidMember & INTERFACE_MASK;
    dispidMember &= DISPID_MASK;
    switch (dwInterface)
    {
    case DISPMASK_IADs:
        return IDispatch_IADs :: Invoke(dispidMember, riid,
            lcid, wFlags, pdispparams, pvarResult, pexcepinfo, puArgErr);
    case DISPMASK_IADsContainer:
        return IDispatch_IADsContainer :: Invoke(dispidMember, riid,
            lcid, wFlags, pdispparams, pvarResult, pexcepinfo, puArgErr);
    case DISPMASK_IADsPropertyList:
        return IDispatch_IADsPropertyList :: Invoke(dispidMember, riid,
            lcid, wFlags, pdispparams, pvarResult, pexcepinfo, puArgErr);
    case DISPMASK_IADsOpenDSObject:
        return IDispatch_IADsOpenDSObject :: Invoke(dispidMember, riid,
            lcid, wFlags, pdispparams, pvarResult, pexcepinfo, puArgErr);
    default:
```

```
        return DISP_E_MEMBERNOTFOUND;
    }
}
```

Simple enough? It looks like a lot of code but that's mostly because of the need to check for all the different interfaces implemented by the namespace object. Basically, GetIDsOfNames() simply tries out all the different IDispatchImpl<> versions of GetIDsOfNames() until it finds one that works. That tells it which bit to set in the returned DISPID. Invoke() looks to see which bit has been set, and deduces from that which version of GetIDsOfNames to call. The only real complication is that we need to treat the IADsContainer::_NewEnum property as a special case. This is because the enumerator object in collections is conventionally assigned a special dispatch ID, 0xfffffffc (that is, 3). As far as our code is concerned, this value is stored in the variable DISPID_NEWENUM, which has been defined in ActiveDS.h. Because this value uniquely has all of our mask bits set, we will need to be careful to catch it correctly – for that reason it's the first DispID that our override of Invoke() checks for. Our override for GetIDsOfNames() checks for this value as well, if it finds that the requested property is an IADsContainer one. This is done in the lines:

```
    hRes = IDispatch_IADsContainer::GetIDsOfNames(riid, rgszNames, cNames, lcid,
rgdispid);
    if (SUCCEEDED(hRes) && rgdispid[0] == DISPID_NEWENUM)
        return hRes;
    else if (SUCCEEDED(hRes))
    {
        rgdispid[0] |= DISPMASK_IADsContainer;
        return hRes;
    }
```

which checks if we're returning the DispID of _NewEnum, and if so avoids encoding it. In this case this isn't really necessary since performing a bit-wise OR of 0xfffffffc with DISPMASK_IADsContainer won't actually have any effect, but I wanted to separate out the case in the code to make it obvious what I was doing.

There are a couple of other special dispatch IDs with negative values that you would need to watch, but you're unlikely to encounter them in the context of ADSI providers. If you're interested, they are documented in Chapter 14 of Craig Brockschmidt's *Inside OLE*, available with MSDN.

Our code first checks that we're not dealing with the enumerator property, _NewEnum. Since this will have the interface flags set, this needs to be treated as a special case. Otherwise, we progress through the interfaces, until we find the method we want, and set an interface flag appropriately. Which bit we set for which interface doesn't matter – as long as we're consistent between GetIDsOfNames() and Invoke() so that Invoke() picks up the correct interface. The real difference here as compared with the previous method is that we are now hard-coding our knowledge of which interfaces are exposed into the source code, as opposed to reading it from the type library. It's this hard coding that makes this method more tedious to implement, since each COM coclass must be treated separately. This is probably good territory for producing some macros to automate the process, though, if anyone feels like doing it!

We've now seen two different ways of using dispatch-ID encoding. What are the advantages of each?

Well, the `IDispatchImplEx<>` technique of using some code that looks data up in the type libraries means you can have a very highly automated process. From that point of view, your code will be a lot easier to maintain. For example, if in a new release, you modify one of your objects, say to support a new interface, then the `IDispatch` implementation will be taken care of automatically. With the technique we use in StarRaiders, we'd have to explicitly change the code in our `GetIDsOfNames()` and `Invoke()` methods to cope with the new interface. There's also a lot less coding to do initially if you use Kjell Tangen's pre-written class.

On the other hand, by doing everything by hand by overriding functions, we don't have to worry about making our own accurate type library, and all the potential problems that raises. You don't have to be so careful about how you install and uninstall your provider.

> *Another corollary of all this is that you shouldn't write any code that depends in any way on your type library being present and being the registered library for any of the standard ADSI interfaces – because that code may stop working if someone later on installs another provider which tries to register its own type library. This is probably a non-issue for most people, but it's something you should be aware of if you start trying to be really clever and hack around with the COM API functions and interfaces that deal with type libraries.*

You've probably gathered by now that this is a deep subject. If you do want to explore further, the SellsBrothers web site, `http://www.sellsbrothers.com`, is a good place to look. You'll find a lot of very ingenious solutions to the problem of making multiple interfaces available to scripting clients there. Some are variants of `DispID`-encoding, but there are other ideas there too. You'll need to bear in mind though, that almost all of these solutions impose some restrictions on the interface definitions. This is fine for normal COM servers that expose only your own interfaces, but makes most of the ideas unworkable for ADSI providers, for which you have to take the Microsoft interfaces as given.

Threading Issues

ADSI providers must mark themselves as supporting the both-threaded model. This means that any COM method must be called up on any thread, so all global data and all member variables of COM objects must be protected against thread synchronisation issues. The fact that the model is 'both' rather than 'free' also means in principle that any callbacks to the client should be performed from the same thread that the method was called on. Since ADSI interfaces do not implement callbacks, that one is a non-issue for us.

But we have got to find a way of protecting our data. This is potentially a minefield for ADSI providers, because of the way you have a large number of directory objects that are linked, and which will often call up methods on each other. Protecting the data itself is not really a problem – you just bung critical sections into the classes that need protecting and call them up around the appropriate sections of code. The problems come if you have more than one critical section, and there is a chance of multiple threads wanting the same critical sections at the same time. In that case you have the risk of deadlocks.

I've decided to hand responsibility for the critical sections to the calling functions rather than trying to enter them within the functions in CPropertyCache for ease of code maintenance. Most of my CPropertyCache functions have a lot of premature exit points arising from error trapping, and I don't want to have to remember to leave the critical section everywhere. It means the critical sections stay locked for longer (the entire duration of a function call rather than just round the places where data gets modified) but I judge that to be a fair trade-off for maintainability. Besides, realistically, most ADSI clients are written in VB or ASP anyway and hence single threaded. For efficiency reasons the COM runtime will normally instantiate the COM objects in the same single-threaded apartment that the VB/ASP client thread runs in so threading issues will only rarely arise anyway.

> *An alternative approach to this problem would be to define a guard class which enters the critical section in its constructor and leaves it in its destructor, and create an instance of this class in the function that needs to be protected.*

So that's how StarRaiders does it. How you handle thread synchronisation will depend a lot on how you architect your own provider. However, in most cases, you will find you will be OK if you give each COM object it's own critical section to protect its own data, and do nothing more. Why am I confident of that? Well let's take a look again at what I wrote a couple of pages back about when deadlocks occur. Here – I'll even reprint it for you, to save you turning the page back:

> *A deadlock occurs when you've got this situation: There are two threads. Thread **A** has taken ownership of critical section **a** and is waiting for critical section **b**. Thread **B** has ownership of critical section **b**, and is waiting for **a** to become free. Neither thread gets anywhere because they are both waiting for each other. The result is your application just hangs.*

How could this situation happen with the thread synchronization scheme I've just described? Well clearly the ADSI object containing critical section a would need to have a method somewhere that calls up a function in the ADSI object containing critical section **b**. At the same time, ADSI object containing critical section **b** would need to have a method somewhere that calls up a function in the ADSI object containing critical section **a**.

You can make sure this situation never occurs by enforcing this rule in your architecture. Methods in ADSI objects should only ever call up methods in their children, never in their parents.

This rule might sound a bit restrictive, but it actually fits in quite naturally with the architecture of the ADSI interfaces. You see, there isn't a single method in any ADSI interface whose definition or specification says that it should do anything with the parent object. To see this, let's look at the main ADSI methods that refer to objects other than the one on which the method has been called.

- ❑ IADs::get_Parent().
- ❑ IADsContainer::get_NewEnum(), and other IADsContainer methods such as Create(), Move(), etc.
- ❑ IDirectorySearch::Execute().
- ❑ IADsGroup methods to create, move, delete, or access specific children.
- ❑ Methods in IADsGroup, IADsMembers and IADsCollection to access members of groups and collections.

I've decided to hand responsibility for the critical sections to the calling functions rather than trying to enter them within the functions in `CPropertyCache` for ease of code maintenance. Most of my `CPropertyCache` functions have a lot of premature exit points arising from error trapping, and I don't want to have to remember to leave the critical section everywhere. It means the critical sections stay locked for longer (the entire duration of a function call rather than just round the places where data gets modified) but I judge that to be a fair trade-off for maintainability. Besides, realistically, most ADSI clients are written in VB or ASP anyway and hence single threaded. For efficiency reasons the COM runtime will normally instantiate the COM objects in the same single-threaded apartment that the VB/ASP client thread runs in so threading issues will only rarely arise anyway.

An alternative approach to this problem would be to define a guard class which enters the critical section in its constructor and leaves it in its destructor, and create an instance of this class in the function that needs to be protected.

So that's how StarRaiders does it. How you handle thread synchronisation will depend a lot on how you architect your own provider. However, in most cases, you will find you will be OK if you give each COM object it's own critical section to protect its own data, and do nothing more. Why am I confident of that? Well let's take a look again at what I wrote a couple of pages back about when deadlocks occur. Here – I'll even reprint it for you, to save you turning the page back:

A deadlock occurs when you've got this situation: There are two threads. Thread A has taken ownership of critical section a and is waiting for critical section b. Thread B has ownership of critical section b, and is waiting for a to become free. Neither thread gets anywhere because they are both waiting for each other. The result is your application just hangs.

How could this situation happen with the thread synchronization scheme I've just described? Well clearly the ADSI object containing critical section a would need to have a method somewhere that calls up a function in the ADSI object containing critical section b. At the same time, ADSI object containing critical section b would need to have a method somewhere that calls up a function in the ADSI object containing critical section a.

You can make sure this situation never occurs by enforcing this rule in your architecture. Methods in ADSI objects should only ever call up methods in their children, never in their parents.

This rule might sound a bit restrictive, but it actually fits in quite naturally with the architecture of the ADSI interfaces. You see, there isn't a single method in any ADSI interface whose definition or specification says that it should do anything with the parent object. To see this, let's look at the main ADSI methods that refer to objects other than the one on which the method has been called.

- ❑ `IADs::get_Parent()`.

- ❑ `IADsContainer::get_NewEnum()`, and other `IADsContainer` methods such as `Create()`, `Move()`, etc.

- ❑ `IDirectorySearch::Execute()`.

- ❑ `IADsGroup` methods to create, move, delete, or access specific children.

- ❑ Methods in `IADsGroup`, `IADsMembers` and `IADsCollection` to access members of groups and collections.

Of these, the only method which refers to a parent, rather than children, is `IADs::get_Parent()`. But this method doesn't involve any interface pointer to the parent – it simply uses the name of the parent object. Provided this name has been cached in the object, which is very easy to do when the object is first instantiated, then `IADs::get_Parent()` can be implemented without accessing the parent at all.

By contrast, the remaining methods, (apart from `IDirectorySearch`), which tend to look at children, do involve interface pointers, so it may be harder to avoid implementing them without actually calling up methods on the children. That's fine.

There is one exception to this reasoning: `IADsMembers::get_NewEnum()` returns an enumerator that will give you interface pointers to members of the group, and there's nothing in the ADSI specification to prevent a group from containing members above it in the directory tree. This is a fairly unlikely scenario, but if your directory structure allows this, then you will need to be more careful about thread synchronization. One way round this problem is by constructing the enumerator dynamically, as calls to `EnumVARIANT::Next()` are made, rather than obtaining the interface pointers when the enumerator is initialized. If you do this, then you will have to write the enumerator class yourself, you won't be able to use the prewritten ATL enumerator classes. But you will ensure that the interface pointers to parent objects aren't accessed until the `IADsMembers::get_NewEnum()` call has safely returned.

The other issue that might theoretically open the possibility of a deadlock is if you access global data, which requires a critical section. I've avoided this in StarRaiders because there is no global data to protect. If you do have any, and need to allow simultaneous access to it – then you'll need to be careful. Good ways to avoid deadlocks include trying to ensure that a given method call only holds one critical section at any one time, or deciding on clear guidelines for the order in which several critical sections will be requested, and ensuring that all method calls that require more than one critical section stick to this order.

To summarize, it's a complex issue. I can't give you global solutions here because every provider has a different architecture. This section has hopefully given you some guidelines that may be useful when you are planning your provider architecture.

One other point. I have to admit I have on occasions been tempted to simply avoid the issue by marking a provider as apartment threaded instead. Provided you don't use the `CComAutoThread` model for your ATL class factory, this will ensure that all methods are always called on the same thread. But doing this does depart from ADSI standards, even though it's hard to see how it could actually cause any client to have problems, so I've avoided it. But I'll mention it just in case you're lazy and not too bothered about standards!

That's covered deadlocks. I should mention the other thread synchronisaton problem – races. A race typically occurs when a thread passes a task on to another thread, then it may need to perform some action after the task is completed, but unwittingly starts the action *before* the other thread's task has actually completed. This problem requires good communication between threads, but it is only going to affect your provider if you are directly spawning extra threads beyond the ones that COM gives you. Since ADSI providers will rarely need to do this, I'll leave that topic.

There's one other issue we need to deal with that's related to this. Strictly it isn't a thread issue, it's an issue about making sure COM objects are up-to-date as far as the state of a directory is concerned. The question is, what happens if you move or delete an object using one of the `IADsContainer` methods, but you already had interface pointers on one or more objects that were affected by the move or delete. If it's a move operation, then you could simply let the affected ADSI objects work normally, but with the updated `ADsPaths`. If it's a delete, then at some point, COM methods that access or modify data on the affected objects will have to fail. You could have the provider check for this, perhaps by setting a variable that indicates that the affected objects are no longer valid, and hence return error codes for any method on the objects, or you could leave the validity checking for the directory, in which case no error code will get returned until a call to `GetInfo()` or `SetInfo()` is made. Incidentally I've avoided this problem in StarRaiders by never getting round to implementing `IADsContainer::Move()` or `IADsContainer::Delete()`!

Direct Access to ADSI Objects: The ADSI Router and Monikers

We've put this off long enough. Not only have we not yet seriously looked at what really goes on when you make that innocent call to `ADsGetObject()`, but we have something missing from our provider. I've happily demonstrated to you how you browse through it. You call up `dsbrowse` and simply start expanding the tree, or you call up `adsvw.exe`, ask to open the new object ADs, and expand that tree. Let's see what happens if we try a more direct approach. I'm going to open `adsvw.exe` and home straight in on the Spice Girls. So let's select New Object in the Active Directory Browser, and type in "StarRaiders://Fans/Simon/Spice Girls". Here's the result:

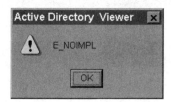

You see, so far I've been really careful with my screenshots in this chapter: in every one of them I've called `ADsGetObject` on the ADSI Namespaces object, `ADs:`, and then enumerated the children of the container to get into StarRaiders. Up until now, I've not passed the `ADsPath` of any object that's actually in the StarRaiders provider to `ADsGetObject()`. `ADsGetObject()` doesn't enumerate the children of a container. In fact it doesn't directly use any ADSI interfaces at all to find the chosen object – it uses a different mechanism, involving COM and monikers to get you the object of your desires. The mechanism uses the provider object, which we haven't yet implemented. So we're going to have to take another theory break here and find out about monikers before we implement the next bit of StarRaiders.

Getting Inside Moniker

So let's make it clear what the problem is that we have to solve. We want to get an interface pointer to a particular COM object – and the only piece of information we've got to work from is some kind of path name. In ADSI, we're talking `ADsPaths` like `StarRaiders://Fans/Simon/Spice Girls`. But there are lots of other names from which you might want to get COM objects. More generally you might be presented with something like `C:\My Documents\DontLetTheBossHere\MyOtherJobApplications.doc` or `http://www.wrox.com`, or even something like `clsid:CDCC2620-9906-11d2-80BF-0000E8DC2D45`.

These obviously look like totally different types of object, and it's here that monikers come in, by providing a unified access mechanism.

Monikers have really evolved to solve two issues in COM. Firstly, a lot of COM objects are persistent: they have an internal state that needs to be stored between invocations. When a client wants to call up a particular object again, it needs a mechanism to specify that it doesn't want COM to just create a new COM object (which is what `CoCreateInstance()` does), but that it wants to bind to an object that already exists. Secondly, we really need a way of naming objects that doesn't involve GUIDs. GUIDs are a great idea, but for some strange reason a lot of people seem to have trouble remembering particular GUIDs – a fact which makes them more awkward to use in user interfaces.

Before we start I will warn you that Monikers isn't the simplest of subjects. There's a lot of information to be taken in at once, so I'm not going to be offended if you need to read the next few pages several times before it starts to make sense.

I'm going to start off with some pseudo-code again. We've gone on enough about how clever the `ADsGetObject` API function is. Let's see what it does. Here's what I think is inside it, but with the error handling removed for clarity.

```
HRESULT WINAPI ADsGetObject(
      LPWSTR lpszPathName, REFIID riid, VOID * * ppObject)
{
   DWORD chEaten = 0;
   IMoniker *pMoniker;
   IBindCtx *pbc;
   HRESULT hRes;

   hRes = CreateBindCtx(NULL, &pbc);
   hRes = MkParseDisplayName(pbc, lpszPathName, &chEaten, &pMoniker);
   hRes = pMoniker->BindToObject(pbc, NULL, riid, ppObject);
   pbc->Release();
   pMoniker->Release();
   return hRes;
}
```

There's some new stuff here, but I can't overemphasize that none of it is ADSI-specific. Well, that's not too surprising really: ADsGetObject() basically emulates the functionality of VB's GetObject(). And GetObject() is a generic COM function, not an ADSI-specific function. After everything I've said about how important the ADSI router is, it might come as a surprise that, internally, ADsGetObject() has anything to do with ADSI. But it's true. So what do we have? Well, our first encounter with the IMoniker interface, and another interface called IBindCtx, as well as two new COM API functions, MkParseDisplayName() and CreateBindCtx(). For the time being, I'll ask you to forget about the bind context. It's there as a convenient store for some data that's gathered during the binding process, but we don't need to bother ourselves with it. You create a bind context object using CreateBindCtx() and MkParseDisplayName() expects an IBindCtx pointer as one of it's parameters but that's as much as we need to know for now. The really interesting line is the call to MkParseDisplayName(). MkParseDisplayName() is a function that is designed to accept a string – the Display Name – and return a pointer to a something called the Moniker. The Moniker isn't the object we want – it's another COM object whose function in life is to retrieve our object, represented by the display name. The actual process of getting the object is handled by that call to BindToObject() in the returned Moniker. That's the line where all the action is – everything else in our bit of pseudo-code is really just tidying up.

So to see what's going on, we're going to need to understand what's happening inside that MkParseDisplayName() call. I'll present you with the diagram of the sequence of operations first, then I'll talk through the process and explain what MkParseDisplayName() is there for in detail.

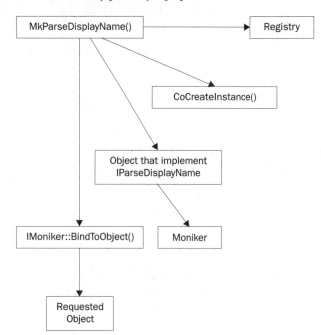

Moniker Exposed Further

The starting point to tracking down an object is the call to MkParseDisplayName(). This is a COM API function, defined in objbase.h. Let's have a look at its definition.

```
WINOLEAPI  MkParseDisplayName(LPBC pbc, LPCOLESTR szUserName,
                ULONG FAR * pchEaten, LPMONIKER FAR * ppmk);
```

Unfortunately, understanding the parameter list isn't helped by Microsoft's tendency to use `#define` directives over most of the variable types! For `LPBC` read `IBindCtx*`, for `ULONG FAR *` read `unsigned long *`, and for `LPMONIKER FAR *` read `IMoniker**`. `LPCOLESTR` for all practical purposes can be considered as `const wchar *` – in other words a UNICODE string. (Technically, it's an ANSI string on 16 bit windows, but that's not going to bother us for ADSI).

So what does `MkParseDisplayName()` do with the name it's been handed? Well, it tries a couple of avenues. It looks to see if the display name could be the name of a file. (It's possible to use COM to create special files known as compound document files. Each of these files has an associated GUID and an associated COM object, and it's possible to use `MkParseDisplayName()` to get to that object.)

Another track that `MkParseDisplayName()` tries – the one that's relevant to us – is that it looks to see if the name might be the `ProgID` of a class in the registry. More precisely, it takes the bit of it that it thinks is relevant – which is the name up to the first, and looks to see if that name matches any `ProgID`. That's the key for us. Remember how fussy I was about changing the `ProgID` of the StarRaiders `Namespace` object to `'StarRaidersNamespace'`? Well the ADsPath of any object in the StarRaiders directory always looks like `StarRaiders://SomePathName`. So `MkParseDisplayName()` will take this name and look for an object with the `progID` `StarRaiders`. At the moment there isn't one, and none of the other tricks `MkParseDisplayName()` uses to get that elusive object succeed, which is why we get that error code back.

So we need to create an object with a `ProgID` of `StarRaiders`. What does this object have to do? Well if `MkParseDisplayName()` finds an object with the required `ProgID`, it will call `CoCreateInstance()` to get an instance of it, and `QueryInterface()` it for the `IParseDisplayName()` interface. `IParseDisplayName()` is a standard COM interface, which implements a single method, `ParseDisplayName()`. `MkParseDisplayName()` will call this method, passing it the complete display name (or in our case, the ADsPath) – basically saying to `ParseDisplayName()` something like 'I've done all I can with this string. You see what you can make of it'. Have a look back at those examples of names from a couple of paragraphs back. Do you notice how every one of them is really a set of names joined together? `MkParseDisplayName()` is there to handle the first bit. Then it's up to a more specialised object to deal with the rest. `IParseDisplayName::ParseDisplayName()` will actually return one of those Monikers, which can be used to bind to the actual object.

We've talked a lot about monikers without actually saying what they are. Well in simple terms they are COM objects that expose the interface `IMoniker`. `IMoniker` is a fairly complex interface defined in `objidl.idl`, but it's got one key method that we're interested in: `BindToObject()`, defined as:

```
[local]
    HRESULT BindToObject(
        [in, unique] IBindCtx *pbc,
        [in, unique] IMoniker *pmkToLeft,
        [in] REFIID riidResult,
        [out, iid_is(riidResult)] void **ppvResult);
```

Monikers are often described as intelligent names, and that is how they can be seen. A Moniker is associated with a particular COM object, and knows exactly where to find the object and how to get an interface pointer on it. Once you've got the Moniker associated with an object, you just call `IMoniker::BindToObject()` to get the object itself. Which for us completes the process. To recap: `ADsGetObject()` calls `MkParseDisplayName()`. `MkParseDisplayName()` tracks down the provider object for our ADSI provider, and hands it the `ADsPath`. The `IParseDisplayName::ParseDisplayName()` method figures out what the object is, hands out a moniker to it, and finally `ADsGetObject()` calls `BindToObject()` on the moniker to retrieve an interface pointer to the object itself. All we've got to do is implement the provider object, and possibly implement the moniker object. I say possibly because there are some standard COM moniker objects that can help us out – but more on that in a bit.

If you've never encountered monikers before, I'm going to guess you're finding this a lot to take in. You'll probably want to read those last paragraphs a couple of times. But do persevere – it'll be worth it in the end.

Once you've understood this far it might strike you that this all seems unnecessarily complicated. I'm guessing here but I reckon it makes sense to you that `MkParseDisplayName()` interprets the first bit of the display name, and passes the rest to an object that implements `IParseDisplayName()`. But what's the point of bringing monikers into it? Why can't `IParseDisplayName::ParseDisplayName()` simply produce an interface pointer to the requested object? Why bother with the extra step? Actually there are several reasons.

The first reason for using a moniker is that actually we were a bit optimistic in our assumption that the object that implements `IParseDisplayName()` knows everything it needs to get to the object. For the StarRaiders provider, that's a good assumption. After all, we're writing the entire provider (actually *I'm* writing the entire provider but I'll let that one pass). So it makes sense that we can write the StarRaiders provider object in a way that can get to any object in StarRaiders. But in general that might not be the case. Look again at some of the display names I gave as examples:

```
StarRaiders://Fans/Simon/Spice Girls.
C:\My Documents\DontLetTheBossHere\MyOtherJobApplications.doc
http://www.wrox.com
clsid:CDCC2620-9906-11d2-80BF-0000E8DC2D45.
```

Notice how some of them are composed of not just two but lots of sections. Isn't it possible that sometimes the object that implements `IParseDisplayName()` might actually not know enough to locate the object? Perhaps it'll be able to figure out a bit more of the display name, and then have to hand the rest on to something else to interpret. After all these are the days of object oriented programming and data hiding! This is where the power of monikers really comes in. Look again at that definition of `IMoniker::BindToObject`. Notice that parameter `ppMonikerToLeft`? Guess what's that for. Yep, you got it; you can actually string monikers along, one after the other. The technical term is composition, and it means you can have one moniker know so much about how to get at an object, then have another moniker take over. We're actually going to see an example of this in StarRaiders – I'm going to use composition to create some of the objects.

Another reason for using monikers as an extra step is that it gives the COM server more flexibility over when to create the object. There's broadly two ways a moniker can work. Firstly, you could create the actual object when the moniker is created. The moniker will probably store a pointer to the actual object, and when you call `IMoniker::BindToObject()`, you'll just get back that pointer. Microsoft has actually implemented a moniker object like that. It's called a **pointer moniker**, and you can create one using the API function `CreatePointerMoniker()`. In ATL, the code would work roughly like this:

```
CComObject<CMyObject> *pNewObject;
CComObject<CMyObject>::CreateInstance(&pNewObject);
IUnknown *pNewUnknown = pNewObject->GetUnknown();
hRes = CreatePointerMoniker(pNewUnknown, ppmkOut);
```

In this code the last line is the one that creates the moniker. The other lines are simply ATL's way of creating a COM object and getting an `IUnknown` interface pointer on it.

And if I produce a bit of pseudo-code, guessing what goes on inside the pointer moniker, I'd guess something like this. The pointer would have this member variable:

```
IUnknown *m_pObject;
```

`m_pObject` will have been initialized when the pointer moniker was created to point to the object the moniker can be used to bind to.

The `IMoniker::BindToObject()` will most likely be implemented like this:

```
HRESULT CPointer::BindToObject(IBindCtx *pbc, IMoniker *pmkToLeft,
                    REFIID riidResult, void **ppvResult)
{
    // bind context and moniker to left not relevent for pointer moniker
    HRESULT hr;
    hr = m_pObject->QueryInterface(riidResult, ppvResult);
    return hr;
}
```

The second option is you could have an moniker that knows enough to be able to create and initialize the object, but doesn't actually do so until you call `BindToObject()`. This could be quite useful if the object actually uses a lot of resources, or is time consuming to create. With ADSI there's probably not that much advantage to this. After all if you call `ADsGetObject()`, you expect (and get) the actual object back. But in another application, you might use `MkParseDisplayName()` just to get something you can use to create the object easily later on. You might want to pass the moniker pointer around, perhaps to another application on another computer, before you actually do anything with the object. Monikers give the server the flexibility to decide when the object is actually going to be created.

For completeness, I should really mention a third possibility for how monikers can work. The object might already exist when the moniker is requested, so the moniker doesn't have to do anything except store an interface pointer to the object. Pointer monikers again fit this idiom beautifully.

Well we've got most of the theory we need. Just to make sure it's clear, here's a time diagram showing the sequence of operations that occurs when `ADsGetObject` is called.

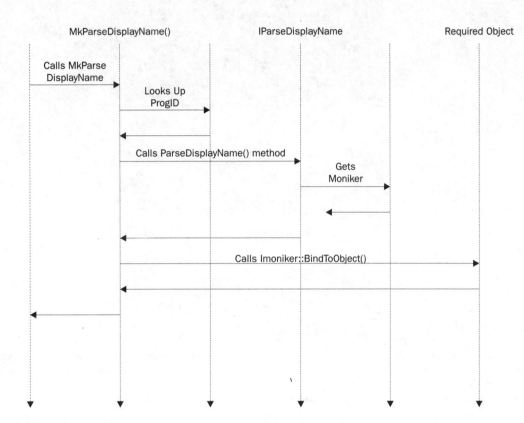

Putting It Into Practice

I think it's time we put together some more code to show how this all works in ADSI. In the process we'll learn more about different types of moniker and what some of those parameters in `IParseDisplayName::ParseDisplayName()` and `IMoniker::BindToObject()` mean.

We'll need to add the provider object to StarRaiders. So bring up Object Wizard, to create an object called StarProvider. Make sure this one is a *custom* object: there's no need for it to be dual, since it will only ever be called by `MkParseDisplayName()`, never directly from ADSI clients. Also – this is important – make sure you change the **Prog ID** to StarRaiders. Remember the name of the object doesn't really matter – that only really affects names inside your code. But the `ProgID` *has* to be correct so that `MkParseDisplayName()`, and hence `ADsGetObject()` are able to locate the object. The name you give the interface doesn't matter.

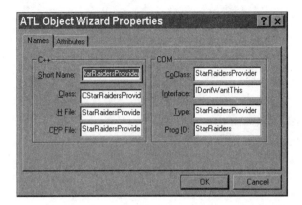

And:

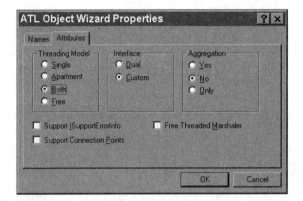

Now go to the idl file and remove the references to the wizard-generated interface. We can't use the implement interface wizard here because `IparseDisplayName()` isn't defined by any type library, so we'll need to add the implementations to the C++ source and header files manually. Go to `StarRaidersProvider.h` and make the following changes.

```
/////////////////////////////////////////////////////////////////////////////
// CStarRaidersProvider
class ATL_NO_VTABLE CStarRaidersProvider :
    public CComObjectRootEx<CComMultiThreadModel>,
    public CComCoClass<CStarRaidersProvider, &CLSID_StarRaidersProvider>,
    public IParseDisplayName
{
public:
    CStarRaidersProvider()
    {
    }

DECLARE_REGISTRY_RESOURCEID(IDR_STARRAIDERSPROVIDER)
DECLARE_NOT_AGGREGATABLE(CStarRaidersProvider)

DECLARE_PROTECT_FINAL_CONSTRUCT()
```

```
BEGIN_COM_MAP(CStarRaidersProvider)
    COM_INTERFACE_ENTRY(IParseDisplayName)
END_COM_MAP()

public:
// IParseDisplayName
STDMETHOD(ParseDisplayName)
    (
        /*[in, unique]*/ IBindCtx *pbc,
        /*[in]*/ LPOLESTR pszDisplayName,
        /*[out]*/ ULONG *pchEaten,
        /*[out]*/ IMoniker **ppmkOut
    );
};
```

Now go to `StarProvider.cpp` and add basic stub code for `ParseDisplayName()`.

```
STDMETHODIMP CStarRaidersProvider :: ParseDisplayName
    (
        /*[in, unique]*/ IBindCtx *pbc,
        /*[in]*/ LPOLESTR pszDisplayName,
        /*[out]*/ ULONG *pchEaten,
        /*[out]*/ IMoniker **ppmkOut
    )
{
    AFX_MANAGE_STATE(AfxGetStaticModuleState())

    return E_NOTIMPL;
}
```

You can compile the code now, and `ADsGetObject()` (and VB's `GetObject`) will be able to hook up to your provider. To test this, put a breakpoint in your `ParseDisplayName()` implementation, at the line:

```
    return E_NOTIMPL
```

Now set the debug executable to be the Active Directory Browser, and run your code in debug mode. In the object dialog box, type in `StarRaiders:`, and you'll see your breakpoint gets hit. Note that this won't work if you're using `dsbrowse` because `dsbrowse` can only browse starting with `ADs:` it doesn't have an option to directly go to an object.

While you're sitting there, take a peek at the variables passed in to `ParseDisplayName()`. You should see the following:

pszDisplayName	"StarRaiders:"
*pchEaten	0x00000000

What does this mean? Well, `lpszDisplayName` is the display name – in other words the `ADsPath`. `MkParseDisplayName()` is telling your provider object that this is the name that needs to be parsed. `pchEaten` is quite interesting. This is the variable that is used to say how many characters in the string have been processed (that is eaten). `MkParseDisplayName()` has set this number to 0, implying that it hasn't processed any of the name. This is perhaps slightly misleading because `MkParseDisplayName()` has in fact interpreted that StarRaiders: means something that our new provider object can handle, but by doing this, `MkParseDisplayName()` is giving our provider object the chance to check the entire name for syntax etc. if it wants to. The important point is that `MkParseDisplayName()` is expecting our implementation of `ParseDisplayName()` to indicate that it has processed the entire string - we do this by setting `*pchEaten` to the total length of the `lpszDisplayName` string before we return.

So far so good. Unfortunately, what we've written won't help `MkParseDisplayName()` much, as all we do is hand it an error code back. If you let the program continue, the Active Directory browser will display a message box telling you that's what happened. If we'd been careless and returned `S_OK` here, we'd probably cause the browser to crash as it tried to process the contents of the memory pointed to by `*ppMoniker`, which we haven't yet set!

So now let's add the code to actually implement `IParseDisplayName::ParseDisplayName()` to track down an object:

```
STDMETHODIMP CStarRaidersProvider :: ParseDisplayName
    (
        /*[in, unique]*/ IBindCtx *pbc,
        /*[in]*/ LPOLESTR pszDisplayName,
        /*[out]*/ ULONG *pchEaten,
        /*[out]*/ IMoniker **ppmkOut
    )
{
    AFX_MANAGE_STATE(AfxGetStaticModuleState())

    // try and obtain the new object
    HRESULT hRes;
    IUnknown *pNewObject;
    pNewObject = CreateADsObjectFromADsPath(pszDisplayName, NULL, NULL);

    // if we haven't got an object back there must have been
    // something wrong with the path name.
    if (pNewObject == NULL)
        return E_FAIL;

    // mark characters eaten to indicate entire display name has been parsed
    *pchEaten = wcslen(pszDisplayName);
    hRes = CreatePointerMoniker(pNewObject, ppmkOut);
    if (FAILED(hRes))
        return hRes;

    return S_OK;
}
```

Pretty simple, huh? The only new point in this code is the function `CreateADsObjectFromADsPath()`. This is a utility function I've written for StarRaiders that does the job of taking a `CString` containing an `ADsPath`, figuring out what object to create, and creating the object and returning an `IUnknown` interface pointer on it. If for any reason it can't create the object (usually because the `ADsPath` supplied wasn't a valid `ADsPath` for any object in StarRaiders) then it'll return `NULL`. How have I implemented `CreateADsObjectFromADsPath()`? Here it is:

```
IUnknown *CreateADsObjectFromADsPath(LPOLESTR pszDisplayName, LPOLESTR pszUserName,
                            LPOLESTR pszPassword)
{
   CStringArray csarrRDNs;
   HRESULT hr = BreakADsPath(pszDisplayName, csarrRDNs);
   if (FAILED(hr))
      return NULL;

   CComObject<CStarRaidersNamespace> *pNamespace;
   CComObject<CStarRaidersNamespace>::CreateInstance(&pNamespace);
   pNamespace->ADsInitialize(pszUserName, pszPassword);

   if (csarrRDNs.GetSize() == 0)
   {
      pNamespace->AddRef();
      return pNamespace->GetUnknown();
   }
   else
   {
      return pNamespace->GetChild(csarrRDNs);
   }

}
```

The first thing we do is break down the `ADsPath`, using another utility function written for that purpose. This function – which I won't reproduce here since it's not really relevant to ADSI – simply converts a StarRaiders `ADsPath` into a string array of the component names. For example, `StarRaiders://Fans/Simon/Spice Girls` would become an array containing three elements – Fans, Simon and Spice Girls.

The next part of `CreateADsObjectFromADsPath()` could actually be quite a good demonstration of the same principles behind composite monikers (OK, I know it doesn't use monikers but the principle is similar). We set about creating the ADSI objects going down the tree hierarchy. Each ADSI object is responsible for looking at the next name in the array of names, creating the appropriate child object, and passing that child the remainder of the StringArray to continue down the tree. So our utility function creates a `Namespace` object, then hands it the array of names to parse. This is done in the `GetChild()` function, implemented by all COM objects in the StarRaiders provider. Notice that if a user name and password has been supplied, this also gets passed down. If at any point an invalid name is encountered, one of the `GetChild()` functions will return `NULL`, which will be passed back up to `CreateADsObjectFromADsPath()`.

After all that explanation of Monikers, that code is all we need to get `ADsGetObject()` working correctly for any object in StarRaiders. We can now see the StarRaiders provider in action, even if we don't go through the ADSI router. This screenshot is taken from `adsvw.exe`, and shows StarRaiders working when I've selected an object inside the directory, StarRaiders://Fans, to bind to directly.

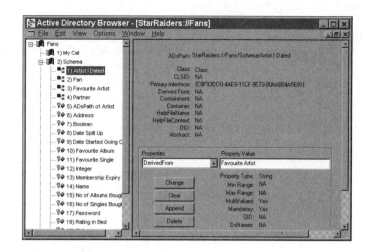

Two Registrations for your Provider

Now we've finished our discussion of binding to ADSI objects, it's worth stepping back for a minute and comparing the two sets of registry entries that need to be made to fully register your provider. Recall that there are two ADSI COM objects that need to be publicly visible: the namespace object and the provider object. Each of these gives access to the directory by a different means. The interesting thing is that these two objects are completely separate. Each has a different means of being fully registered, and neither is dependent on the other in any way. So when we talk about registering an ADSI provider, we are actually talking about two distinct registrations. Even the convention that if the provider object is called XXX then the namespace object is called XXXNamespace is just that: a convention. You don't have to follow it, and it won't stop your provider working if you don't. The only point you have to watch is that it is the ProgID of your provider object that determines the name of your provider (That is, the RDN of the namespace object) when it is used to bind to ADSI objects. However, the text displayed in ADsPaths as the name of the provider is determined by the get_Name() method of the namespace object and the get_ADsPath() method of all other objects. These strings giving the provider name had better all be the same, otherwise you will cause a lot of confusion (and probably a few crashed clients)!

Just to make things clear, the following table compares the two different sets of registry entries needed.

Object Registered	Namespace Object	Provider Object
Usual convention for `ProgID` in registry	*ProviderName*Namespace	*ProviderName*
Function	Allows binding to namespace object by enumerating children of the ADSI router, ADs:	Allows binding to any object by specifying its ADsPath in a call to GetObject(), ADsGetObject(), or MkParseDisplayName().

Object Registered	Namespace Object	Provider Object
Registry entries needed	Usual COM CLSID and `ProgID` entries, plus entry in `HKLM/Software/Microsoft/ADs` specifying the `ProgID`	Usual COM CLSID and `ProgID` entries only. `ProgID` *must* have same name as the `ADsPath` of the namespace object (without the trailing :)
Interfaces that MUST be implemented	`IADs` `IADsContainer`	`IparseDisplayName()`

Summary

You've probably figured by now that writing an ADSI provider is a fairly major task, and if you do it in ATL you will need a good understanding of some of the more advanced features in ATL. You'll also need to think carefully about how you architect your provider (but that goes without saying for any project...). In this chapter I've covered the areas that are likely to catch you out if you're not careful, and the areas for which you need a reasonably advanced understanding of COM and ATL to implement correctly. The one message I would like to leave you with is that if you are going to write a provider, then do make sure you are *very* familiar with the specifications of ADSI. Don't just take it from this book, but do go over the ADSI MSDN documentation very carefully. When you write an ADSI provider, you're not just writing any old custom COM server, for which you are free to define the rules of how to use it. An ADSI provider probably won't only be accessed by your own clients – there's going to be a lot of other Microsoft and third party clients out there that will think they can access it too. When you make that innocent registry entry in `HKLM/Software/Microsoft/ADs/Providers` that announces your provider to the world, you are implicitly declaring that your provider will follow all the rules Microsoft have defined for how ADSI providers will behave. If your provider deviates at all from these rules you can pretty much guarantee that sooner or later you'll cause an unsuspecting client application to crash. And you really wouldn't want that would you?

Anyway, that completes what I believe will be technically the hardest chapter in the book. We've also now completed examining most of the main topics in ADSI. In the next chapter we're going to step back a little by looking at the principles of LDAP which underpin a lot of the design of ADSI, before completing our discussion of ADSI itself by looking at various miscellaneous advanced topics in Chapter 11.

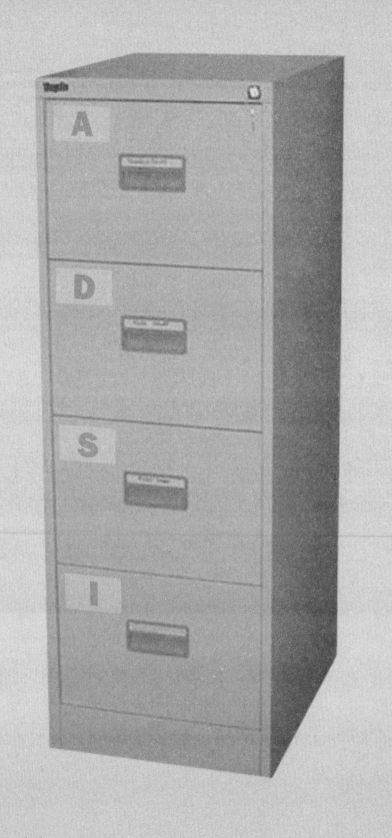

10

LDAP

In this chapter you'll learn:

❑ About the definition of LDAP version v3, and what requirements LDAP v3 directory services must satisfy to function

❑ How LDAP v3 directories are structured

❑ What LDAP APIs (which come with Windows 2000) and directories are available

❑ How to program LDAP clients using the Microsoft LDAP API to develop an LDAP directory browser.

I've hinted that ADSI has a strong LDAP heritage, and we've seen that Active Directory needs to be accessed through the ADSI LDAP provider. When we go over the actual definition of LDAP version 3, you'll see how much of the ADSI schema has been taken from LDAP. In this chapter, we're going to have a look at this in closer detail. In fact, we'll see how the Microsoft LDAP API can in fact be used as an alternative to ADSI to bind to Active Directory, or any other LDAP directory.

If you look at a lot of the available material about LDAP, you'll find quite a lot of historical detail about how LDAP evolved from the X500 DAP protocol, and how LDAP removed a lot of the complications of DAP. You'll also learn that certain key features were missing from LDAP v2, which led to the development of LDAP v3. I'm going to take a slightly different approach here. The ADSI LDAP provider is LDAP v3 compliant, and to be honest you're not very likely to find an LDAP server these days that doesn't understand LDAP v3.

Now it's possible to understand C++ without learning C or how C evolved. Similarly, you don't need to understand all the OLE background before you learn DCOM – and by the same principle, you don't really need a history lesson in order to understand how LDAP v3 works. So in this chapter I'm simply going to explain the LDAP v3 specification – we won't cover LDAP v2. If you need to understand how version 3 has evolved from earlier versions of LDAP, there's plenty of other material out there.

In this chapter, I'll go over the theory you need to understand how LDAP works first. Then I'll go on to some coding samples using Microsoft's LDAP API to access Active Directory. The coding samples are all in C++, since the LDAP API is a C API. It's not really intended for VB use. It is of course possible to call it from VB since VB can in principle be used to call API functions, but it's really much more recommended that if you code up in VB then you use the API that was intended for VB use to talk to LDAP directories. That would be ADSI itself. As far as the theory is concerned, we won't need to spend too long on it. If you've got this far in the book, you'll have picked up a lot of the ideas of LDAP just by following the ADSI samples. What's more, you'll find the code involved in the samples isn't too complex, so you probably would be able to follow it without most of the detailed theoretical background. So if you're impatient, or just want to see some samples, then you do have my permission to skip the first half of this chapter.

The Basics of LDAP

LDAP is based on the client-server model, which should be pretty familiar to you: It's based on a client performing operations against a server: In other words, the client requests to access information in the directory, and the server carries out the requested operation and returns any results. Something like this:

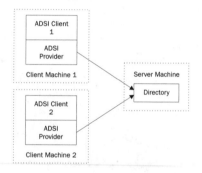

Notice that in this diagram, I've had the client direct its requests through the LDAP API, and the request goes to any of several servers. You shouldn't have any trouble recognizing this structure – it's pretty much how ADSI works. Just replace LDAP API by ADSI COM interfaces, and LDAP server with directory service, and you're there.

Communication over the network is done by messages. The structure of a message is fairly precisely defined in RFC 2251. It includes a message ID, which is chosen by the client when it initiates a request, and which must be used in all subsequent messages related to that request. It also includes the type of request (bind, search, modify, etc.) and any accompanying data, for example, to identify the search base and scope etc.

The only snag is that this diagram is a bit of a fudge, mostly because I'm trying to highlight the bits of LDAP that are relevant to us as high level programmers. Technically, none of the available LDAP APIs are part of LDAP. You see, LDAP really defines the protocol for how the client and server communicate. It tells you how the LDAP servers respond to requests over TCP/IP. It tells you what the servers should be able to do. It even defines an LDAPMessage structure, which you can think of as the basic packet of information that contains all the data needed for the client to tell the server what it wants, and the server to respond.

I don't know about you, but personally I've never fancied doing basic TCP/IP programming. Not that I've anything against it mind – I'm very grateful that other programmers have written enough high level APIs and similar packing around it that I don't need learn it myself. I like doing the kind of programming where I don't have to write more than 10 or 20 lines of code before I can see the results displayed on the screen.

As a result, we're not going to pay much attention to the low level LDAP protocols in this chapter. We'll concentrate instead on the parts of the LDAP definitions that have a direct effect on how any higher level APIs work.

What I do want you to notice, however, is that LDAP defines the protocols at a slightly different point in the client-server architecture than ADSI does. LDAP deals with everything behind the API that the client uses to talk to the directory service. From the protocols for communicating over the network to defining what operations the directory service is capable of. ADSI on the other hand deals largely with the API itself – it defines the interfaces that ADSI providers expose and says something about what the various methods should do. ADSI says nothing about network protocols – that's up to the individual ADSI provider to implement and hide from the client. That's why in Chapter 1 I described ADSI as a client-side API.

So although it might appear at first sight that ADSI and LDAP are to some extent duplicating each others functionality, this isn't really the case. It's more true to say that ADSI and LDAP are able to complement each other

The LDAP APIs

Luckily for us, there are several C APIs out there which convert the low-level stuff into actual, useful function calls, and many of them are now also open source. APIs that have been around for some time include offerings from Netscape, the University of Michigan, and the openLDAP API. Naturally, Microsoft has one too. This last statement might come as a surprise. The Microsoft LDAP API has been around for a while now, but Microsoft hasn't pushed it very hard – until ADSI arrived.

These APIs all consist of a low level set of C-style function calls, and in principle, any of these APIs may be used to access any LDAP server. We're going to use the Microsoft LDAP API in this chapter, but you will find that the other APIs are *extremely* similar – to the point where even the names of many API functions are identical. So even if you prefer to use the Netscape or University of Michigan versions, you will still get a good idea of how to use your chosen API from the samples in this chapter.

Although I'm concentrating on the C APIs, it's worth pointing out that there are quite a number of others:

- ❑ Netscape have released a Java Directory SDK

- ❑ You can download PerlDAP, which lets you write LDAP clients in Perl, from a couple of web sites

- ❑ Sun have produced the Java Naming and Directory Interfaces – another SDK that you can use to access LDAP directories using Java

- ❑ Microsoft have released something called the LDAP provider for Active Directory Services Interfaces (ADSI), which you may have heard of

If you are interested in any of these products, Appendix H gives you the appropriate URLs. They are all free.

The book, Implementing LDAP, by Mark Wilcox, ISBN 1-861002-21-1, published by Wrox, goes into more detail of the various different LDAP APIs available.

The reason I'm going to cover a C API in this chapter is that the LDAP C APIs perform very little translation between the operations you can do in LDAP and the API function calls. All the other APIs are designed to make your life easier by hiding a lot of the basic ideas of LDAP from you, but the C ones don't. So that's the API we need to use if we want to really dive in and understand LDAP. (Which hopefully you want to do.)

I should point out by the way that all the APIs are – like ADSI – **client-side** APIs. They sit in the process space of the client and handle all the business of communicating using the LDAP protocols to a specified server. They won't help you write LDAP directory services. If you want to do that, you've no alternative but to start learning all the low level protocols and write code in a relatively low level language like C or C++ to handle them from scratch.

What the LDAP Definition Covers

So what does LDAP cover precisely? Well, the LDAP definition specifies:

❑ **Directory Structure**. LDAP defines how a directory can be divided into naming contexts, with a rootDSE object at the top that lets you find out what the naming contexts are. Much as we found for Active Directory.

❑ **Operations**. How a client interacts with the server. What operations may be performed, and how the client and server communicate over TCP/IP.

❑ **Schema**. There is a basic LDAP schema, which includes definitions of objects and attributes which are likely to be in common use. This schema may be extended, though in general the aim is that objects in the basic schema have so many optional attributes that most uses should be covered.

❑ **URLs**. LDAP defines a format for URLs that may be used to search LDAP directories. These URLs are recognized by Netscape Communicator, though not at present by Internet Explorer.

The LDAP models

If you've read much about LDAP before, you might be a bit puzzled by the list I've just given above. You see, LDAP v3 specifies both the protocol for talking to directories, and something of the directory structure. The guys who wrote the specification actually formally divided it into four so – called **models** – which means you'll often hear people talk about the LDAP models.

❑ **The Information Model** tells you what can be stored in the directory

❑ **The Naming Model** defines how objects should be identified

❑ **The Functional Model** defines the operations that can be carried out

❑ **The Security Model** tells you how security works

You can think of these models in the same way you think of the categories Microsoft have defined for the ADSI interfaces (persistent object interfaces, core interfaces etc.) – as a way of categorizing the specifications, which may or may not be useful, but which doesn't in the end have any real effect on how you do your coding.

Personally however, I don't find the LDAP models remotely helpful in explaining how LDAP actually works, so I'm going to ignore them. The following sections are divided according to my own earlier list of LDAP features.

Directory Structure

The structure of an LDAP directory can really be thought of as this

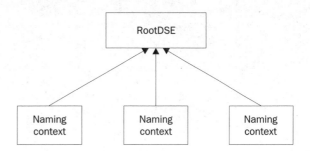

So you have an object called the `root dse` (root directory-specific entry) which acts as the gateway into the rest of the directory. By gateway, I don't mean in any security-related sense, but in the sense that it tells you what the distinguished names you need are to get to the objects at the roots of the naming contexts.

To understand this, and to understand what a naming context is, we need to understand that although an LDAP directory will have a hierarchical structure, there doesn't have to be only one tree in the hierarchy. It is possible to have several trees, each with its own root node. For example, my Active Directory installation has three trees, with roots

```
DC=TopOfThePops,DC=Fame,DC=Com
DC=Configuration, DC=TopOfThePops,DC=Fame,DC=Com
DC=Schema, DC=Configuration, DC=TopOfThePops,DC=Fame,DC=Com
```

It might look from their distinguished names like the latter two roots ought to be buried somewhere first tree, but as we saw in Chapter 4 they aren't – it's little more than a coincidence that that is how their names look. It is not possible to reach either of these objects by browsing down the tree from `DC=TopOfThePops,DC=Fame,DC=Com` in Active Directory (though it is possible in the global catalogue, which is technically a different directory).

Each tree is a naming context. Notice also that just because a node is at the top of a naming context, that doesn't prevent it from having a distinguished name with more than one component in it.

There doesn't seem to be any standard for how 'root DSE' is written. The LDAP RFCs tend to use root DSE (two words) and since this is a chapter about LDAP I've taken my lead from there in this chapter. The ADSI documentation, on the other hand, more commonly writes 'rootdse' or 'rootDSE' (one word), and rootdse must be given as one word (case insensitive) in `ADsPaths` when binding to this object.

> **You can think of a** naming context **as a complete tree of directory objects, although it may only form a portion of the entire directory.**

You can find out what the naming contexts are by looking at the attribute `namingContexts` on the root DSE. `namingContexts` is a multi-valued attribute, whose values are the distinguished names of the objects that sit at the root nodes of the naming contexts. For example, in my Active Directory installation, the `namingContexts` attribute of the `root DSE` has the values.

```
DC=TopOfThePops,DC=Fame,DC=Com
DC=Configuration, DC=TopOfThePops,DC=Fame,DC=Com
DC=Schema, DC=Configuration, DC=TopOfThePops,DC=Fame,DC=Com
```

There is a list of attributes, defined in RFC2251, which the `root DSE` must have. This includes such things as a list of alternative servers that may be used if this one is down, (this presumably relies on the client having read and remembered the list on a previous occasion when this server wasn't down!) and which versions of LDAP this directory service supports. Individual directory services may add other attributes.

Names

A word about naming objects in the directory. All objects have a unique distinguished name. Unlike ADSI ADsPaths, the distinguished name does not include any reference to the server or port number, since that information will have been sorted out when the connection to the server was established.

The format of the distinguished name is exactly the format of Active Directory names that we've been using, but with the extra ADSI server information stripped off, for example, `CN=Users,DC=TopOfThePops,DC=Fame,DC=COM`. Distinguished names are case insensitive.

> *The distinguished name of the* `root DSE` *is an empty string. In LDAP, don't go trying to bind to an object with the distinguished name 'rootDSE' the way you would do with ADSI, as it won't work. The name, rootDSE, is added by the ADSI LDAP provider to make it easier to see what's going on. This is the one exception to the general rule that LDAP ADSI ADsPaths are just the LDAP distinguished name, prefixed by* `LDAP://[server name[:port]/]`.

Operations

LDAP specifies the following operations that you may choose to do against a server:

- ❑ Binding
- ❑ Searching
- ❑ Adding Entries
- ❑ Modifying Entries
- ❑ Deleting Entries

We don't need to say anything more about adding, modifying, and deleting entries, as those operations simply do what they say. Binding and searching are more interesting though.

Binding

LDAP does not distinguish between binding and authenticating. When you bind to a directory server, you simultaneously indicate two things: that you want to talk to the specified server, and who you are (supplying a password if necessary).

One aspect of LDAP that can be confusing if you're not used to thinking in the right way is that who you are should be one of the entries in the directory. There's an inbuilt, unstated, assumption that the directory includes details of all the people authorized to access it, though a directory might choose to allow guest access as well. What this means in practice is that when you bind, the username that you give will usually be the distinguished name of an object in the directory. There may also be a special administrative account, `cn=Directory Manager`, which has unlimited read/write access to the directory.

> *People familiar with TCP/IP connections will be aware that setting up an initial connection is much more time consuming than maintaining it. LDAP responds to this by reusing connections as far as possible. If you rebind to an LDAP server, you will most likely be reusing the same TCP/IP connection. However, this detail is something that high level programmers do not need to be aware of, and should not rely on even if they do.*

Searching

If you read through the list of operations carefully, you might notice that it doesn't mention browsing or reading an object. Operations are defined to let you modify, add or delete objects, but not to simply read them.

The reason is that LDAP does exactly the same thing as the ADSI `IDirectorySearch` interface: It merges the ideas of reading, browsing, and searching. Just as for `IDirectorySearch`, if you perform a search, you must pass in a parameter that specifies the scope of the search. The possible values are:

Value	Description
LDAP_SCOPE_BASE	The base object only
LDAP_SCOPE_ONELEVEL	The immediate children of the base object
LDAP_SCOPE_SUBTREE	Base object and all children below it

> *Notice the careful wording here. If you ask for a one-level search, the base object will be excluded. This is not the case for the other scopes.*

If you want to do a real search for an object that you know is somewhere in the directory, then you will specify `LDAP_SCOPE_SUBTREE`. The other options are technically known as searching, but don't really correspond to what you'd normally imagine searching to involve. `LDAP_SCOPE_ONELEVEL` allows you to enumerate the *immediate* children of an object – or at least those children satisfying certain conditions. This really corresponds to browsing. When I say *immediate children*, I mean those objects that are one level below the object in question in the directory tree.

`LDAP_SCOPE_BASE` is the one you would use to obtain details of the properties of the named object.

LDAP URLs

These have been defined in recognition of the importance of the Internet, and of web browsers. The idea of LDAP URLs is to make it easy for someone using a web browser to be able to carry out a search of a directory, just by typing in a URL in the same way that you'd type the URL of a web page that you want.

This means that an LDAP URL has to convey quite a lot of information. It must specify:

❑   The directory to be searched

❑   The base object for the search

❑   The search scope

❑   The filter

❑   Which attributes are to be returned

That's quite a tall order for one string, and you can imagine it leads to some quite long URLs. Here's the format that is used:

```
ldap://<Server Name>/<DN of Search Base>?<Requested Attributes>
                              ?<Scope>?<Filter>?<Extensions>
```

For anything inside angled brackets, insert the appropriate text.

So an LDAP URL has a similar format to any other URL, except that the protocol is ldap (as opposed to – say – http or ftp), and all the different fields are separated by question marks (apart from the / separating the server name from everything else).

To simplify the URLs, it's fine to cut off the URL at any point after the Search Base. Default values will be assumed for any omitted items. The default values are * for Requested Attributes, base for the Scope, (objectClass=*) for the filter, and nothing for the extensions. This means that if you just want to look at all the attributes for any one object, the URL is very simple:

```
ldap://<Server Name>/<DN of required object>
```

Actually it is possible to simplify this even more. The Server Name can be omitted, provided the browser (or whatever LDAP client is processing the URL) has some default server (and port) it can connect to. Usually, the default is the local host, port 389.

By the way, did you notice that I said LDAP client? That's one oddity about LDAP URLs: Pretty much everything else in the LDAP definition is intended to be supplied by the client and processed by the server. The whole idea of LDAP is, after all, that the client makes requests to the server. But LDAP URLs are there to be processed by a client (e.g. a web browser) and converted to the actual LDAP requests to be sent to the server.

Anyway, that all looks simple enough so far, but there is a complication. As usual for LDAP names, any character which might be misinterpreted as a command needs to be escaped by preceding it with a % sign. Unfortunately, the characters that need to be escaped in LDAP URLs include not only our old friends from search filters, but a couple of new – and common – characters. Most awkwardly, it includes the space character – which has to be replaced by %20. As you can imagine, this can lead to some awkward looking names.

Strings

LDAP v3 uses what are described as Unicode strings. However, if you've been using COM and such things as BSTRs before, then don't be fooled – the Unicode strings that LDAP uses aren't the same as the Unicode strings you're used to.

In COM, Unicode means that every character occupies 2 bytes, allowing almost all of the characters in use in any of the languages across the world to be represented. This is the usual definition of Unicode. It can be wasteful of memory if you're working mostly or entirely in languages with the Latin alphabet, since in that case, almost every other byte is a zero. But it's easy to process strings in this format, so (for example) working out how long a string is or getting to the 235th character in a given string are both fairly trivial.

By contrast, the Unicode that LDAP uses is UTF-8 format. In this format, Latin characters are still represented by only one byte, using ANSI. Essentially, what happens is that the highest order bit is checked. If it is zero (which it will be for all alphabetic characters, since these have an ASCII code less than 128), then the character is assumed to be represented by one byte. If, however, the highest level bit is one, then the character spans at least two bytes, so the next byte is assumed to be part of the same character.

This is going to sound confusing to experienced C++ and COM programmers, who will probably tell me that what I've just described is more similar to the multi-byte character set (MBCS) than to Unicode. MBCS is a convention for representing characters which also uses either 1 or 2 bytes per character depending on the character to be represented. Nevertheless, the UTF-8 format is commonly referred to as *a* Unicode format.

As you can probably guess UTF-8 is more efficient memory wise, but does make operations like calculating the length of the string harder. One of the reasons for using this format is that old ANSI data can be recognized without any conversion: LDAP version 2 specified that strings should be ANSI strings, so using double-byte strings throughout would have caused backwards compatibility problems.

Again, this is a detail that you don't need to be aware of, since we will be using LDAP by calling an LDAP API. The LDAP APIs will generally expect ANSI or COM-style Unicode strings, and do any necessary conversions internally. For example, the ADSI LDAP provider expects normal Unicode strings.

Binary Data

LDAP is based heavily on strings – almost all data is represented as strings, and in fact all data is to be transmitted as strings as well. Occasionally, however, you do need to handle data which is binary – for example security key certificates, or photographs of people. When this occurs, LDAP uses what are known as **Basic Encoding Rules** (**BER**), which specify a format for transmitting the data. BER also makes it possible for the binary data to be encoded as strings, which makes it possible for clients to store the data in text files.

Once again, this is a detail you probably won't need to know about when programming clients, though if you wonder why you're handling variables and variable types with ber *in their names, now you know why!*

Other LDAP Features

The LDAP specifications are fairly comprehensive. In this chapter we only have space to touch on some of its most basic features. However, it's worth pointing out that the following are also defined by LDAP:

❑ **Schema** As mentioned above, there is a basic LDAP schema. This schema covers commonly used attributes, and is intended as a base schema to which other directories will add their own attributes. It includes such properties as CN (common name), objectClass and ou (organizational unit).

❑ **Object IDs** In the LDAP schema, syntaxes are identified using object IDs as described in Chapter 2. There are standard recognized object IDs, and their use allows the LDAP definitions to specify how data with a certain object ID is to be interpreted and also how to perform comparison operations (such as case sensitive or not case sensitive). This also means that by creating your own object IDs you can specify new ways of carrying out comparisons. (For example, you might define an object ID for locations in your company building, in which location is identified by an ID assigned to a cubicle, but cubicles in the same room are considered to be in the same location, so their location attributes should be considered equal in comparisons).

❑ **Controls** LDAP supports the notion of controls, which allow extended operations to be defined on particular directory services. This can be used to give directory objects extra functionality, as if it was possible to call methods on them as well as setting attributes. Note however that controls are directory-specific.

The Definition of LDAP

LDAP is formally defined in RFCs 2251-2256. If you are interested in looking anything up, you'll find the following:

❑ RFC 2251. Lightweight Directory Access Protocol (v3). This defines LDAP itself.

❑ RFC 2252. Lightweight Directory Access Protocol (v3): Attribute Syntax Definitions.

❑ RFC 2253 Lightweight Directory Access Protocol (v3): UTF-8 String Representation of Distinguished Names.

❑ RFC 2254. The String Representation of LDAP Search Filters.

❑ RFC 2255. The LDAP URL Format.

❑ RFC 2256. Summary of the X.500 User Schema for use with LDAPv3.

Using the Microsoft LDAP C API

OK, we've covered enough of the theory of LDAP, it's time for some coding practice. We're going to have a go at looking at Active Directory using an LDAP API.

We're going to use the Microsoft LDAP API here. If you want to use another API (such as the Netscape or University of Michigan ones), you'll find the names of some of the functions may be different, but all the general principles of how you write your client application remain the same. This file can be found in the .lib subfolder of the folder in which you have installed the Platform SDK, provided you have selected the correct options.

In order to use the Microsoft LDAP API in C++ code, you will need to #include the file winldap.h. You will also need to link to the library wldap32.lib.

A word of warning here. There's a problem with the version of wldap32.lib that is supplied with Visual Studio 6, and you'll very quickly find your app crashing if you use it. Make sure you set up your paths so you link to the version of wldap32.lib that is supplied with the latest Platform SDK instead.

The Microsoft LDAP API does NOT use Unicode strings. Internally, data is passed to the server in UTF-8 format, but the API itself simply takes standard ANSI string and converts them internally to UTF-8. For this reason I haven't done a Unicode compile of any of the projects in this chapter. The builds are all standard ANSI ones.

The samples I'm going to work through aren't exhaustive. There's a huge list of functions in the Microsoft LDAP API and there's no way I could cover them all without boring you silly. What I'm trying to do in this chapter is give you a flavor of how to use the API. MSDN will give you a very comprehensive function-by-function reference guide to everything you can do with the API, and there'd be little point in me repeating that here.

LDAP API – General Principles

Before we look at some sample code, I just want to point out some of the general principles that the API follows.

Asynchronous and Synchronous Calls

Most calls in the LDAP API come in **synchronous** and **asynchronous** varieties. Synchronous calls are exactly what they say: The call blocks until all the results have been returned.

Asynchronous calls are slightly more interesting. They don't work in the way that you might have expected if you're used to COM, and are used to using connection points to simulate asynchronous operations. In COM, the server will normally call the client back when the result is ready. LDAP asynchronous calls work by the client polling the server, using an API function ldap_result() to find out whether the result is ready.

This has the advantage that you don't need to manually sort out implementing a separate thread, or a message loop, to receive the result. The disadvantage is that you use asynchronous operations in order to be able to perform other tasks while you are waiting for the result, then you will have to keep interrupting your other tasks to check if a result is ready.

If you have requested an asynchronous operation, you can cancel it at any time by calling the `ldap_abandon()` function.

> *You need to be careful if you're using asynchronous functions in a multi-threaded client, because not all of the asynchronous functions are thread safe. The MSDN documentation indicates which ones are not thread safe.*

You can easily spot the synchronous versions of functions, since they end in `_s`. For example, `ldap_bind()` binds to an LDAP server asynchronously, while `ldap_bind_s()` does the same thing synchronously.

Return Codes

Many LDAP functions return a code to indicate the status of the operation. This is a `ULONG`. It works in much the same way as the `HRESULT`s familiar from COM, except that the actual values for the different error codes are different.

The success code is called `LDAP_SUCCESS`. Like `S_OK`, it does have the value 0, but the error codes are generally small non-zero numbers. Don't try to use the COM `SUCCEEDED()` or `FAILED()` macros on these results, as even the errors will pass a `SUCCEEDED()` test. This is because the error codes are actually not Microsoft-specific. They are defined within LDAP, in RFC 2251.

LDAP Structures

LDAP uses a number of C-style structures to store information between function calls. Although they are C-style structures, so technically the member variables are public, in most cases you are strongly advised not to access the member variables directly. There will be functions available to do all the tasks you are likely to want to with the structures. And just to give you an extra incentive to treat the member variables of the structures concerned as private, Microsoft are not guaranteeing to keep the internal member variables the same in future versions of the API.

The two main structures you will encounter are:

❑ **LDAP**: This is used to maintain details of a session with an LDAP server. Generally, a session means a connection to one server, but if a server generates referrals to other servers, then the session will encompass those too. Virtually every function in the API requires a pointer to an LDAP structure to be passed in as a parameter, so the function knows which session the call refers to. You should treat member variables of this structure as private.

❑ **LDAPMessage**: This structure is used almost universally to store the results of a wide variety of operations. In many cases, you will call one function which returns an LDAPMessage, then pass the LDAP Message into other functions to return details of the results. Search requests return their results as LDAP Message structures, as do requests for attributes on directory objects. An LDAPMessage is even the structure that you get back from an `ldap_result` call, if the result is now available.

We're going to look at a couple of samples now. First of all, we'll do a couple of small samples that show how to bind to a directory service in the first place, and how to use asynchronous operations. Then we'll do the main sample of this chapter – a C++ dialog-bases application that lets you browse an LDAP directory.

Synchronous Bind

This is a really simple sample that illustrates the process of binding to an LDAP server. The sample requests a simple bind to Active Directory, and displays the result of the bind (that is to say, whether the bind succeeded). As in all the samples, I'm using an MFC dialog project.

The code to perform the bind is in the `OnInitDialog()` function. Here it is:

```
BOOL CCPPSynchBindDlg::OnInitDialog()
{
    CDialog::OnInitDialog();

    // MFCwizard-generated code not shown

    ULONG ulres;
    LDAP *ld = ldap_init("BiggyBiggy", 389);
    unsigned uiVersion = LDAP_VERSION3;
    ulres = ldap_set_option(ld, LDAP_OPT_VERSION, &uiVersion);
    ASSERT(ulres == LDAP_SUCCESS);

    char pszDN[] = "CN=Administrator,CN=Users,DC=TopOfThePops,DC=Fame,DC=com";
    m_listbox.AddString(CString("Attempting to bind synchronously to ")
                        + pszDN);
    ulres = ldap_simple_bind_s(ld, pszDN, "mypassword");
    m_listbox.AddString(CString("Result is :") + ldap_err2string(ulres));

    return TRUE;  // return TRUE  unless you set the focus to a control
}
```

It's a fairly short bit of code, but illustrates a number of points about using the API.

We start off with two variable declarations – an unsigned long to hold results returned from function calls, and that LDAP structure I mentioned. When you're using an LDAP API, the first thing you will almost always do is declare and initialize an LDAP structure which you will maintain in memory for the entire session. In this case we've initialized it using the `ldap_init` function to indicate that we want to connect to the server BiggyBiggy using port 389. `ldap_init()`, by the way, simply initializes the `ld` variable – it doesn't attempt to open a connection to the server, so there's no point having separate synchronous and asynchronous versions.

> *You might notice that I've abandoned my usual Hungarian notation for variable names here, and called my LDAP pointer `ld` instead of something more logical, like `pldap`, or `pldapSession`. The reason is that `ld` has become so entrenched as a standard variable name in this context that it would probably cause some confusion if I used anything different. You'll notice a few other places in these samples where I've used similarly illogical variable names for the same reason.*

The next lines make sure that we inform the server that we are an LDAP version 3 compatible client. The Microsoft API can work as either a version 2 or a version 3 client, but the default is version 2. So, we need to explicitly set the version, which is done using the `ldap_set_version()` function.

This function takes three parameters, the obligatory LDAP pointer, an integer which indicates which option we wish to set, and a void* to indicate the value of the option (void* because different options take different data types). The fact that the third parameter is a pointer explains why I've had to set a variable equal to the required constant, `LDAP_VERSION3`, rather than simply passing in the constant. `LDAP_VERSION3`, by the way , is `#defined` to be 3. Use the name, `LDAP_VERSION3` if you fancy doing more typing than you need to!

At present, the `ldap_set_option()` function simply sets some of the member variables in the supplied LDAP structure. You can find a full list of the options you can set using it in MSDN. They include things like the maximum page size, and whether the LDAP API should automatically follow referrals sent from the server.

Then we get to the key line:

```
ulres = ldap_simple_bind_s(ld, pszDN, "mypassword");
```

This line actually opens the connection to the server and attempts to authenticate using the supplied distinguished name and password. Note that I say distinguished name, rather than user name, because LDAP requires that clients authenticate as an entry in the directory. I've chosen the DN and password of the Administrator account on the domain controller.

Because we are opening a connection here, this operation could take a while – hence the _s on the end of the function name, indicating that separate synchronous and asynchronous versions of this function are available, and this is the synchronous version.

It's called `simple_bind` because the authentication is done in clear text. If I'd wanted to do a more secure bind, there are two other API functions, `ldap_bind` and `ldap_bind_s`, which will use encryption, or attempt to use the underlying security provided by the operating system. We won't cover those functions here, but they are documented in MSDN.

Finally, we use the function `ldap_err2string()` to convert the status code returned from `ldap_simple_bind_s` to a string that gives us an indication of whether the attempt to bind to the object succeeded.

If I run this sample I get this:

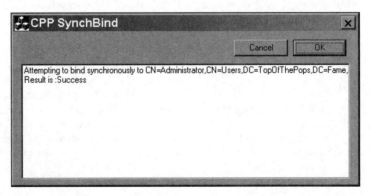

Asynchronous Bind

So that's how we bind synchronously. The next example will do the same thing, except that we will bind asynchronously. This will give us the chance to perform other tasks while the bind is going on the background.

This sample will request a bind, then print out status reports until it hears that the bind attempt has returned a result. The status reports will simply consist of the time elapsed since the bind attempt was started. As before, we will display the result from the bind attempt at the end.

Since we are using MFC, we already have the benefit of a message loop which we can use for displaying status reports. We can request the bind in our dialog box's `OnInitDialog` function, then set a timer and check the status of our bind attempt in the message handler for the timer, `OnTimer()`. If we had some real work to be done in the meantime, we could perform that in MFC's `CWnd::OnIdle()` function, making sure we broke it into sufficiently short segments that we returned to the message loop frequently.

Since we are spreading our work across a couple of member functions of our dialog class, we need to declare a couple of member variables to hold the data for our session across function calls:

```
class CCPPAsynchBindDlg : public CDialog
{

// wizard stuff not shown (again)

private:
    UINT m_iTimer;
    LDAP *m_ld;
    ULONG m_ulMesgID;
    int m_iTime;

};
```

❑ `m_ld` is our usual **LDAP** structure to maintain details of the session

❑ `m_iTime` stores the time elapsed since the bind request

❑ `m_iTimer` is the ID of the timer we've set up

❑ `m_uIMesgID` is an identifier that we can use to identify the request we've made to the server: it's returned from the call to bind asynchronously, and must be passed in to `ldap_result()` to indicate which request we are seeking the result for

We also want to define the interval with which we check the timer. This line can go anywhere outside the class definitions. I'm anticipating that the bind will happen quite quickly so I'm going to go for the smallest possible interval: one millisecond:

```
const int TIMER_INTERVAL = 1;
```

Now we can set up our bind request:

```
BOOL CCPPAsynchBindDlg::OnInitDialog()
{
    CDialog::OnInitDialog();

// wizard stuff not shown

    m_iTimer = SetTimer(20, TIMER_INTERVAL, NULL);

    ULONG ulres;
    m_ld = ldap_init("BiggyBiggy", 389);
    unsigned uiVersion = LDAP_VERSION3;
    ulres = ldap_set_option(m_ld, LDAP_OPT_VERSION, &uiVersion);
    ASSERT(ulres == LDAP_SUCCESS);

    char pszDN[] = "CN=Administrator,CN=Users,DC=TopOfThePops,DC=Fame,DC=com";

    m_listbox.AddString(CString("Attempting to bind to ") + pszDN);
    m_ulMesgID = ldap_simple_bind(m_ld, pszDN, "mypassword");

    return TRUE;  // return TRUE  unless you set the focus to a control
}
```

This is the same as the code for a synchronous bind, except that `ldap_simple_bind()` does not return a status code: it can't, because when the function returns the bind hasn't yet completed. Instead, it returns a message ID, which can be used later to check on the status of the bind request.

OK, now the timer function to check the progress of our bind request:

```
void CCPPAsynchBindDlg::OnTimer(UINT nIDEvent)
{
    CDialog::OnTimer(nIDEvent);

    LDAPMessage *ldmesgResult;
    l_timeval timeout = {0, 0};
    ULONG ulres = ldap_result(m_ld, m_ulMesgID, 0, &timeout, &ldmesgResult);
    if (ulres == 0)
    {
        TCHAR pszText[30];
        _itot(m_iTime, pszText, 10);
        m_listbox.AddString(CString(pszText) + " ms");
        m_iTime += TIMER_INTERVAL;
        return;
    }

    ASSERT(ulres == LDAP_RES_BIND);
    m_listbox.AddString("Bind result returned");
    KillTimer(m_iTimer);
    ulres = ldap_result2error(m_ld, ldmesgResult, true);

    m_listbox.AddString(CString("Result is :") + ldap_err2string(ulres));
}
```

This function will be called every `TIMER_INTERVAL` milliseconds. The important line is the one that calls the `ldap_result()` function:

```
ULONG ulres = ldap_result(m_ld, m_ulMesgID, 0, &timeout, &ldmesgResult);
```

The function can be used to check on the status of any asynchronous operation, not just bind requests. It returns a status result, which is zero if no result is yet available, and a value that indicates the type of operation if the operation has completed. In our case, this value is `LDAP_RES_BIND`. If the operation has completed, the result will be returned via an `LDAPMessage` structure.

Besides the LDAP structure to identify the session, `ldap_result()` needs the MessageID that identifies the operation and an `LDAP_TIMEVAL` structure (also known as an `l_timeval` structure) that tells `ldap_result()` how long to wait for the result. The `LDAP_TIMEVAL` structure is defined as:

```
typedef struct l_timeval {
    LONG     tv_sec;
    LONG     tv_usec;
} LDAP_TIMEVAL, * PLDAP_TIMEVAL;
```

In this case, we can treat the member variables as public. This is not one of the structures where Microsoft have advised against using the member variables directly. They respectively give the time in seconds and any milliseconds left over. In our sample, since we're just polling for a result we don't want `ldap_result()` to wait at all, so we'll set the structure to zero. If we wanted to tell `ldap_result()` to wait indefinitely, we could pass in a NULL pointer.

And once we've got a return value from `ldap_result()`? Well, if the value is zero (indicating no result is ready) then we just display the elapsed time in the listbox and increment it. Otherwise, we need to kill the timer and display the result status. We can't use the `ldap_err2string()` result directly for this. It requires an integer error code, whereas what we've got back from `ldap_result()` is an `LDAPMessage` structure. So we first use another API function, `ldap_result2error()`, which extracts the error code from the message. This function has the additional bonus that if we set the last parameter to `True`, it'll free up the memory from the structure for us as well. We take advantage of that, since we won't be wanting this structure again.

Now we're ready to try the code. Unfortunately, it's not very successful, because even with a timer interval of just one millisecond, the performance of the bind operation is too good for us:

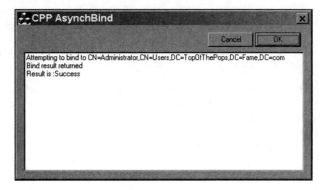

494

Well it's nice to know my computer is fast, but I'd rather like to demonstrate the fact that you can do other work during an asynchronous operation in principle. I'll cheat a bit, and attempt to authenticate with the wrong password – or, more precisely a username and no password. I'm not clear why, but that really confuses my machine, so much so that I'll need to change the timer interval to half a second:

```
const int TIMER_INTERVAL = 500;
```

And the command to perform a simple bind becomes:

```
m_ulMesgID = ldap_simple_bind(m_ld, pszDN, NULL);
```

Now when I attempt to bind, this happens:

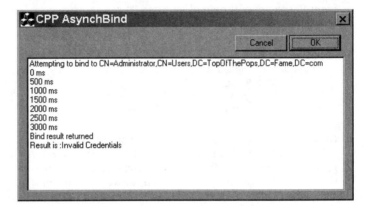

An LDAP Directory Browser

Now we come to the big main browser. This application will let us take a little tour around any LDAP v3 directory. Its only restriction is that it's a read-only application – it won't let you modify anything.

Modification is a bit harder to demonstrate in samples, since some attributes are multi-valued, and you need a much more sophisticated user interface to modify multi-valued attributes. Plus there's the fact that modification tends to require higher security permissions than reading directory objects. I don't want to get caught up in issues like writing user interfaces – that'll detract from the main point of the samples. Since I'm only trying to give you a feel for how the LDAP API is designed, browsing is enough to do that, which is why I've kept this browser read-only.

This sample is also our chance to have some fun by doing something that looks impressive, but is surprisingly simple to develop.

So let's see what our browser will look like. The project is called CPP LDAPBrowse, and when you run it you get a little dialog asking which server and port you want to bind to:

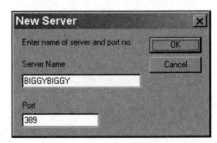

You don't get asked for credentials – I've hardcoded my credentials in...

The initial dialog is quite friendly – it attempts to put default values in for the server and port – the name of the machine you're running on , and the default LDAP port of 389. But you can change those if you want to.

Once you've chosen your server, you get the real dialog:

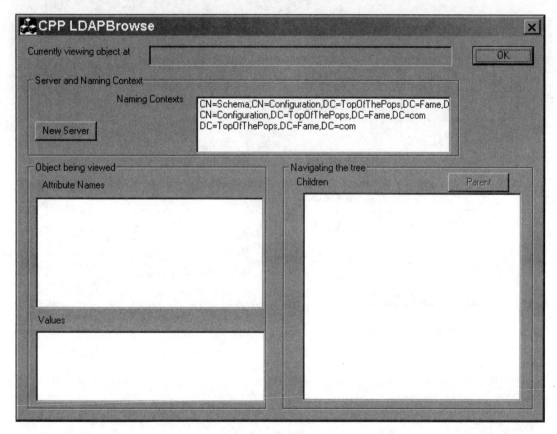

Initially, all the list boxes are blank, apart from the top one marked Naming Contexts. This list box gives you all the naming contexts for the directory service you have bound to. If you double-click on one of the naming contexts in this list box, the LDAP browser will bind to the object at the root of that naming context, and display the names of all its attributes and all its children in the appropriate list boxes.

If you double-click on the name of an attribute, its values will appear in the list box marked Values. If you double-click on the name of a child object, then the browser will bind to that child instead. You can also navigate back up the tree by clicking the button marked Parent. This will take you back to the parent of the object currently being viewed. In this way you've got complete freedom to navigate round the directory.

Clicking on the New Server button will take you back to the dialog box that asks you to choose a new directory server and port, so you can look at a different directory service. When the browser is in full swing, it'll look something like this. Here I'm using the browser to look at the container object that holds most of the user accounts:

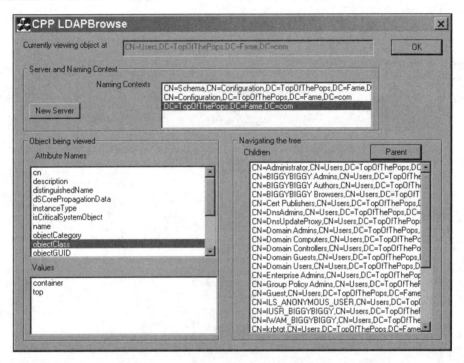

Getting Attributes and Values

Before we go over the code for the LDAP browser, I just want to go over the principles behind how you use the LDAP API to look at objects and attributes. Unlike in ADSI, there's no concept in LDAP of binding *to* a specific object. You might authenticate *as* an object in the directory, but the only thing you can bind *to* is the directory service itself. Instead of binding to an object, requests for operations pass in as a parameter the DN of the object concerned.

Recall that in LDAP, all read access to objects is carried out by performing a search – because there's no separate concept of browsing or reading one object in LDAP. When you do a search, the thing you get back is an LDAPMessage, which will contain all the information you asked for in the search. You can use the ldap_first_entry() and ldap_next_entry() functions to enumerate the directory objects returned by the search. These functions also each return an LDAPMessage. You can start to see how ubiquitous this LDAPMessage structure really is.

Once you've got the LDAPMessage which refers to a given entry, you'll use the ldap_first_attribute() and ldap_next_attribute() functions to enumerate the attribute names. These take an LDAPMessage and simply return strings – the actual names of the attributes.

Given the name of an attribute, you use the ldap_get_values() function, which returns any values as an array of strings. Got it? You'll see how this works when we go through the examples. Notice that whatever the actual data type of the value, it always gets returned as a string.

The Sample Code: The LDAP Browser

Apart from the little dialog that asks for the server and port, all the action takes place in the main MFC dialog class, `CCPPLDAPBrowse`. So we'll start off there, by looking at the extra member variables I've defined.

```
private:
    LDAP *m_ld;
    ULONG m_ulPort;
    CString m_csServer;
    CStringArray m_csarrBoundDNs;
```

`m_ld` is the LDAP structure that gets everywhere and stores information about our LDAP session.

`m_ulPort` and `m_csServer` are the port number and server name we are currently bound to. The only reason for storing them is so we can feed them back into the New Server dialog box as friendly default values if the user requests to bind to a new directory service.

`m_csarrBoundDNs` is an array that stores all the distinguished names of the objects we've bound to, heading down the directory tree. We need this array so we know the DN of the parent object if the user clicks the parent button, since there's no LDAP function that will let you find out the parent of a given object. `CStringArray` is a nice choice of variable type here because it automatically adjusts its size to accommodate how many variables we put in it (such as how far down the tree we are), while allowing the advantage of keeping the same simple syntax we use for ordinary arrays. That said, we should note that it is not very efficient – in production code you'd probably opt to use some linked list-based class rather than an array-based class instead.

There are also the member variables that class wizard has generated for us to control the various list boxes in the main dialog:

```
class CCPPLDAPBrowseDlg : public CDialog
{
// Construction
public:
    void BindToChild(LPSTR pszDN);
    void BindToNamingContext(LPSTR pszDN);
    void BindToObject(LPSTR pszDN);
    void GetNamingContexts();
    void BindToServer(LPCSTR pszServer, ULONG ulPort);
    CCPPLDAPBrowseDlg(CWnd* pParent = NULL);    // standard constructor

// Dialog Data
    //{{AFX_DATA(CCPPLDAPBrowseDlg)
    enum { IDD = IDD_CPPLDAPBROWSE_DIALOG };
    CEdit       m_editCurrentObject;
    CButton     m_buttonParent;
    CListBox    m_listboxChildren;
    CListBox    m_listboxValues;
    CListBox    m_listboxAttribs;
    CListBox    m_listboxContexts;
    //}}AFX_DATA
```

This snippet shows both the names of the control variables, and also the functions that I've added to the main dialog class to do the work of browsing. For these variables, I think it should be obvious from the names which control each variable refers to.

As far as the functions are concerned, `BindToObject()` is the one that gets called when you we need to access and store the details of a new object in the directory. (OK, OK, I know LDAP doesn't really have a concept of binding to an object, but I've adopted the notion of binding in my code to mean storing the details of a directory object in the various member variables in the code). It takes the distinguished name of the required object as a parameter, and sorts out sticking all the appropriate information in the attributes and children list boxes.

`BindToNamingChild()` is a wrapper around `BindToObject()`. It calls `BindToObject()`, and does any other stuff needed if the new object is a child of an existing object (basically adding the name of the new object to the `m_csarrBoundDNs` array).

`BindToServer()` is what gets called when you actually need to connect to a new server, and hence reinitialize everything – including the list of naming contexts. `GetNamingContexts()` is a helper function that sorts out the list box containing the naming contexts. `BindToNamingContext()` is what happens when you double-click on a naming context to ask to view the root object in that naming context. It basically does a bit of initialization – clears out the `m_csarrBoundDNs` array, and calls `BindToObject()`.

Initialization

OK – that's the structure of the program. We need one bit of initialization in the constructor to the main dialog:

```
CCPPLDAPBrowseDlg::CCPPLDAPBrowseDlg(CWnd* pParent /*=NULL*/)
    : CDialog(CCPPLDAPBrowseDlg::IDD, pParent),
    m_ld(NULL)
{
```

Now let's check out what happens when the main dialog appears:

```
BOOL CCPPLDAPBrowseDlg::OnInitDialog()
{
    CDialog::OnInitDialog();

    // wizard generated stuff not shown
    m_buttonParent.EnableWindow(false);

    // display dialog box to ask for server and port
    char pszComputerName[MAX_COMPUTERNAME_LENGTH+1];
    DWORD dwLength = MAX_COMPUTERNAME_LENGTH+1;
    memset(pszComputerName, 0, dwLength);
    BOOL bSucceeded = GetComputerName(pszComputerName, &dwLength);
    ASSERT(bSucceeded);

    m_csServer = pszComputerName;
    m_ulPort = 389;
    CDialogNewServer dlgServer(pszComputerName, 389);
    if (dlgServer.DoModal() == IDOK)
        BindToServer(dlgServer.m_csNewServer, dlgServer.m_ulNewPort);
    return TRUE;  // return TRUE  unless you set the focus to a control
}
```

We disable the **Parent** button since we're not yet viewing an object that has a parent (or any object at all for that matter!). Next we do a bit of processing to find out the name of the machine we're running on – that bit's nothing to do with LDAP, just standard Windows API. Then we call up the dialog box to ask for the name of the server (I'm not going to show you the code for that dialog, since that is just standard MFC stuff – the full code is, as ever, n the download sample from the Wrox web site).

Finally, we call `BindToServer()` to do the work.

Connecting to a Server

This is where it starts getting exciting:

```
void CCPPLDAPBrowseDlg::BindToServer(LPCSTR pszServer, ULONG ulPort)
{
    ULONG ulres;
    LDAP *ld = ldap_init(const_cast<LPSTR>(pszServer), ulPort);
    unsigned uiVersion = LDAP_VERSION3;
    ulres = ldap_set_option(ld, LDAP_OPT_VERSION, &uiVersion);
    ASSERT(ulres == LDAP_SUCCESS);

    char pszDN[] = "CN=Administrator,CN=Users,DC=TopOfThePops,DC=Fame,DC=com";
    ulres = ldap_simple_bind_s(ld, pszDN, "mypassword");

    if (ulres == LDAP_SUCCESS)
    {
        if (m_ld != NULL)
            ulres = ldap_unbind(m_ld);

        ASSERT(ulres == LDAP_SUCCESS);
        m_ld = ld;
        m_ulPort = ulPort;
        m_csServer = pszServer;

        GetNamingContexts();
    }
    else
    {
        AfxMessageBox(CString("Failed to bind to this server and port\n")
                    + ldap_err2string(ulres));
    }
}
```

OK, so it's not very exciting – just a standard simple bind. If it worked, we replace any information from previous binds by the new bind, and call `GetNamingContexts()` to sort out the naming contexts list box.

Notice the special function, `ldap_unbind()`. This is the standard way of freeing resources associated with an LDAP structure and telling the server that you've finished with it. You should always call this function, eventually.

Listing Naming Contexts

Let's check out `GetNamingContexts()`:

```
void CCPPLDAPBrowseDlg::GetNamingContexts()
{
    ULONG ulres;
    LDAPMessage *res;
    LPSTR ppszAttribs[] = {"namingContexts",NULL};
    ulres = ldap_search_s(m_ld, "", LDAP_SCOPE_BASE,
            "(objectClass=*)", ppszAttribs,
            0, &res);
    ASSERT(ulres == ERROR_SUCCESS);

    LDAPMessage *e;
    e=ldap_first_entry(m_ld, res);
    char **ppContexts = ldap_get_values(m_ld, e, "namingContexts");
    for (int i=0 ; ppContexts[i]   != NULL ; ++i)
        m_listboxContexts.AddString(ppContexts[i]);

        // free memory
        ldap_value_free(ppContexts);
        ldap_msgfree(res);

}
```

Here's where we meet some new LDAP API stuff. And here's our first encounter with a search:

```
ulres = ldap_search_s(m_ld, "", LDAP_SCOPE_BASE,
            "(objectClass=*)", ppszAttribs,
            0, &res);
```

although it's not much of a search – we're only looking in the root DSE object. The second parameter to `ldap_search()` is the DN of the base object from which we want to start the search. We've passed an empty string – the DN of the root DSE.

We've specified a base search, a filter of `(objectClass=*)` – meaning 'everything'. That's the way you should look for attributes of the root DSE.

The next parameter is the list of attributes that we'd actually want NULL if we want all attributes. In this case, we're specifically looking for the `namingContexts`, so we pass a NULL-terminated array of strings with this name as the only non-NULL entry.

This is followed by a Boolean, which we can set to 1 to improve performance if we want the attribute names rather than the values. We do want the values – the values of the `namingContexts` attribute are what are going to go in the naming contexts list box – so we'll set this parameter to zero.

The final parameter is the `LDAPMessage` structure that will contain our search results.

Now we need to get at the values. Well, the LDAPMessage we've got back from the ldap_search_s() call is a complete set of search results. We need the ldap_first_entry() function to actually retrieve the first entry from the list. Since we've done a search with a scope of base, we know there'll only be one entry in it anyway! Finally, ldap_get_values(), applied to the LDAPMessage structure that contains this entry, will retrieve the named values as a NULL-terminated array of strings, which we can place in the list box. We also need to free the memory that the LDAP API allocated for us.

So now let's see what happens if we double-click on a naming context. Here's the message handler for that event:

```
void CCPPLDAPBrowseDlg::OnDblclkListNamingContexts()
{
    // TODO: Add your control notification handler code here
    int index = m_listboxContexts.GetCurSel();
    CString csDN;
    m_listboxContexts.GetText(index, csDN);
    BindToNamingContext(const_cast<LPSTR>(LPCSTR(csDN)));
}
```

This retrieves the actual text that we've double-clicked on – which is the distinguished name of the root of the naming context we're interested in – and calls BindToNamingContext() to do the work:

```
void CCPPLDAPBrowseDlg::BindToNamingContext(LPSTR pszDN)
{
    m_csarrBoundDNs.RemoveAll();
    m_buttonParent.EnableWindow(false);
    m_csarrBoundDNs.Add(pszDN);
    BindToObject(pszDN);
}
```

And let's follow that through…

```
void CCPPLDAPBrowseDlg::BindToObject(LPSTR pszDN)
{
    ULONG ulres;
    LDAPMessage *res;

    // clear list boxes
    m_listboxAttribs.ResetContent();
    m_listboxChildren.ResetContent();
    m_listboxValues.ResetContent();

    // show the name of the object we are bound to
    m_editCurrentObject.SetWindowText(pszDN);

    // list the children
    ulres = ldap_search_s(m_ld, pszDN, LDAP_SCOPE_ONELEVEL, "(objectClass=*)",
                          NULL, true, &res);
```

```
    if (ulres != ERROR_SUCCESS)
    {
        AfxMessageBox(ldap_err2string(ulres));
        return;
    }

    LDAPMessage *e;
    for(e=ldap_first_entry(m_ld, res); e != NULL; e=ldap_next_entry(m_ld, e))
    {
        LPSTR pszDN = ldap_get_dn(m_ld, e);
        m_listboxChildren.AddString(pszDN);
        ldap_memfree(pszDN);
    }
    ldap_msgfree(res);

    // list the attributes
    ulres = ldap_search_s(m_ld, pszDN, LDAP_SCOPE_BASE, "(objectClass=*)",
                        NULL, true, &res);

    if (ulres != ERROR_SUCCESS)
    {
        AfxMessageBox(ldap_err2string(ulres));
        return;
    }

    BerElement *ber;
    char *pszAttribName;
    e=ldap_first_entry(m_ld, res);

    for (pszAttribName = ldap_first_attribute(m_ld, e, &ber);
        pszAttribName != NULL;
        pszAttribName = ldap_next_attribute(m_ld, e, ber))
        {
        m_listboxAttribs.AddString(pszAttribName);
        ldap_memfree(pszAttribName);
    }

    ldap_msgfree(res);
}
```

Now we've got into the action. We clear out the list boxes, then write stuff into both the children and attributes boxes.

We'll deal with the children first. Basically, we need to do a one-level search, and get the distinguished names of all the entries returned. Next, we'll get the attributes. This involves a base search, followed by an iteration through the attributes of the one object returned.

Notice there's a new structure rearing its head here: the BerElement, the first occurrence of something related to the BER rules that we mentioned earlier, in the section on Binary Encoding. We don't actually need to worry about it. It's just used internally by ldap _first_attribute() and ldap_next_attribute() to keep track of where we are in enumerating the attribute names. If this was a C++ API, we'd probably never see this as it would be a private member variable stored in some class that we call up. Unfortunately, raw C APIs don't have the option to store information between function calls in this way, so sometimes we have to get our hands dirty and pass round information between function calls that we're not actually interested in ourselves, but which the functions need to be able to work. In this case, the BerElement falls into that category.

Listing Children

So that's sorted out viewing the root object in a naming context. What happens if we double-click on the DN of a child in the **Children** list box? (Recall that this indicates we want to view the child.) Well, what happens is this:

```
void CCPPLDAPBrowseDlg::OnDblclkListchildren()
{
    // TODO: Add your control notification handler code here
    int index = m_listboxChildren.GetCurSel();
    CString csDN;
    m_listboxChildren.GetText(index, csDN);
    BindToChild(const_cast<LPSTR>(LPCSTR(csDN)));
}
```

Followed by this

```
void CCPPLDAPBrowseDlg::BindToChild(LPSTR pszDN)
{
    m_csarrBoundDNs.Add(pszDN);
    m_buttonParent.EnableWindow(true);
    BindToObject(pszDN);
}
```

And with the call to `BindToObject()`, we're back where we started.

Listing Parents

Then, suppose we click on the **Parent** button to move back up the tree:

```
void CCPPLDAPBrowseDlg::OnButtonParent()
{
    int iDepth = m_csarrBoundDNs.GetSize();
    ASSERT(iDepth >= 2);

    m_csarrBoundDNs.RemoveAt(iDepth-1);
    BindToObject(const_cast<LPSTR>(LPCSTR(m_csarrBoundDNs[iDepth-2])));

    if (iDepth == 2)
        m_buttonParent.EnableWindow(false);
}
```

Clear enough? The only significant bit here is the check on how far down the tree we are, to see if the **Parent** button should still be enabled. It should only be enabled if we are viewing an object which has a parent. In that case, there will still be at least two distinguished names in the list stored in `m_csarrBoundDNs` which walks us down the tree.

Binding to a New Server

We also need to check out what happens if the user decides to view a new server:

```
void CCPPLDAPBrowseDlg::OnButtonNewServer()
{
    CDialogNewServer dlgServer(m_csServer, m_ulPort);
    if (dlgServer.DoModal() == IDOK)
        BindToServer(dlgServer.m_csNewServer, dlgServer.m_ulNewPort);

}
```

Listing Attribute Values

And finally, the last possible action – what if the user double-clicks on an attribute name in the Attributes dialog box, to request to view the value(s) of an attribute?

```
void CCPPLDAPBrowseDlg::OnDblclkListAttribs()
{
    ULONG ulres;
    LDAPMessage *res;

    // clear values list box
    m_listboxValues.ResetContent();

    // list the values

    // first get hold of the object being viewed again
    CString csDN = m_csarrBoundDNs[m_csarrBoundDNs.GetSize()-1];
    ulres = ldap_search_s(m_ld, const_cast<LPSTR>(LPCSTR(csDN)),
            LDAP_SCOPE_BASE, "(objectClass=*)",
            NULL, false, &res);

    if (ulres != ERROR_SUCCESS)
    {
        AfxMessageBox(ldap_err2string(ulres));
        return;
    }

    // now get the attribute name
    int index = m_listboxAttribs.GetCurSel();
    CString csAttribName;
    m_listboxAttribs.GetText(index, csAttribName);

    // now got enough info to list its values
    LDAPMessage *e;
    e=ldap_first_entry(m_ld, res);
    ASSERT(e != NULL);

    char **ppValues =
            ldap_get_values(m_ld, e, const_cast<LPSTR>(LPCSTR(csAttribName)));
    ASSERT(ppValues != NULL);
```

```
    for (int i=0 ; ppValues[i] != NULL ; ++i)
        m_listboxValues.AddString(ppValues[i]);

    ldap_value_free(ppValues);

    // free memory
    ldap_msgfree(res);
}
```

We need to find out the name of the object being viewed so we can do a base level search to get the attribute value. The name will be stored in our m_csarrBoundDNs array – which *is* proving very useful. Once we've done the search, we want the attribute name – this is just the text that's been selected in the listbox, and we can use ldap_get_values() to find out the values.

And that's it! Once you get used to the feel of LDAP API programming, it's not hard! Like I said, we're not covering adding, deleting or modifying entries, because I think you've got enough of a feel for how the API works now. If you need to do any of those operations, the functions to check out are ldap_add[_s](), ldap_modify[_s]() and ldap_delete[_s](). There are also extended versions of all those functions which give you a few more options, and have names like ldap_modify_ext() and ldap_modify_ext_s().

Summary

This has been a very brief introduction to LDAP – enough to give us a flavor of how the LDAP protocol works and what kinds of operation it covers. If you are coding ADSI clients then you won't normally need to be aware of the details of LDAP, since to a large extent they are hidden by the ADSI LDAP provider. Nevertheless, some understanding of LDAP is important in order to appreciate aspects of the design of the ADSI interfaces where they have been influenced by the LDAP protocols. Also, since Active Directory is an LDAP compliant directory, understanding the LDAP specifications is important for understanding the design of Active Directory.

In this chapter we've emphasized the way the LDAP directory trees are split into naming contexts, who's paths must be determined from the root directory service entry object, and we've shown how to use this in a sample client that browses an LDAP directory. That and the fact that LDAP has no separate concept of browsing are the key points to understand when using LDAP directories. If you need more information, the RFCs are the definitive place to start for the definition of the LDAP protocols themselves, and Mark Wilcox's book *Implementing LDAP* (ISBN 1-861002-21-1) also goes into both LDAP and the various LDAP APIs available to clients in some detail.

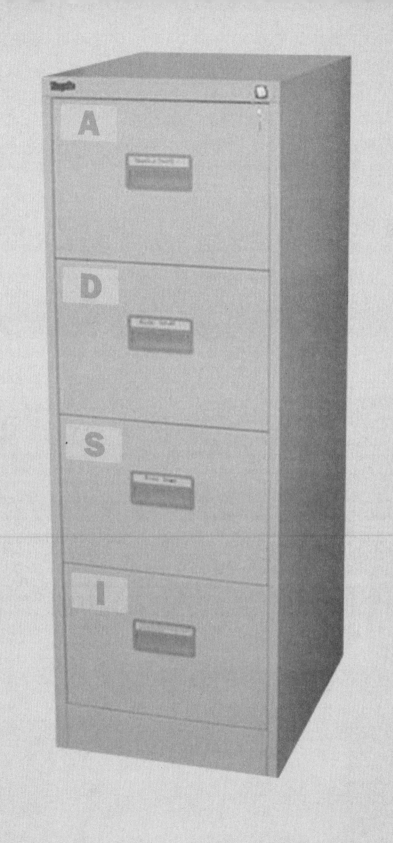

11

Advanced ADSI Topics

In this chapter you will learn

- ❑ How to optimize ADSI calls
- ❑ How to use the StarRaiders provider to investigate what MS expects providers to handle
- ❑ About provider-specific extensions

We've covered all the major topics in ADSI now. The purpose of this chapter is to wrap things up by going over a couple of miscellaneous areas which don't seem to have fitted in anywhere else, but which are useful to know.

Optimizing ADSI Calls

If you've played around with the sample code for this book, you'll have noticed one quite annoying thing; binding to an ADSI object can be slow – especially the first time you bind to an object exposed by a particular provider and on a given server; WinNT appears to be the worst culprit here. So is there anything you can do to help speed things up? Yes there is – you can try to keep connections with the server open.

Let me explain. The ADSI provider is an in-process COM server so communication between the client and the provider is very fast. (For ASP pages, the client I'm talking about is the ASP script being run on the machine that hosts the web site. Obviously, here, there's the additional factor of the time for the web browser to talk to IIS – and that's something you can't do anything about – at least, not with ADSI!). As far as we're concerned, it's the communication between the ADSI provider and the back-end directory – or the server that hosts the actual object – that takes the time.

Here we need to introduce the concept of a **connection**. We're going to leave the concept a bit vague because we don't want to start going into low level communications protocols, but basically when you first attempt to bind to an object in WinNT or LDAP which is hosted on another machine, the ADSI provider will attempt to open a connection with the remote machine. In other words, it will tell the remote machine it wants to talk to it, and set up a channel by which it can ask for and receive information. This connection is not necessarily tied to a particular ADSI object. If you subsequently bind to other objects hosted on the same server and implemented by the same provider, the chances are that the ADSI provider will simply reuse the same connection to get information about the new objects from the server. (This is not necessarily true if you use different authentication credentials for the new objects: in that case, the ADSI provider may need to open a new connection that uses the new credentials).

Now once a connection is established, communication can be fairly fast. It's opening the connection in the first place that takes time. Even if you don't supply any authentication credentials to ADSI, your computer will still need to locate the remote server machine, and to authenticate to it with an account name and password. If your domain is an NT4 domain, and uses NTLM security, the remote server may want to contact the domain controller to verify your machine's (or your account's) credentials. If it's a Windows 2000 domain, then your machine may need to obtain a Kerberos ticket from the domain controller. Clearly, the whole process isn't trivial and you will have to wait while it takes place. But the key here is that the same connection can be used for different ADSI objects. That's why you'll often notice that the first time you bind to an object on a certain server, it may take several seconds to do it, but subsequent binds to objects on the same server are pretty much instantaneous. So if you want good performance, you need to try to keep connections that you are going to reuse later on open, rather than allowing them to be closed and then reopening them.

Unfortunately, keeping the connections open is a bit of a hit and miss affair, since how the connections are implemented is up to the particular provider and – at least in the case of the Microsoft providers – not documented. However, you can normally expect that as long as you have an outstanding reference count on an ADSI object that refers to a certain server, then a connection to that server is likely to be open. If you release all your reference counts to ADSI objects associated with a certain server then you can expect that any connections to that server will soon get closed – though my own experiments with the WinNT provider suggest this doesn't happen instantly.

What this means in practice is that, for as long as you think your client application might want to bind to other objects on a given server, it's a good idea to have an outstanding reference count to at least one ADSI object associated with that server. That forces the connection to stay open. The following code is potentially bad from the point of view of efficiency:

```
Dim oObj1 As IADs
Dim oObj2 As IADs
Set oObj1 = GetObject("WinNT://<ComputerName>/<Something>"
' do processing
Set oObj1 = Nothing
'more lengthy processing
Set oObj2 = GetObject("WinNT://<SameComputerName>/<SomethingElse>"
' more processing
Set oObj2 = Nothing
```

While this code will probably perform better:

```
Dim oObj1 As IADs
Dim oObj2 As IADs
Set oObj1 = GetObject("WinNT://<ComputerName>/<Something>"
' do processing
 'more processing
Set oObj2 = GetObject("WinNT://<SameComputerName>/<SomethingElse>"
Set oObj1 = Nothing
 ' more processing
Set oObj2 = Nothing
```

Though on the other hand you might regard the second version as less easily maintainable.

Using StarRaiders to Investigate ADSI

Microsoft has provided reasonably complete documentation for ADSI, however documentation in general has a way of never being completely comprehensive. Which is one reason why so many programmers prefer to see sample code when they want to know how something is done. That's all very well when you're writing ADSI clients because they are short and simple – so it's relatively easy to look at a sample. If you're coding a provider, or if you want to see in more detail which sorts of method calls with which parameters might be made to providers, then it's another matter. There is the sample provider available with the ADSI SDK, and now you have this book, and (presumably) access to the Wrox web site, you also have the StarRaiders provider. However, both of these providers have a very limited functionality – simply because writing a provider is a sufficiently big project that it would be impractical to provide a complete working sample that shows how to do everything.

In this section I'm going to show you how you can use your provider to get additional information about how Microsoft expects ADSI to work. The principle is simple – you set break points in your provider, set the Active Directory browser, adsvw.exe, to be the working executable, and then use adsvw.exe to browse round your provider. Your breakpoints will then tell you exactly what methods are getting called in which circumstances. It doesn't of course have to be breakpoints. In principle, any statement that records that a certain part of the code is getting executed will do – for example the MFC or ATL TRACE macros or simple OutputDebugString() statements. But breakpoints do have the advantage that they give you the chance to easily investigate the contents of any variable or parameter to a method call that you choose.

To demonstrate this technique, we'll see what happens when we try to view the value of a property. For this we need to set breakpoints at the beginning of all the method calls which might be used to get a property, that is to say `IADs::Get()`, `IADs::GetEx()`, `IADsPropertyList::Next()`, `IADsPropertyList::Item()` and `IADsPropertyList::GetPropertyItem()`. For this I'm going to use the `CStarRaidersLeaf` C++ class, which encapsulates a favorite artist, and use `adsvw.exe` to browse down to a favorite artist:

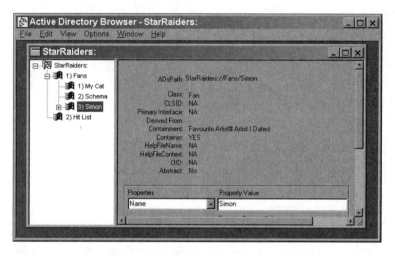

If you do this you'll find that `adsvw.exe` always uses `GetEx()`, never `Get()` or any of the property cache interface methods, to obtain properties. You'll also find, if you put breakpoints on the `CStarRaidersClass` methods, that `adsvw.exe` uses the class schema object to find out what mandatory and optional properties to display (though that's perhaps fairly obvious, since there's no other way to get that information!)

So far that hasn't told us anything particularly exciting. It gets more interesting if you try to use the buttons in the right hand pane of `adsvw.exe` to set properties. If you do that you'll find that `adsvw.exe` always uses `IADs::PutEx()` to set properties. More importantly, `adsvw.exe` makes no attempt to interpret the data type of the property: No matter what the actual data type is, or whether or not it is multi-valued, `adsvw.exe` will always pass in the new property values as a `VARIANT` containing a `SAFEARRAY` of `VARIANT`s of `BSTR`. That tells us something that is significant, and undocumented: It is up to the provider to accept new property values in any of the `VARIANT` formats , and convert it to whatever data format that particular property is supposed to be stored as. That's the reason why in Appendix C I go to so much trouble to write a utility function for StarRaiders which can convert *any* `VARIANT` data type (within reason), including arrays, into any other type.

Incidentally, this was the technique I used to investigate how `IDirectorySearch` worked. When I first read the documentation for `IDirectorySearch`, I didn't find it that clear. So I rigged up a very simple provider, which exposed basic, do-nothing methods for `IDirectorySearch`. Then I used `adsvw.exe` to perform a search with breakpoints on all the `IDirectorySearch` method calls in the provider. That told me fairly quickly what the sequence of method calls was intended to be. As a useful by-product, it also told me more about the (undocumented) data required in the various text boxes in the `adsvw.exe` search dialogs – that's where a lot of the information in the early part of Chapter 7 of this book came from!

It's worth bearing in mind that doing the kind of reverse engineering that I've just presented can generally be dangerous since it brings up things that, by virtue of being undocumented, may be subject to change in future releases of software. That shouldn't be a problem in this particular case since we are using `adsvw.exe` to find out about the kinds of requirements that Microsoft expects providers to be able to satisfy – those are unlikely to change even though the implementation of `adsvw.exe` may do.

OK, this section isn't here to tell you everything there is to know about advanced ADSI. It's here to give you the motivation to go away and play with providers for yourself. So I'll leave it there.

Provider-specific Extensions

I have to admit that when I first heard extensions were one of the new features in ADSI 2.5 I was sceptical. My immediate reaction went something like, '*So what? If I want to do a provider with extra non-ADSI interfaces in it, what's to stop me just doing that anyway?*' As it turns out, at the time I'd rather misunderstood the point of provider-specific extensions. The provider-specific bit in the name doesn't mean that you have to write your own provider – it means that you can extend a specific provider that's already there, including WinNT, IIS and LDAP. Granted, you can choose to use extensions on your own provider, but the real purpose of them is to let third parties extend what a provider that already exists can do.

I also have to admit that usually I'm one of the first people to criticize Microsoft. There are a lot of things that Microsoft have designed or ways that Microsoft have used their market power that I don't like. I've also wasted a lot of time over the last few years struggling with poorly written documentation. Strangely, that kind of thing never endears me to a company. But when I started investigating ADSI extensions and what you could do with them, boy, was I impressed! The idea is extremely clever.

So what do extensions do? Well, let's suppose that you decide you want all your user objects in either Active Directory or WinNT to do something different. Perhaps you're writing an ADSI client that prints summary information about all your user accounts. You can get all the information you want from ADSI, *except* that list of which files in source safe each user has still got checked out, preventing other users from using those files. Your boss is sick to death with people forgetting to check files back into source safe when they've used them, and he badly wants that list to use to rap people over the head with.

Or perhaps, you're feeling a bit fed up and overworked and just wish that while running your ADSI client you could get the computer to print out a nice message to cheer you up.

Anyway, the point is that you can't usually do those sorts of things with ADSI. So, the following VB code that I've just typed in won't work.

```
Private Sub Form_Load()


Dim oADs

Set oADs = GetObject("WinNT://BiggyBiggy/Simon")
oADs.TellMeImGorgeous
Set oADs = Nothing


End Sub
```

This code can't possibly work because we've just bound to an ADSI user object using the WinNT provider. The user object exposes the standard ADSI interfaces, like `IADs` and `IADsPropertyList`. ADSI objects do not implement a method, `TellMeImGorgeous()`. That would be silly. And just to prove it doesn't work, here's the screenshot from when I ran that little application.

Oh, so it did work. There's obviously something funny going on.

Now seriously, are you interested in the idea of being able to extend an object in either Active Directory or the WinNT provider, so that besides the standard ADSI interface methods, you can call up some other methods that you or a third party have written, and which could theoretically do anything? If the idea has whetted your appetite, you'd better read on.

Extension Architecture.

The name of the game when it comes to extensions is writing your own COM objects and making them appear to merge with ADSI COM objects so that the ADSI client gets fooled into thinking that your object and the ADSI object it's just bound to are the same object. What happens is you decide on some additional functionality that you would like certain objects in ADSI to be able to do. You write a COM component – known as an **extension** – that exposes appropriate interface(s) which implement methods to do whatever you want to do. In order to make the extension architecture work completely, you'll also need to implement an extra interface, `IADsExtension`. (You don't *have* to do this bit but if you don't then your extension won't be available to scripting clients). So far, so good. Trouble is, so far you've got a separate COM object that has nothing to do with ADSI, beyond the fact that it happens to implement an ADSI interface. Somehow, we've got to make it look like it's an object in the appropriate directory, to the extent that when a client binds to an object using that ADSI provider, it ends up unknowingly binding to your object as well.

COM, of course, does have a mechanism to make objects look like they are merged together. It's called aggregation. I don't want to go into the technical details too much here, but you can think of aggregation as being something like when one COM object (the **aggregatee**) ends up getting contained inside another COM object (the **aggregator**). As in this diagram,

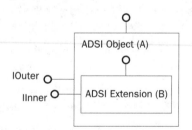

Here we see an outer object, A, the aggregator, which aggregates an inner object, B, the aggregatee. A exposes the interface `IOuter` and B exposes `IInner`.

So a COM client binds to the outer object, A, but because A aggregates B, the client can actually access the `IInner` interface exposed by B as well as the `IOuter` interface exposed by A. In this case, if the client asks for the interface `IOuter`, by calling `QueryInterface()` on the outer object A, then A will check to see if it implements the required interface. Since A does implement `IOuter`, A can simply return a pointer to this interface. But A also knows what interfaces B exposes. So if a client asks A for an `IInner` interface pointer, A will know how to cope with this. It will ask B for the `IInner` pointer, then return the pointer it gets from B back to the client. The client has got the interface pointer it wants, without having been aware that it is actually dealing with two COM components.

This works because in COM, clients never really see objects. They only see the interface pointers exposed by the objects. So far so good. Unfortunately, the other reason why this works is because the same company has usually coded up both components, so the components have quite a lot of knowledge about each other hard coded into them. The outer object knows all about which interfaces the inner object exposes, and in turn, the inner object knows to delegate `IUnknown` calls to the outer object so that they will work properly. For the whole setup to work, the outer object needs to know all about the inner object, and the inner object needs to know that it is running as an aggregatee. That's a problem for us, because we want to be able to write our own extension, which the guys who wrote the Microsoft ADSI providers know nothing about. So we're effectively writing inner objects that the outer objects don't know about. We want to simulate the effects of aggregation, but the normal way of implementing aggregation just won't work here.

The way that ADSI gets round this problem is your extension object writes some registry entries that tell the provider about itself and which interfaces it supports. When any provider that supports extensions starts up, it reads these entries and will then know enough to be able to aggregate your object. Basically, your object needs to write entries for its own CLSID – so the ADSI provider can use `CoCreateInstance()` to call up your object, and for its interface IIDs – so the provider is able to `QueryInterface()` for them and return those interface pointers to your client. As for the method calls – well that's up to the ADSI client to know what methods it might want to call up. The registry entries made, incidentally, are grouped by class of object, so that your extension is added to a class. You can choose to extend – say – all users, or all print queues, but you can't arrange to extend a particular user. That's reasonable, since the whole point of having a class of objects is that instances of that class all expose the same properties and methods.

The great thing about this architecture is that not only can you write a COM object which ADSI objects will then happily aggregate, even though they don't have any knowledge of your object hard coded into them – but someone else can later come along and write another COM object which they also intend to be used to extend the same ADSI objects. The provider will aggregate both of these COM objects, so ADSI clients can get at the extra functionality exposed by both objects, even though neither object knows anything about the other.

> *If you want to find out a bit more about aggregation in general, then you might want to read either. Beginning ATL COM Programming (ISBN 1-861000-11) or Professional ATL COM Programming (ISBN 1 861001-40-1), both published by Wrox.*

Now we've covered the basic architecture of the extension mechanism, we're going to look in more detail at how it works and what the advantages of using extensions are, then we're going to go over writing a small extension using ATL. I promise you'll be surprised at how little work it takes.

Why Use Extensions?

ADSI COM components are really components that wrap certain objects – such as computers or user accounts. One of the most common situations in which you'd think of writing an extension is when you need to write a COM object which also provides a wrapper round the same objects. In this situation, extensions offer advantages both for the ADSI client and for coding up the extension

To see what I mean by that, let's say you want to be able to easily back up files on your computer, and you are writing a COM coclass that let's you do that. Each instance of this class that gets created using `CoCreateInstance` presumably wants to be associated with a computer. So I guess you might have a method that sets which computer the instance refers to, and methods to backup and restore. Well if you make this object an ADSI extension, which extends computer objects, then you don't need a method to set the computer. An instance that is created and aggregated by an ADSI computer object will automatically be associated with a computer. All the extension needs to do is find out which computer by calling ADSI methods on the object which aggregated it. This is easy, since COM provides aggregates with an `IUnknown` interface pointer to the aggregator (it's the `pUnkOuter` parameter in `CoCreateInstance()` that you normally set to NULL). So actually implementing the extension – that is, the aggregatee – is easier because it has easy access to all the `IADs` and methods that it can use to find out about or modify the object it's associated with. And writing a client to use it is easier, because the client can bind to your object using the normal ADSI methods.

This also means there's slightly less for developers writing client applications to have to learn in order to use your component. All they need to know is what additional interfaces, methods and automation properties your component exposes. (And as usual, scripting clients and VB clients that use late binding don't even need to know the interfaces. They call the methods using `IDispatch`). The process of binding to the object is done using standard ADSI methods. There's also the additional advantage that all the custom methods that you implement appear to be exposed by the same object which exposes all the ADSI properties and methods.

Other examples of cases for which you'd use extensions might include:

❑   If you want to be able to set a large number of ADSI properties simultaneously, you could write an extension that exposes a method to do this.

❑   A component that manages services. The `IADsService` and `IADsServiceOperations` only expose a subset of the functionality of services that you can get to, using the Windows API functions. You could implement an extension component that fills in the gaps.

❑   An extension which connects Exchange mailboxes to user accounts, so that when a user account is created, you can use it to automatically add a corresponding Exchange account.

❑   We saw in chapter 2 that displaying all the mandatory and optional properties of an ADSI object isn't trivial – as you have to explicitly bind to the schema object in the process. You could write an extension object that exposes a method that does this automatically and returns all the properties.

❑   Many of the properties of, for example, user objects and access control lists, are returned via flags that are constructed by bit-wise operations. An extension object could retrieve certain flags that you know in which you are often going to be interested in a friendlier format.

You can doubtless think up more examples. You'll notice that these examples all tend to fall into one of two categories. Either they are exposing functionality that is not directly available through the normal ADSI interfaces, or they are automating some of the work that you could do using the usual ADSI interfaces in order to return particular information more conveniently. Whenever you have a task that falls into one of those categories, you have a possible candidate for an ADSI extension.

How Extensions Work

In this section, we'll have a look under the covers at what goes on when you use extensions.

Registry Entries

First up, let's check what those registry entries you have to make are. For Microsoft's providers, the entries are made under the same registry keys by which the providers register themselves as ADSI providers, in `HKLM/Software/Microsoft/ADs/Providers`. Under the name of the provider there should be a key called Extensions. This in turn should contain a series of keys, one key for each class that you want to extend. Under this key should go a key named by the CLSID of your extension object. This key should have a value named *Interfaces*, whose value is a list of the interface IIDs, in multi-string format.

If that all sounds confusing, it'll probably be clearer if we look at how that actually looks in the registry editor. Here's the registration entry for a Microsoft-supplied extension to the Computer class in LDAP. The entry is under `HKLM/Software/Microsoft/ADs/Providers/LDAP`.

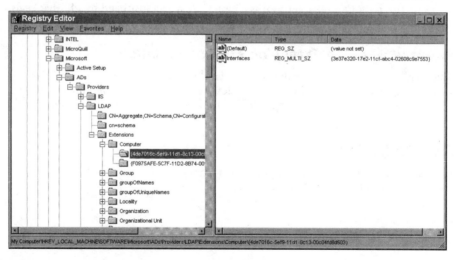

A couple of points you need to note:

If you haven't encountered multi-string format before, it's one format that registry keys can be stored in. It consists of the strings, in sequence, each one terminated by a single NULL as normal. The entire set of strings is terminated by two consecutive NULL characters.

You can extend any class exposed by these providers. If you are dealing with an LDAP directory that supports schema extension (eg. Active Directory), then this can include classes that you have defined, if you have extended the schema. Obviously, no such classes would exist in WinNT or IIS because you cannot extend these schemas. It's interesting to note, however, that adding extensions does provide a back-door route to simulate many of the benefits of schema extension.

> It is important to understand that ADSI extensions are NOT the same thing as schema extensions. ADSI extensions are where you effectively add new methods (or automation properties) to an ADSI object using aggregation. Schema extensions are where you actually modify the definitions of the classes in the schema so that they support additional (schema-defined) mandatory and optional properties. Schema extension does not involve supporting new interfaces, whereas ADSI extension does.

A given extension can expose as many interfaces as it wants for aggregation. There are also no problems with using the same object or interfaces to extend different ADSI classes – you just need to make sure the appropriate registry entries are present. For example, if you had an extension that supplied information about all registered user accounts on computers or domains, you'd probably want to register this extension so that it extended both computer and domain objects.

It's worth noting, by the way, that this way of registering extensions using registry entries applies to the LDAP, IIS and WinNT providers. If you write your own provider and arrange for it to support extensions, then strictly speaking you can use any other means you want for the extensions to tell your provider about themselves – though clearly it makes things a lot simpler for everyone if you follow the same arrangement as Microsoft have for their providers.

By the way, the default install for WinNT doesn't give you an Extensions key under the `HKLM/Software/Microsoft/ADs/Providers/WinNT` key. Don't worry about this – that just shows that nothing has registered itself by default to extend WinNT. If you want to extend WinNT objects– as we do in the sample later in this chapter, then you just need to add that registry key. The LDAP provider, by contrast, comes by default with a number of extension entries.

What Happens when an Extension Method is Called

What happens depends on whether the ADSI client has requested the interface directly, using vtable or early binding, or whether – as in scripting clients – it has simply called up a method directly, relying on the less efficient late binding. We'll cover early binding in this section, and late binding in the next section.

VTable and Early Binding

For vtable and early binding, what happens is the same as what happens in standard COM aggregation.

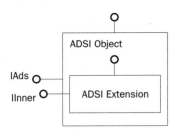

The figure shows an ADSI object which has aggregated an extension. (Notice that I say *an* extension because there may be more than one extension aggregated by the ADSI object). The object exposes the usual ADSI interfaces – for the sake of the discussion we've taken IADs as an example. The extension exposes an interface you've defined, which we'll call IInner. Note that in this situation, the ADSI provider is often termed the **extension client**, since it is acting as a client by calling up the services of the extension.

Suppose an ADSI client requests a pointer to `IInner`. This works in a similar way to normal COM aggregation – the provider will know that it needs to create an extension object and get the interface pointer from it. So it creates an instance of the extension, and calls `IUnknown::QueryInterface()` on the extension, asking for `IInner`. The extension supplies this interface pointer back to the provider, which in turn passes it on to the client. The only difference between this and normal COM aggregation is that the provider didn't have any knowledge of the extension hard coded into it – rather, it knows about the extension because it read in the appropriate registry entries when it initialized itself.

If a subsequent call to `QueryInterface()` comes in to the interface pointer that was handed out by an extension in our example, the `IInner` interface pointer, then the extension must respond by calling up `IUnknown::QueryInterface()` on the provider. In other words, it never handles `QueryInterface()` calls itself in this situation – it delegates them back to the aggregator. The aggregator – the provider – is responsible for returning the interface pointer to the ADSI client. This is a requirement for aggregation in COM, not something specific to ADSI.

There is one thing I've missed out of all this. Remember, I mentioned earlier that the extension might choose to implement the interface `IADsExtension`. `IADsExtension` actually exposes three methods:

Methods	Names
Operate	Instructs the extension to carry out any initialization
PrivateGetIDsOfNames	Gets dispIDs from method names
PrivateInvoke	Invokes the method specified by the dispID supplied as a parameter

Of these, `PrivateGetIDsOfNames()` and `PrivateInvoke()` are there to support late binding, so we'll cover those in the next section. If you don't want to support late binding, then these methods can just return E_NOTIMPL, but support for scripting clients is really a fundamental part of the principles of ADSI so I'd suggest you really ought to support late binding unless you have a good reason not to.

`Operate()` is an initialization function. It's always called by the providers when they first create your object, in order to give your extension a chance to initialize itself. It takes four parameters, an unsigned long and three VARIANTs. The IIS, LDAP and WinNT providers will always pass in the value ADS_EXT_INITCREDENTIALS for the long and nothing for the VARIANTs. If you don't want to do any initialization, you can just return E_NOTIMPL. The reason for all the parameters is to give other providers that third parties might write a chance to ask extensions to carry out more sophisticated initialization and processing. They are not used by Microsoft, but parameters are there if you want to write an ADSI provider that passes in a value other than ADS_EXT_INITCREDENTIALS, and some other data besides. It also means other providers might choose to call this method at other times other than to initialize the extension – for example they might do so in order to notify an extension of certain events.

Late Binding

Late binding is where we come into territory that is specific to ADSI extensions. In general, COM aggregation doesn't define any general framework for using aggregation with late binding, so Microsoft's ADSI team appear to have implemented their own solution – and I think it's quite a neat one.

The basic idea is fairly simple. For vtable binding, the interface pointer is handed out by `IUnknown`. `IDispatch` plays a corresponding role for late binding, though instead of handing out an interface pointer, it goes further and actually calls the method. For vtable binding, the aggregatee is supposed to delegate its `IUnknown` implementation to the aggregator. So what happens here is it has to do the same with its `IDispatch` interface.

What happens is this. The ADSI client has an object bound to a directory object. This means the ADSI client is actually holding an `IDispatch` pointer on the ADSI object. The client attempts to call up a method, by calling `GetIDsOfNames`, followed by `Invoke`. For both function calls, the provider finds that it's not one of its own methods that is required. So it needs to find out if it's a method implemented by an extension. Now it can't call an `IDispatch` method on an extension, because – for reasons that will become clear in a moment, the extensions' implementations of `IDispatch` must simply call up the ADSI provider's implementations of the corresponding methods. So what can it do? This is where those `PrivateGetIDsOfNames()` and `PrivateInvoke()` methods of the `IADsExtension` come in. In response to a call to `IDispatch::GetIDsOfNames()` which the provider is unable to satisfy itself, it will call up the `IADsExtension::PrivateGetIDsOfNames()` methods on each of the available extensions until it finds a match for the name. Internally, the provider will carry out some DispID-encoding on the DispID returned by the extension (DispID–encoding was explained in Chapter 9 of this book), so that when the call to `Invoke` comes in, the provider will know from the encoded DispID whether that DispID is intended for itself or an extension. If it is a DispID that has been encoded for an extension, the provider will decode it and pass it to the `IADsExtension::PrivateInvoke()` method of the extension.

This means that the extension has to implement `PrivateGetIDsOfNames()` and `PrivateInvoke` to act exactly like the corresponding `IDispatch` methods, but using the extension's own type library rather than the ActiveDS one.

You might wonder why we have to implement these methods on a separate interface. Why can't the extension just implement its own `IDispatch` methods in the normal way. Well the reason here is exactly the same reason that `IUnknown` must be delegated to the aggregator. What if a client is holding an interface pointer that was actually supplied by the extension and calls an `IDispatch` (or `IUnknown`) method? There's no way that a scripting client can get into this situation, but a C++ or VB client could theoretically do so. If such a client calls an `IDispatch` method on an interface pointer that is actually a pointer to the extension, the client might actually be requesting a method that is implemented by the extension, the ADSI provider, or any other extension that has been aggregated by the same ADSI provider object. The extension cannot possibly resolve that issue – only the aggregator knows enough to do that, so it's essential that `IDispatch` methods are referred back to the aggregator. That way it is guaranteed that the client will see something that appears to be a single `IDispatch` interface, and which knows about all the methods exposed by the provider and all the extensions.

Resolving Name Clashes

I've made a big point of the fact that it is possible for two or more extensions to register themselves to be aggregated by the same ADSI object. These extensions might have been written by completely different companies, neither of which knows of the existence of the other company's extension. Because of this it's possible that there could be name clashes: two extensions might happen to implement a method of the same name. It's less likely, but theoretically possible, that two extensions might implement the same interface. (For example, they might both have a reason to implement a standard COM interface, such as IMoniker). So we need a means to resolve such conflicts.

The way the IIS, WinNT and LDAP providers handle that situation is this. They first look at the methods and interfaces that they implement themselves. If a provider implements a method or interface which is also implemented by the ADSI object, then the ADSI object gets priority. The provider won't get a look-in when such a method is requested by late binding, or an interface is QueryInterface()d for. It may seem that there's therefore no point in implementing any methods or interfaces like that in an extension. However you might want to write an extension which is also able to function as a standalone COM object – in which case it might be meaningful for it to implement its own automation properties like Name or Class. You just need to remember when writing an extension that those properties will be inaccessible when your object is used as an extension.

If a name clash between extensions occurs, then the extension which takes priority will be the one which appears first in the list of extensions for that ADSI class in the registry.

Coding an ADSI Extension

In this section, we're going to use ATL to write a little COM component which will extend user objects in Active Directory and WinNT. Unfortunately for VB guys, extensions do need to be written in C++ since at present VB doesn't offer any way of building components that can act as aggregates.

I guess I could have written an extension to do something like manage an NT Service or print information about a user. However, the important point here is how you do the extension so it can get aggregated by ADSI objects – we're not concerned with implementing the actual methods in the extension's interfaces, so we really want an extension that will do something very simple.

Although my example is fairly trivial, I'm going to trust you to use it to write an extension that actually does something useful. My extension has the (clearly worthless) purpose of making software developers who use it happy, so I've called it my Happifier, and it exposes the interface IHappifier.

Actually there is a teeny bit more in my extension. It does take the trouble to obtain an IADs interface pointer on the aggregating ADSI object, and uses it to find out the username of the object – just so I can demonstrate how you do this. I've also implemented a read-only property, LovelyMessage, which returns a nice message. Again, just to show that you can do automation properties as well as methods.

Anyway, before we write the extension, let's check out the VB ADSI client that I've written to check it works. Here it is:

```
Private Sub Form_Load()

' test the Happifier extension using the LDAP provider
' and using early binding
Dim oADsLDAP As IADs
Dim oHappy As Happifier
Set oADsLDAP =
GetObject("LDAP://CN=Administrator,CN=Users,DC=TopOfThePops,DC=Fame,DC=com")
List1.AddItem "Name of LDAP object is " & oADsLDAP.Name

Set oHappy = oADsLDAP
List1.AddItem "Lovely message is : " & oHappy.LovelyMessage
oHappy.TellMeImGorgeous
Set oHappy = Nothing
Set oADsLDAP = Nothing


List1.AddItem ""

' now test the Happifier extension using the IIS provider
' and using late binding
Dim oADsIIS
Set oADsIIS = GetObject("IIS://BiggyBiggy/W3SVC/3")
List1.AddItem "Name of IIS object is " & oADsIIS.Name
List1.AddItem "Lovely message is : " & oADsIIS.LovelyMessage
oADsIIS.TellMeImGorgeous
Set oADsIIS = Nothing


List1.AddItem ""


' now test the Happifier extension using the WinNT provider
' and using late binding
Dim oADsWinNT
Set oADsWinNT = GetObject("WinNT://BiggyBiggy/Simon")
List1.AddItem "Name of WinNT object is " & oADsWinNT.Name
List1.AddItem "Lovely message is : " & oADsWinNT.LovelyMessage
oADsWinNT.TellMeImGorgeous
Set oADsWinNT = Nothing


End Sub
```

This client first binds to an LDAP user object. It calls an IADs method to get and display the name of the object, then calls the IHappifier property LovelyMessage to display the message. It also calls the method TellMeImGorgeous which displays a dialog box to cheer you up.

Having done that, the client does the same thing first using a web server object exposed through the IIS provider, then using a user object exposed through the WinNT provider, in both cases using late binding. There's no particular reason for using early binding with LDAP and late binding with WinNT and IIS – I could have done it the other way round, but that's just how I chose to do it in order to demonstrate all the different possibilities using as little code as possible.

Notice that when using early binding, I need to declare two variables, one as IADs, and one of the appropriate type for my extension object. Since IHappifier is the default interface for the Happifier object, I could have declared the second variable using either the object name or interface name – I've plumped for the object name here. Also, in order to use early binding, I need to have added the type library for my extension to the project references, in addition to the ActiveDS type library. For this sample, the type library is called Extension.

As usual, late binding is less efficient, but saves you from having to reference either type library. It also means I only need to declare one variable for each provider, oADsIIS and oADsWinNT, to access methods on both the IADs and IHappifier interfaces. (actually I didn't even need to do that – I could have reused the same variable for both providers if I'd wanted to). If you think about it, that really is powerful. Remember that the IHappifier interface isn't just a different interface – it's a different interface on a different COM object. VB, helped by COM aggregation, has actually hidden what's going on under the covers so well that one variable can be used to call methods on two different objects, without you, the developer, needing to be aware that that's what's actually happening.

Anyway, let's quickly ensure everything works OK when you run the client. If we do, we get this dialog box:

followed by this dialog box:

then this one

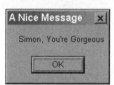

and finally followed by this appearing in the list box:

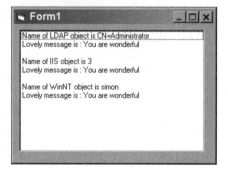

So everything appears to be OK there – and the Happifier is happily able to pick up the name of the ADSI object that's aggregating it to put it in its message.

Coding the Extension Itself

The extension itself is a normal ATL DLL
project called Extension – so we'll create one
using Visual Studio's AppWizard. We're not
using MFC in it. To create the object, make
sure that we create a dual object that supports
aggregation:

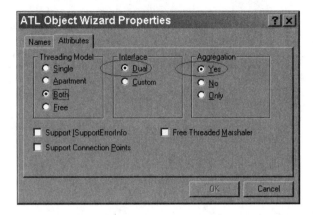

Once we've got the Happifier object, use the wizard to add one method, TellMeImGorgeous,
and one read-only automation property, LovelyMessage, to the IHappifier interface. There are
no problems, by the way, with having read/write automation properties. It's just that I've chosen not
to do so. I don't want any vindictive ADSI clients in and changing LovelyMessage so it isn't as
lovely anymore.

First the easy bit – we'll add our implementations to the methods:

```
STDMETHODIMP CHappifier::TellMeImGorgeous()
{
    CComPtr<IADs> spADs;
    HRESULT hr;

    hr = OuterQueryInterface(IID_IADs, (void**)&spADs );
    if ( FAILED(hr) )
        return hr;

    CComBSTR bstrText;
    CComBSTR bstrText;
    hr = spADs->get_Name(&bstrText);
    if ( FAILED(hr) )
        return hr;

    bstrText += L", You\'re Gorgeous";
    MessageBox(NULL, bstrText, L"A Nice Message", MB_OK);
    return S_OK;
}

STDMETHODIMP CHappifier::get_LovelyMessage(BSTR *pVal)
{
    *pVal = SysAllocString(L"You are wonderful");
    return S_OK;
}
```

The new bit here is the call to `OuterQueryInterface()`. This is an ATL method, implemented in the `CComObjectRootEx<>` template, which simply grabs the `IUnknown` interface pointer for the aggregator and does a `QueryInterface()` on it. That's how we get the `IADs` pointer that we can use to tell us where in the directory tree we happen to be.

That's almost it. The only other thing we need to do is register our object as an ADSI extension. Now here's where we encounter a slight problem, because the easiest way in ATL to add registry entries would normally be to modify the registry script, and let the registrar handle it. Unfortunately, we need to put the interface IID in multi-string registry format, and the registrar supplied with Visual Studio 6.0 can't cope with that. Microsoft have promised that in Visual Studio 6.1 (if/when that is ever released) we will be able to – but for now we're going to have to rely on raw API registry calls.

We'll put the registration calls in the function `DllRegisterServer` which is called up by `Regsvr32.exe`, which will ensure that these registrations are performed along with the COM registration. This also means that our extension will automatically register itself as an ADSI extension as well as a COM server when we compile it.

So we'll open the `Extension.cpp` file, where the registration stuff is, and modify `DllRegisterServer` as follows

```
/////////////////////////////////////////////////////////////////////////////
// DllRegisterServer - Adds entries to the system registry

STDAPI DllRegisterServer(void)
{
  // registers object, typelib and all interfaces in typelib
  HRESULT hr = _Module.RegisterServer(TRUE);
  if (SUCCEEDED(hr))
  {
    // register ourselves as an ADSI extension
    HKEY hKey;
    DWORD dwDisposition;

    hr = RegCreateKeyEx( HKEY_LOCAL_MACHINE,
        L"SOFTWARE\\Microsoft\\ADs\\Providers\\LDAP\\Extensions\\"
        L"User\\{BB199110-2DA0-11D3-92E1-0080C8D38C55}",
        0, NULL, REG_OPTION_NON_VOLATILE,
        KEY_WRITE, NULL, &hKey, &dwDisposition );
    const wchar_t pszIID[] = L"{BB19910F-2DA0-11D3-92E1-0080C8D38C55}\0\0";
    hr = RegSetValueEx( hKey, _T("Interfaces"), 0,
        REG_BINARY, (const BYTE *) pszIID, sizeof(pszIID));
    RegCloseKey(hKey);
    hr = RegCreateKeyEx( HKEY_LOCAL_MACHINE,
        L"SOFTWARE\\Microsoft\\ADs\\Providers\\WinNT\\Extensions\\"
        L"User\\{BB199110-2DA0-11D3-92E1-0080C8D38C55}",
        0, NULL, REG_OPTION_NON_VOLATILE,
        KEY_WRITE, NULL, &hKey, &dwDisposition );
    hr = RegSetValueEx( hKey, _T("Interfaces"), 0,
        REG_BINARY, (const BYTE *) pszIID, sizeof(pszIID));
     hr = RegCreateKeyEx( HKEY_LOCAL_MACHINE,
        L"SOFTWARE\\Microsoft\\ADs\\Providers\\IIS\\Extensions\\"
        L"IISServer\\{BB199110-2DA0-11D3-92E1-0080C8D38C55}",
        0, NULL, REG_OPTION_NON_VOLATILE,
```

```
            KEY_WRITE, NULL, &hKey, &dwDisposition );
        hr = RegSetValueEx( hKey, _T("Interfaces"), 0,
            REG_BINARY, (const BYTE *) pszIID, sizeof(pszIID));
    RegCloseKey(hKey);

        if (hr != ERROR_SUCCESS)
            return E_FAIL;
    }
    return hr;
}
```

We're making three entries here – one for the LDAP provider, one for WinNT, and one for the IIS provider, For the LDAP and WinNT providers, we're adding our extension to the User class, for the IIS provider it's the WebServer class. Note by the way, that in the case of LDAP it's the objectClass name we use to name our new registry key, not the objectCategory name. Another point to be aware of is that in general, we are using the class name to name the registry key. However, in the case of IIS, the registry key is named slightly differently, I've used a registry key

```
SOFTWARE\Microsoft\ADs\Providers\IIS\Extension\IISServer
```

naming the key IISServer – whereas in fact the class name is IISWebServer. If you want to add extensions to other IIS classes, you can find out the key to use by inspecting the registry – the relevant keys with the class names in are all already there because some of the extra IIS interfaces that we discussed in Chapter 6 are actually implemented as extensions!

Also notice that the error codes returned by the registry API functions are NOT the same as the HRESULTs used by COM method calls (though the success code, ERROR_SUCCESS, does happen to have the same value, zero, as S_OK.) Some failure codes returned by the registry API functions would actually pass a SUCCEEDED(hr) test, so I take the trouble to convert a failure to E_FAIL. Not that we're seriously expecting our extension to fail on registration of course. That would indicate some serious problems!

While we're at it, we'd better modify the DllUnregisterServer() function to make sure we remove those entries when we unregister ourselves.

```
/////////////////////////////////////////////////////////////////////////////
// DllUnregisterServer - Removes entries from the system registry

STDAPI DllUnregisterServer(void)
{
    RegDeleteKey(HKEY_LOCAL_MACHINE,
            L"SOFTWARE\\Microsoft\\ADs\\Providers\\LDAP\\Extensions\\"
            L"User\\{BB199103-2DA0-11D3-92E1-0080C8D38C55}");
    RegDeleteKey(HKEY_LOCAL_MACHINE,
            L"SOFTWARE\\Microsoft\\ADs\\Providers\\WinNT\\Extensions\\"
            L"User\\{BB199103-2DA0-11D3-92E1-0080C8D38C55}");
    RegDeleteKey(HKEY_LOCAL_MACHINE,
            L"SOFTWARE\\Microsoft\\ADs\\Providers\\IIS\\Extensions\\"
            L"IISServer\\{BB199103-2DA0-11D3-92E1-0080C8D38C55}");  return
_Module.UnregisterServer(TRUE);
}
```

This code will actually leave the *Extensions* and *User* keys in place, even if we added them on registration. That's harmless – and essential – since we don't want to delete that key in case any other extensions have registered themselves under them.

That has actually completed the registration process – our extension will now work OK, but only for clients that use vtable or early binding. We need to make some more changes to ensure that our extension will work for clients that use late binding.

First, let's sort out our implementation of `IDispatch`. We need to get rid of the ATL-supplied `IDispatch` implementation, by changing our `CHappifier` class so it is derived from `IHappifier` rather than `IDispatchImpl<IHappifier>`

```
class ATL_NO_VTABLE CHappifier :
    public CComObjectRootEx<CComMultiThreadModel>,
    public CComCoClass<CHappifier, &CLSID_Happifier>,
    public IHappifier,
{
public:
    CHappifier();
```

Now we need to add our own `IDispatch` methods, again to the `CHappifier` class. First the definitions

```
// IDispatch
STDMETHOD(GetTypeInfoCount)(UINT* pctinfo);
STDMETHOD(GetTypeInfo)(UINT itinfo, LCID lcid, ITypeInfo** pptinfo);
STDMETHOD(GetIDsOfNames)(REFIID riid, LPOLESTR* rgszNames, UINT cNames,
    LCID lcid, DISPID* rgdispid);
STDMETHOD(Invoke)(DISPID dispidMember, REFIID riid,
    LCID lcid, WORD wFlags, DISPPARAMS* pdispparams, VARIANT* pvarResult,
    EXCEPINFO* pexcepinfo, UINT* puArgErr);
```

Now the implementations. Basically some boilerplate code that calls back the aggregator's `IDispatch` methods.

```
STDMETHODIMP CHappifier::GetTypeInfoCount(UINT* pctinfo)
{
  CComPtr<IDispatch> spDisp;
  HRESULT  hr;
  hr = OuterQueryInterface( IID_IDispatch, (void**) &spDisp );
  if ( SUCCEEDED(hr) )
  {
     hr = spDisp->GetTypeInfoCount( pctinfo );
  }
  return hr;
}


STDMETHODIMP CHappifier::GetTypeInfo(UINT itinfo, LCID lcid, ITypeInfo** pptinfo)
```

```
{
  CComPtr<IDispatch> spDisp;
  HRESULT  hr;
  hr = OuterQueryInterface( IID_IDispatch, (void**) &spDisp );
  if ( SUCCEEDED(hr) )
  {
    hr = spDisp->GetTypeInfo( itinfo, lcid, pptinfo );
  }

  return hr;
}

STDMETHODIMP CHappifier::GetIDsOfNames(REFIID riid, LPOLESTR* rgszNames, UINT
cNames,
      LCID lcid, DISPID* rgdispid)
{
  CComPtr<IDispatch> spDisp;
  HRESULT  hr;
  hr = OuterQueryInterface( IID_IDispatch, (void**) &spDisp );
  if ( SUCCEEDED(hr) )
  {
    hr = spDisp->GetIDsOfNames( riid, rgszNames, cNames, lcid, rgdispid);
  }

  return hr;

}

STDMETHODIMP CHappifier::Invoke(DISPID dispidMember, REFIID riid,
      LCID lcid, WORD wFlags, DISPPARAMS* pdispparams, VARIANT* pvarResult,
      EXCEPINFO* pexcepinfo, UINT* puArgErr)
{
  CComPtr<IDispatch> spDisp;
  HRESULT  hr;
  hr = OuterQueryInterface( IID_IDispatch, (void**) &spDisp );
  if ( SUCCEEDED(hr) )
  {
    hr = spDisp->Invoke( dispidMember, riid, lcid, wFlags, pdispparams,
pvarResult,
                pexcepinfo, puArgErr);
  }

  return hr;
}
```

Now we've ensured that any calls to IDispatch will simply be delegated back to the aggregator, we need to implement our own dispatch methods in IADsExtension. Firstly, we need to derive our CHappifier class from IADsExtension.

```
class ATL_NO_VTABLE CHappifier :
    public CComObjectRootEx<CComMultiThreadModel>,
    public CComCoClass<CHappifier, &CLSID_Happifier>,
    public IHappifier,
    public IADsExtension
{
public:
    CHappifier();

DECLARE_REGISTRY_RESOURCEID(IDR_HAPPIFIER)

DECLARE_PROTECT_FINAL_CONSTRUCT()

BEGIN_COM_MAP(CHappifier)
    COM_INTERFACE_ENTRY(IHappifier)
    COM_INTERFACE_ENTRY(IDispatch)
    COM_INTERFACE_ENTRY(IADsExtension)
END_COM_MAP()

// IADsExtension
    STDMETHOD(Operate)(ULONG dwCode, VARIANT varData1, VARIANT varData2, VARIANT
varData3);
    STDMETHOD(PrivateGetIDsOfNames)(REFIID riid, OLECHAR ** rgszNames,
        unsigned int cNames, LCID lcid, DISPID * rgdispid);
    STDMETHOD(PrivateInvoke)(DISPID dispidMember, REFIID riid,
        LCID lcid, WORD wFlags, DISPPARAMS * pdispparams,
        VARIANT * pvarResult, EXCEPINFO * pexcepinfo, UINT * puArgErr);
```

We're also going to need a member variable in our `CHappifier` class, an `ITypeInfo` smart pointer, which I'll explain in a moment.

```
private:
    CComPtr<ITypeInfo> m_spTypeInfo;
```

The `ITypeInfo` pointer needs to be initialized, which we'll do in the constructor.

```
CHappifier :: CHappifier()
{
    HRESULT hr;
    CComPtr<ITypeLib> spTypeLib;
    hr = LoadRegTypeLib( LIBID_EXTENSIONLib, 1, 0,
        PRIMARYLANGID(GetSystemDefaultLCID()), &spTypeLib );
    if ( SUCCEEDED(hr) )
        hr = spTypeLib->GetTypeInfoOfGuid( IID_IHappifier, &m_spTypeInfo);

}
```

Finally we can implement our `PrivateGetIDsOfNames` and `PrivateInvoke` methods.

```
STDMETHODIMP CHappifier :: PrivateGetIDsOfNames(REFIID riid, OLECHAR ** rgszNames,
unsigned int cNames, LCID lcid, DISPID * rgdispid)
{

    if (rgdispid == NULL)
        return E_POINTER;

    return DispGetIDsOfNames(m_spTypeInfo, rgszNames, cNames, rgdispid);
}



STDMETHODIMP CHappifier :: PrivateInvoke(DISPID dispidMember, REFIID riid, LCID
lcid, WORD wFlags, DISPPARAMS * pdispparams, VARIANT * pvarResult, EXCEPINFO *
pexcepinfo, UINT * puArgErr)
{
    return DispInvoke( (IHappifier*)this, m_spTypeInfo, dispidMember,
        wFlags, pdispparams, pvarResult, pexcepinfo,
        puArgErr );
}
```

Let's explain that lot. There's actually nothing special about our implementations of these two `IDispatch` methods. What I've just done is the standard way of implementing `IDispatch`, as recommended by Microsoft. `DispGetIDsOfNames()` and `DispInvoke()` are COM API functions which do all the work. `DispGetIDsOfNames()` accepts the names passed in as a parameter, and figures out what the corresponding DispIDs are by looking in the specified type library. The type library is specified by passing in a parameter to an `ITypeInfo` interface pointer. Apart from this pointer, the function takes the same parameters as `IDispatch::GetIDsOfNames()`, apart from the locale ID and interface IID. Similarly, `DispInvoke()` takes the supplied `DispID` and calls the corresponding method. Apart from the parameters passed to `IDispatch::Invoke()`, it needs the interface pointer on which it is going to call the method, as well as the `ITypeInfo` pointer that it can use to locate the type library.

I mentioned that both of these API functions need to be told which type library they should look in for the information. The way they get told is via an `ITypeInfo` pointer. `ITypeInfo` is a standard COM interface which can be used to obtain information about type information. The bit of the code in the constructor is simply the normal way of initializing an `ITypeInfo` pointer, using another COM API function, `LoadRegTypeLib()` and interface, `ITypeLib`.

Finally, we need to implement our `IADsExtension::Operate()` method. We don't actually need to do anything here – we could just return `E_NOTIMPL`. But just so I can show you an implementation that's ready for you to fill in any real implementation that you need to do in your extension, we'll be a bit more sophisticated:

```
// IADsExtension
STDMETHODIMP CHappifier :: Operate(ULONG dwCode, VARIANT varData1, VARIANT
varData2, VARIANT varData3)
{
    HRESULT hr = S_OK;
```

```
    switch (dwCode)
    {
    case ADS_EXT_INITCREDENTIALS:
        break;

    default:
        hr = E_FAIL;
        break;
    }
    return hr;

}
```

All I've done here is picked out the one value of the parameter that will actually be passed in by the WinNT and LDAP providers, `ADS_EXT_INITCREDENTIALS`, and returned a success code if this is what was passed in. The default clause in the switch statement will pick out any other parameters that may be passed in by other providers, if you implement an extension to your own or to third party ADSI providers.

Well that's it. We now have a working ADSI extension. You can download the code from the Wrox web site and run it whenever you feel like you need cheering up.

There is a fair bit of code there, but the nice thing is it's virtually all boilerplate code. The only bits you will need to customize are the registry entries, and the implementations of your own methods. Apart from that, you can basically just cut and paste it all in from this sample! Microsoft's equivalent sample, by the way, is in the `Samples\Extension` folder in the ADSI SDK.

Summary

In this chapter we've briefly covered some of the more advanced topics in ADSI, including some guidance on how to keep connections to servers open, thus improving performance, and going over how you can use your own providers (or the StarRaiders provider) to find out more about both ADSI clients and some of the less well documented requirements of the ADSI specifications.

But we've spent the bulk of the chapter studying ADSI extensions. These are an extremely powerful way of enhancing the functionality of not just your own providers (if you write any) but the Microsoft providers. It also opens up a new software market – where at present there is already a large market for COM components that perform generically useful tasks in general, it also means that it would be conceivable to write, market, and sell ADSI extensions that perform useful tasks.

Anyway that's the ADSI part of the book out of the way. We've now covered all the important topics in ADSI itself. However, I've made it clear from the start that this book isn't just about ADSI, but is here to help you get the best of all the new technologies you need to use to correctly directory-enable your software in Windows 2000. For that we also need to talk about Microsoft Management Console, the Windows Installer and Windows Management Instrumentation. In the final three chapters of this book we'll move on to look at those three topics.

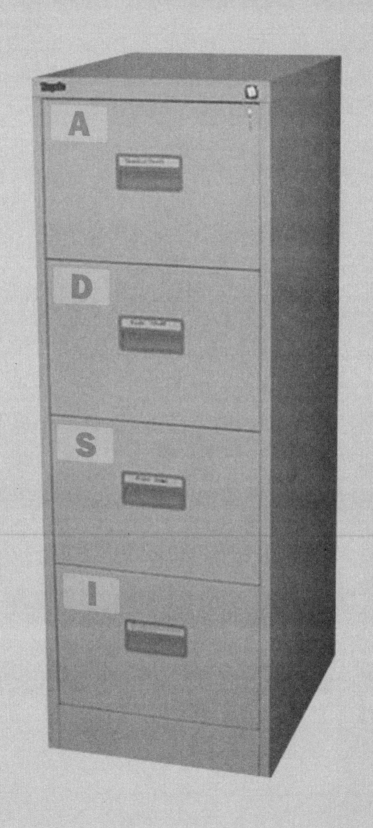

Section 3: Writing Directory Enabled Applications

Having looked at ADSI in depth, in the final section of the book we're going to broaden the scope to look at what you need to create and deploy a professional ADSI application. As such, we'll be looking at several fairly heterogeneous topics, including...

Chapter 12 - Microsoft Management Console

In this chapter we go over what the MMC console and snap-ins actually are, and how the relevant COM interfaces are designed. We explain some of the C++ classes written for ATL that help you write snap-ins, show you how to write a snap-in using ATL, and go on to develop an administration snap-in for the StarRaiders provider.

Chapter 13 - The Windows Installer

The first thing about your application that most of your customers are going to see is how to install it – and the Windows Installer is great for making sure that that is a pleasant experience! We go over what the Windows Installer is and what benefits it will bring. We cover the features Windows 2000 expects an installation package to handle, examine the installer's architecture, then go on to develop a small installation package for StarRaiders.

Chapter 14 - WMI and the CIM Repository

Most applications need to be managed at some point, and WMI is Microsoft's attempt to ensure that other applications have a unified way of being managed – by storing management and configuration data in a special directory called the WMI repository. Making your applications WMI-compliant will be a Windows Logo requirement in Windows 2000. This chapter explains how the CIM repository works and shows you how to use it.

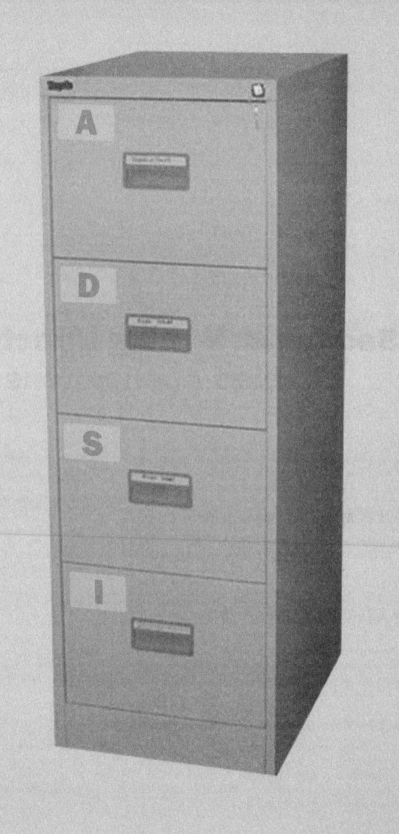

12

Administering Applications: Microsoft Management Console

In this chapter you will learn

- ❑ What MMC is and what you can do with it
- ❑ How the MMC interfaces are structured
- ❑ How ATL implements the MMC interfaces
- ❑ How to write a simple snap-in using ATL

For the final three chapters of this book we're going to move away from ADSI. As I've said before, this is a very application-centric book. My aim is to teach you what you need to know to be able to write good, directory-enabled applications for Windows 2000. The first requirement for this is to understand and use ADSI. We've now covered all the basics and many of the more advanced topics in ADSI, and are ready to move on to the other big new areas which you need to make your applications compatible with Windows 2000. Above all, Windows 2000 changes how you administer and deploy your application. Put bluntly, if your application doesn't install itself using the new Windows 2000 Windows Installer then, according to Microsoft at any rate, it won't meet user expectations for a professional application. No matter how good the content of your software is, it'll look amateurish, and it certainly won't qualify for the Windows logo. Likewise, Microsoft believe that your application should be administered in a particular way, and that way is using the Microsoft Management Console. Finally, if your application has identifiable management data, that data should be exposed via the Windows Management Instrumentation (WMI) services, to allow third parties to write applications which can manage your software using a standard set of interfaces. Failure to meet all three requirements will mean your software won't qualify for the BackOffice Logo.

By the way, although I'm emphasizing Windows 2000, all this stuff is still relevant to NT4. Management Console, Windows Installer and WMI are all available for NT4 as add-ins, although they come as standard with the operating system in Windows 2000.

We're going to look at the MMC in this chapter, then Windows Installer in Chapter 13 and finally the WMI in Chapter 14.

We'll start off by going over exactly what MMC is, how you can get it, and what you can do with it. MMC is implemented by means of a number of COM interfaces. Quite a large number in fact – far too many to cover in one chapter, but we'll go over how to use the most important ones. Once we've done that, we'll be in a position to write the StarAdmin administration tool for StarRaiders, which we will do using the new ATL C++ classes specially developed in ATL 3.0 to write MMC snap-ins with. In the process we'll learn quite a bit about the internal architecture of these snap-in classes.

What Is Microsoft Management Console?

So what is MMC then? Let's take a look. Here's the basic MMC console.

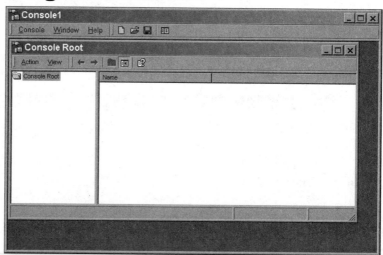

We've seen a few examples of snap-ins already in this book, but just so we are clear what we're talking about, here's a console with a snap-in loaded. This is the Event Viewer, which you'll find in the Start Menu, under the Programs | Administrative Tools in Windows 2000. I've also maximized the child window in this screenshot.

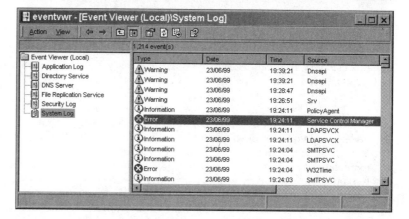

The next screenshot is the console with a couple of different snap-ins loaded. For this one I decided that I just *had* to have a application from which I could defragment my disk, look at my NT Services, visit the COMDeveloper website, and manage my Active Directory sites and services, all at once. Perhaps not the most likely combination but it does show how flexible the MMC console is. This screenshot also shows that the right hand pane doesn't always have to just be a boring looking listview control.

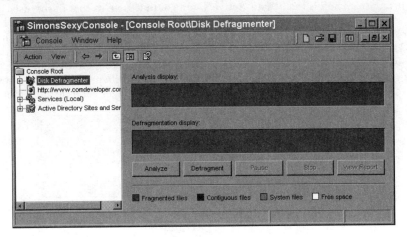

What is MMC There For?

You'll have gathered that what you're looking at are administrative tools. Think how the control panel works. You choose which tool you want and up pops the corresponding dialog box to let you carry out your chosen task, be it install or remove some software or manage your network settings. MMC is similar, but a lot more powerful and flexible, and for many purposes it's replacing the control panel in Windows 2000. The big difference you'll notice between MMC and the control panel is that instead of dialogs, we've got a Windows Explorer type window. Or rather windows, since MMC runs as a multiple-document interface app. It doesn't matter which particular administrative tool you want, you'll get roughly the same Explorer-style interface with a tree control on the left.

The idea is that MMC will be used for the type of administration that systems administrators do – changing security permissions, adding users, or looking at Active Directory. That way, systems administrators get a more consistent interface – there's less work to do to learn how different admin tools work. End users are less likely to have much contact with MMC because the customization tools they use, such as changing the screen colors and backdrops, are staying in the control panel. This means that the control panel in Windows 2000 is very much slimmed down compared to the one in NT4. I have to confess one of my favorite hobbies over the last few months has been to watch people trying out one of the beta versions of Windows 2000 for the first time – it's never long before they bring up the control panel to change some setting or add a new user, and start wailing about the missing control panel applets...

Eventually, they realize many of the admin tools now appear under the Administrative Tools item of the start menu.

So that's what MMC is for. How does it work? Well, it comes in two parts. The console provides a basic Windows Explorer-style interface in that it usually has a tree view on the left and (usually) a list view on the right. Unlike Windows Explorer however, although the default is a list view in the right hand pane, it is possible to put other types of views there. Apart from the list view, MMC will happily cope with HTML pages (specified by a URL – so you can display web pages), ActiveX Controls, and **Taskpads**. Since an ActiveX control can look like anything, that gives you quite a bit of flexibility. In fact, my strong suspicion is that it's an ActiveX control that gave us that flashy user interface we've just seen in the disk defragmenter screenshot. You may not have heard of taskpads before, though you've probably used them when you've been surfing the web. Roughly speaking, they are a kind of dynamic HTML page that displays a series of options for different actions you can take, and which supports events so that when you take some action such as clicking on a button, the page can call up code that could be written in any language, including C++. Perhaps the best known example of a snap-in which uses taskpads is the Microsoft SQL Server manager snap-in, shown here

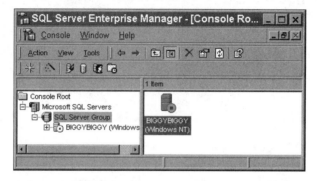

There's only one option in the taskpad here – the BiggyBiggy icon, since the options correspond to the servers and I only have one server – but in principle there could be more.

Taskpads and ActiveX controls, although a useful and important extension of the MMC theme are taking us away from the core information you need for ADSI and directories, so for the moment we'll stick to programming list views.

By the way, I mentioned that the console is an MDI interface. You can add more windows. The first window always contains both a scope and a results pane, but if your snap-in asks the console to add more windows, it can ask for the scope pane to be suppressed in these. By opening another window with only a results pane, displaying an ActiveX control, you really can have almost complete flexibility over what that window looks like and how it behaves.

What actually goes in the views is determined by the snap-in. The snap-in is the actual administrative tool, and will be written by Independent Software Vendors (ISVs - that's you!), possibly along with the applications that need to be managed. It hooks up to the console by means of some COM interfaces, which – in theory at least – saves you from having to write much user interface code. You can just concentrate on the guts of administering your application. For example, you don't have to write a tree control for the scope pane – you just need to implement an interface method that tells the console how many items to add when the user expands a particular node, and what text and icons to display with them. Windows 2000 comes with quite a few snap-ins Microsoft have written to control various aspects of Windows, and such tools as Transaction Server and SQL Server are starting to come with their own snap-ins too.

That's not quite all yet. When you run MMC, for example to change some settings on your software, it won't actually be a snap-in that you run – it'll be a Management Saved Console (.msc) file. In fact, it's the mmc.exe executable with a .msc file specified as a parameter. Management Saved Console files have a file association set up so that mmc.exe is the program that will be used to open them if you click on them.

A Management Saved Console file is a console in which one or more snap-ins have been loaded. This means if you think a couple of tools would go well together, you can just place them together in the same .msc file. A saved console file can have as many snap-ins as you want (though in practice more than one or two would be rare), and a snap-in can be loaded into as many .msc files as you want. The different tools in the in the Start | Programs | Administrative Tools menu in Windows 2000 are all actually .msc files. You can create more .msc files by simply running MMC (type in mmc at the command prompt) without specifying any parameters – this loads an empty console. Then you just use the menu items in the console to add snap-ins and save the results.

MMC Architecture

Up to now, I've been talking loosely about the console, and I will continue to do so throughout this chapter. But in fact there are two parts here. The actual **MMC console** itself is the executable that contains code for the user interface. The **Node Manager** is an in-process COM server, which houses the COM interfaces that will talk to snap-ins. It is always the node manager that your snap-ins interact with, but as this distinction doesn't actually have any effect as far as you're concerned (your snap-in only ever talks to the interfaces exposed by the console – in accordance with the basic principles of COM you don't know or care exactly what the object that exposes those interfaces is), I'll often just refer to them both as the console. Architecturally, we've got the structure shown below.

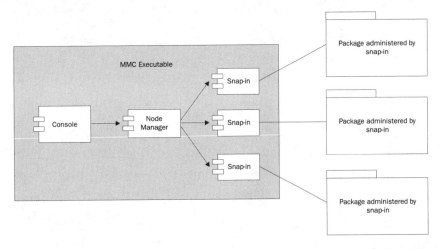

Your snap-in will also be a COM server though, as with ADSI providers, I should qualify this. Any snap-in is there to manage something, which presumably means it is also acting as a client (possibly a COM client) to the object it is managing. Also, the traffic between the snap-ins and the node manager isn't all one-way. The snap-ins expose some interfaces which the node manager uses and the node manager exposes some interfaces which the snap-ins use. (Or as Jonathan Pinnock puts it in his book, *Professional DCOM Application Development*, 'I'll expose my interface to you if you expose your interface to me'.) What this means for you, the snap-in writer, is that there are some interfaces you have to implement yourself and other interfaces you have to know how to use as a client.

There are a couple of other architectural features worth mentioning. MMC does use MFC, which is worth bearing in mind because if you're tempted to use MFC in your snap-ins but worry about the size of the MFC dlls then don't worry, because you'll use them anyway. Also, MMC uses the apartment-threaded model, so you don't have to worry about debugging impossible-to-debug thread synchronization bugs.

What Snap-ins Can Do.

MMC is very flexible, but with the console handling a lot of the user interface features there are inevitably some restrictions on what you can do with your snap-in. Before we say what the restrictions are we're going to need some terminology. The left hand pane of the window – the one with the tree control – is called the **scope pane**. The right hand pane is the **results pane**.

Conventionally the results pane displays the detailed contents of whatever item is selected in the scope pane. If the item selected is really a container for other items, then this will normally be a list of its children. Otherwise the results pane will display data associated with that item (the screenshot of the event viewer shows this situation). Once you've iterated down through the containers and only have lots of leaf objects left, then it's customary *not* to display those in the scope pane. This again is similar to how Windows Explorer works. In Windows Explorer, folders will normally appear in either the tree or list view as appropriate, but files only ever appear in the list view. ADSIEDIT, incidentally, is one MMC snap-in which doesn't follow this guideline. In ADSIEDIT, all Active Directory objects appear in both panes – as shown in the screenshot. However, in general the advice is *not* to design your snap-ins like that since it can result in scope pane with huge numbers of items in the tree control and which is therefore hard for users to navigate around.

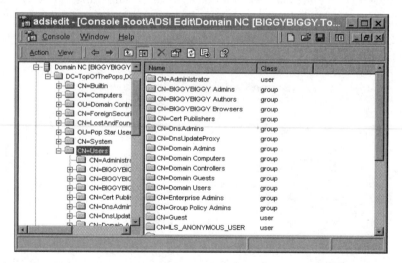

As far as the tree structure of the scope pane is concerned – that is to say, where the items managed by a snap-in get placed in the tree – Snap-ins have complete freedom to determine this for themselves, but with one exception: the children of the root node in the tree will always be the snap-ins loaded into the console. (And obviously, you can only place items under the node that represents *your* snap-in, not under someone else's snap-in!). The nodes which represent the snap-ins are termed **static nodes** – nodes determined by the console, to distinguish them from the **enumerated nodes** below them, which are determined by the snap-ins. The console can also display html pages, ocxs and shortcuts which don't interact with any snap-ins. These are termed **built-in** nodes, and like the snap-ins are specified in the .msc file for that console.

Snap-ins may be **standalone** (**primary**) or **extended**. A standalone snap-in is just what it says – you can load it on its own into a console. An extended snap-in is designed to extend the functionality of another snap-in, and can only be loaded into the console if the corresponding primary snap-in is already loaded. In addition, primary snap-ins can insist on specified **required extension** snap-ins being loaded when they are loaded.

As far as menus are concerned, the main menu items C̲onsole, W̲indow, H̲elp, A̲ction and V̲iew, are fixed by the console. The snap-in is free to add items to these menus in four places: at the top of the A̲ction menu, at the bottom of the V̲iew menu, and into two sub-menus of A̲ction, N̲ew and T̲ask. Most of the options on the A̲ction menu also appear on context menus (The menus that appear when you right-click the mouse over an item, if you have your mouse set up as a right-handed mouse). The snap-in can also tell the console whether or not to include a Properties option with the Action menu, and if so, will supply the property pages to display. Note that sometimes in other areas you will see a tabbed dialog referred to as a **property sheet** and each tab referred to as a **property page.** When we use these terms in the context of MMC, we are always specifically referring to the tabbed dialog box that comes up when you select *Properties* from a menu to view the properties of an object. In MMC, these terms are not used to indicate any other dialog box.

Snap-ins may also add items to the toolbar. The MMC documentation refers to the **control bar**. This is like a generalized toolbar, which can also include menu items and drop-down list boxes, and is normally located beneath the menus in the console.

You can provide help for your snap-in by means of a compiled html help (.chm file). If you do so, the console will merge your .chm file with its own one, so that the users see a combined table of contents that covers all the snap-ins loaded, as well as the help for MMC in general when they click on H̲elp.

How to Install MMC

If you have Windows 2000, you'll have MMC automatically, but if you are running NT4 or Windows 9x, you'll need the NT Option pack and SP3, both available from Microsoft's web site. You'll also find that quite a lot of Microsoft software these days is administered using MMC snap-ins. If you install any of this software, you'll find the installation process installs MMC for you if you don't already have it. Examples include SQL server, and IIS 4 (if you include the MMC snap-in admin tool with the installation options).

In order to write MMC snap-ins you'll need the relevant SDK. All the MMC header files are included with Visual Studio 6, but you probably won't want to use these: they are for MMC 1.0, whereas MMC is currently at version 1.2. There are quite a few additional features and interfaces that have been added since 1.0, so you'll want the latest header files. They are included with the Platform SDK, or can be downloaded from Microsoft's web site.

Since people running Windows NT4 or 9x might not have MMC installed, you can freely redistribute MMC with any software you sell that depends on it. The only proviso is that you should distribute the installation file only, and have that file run during installation of your software: Don't try and do anything clever, like redistributing the actual installed MMC dlls.

Writing MMC Snap-ins.

For snap-in development, you've in principle got the usual choice between VB and C++. However, at the time of writing there's not too much information available about snap-in development in VB – which gives me the perfect excuse to show off some more nifty ATL code!

Microsoft have been promising for a while to provide a tool that allows writing snap-ins in VB. Unfortunately at the time of writing it still hasn't showed up. If it's appeared by the time you read this, and you like programming in VB, then it'll be worth checking out.

If by any chance you're running ATL 2.1 then you're basically on your own for snap-in development. Assuming you're on ATL 3.0, then you'll be able to use the snap-in option within the object wizard (note: object wizard, not AppWizard), which will generate classes to give you a basic MMC snap-in. And they are non-trivial classes; they actually do a lot of work for you, in addition to the generic boilerplate code ATL generates for basic COM classes. This will save you a lot of code writing, but does give you some extra learning to do. You'll have to learn not only the MMC COM interfaces, but how the classes that ATL implements to wrap these interfaces work. The fact that the ATL classes are at present almost completely undocumented in MSDN can serve to heighten the sense of challenge involved, and the sense of achievement when you've done it. One other point to bear in mind – the ATL snap-in classes do a lot of work, but it's at the cost of imposing a particular architecture on your snap-in. We'll go over this architecture over the next few pages, and if you don't like the way wizard-generated snap-ins work, then you may feel justified in by-passing the wizard altogether, and implementing a snap-in using the generic ATL COM classes.

The MMC Interfaces

OK – let's have a look at the interfaces you need. There are about twenty, roughly half of which are implemented by the snap-in and half by the node manager. First, here's a summary of which interfaces do what, and I'll go over some of them in more detail afterwards.

This summary is provided for MMC 1.1, because at present Microsoft haven't provided any documentation concerning new features in MMC 1.2. It's probably worth while checking the MS web site or the latest MSDN to check if any new stuff has been added.

Basic Interfaces you'll always need to implement:

- ❑ IComponentData – Tells the console what to display in the scope pane
- ❑ IComponent – Tells the console what to display in the result pane

When the console asks for instances of these interfaces, in return it will supply an interface pointer to itself, which the snap-in is expected to store. The snap-in will want to QueryInterface() this pointer for IConsole2 and IConsoleNamespace2. These are the two interfaces implemented by the console which let the snap-in manage the data displayed. IConsoleNamespace2 lets you navigate round the tree control in the scope pane, and add and remove items from it. IConsole2 lets you do things like select an item in either pane, and exposes methods to give you pointers to some other interfaces.

The interfaces you implement to manage the control bars and property sheets include

- IExtendControlbar, called by the console to give you the chance to add control bars to the main window. You'll probably implement the IExtendControlbar methods so called to respond by calling methods in IControlbar, which is exposed by the console and exposes methods to actually add control bars.

- IExtendPropertySheet2 is called by the console when it is ready to display a property sheet. You'll probably respond by calling methods in IPropertySheetCallback and IPropertySheetProvider to add pages to the property sheet.

While if you want to display taskpads, you'll implement

- IExtendTaskPad, which lets you display a taskpad in the results pane and receive notifications from it.

- IEnumTaskPad, which lists the taskpads you might want to display.

If you are writing a primary snap-in which has some required extensions, then you'll implement IRequiredExtensions. This is called by the console when your snap-in initializes, to ask whether your snap-in needs certain extension snap-ins to be loaded.

If you decide to implement a virtual list, you'll need to implement IResultDataCompare and IResultOwnerData. The console implements IResultData, which these interfaces will call up. If you're wondering, by the way, a virtual list is a list in which you don't tell the console at the outset what stuff goes in the list. Rather, you can dynamically generate the text to go in each row and column when the console decides it needs to display that particular data.

You can specify the .chm help file for your snap-in by implementing ISnap-inHelp.

Implement ISnap-inAbout to tell the console what to display in the About dialog box.

And finally, you can implement IExtendContextMenu, which is called by the console to let you know when it's going to display a menu and do you want to add any of your own stuff to it? You'll probably respond by calling methods in IContextMenuCallback to actually add menu items. Despite the names, these interfaces apply to any of the menu locations where you are allowed to add menu items, not just context menus.

There are a number of other MMC interfaces implemented by the console, to which your snap-in may want to act as a client:

- IConsoleVerb lets you get and set the status of verbs. (To understand what a console verb is, think in terms of Windows Explorer. When you click on an item, you select it, and (if you have the normal Windows color scheme) it'll appear as white text with a dark background. If you click again on the item, it'll have the focus. it'll appear to be surrounded by a box, and you'll be able to directly edit its name. If you press *Ctrl+X* over the item, it'll appear grayed, and be ready to be cut and pasted somewhere else. These different states represent different verbs.) IDisplayHelp lets you tell the console to display a particular topic in the help file.

- IHeaderCtrl lets you manipulate the headers for the list view in the result pane.

❏ IImageList lets you tell the console about bitmaps you want to use as images in the scope and results panes.

❏ IMenuButton lets you add menu buttons.

❏ IToolbar implemented by console to add items to toolbars.

Finally, MMC uses several other standard COM interfaces, which the snap-in will implement.

❏ IDataObject is used to transfer some data between console and snap-in.

❏ IPersistStream, IPersistStorage and IPersistStreamInit are implemented if your snap-in needs to persist some data – in other words store it, most likely in a file. The data concerned will normally be data concerning the state of the snap-in just before you exited the console – which node you were looking at etc., so the next time the snap-in starts up, it can start up in the same state. If you need to do this, you can choose any of these interfaces to implement.

That's a fair few interfaces, and unfortunately, if you are writing a commercial grade snap-in you will need almost all of them. Since I'm just doing an example for a book, not writing a commercial grade snap-in, the StarAdmin example is going to be a fairly basic snap-in which will only implement some of the interfaces. At any rate, it'll be enough to get you started and give you an idea of how the whole thing works.

The most basic thing you will do is put data in the scope and results panes. So let's go over the sequence.

IComponentData and IComponent

The most important interfaces that you will implement are IComponentData and IComponent. IComponentData is the interface that controls everything in the scope pane, and IComponent controls everything in the results pane. The naming of them is a bit unfortunate, since you'd really associate data with the results pane, and so expect them to be named the opposite way round. There's also no agreed name for the COM objects that implement these interfaces. Some authors relate them to the interfaces and call them the ComponentData and Component objects, but personally I prefer to think in terms of their functionality, so in this book we'll respectively call these objects the scope pane and results pane objects.

The most important point about these objects is that they are associated with the panes rather than with any particular item controlled by the snap-in. So you get just one instance of these objects for each window that uses your snap-in. Incidentally, there's no obligation to have separate scope pane and results pane objects. You *could* have both interfaces implemented by the same object, but the convention seems to be two objects, and that's certainly how ATL's implementation of snap-ins works – so that's what we'll do here.

> There's no COM object or interface that is associated with a particular item in the scope or results panes. Instead, cookies are used and passed as parameters in the method calls to identify the relevant item when data needs to be transferred between console and snap-in. For MMC, a cookie is just an integer, unlike HTTP usage, where a cookie is a small binary file stored on the client machine.

The figure shows how a typical snap-in might be built. It shows the scope pane and results pane objects, along with the node manager, and shows the interfaces exposed by each. Since the node manager is implemented by Microsoft, the interfaces it implements are fixed, but those implemented by the snap-in will vary according to the individual snap-in. So you shouldn't take the architecture I've shown as gospel – think of it as a model that you can use to get your bearings from when I discuss the different interfaces over the next couple of pages.

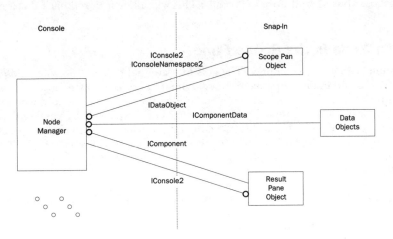

IDataObject

The figure also shows a number of boxes marked `DataObject` objects. What are these? Well in the days when COM was just being put together – when people weren't even really talking about it much as COM, they were talking about it as OLE, one of the problems that needed to be solved was how to define some kind of standard for transferring data between COM objects. What Microsoft came up with was an interface called `IDataObject`. This interface contains a number of methods for defining data formats and copying data. `IDataObject` is also the chosen interface for passing some data between snap-in and console. It's a fairly complex interface, but fortunately for us, the console only ever tries to call up one method on it, `IDataObject::GetDataHere()` – so we've only got one method to implement. Data Objects are transient entities – in MMC at least, they tend to get created, used once, then discarded. You'll find the pattern is that when the console needs to perform certain tasks, it will ask either the scope pane or result pane object for an `IDataObject` interface (by calling `IComponentData::QueryDataObject()` or `IComponent::QueryDataObject()`). It will then immediately use the `IDataObject` interface, then `Release()` the data object. So it's up to us to implement `QueryDataObject()` to create a data object and initialize it to refer to the particular snap-in item that the console wants. We also need to implement `IDataObject::GetDataHere()` to return the appropriate data.

Being a good C++ object-oriented developer, you'll probably want to design some C++ class that wraps the actual items that the snap-in manages. You'll probably have one instance of this class for each item in the tree structure that you can see in the scope pane, and have `IComponent` and `IComponentData` refer to instances of this class. Note that individual items may be displayed in either the scope or results pane, so the corresponding C++ class must be able to interact with both interfaces.

So that's the objects sorted out. With 20-odd interfaces and an average of 4 to 5 methods in each, there's obviously no way we can cover everything. But to give you a flavor of what goes on, I'm going to run through the sequence of what happens when the user performs certain actions.

Initializing a Snap-in.

When you first click on a snap-in in the scope pane, the console reacts by trying to create an instance of the scope pane object. In a very real sense the scope pane object could be seen as being *the* snap-in object. The console will call `IComponentData::Initialize()` on the object, passing in a pointer to itself. The snap-in will probably `QueryInterface()` this pointer for `IConsole2` and `IConsoleNamespace2` and store the results. This will allow it to call back the console when it wants to.

Expanding a Node in the Scope Pane

This operation is a lot more complex. The guts of it are that the console will need to know what new nodes it needs to add in the scope pane. It will attempt to find out by calling `IComponentData::Notify()`. This method allows the snap-in to be told when various events happen. The console will tell the snap-in a node has been expanded by passing in the flag `MMC_EXPAND` – one of a number of MMC enumeration values for different events. What the snap-in does in response is up to it, but the most likely action is that it will repeatedly call `IConsoleNamespace2::InsertItem()` to progressively add text for all the child items of the node to be expanded.

That's the basics, but there's a lot more to it than that. I'm afraid this is one of those cases where there's a lot going on that we need to understand. So first, here's a time diagram that shows the sequence of actions, and I'll go through it all in detail afterwards.

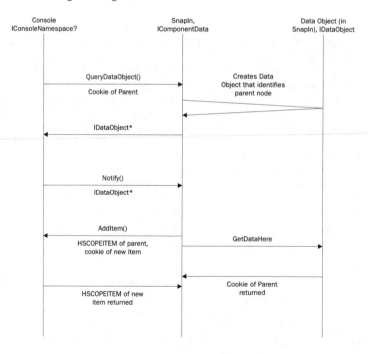

The problem here is we also need a way for the console and snap-in to tell each other which node we're talking about. Let's be more precise. The console here is thinking of the node in the scope pane. The snap-in doesn't really know about nodes in the scope pane – it doesn't manage the tree control. It will be thinking about the particular snap-in item that the node represents – in other words, the underlying object, if any, that is represented and administered by that node. So we've got two identifiers here to think of.

The node is easiest to deal with. Along with the MMC_EXPAND flag, the console will also pass to IComponentData::Notify() a handle – a variable of type HSCOPEITEM – that it can use to identify the node. The snap-in must pass this handle back when it calls IConsoleNamespace2::InsertItem().

The snap-in item is more complex. It's going to be identified by a cookie, and – because the snap-in item is something that the snap-in is responsible for, the cookie will have to have been supplied originally by the snap-in. How can this work? Well, if you think about it, the only way a node can be expanded is if it was created by its parent having been expanded at some point. And so on back to the root node for the snap-in. So the first time a console encounters a node is when it gets told about it by the snap-in calling IConsoleNamespace2::InsertItem(). The snap-in passes the cookie of the item in along with the HSCOPEITEM of its parent in this method. That covers us for everything except the root node. By convention, the snap-in and console agree that a NULL cookie identifies the snap-in item represented by the root node. So whenever the console calls IComponentData::Notify(), it must already know the cookie for the snap-in item corresponding to the node being expanded. Either, the root node is being expanded, in which case it uses a cookie value of NULL, or the console was told the cookie in a previous call to IConsoleNamespace2::InsertItem(). Either way, we're clear.

Well, almost clear. There's one extra complication though. Remember what I said about how DataObjects are used for passing data around? Well, IComponentData::Notify() doesn't have any parameter that's a cookie: it wants a pointer to an IDataObject interface that it can use to identify the snap-in item.

How's the console going to get one of them? Well, as I've mentioned, it calls the method IComponentData::QueryDataObject() to ask for a data object that represents the required snap-in item. And to this method it passes the cookie. Right? No, sorry, wrong. Instead, it passes in a big C-style structure called a SCOPEDATAITEM. The SCOPEDATAITEM structure is defined as:

```
typedef struct _SCOPEDATAITEM
  {
  DWORD mask;
  LPOLESTR displayname;
  int nImage;
  int nOpenImage;
  UINT nState;
  int cChildren;
  LPARAM lParam;
  HSCOPEITEM relativeID;
  HSCOPEITEM ID;
  }  SCOPEDATAITEM;
```

The SCOPEDATAITEM is *the* structure for telling the console about nodes in the scope pane.

The lparam member is the one we're interested in. This is the member variable that is intended to store the cookie. So the console sets this to the required cookie. The member variable, *mask*, is a bit-wise mask that indicates which of the other member variables contains valid data. So the console also sets the appropriate bit in the mask to indicate the lparam is now valid, and then passes the whole structure back to to `IComponentData::QueryDataObject()`. The other fields aren't really needed here, but for reference, the complete list is:

Name	Description
mask	A flag that indicates which other member variables are valid or need to be filled in.
displayname	The name that actually appears for this node in the scope pane. This value may be set to the special value MMC_CALLBACK (the number 0xffffffff – this can't be a pointer to anything!), indicating the console must call the snap-in back to obtain the name.
nImage	An index to the bitmap (actually a part of an imagelist) displayed with the item.
nOpenImage	As for nImage, but for the image displayed when the item is selected.
nState	Whether this item has ever been expanded
cChildren	The number of children the item has
lParam	The cookie that identifies the snap-in item associated with this node
relativeID	This is the HSCOPEITEM of a node. Depending on the value of mask, this may point to the parent node or to one of the siblings next to which this item resides in the tree.

If the console needs any of the information stored in these variables, it'll pass a SCOPEDATAITEM with the lparam initialized to the required cookie and the mask initialized to indicate which member variables it wants, to the method, `IComponentData::GetDisplayInfo()`, and expect the fields specified in mask to be filled in. But that's another story, and needn't concern us for what we want to do.

Feeling confused yet? Don't worry, what we've just covered is one of the hardest parts of how snap-ins work. To summarize:

The console calls `IComponentData::QueryDataObject()` to get a data object. It passes in a SCOPEDATAITEM structure with either a NULL cookie or one it got from a previous call to `IConsoleNamespace2::AddItems()`.

The console calls `IComponentData::Notify()` passing in an HSCOPEITEM of the node to be expanded, along with the newly acquired IDataObject pointer, which the snap-in can use to figure out exactly what snap-in item the HSCOPEITEM is referring to.

The snap-in will probably call `IConsoleNamespace2::AddItem()` to add the items. For each call, it passes the HSCOPEITEM of the parent node, to which items must be added, and the cookies of the new child items, which the console can use later on when it asks for information or wants to pass messages about those items.

The call to `IComponentData::Notify()` returns, and the console expands the node. If the user expands any of the new child nodes, the cycle can repeat itself.

Selecting an Item in the Scope Pane

The console will need to display the data associated with that item in the results pane. If it doesn't already have an `IComponent` interface, it'll QI the scope pane object for one, and call `IComponent::Initialize()` on it, again passing it an `IUnknown` pointer to itself. The result pane object will probably also use this to store an `IConsole2` pointer so it can talk to the console.

The sequence for displaying the item in the results pane is very similar to expanding an item – and hence displaying items in the scope pane. The difference is threefold.

Firstly, it is `IComponent` rather than `IComponentData` which will receive the Notify call. (`IComponent` and `IComponentData` actually expose nearly identical sets of methods – and both implement `Notify()`). The messages `IComponent` receives are `MMCN_SHOW` and `MMCN_ADD_IMAGES`, to allow the snap-in to take any custom action it wishes in respect of these events.

Secondly, because the console needs information about displaying an item in the results pane, it will call `IComponent::GetDisplayInfo()` instead of `IComponentData::GetDisplayInfo()`. This will return the cookie to the snap-in item, but this time as part of a `RESULTDATAITEM` structure. The `RESULTDATAITEM` structure contains information relevant to a list view rather than a tree view. Its definition is:

```
typedef struct _RESULTDATAITEM
  {
  DWORD mask;
  BOOL bScopeItem;
  HRESULTITEM itemID;
  int nIndex;
  int nCol;
  LPOLESTR str;
  int nImage;
  UINT nState;
  LPARAM lParam;
  int iIndent;
  }   RESULTDATAITEM;
```

By the way, you can find the definitions of `SCOPEDATAITEM`, `RESULTDATAITEM` and all the other structures, enumerations etc. relevant to MMC in the header file `mmc.h`. This structure works in the same way as `SCOPEDATAITEM` to the extent that `lParam` contains the cookie that points to the snap-in item and mask is a bit-wise flag that indicates which of the other members contain valid data. You'll notice as you read through the list that not all variables are meaningful in all circumstances.

The meanings of the different members in detail are:

Name	Description
mask	Flag that indicates which of the other members contain valid data or need to be filled in.
bScopeItem	This is set to 1 if the item is an item in the scope pane (ie. a scope pane node was selected and its contents need to be displayed), or 0 if an item in the list view in the result pane was selected.
itemID	Another unique identifier!
nIndex	Roughly translates to the row an item is located at in the listview
nCol	The column an item is at in the listview
str	The text to be displayed for the item
nImage	As for SCOPEDATAITEM::nImage. The icon to be displayed next to the item's name. Note that here there is only one possible image. No Separate nOpenImage.
nState	Whether the item has been selected, focussed, or marked for a cut-and-paste operation.
lParam	The cookie that identifies the corresponding snap-in item
iIndent	Reserved for future use.

Note the need for another identifier. The cookie will probably only narrow down the item to an object managed by the snap-in, something that might reasonably be a node in the scope pane. This item may have a lot of properties and so on. which may well be displayed as separate rows in the list view, and may be represented by sub-items. Hence we may need an extra identifier, itemID, which you can often interpret as the number of the row being displayed.

Before we move on to actual coding, I do have one confession to make: I suspect that after reading the last couple of pages, you might not believe this – but I actually have oversimplified the events of expanding or selecting an item. The main thing I've missed out is that the console actually makes quite a number of calls to IComponentData::QueryDataObject() during the sequences. It then calls IDataObject::GetDataHere() on the data objects to obtain such information as the CSLID of the node, etc. This stuff isn't going to concern us, and is fully implemented by ATL, so we'll ignore it.

The StarRaiders Administrative Snap-in

We're going to write the snap-in that can be used to administer StarRaiders. Actually I have to admit, as far as administering the StarRaiders provider is concerned, this snap-in isn't too useful. I was more concerned with showing you how to write a snap-in and get it into the console than with writing a lot of back-end code inside the snap-in which doesn't actually have anything directly to do with MMC. So what we've ended up with as a snap-in that calls itself the StarAdmin snap-in, but whose functionality is to (1) display a list of the currently registered fans in the StarRaiders directory (in a standard list view), and (2) display Wrox Press's web page. I added this last feature in order to demonstrate how you can display a URL in StarRaiders.

We will separate out these two operations into two different enumerated nodes, StarRaider Fans and Wrox web site. There is also a context menu for the Star Admin static node, which displays a message box.

All this means that our snap-in will look like this when you select the fans

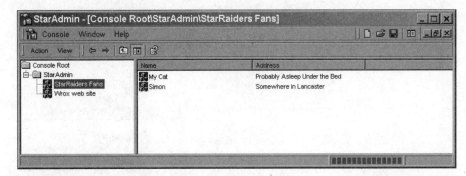

and like this when you select the web site

Let's get coding!

Building a Snap-in with ATL Object Wizard

We've now seen how the MMC interfaces work. We need to look at how ATL implements these, and I'm going to do that by writing the administrative tool for StarRaiders, and seeing what code it throws up for us. So let's get our developer studios out and go!

We want to start the developer studio, and as usual create an ATL dll project called StarAdminTool, supporting MFC. It's not essential to support MFC if you'd prefer not to in your projects, but since the console uses MFC internally anyway, we're not going to lose anything performance-wise by using it. The only reason I've specified this option for this project is so I can use the MFC collection classes, which I happen to like. Once you've got the project up and running, we'll need a snap-in object.

So bring up the object wizard, and select an
MMC snap-in object.

We'll call the object StarAdmin. Because we've
selected an MMC snap-in, we get an extra tab
on the object wizard, asking which MMC
interfaces we want. We make sure that
standalone snap-in is selected. We don't want
this to depend on any other snap-ins, and we'll
also take the chance to add a context menu
extension, so we'll make sure the
IExtendContextMenu check box is checked. On
the other hand, this snap-in is not going to
support persistence, so uncheck the Supports
Persistence box.

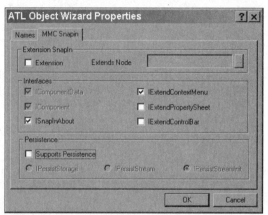

And that's it. The object wizard has given us all the classes we need.

This snap-in is actually ready to build. It won't
do much – it'll just display the main static node
in the scope pane, but it works. So make sure
you have MMC installed, and then build the
snap-in (as usual for ATL, it'll be registered
automatically from registry scripts when you
build it. The usual COM entries plus an entry
under HKLM/SOFTWARE/Microsoft/MMC to
tell mmc that your dll is an MMC snap-in).
That's the easy part. Running it is a bit harder
because the console expects to run a .msc file,
and you've only built a dll. So we'll need to
create a management saved console file. Go to
the command prompt and run mmc. This will
bring up a blank console. On the console menu,
select Add/Remove Snap-in. This will bring up
a dialog box.

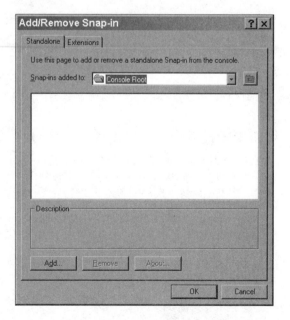

Click on the Add button. This will bring up a second dialog box that lists all the registered snap-ins. Locate the StarAdmin one and click to select it. If you're running Windows 2000 you'll have to scroll through a *lot* of Microsoft-supplied snap-ins. If you're on NT4, StarAdminTool will be virtually the only one there. If you want, you might like to guess which operating system I built the StarAdminTool on…

Click on Add, then Close, then click OK to close the first dialog box. Congratulations! You now have a console with the StarAdminTool snap-in.

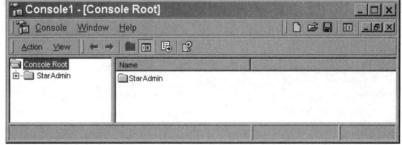

We need to save this. So on the console menu, select Save, and type in a suitable name for the console. StarAdmin is a good one, though it doesn't have to be the same name as the snap-in (the console can after all have more than one snap-in loaded!). You'll probably find that by default, MMC will suggest putting your snap-in in either the desktop or the start menu, though you don't have to accept this choice.

You can now safely close the console. We can run it any time later by typing 'mmc StarAdminTool.msc' at the command prompt, or by double clicking on the .msc file in Windows Explorer; MMC is the application associated with .msc files.

We haven't quite finished yet, because we need to tell the developer studio how to run our dll when we are debugging. So open the Project Settings tabbed dialog box and select the Debug tab. Choose 'All Configurations' in the drop-down list box and enter mmc.exe, with the full path name, as the executable, and the name of the new management saved console file you just created, also supplying the full path name for the parameter. I've also added the parameter -s, which stops the annoying MMC splash screen from appearing when mmc starts. You can't see the full set of program arguments in the screenshot because the pathname is too long, but the actual contents of that particular text box is

```
-s "f:\winnt\Profiles\Simon\Start Menu\Programs\My Administrative
Tools\StarAdmin.msc"
```

which is the path to the management saved console file I just created.

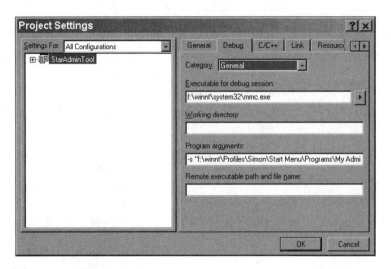

StarAdminTool will now run correctly, but we need to make a small change before we can debug it. Go to the `StarAdmin.cpp` file, and comment out the line that registers the `CSnap-inAbout` class in the object map.

```
CComModule _Module;

BEGIN_OBJECT_MAP(ObjectMap)
OBJECT_ENTRY(CLSID_StarAdmin, CStarAdmin)
//OBJECT_ENTRY(CLSID_StarAdminAbout, CStarAdminAbout)
END_OBJECT_MAP()
```

This will prevent the About box from working. There is a good reason behind my apparent sabotage of my own snap-in. There is a bug in the wizard-generated code. The About dialog box is registered using long file names. The remaining COM objects are registered using short Windows 3.1-style file names. The result is that when the operating system loads up everything, it thinks it's looking at two separate `dll`s. So StarAdminTool gets loaded up in two different locations in memory. The result is that any attempt to set a breakpoint will usually fail because we'll set the breakpoint in one memory-mapped copy of the `dll`, while execution happily takes place in the other copy. The breakpoint simply gets ignored. Since debugging programs without being able to set breakpoints isn't my idea of fun, I solve the problem by disabling the About dialog box until I've finished debugging. Other workarounds are to give the `dll` a short filename in the first place, to dive into the registry script code that registers the objects to make sure that the file names match, or to hard code breakpoints instead of setting them from the developer studio,. If you choose this last option, one way of doing this is to add the statement

```
_asm int 3
```

wherever you want a breakpoint. `_asm` causes the specified assembly language command to be inserted directly in the code. `int` is an assembly-language interrupt, and `3` specifies the type of interrupt. Just take my word for it that `3` is the value you need if you want to hit the debugger.

The snap-in is now ready to be debugged. But before we do that we need to add some code that we can debug. And before we can do that, we need to understand a bit about the wizard-generated code we've got.

ATL Snap-in Classes

Which classes you get given by the object wizard depends to some extent on which options you checked for your snap-in to support. Let's take a look at the classes we've been given to customize for our case.

Class	Interfaces implemented	Function
CSnap-inAbout	ISnap-inAbout	Manages the about dialog box
CStarAdmin	IComponentData	The scope pane object
	IExtendContextMenu	
	IExtendPropertySheet	
CStarAdminComponent	IComponent	The results pane object
	IExtendContextMenu	
	IExtendPropertySheet	
CStarAdminData		The snap-in items

One of these classes, CstarAdminData, isn't actually a COM object: it is simply a useful C++ classes for internal use within the snap-in. Though, as we're going to see, it is an extremely useful class, which does most of the actual work. The other three are implemented as COM objects in the usual way, by deriving the template class CComObject<> from them.

We also have another class, CStarAdminToolApp – the only class which takes its name from the project name rather than the snap-in name. We won't worry about it – it's an MFC application there to act as a wrapper for the application, and is there as a by-product from my having opted to support MFC.

The big three classes are CStarAdmin, CStarAdminComponent and CStarAdminData. CStarAdmin implements IComponentData, so in a real sense it is *the* object that represents your snap-in. The snap-in object is the one which is registered, and it is the COM object that will be called up by the console using CoCreateInstance() in order to load the snap-in.

CComObject<CStarAdminComponent> implements the COM objects that expose IComponent: These objects are created indirectly, via CStarAdmin::CreateComponent(), never using CoCreateInstance().

CStarAdminData, even though only an internal C++ class, is actually where almost all the processing occurs. It's the class that represents the underlying snap-in items that can be displayed in either the scope or result panes. Most of the methods in ATL's implementation of IComponentData and IComponent end up deferring to methods in the C<ProjectName>Data class where <ProjectName> is the name of your project – in this case, StarAdmin.

Here are the respective class definitions, for the scope pane object

```
class CStarAdmin : public CComObjectRootEx<CComSingleThreadModel>,
public CSnap-inObjectRoot<1, CStarAdmin>,
    public IComponentDataImpl<CStarAdmin, CStarAdminComponent>,
    public IExtendContextMenuImpl<CStarAdmin>,
    public CComCoClass<CStarAdmin, &CLSID_StarAdminTool>
{
public:
// constructors removed for clarity

BEGIN_COM_MAP(CStarAdmin)
COM_INTERFACE_ENTRY(IComponentData)
  COM_INTERFACE_ENTRY(IExtendContextMenu)
END_COM_MAP()

DECLARE_REGISTRY_RESOURCEID(IDR_STARADMINTOOL)

the results pane object

class CStarAdminComponent : public CComObjectRootEx<CComSingleThreadModel>,
    public CSnap-inObjectRoot<2, CStarAdmin >,
    public IExtendContextMenuImpl<CStarAdminComponent>,
    public IComponentImpl<CStarAdminComponent>
{
public:
BEGIN_COM_MAP(CStarAdminComponent)
    COM_INTERFACE_ENTRY(IComponent)
  COM_INTERFACE_ENTRY(IExtendContextMenu)
END_COM_MAP()
```

and the snap-in object

```
class CStarAdminData : public CSnap-inItemImpl<CStarAdminData>
{
public:
    static const GUID* m_NODETYPE;
    static const OLECHAR* m_SZNODETYPE;
    static const OLECHAR* m_SZDISPLAY_NAME;
    static const CLSID* m_SNAP-IN_CLASSID;
```

There are a lot of
base classes here. To
understand what's
going on, let's look at
the inheritance tree.
The first figure shows
the inheritance tree
for the scope pane
object:

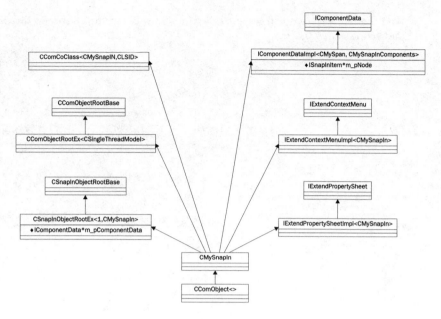

The next, the
equivalent tree for
the results pane
object,

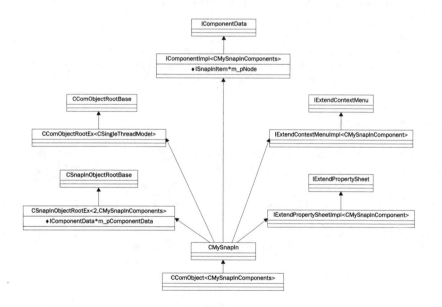

And the figure here, the trees and containment relationships between the data object, snap in item and scope pane objects.

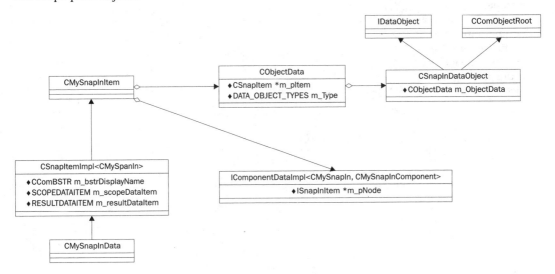

Note that in these figures only those member variables that are significant to our discussion, and not member functions, have been shown.

The Scope and Results Pane Objects

If we take the scope and results pane objects first, we see almost what you'd expect for plain COM objects. Both classes derive from the appropriate interfaces and from CComObjectRootEx<>. As usual, the component data object also derives from CComCoClass<>. The component object doesn't derive from this class, which is what you'd expect for a coclass that isn't externally creatable. This class also doesn't declare a registry resource ID. In fact, if you look at the generated StarAdminTool_i.c file that contains the GUIDs, the only ones you'll see that have been defined are the ones for the component data object and the about box object. There's also a GUID for the type library generated by the MIDL compiler.

```
const IID LIBID_STARADMINTOOLLib =
{0x64BD8931,0x2CBF,0x11D3,{0x92,0xDD,0x00,0x80,0xC8,0xD3,0x8C,0x55}};

const CLSID CLSID_StarAdmin =
{0x64BD893E,0x2CBF,0x11D3,{0x92,0xDD,0x00,0x80,0xC8,0xD3,0x8C,0x55}};

const CLSID CLSID_StarAdminAbout =
{0x64BD893F,0x2CBF,0x11D3,{0x92,0xDD,0x00,0x80,0xC8,0xD3,0x8C,0x55}};
```

Both the scope and results pane COM objects derive through another set of classes that parallel CComObjectRootBase and CComObjectRoot<>: CSnap-inObjectRootBase and CSnap-inObjectRoot<>. These latter classes actually contain almost no significant methods and only a couple of data items. There is a map of tool bar items, a pointer to the control bar object, and – somewhat more significantly for us – a pointer to a CSnap-inNameData class – which actually gets initialized to point to the scope pane object. This allows the result pane object to contact the scope pane object if it needs to. The integer passed in the CSnap-inObject<> template simply serves to identify the type of object – 1 for scope pane, 2 for results pane.

Given the simplicity of these classes, you might be forgiven for wondering what the point of having two base classes is. The reason is to separate out the functionality which requires knowledge of your derived class – as supplied in the template parameter to `CSnap-inObjectRoot<>`, from the functionality which doesn't. The standard ATL code in `ATLSnap.h` cannot have any knowledge of your snap-in, so if it needs to access a pointer to your scope and results panes, it needs to have the `CSnap-inObjectRootBaseClass` available so it can have a base class to point to.

Now we move on to those strange templates with names ending in `Impl<>`. Apart from `CSnap-inItemImpl<>`, these are ATL's implementations for the relevant interfaces. They all take as a template parameter your class that object wizard has given to you to customize. There are several of them, not all of them covered here. The complete list is:

Interface	ATL Class
`IComponent`	`IComponentImpl<>`
`IComponentData`	`IComponentDataImpl<>`
`IExtendContextMenu`	`IExtendContextMenuImpl<>`
`IExtendControlbar`	`IExtendControlbarImpl<>`
`IExtendPropertySheet`	`IExtendPropertySheetImpl<>`

You'll notice that in the figures these classes are derived from the interface they implement. As usual the interface C++ class itself (`IComponent`, `IComponentData` etc.) is simply an abstract base class generated by MIDL.

The Data Object

The implementation of the Data Object isn't going to concern us much because we don't have to fiddle with it at all: ATLs implementation is complete, and not related to our own customizable classes. However we will note that the data object references, indirectly via an `ObjectData` structure, a `CSnap-inItem` instance. Recall that the data object exists only for the transfer of data and is always based on a particular snap-in object. Well the simplest way to do it is to have the data object contain a pointer to a snap-in object, from which the object can be retrieved in calls to `GetDataHere()`. The `CObjectData` class is literally a structure that contains no methods: it's simply a convenient way of wrapping a snap-in item with an integer that gives information about its type.

The Data Object is also used by the node to obtain some information about the node types – the CLSID of a node. This won't concern us, but we will note that in general `IDataObject` passes data using clipboard formats, a relic from its use in OLE. This means that a number of standard MMC clipboard formats need to be registered. This is done by means of a static initialization function in `CSnap-inItem`, and the formats are stored in some static variables in `CSnap-inItem`.

The Snap-In Item

CMySnap-inData, inherited through CSnap-inItemImpl<> is where almost all the action happens. The idea is that an instance of CMySnap-inData really encapsulates an instance of the underlying object represented by a node. Since this object may at different times be displayed in either the scope or the result pane, it wouldn't be appropriate to associate the object too closely with either the scope or result pane objects. The scope pane object does however contain a public pointer to one CMySnap-inData instance. This is best interpreted as the snap-in item represented by the root node. Since the CMySnap-inComponent instance contains a pointer to the scope pane object, the results pane object can get access to this root snap-in item as well.

Many of the methods in IComponentData and IComponent take the cookie that identifies the appropriate snap-in item as an [in] parameter. The ATL implementations of these methods in IComponentDataImpl<> and IComponentImpl<> generally simply track down the appropriate snap-in item identified by the supplied cookie (or the supplied data object) and call up corresponding methods in the CMySnap-inData instance. In ATL, the cookie is simply a pointer to a CSnap-inItem, cast to an LPARAM, so recovering the snap-in item from the cookie is trivial. If the cookie supplied is NULL, then according to the MMC convention that a NULL cookie references the root item, the appropriate CSnap-inItem is the one referenced by the m_pNode variable of CSnap-inObjectRoot. Otherwise, we simply dereference the cookie by using the C++ * operator on the pointer.

I've mentioned that SCOPEDATAITEM and RESULTDATAITEM structures are used quite a bit in data transfer. The CSnap-inItemImpl<> class makes this easy for us by keeping a member variable of each type, m_scopeDataItem and m_resultDataItem. These variables are initialized in the wizard-generated constructor of CMySnap-inData, with the lparam set to *this so that the cookie points to its containing snap-in item. Stepping forward a bit and seeing how that works in the StarAdminTool, we find this wizard-generated code:

```
CStarAdminData()
{
    // Image indexes may need to be modified depending on the images specific to
    // the snap-in.
    memset(&m_scopeDataItem, 0, sizeof(SCOPEDATAITEM));
    m_scopeDataItem.mask = SDI_STR | SDI_IMAGE | SDI_OPENIMAGE | SDI_PARAM;
    m_scopeDataItem.displayname = MMC_CALLBACK;
    m_scopeDataItem.nImage = 0;          // May need modification
    m_scopeDataItem.nOpenImage = 0;      // May need modification
    m_scopeDataItem.lParam = (LPARAM) this;
    memset(&m_resultDataItem, 0, sizeof(RESULTDATAITEM));
    m_resultDataItem.mask = RDI_STR | RDI_IMAGE | RDI_PARAM;
    m_resultDataItem.str = MMC_CALLBACK;
    m_resultDataItem.nImage = 0;         // May need modification
    m_resultDataItem.lParam = (LPARAM) this;
}
```

Without going into too much detail (you can look up the precise meanings of all the parameters in MSDN), notice how the mask is set to indicate those member variables which are being explicitly set.

The Snap-inAbout object

CMySnap-inAbout is the simplest to deal with. It's the classic ATL object model, of a customizable class derived from CComObjectRoot<>, CComCoClass<>, and the COM interface, in this case ISnap-inAbout. There's no difference here from the structure you'd get if you created a plain vanilla COM object using object wizard.

Adding a Snap-in Item Hierarchy

This snap-in really has just four underlying types of item: the list of fans, the web page, the root node (representing the snap-in itself), and the individual fans. We need to represent all these by CSnap-inItem-derived classes – and since these all behave in slightly different ways we're going to implement them using virtual functions. We'll treat the CStarAdminData class as an abstract base class and derive four other classes from it:

- ❑ **CStarAdminRoot** represents the root node
- ❑ **CStarAdminWroxPage** represents the web page item
- ❑ **CStarAdminFans** represents the node which contains the fans
- ❑ **CStarAdminFansRow** represents each individual fan – in other words one row in the results pane when we're displaying the fans.

In most of these classes we will need to override CStarAdminData::Notify() to respond correctly to notifications. In addition, CStarAdminWroxPage will need to override the GetResultViewType method. This is a method in IComponent called by the console to check what needs to be displayed in the result pane for that item. The implementation in CSnap-inItemImpl<> tells the console to display a list view, but CStarAdminWroxPage needs to tell the console to display a web page.

Individual fans are only displayed in the results pane, not the scope pane – so for them we don't need to override the do-nothing implementation of Notify(). But we do need to override another function, which tells the console what text to display in the different columns of the results pane, GetResultPaneColInfo().

We'll need to sort out the constructors and destructors of these classes as well. The way it's going to work is that when an instance of CStarAdminRoot is created, it will automatically create the complete tree of snap-in items, corresponding to the tree displayed in the scope pane. This tree will automatically be destroyed in the destructors for our derived snap-in items.

To achieve all this, we create new files called `StarAdminDerived.h` and `StarAdminDerived.cpp`. These files will contain the definitions and implementations of all the new classes. The definitions in `StarToolsDerived.h` are:

```cpp
// CStarAdminRoot

class CStarAdminRoot : public CStarAdminData
{

public:
   CStarAdminRoot();
   virtual ~CStarAdminRoot();

   STDMETHOD(Notify)( MMC_NOTIFY_TYPE event,
       long arg,
       long param,
       IComponentData* pComponentData,
       IComponent* pComponent,
       DATA_OBJECT_TYPES type);

// the child snap-in items
   CStarAdminWroxPage *m_pWroxPage;
   CStarAdminFans *m_pAdminFans;
};


// CStarAdminWroxPage

class CStarAdminWroxPage : public CStarAdminData
{
public:
   CStarAdminWroxPage();
   virtual ~CStarAdminWroxPage();

  STDMETHOD(GetResultViewType)(LPOLESTR *ppViewType,
     long *pViewOptions);
};


// CStarFansRow

class CStarAdminFansRow : public CStarAdminData
{
public:
   CStarAdminFansRow();
   CStarAdminFansRow(LPOLESTR pszName, LPOLESTR pszAddress);
   virtual LPOLESTR GetResultPaneColInfo(int nCol);

private:
   CComBSTR m_bstrAddress;
};


// CStarFans
```

```
class CStarAdminFans : public CStarAdminData
{
public:
    CStarAdminFans();
    virtual ~CStarAdminFans();

    STDMETHOD(Notify)( MMC_NOTIFY_TYPE event,
        long arg,
        long param,
        IComponentData* pComponentData,
        IComponent* pComponent,
        DATA_OBJECT_TYPES type);

private:
    CTypedPtrArray<CPtrArray, CStarAdminFansRow*> m_arrTheFans;
};
```

Responding to Notifications

Let's have a look at the Notify() function. This will actually have calls from the console to both
IComponentData::Notify() and IComponent::Notify() passed through to it, so it needs to
be able to handle notifications sent to the scope and results panes. The wizard has generated a fairly
large Notify() method in CStarAdmin, the guts of which are a large switch statement that
distinguishes the more important messages. It looks like:

```
HRESULT CStarAdminData::Notify( MMC_NOTIFY_TYPE event,
    long arg,
    long param,
    IComponentData* pComponentData,
    IComponent* pComponent,
    DATA_OBJECT_TYPES type)
{
    // Add code to handle the different notifications.
    // Handle MMCN_SHOW and MMCN_EXPAND to enumerate children items.
    // In response to MMCN_SHOW you have to enumerate both the scope
    // and result pane items.
    // For MMCN_EXPAND you only need to enumerate the scope items
    // Use IConsoleNameSpace::InsertItem to insert scope pane items
    // Use IResultData::InsertItem to insert result pane item.
    HRESULT hr = E_NOTIMPL;


    _ASSERTE(pComponentData != NULL || pComponent != NULL);

    CComPtr<IConsole> spConsole;
    CComQIPtr<IHeaderCtrl, &IID_IHeaderCtrl> spHeader;
    if (pComponentData != NULL)
        spConsole = ((CStarAdmin*)pComponentData)->m_spConsole;
    else
    {
        spConsole = ((CStarAdminComponent*)pComponent)->m_spConsole;
        spHeader = spConsole;
    }
```

```
    switch (event)
    {
    case MMCN_SHOW:
        {
            CComQIPtr<IResultData, &IID_IResultData> spResultData(spConsole);
            // TODO : Enumerate the result pane items
            hr = S_OK;
            break;
        }
    case MMCN_EXPAND:
        {
            CComQIPtr<IConsoleNameSpace, &IID_IConsoleNameSpace>
spConsoleNameSpace(spConsole);
            // TODO : Enumerate scope pane items
            hr = S_OK;
            break;
        }
    case MMCN_ADD_IMAGES:
        {
            // Add Images
            IImageList* pImageList = (IImageList*) arg;
            hr = E_FAIL;
            // Load bitmaps associated with the scope pane
            // and add them to the image list
            // Loads the default bitmaps generated by the wizard
            // Change as required
            HBITMAP hBitmap16 = LoadBitmap(_Module.GetResourceInstance(),
MAKEINTRESOURCE(IDB_STARADMINTOOL_16));
            if (hBitmap16 != NULL)
            {
                HBITMAP hBitmap32 = LoadBitmap(_Module.GetResourceInstance(),
MAKEINTRESOURCE(IDB_STARADMINTOOL_32));
                if (hBitmap32 != NULL)
                {
                    hr = pImageList->ImageListSetStrip((long*)hBitmap16,
                    (long*)hBitmap32, 0, RGB(0, 128, 128));
                    if (FAILED(hr))
                        ATLTRACE(_T("IImageList::ImageListSetStrip failed\n"));
                }
            }
            break;
        }
    }
    return hr;
}
```

The lines at the top of this function grab a pointer to the `IConsole` interface in the console. The
reason why it looks in `pComponent` and `pComponentData` for it is that
`IStarAdminToolData::Notify()` can be called through from either
`IComponentImpl::Notify()` or `IComponentDataImpl::Notify()`. Let's take a quick look at
the definition of `IComponent::Notify()`. (The definition of `IComponentData::Notify()` is
identical.)

```
STDMETHOD(Notify)(LPDATAOBJECT lpDataObject,
        MMC_NOTIFY_TYPE event, long arg, long param) = 0
```

The parameter list is quite similar to that of `IStarAdminToolData::Notify()`. What happens is that the scope pane object figures out which snap-in item is required from the parameter `lpDataObject`, and passes the remaining parameters to `IStarAdminToolData::Notify()`. It also passes a pointer to itself in `pComponentData`, to allow the snap in object to get to the console. The result pane object does the same, except it passes a pointer to itself via `pComponent`. So the first thing the snap-in item has to do is figure out which pointer contains valid data so it can grab a pointer to the console.

We then enter the switch statement. The one case for which ATL has provided an implementation for us is when the console is asking for the indices of the images to be displayed next to an item. ATL has generated a couple of nice ATL icons for us – pictures of ATL made from blocks, which you can see in the StarAdminTool screenshots.

ATL has also added some comments for us reminding us to add our own message handlers for when we are asked to display an object (`MMCN_SHOW` notification) and expand a node in the tree view (`MMCN_EXPAND` notification). We're not going to modify this function as ATL suggests. Instead we'll override it, since we've got several different C++ classes that need different implementations of this function.

For `CStarAdminRoot`, the override needs to tell the console about the other two nodes below it. It does this by calling the method `IConsoleNamespace::InsertItem()`. Recall that `IConsoleNamespace` is one of the interfaces exposed by the console. Here's how we do it:

```
STDMETHODIMP CStarAdminRoot :: Notify( MMC_NOTIFY_TYPE event,
    long arg,
    long param,
    IComponentData* pComponentData,
    IComponent* pComponent,
    DATA_OBJECT_TYPES type)
{
    // this stuff - getting a pointer to the IConsole is just cut and
    // pasted from the code in CStarAdminData
    HRESULT hr = E_NOTIMPL;

    _ASSERTE(pComponentData != NULL || pComponent != NULL);

    CComPtr<IConsole> spConsole;
    CComQIPtr<IHeaderCtrl, &IID_IHeaderCtrl> spHeader;
    if (pComponentData != NULL)
        spConsole = ((CStarAdmin*)pComponentData)->m_spConsole;
    else
    {
        spConsole = ((CStarAdmin*)pComponent)->m_spConsole;
        spHeader = spConsole;
    }
```

```
    switch (event)
    {
    case MMCN_EXPAND:
    {
        CComQIPtr<IConsoleNameSpace, &IID_IConsoleNameSpace>
spConsoleNameSpace(spConsole);
        AddScopeItem(spConsoleNameSpace, param, m_pAdminFans);
        AddScopeItem(spConsoleNameSpace, param, m_pWroxPage);
        hr = S_OK;
        return hr;
    }
    default:
        return CStarAdminData::Notify(event, arg, param,
            pComponentData, pComponent, type);
    }
}
```

There's no need to provide any overrides to MMCN_SHOW in this case because the root node has nothing to display in the results pane. The console will by default show a list of its children. In order to tell the console about the child items, I've used a little helper function I've written called AddScopeItem(). It's definition looks like:

```
void CStarAdminRoot :: AddScopeItem(
        CComQIPtr<IConsoleNameSpace, &IID_IConsoleNameSpace> spConsoleNameSpace,
        HSCOPEITEM param,
        CStarAdminData *pNewData)
{
    HRESULT hr;
    pNewData->m_scopeDataItem.mask |= SDI_PARENT;
    pNewData->m_scopeDataItem.relativeID = (HSCOPEITEM)param;
    pNewData->m_bstrDisplayName = SysAllocString(pNewData->m_bstrDisplayName);
    hr = spConsoleNameSpace->InsertItem(&pNewData->m_scopeDataItem);
    _ASSERTE(SUCCEEDED(hr));
}
```

This calls the InsertItem() method of IConsoleNamespace. InsertItem() needs to be told about the new item by means of a SCOPEDATAITEM structure, so we just grab the one out of the snap-in item corresponding to the child node we want to add. We do a bit more initialization on it to make sure the console gets all the right information. The SDI_PARENT flag in the mask tells the console to insert the node as a child of the one with the supplied HSCOPEITEM (as opposed to – say, immediately before or after it).

CStarAdminWroxPage doesn't need to provide any override for Notify(); it's got no children below it to expand when it receives an MMCN_EXPAND message, and nothing to display in response to MMCN_SHOW because it's displaying a web page.

That leaves CStarAdminFans. This one is a bit more complicated because we need to actually fill in the data in the list view.

Showing a ListView in the Results Pane

We'll only show the code here for `CStarAdminFans` since the response to the way we do this is pretty much identical for both classes. It must respond to `MMCN_SHOW` by adding the list of fans to the list view. That means it has to generate the list of fans in the first place.

We've said each fan is represented by another `CSnap-in` derived object, `CStarAdminFansRow`. You might wonder why we're doing this for an object that isn't ever displayed in the tree hierarchy of the snap in. The reason is to do with the way the ATL snap-in classes work: When the console tries to display the list view, it will expect to call a method, `IComponent::GetResultData()`, for each row. `GetResultData` receives a `RESULTDATAITEM` structure, to be filled in. In theory, we could use the `nItem` and `nCol` parameters of this structure to uniquely identify the row and column for which data is required. However, ATL is a bit awkward in this regard. It internally routes the call to a function, `CStarAdmin::GetResultColInfo()`, and loses all the identifiers except for the column number on the way. This means that the only possible way we can uniquely identify the row for which the text is being requested is by having a separate snap-in item for each row.

The `CStarAdminFansRow` class is very simple. It internally stores the fan's address, as well as the name, which is wrapped up in the `m_bstrDisplayName` variable declared in `CSnap-inItemImpl<>`. `GetResultPaneColInfo()` is the function that returns the text for the given column, and is called internally by ATL.

The implementation of `CStarAdminFansRow` looks like:

```
CStarAdminFansRow:: CStarAdminFansRow(LPOLESTR pszName, LPOLESTR pszAddress)
:    m_bstrAddress(pszAddress)
{
    m_bstrDisplayName = pszName;
}


LPOLESTR CStarAdminFansRow::GetResultPaneColInfo(int nCol)
{
    if (nCol == 0)
        return m_bstrDisplayName;
    else
        return m_bstrAddress;
}
```

To get this class working we need to make one change to the wizard-generated code in `CStarAdminData`. The function `CStarAdminData::GetResultPaneColInfo()` is actually NOT defined as virtual. (Ironically, since if you look at the implementation, you'll see that essentially it returns a string reminding you to override the function!) So we look for its definition in `StarAdminTool.h` and change it to virtual, so that our override to it will correctly be called:

```
virtual LPOLESTR GetResultPaneColInfo(int nCol);
```

That's the class that prints the individual rows sorted out. We just need to set up `CStarAdminFans` so that it initializes itself with data from the StarRaiders directory, creates all the `CStarToolCustomerRow` instances, and tells the console about them when it's asked about what to display in the results pane.

To store the `CStarAdminFans` instances, we'll create a new member variable in `CStarAdminFans`:

```
class CStarAdminFans : public CStarAdminData
{
public:
// stuff commented out for clarity

private:
    CTypedPtrArray<CPtrArray, CStarAdminFansRow*> m_arrTheFans;
};
```

This variable is the sole reason why I wanted this snap-in to support MFC!

We need to fill this array when the `CStarAdminFans` class is created. This is the one part of the snap-in that makes use of ADSI.

```
CStarAdminFans :: CStarAdminFans()
{
    // set the name
    m_bstrDisplayName = _T("StarRaiders Fans");

    // load the data from the StarRaiders directory
    CComQIPtr<IADs, &IID_IADs> spADsFan;
    CComQIPtr<IADsContainer, &IID_IADsContainer> spADsFanContainer;
    CComQIPtr<IEnumVARIANT, &IID_IEnumVARIANT> spEnumerator;
    HRESULT hr;
    hr = ADsGetObject(L"StarRaiders://Fans",
        IID_IADsContainer, (void**)&spADsFanContainer);
    _ASSERTE(SUCCEEDED(hr));
    hr = ADsBuildEnumerator(spADsFanContainer, &spEnumerator);

    // enumerate through all the fans
    CComVariant var;
    ULONG cElementsFetched;
    CStarAdminFansRow *pRow;
    do
    {
        hr = ADsEnumerateNext(spEnumerator, 1, &var, &cElementsFetched);
        _ASSERTE(SUCCEEDED(hr));
        if (hr == S_OK)
        {
            // extract the name and address from the ADSI object
            spADsFan = var.pdispVal;
```

```
            CComBSTR bstrName;
            hr = spADsFan->get_Name(&bstrName);
            hr = spADsFan->Get(L"Address", &var);
            if (SUCCEEDED(hr))
            {
                // create a new CStarAdminCustomerRow object and add it to the list of
rows
                pRow = new CStarAdminFansRow(bstrName, var.bstrVal);
                m_arrTheFans.Add(pRow);
            }
        }

    }
    while (hr == S_OK);

}
```

The final thing to do to get the list view to display is to tell the console that two rows are needed in the list view, and to give it the cookies for all the `CStarToolCustomerRow` instances. The console needs this information when it sends the `CStarAdminFans` instance an `MMCN_SHOW` message. So here's how we respond:

```
STDMETHODIMP CStarAdminFans :: Notify( MMC_NOTIFY_TYPE event,
    long arg,
    long param,
    IComponentData* pComponentData,
    IComponent* pComponent,
    DATA_OBJECT_TYPES type)
{
    // Add code to handle the different notifications.
    // Handle MMCN_SHOW and MMCN_EXPAND to enumerate children items.
    // In response to MMCN_SHOW you have to enumerate both the scope
    // and result pane items.
    // For MMCN_EXPAND you only need to enumerate the scope items
    // Use IConsoleNameSpace::InsertItem to insert scope pane items
    // Use IResultData::InsertItem to insert result pane item.
    HRESULT hr = E_NOTIMPL;


    _ASSERTE(pComponentData != NULL || pComponent != NULL);

    CComPtr<IConsole> spConsole;
    CComQIPtr<IHeaderCtrl, &IID_IHeaderCtrl> spHeader;
    if (pComponentData != NULL)
        spConsole = ((CStarAdmin*)pComponentData)->m_spConsole;
    else
    {
        spConsole = ((CStarAdminComponent*)pComponent)->m_spConsole;
        spHeader = spConsole;
    }
```

```
        switch (event)
        {
        case MMCN_SHOW:
            {
                CComQIPtr<IResultData, &IID_IResultData> spResultData(spConsole);
                // TODO : Enumerate the result pane items
                // the case MMCN_SHOW only occurs when the console is asking
                // to be told what to display in the results pane, and only then in
                // the case where it has to display a list view. Since we've only
                // got one object for which this can happen, we just display the
                // stuff for that object

                // this stuff sets up two columns in the results pane, for the
                // person's name and phone extension

                spHeader->InsertColumn(0, _T("Name"), LVCFMT_LEFT, 200);
                spHeader->InsertColumn(1, _T("Address"), LVCFMT_LEFT, 200);
                // and these lines actually add the sample data to the list view
                for (int i=0 ; i<m_Customers.GetSize() ; i++)
                    spResultData->InsertItem(&m_Customers[i]->m_resultDataItem);
                hr = S_OK;
                return hr;
            }
        default:
            return CStarAdminData::Notify(
                event, arg, param, pComponentData, pComponent, type);
        }
    }
```

Although it's buried in quite a large function, the code to do all this is fairly simple. We first obtain a pointer to the `IHeaderCtrl` interface on the console. This is the interface that allows us to tell the console what to put in the headers for the list control. We insert two columns, both of width 200 pixels, using `IHeaderCtrl::InsertColumn()`. The first parameter to this function is the index of the column and the second is the text to be displayed in the header. The `LVCFMT_LEFT` parameters simply indicate that the columns should be left-justified.

Once we've added the headers, we simply add all the items using another interface on the console, `IResultData`. This interface lets us control the individual rows in the results pane, to perform tasks such as inserting or deleting rows. In this case `InsertItem()` is the method we want, and as I mentioned it takes a `RESULTDATAITEM` structure that describes the row.

Displaying a Web Page

We need to sort out the node which displays a web page. This is done by overriding the `GetResultViewType()` method. This is another method which is exposed by `IComponent`, but ATL's implementation hands the implementation of it to the snap-in item class. When the console calls this method, it expects the values of two parameters to get filled in: an integer, `*pViewOptions`, which should have an enumeration value placed in it to indicate the type of view to be displayed, and a string that should have any additional information put in it. In addition, the console expects the method to return `S_FALSE` if a standard list view is to be displayed, and `S_OK`, if the snap-in wants to display another type of view.

ATL's implementation of this function, in `CSnap-inItemImpl<>`, looks like this:

```
STDMETHOD(GetResultViewType)(LPOLESTR *ppViewType,
  long *pViewOptions)
  {
    ATLTRACE2(atlTraceSnap-in, 0, _T("CSnap-inItemImpl::GetResultViewType\n"));
    *ppViewType = NULL;
    *pViewOptions = MMC_VIEW_OPTIONS_NONE;
    return S_FALSE;
  }
```

Apart from the trace statement used for debugging to record that this method has been called, this implementation simply sets the parameters to indicate that this item wants a list view to be displayed. The full list of options you can set in `ppViewType` is (from MSDN)

Value	Meaning
MMC_VIEW_OPTIONS_NOLISTVIEWS = 0x0001	Tells the console to refrain from presenting standard list view choices in the View menu. Allows the snap-in to display its own custom views only in the result view pane.
MMC_VIEW_OPTIONS_OWNERDATALIST = 0x0002	Specifies that the result pane list view should be a virtual list.
MMC_VIEW_OPTIONS_MULTISELECT = 0x0004	Allows multiple item selections in the result pane view.
MMC_VIEW_OPTIONS_NONE = 0	Default value. Displays a standard list view.

Armed with this knowledge we can now write our override for `GetResultViewType` to display a web page. Here it is:

```
STDMETHODIMP CStarAdminWroxPage :: GetResultViewType(LPOLESTR *ppViewType,
    long *pViewOptions)
{
  CComBSTR bstrURL = L"http://www.wrox.com";
  *ppViewType = (LPOLESTR)CoTaskMemAlloc(sizeof(OLECHAR)*(bstrURL.Length()+1));
  wcscpy(*ppViewType, bstrURL);
  *pViewOptions = MMC_VIEW_OPTIONS_NOLISTVIEWS;
  return S_OK;
}
```

The one other significant point to note about this is that, although we are returning a string in the parameter `ppViewType`, we need to use `CoTaskMemAlloc()`, *not* `SysAllocString()` to allocate it. The string is `NULL` for a standard list view, or the URL for a web page. If you want to display an ActiveX control instead, you can do this by simply passing the CLSID of the control in the string here – you won't need to do anything else beyond make sure your control is registered.

Initializing the Root Node in the Scope Pane

We're not quite done yet. We still have to write the constructor for the root snap-in item. But the code for that is pretty simple.

```
CStarAdminRoot :: CStarAdminRoot()
{
    // set the name
    m_bstrDisplayName = _T("StarRaiders Admin Tool");
    // create the child objects
    m_pAdminFans = new CStarAdminFans;
    m_pWroxPage = new CStarAdminWroxPage;
}
```

We also need to modify the constructor of the scope pane object so that it creates an instance of CStarAdminRoot instead of CStarAdminData. So locate the function in StarAdminTool.h and make the changes:

```
CStarAdmin()
{
    m_pNode = new CStarAdminRoot;
    _ASSERTE(m_pNode != NULL);
    m_pComponentData = this;
}
```

At this point the StarAdminTool is in a position to be compiled. If you build it, you will find you can navigate around the tree control quite comfortably. The one thing we haven't yet done is add our context menu item. That's our next task.

Cleaning Up

Finally we need to remove all the extra memory we've allocated for the various CSnapInItem-derived classes that we've created to populate the tree. This is done in the destructors.

```
CStarAdminFans :: ~CStarAdminFans()
{
    while (m_arrTheFans.GetSize() > 0)
    {
        delete m_arrTheFans.GetAt(0);
        m_arrTheFans.RemoveAt(0);
    }
}

CStarAdminRoot :: ~CStarAdminRoot()
{
    delete m_pAdminFans;
    delete m_pWroxPage;
}
```

Adding Menu Items

MMC is quite flexible in letting us add menu items, but it does have guidelines. We can't just add whatever we want wherever we want: if that was the case, MMC would lose a lot of the consistency between snap-ins that is one of its best selling points.

If you look at a blank MMC console you'll see five menus: Console, Window and Help, which are supplied by the main window, and Action and View, which are supplied by the child windows. Console, Window and Help are out of bounds as far as snap-ins are concerned. Console and Window are concerned with operations affecting the console as a whole, rather than any individual snap-in. The Console menu contains items to do with adding and removing snap-ins and saving Management Saved Console files. The Window menu contains options to do with the management of windows (such as whether they are tiled or cascaded). The meaning of help should be obvious!

The View menu is somewhat more interesting. It has options to allow the user to choose how the views display information, such as whether a list view is displayed in list, large icon, small icon or detail mode. The user can also use this menu to close the scope pane completely, and look at only the results pane. Snap-ins are allowed to add menu items to the end of the View menu. They might wish to do this, for example to allow the user to select between viewing an item using a listview or a taskpad. We won't be doing this however.

As far as we are concerned, the Action menu is where all the action is. Let's have a look at it in more detail. This is the Action menu as displayed by the event viewer snap-in. I'm using an existing snap-in rather than the StarRaiders admin one for this screenshot so you can see a menu with items added by the snap-in.

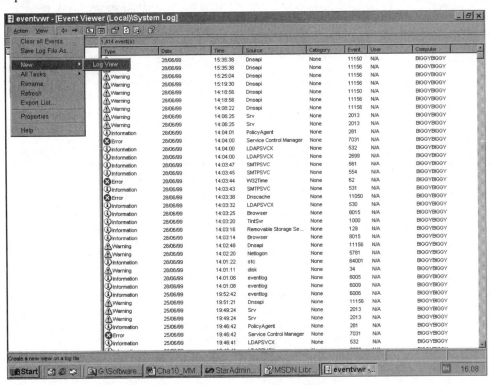

There are three places we are allowed to add menu items here. At the top of this menu, and as submenu options of the New and All Tasks items. Items that go at the top of the Action menu should be those operations that need to be highly visible. Items that are used less frequently, or which you want to be slightly more hidden, go in the All Tasks submenu. Actions that involve creating new objects should go in the New submenu. In the example shown above, Clear All Events and Save Log File As have been added by the Event Viewer snap-in, while the other menu items were supplied by the console.

There is one other respect in which the Action menu is interesting: items on it are reproduced in the context menu. Consequently, we don't need to add items to the Action menu and the context menus as separate tasks.

Snap-ins can also make one more change to the Action menu. They can determine whether or not the Properties item should be there. If it is there, then the snap-in needs to supply property sheets for the selected object. But we'll cover that in more detail in the next section.

To go over how to add menu items, we'll go over the process for adding a new customer. We want the administrator to be able to do this by right clicking whilst the Customers node is selected in the scope pane. To see how to do this, we need to know both how to implement context menus in MMC, and how ATL helps us to implement them.

Context Menus in MMC

If the user right clicks over an item in the scope pane, then the console will `QueryInterface()` the scope pane object for `IExtendContextMenu`. (If the user right-clicks in the result pane, it'll be the result pane object that gets that dreaded `QueryInterface()` call...). If the object supports that interface, then the console will call the method `IExtendContextMenu::AddMenuItems()`. The definition of this method in IDL is:

```
[helpstring("Extension may add context menu items via callback interface")]
    HRESULT AddMenuItems([in] LPDATAOBJECT piDataObject,
               [in]  LPCONTEXTMENUCALLBACK piCallback,
               [in,out] long *pInsertionAllowed);
```

Calling this method is the console's way of asking the snap-in for the menu items. It passes in a pointer to an `IContextMenuCallback` interface, which the snap-in can use to call back if it wants to add the menu items. The `LPDATAOBJECT` and `LPCONTEXTMENUCALLBACK`, are just alternative names for the interface pointers `IDataObject*` and `IContextMenuCallback*`.

`IContextMenuCallback` exposes a method, `AddItem`, defined as:

```
[helpstring("Adds one item to context menu")]
    HRESULT AddItem([in] CONTEXTMENUITEM* pItem);
```

The parameter is a pointer to another C-style structure, `CONTEXTMENUITEM`. We don't need to go into this in detail, but suffice to say that among its members are a string, which will be the text displayed for that menu item, an ID to identify the item, and an integer that indicates to which of the four locations in which the snap-in is allowed to add menus this item should go.

That takes care of adding the items. What happens if the user actually selects one of the snap-in's menu items? In this case, the console informs the snap-in by calling the method `IExtendContextMenu::Command()`. This method takes a single parameter, the ID of the menu item that was originally passed to the console inside the `CONTEXTMENUITEM`:

```
[helpstring("Extension context menu item was selected")]
    HRESULT Command([in] long lCommandID, [in] LPDATAOBJECT piDataObject);
```

The snap-in will use this ID to determine what menu item was selected and take the appropriate action.

Context Menus in ATL

ATL actually does almost all the work for you in adding menu items. The only snag is that the process of calling up a context menu involves a couple of functions in the snap-in item base classes. We will need to override these functions, but they have *not* been declared as virtual in the ATL code; our decision (oh OK, I'll admit it, my decision) to derive classes from `CStarAdminData` will muck up the context menus – we'll need to work around that, but that's not too hard to do.

Before we start on our workaround, let's see what would normally happen:

The ATL MMC Object Wizard creates a menu resource for you:

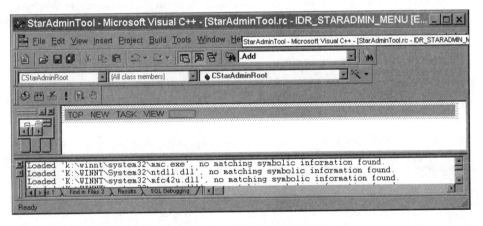

The menu contains four items, TOP, NEW, TASK and VIEW. These are supposed to correspond to top of the action menu, inside the New and All Tasks submenus of the Action menu, and at the bottom of the View menu. All you have to do is add menu items below these headers, just as you would do for any other menu resource, and ATL, by means of code in `CSnap-inItemImpl<>`, will make sure that these items get added to the appropriate place when `IExtendContextMenu` is called.

The only other thing you've got to do is add your command handlers. ATL makes this easy for you with a couple of macro definitions. If you look in your definition of `CStarAdminData`, you'll see the following:

```
class CStarAdminData : public CSnap-inItemImpl<CStarAdminData>
{
public:
    static const GUID* m_NODETYPE;
    static const OLECHAR* m_SZNODETYPE;
    static const OLECHAR* m_SZDISPLAY_NAME;
    static const CLSID* m_SNAP-IN_CLASSID;

    CComPtr<IControlbar> m_spControlBar;

    BEGIN_SNAP-INCOMMAND_MAP(CStarAdminData, FALSE)
    END_SNAP-INCOMMAND_MAP()

    SNAP-INMENUID(IDR_STARADMIN_MENU)
```

The line `SNAP-INMENUID` indicates which menu to use. The integer `IDR_STARADMIN_MENU` is the ID of the menu that object wizard has generated for you. The lines `BEGIN_SNAP-INCOMMAND_MAP` and `END_SNAP-INCOMMAND_MAP` delimit a map, in which you add macros to direct particular menu items to particular command handling functions.

For example, say I'd added two menu items somewhere (it doesn't matter whether they're under TOP, NEW, TASK, or VIEW), **Big Hug**, with the ID `IDR_MENU_BIGHUG`, and **SayTubbyByeBye**, with the ID `IDR_MENU_SAYTUBBYBYEBYE`. Then in order to process these you'd change the command map to something like:

```
BEGIN_SNAP-INCOMMAND_MAP(CStarAdminData, FALSE)
    SNAP-INCOMMAND_ENTRY(IDR_MENU_BIGHUG, CommandBigHug)
    SNAP-INCOMMAND_ENTRY(ID_MENU_SAYTUBBYBYEBYE, CommandSayTubbyByeBye)
END_SNAP-INCOMMAND_MAP()
```

Internally, the command map macros expand out to a function called `ProcessCommand()` containing a big switch statement that calls up the appropriate command handler function depending on the command ID. You need to supply the command handler, which must take the form:

```
HRESULT CMySnap-inData :: CommandHandler(bool &bHandled, CSnap-inObjectRootBase
*pObj)
```

The parameter `bHandled` indicates whether or not command processing can be regarded as now complete. If it is false on return from the function, command processing will carry on through the command map, otherwise `ProcessCommand()` will return. The `SNAP-INMENUID` macro expands to a static function `GetMenuID()`, which returns the supplied resource ID.

So in theory, the work you have to do to implement this is very simple. Edit a resource, add a couple of macros, and supply your command handler function to do whatever you want.

The trouble with this is that it gives you a command handler in the wizard-generated `CMySnap-inData` class. This doesn't let you either to provide command handlers in derived classes, or arrange for different nodes to expose different context menus. So the next step is for us to be clever and implement context menus in StarAdminTool that gets around both limitations.

Coding up Context Menus

We're going to add a context menu which we want to be available *only* to the root snap-in item (the one represented by the static StarAdmin node, not to any of the dynamic nodes below it. I'm going to call this menu **Add Fan**, on the pretext that this is supposed to be the StarRaiders administration tool, and one of the tasks you might want to do is add a new fan to the directory whenever someone else subscribes. But because I'm only really interested in showing you how to add a message handler, all the command handler will do is display a message box – it won't actually do anything.

The first step is to provide a context menu that will only be available to the root snap-in item. Actually this part is quite easy. We simply create a new menu in the resource editor, with the same TOP, NEW, TASK and VIEW items. We want to provide a command to add new customers. This is a prominent task, so we'll add it to the TOP menu. So under TOP, add a menu item with the text Add Fan, and the ID `IDR_MENU_ROOT_TOP_ADDFAN`.

Now we need to add a `SNAP-IN_MENUID` macro to our `CStarAdminRoot` class to identify this new menu. Or hang on, do we? Remember what I said about ATL's implementation not being able to handle derived classes? Let's examine the definition of `SNAP-INMENUID` in more detail. It's in `atlsnap.h`:

```
#define SNAP-INMENUID(id) \
public: \
   static const UINT GetMenuID() \
   { \
      static const UINT IDMENU = id; \
      return id; \
   }
```

So this macro simply defines a function, `GetMenuID()` which returns the ID of your context menu. This function is called during the processing of menus. Unfortunately, it's *not* virtual. If we trace back through the ATL code, we find that `GetMenuID()` is called during the process of adding context menu items, via pointers to the *base* class. So if we attempt to add a new `GetMenuID()` function to `CStarAdminRoot`, it'll simply be missed.

The easiest way to get round this is to define a new macro. So go to `CStarAdmin.h` and add the following code somewhere near the top of the file.

```
#define STAR_SNAP-INMENUID(id) \
public: \
   virtual const UINT GetMenuID() \
   { \
      static const UINT IDMENU = id; \
      return id; \
   }
```

This new macro is identical to the old one, except I've changed the static function to a virtual one. now we're OK. All we need to do is add the macros to our definition of CStarAdminRoot:

```
BEGIN_SNAP-INCOMMAND_MAP(CStarAdminRoot, FALSE)
    SNAP-INCOMMAND_ENTRY(ID_ROOT_TOP_ADDFAN, CommandAddFan)
END_SNAP-INCOMMAND_MAP()

STAR_SNAP-INMENUID(IDR_STARADMINROOT_MENU)
```

We'll also need to replace the SNAP-INMENUID() macro in CStarAdminData with our new macro:

```
BEGIN_SNAP-INCOMMAND_MAP(CStarAdminData, FALSE)
END_SNAP-INCOMMAND_MAP()

STAR_SNAP-INMENUID(IDR_STARADMIN_MENU)
```

We now need to add the command handler to add the new user. This is the function, CommandAddFan, which I've referred to in the SNAP-INCOMMAND_ENTRY macro. This function needs to have the signature:

```
HRESULT CommandAddFan(bool &bHandled, CSnap-inObjectRootBase *pObj);
```

and our implementation is about as easy as you can get...

```
HRESULT CStarAdminRoot :: CommandAddFan(bool &bHandled, CSnap-inObjectRootBase
*pObj)
{
    AfxMessageBox(L"This is the Add Fan handler");
    bHandled = true;
    return S_OK;
}
```

Incidentally, it is worth pointing out that this code, simple though it may be, actually breaks the Microsoft guidelines for using MMC. Dialog boxes should always be modeless and created on separate threads. The reason is that your snap-in may not be the only one loaded, and a modal dialog box on the user interface thread will prevent the user from getting access to not just your snap-in but any other snap-ins that happen to be loaded as well, until the dialog is dismissed.

We're almost finished, but not quite. In fact, if you compile and run the code at this stage, you'll find the context menu item does behave correctly in that it gets added to the top of the context menu, but only if the root item is selected, not if any other item is selected. That's what we want. Unfortunately, if you select this context menu item, our command handler doesn't get called. So we've clearly missed something.

The one missing link in our change is another function that hasn't been declared as virtual. When we select a menu item, ATL ends up executing the CSnap-inItemImpl<>::Command function, which looks like:

```
    STDMETHOD(Command)(long lCommandID,
        CSnap-inObjectRootBase* pObj,
        DATA_OBJECT_TYPES type)
    {
        ATLTRACE2(atlTraceSnap-in, 0, _T("CSnap-inItemImpl::Command\n"));
        bool bHandled;
        T* pT = static_cast<T*>(this);
        return pT->ProcessCommand(lCommandID, bHandled, pObj, type);
    }
}
```

ProcessCommand is a function that is constructed from the menu macros, and it's not virtual. This implementation of Command will therefore always pick up the version defined in the wizard-generated snap-in class, in our case CStarAdminData, referred to as T in the above code.

Our solution relies on the fact that although ProcessCommand isn't virtual, Command is. So we put an override to the Command function in our CStarAdminRoot class:

```
    STDMETHODIMP CStarAdminRoot::Command(long lCommandID,
        CSnap-inObjectRootBase* pObj,
        DATA_OBJECT_TYPES type)
    {
        ATLTRACE2(atlTraceSnap-in, 0, _T("CStarAdminRoot::Command\n"));
        bool bHandled;
        return ProcessCommand(lCommandID, bHandled, pObj, type);
    }
```

This ensures that the correct version of ProcessCommand is called – and our menu handlers, customized for particular snap-in items, will work correctly.

Summary

Well that's MMC for you. We have only skimmed the surface – if you really want to write sophisticated MMC snap-ins, you'll need to investigate most of the other 15-odd MMC interfaces. I've tried to show you what MMC is, and what you can do with your snap-ins. We've seen how the main MMC interfaces work together and pass data around, and how this gets implemented in ATL. We've covered how to write snap-ins using ATL, and even a bit about how to get round some of the more awkward parts of ATL's implementation. We haven't covered stuff like control bars and property sheets, but you'll find they're implemented in ATL in a fairly similar manner to context menus.

But so far we've only covered part of the battle to make sure our apps look like sophisticated software that's ready for the 21st century. The next couple of chapters continue that story by showing you how to make your applications aware of the Windows Installer and the WMI repository.

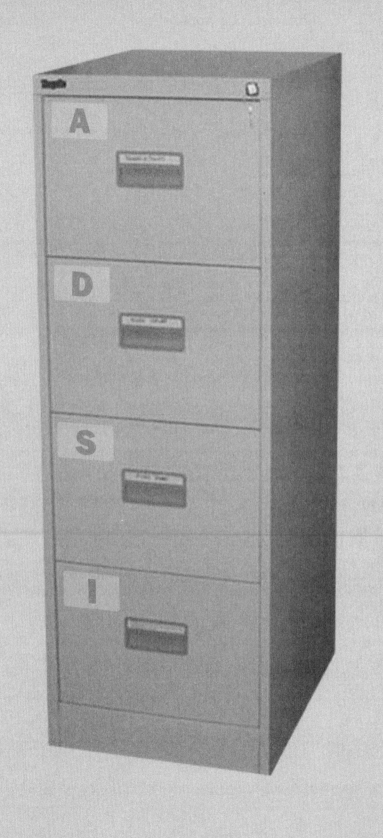

13

Windows Installer

In the last chapter, we looked at how to manage your applications in a standard way in Windows 2000, using Microsoft Management Console. In this chapter, we move on to look at how to install your products in a standard way, using the Windows Installer. You will learn:

❑ What the Windows Installer is and why it is useful

❑ How to write simple installation databases using the Orca tool

❑ About the Windows Installer API

The Windows Installer is a package designed to help with the installation and maintenance of all the software on your system. At its heart is a database for each software package on your system or network that lists all the files and registry entries that package requires. Each database is stored in a binary file in a format the Windows Installer understands.

Notice that I emphasize network here. This is important, since the Windows Installer is quite comfortable with installing a package on a domain as a whole, then letting individual users on the member workstations use this master installation to pick out, install on their own machines, and use the bits that they want.

The Windows Installer comes as an integral part of the operating system with Windows 2000, although it is also available as a separate package for Windows NT4 and 9x. In fact, many of the most recent Microsoft products already use the Windows Installer to install themselves – for example Office 2000 does so, as does the Platform SDK from the June 1999 edition onwards. If you install any of these packages on a pre-Windows 2000 machine, you'll find you get the Windows Installer installed on your system anyway – since these products couldn't install if they didn't put Windows Installer on your system first.

In this chapter, we're going to do three things:

- ❑ Firstly, we're going to take a more detailed look at what is wrong with the process used previously to install software

- ❑ Then we'll take a tour of how the Windows Installer works and how it solves the problems that we'll uncover

- ❑ Finally we'll get down to some coding

We'll show how to use the Windows Installer by writing a small C++ application that uses the Installer API to find out about the products installed on your system. Then we'll actually make sure this application is itself installed correctly, by writing an installation database that the Installer can use to install it.

Why Do We Need Windows Installer?

OK, let's take a look at some of the things that are wrong with the previous system. In other words the way that pre-installer packages install themselves.

Deciding What Components You Want

Say I'm just about to install Office 97 – that's the last version of Microsoft Office that didn't use the Windows Installer. When I try to install it, I get this dialog box, asking me exactly what I want to install:

So far, so good. I know I'm going to use Word, but my disk space is incredibly restricted, so I don't want to install any more stuff than I really need.

So, I click on Change Option to see what components of Word I should install:

Now, here's where my problems start. Text Converters? I remember once I needed to save a document specifically in Word for Windows version 2 format, so an old version of Word on a very old computer could look at it. Unfortunately, I couldn't save the file in the right format because I hadn't installed the right component of Word. I don't want to repeat that problem. Is Text Converters what I need?

The text in the Description in the above screenshot suggests it might be, but I'm really not certain. So what do I do? Do I install it and risk wasting disk space on an unnecessary component, or do I leave it and find later on I need to break off and install it (even then, not knowing if I've correctly identified the component I need).

Of course, at least in that case I'll know if I don't have the right component – Word will simply not present the file type I want as an option in the dialog box that asks me what file types I can save a document as. However, sometimes you don't even have that advantage. For example, if you install Visual Studio 6 in order to write some MFC code, the Unicode libraries are not installed by default – you have to explicitly select to install them. If you don't install them, and attempt a Unicode compile, you'll be met by a series of link errors, which give no indication that the real problem is you didn't install the components of Visual Studio that you need. I've known more than one developer get thrown by that.

The real problem here is that you need to decide what components you need upfront. If you think about it that doesn't make a lot of sense: if you're installing a brand new software package, the chances are you don't yet know all the details of what that package does – you haven't used it yet! So what chance have you got of knowing precisely what bits of it you'll need, in order to do whatever you'll want to do? Not a lot, really.

So one of the first things that it would be nice for an Installer package to do is to offer you some way that you can automatically have things installed when it becomes apparent that you need them – without your having to decide in advance what you want.

Repairing Files

With the best will in the world, files do occasionally get corrupted or lost. Users – dare I say it – have been known to accidentally go in and delete folders that contain essential files needed for software packages. When that happens, things start to get nasty.

Clearly, the packages affected won't work, but it may not be clear why they don't work. The package may complain about a file not being found – or it may simply crash. Even worse, if you try to reinstall it, there's no guarantee of success. Depending on exactly what's been corrupted, and how intelligent the installation/uninstallation program is, it may no longer be possible to reinstall – or even to uninstall – the application. I'm sure there can't be many developers who haven't got into this situation at one time or another. I know there's a few times when I've been driven to reinstalling Windows from scratch in order to get some application (usually Visual Studio...) working again.

Once again, it would be nice if we could have a system in which it was guaranteed that applications would be able to cope somehow with damaged files, so that the package could be repaired. Of course, it would be even nicer if this happened automatically!

Failed Installs

This can have a similar effect to installations getting corrupted later on. The problem will usually involve a network going down, or you running out of disk space during a lengthy install. On occasions, it's happened to me due to faulty MSDN CDs that have some file on them that can't be read. At any rate, the installation fails halfway through for some reason, and you end up with a half-installed package.

Life being what it is, you'll probably find you can't reinstall it because the setup program will think it's already installed. And you can't uninstall it, because the uninstall program can't cope with the package being in this funny half-installed state. Your choice probably comes down to trying to guess which files and registry entries the setup program has made and removing them. Or of course, reinstalling Windows.

In short, the problem really is that there is usually no transaction monitoring: most setup programs don't have any facility to rollback failed installs, and leave your computer in exactly the state it was originally in. We'll add that to the list of improvements we need.

Knowing What's Happening to your Machine

Setup applications written before the Windows Installer are completely custom – in other words they are written by the same third party that wrote the application to be installed. Ideally they follow the Windows guidelines, and they may have been written using a well known package designed to help write installer programs (eg. InstallShield). But the bottom line is that they don't have to follow any standard procedures, and you've no way of knowing what's going on inside the setup program (unless you happened to be the one who wrote it!). The Microsoft documentation likes to describe them as black boxes to indicate this fact. Personally, I think that's not quite accurate. The idea of a black box is that you know exactly what it does – you just don't know (or care) how it does it. That's the idea of COM components and interfaces. You know that if you call a certain method on an interface, it will produce certain results. You're not remotely bothered about what algorithm it goes through to get those results, as long as it works. This is in contrast to a white box, in which you are aware of the internal workings.

Well, with custom setup applications, you're worse off than that – you don't actually know what the setup.exe does. OK, at one level, you might know that it installs a certain product according to specifications you selected, probably by checking various check boxes to indicate which options you wanted. But when it comes to what the application has done to your machine, you don't know anything. There's simply no general way of telling what files it's added to your computer, what other files it may have replaced, or what registry keys it may have written. If the uninstall doesn't quite work properly, and actually leaves stuff on your machine, you're in trouble.

If you're a systems administrator, this isn't too convenient. Usually, it's quite nice to know what is actually on the machines in a domain – what state they're in. At present, there's not even any sure way of finding out what products have been installed on a computer at all! So that's another requirement for the ideal installation package – it should leave some record of what changes it's actually made to the system.

Interaction Between Packages

To some extent, this is related to the problem of not knowing what a given setup program does to your system. The problem is that if you, as the administrator, don't know what a given setup routine does to the computer, then neither does any other setup program for any other product. Each program works pretty much independently.

In principle, things should work as long as every setup program is well behaved. Packages should have no trouble interacting with each other, provided that

1. Each installation program always refcounts every resource it uses, and decrements that refcount on uninstallation

2. Every time a setup program upgrades a resource, the new version is completely backwards compatible with any other applications that may have been using the old version.

Unfortunately when setup programs can be written by anyone, those requirements are difficult to achieve. If any individual setup program is badly written, then you leave yourself open to problems where installing or uninstalling one product causes another product to no longer work.

This is an area that will hopefully improve if installer packages do leave details of what changes have been made to the system.

Locked Down Desktops

A lot of organizations like to lock down their computers. This roughly means that they try to give each user only limited permissions, so that users can't start making too many changes to the configurations of individual computers. That way, the network administrators can make sure that all the computers stay in the same state, which makes for easier administration. It's also important in companies that use roaming computers. In that case, employees don't each have a fixed computer: rather, each employee logs on to the most convenient computer, and expects all the services they normally use to be available on it.

This is fine, except when it comes to installing new software. You see, installing software almost invariably requires administrator privileges on the machine on which the software is to be installed. Registry entries need to be modified, and shared resources, such as dlls, may need to be updated. That means, if your desktops are locked down, it becomes difficult for users to add any new software they need. It's not implausible that one of the network administrators will have to walk round and install the software for the users on all machines that might be used by the people who need that software.

The problem could potentially get worse on Windows 2000, because W2K allows administrators to set quotas on the disk space owned by individual users. If a user is installing an application, and it will be a shared application on a machine that lots of different people use, then you probably don't want that user to have ownership of the files. As well as all the security implications, there's the problem of those files unfairly taking up part of that user's quota.

So we need some mechanism whereby installing products can take place at a higher privilege level than the user doing the installation normally has – so that users with low privileges can still install software.

Introducing the Windows Installer

Well, the Windows Installer does actually solve all the problems we've just mentioned above, and it does this in a very simple way. Before the Installer, each third party (or Microsoft) product would have its own custom-written setup program. With the Windows Installer, it doesn't work like that. Instead, there's a standard program – the Windows Installer itself – which can install or uninstall everything, and each product supplies a database that contains full details of what needs to happen in order for that product to be installed.

> *The Windows Installer runs as an NT Service on Windows NT and Windows 2000, and as a COM server in Windows 9x. (Windows 9x doesn't support NT Services, but for the sake of argument, I'm going to refer to the Installer as a service in this chapter.) Strictly, of course, it is only in Windows 2000 that the installer really is part of the operating system, in the sense that it is supplied with Windows 2000 and the operating system has a special awareness of the existence of this service.*

As far as internal format is concerned, the database is a specialized relational database. It is contained in a file with a .msi (Microsoft Installer) extension. It contains all the information that Windows Installer needs, including what options to offer the user at installation time, and what changes need to be made to the system, to actually do an install according to the options the user selects. The database also gives information on the user interface to be offered to the user during installation.

We're going to quickly go over how this solves all the problems mentioned above, and then we'll take a look at how the Installer actually works.

Deciding What Components You Want

The Installer supports the ability to install on demand (also known as **Just In Time installation**). The details of which files are needed for a certain feature can be put on the system, without those files actually being copied across.

The installer will detect when the user does something that requires those files (or registry entries), and will install them automatically. The most inconvenience the user will suffer is the Installer asking for the CD (or, if the product is installed on a server, connecting to the server) that the product was installed from to be inserted. The installer will then handle everything automatically – the user won't get presented with another dialog box asking what things to install.

Repairing Files

When a certain feature of a product is used, the installer can check that all the required files and registry entries. are present. If anything seems to be missing, the installer will automatically reinstall the affected components. It can do this quite easily because it has access to the `.msi` file that says what should and shouldn't be there.

Failed Installs

While the Installer carries out an install or uninstall, it maintains a record of exactly what it is doing (not too hard really, since that record is already there in the `.msi` file!). Files to be deleted are temporarily moved, and only actually deleted once the process has run to completion. This way, if anything goes wrong, the Installer can simply rollback the system to the exact state it was in at the start. In other words, the installer treats the installs as a **transaction**.

Note, however, that this is only true during the installation (whether an initial installation, or a later maintenance or expansion installation). Once an install has successfully completed, the transaction is closed and old files etc. really are deleted. From that point, it's no longer possible to reverse the install, except by doing an uninstall. (It has to be like that really – otherwise think how rapidly your disk would fill up, with copies of every file that ever got installed to your machine....)

Knowing What's Happened to your Machine

That's easy. The installer doesn't have to do anything for this. Details of the changes that have been made to your computer are readily available, along with the installer's own record of what bits of which products have been installed.

Interaction between Packages

Again, since the system has full knowledge of what changes it has made there are no problems due to different install programs not knowing what other programs have done. In fact, this problem no longer exists anyway, because there is *only* one installation program – the Windows Installer. There is simply no reason for software vendors to write their own setup programs any more! It's worth pointing out, however, be pointed out that this argument assumes that *all* software will be installed using the Installer. If you have legacy applications installed which do not use the Installer – and which Windows Installer therefore knows nothing about, then you may still have problems.

Locked Down Desktops

This problem is solved because the Windows Installer can run as a service, under an account with elevated privileges. So even if the user currently logged on doesn't have permission to write to certain folders or registry keys, the Installer will have those permissions and can install the software. Administrators can safely lock down computers, yet know that any software the users need can be installed without the administrators having to spend their time on it.

As you can see from this list, some of the new benefits of the Installer are a result of the existence of the `.msi` files. Others are because the Installer service itself implements those facilities.

Installing with the Windows Installer

So let's check out how this all looks from the end user's point of view. Office 2000 is the next version of Microsoft Office on from Office 97, and Office 2000 does use the Windows Installer.

Here's what happens if I try to install Office 2000. After the usual standard dialogs, asking me such things as where I want the installation and do I accept the license agreement, I end up with this:

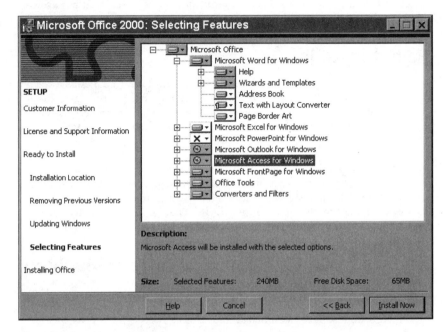

It's now a very standard user interface – remember it's the Windows Installer in charge here, not some custom setup program. The old style of clicking on a feature in order to bring up another dialog to view its details has been replaced by a more friendly tree control.

More interestingly, there are quite a few different options for how each feature is to be installed, as shown by the different icons next to each node in the tree. At the top level, Microsoft Office itself has a gray icon next to it. This indicates that different subcomponents have different installation options.

If we dive into Microsoft Word for Windows, we see that I've chosen to install the Address Book and Page Border Art completely to my disk. Hence, they have a white icon with a picture of a hard drive. The Text with Layout Converter is one that I'm not sure about. I just don't know whether it's something that I need, so I've set it to install on first use – marked by a yellow **1** in the icon. That option is the new, interesting, one. It means that the Text Converter won't be installed now, so it won't take up any valuable disk space. However, details of what is needed in order to install it will be made available, and if in a couple of months I try to do something in Word which requires the text converter, then the Windows Installer will get it for me. (It may ask me to insert the CD with the files on it, but I won't get any nasty dialogs asking me to select things to install: once it has the source media, the Installer can automatically install the stuff it's detected that I need).

Amongst the other options in the above screenshot, Microsoft PowerPoint is not going to be available. I'm pretty confident that I will never want to use it. Outlook and Access are to be run from source – in this case the CD ROM.

So at this stage the main benefit to me as an end user is I don't have to worry too much about what features of Office I'm going to use.

The benefits increase when files start getting corrupted. The first time I installed Office 2000, I decided to test this auto-repair facility. I could have gone for the small fry, and just deleted an odd file. I thought I'd try it big time– I renamed the entire folder to which I'd installed Office, thus preventing Windows from finding *any* of the Office files. (Notice I renamed rather than deleted it – I wasn't quite ready to take chances!). Then I went to the start menu and attempted to launch Word 2000.

Well there was no need to worry about anything. On any pre-installer product, what I'd done would probably have resulted in the usual Missing Shortcut dialog box. But with the installer, I got this:

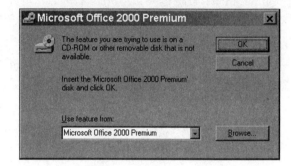

When I inserted the CD and clicked OK, the Installer chugged away for a bit, then Word started up as normal. All I had to do afterwards was delete my renamed folder of Office files, which was now redundant.

Windows Installer Architecture

We've seen what the Installer can do. Now it's time to take a look at how it does it. This section really gives you the background material and concepts that we're going to need in order to understand how to write installer databases.

What's in Windows Installer

There are a fair number of bits that make up the Windows Installer. They are:

- ❑ The .msi files that tell the system how to install a product

- ❑ The Installer runtime – the NT Service that actually does all the work in installing things

- ❑ The registry and Active Directory entries that indicate what state each product is in, and what has actually been installed

- ❑ An API that allows applications to perform operations using the installer and query their states. This API comes in two varieties, a set of API functions for C and C++ products, and a set of automation COM interfaces for scripting and VB products, and together they allow you to programmatically carry out tasks like finding out what software is actually installed, and arranging for other components to be installed or uninstalled.

- ❑ The enhanced shell

- ❑ The COM runtime (this and the enhanced shell are not really part of the Windows Installer but I've put them in the list because it is important that the shell and the COM runtime are installer-aware in Windows 2000).

The API is important, and it shows up the one thing we haven't yet mentioned: all this great new functionality comes at a price, since you'll need to make your applications aware of the Windows Installer, by having them use Installer API functions for certain tasks.

I should qualify that last statement. In principle, you could get away without making your applications installer-aware. You *could* leave your pre-installer products exactly as they are, and simply replace the `setup.exe` program with an Installer `.msi` file. However, if you do that, your product won't be able to take advantage of most of the features of the Installer. For example, you might want to use Install On Demand, so that when the user selects a certain menu item, your application is able have the Installer check whether the relevant feature is installed, and install it if necessary. If so, your application will have to use the Installer API functions to do this.

The Enhanced Shell and the COM Runtime

It may come as a surprise that I've stuck the shell and the COM runtime in the above list as components. What the heck have they got to do with the Installer?

> *In case anyone hasn't encountered the term before, the **shell** is the program that runs the desktop on your computer. It's responsible for displaying all the icons on your desktop, responding to mouse clicks and key presses, and it also handles Windows Explorer.*

In the case of the shell, the answer comes in the shortcuts that appear on your desktop and the start menu. In pre-installer days, these shortcuts were always shortcuts to *files* – you ran the shortcut, and the file would get launched. But now, with the Installer, it is possible for applications to be installable on first use. That means it's possible to have a shortcut that leads to a product or feature that hasn't been installed yet, so the files won't actually be there.

If that was all there was to it, it would be a bit silly since a shortcut must point to *something*! So there must be something a bit cleverer going on behind the scenes. In fact, such shortcuts will now lead to Windows Installer instructions for installing the relevant software. That really means we're talking about a new type of shortcut, which the shell has to be aware of. The shell in Windows 2000 and Windows 98 uses Active Desktop, and does understand Windows Installer shortcuts. In Windows 95 and NT4, you will need to install at least Internet Explorer 4.01 Service Pack 1 to take advantage of Installer shortcuts.

It's the same thing with COM. It is possible to have a COM component that is installed on demand. Hence CLSIDs that the COM runtime (actually the COM Service Control Manager) encounters on a call to `CoCreateInstance()` may actually lead to the Windows Installer, in order for a component to be installed. In Windows 2000, COM is Windows-Installer aware, and can cope with this.

What's in a Product

I've said a few times that a `.msi` file contains all the
information that is needed to install a product, and
up till, now we haven't really looked in detail at
what this information is. Not only that, I've been
carelessly bandying around a few terms like
product, **feature** and **component**, assuming that
you'll understand roughly what I mean. In fact,
these terms have fairly precise technical meanings
in the Windows Installer, and in order to
understand how the Installer works, we need to go
over exactly how these terms are used. So here
goes:

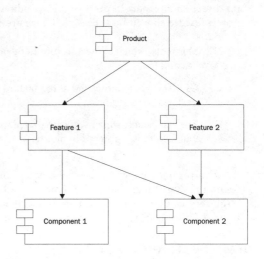

This figure shows how a product might be arranged.

The **product** is the entire thing you're installing. It is a complete package, described by a `.msi` file,
and which can act independently of other products. In the earlier Microsoft Office Windows Installer
screenshot, it is the thing at the top of the tree in the dialog box – Microsoft Office itself.

A **feature** is any part of a product that might be presented to the user as something they want to
install. It is possible for features to be contained within each other. For example, Microsoft Word is a
feature of Microsoft Office. It contains other features, such as the Address Book and the Text with
Layout Converter. A feature is the smallest unit that can be independently installed or uninstalled.

A **component** might appear at first sight to be similar to a feature. The difference is that a feature is
what the user sees as something that can be installed. A component is a set of files and registry
entries, which are needed by that feature. So the end user will generally not be aware of components,
but as far as the system is concerned, they are crucial.

The reason for separating out components and features is that different features may sometimes use
the same components. For example, it's a fair guess that the spellchecker feature in word actually uses
the same files as the spellchecker feature in Excel. If the feature you are installing uses components
that have already been installed, as a result of their having been used by another feature, then you
don't want the components reinstalled! We simply need them to be marked as now being used by
more than one feature.

From this discussion, you'll have figured out that a component can be used by more than one feature.
Similarly, a feature can use more than one component.

A **resource** is the most basic entity: it can be a file or a registry entry. A component is made up of one
or more resources. It's important not to include the same resource in more than one component, since
doing so will result in the resource being installed twice in the event that both components are
installed. Rather, if a resource is to be used by multiple features, it should be contained in its own
component, and that component should be made a part of both features. This is because it is only at
the level of the component that the installer will check whether something is already in use, and
therefore doesn't need to be reinstalled.

An **entry point** is perhaps the object in the hierarchy that will appear most unfamiliar to you, as it has no direct counterpart in pre-installer product setup. It can be thought of as an object that indicates how a feature should be accessed. There are three basic types of entry point:

❑ **Shortcuts**, which allow a feature to be accessed by the user running it from the start menu or a desktop icon

❑ **CLSIDs**, which indicate that the feature can be called up as a COM object, for example, using `CoCreateInstance()`.

❑ **File extensions**, which will cause a feature to be accessed if an attempt is made to open a file which that feature is registered to handle.

All features must have at least one entry point, and they may have more than one. Entry points are really the new things that the enhanced shell and the COM SCM (the COM service control manager – the service that responds to requests to instantiate COM components) need to understand in order to be installer-aware. They are the objects that installer shortcuts actually lead to.

How a Feature Can be Installed

As I've indicated, installation really takes place at the level of features, in the sense that it is features that can be individually installed. There are five main states a feature can be in on a particular computer on a network:

❑ **Not Installed** – the feature is simply not available

❑ **Installed** – the feature is fully installed on a local disk

❑ **Run from source** – the feature is available for use, but must be run from its source media. This may be the CD-ROM, but it may also be a network drive, when a feature has been installed on a domain controller of a network.

❑ **Assigned** – this is the first of the new possible states that are introduced, and corresponds to just-in-time installation. The feature will be installed on demand. What happens under the covers is that the entry points are installed, but nothing else. The Windows Installer is able to use the entry points to carry out the actual installation as soon as an entry point is activated.

❑ **Published** – this is actually very similar to assigned. The difference is that if a feature is published, then only the CLSID and file extension entry points are installed: the shortcut entry points are not. This means that the feature is not obviously available on a user's desktop, but is still available to be installed if the user indirectly tries to access it – by opening a file that requires that feature, or if the application calls up the feature while running.

In order to understand how these states can be used, it's important to appreciate that Windows Installer was designed to work on networks. What this means is that an entire product – or most of a product – can be installed on a domain controller, and it can then be assigned or published to all the users in the domain. Then each feature of the product will automatically only be installed on those computers on which it is actually needed. Conversely, users gain the benefit of having all the software that is installed to the domain controller available to use, without their having had to install it themselves.

Writing Installer Databases – Introducing Orca

So far, we've covered a lot of the basic architectural theory of the Installer, without saying anything about how you actually write the databases that the Installer needs to install your product. In fact, the .msi files are stored in a binary format, which means we're going to need a special editor to edit them. Microsoft has provided such an editor – it's called Orca. However, it's important to point out that Orca is NOT the recommended way of authoring .msi files.

You see, in the past there were a number of tools available that would write setup applications for you – saving you a lot of the drudgery of writing the raw code for them. Perhaps the most well known example was InstallShield, though there are other products that do the same thing. This is going to carry on: InstallShield and other third party products have been, or are being, updated, so they can produce .msi files, rather than custom setup routines. If you're a developer who uses these tools already, then, to some extent, you won't see too much difference in how you sort out installation now that the Installer is here. The main difference is that you will need to work within the framework of the Installer, so, for example, you'll need to think more formally about which parts of your software constitute a feature, and which constitute a component.

In this chapter, I'm not going to go over using any particular independent software vendor's product to write an installation database. This is really because I want to show you how everything is working at a low level. The install programs hide a lot of those details behind neat user interfaces and wizards – after all, that's the whole point of having a program to help write your installation routine!

What we are going to do is have a closer look at that database in the .msi file, and we're going to do this using Orca. Orca.exe is the program that lets you create and edit the databases used by the Windows Installer. It's quite a low level program – when you use it, you will find you are directly editing the various tables and rows in the database. That means it's good for playing with in order to understand what's going on, but if you actually want to write a real life .msi file, you'll probably be better off with one of the those ISV's packages. Installer databases can become extremely complex the moment you have a reasonable sized app.

Installing Orca

Orca is supplied with the Windows Installer SDK, which you can either download from Microsoft's web site, or get off your Platform SDK CD. You'll need to install the SDK anyway, if you want to write software that uses the Installer API.

One of the great things about Orca is that it illustrates the Windows Installer beautifully when you try and install it. That's because you don't get the Orca executable with the SDK. Rather, you get the .msi file that you can use to install Orca with.

After you've installed the SDK, you'll need to locate and run the Orca.msi file. .msi files are associated with the Windows Installer itself, so attempting to open one will, by default, cause Windows Installer to open the file and carry out the installation instructions it finds in it. In the case of Orca.msi, it's not quite a bootstrap program, but it definitely reminds me of the concept – installing Orca so that you can use it to edit its own installation file!

Once you've installed Orca, you will have an Orca.exe executable. You can either run it directly to create a new or edit an existing .msi file, or find a .msi file in Windows Explorer, right-click on it, and select Edit with Orca from the context menu. Obviously, double-clicking on the .msi file is not going to work, since the default action is still to run the Installer on the file, not to run Orca.

So let's see what it looks like. In this screenshot, I've started Orca and actually used it to look at its own .msi file, Orca.msi:

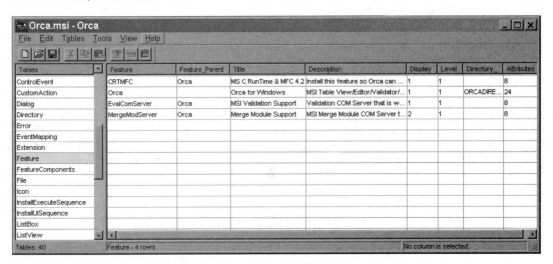

What we see is a something that looks like a treeview/listview, but it's not quite. The left hand pane lists all the tables in the database, while the right-pane lists the data in that table, by row. I've selected the Feature table on the left, so that's what we can see in the main right hand pane.

Talking of which, we're starting to use concepts from relational databases here, so before we move on any more, we'd better make sure we're clear what we're talking about.

Relational Databases and using Orca

Whole books have been written on the subject of how relational databases are structured, and there's quite a bit of mathematical theory behind it as well. I don't want to get sidetracked, so I'm going to compress the essentials of databases down to a couple of paragraphs – just enough that we can understand what's going on inside Orca. And I'm going to introduce relational databases using Orca.msi as an example, so you'll start to get a feel for what stuff needs to go in to Installer databases.

A relational database is divided into **tables**. A table of data is just that: a table of data. For example, check out that previous screenshot of the Feature table in Orca. The Feature table, oddly enough, tells us what features the product has.

A table is divided into **rows**, and in a lot of cases, a row tells us about a distinct data item. The columns (or **fields**) tell us about different properties of that data item.

I say that each row corresponds to a distinct item *in a lot of cases*, since one of the rules of relational databases is that each cell can only have one value. Hence, if we need to store any multi-valued properties, the only way to do so is to use more than one row for that data item, which will mean duplicating some data. This might sound inefficient, but there are good reasons for doing things this way since it makes processing the database a lot easier and more efficient – and usually tables will be designed in such a way that very few data items need to be duplicated.

Going back to the previous screenshot, since I've selected the *Features* table, Orca has displayed the features that it (Orca) is comprised of. So we can see that Orca has four features:

❑   Orca itself

❑   CRTMFC, a private copy Orca maintains of the MFC C run-time library

❑   `EvalComServer`, the MSI Validation support that can be used to check the consistency of files

❑   `MergeComServer`, a feature to allow merging of components

In fact, when you install Orca, these are the features that you're offered if you select the custom install option:

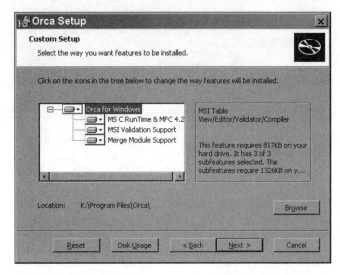

Looking back at the Feature table, we can see that each column in the table corresponds to a named property of the feature – these are the fields of the table in the database. We can tell that Orca is the product itself, because it does not have a parent (The Feature_Parent property doesn't contain anything). The other features have Orca as their parent.

Without going into all the details of what each property means, we can also start to see how this table is used by the Installer. For example, the Feature_Parent property is used to construct the tree control displayed in the user interface, and to select where in the tree to place each feature. The Title property is used for the text displayed in the tree control.

Linking Tables Together

The Feature table is just one of a large number of tables in `Orca.msi`. There are a large number of tables because there's a lot of interrelated data to be stored, and this means that we need to have some way of connecting the data in different tables. The usual way of doing this is by means of fields known as **keys**.

Let's look again at the Feature table. The first column, the one called Feature, is really the one that tells us which feature we are talking about. In some ways, it's analogous to the name of an item in a directory. This field is the **key**, or **primary key**. Its value must be unique: no two rows may have the same primary key.

So how does that help us to link tables together? Well, another table in Installer databases is the Component table. You might guess that this table stores details of the components contained by a product. Let's have a look at the Component table for Orca.msi:

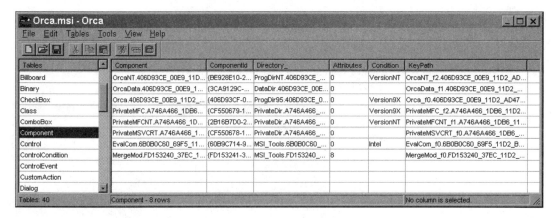

This table tells us that Orca has 8 components. Again, we don't need to understand what all the fields mean. The main ones are:

❑ Component is the name of the component

❑ ComponentID is a GUID that uniquely identifies the component

❑ Directory and KeyPath tell us about the actual resource that makes up the component

Component is the primary key for this table.

So we have a table of components, and a table of features. But we know that features are made up of one or more components, so the Installer must have some way of knowing which features require which components. That's something we haven't got yet – so far, the two tables are totally unconnected.

What we need is a third table, that tells us how the components and features are related. Here it is – it's called the FeatureComponents table:

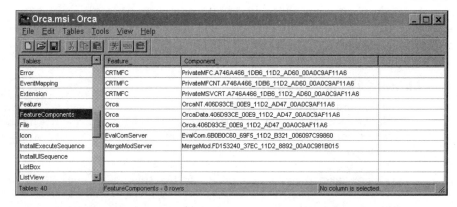

Each row of this table tells us that a certain feature contains a certain component. But do you recognize the values in these two columns? The ones in the Feature_ column are the same as the values in the primary keys from the Feature table. Similarly, the values in the Component_ column are taken from the primary keys in the Component table.

> **This is how rows in different tables are linked in relational databases: primary keys from one table are copied into another table. Keys taken from other tables in this way are known as** foreign keys.

Note that foreign keys don't need to be unique. For example, the CRTMFC feature actually needs three components, as does the Orca top-level feature. Hence, both of these foreign key values appear three times in the FeatureComponents table.

This table happens to have nothing but foreign keys in it, but, in principle, that's not a problem – we can have tables that contain any combination of foreign keys, primary keys and other fields. Many of the tables in .msi files do so. For example, if we look back at the Component table, the field, Directory_ is actually a foreign key that's taken from another table, the Directory table. The Directory table gives information about the folders used in the installation.

Note that .msi files use the term directory to refer to Windows folders. Directory, in this context, doesn't have anything to do with the directories that we've been studying throughout this book. Also, note that .msi files follow the convention that foreign keys have names ending in an underscore. This is something unique to the Windows Installer database format – it's not necessarily true of relational databases in general.

Structure of the Installer Databases

We've now covered all the theory of relational databases that we need, and we're ready to look in a bit more detail at how that gets put into practice in .msi databases.

We've already mentioned three of the tables used. In fact, there are a huge number of tables that can be stored in Installer databases, and there's no point in us going through all of them. Not all applications will need all of the tables. Orca uses 40 of them. The .msi file that we're going to create later in this chapter is a lot simpler, and only contains 8 tables.

All I want to do here is give you a flavor of what's in the databases – and I can do that by looking at a small group of tables that Microsoft have dubbed the **core tables**. These include important tables that tell the Installer about the features and components to be installed, and which will be needed by almost all applications. Here's the diagram of the core tables, taken from MSDN:

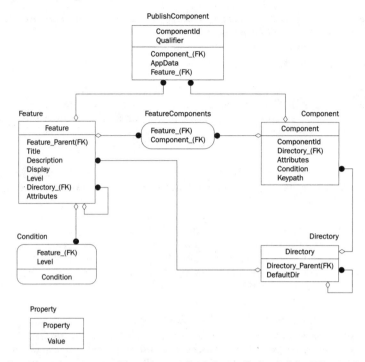

In the figure, each table is represented by a box, which lists all the fields. Where there is a horizontal line, the field above it is the key. A lot of the tables are linked by dashed lines with a diamond at one end and a black circle at the other. This indicates that the primary key in the table with the diamond has been copied into the table with the black circle, where it has become a foreign key.

We've already explained the relationship between the **Feature**, **Component** and **FeatureComponents** tables. Amongst other links, the directories defined in the **Directory** table are used by the **Component** table. The **PublishComponents** table also uses data from the **Component** and **Feature** tables, to show how to publish components. The **Condition** table allows the user to define certain conditions, governing when features should be presented as options to install.

> *You may be wondering, by the way, why we're using a relational database here, rather than a hierarchical directory. Well, the relationship between the different core tables in the diagram gives us a strong clue: the real strength of relational databases lies in their ability to represent data where there is a complex set of relationships between the different data items in the database. That is exactly the situation we are in here, and that is the area for which hierarchical data structures are weak. With a hierarchical directory, we are restricted to objects being children of other objects, along with some group membership associations. That is completely inadequate for Installer databases, with their complex interrelationship of features, components, entry points, files, registry entries, and various actions and user interfaces that need to be presented. Here, we need a relational database.*

That has given us a look at a small number of the tables used in Installer databases. Documentation for the full set of tables can, of course, be found in MSDN. We're going to take a break from databases now, in order to do some programming. We'll develop a small C++ application that illustrates some very elementary use of the Windows Installer API. Once we've done that, we'll return to the subject of `.msi` files, in order to write a database that can be used to install our application correctly.

The EnumProducts Application

The Installer API comes in two varieties. There is one set of API functions which can be used by C++ programs, while for VB and scripting clients, there is a set of COM objects which expose dual interfaces. The API is quite rich, allowing programs to find out about their installed state, and ask the installer to make repairs, or to install or uninstall features. It is also possible to use the API to obtain information about the folders to which applications are installed.

In this section we're going to use the C++ variant of the API. We're barely going to scratch the surface of it – doing no more than use a couple of functions to illustrate use of the API. We're going to write an application called EnumProducts, which will list all the products currently installed on your system, as well as listing the features that make up a selected product. EnumProducts is a standard dialog app written in C++ using MFC.

Here's what it looks like when it's in action:

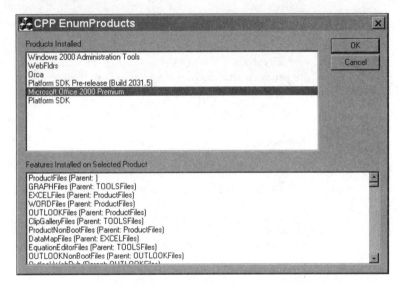

It contains two list boxes. The top list box shows all the products that have been installed. If you double-click on any product in this list box, the lower list box will display all the installed features that make up that product. In this screenshot, I'm examining the installation of Microsoft Office 2000. Notice that EnumProducts does not yet show up on the list of products, because we haven't yet written the database to install it.

OK – now to the coding. We need to #include the file msi.h, and link to the library msi.lib. The Installer API functions come in both Unicode and ANSI varieties, so it doesn't matter whether you do a Unicode compile or not.

All the action takes place in the main dialog class for this project. We need one member variable besides the stuff the wizard has given us:

```
class CCPPEnumProductsDlg : public CDialog
{

// wizard stuff deleted for clarity

// Dialog Data
    //{{AFX_DATA(CCPPEnumProductsDlg)
    enum { IDD = IDD_CPPENUMPRODUCTS_DIALOG };
    CListBox     m_listboxFeatures;
    CListBox     m_listboxProducts;
    //}}AFX_DATA

private:
    CStringArray m_csarrProductCodes;
};
```

The two `CListBox` variables control the list boxes. The string array is there to store the product codes for all the products that we find are installed on the computer. The product codes themselves are GUIDs – each product has a GUID that uniquely identifies it.

Displaying the list of products takes place in the `OnInitDialog()` function. Here's the code:

```
BOOL CCPPEnumProductsDlg::OnInitDialog()
{
    CDialog::OnInitDialog();

// wizard generated stuff removed for clarity

    UINT uiResult = ERROR_SUCCESS;
    DWORD dw = 0;
    TCHAR pszProductCode[40];

    while (uiResult == ERROR_SUCCESS)
    {
        uiResult = MsiEnumProducts(dw, pszProductCode);
        ++dw;

        if (uiResult == ERROR_SUCCESS)
        {
            UINT uiRes2;
            TCHAR pszValue[201];
            DWORD dwLength = 200;
            uiRes2 = MsiGetProductInfo(pszProductCode, "ProductName",
                    pszValue, &dwLength);
            ASSERT(uiRes2 == ERROR_SUCCESS);
            m_listboxProducts.AddString(pszValue);
            m_csarrProductCodes.Add(pszProductCode);
        }
    }

    return TRUE;  // return TRUE  unless you set the focus to a control
}
```

The key new bits here are the calls to the Installer functions, `MsiEnumProducts()` and `MsiGetProductInfo()`.

`MsiEnumProducts()` is a function which enumerates over the installed products. It takes two parameters: an index to indicate whereabouts in the enumeration we are, and an LPTSTR into which the product code is placed. Note that the second parameter is an LPTSTR – in other words it can be a Unicode or ANSI string. Microsoft are doing their usual trick here: `MsiEnumProducts()` is a generic function, which will map on to either an ANSI function, `MsiEnumProductsA()`, or on to the equivalent Unicode version, `MsiEnumProductsW()`, according to whether the _UNICODE preprocessor symbol has been set. All the Installer functions work the same way.

The way `MsiEnumProducts()` works is simple: you keep calling it, incrementing the index by one, until it returns ERROR_NO_MORE_ITEMS. What it returns is a product code – a GUID, which isn't exactly friendly for displaying in a list box. That's where the second API function, `MsiGetProductInfo()` comes in.

`MsiGetProductInfo()` accepts the product code, and looks up any of the named properties. These named properties are contained in another table in the `.msi` file – the **Property** table. This table contains data such as the name of the product, the manufacturer and the version. We want the `ProductName` property here, so we pass that into the function and get the name back as a string, in memory that we've allocated. `MsiGetProductInfo()` also expects a DWORD to tell it how much memory we've actually allocated, so it can fail if we haven't allocated enough. I've played safe here – 200 characters should be ample for almost any product name!

The one other thing we've done is to add the product code to the string array, `m_csarrProductCodes`. The reason for doing this is that the function to enumerate the features expects to be given the product code rather than the name to identify the product – so we need to have the product codes on hand somewhere.

Next let's check what happens if we double-click on an item in the products list box:

```
void CCPPEnumProductsDlg::OnDblclkList1()
{

    CString csCurSel;
    int i = m_listboxProducts.GetCurSel();
    m_listboxFeatures.ResetContent();

    if (i >= 0)
    {
        EnumFeatures(const_cast<LPTSTR>(LPCTSTR(m_csarrProductCodes[i])));
    }
}
```

Nothing too exciting here – we just figure out which item has been selected, grab the corresponding product code, and hand it to another function that I've written, `EnumFeatures()`, which does the job of populating the features list box.

Note that this code depends on the product names in the products list box being in the same order as the product codes in our member array. For this to work, the list box should *not* be set to sort its data.

The `EnumFeatures()` function is fairly simple:

```
void CCPPEnumProductsDlg::EnumFeatures(LPTSTR pszProductCode)
{
    UINT uiResult = ERROR_SUCCESS;
    DWORD dw = 0;
    TCHAR pszFeatureCode[40];
    TCHAR pszParentCode[40];

    while (uiResult == ERROR_SUCCESS)
    {
        uiResult = MsiEnumFeatures(pszProductCode, dw,
                    pszFeatureCode, pszParentCode);
        ++dw;

        if (uiResult == ERROR_SUCCESS)
        {
            m_listboxFeatures.AddString(CString(pszFeatureCode)
                    + CString(" (Parent: ") + CString(pszParentCode) + ")");
        }
    }
}
```

This function uses the `MsiEnumFeatures()` API function, which works in pretty much the same way as `MsiEnumProducts()`: you keep calling it until it complains, via its return parameter, that there are no more features. There are two differences. Firstly, it needs the GUID for the product code as a parameter. Secondly, it actually returns two strings: the name of the feature and the name of its parent feature. Although I've called these variables `pszProductCode` and `pszFeatureCode`, they are actually the names, not GUIDs, so we can stick them straight in the features list box.

Installing the EnumProducts Application

In this last section we'll write the `.msi` file that can be used to install `EnumProducts`.

`EnumProducts` is as simple as an application can get. It consists of one executable, there is only one feature (the application itself), and no custom registry entries need to be made to install it. Even so, we're going to need to stick a fair amount of entries in the `.msi` database. I'll explain enough to give you an idea of how the database and the installation procedure works, but a few of the entries we need are a bit esoteric. You're unlikely to encounter them if you use a higher level ISV product to write an installation package, so in those cases, I'll leave them and let you look up the explanations in MSDN if you're curious.

The first thing we need to do is create the folder structure. We need a folder that contains the `.msi` file, and below that, the actual folder structure of the package. By default, this folder structure will be copied, unchanged, to the target folder when the product is installed.

So we create a folder that will contain the `.msi` file. The name of this file doesn't matter, but I've called it `EnumProducts Install`. Create another folder inside this one, called `EnumProducts`. This is the folder that will be copied to the destination directory on installation. Make sure that the compiled executable for `EnumProducts` is placed in this folder.

We now need to create a new .msi file, which must be saved in the EnumProducts Install folder. To do this, run Orca.exe, and use the File|New menu to create a new .msi database. Depending on the options you have installed you may get a new empty database, or you may have to go through an additional step of specifying what you want to create:

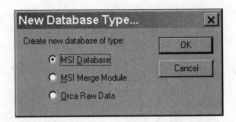

Now we need to add the tables. Go to the Tables | Add Table menu item. This brings up a dialog box asking you to select the tables you want. We need the following tables:

- Component
- Directory
- Feature
- FeatureComponents
- File
- InstallExecuteSequence
- Media
- Property

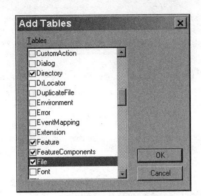

Now we simply need to add the rows to each table. This can be done by double-clicking on the relevant table in the left hand pane to display the contents of that table in the right hand pane. Then, double-clicking on an empty row in the right hand pane will bring up a dialog box, asking you to fill in the data for that row. Orca completely understands the Installer database format, and knows what fields to ask you for in each table. For example, for the Feature table, you will need to fill in this data:

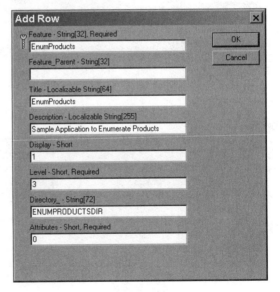

The following screenshots show the complete set of data you will need in the different tables. Note that since there's a lot of data here we won't explain what all the fields are for – that's all documented in MSDN – we'll simply go over the ones that are important for understanding the overall process.

Component Table

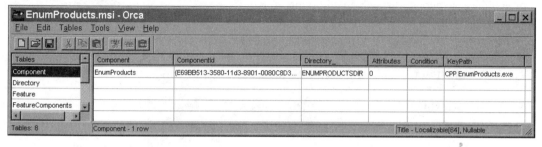

For this, the ComponentID is a GUID – for which it's probably easiest to generate your own one using GuidGen. The value in Directory_ is a foreign key into the Directory table.

Directory Table

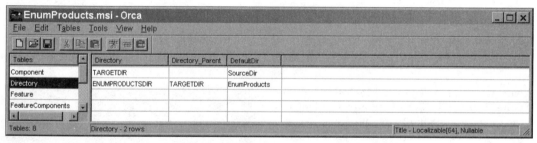

This table tells the installer about the directories to use. SourceDir will be evaluated at run-time.

Feature Table

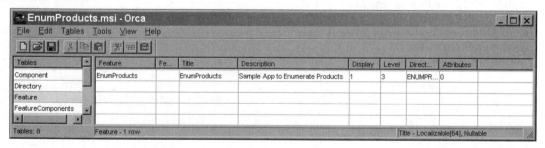

We've already discussed this table, which tells the Installer what features your product is composed of.

FeatureComponents Table

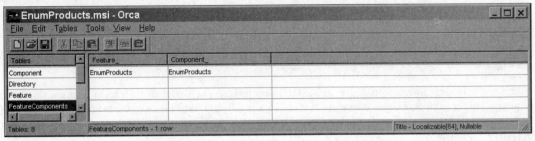

Again as discussed earlier, this table indicates which feature uses which components. Since we only have one feature and one component, it makes for a very simple table.

File Table

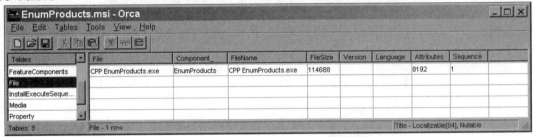

This table indicates the details of the file to be used. The only significant point about this is the FileSize, which must be the actual size of the file, in bytes. This information is used by the Installer to check that there is sufficient disk space to do the install. The easiest way to get this information is to right-click on the file in Windows Explorer and look at its Properties.

InstallExecuteSequence Table

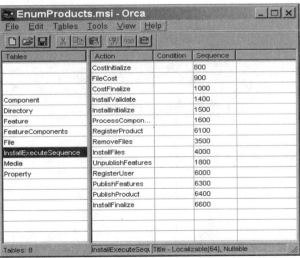

This table indicates the actions to be taken during the install (though some actions, such as RemoveFiles, are only relevant during Uninstall).

The Action field of this table indicates the action – the choice to be taken from a defined set of actions (although it is possible for .msi files to define custom actions as well). The condition gives us a chance to indicate that the action should only happen if certain conditions are met – we're not doing that here, as it's a simple install.

The sequence is a number (defined in MSDN) that tells us the order in which the actions should be taken. This is important, since rows in a table in a relational database are unordered.

Property Table

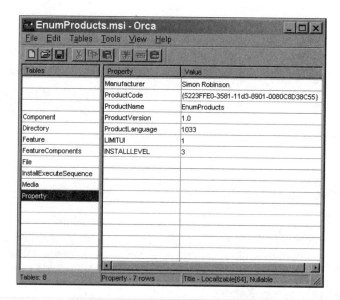

This table simply gives us some basic information about the product.

Media Table

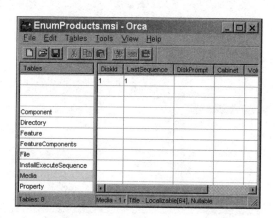

The values in this table tell us about the storage media on which the files are stored.

If you add all these values to the database, it will now be ready for use. Simply save the .msi file, and double-click on it to run Windows Installer. You'll have to quit Orca in order to do that, by the way. The Installer will install the application, which you can then check by running the application itself:

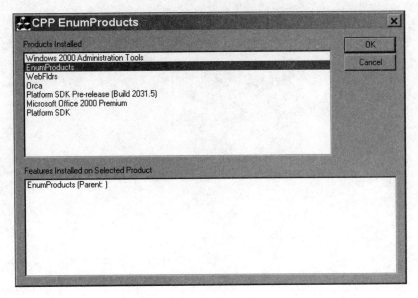

This shows that EnumProducts is now installed, with its one top-level feature. The EnumProducts project and the completed .msi file are downloadable from the Wrox web site.

Summary

This has been a very brief introduction to the Windows Installer that covers how the Installer works, what it is and how to use the C Installer API. We've also had a look at the kind of information that gets stored in an Installer database and how to access the database at a low level. I hope that has given you an idea of how much information needs to be stored to ensure a successful installation of even a simple software package. For a more typical package you are more likely to use higher level software produced by a third party to write the database.

The Installer also features an easy to use scripting API so that it is possible to carry out installations and check the install state of packages from scripting languages (and VB) just as easily as it is using C++. This API consists of a set of COM components that expose dual interfaces, although due to lack of space we haven't covered that in this chapter.

I also hope this chapter has given you a flavour of how powerful the Windows Installer is in its ability to ensure that the software installed on your system corresponds more exactly to what you actually need to be installed on it and its ability to prevent bugs that would previously have occurred due to the installation of software having been damaged.

We've one more new technology to go over before we've finished the book. In the next chapter we'll take a look at the Windows Management Instrumentation (WMI).

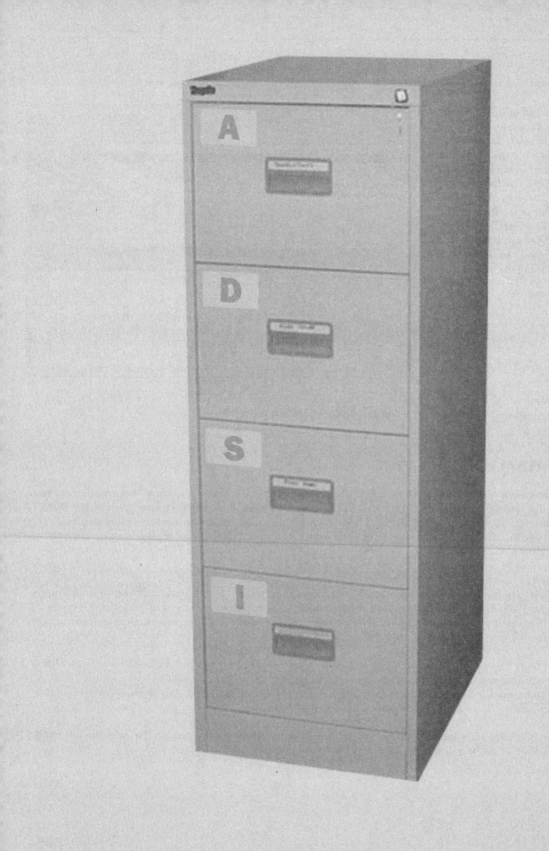

Windows Management Instrumentation (WMI)

In this chapter you will learn

- ❏ What **WBEM** and **WMI** are
- ❏ About the **CIM** schema
- ❏ Why you might want to set your software up as either a WMI client or a WMI provider.
- ❏ How to explore the **WMI** providers on your system using the CIM studio and the WBEM object browser.

We're almost there now. We've covered all the main ADSI topics, as well as two of the new technologies that you are going to need to write good, manageable, applications in Windows 2000. We just have one more technology, to look at, and this is the one that actually allows you to expose the management and configuration data from your applications, as well as allowing hardware devices to do the same thing.

WMI is still to some extent evolving. At the time of writing, the latest SDK available is the WMI 1.01 SDK, which is fine to use on Windows 2000 beta 3, but which Microsoft have stated will not work on Windows 2000, due to some changes in WMI. For this reason we're only going to give a brief introduction here – enough to give you an idea of what you'll be able to do using WMI and WBEM and why you would want to use it. We won't go into any actual code samples in this chapter.

What is WMI?

So what the heck is WMI, apart from another in a long line of acronyms you need to learn about in order to comply with the Windows 2000 logo? Well I like to compare it with Microsoft Management Console, and think of it a bit like this:

With MMC you have a standard user interface that you can use to manage your application. Something like

(In this and the next few diagrams, the arrows should be interpreted as meaning *uses*).

Well suppose I added another layer in there:

I've separated the actual data (for example registry entries) that form the management and configuration data of the application from the application itself. What's that gained us? Well, if we agree that there will be a standard method – like a standard API - for getting to this data, then that means my MMC snap-in could in principle start to be a lot more flexible. Like, it could start being used to manage someone else's application – because it can just use the same standard API to do so. So you end up with this.

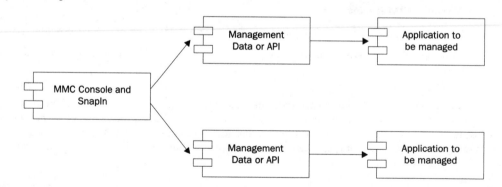

Where does that leave us? Well, if we have a standard API to get to the management data, then we don't actually need to use an MMC snap-in to get to it! We may as well use a web page or any other user interface that you might choose to write, which can act as a client to this API.

We'll also extend the things we're going to manage – besides software, we'll say it can include hardware devices too – things like your cdrom drive. Actually there's nothing particularly exciting about that move: there's no reason for not writing MMC snap-ins that manage hardware devices too – I just draw attention to the existence of hardware here because that was one of the most important motivations behind the development of WMI, whereas most documentation about MMC doesn't even mention hardware!

Because we now have a wider definition of things that you might want to manage, we'll introduce a new term, **managed object**. This term is hopefully self-explanatory, indicating anything, be it application, software, or hardware, which may expose management data.

Management data can mean anything that affects how an application, service, or device, operates. For example, in StarRaiders it would be the registry entries that control the security settings on StarRaiders and the location of the backend Access database behind the directory

All we need now is a name for our new management data stuff, and of course, that name is WMI.

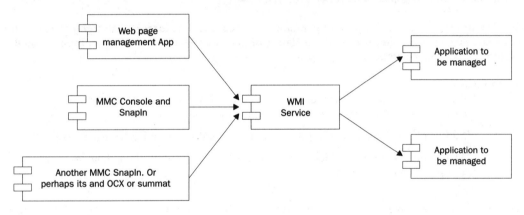

And that's it!

Now before I start to get lots of complaints about misleading you, let me make it clear that there is no direct link between WMI and WBEM on the one hand, and MMC on the other. They are completely independent technologies that evolved separately. It's just that I can't resist making the comparison. Management Console is a Microsoft standard for the user interface. WMI is a standard that takes one step back from that and defines how to expose management data. The two technologies do seem to complement each other rather well. I should also point out that the fact that the two technologies do appear to fit together so well does not excuse you from writing your own MMC snap-ins to administer your software. For a start, a generalized management application that can manage any applications is never going to be as good for managing your own software as a snap-in that was specially written *for* your software. Anything that WMI provides is additional to, not instead of, your own snap-ins. Also there will be some performance loss associated with the extra layer of going through WMI rather than a snap-in talking to your software directly.

As a final point, note that the API I've describe goes both ways. The clients – the applications on the left of the above diagram – will use it to request data from WMI, but the managed objects will also use another part of the same API to supply data to WMI.

Relationship between WMI, WBEM and CIM

That should have clarified what WMI is. However, in this chapter I've also referred to WBEM. So we need to explain what the difference is.

The key point is that WMI is Microsoft-specific. However Microsoft didn't develop WMI from scratch. It's actually based on an industry standard known as **WBEM** (**Web Based Enterprise Management**). WBEM has been developed by a body known as the Distributed Management Task Force (DMTF). (The DMTF was renamed in September 1999 – you may have heard of them by their original name of Desktop Management Task Force). The DMTF is a consortium of several large companies, including Microsoft, Intel, Cisco, Compaq and BMC.

WBEM is an industry standard for how to expose management data. As a standard it is applicable cross-platform (Windows, Unix, etc.), but needs to be actually implemented on each platform. WMI is Microsoft's implementation of WBEM for Windows.

WBEM also contains as an important component the **common information model** (**CIM**), which defines a schema – in other words which classes of object are defined, and what properties and methods those objects implement.

To summarize all this:

❑ **WBEM** is an industry wide standard that has been developed by the DMTF in order to define how applications and hardware devices should expose their management data.

❑ **WMI** (Windows Management Instrumentation) is Microsoft's own implementation of WBEM.

❑ **CIM** (Common Information Model) is a schema that defines some of the standard objects that may be stored. It can be extended.

Let's have a look at how this works in practice. You'll have gathered that WBEM, WMI and CIM are not independent. It may be easiest to think of the relationship between them as a containment one:

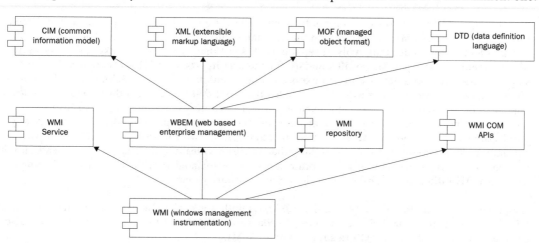

In this diagram, the arrows imply a parent relationship – so WMI contains the WMI services and the WMI Repository and so on.

At the lowest level is CIM, the schema. WBEM is the standard that completely encompasses how management data is exposed. WBEM includes CIM, as well as the **MOF** (**managed object format** language), which can be used to define MOF files to initialize management data and define the schema. The relationship between CIM and MOF files is analogous to that between the LDAP schema and LDIF files in LDAP: recall that in LDAP, the schema starts to define what sorts of classes of object can be stored, and LDIF files can be used to populate a directory with initial data. Also included inside WBEM are the extensible markup language, XML, along with the data definition language (DTD) associated with XML.

WMI extends WBEM by adding the following:

- ❑ A new schema, the **Win32 schema** containing objects relevant to Windows. The CIM schema allows classes to be derived from other classes, and the Win32 schema contains classes derived from classes in the CIM schema.

- ❑ An actual database that holds the schema and some information about instances of WMI objects. This database is known as the WMI repository.

- ❑ An NT/Windows 2000 Service, the WMI service to manage the repository and respond to queries against the repository and the WMI providers.

- ❑ A COM-based API and COM components to allow other programs to access the repository and WMI service. The COM components expose dual interfaces, which means they are accessible from scripting clients as well as VB clients.

Until recently, the WMI repository was known as the CIM repository, and the WMI service as CIMOM (the CIM object manager). You may still find these terms in some of the Microsoft documentation. The acronym CIM is still in use to denote the schema defined by the DMTF, but Microsoft are moving away from using it to refer to any of their own software.

The DMTF maintains details of the WBEM specification and the CIM schema at its website, `http://www.dmtf.org`.

Note the order of the initials – DMTF, not DTMF. Apparently sufficiently many people have been confused that the completely unrelated website, `http://www.dtmf.org` *actually has a link back to the DMTF's site for people who visited that site by mistake!*

The Architecture of WMI

When you add all the components of WMI together, you get something like this (where in this diagram the arrows imply that the connected components talk to each other).

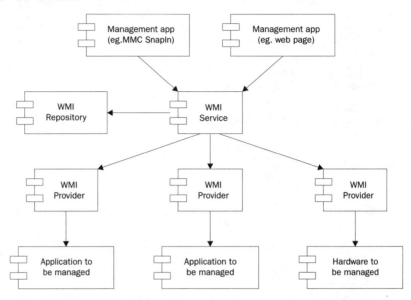

Besides the components I've already mentioned I've added the applications that will use the services of WMI to the diagram. On the one hand, there are the WMI providers. These are the programs that will supply management data. I've actually drawn the providers separately from the sources of the data, though if you are writing an application that exposes management data, you might want to make the provider part of your application. At the other end of the chain are the clients. These are management programs which manage or otherwise use the managed objects.

There are a couple of useful general purpose WMI clients supplied by Microsoft, by the way. The most important ones are:

❑ The **WMI object browser**. A general purpose browser that let's you hunt around WMI. It serves a very similar function to adsvw.exe in ADSI, and we've already encountered this browser in most of our screenshots.

❑ The **CIM studio**, a similar browser.

The difference between the object browser and the CIM studio is that the CIM studio is there to let you look at the schema – in other words at what classes are around and what methods and properties are defined for those classes, whereas the WBEM object browser lets you look at instances of objects.

Why Use WMI?

Now we've seen what WMI is. We'll look at how and why you'd want to WMI-ify your software. There are really two reasons:

❑   To use data exposed by other WMI providers.

❑   To expose your management and configuration data to WMI

Using WMI as a Client

Let's look at the first reason. If you want to use data exposed by other WMI providers, then you are basically using WMI as another directory – in other words as another source of information, in this case about your local computer or other computers on the network. Since there's at present no ADSI provider for WMI, you cannot use ADSI here – you need to use another set of COM components and interfaces supplied by WMI to get to the information. Since this is only an introductory chapter we won't go into how to use these interfaces – that is all detailed in MSDN. We will say, however, that you can use these interfaces from any COM aware language including scripting languages. You can get an idea for the kind of information you can get to in this way by looking at the list of WMI providers that are currently available:

❑   The **Registry Provider**. Lets you use WMI to access registry entries.

❑   The **Win32 Provider**. Lets you look in more detail at some of the base NT services.

❑   The **Windows Installer Provider**. Gives access to data concerning which applications have been installed (though it will only cover applications that have been installed using the Windows Installer).

❑   The **Event Log Provider** lets you look at data in the event log.

❑   The **Performance Monitor Provider** supplies performance information about managed objects.

❑   The **WDM (Windows Driver Model) Provider** gives access to hardware devices.

❑   The **Security Provider** lets you get to the security settings on files, folders and file shares.

❑   The **SNMP Providers** (two of them) give you access to SNMP tools.

❑   The **View Provider**. This is only available in Windows 2000, and allows you to combine information returned from other providers. You can use this, for example, if the information you need is not exposed by one single WMI provider, but spread across several providers, in order to give you a single unified point of access to the information.

❑   The **Directory Services Provider** makes the information in Active Directory available to WMI. Again, this is only available in Windows 2000. This is the provider we used in our earlier screenshots of the root/directory/LDAP namespace.

All of this demonstrates that you can access system software (such as the registry and Active Directory) as well as hardware devices. If you are coding in C++ then a lot of this information will be readily available anyway using the Windows API functions. If you are using VB then using those functions is possible although harder, and if you are using VBScript you can't get to them at all. That's when WMI really comes into its own. With WMI you can write ASP pages that lets you – say – report what's in the Event log, or examine the status of device drivers. Combine this with ADSI in the same ASP page and there's not much information left concerning Windows that you can't get hold of from the script. You can see that this could lead to some very powerful web pages!

Using WMI as a Provider

You'll do this if you want to expose any management or configuration data of your own through WMI. Doing this is helpful to your customers, since it means they can use the WMI API or any of the standard WMI browsing tools that Microsoft have supplied to view or configure settings for your software. If your applications are in any way related to the hardware of your computer or to the operating system then making them into WMI providers will be extremely important. If they are not, then it is still very useful for them to be WMI providers.

You can code your software up to be a WMI provider by implementing a number of WMI interfaces defined by Microsoft, which will be called up by the WMI service as required. You will also need to call up certain other WMI interface methods in order for your software to register itself as a WMI provider. Depending on precisely how your software works you may also want to write a MOF file that defines any additional schema you supply as well as the values of properties of class instances. Once again, we're not going to go into the interfaces here – the purpose of this chapter is to show you what WMI can be used for. But also, once again, you should note that it is possible for VB or C++ applications to set themselves up as WMI providers.

Note that even if your software has registered itself as a WMI provider, you will probably still want to write a separate MMC snap-in to manage it. This snap-in might for performance reasons not use WMI at all but communicate directly with your software.

We've now explained in fairly abstract terms what the architecture and aims of WMI are. What we haven't yet done is given much in the way of specific examples of the sort of information that can be stored. We're going to do this by looking in some more detail at some of the objects in the CIM and Win32 schemas. To do this we'll also need to understand something of how the CIM schema works.

The CIM Schema

The **CIM schema** is a definition of classes, and so it's probably best to understand it by comparing it to any directory schema. For example the Active Directory schema defines a large number of classes, as well as a number of attributes that can be stored by each attribute. The CIM schema is similar, but there are a number of differences between how the CIM schema works and how an ADSI or LDAP-compliant directory schema works.

Methods

Classes in CIM need to have methods as well as properties, since (for example) you may want to be able to start or stop a service, or tell a cdrom drive to eject. Methods can take any number of parameters. CIM does however define a fairly limited number of data types (integers of different sizes, floating points, strings and dates) and all properties and parameters to all methods have to be of one of these data types.

Single Inheritance

Classes in CIM can derive from other classes – however there is nothing corresponding to multiple inheritance in C++ or Auxiliary classes in ADSI/LDAP. There is only single inheritance – that is, a class can only inherit from one other class, though any number of classes can inherit from it. As with directories, the base class is known as a **superclass** and any inherited class are known as **subclasses**.

Association Classes

Association classes are a concept that has no equivalent in directories. An association class is a class whose sole purpose is to link instances of other classes together. An example which we'll encounter later in this chapter is that of processes running in Windows. A process will generally be running a certain executable file, and may have some dlls loaded. That means that there is a link between the WMI object that represents the process and each of the WMI objects that represent these files. This link is formalized by creating instances of association classes which link the process to the relevant files.

Another use for association classes is with multiple inheritance. We've mentioned that the CIM schema supports only single inheritance – this means that if you want to define an object of your own that you'd like to be derived from more than one existing class, you've got a problem. Say you've created an NT service which manages disk partitions, and you'd like to create a class which represents this service. You want this class to derive from the class representing a service and the class that represents a disk partition (for Windows you'll probably be thinking of the classes `Win32_Service` and `Win32_DiskPartition`). You can't directly do that, but what you can do is create an association class that links an instance of `Win32_Service` and `Win32_DiskPartition`, so an instance of your new service will actually be represented by three instances of WMI classes – two main classes and one association class.

Singleton Classes

From our work with ADSI we are familiar with the fact that classes can be structural (in which case they can be instantiated) or abstract (in which case they cannot be instantiated) (or auxiliary – in which case they cannot be instantiated either – but there's no equivalent to auxiliary classes in WBEM).

WBEM allows for another type of class – the **singleton class**. Such a class can be instantiated, but only once. It can only ever have one instance and there's no really analogy to this in directory services.

CIM Schema Models and Deriving New Schemas

WMI is not limited to one schema. In fact, although the last section was headed the CIM schema, and discussed the architecture of the CIM schema, the actual examples in it were taken from Microsoft's Win32 schema. How is this? Well, in WBEM, a schema is considered to be a set of classes that are owned by the same organization. So WBEM starts off with the CIM schema, which contains everything that is in the WBEM standard. Microsoft have then added the Win32 schema which contains classes derived from classes in the CIM schema. For example, `Win32_Service` is derived from `Win32_BaseService`, which in turn is derived from `CIM_Service`, which is derived from... and so on. Anyone is welcome to add new schemas that define new types of object, with the proviso that classes in these new schemas MUST be ultimately derived from classes in the CIM schema.

The CIM schema is itself divided into two models:

- ❑ The **core model** consists of those classes which are considered as likely to be common to many technologies and management applications.

- ❑ The **common model** consists of those classes which are relevant only to specific technology areas.

Note that at this point we are not dealing with anything that is Windows-specific. We are talking about industry standard schemas. The common areas are systems, applications, devices, network and databases.

We can see how this hierarchy works by looking at the inheritance diagram leading to two common objects – the disk partition and the NT (W2K) service in Windows. Here it is.

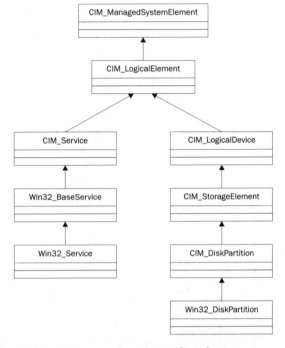

At the top of the hierarchy is CIM_ManagedSystemObject – a pretty generic class that can represent most managed objects. Incidentally, you should notice how the name of the class is always preceded by the name of the namespace of which it is a part. Next down the hierarchy is CIM_LogicalElement, which represents any object which has a logical, rather than a physical existence. There is an equivalent class, CIM_PhysicalDevice, which would represent such devices as keyboards and mice.

So far we are in the CIM core model – the classes that are extremely generic. Now we move into the common model, and reach classes that are related more to specific technologies – CIM_Service on the one hand and CIM_LogicalDevice, CIM_StorageElement and CIM_DiskPartition down the other branch of the tree. That's as far as CIM itself will take us. The CIM schema has taken us to the point of defining a generic service (something that in Windows would be a service, but in unix would more likely be a unix daemon) and a generic disk partition. Then it's up to Microsoft to take over and define classes that add specific properties relevant to Windows – so we reach Win32_Service and Win32_DiskPartition.

WMI Browsers

It's time we actually dived in and had a look at what data is actually on a typical computer. For this Microsoft have supplied a couple of browsers, the **CIM Studio** and the **WBEM Object Browser**, which serve much the same role in WMI as adsvw.exe does in ADSI. Before we can use them to go exploring, however, we need to have WMI installed. There's two parts to this:

Installing WMI and WBEM

There are two parts to installation; first, the WMI and the WBEM core. If you are running any version of Windows 2000 then you will have this automatically as part of the operating system. It contains the WMI service and the CIM repository, as well as various WMI providers. If you are running NT4 you will need to download this from Microsoft's website, off `http://msdn.microsoft.com/developer/sdk/wmisdk/default.asp`.

You'll also need the WMI SDK. This is also available for download, from the same URL. You need to install the core before you can install the SDK . At the time of writing Microsoft have promised that the WMI SDK will be supplied with the Platform SDK in the near future. The SDK contains most of the documentation, as well as the necessary header files and libraries needed to develop code that uses WMI, and some useful tools to browse the information available through WMI – the CIM Studio and WBEM Object Browser, as well as a couple of other useful ActiveX controls.

Note that due to changes in WMI, the version of the SDK that is used with Windows 2000 Beta and Windows NT, will not work with Windows 2000 – you will need a newer version of the SDK to match the upgraded version of WMI.

The WBEM Object Browser

The WBEM Object Browser is used to explore the various WMI objects on your computer. It uses a web interface. When you first start it up you will be asked to authenticate, and to choose a namespace to bind to. Using default authentication will be adequate for our purposes. The namespace we want is `root/CIMv2`, which is where most of Microsoft's objects are. A namespace, by the way, has much the same meaning as in LDAP: in LDAP it's a contiguous part of the directory tree, in WMI it's a way of grouping objects together.

Here's what the object browser looks like when it's running.

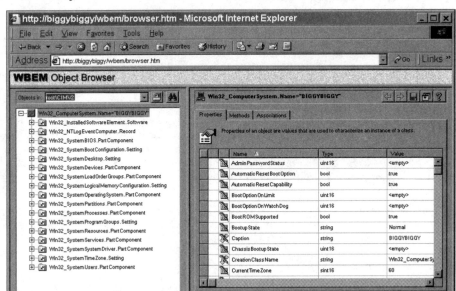

It's the usual kind of interface we're accustomed to from Windows Explorer and MMC – a tree view on the left and a list view on the right that displays the properties of the object selected on the left. In this case, however, the 'list view' contains several tabs, which you can use to look at either the properties or call methods on the object, or find out what other objects this object is linked to through association classes.

You should also be careful not to be fooled by the tree view. The fact that object viewer uses something that looks like a tree control to display all the objects doesn't mean its viewing a directory with a treelike structure – it's not. WMI doesn't really have any concept of a tree structure with objects having parents. Instead, the object browser is using the associations between objects to construct a reasonable looking tree structure.

> *Speed is not one of the object browser's biggest advantages. Don't be surprised if when you attempt to open some of the nodes in the tree control, your computer virtually hangs for several seconds – or in some cases minutes, while the object browser gathers the required information together. The CIM studio has a similar problem.*

This is where we can really start to see what sort of information can be accessed using WMI. Amongst the nodes in the above screenshot, you can see ones that represent

❏ The Event Log

❏ Registered Windows 2000 (NT) Services

❏ Currently running processes

❏ The system clock

❏ Users

❏ Disk partitions

Remember all these are being accessed from a *web browser* – in other words a scripting language – using a single COM-based API. This should start to give you an idea of the potential power of WMI.

To look at some objects in a bit more detail, let's examine the currently running processes:

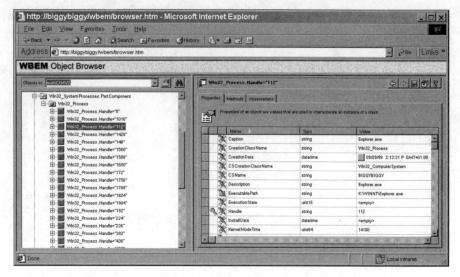

In this screenshot I've opened the System Processes node to reveal the currently running processes. In the tree control, the nodes with the box icons (which will be blue on screen) represent actual WMI objects, while those with the folder-like icons (yellow) are really just the associations that the object browser has used to build the tree.

Unfortunately, the processes are identified in the tree view by their handles, which isn't that helpful, but after some browsing I've located and selected the process that happens to be the Windows Explorer – as you can see by checking the value of its Description property in the list of properties. The executable path gives the name path to the file from which this process is running – K:/WINNT/Explorer.exe. If I browse down the list view a bit I can also discover that explorer has so far generated 29320 page faults (lucky page faults aren't serious), is running on a Windows NT5.0 operating system (someone at Microsoft forgot to change some string from 'NT5.0' to 'Windows 2000' somewhere…) and is running at a priority of 32.

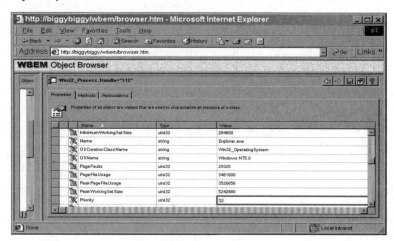

Let's have a look at the methods available:

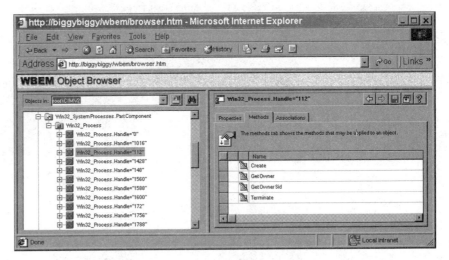

This tells us that we can use WMI to actually terminate the process as well as get some information about it.

The associations tab tells us what other WMI objects are associated with this process object.

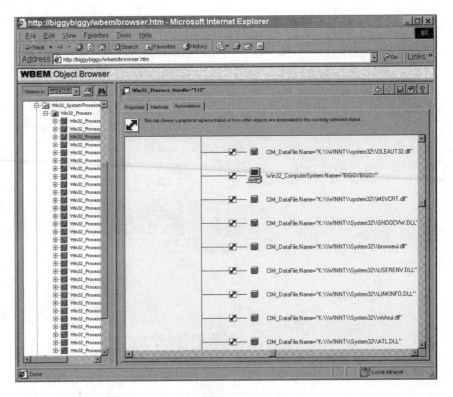

The size of the scroll bar on the right tells us that this process is associated with a *huge* number of other objects. In fact, one of these objects is a computer object, which identifies the computer on which the explorer is running on (shown in the screenshot). All the other objects are the various dlls that this executable is dependant on, and have been brought in. The computer is represented by an instance of the class `Win32_ComputerSystem`, while the files are represented by instances of the class `CIM_DataFile`. You might be a bit surprised by how many associated files there are if you are used to thinking of the Windows Explorer process as being simply the window that pops up when you try to run Windows Explorer to browse around your file system. That's a common misperception – in fact the explorer is the shell that controls the entire user interface to Windows. The Windows Explorer windows you can bring up are simply extra threads running in the Explorer process. That's why this particular process is linked to so many files – most of the processes in the tree control in the previous screenshots wouldn't have anything like as many files associated with them.

Incidentally, just to confirm the point I made about the WBEM object browser using association classes to construct its tree control, if you open up the node that represents the explorer process, you find the file instances it is associated with:

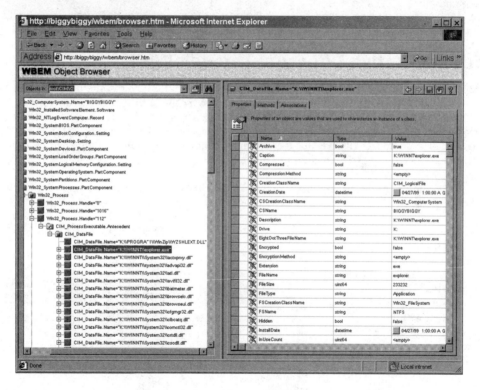

Looking at Different Namespaces

It's possible to use the object browser to examine objects in different namespaces. So far we've looked in the `root\CIMV2` namespace in which all the Windows system objects are located. In order to see what other namespaces are available, click on the toolbar button with the computer icon above the tree control. This brings up an extra window allowing you to select a namespace:

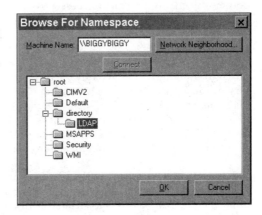

The Machine Name text box and Network Neighbourhood button in this screenshot should remind us that we can use WMI to look at WMI objects on remote machines across the network as well.

Accessing Active Directory Through WMI

Since this is a book about ADSI, we're going to take a special interest in the directory/LDAP namespace. This is a namespace that is made available by the WMI provider for Active Directory – so it enables us to use WMI to access objects in Active Directory. Doing so gives quite a big performance hit, as compared to accessing these objects more directly using ADSI, the ADSI LDAP provider, or even an LDAP API, but the fact that we have the option available can be useful if data in Active Directory is used to manage other objects.

We're not going to try to do anything fancy here – we're just going to use the object browser to look at Active Directory – to show you that it can be done.

After selecting the directory/LDAP namespace, we get a dialog box asking us to browse for an object to view. We can also bring up this dialog by clicking on the toolbar item with the binoculars icon above the tree control.

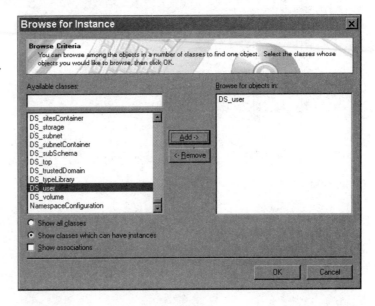

The left hand list view gives the WMI classes corresponding to different Active Directory classes – you use the **Add** button to add classes to the list of classes to browse in. I've decided to try and hunt down my own user account, so I've selected the user class. (WMI class: `DS_user`).

Clicking on OK brings up another dialog box asking you to select which of the instances of the selected class(es) you wish to view.

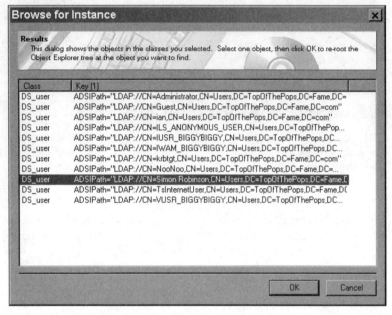

Notice that in keeping with the aims of WBEM the instances are identified by a key property rather than a name. For Active Directory, the key property is quite sensibly the `ADsPath` – or as WMI describes it, the `ADSIPath`.

Finally clicking **OK** to this user gives us our view of this object.

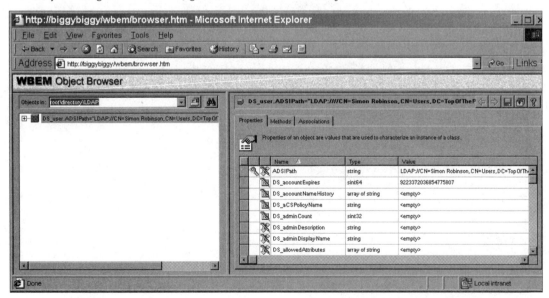

Not that exciting, admittedly. We can see a lot more, and a lot more easily, using `adsvw.exe` or any of the tools we developed in Chapter 2 to view directory objects directly using ADSI. But the point here is not to demonstrate the user interface tools that Microsoft have produced to allow you to browse WMI, but to show you what information can be obtained using WMI. The WBEM object browser uses the same COM components internally that you would call up in any WMI clients you write. It's beyond the scope of this chapter to go into the various components and interfaces available – that's all described in the WMI MSDN documentation. But you can take my word for it that they are perfectly normal COM objects, which you would call up from C++, VB or scripting languages in the normal way and use to get to any of the information that the object browser can access.

More About WMI Architecture

That's completed our tour of the types of object that are represented in WMI. Before we leave off, I want to explain a little more about the structure of WMI and some of the components of the WMI service.

The WMI Repository

If you look back at the diagram we presented earlier, in the *Architecture of WMI* section, you'll see that there are two possible sources of management data that the management applications might want to see: the individual WMI providers, and the WMI repository. So why have both of these?

Well, the point is that querying a provider for data or asking a provider to modify data is potentially not a very efficient operation. The provider may be running in a separate process – it may even be servicing a managed object that resides in yet another process. Now there's some data for which you've little choice but to accept this. If – say – your WMI provider is responsible for monitoring the state of certain network connections, then whenever the management application needs to query the state of those connections, there's not really any alternative but to ask the provider to go away and check out what the current state is – no matter how long it might take the provider to do so.

But there's a lot of data that doesn't change regularly. For example, if you wrote a WMI provider for almost any application, it's not often that you'd need to change the configuration settings for it. For that sort of data, it works best if the provider simply tells WMI when it first registers itself what the data is, then WMI can simply store its own local copy of the data, and save having to bother providers with repeated requests for the same data. That's what the WMI repository (formerly the CIM repository) is there for. It's a store for all the management data that rarely or never changes.

In many ways you can think of the WMI repository as being quite analogous to the local property cache on ADSI providers. The difference is that whereas the ADSI property caches store *everything*, the WMI repository only stores the data which the providers deem is more appropriate to be cached.

The actual definitions of classes are normally stored in the repository, since class definitions rarely change. Property values for class instances are more likely to be supplied dynamically by the provider, since they may change more frequently, though it is also common for these to be stored in the repository.

If you're coming from a directory background, you might be surprised at the concept that a class definition can *ever* change – in WMI this is possible: WMI supports the notion of dynamic classes, where the class definition is supplied on request by the provider. This means that even the definition of a dynamic class may frequently change.

Comparing WMI and Active Directory

In this section we'll round off by asking – and providing a few answers to – one question that has probably occurred to you. What's the point of having WMI and the CIM repository separate from Active Directory?

In pre-W2K Windows, we had the registry. Windows 2000 has added Active Directory to that. With the WMI Directory Service provider, the information in Active Directory will be made available through WMI. However, you might be wondering what the point of adding yet another directory is. After all, couldn't the WMI repository just have been absorbed into Active Directory, instead of linking them via a WMI provider? Wouldn't that make things a lot simpler for the likes of us poor developers? Well, yes, it probably would make our lives simpler if having just one directory were possible. Unfortunately there are a couple of good reasons why merging the two isn't practical.

The most important point is that Active Directory is very much a domain-based directory. It is stored on domain controllers, and handles information pertaining to the domain as a whole. For example, even something like local user accounts on member workstations are not by default stored in Active Directory. By contrast, the WMI repository is machine-based. Each computer running Windows 2000 will have its own WMI repository. The repository would normally be active and working even if the computer is a standalone machine, and not a member of a domain at all. This is clearly essential since even standalone machines have devices such as disk drives attached to them, and these are exactly the kinds of objects WMI is designed to manage.

The second point is that WMI is based on an industry wide standard. WMI is Microsoft's own implementation of WBEM, just as you could perhaps view Active Directory as an implementation of the LDAP standard – to the extent that Active Directory is an implementation of an LDAP directory. But here Microsoft's hands are tied. If you want to implement industry standards then you have to follow those standards, and the WBEM standard evolved separately from the LDAP standard. With hindsight, that's perhaps regrettable since it does mean we have a standard for a directory service, and a completely different standard for exposing information that really could have been stored in a directory service. That's evolution for you.

The problem is that even exposing CIM data using an LDAP directory would be quite awkward: LDAP has its own schema defined, while CIM is another schema. As we've seen the two schemas are pretty much incompatible because of the different ways they work. LDAP supports auxiliary classes where WBEM uses associations, for example.

Similarly, WMI lets you get at not only data but also method calls on the providers. LDAP does have the LDAP controls, which are designed to do something similar, but LDAP is really intended to store information – the controls are very much an add-on, whereas the ability to call methods is a fundamental part of WBEM and WMI.

It's problems like these that ensure that the WMI repository has to be independent of Active Directory.

Having said that, even if WMI and Active Directory are independent, it would clearly be desirable to allow some association between WMI and ADSI. After all, ADSI is a standard for accessing any directory, while the WMI repository is a kind of directory. It's not hard to see the link.

In fact, at the time of writing, although there is a WMI provider for Active Directory, Microsoft are still formulating their strategy for how to link WMI and ADSI, so it's really a case of wait-and-see here. When NT5 beta 2 was released, it did actually ship with an ADSI provider for WMI, which allowed the management data exposed by WMI to be accessed using the ADSI interfaces. However, with Windows 2000 beta 3, this provider was withdrawn. I'd suggest you check the current documentation to see if Microsoft have released any replacement since this book was published - again, the WMI SDK page is likely to be your best source of up-to-date information.

Summary

In this chapter we've had a very brief introduction to WMI, WBEM and CIM. We haven't presented any code samples because the emphasis was on giving you a feel for what the capabilities of WMI are and how you might want to make your applications WMI-aware. If you do decide to start coding WMI-aware applications, the WMI API is well documented in MSDN.

We've seen that WMI effectively exposes a type of directory, albeit one with a rather different structure from the type of directory you'd normally use ADSI to look at. Accordingly, you don't access it with ADSI but with a different COM-based API, the WMI API. We've also seen that you might want your application to act as either a client to WMI (requesting information) or as a provider (supplying information that other WMI-aware applications can then use). The information available through the Microsoft-supplied WMI providers is already fairly extensive, covering both the Windows operating system and the hardware devices attached to your computer. Making your software WMI-aware allows it to take advantage of all this information.

Conclusion

That's it! We've done not only ADSI but also the other new technologies you are going to need in Windows 2000. Hopefully if you've got this far you'll agree ADSI is quite simple to use at a basic level, but does have some quite useful subtleties and is undeniably powerful. I believe it's destined to become one of those technologies that will end up getting everywhere in the next few years – especially because it's the most convenient way to access Active Directory. In the future, I can even imagine people merrily sticking ADsPaths in calls to VB's `GetObject()` function, without even being aware that they are using ADSI, something that was once a revolutionary technology.

In this book we've seen how to write both ADSI clients and ADSI providers, as well as seeing something of the structure of Active Directory and how to use the LDAP, WinNT and IIS providers to perform administrative and other tasks. We've also gone on to examine Microsoft Management Console, the Windows Installer, and – finally in this last chapter, WMI, WBEM and CIM. They are all at first sight very different technologies, but are ones which do complement one another. In the years to come, a typical large enterprise software package is likely to

- ❑   Include a Windows Installer `.msi` database to let the Windows Installer install and uninstall itself.

- ❑   If it is to fill a sufficiently important role in managing your network or computers, expose the WMI interfaces to register itself as a WMI provider

- ❑   Come with an MMC snap-in to allow users to configure it using MMC

- ❑   Make extensive use of the ADSI interfaces to obtain and modify relevant data.

Hopefully you've now got a sufficient understanding ADSI to go away and start writing ADSI-aware applications and of the other related technologies to at least understand where they might usefully fit into your software. We're going to conclude this book by briefly going over the topics we've covered and seeing how they all fit together.

First ADSI itself. We've seen that ADSI features a large number of interface definitions as well as some prewritten COM components (providers, the router, and certain directory-independent components) that let you access directories from any COM-compliant language (including scripting languages). The ADSI interfaces have been carefully designed to allow you to easily

- ❑   browse around the directory tree

- ❑   examine and modify properties and objects in the directory

- ❑   create, move, copy and delete objects in the directory

- ❑   search for directory objects satisfying certain criteria (possibly using the help of ADO)

- ❑   examine and modify access control entries associated with objects

- ❑   control other resources, such as starting and stopping services and controlling print queues.

There is a range of ADSI providers available, which between them allow you to access a wide number of directories

❑ Active Directory – giving you access to domain resource and security information as well as any other information which your domain administrators choose to store in Active Directory

❑ The Exchange Directory, containing details of recipients and configuration information for Exchange Server

❑ The Site Server Membership Directory, with its database of users of your web site

❑ The IIS Metabase, allowing you to configure your web site itself

❑ Netscape Directory Server and the openLDAP Directory Server – and so all the information that may have been stored in these directories if they are installed

❑ Novell Directory Services (NDS) so you can access information about networks controlled by NDS

❑ The WinNT provider – although not strictly a directory – gives you access to many resources on your network, for example NT services, user and group accounts, and print queues

Collectively, these let you access a huge number of objects, and cast amounts of data. The remarkable thing is that you can use the same interfaces for each one of them – and for the most part you only need to be familiar with a small number of the ADSI interfaces as well. All you need to do is supply the appropriate ADsPath to bind to the appropriate object. This is a powerful technology you're dealing with.

Not only that but the whole thing is extensible, both in terms of the objects you can access and what you can do with them. The range of objects and data accessible through ADSI can grow through the process of writing new ADSI providers, while you can expand what you can do with the objects by writing extensions for existing providers (in a couple of cases you may be able to do this by extending the directory schemas). Writing extensions is very easy using ATL (although you do need to be familiar with C++). Writing new providers is harder since a new provider is a large project involving a lot of interacting COM components. But it is perfectly possible, and several companies have started doing so in order to use ADSI to allow access to directories associated with their own products.

OLE DB is widely recognized as *the* way to access a wide variety of data sources, particularly relational databases. ADSI promises to achieve the same importance for those data sources that count as directories. As an added bonus, it's easier to learn than OLE DB, and in the future will probably support ADO or ADO-like interfaces to make its use even simpler. In short, if you are writing any enterprise application, it's quite likely that you will find it useful to use ADSI at some point. There aren't that many applications for large enterprises that don't involve some directory somewhere – be it a directory of employees, of customers, of products, or of network resources.

But using ADSI is only half the story. Your application, by acting as an ADSI client, is taking advantage of a lot of software that has been written by Microsoft for you. But your application will look even more impressive when it lets other Microsoft software take advantage of its own services. I'm talking here about Management Console and the Windows Management Instrumentation (WMI). Both of these are sitting there on Windows 2000, and many NT4 installations, waiting to be able to access the management data that configures your software so that they can expose it to the users and administrators in a convenient way. By coding up your application to expose all the interfaces that allow it to act as a WMI provider, and writing an MMC snap-in to interact with your software, you can let them do this.

The result is that the people who buy your software will find it a lot easier to manage, using tools that they will be familiar with. (OK, perhaps not everyone is yet familiar with MMC or WMI, but it's early days yet. That will change.) As a result your software will stand out as a truly professional product.

It's the same story for Windows Installer – though this one really *is* essential. If you don't write a .msi database for your software, allowing Windows Installer to do all the work of installing and uninstalling it, then you'll not only make more work for yourself, but your software will again stand out – although not for its professionalism...

There's a nest of technologies here. We've gone over ADSI in a lot of detail, and briefly introduced you to the other technologies – enough to give you a good springboard to investigate and use them further. Now you've read this book you've almost certainly put yourself in a very good position to take advantage of these latest technologies and produce high quality applications for Windows 2000 – good luck!

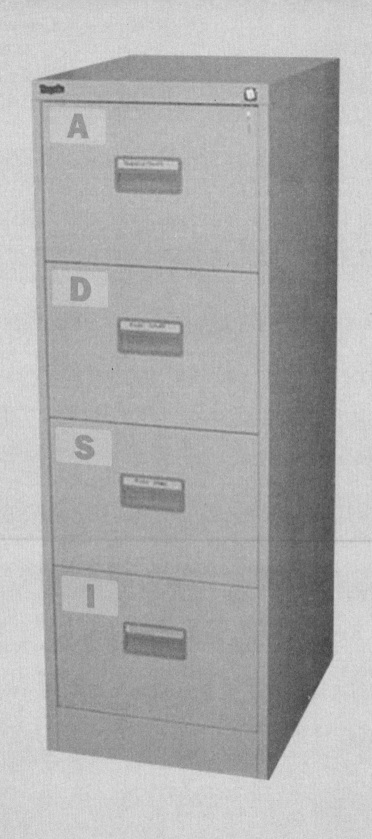

Sources of Information

Microsoft Documentation

At the time of writing, ADSI is at version 2.5. The documentation is available with the ADSI 2.5 SDK, at `http://www.microsoft.com/adsi`. It should also be available with the platform SDK.

All the topics listed below are also covered at Microsoft's web site.

Web Sites

This section lists those web sites where you can find useful material related to the content of this book. This includes articles and sample code, as well as listservers and newsgroups.

Bear in mind that web sites change frequently, so some of this information may get out of date. However, all the sites I've quoted here appear to be fairly stable.

ADSI in General

Without wanting to sound pretentious, a good place to start is my own web site. I keep (hopefully) up-to-date lists of useful sites there, covering not only ADSI, but also MMC and the Windows Installer. There are also guides to the more useful books I've read covering these areas, as well as COM. The URL is `http://www.SimonRobinson.com`.

The ADSI listserver discussion groups are at `http://www.15seconds.com`, while the Microsoft ADSI newsgroup is at `http://support.microsoft.com/support/news/Ngresults.asp?D=sdk`.

COM

The main website for COM at the moment is the COMDeveloper site,
`http://www.COMDeveloper.com`, (which is also sponsored by Wrox Press). You'll find a large
number of articles covering all aspects of COM for C++, VB and Java programmers, including a
couple of articles by me!

There are a lot of sites with information about COM. Other good sites to check out are the Vivid
Creations site (which includes resources to download), `http://www.vivid-creations.com`,
and Chris Sells' site, `http://www.sellsbrothers.com`.

Listservers covering COM and ATL are at `http://discuss.microsoft.com`. These listservers
are extremely useful for swapping hints and ideas with other developers. They are used by all ranges
of ability, from beginners to gurus.

There's also a similar group maintained by the COMDeveloper site, but hosted at egroups at
`http://www.egroups.com/list/comdeveloper`.

> *Please do try to research problems and find out the answers to your questions before asking them
> on the listservers. You'll find that the users of the listservers are generally very helpful, but there's
> no surer way to irritate people than to look like you want them to do your work for you because
> you can't be bothered to make the effort yourself!*

LDAP

For LDAP, there are quite a large number of links available. Good starting points are the University
of Michigan site, `http://www.umich.edu/~dirsvcs/ldap`, and Jeff Hodge's LDAP roadmap
page, `http://www.kingsmountain.com/ldapRoadmap.shtml`, which contains a huge number
of links to other LDAP related sites.

You can also download the University of Michigan's LDAP implementation at their web site, while
the Netscape implementation is available at (guess what) Netscape's web site,
`http://www.netscape.com`.

For definitions relating to LDAP, the RFC's are the standard resource. These are covered in
Appendix B of this book.

Kerberos

Most useful information can be found at the Massachusetts Institute of Technology Kerberos web
page, `http://web.mit.edu/kerberos/www/`. There's also some stuff at
`http://gost.isi.edu/brian/security`.

WBEM

The best site at which to find out about WBEM is the desktop management taskforce's site,
`http://www.dmtf.org`.

MMC

There's not too much on MMC so far, though I am maintaining a list of MMC resources at my own web site, `http://www.SimonRobinson.com`. The COMDeveloper site, `http://www.COMDeveloper.com`, also has some stuff related to MMC.

Christian Beaumont's sample snap-in, which demonstrates using the ATL MMC classes to code a snap-in, is at `http://www.geocities.com/~chrisbe/client.htm`. This sample takes a different approach from the one I develop in Chapter 12. In Chapter 12, I use C++ inheritance to derive snap-in item classes, whereas Christian Beaumont's sample uses templates to achieve the same result. The sample snap-in at my website is closer to the one developed in Chapter 12.

LDAP SDKs

You can download the SDKs at:

- ❑ Netscape SDKs: `http://developer.netscape.com/directory`
- ❑ Perl: `http://www.perl.com/CPAN/index.html`
- ❑ JNDI (Java Naming and Directory Interface): `http://java.sun.com/products`

Object IDs

You can get an object ID prefix for your organization at `http://www.isis.edu/cgi-bin/iana/enterprise.pl`.

Bibliography

This bibliography covers books I found useful, which contain sections relevant to the material I've covered in this book.

Steven Hahn, *ADSI ASP Programmer's Reference*, Wrox Press, ISBN 186100169X.
A basic introduction to ADSI programming with ASP (though you might have done better to have read it *before* you attempted this book). It covers the basics of using the WinNT provider in detail, with some coverage of LDAP and IIS.

Mikael Freidlitz and Todd Mondor, *Professional ADSI CDO Programming with ASP*, Wrox Press, ISBN 1861001908.
The book to get if you want to use ADSI in conjunction with CDO. Shows how you can combine the two technologies, along with the Windows Scripting Host. Ever had the feeling Wrox has a monopoly on books on ADSI?

Jonathan Pinnock, *Professional DCOM Application Development*, Wrox Press, ISBN 1861001312.
This book has a chapter introducing ADSI, and another introducing MMC. It is intended for people who are already reasonably familiar with COM. The MMC chapter only covers ATL 2.1, so you should use it to understand the MMC interfaces themselves rather than how to implement them in ATL.

Richard Grimes, *Professional DCOM Programming*, Wrox Press, ISBN 186100060X.
One of the standard references for DCOM programming, though a little dated now.

Richard Grimes, George Reilly, Alex Stockton and Julian Templeman, *Beginning ATL COM Programming*, Wrox Press, ISBN 1861000111.
Good introduction to both COM and ATL – I'd say one of the best books to buy if you're a C++ programmer, new to COM.

Smith and Tim Howes, *LDAP: Programming Directory Enabled Applications with the Lightweight Directory Access Protocol*, MacMillan, ISBN 1578700000.
Slightly dated now, as it was written before LDAP 3 was approved, but a good introduction to programming with the LDAP C APIs.

Mark Wilcox, *Implementing LDAP*, Wrox Press, ISBN 1861002211.
A good guide to the available SDKs in the different programming languages available for writing LDAP clients. Also explains the principles of LDAP 3.

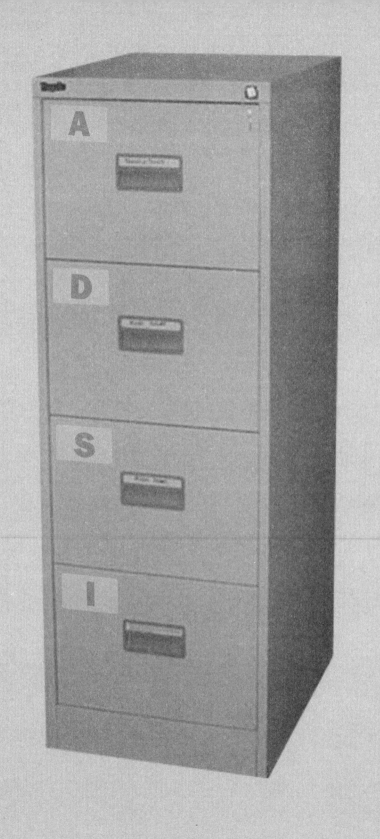

Requests For Comments

Requests For Comments, or **RFCs**, are the standard means of developing Internet standards. A Request For Comments suggests a definition for a standard, and after a suitable period of comments and field trials, the standard may be approved by the Internet Engineering Task Force (IETF). Most are available from the IETF webpage, `http://www.ietf.org/rfc/`.

In this event, the RFCs are still left with their original text – including all the warnings that they are only suggestions, not to be relied upon. So if you do look up any of these RFCs, don't be put off by all the statements to the effect that developers are hereby warned not to use them!

The one point to bear in mind is that the RFCs are proposed as standards. This means that they need to be fairly rigorous – or even mathematical – in their definitions, which can make them quite hard to read. If you don't need to see the exact definitions, you may be better off reading books!

Useful RFCs

There are a few RFCs relevant to LDAP and X500. The important ones are:

- ❏ **RFC 1777: Lightweight Directory Access Protocol.**
  This RFC is *the* definition of LDAP version 2. However, it needs to be read in conjunction with RFCs 1778 and 1779.

- ❏ **RFC 2251: Lightweight Directory Access Protocol.**
  This is *the* definition of LDAP version 3. It's complete in that it includes all the version 2 stuff – you can pretty much tell where the relevant sections of RFC 1777 must have been cut and pasted into this one! Read it in conjunction with RFCs 2252-2256.

- ❏ **RFC 1510**
  You might want to check out RFC 1510 for the definition of Kerberos V 5.

RFC Terminology

Most of these RFCs do assume that you're already familiar with some basic concepts and terms. The main ones are:

❑ **Octet Strings**. These are basically ANSI strings, except that they can store binary values. This means that some characters may have the value, zero, so the strings need to be accompanied by an integer giving their length.

❑ **IA5 strings**. Again, these are ANSI strings, but these have a much more restricted character set.

❑ **ASN1 Notation**. This is a standard for how data is formatted when it is transmitted over the Internet. For high-level programming, you don't need to worry about it. Basically, it means that, if you see something like a statement that a message consists of an integer followed by a string, etc. ASN1 means that that is sufficient to determine how the data is formatted at a low level.

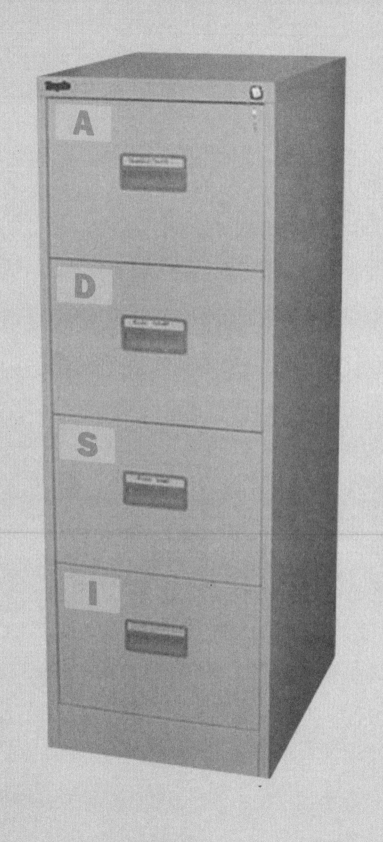

VARIANTs and SAFEARRAYs in ADSI

In this appendix, we will cover how to write code that uses VARIANTs in C++, and how VARIANTs are used in ADSI.

If you program in VB or VBScript, you use VARIANTs all the time, but you don't need to understand how they work. C++ works at a lower level, and in order to manipulate VARIANTs in C++, it's necessary to delve into their internals. If you use COM in C++, then you may have encountered VARIANTs already. Even without COM, you may have found them useful for storing variables that may be of different data types.

ADSI uses VARIANTs a lot, so in order to write ADSI clients and providers with C++, you need to be very familiar with how to use the automation data types – hence this Appendix.

Firstly, we'll quickly go over, at an intuitive level, what kinds of VARIANT combinations you will encounter with ADSI. You won't need to know any of the technical details of VARIANTs to do this. Then we'll run through how VARIANTs and SAFEARRAYs are defined in detail, and the API functions available to manipulate them. Finally, we'll apply our knowledge by developing some of the utility VARIANT conversion functions that we need to write as part of the StarRaiders provider.

Most of this appendix contains reference material, so if you'd rather go straight in and see how to write code that uses VARIANTs, you might be best off skipping to the sample code at the end of the appendix.

How ADSI Uses VARIANTs

ADSI `IADsXXX` **interface methods use** `VARIANTs` **whenever any variable that is to be passed in or out as a parameter in a method call is not of a simple known data type, such as string or integer. This means that** `VARIANTs` **are used to pass arrays, interface pointers, and any parameter that may be of a variable data type.**

You will encounter `VARIANTs` in ADSI in one of three broad formats:

❑ **Simple** `VARIANT`. This is a `VARIANT` that contains one instance of a simple data type, such as an integer or an interface pointer. It's used whenever that's what needs to be passed.

❑ **Array**. This is a `VARIANT` that contains a `SAFEARRAY` of `VARIANTs`, which contains the actual data. It is used to pass a simple data type that is either multi-valued, or might be multi-valued (as in, for example, `IADs::GetEx()`, which makes no assumptions about whether data is single-valued). You need to note the format carefully here, as it's possible for a `SAFEARRAY` to exist as a `SAFEARRAY` of any automation data type, such as `BSTR` or `LONG`. In other words, you could have, say, a `SAFEARRAY` of `BSTR` or a `SAFEARRAY` of `LONG`. ADSI *never* does that (apart from the exception mentioned below). It always imposes an extra level of containment. The `SAFEARRAY` is always a `SAFEARRAY` of `VARIANTs`, and each `VARIANT` contains an actual value. This means that for data in this format, you've got three levels of containment/indirection to get through before you can get at the actual data.

❑ **Byte array**. This is a `VARIANT` containing a `SAFEARRAY` of bytes (`VT_UI1`). It is the only case in which a `SAFEARRAY` will directly contain anything other than `VARIANTs`. This data type is used whenever we need to pass binary data. Incidentally, this means that it is not possible to have multi-valued binary data, since the `SAFEARRAY` has already been used to store the data itself. Hence, if a property is of type binary, it must be single-valued.

❑ These are the only formats in which the ADSI interfaces use `VARIANTs`. Luckily for us, this does mean that there are a couple of potential complications we won't encounter with ADSI: The `SAFEARRAYs` only ever have one dimension, and values are never stored by reference (`VT_BYREF`).

What's Inside a VARIANT

So let's go over the basics. A `VARIANT` is defined as follows:

```
struct   tagVARIANT
{
    union
    {
        struct  __tagVARIANT
        {
            VARTYPE vt;
            WORD wReserved1;
            WORD wReserved2;
            WORD wReserved3;
            union
```

```
        {
            LONG lVal;
            BYTE bVal;
            SHORT iVal;
            FLOAT fltVal;
            DOUBLE dblVal;
            VARIANT_BOOL boolVal;
            _VARIANT_BOOL bool;
            SCODE scode;
            CY cyVal;
            DATE date;
            BSTR bstrVal;
            IUnknown __RPC_FAR *punkVal;
            IDispatch __RPC_FAR *pdispVal;
            SAFEARRAY __RPC_FAR *parray;
            BYTE __RPC_FAR *pbVal;
            SHORT __RPC_FAR *piVal;
            LONG __RPC_FAR *plVal;
            FLOAT __RPC_FAR *pfltVal;
            DOUBLE __RPC_FAR *pdblVal;
            VARIANT_BOOL __RPC_FAR *pboolVal;
            _VARIANT_BOOL __RPC_FAR *pbool;
            SCODE __RPC_FAR *pscode;
            CY __RPC_FAR *pcyVal;
            DATE __RPC_FAR *pdate;
            BSTR __RPC_FAR *pbstrVal;
            IUnknown __RPC_FAR *__RPC_FAR *ppunkVal;
            IDispatch __RPC_FAR *__RPC_FAR *ppdispVal;
            SAFEARRAY __RPC_FAR *__RPC_FAR *pparray;
            VARIANT __RPC_FAR *pvarVal;
            PVOID byref;
            CHAR cVal;
            USHORT uiVal;
            ULONG ulVal;
            INT intVal;
            UINT uintVal;
            DECIMAL __RPC_FAR *pdecVal;
            CHAR __RPC_FAR *pcVal;
            USHORT __RPC_FAR *puiVal;
            ULONG __RPC_FAR *pulVal;
            INT __RPC_FAR *pintVal;
            UINT __RPC_FAR *puintVal;
            struct  __tagBRECORD
            {
                PVOID pvRecord;
                IRecordInfo __RPC_FAR *pRecInfo;
            }__VARIANT_NAME_4;
        }__VARIANT_NAME_3;
    }__VARIANT_NAME_2;
    DECIMAL decVal;
}__VARIANT_NAME_1;
};
```

❑   This looks more complex than it really is. Basically, it's a union of a large number of data types, along with a VARTYPE, vt (VARTYPE is defined as unsigned short), which indicates which of the members of the union actually contains valid data. Since the members of a union all occupy the same memory space, the size of a VARIANT is quite small: 16 bytes. There are also a few unused reserved members.

For our purposes, we can ignore quite a fair bit of the definition – everything after the member

```
UINT uintVal;
```

is irrelevant for ADSI.

The way the vt member has its contents determined is a bit of a hybrid. Its value is mostly taken from the VARENUM enumeration, which is defined in the file wtypes.h. However, there may also be a bitwise operation going on. If the VARIANT contains an array or a reference, then the values VT_ARRAY and VT_BYREF will respectively be logical ORed with the vartype.

The vartype enumeration is quite long, but the values relevant to ADSI are:

```
enum VARENUM
{    VT_EMPTY          = 0,
     VT_NULL           = 1,
     VT_I2             = 2,
     VT_I4             = 3,
     VT_R4             = 4,
     VT_R8             = 5,
     VT_CY             = 6,
     VT_DATE           = 7,
     VT_BSTR           = 8,
     VT_DISPATCH       = 9,
     VT_ERROR          = 10,
     VT_BOOL           = 11,
     VT_VARIANT        = 12,
     VT_UNKNOWN        = 13,
     VT_DECIMAL        = 14,
     VT_I1             = 16,
     VT_UI1            = 17,
     VT_UI2            = 18,
     VT_UI4            = 19,
     VT_I8             = 20,
     VT_UI8            = 21,

     // most of the types not relevant to ADSI removed for clarity

     VT_VECTOR         = 0x1000,
     VT_ARRAY          = 0x2000,
     VT_BYREF          = 0x4000,
     VT_RESERVED       = 0x8000,
     VT_ILLEGAL        = 0xffff,
     VT_ILLEGALMASKED  = 0xfff,
     VT_TYPEMASK       = 0xfff
};
```

A couple of examples:

- ❑ If vt contains VT_BSTR, then the valid data member is bstrVal, which will contain a BSTR.

- ❑ If vt contains VT_BSTR | VT_ARRAY, then the valid data member is parray, which points to a SAFEARRAY. The data type stored in the SAFEARRAY is BSTR. This combination isn't seen in ADSI.

- ❑ If vt contains VT_BSTR | VT_VARIANT then the valid data member is again parray, but this time it points to a SAFEARRAY of VARIANTs. Note that in this case, the vt member doesn't give us any indication of the data type that is ultimately stored. For that you need to look at the vt member of each VARIANT inside the SAFEARRAY.

The vt member is also important in that it implicitly tells you how the memory for the union should be freed in the event that the variant is deleted. (For example, if the valid member of the union is actually a pointer to more memory, then that memory should also be freed.)

What's Inside a SAFEARRAY

A SAFEARRAY is intended as a normal array. However, it is an array that can have an arbitrary number of dimensions, arbitrary size for each dimension, and store any automation data type. That means it needs a lot of associated member variables to indicate what is actually being stored. Hence, a SAFEARRAY has a more complex definition. It is:

```
typedef struct  tagSAFEARRAY
{
    USHORT cDims;
    USHORT fFeatures;
    ULONG cbElements;
    ULONG cLocks;
    PVOID pvData;
    SAFEARRAYBOUND rgsabound[ 1 ];
} SAFEARRAY;
```

Incidentally I've simplified this definition somewhat by removing a #ifdef clause that modifies the definition if you're running Windows 3.1 or earlier. I've never heard of anyone attempting to run ADSI on Windows 3.1, so I think we can safely ignore that bit!

The SAFEARRAY definition includes another structure, the SAFEARRAYBOUND, so let's have a look at that:

```
typedef struct  tagSAFEARRAYBOUND
{
    ULONG cElements;
    LONG lLbound;
} SAFEARRAYBOUND;
```

That's an awful lot of data to define an array.

Let's start off by looking at the SAFEARRAYBOUND. This simply indicates how many elements there are in any one dimension of the array. There are two numbers in it because it's possible that the array might not be zero-based (VB supports arrays with any arbitrary base, and this is achieved with the lLbound member). cElements contains the number of elements, and lLbound stores the index of the lowest element. For SAFEARRAYs created in C++, there's really no reason to set lLbound to any value other than zero, so we'll generally ignore it.

Since the SAFEARRAYBOUND gives the size of only one dimension, we need an array of them to allow for the possibility of a multidimensional SAFEARRAY. If we turn to the definition of a SAFEARRAY, we find the member cDims, which stores the number of dimensions. Then rgsabound is a pointer to the start of the array of SAFEARRAYBOUND structures. Don't be fooled by the [1] in its definition. Strictly, it would have been more accurate to declare this variable as *SAFEARRAYBOUND instead of SAFEARRAYBOUND[1], although both declarations have a similar effect.

pvData is a pointer to where the data is actually stored – it's declared as a void because we don't know what data type is actually there. Since we don't know what the data type is, we need to know how many bytes each element of the array occupies. This is provided in the member cbElements. This is another slightly misleading name – cbElements does NOT store a count of the elements, it stores a count of how many bytes each element occupies.

That leaves us with two elements. cLocks is there because the API functions that manipulate SAFEARRAYs use a system of locking the array to prevent it being modified through the API functions. cLocks is a count of how many times locks have been applied.

fFeatures contains some information which basically tells us how the memory for the array has been allocated. It's needed for the benefit of the API functions that clean up SAFEARRAY memory.

API Functions

We're not entirely on our own when it comes to manipulating SAFEARRAYs and VARIANTs – there are a fair few API functions to help us out. For the VARIANTs, we've got the following:

Name	Description
VariantInit	Initializes a variant, by setting the vt member to VT_EMPTY.
VariantClear	Roughly the equivalent of a destructor. This sets the vt member to VT_EMPTY, but also checks to see if the VARIANT contained pointers to anything that needs to be freed. Memory for SAFEARRAYs will be freed, and interface pointers will have their reference counts decremented.
VariantCopy	Copies a VARIANT. This performs a deep copy, so, for example, contained SAFEARRAYs or strings will be copied in full, while the function will call AddRef() on any interface pointers copied.
VariantCopyInd	Same as VariantCopy, but if the source data contains references, these will be chased so that the destination doesn't need to contain references.

Name	Description
VariantChangeType	This attempts to change the type of data to the specified type. It'll handle simple data types, like integer or floating point to string, but it won't handle complex data types like SAFEARRAYs. Interestingly, it will handle IDispatch pointers. It will attempt, for example, to convert an IDispatch pointer to a string by obtaining the default automation property and converting that to a string.
VariantChangeTypeEx	Similar to VariantChangeType, but will also swap locales if required.

For SAFEARRAYs, using the API functions become a necessity rather than a convenience, since trying to do tasks like allocate memory for an array and fill all the data members would be very complex without some helper functions. There are a huge number of API functions for SAFEARRAYs – too many to list here – but I've listed the most important ones. Full details are in MSDN.

Name	Description
SafeArrayCreate	Allocates memory for and creates a new SAFEARRAY of given variable type, number of dimensions and number of elements in each dimension. This function is all you'll need to create a SAFEARRAY, though you'll need to separately fill in the initial data, either using SafeArrayAccessData or SafeArrayPutElement.
SafeArrayCreateVector	Similar to SafeArrayCreate, but offers a simpler way of creating a SAFEARRAY that only has one dimension.
SafeArrayCopy	Performs a deep copy of a SAFEARRAY.
SafeArrayAccessData	Lets you get at the raw memory (as a void* pointer) in the array. This is usually the most efficient way of reading from or writing to the array, since you can then treat the memory as an ordinary array of the appropriate C++ data type. Also increments the lock count cLocks, which prevents other SAFEARRAY API functions from using the same memory while you are accessing it.
SafeArrayUnaccessData	Releases the lock count. Always call this function after calling SafeArrayAccessData, when you have finished manipulating the memory.
SafeArrayGetElement	Retrieves (as a void*) the element of the array specified by its index or indices.
SafeArrayPutElement	Lets you set the specified element of the array.

ATL CComVARIANT Class

ATL comes to our aid further with VARIANTs (but not SAFEARRAYs) by defining a class, **CComVariant**. The CComVariant class is derived from the VARIANT, and doesn't add any new member variables, so each instance doesn't take up any more space. It does add a large number of constructors, some useful conversion functions and operators, and a destructor. I find it most useful because it saves the need to call VariantInit() to initialize your VARIANT and VariantClear() before it goes out of scope.

At present, the documentation for CComVariant consists of – the source code! However, it is still worth flicking through the code to check what's there. You can find the full definition in atlbase.h. You will find all the main VARIANT API functions are pretty much rendered obsolete by the CComVariant class.

In the code for StarRaiders and the other samples, I tend to swap between VARIANTs and CComVariant, depending on what's most convenient. You might think that with CComVariant available, there's no need to use VARIANTs at all. Unfortunately, for interface methods, you will still need to pass VARIANTs because IDL knows how to marshal them – which it doesn't for CComVariants.

ADSI API Functions

In addition to the standard VARIANT API functions, a couple of other useful ones are implemented by the ADSI runtime. They are defined in adshlp.h, and they are:

Name	Description
ADsBuildVarArrayInt	Takes an array of integers and converts it to a VARIANT containing a SAFEARRAY of VARIANTs of integers.
ADsBuildVarArrayStr	Takes an array of BSTR and converts it to a VARIANT containing a SAFEARRAY of VARIANTs of BSTR.

Working with VARIANTs and SAFEARRAYs in StarRaiders

In this section, we're going to develop a couple of utility functions to convert between VARIANT formats. These functions are used in the StarRaiders provider, but the tasks they perform are quite general, and will almost certainly be required in other ADSI providers – or in some cases in ADSI clients.

As usual, the source code can be downloaded from the Wrox web site. However, for these functions, the code is not available separately: it is contained within the StarRaiders provider. You will need to download StarRaiders, and look in the Utilities.h and Utilities.cpp files.

A General Conversion Function

First up, we'll look at a general function to convert between any given data types. You might think that this functionality is already covered by the VariantChangeType API function, or the equivalent CComVariant::ChangeType member function, but it isn't. These functions will convert between *simple* data types. In other words, they will automatically convert a VARIANT of type VT_I4 to one of type VT_BSTR, but they will give up instantly if they encounter something that contains – say – a SAFEARRAY.

Since a large number of ADSI interface methods involve VARIANTs containing SAFEARRAYs, this isn't really good enough for us. We need something that can cope with simple data types, as well as VARIANTs containing one-dimensional arrays. That's where the ConvertVariantType() function comes in.

I've simplified this somewhat. The StarRaiders provider does not define any binary properties, so we don't need to worry about encountering an array of UI1. The only types we need to worry about are simple data types, and SAFEARRAYs of VARIANTs. Any other formats will trigger an ASSERT. Even so, the general conversion function is a fair sized bit of code. This is how it starts:

```
HRESULT ConvertVariantType(VARIANT &varNewValue, const VARIANT &varOldValue,
                           VARTYPE vtOuter, VARTYPE vtInner)
{
    HRESULT hr;
    hr = VariantClear(&varNewValue); ASH;
```

Let's start off with the parameters. varNewValue is the VARIANT where we will put the result, and varOldValue is the value in the original format. We assume these values are both different. ConvertVariantType() won't do in-place conversion.

The two VARTYPEs, vtOuter and vtInner, indicate what data type we want to convert to. If it's a simple value, vtOuter will contain that type and vtInner will be zero. If it's an array of VARIANTs, vtOuter will be VT_ARRAY | VT_VARIANT, and vtInner will be the data type actually to be stored in the VARIANTs.

Checking Data Types

The first thing ConvertVariantType() does is go through a few ASSERTs to make sure we've been given data types that we can handle. If the parameter varOldValue itself contains an array, we need to delve inside the contained SAFEARRAY and check out the data type of its first element, to make sure it's OK.

```
    // check outer VARTYPE for recognised type
    VARTYPE vtOldOuter = varOldValue.vt;
    ASSERT(!(vtOldOuter & VT_BYREF));
    if (vtOldOuter & VT_ARRAY)
        ASSERT(vtOldOuter == (VT_VARIANT | VT_ARRAY));

    ASSERT(!(vtOuter & VT_BYREF));
    if (vtOuter & VT_ARRAY)
        ASSERT(vtOuter == (VT_VARIANT | VT_ARRAY));

    VARTYPE vtOldInner = 0;
    if (vtOldOuter == (VT_VARIANT | VT_ARRAY))
    {
        SAFEARRAY *psa = varOldValue.parray;

        if (psa->rgsabound->cElements == 0)
            return E_FAIL;

        VARIANT *pvarFirstInArray;
        hr = SafeArrayAccessData(psa, (void**)&pvarFirstInArray);
        vtOldInner = pvarFirstInArray->vt;
        hr = SafeArrayUnaccessData(psa);
    }
```

```
        ASSERT((!(vtInner & VT_ARRAY)) && (!(vtInner & VT_BYREF)));
        ASSERT((!(vtOldInner & VT_ARRAY)) && (!(vtOldInner & VT_BYREF)));

        //got all the relevant VARTYPEs and established we can work with them
```

Converting Data Types

OK – so we've established we should be able to work with the data types we've been given. We now deal separately with the four possibilities for what we have to do. These possibilities are (in order), to convert:

❑   Simple VARIANT to simple VARIANT

❑   Simple VARIANT to array

❑   Array to simple VARIANT

❑   Array to array

Simple VARIANT to Simple VARIANT

The first case is easy to handle: The API function VariantChangeType will cope with it, so we can leave that function to deal with the conversion.

Notice the const_cast<> in the code. That's there because I'm very careful with my code to declare parameters as const if I know the function isn't going to modify them. Unfortunately, Microsoft isn't as careful (possibly for compatibility with ANSI C?), and VariantChangeType doesn't declare the source VARIANT as const.

```
    if (!(vtOuter & VT_ARRAY) && !(vtOldOuter & VT_ARRAY))
    {
        return VariantChangeType(&varNewValue, const_cast<VARIANT*>(&varOldValue),
                                 0, vtOuter);
    }
```

Simple VARIANT to Array

The second case, simple variant to array, is more complex, because we need to create the SAFEARRAY inside the destination VARIANT. This array will be of size 1.

```
    else if ((vtOuter & VT_ARRAY) && !(vtOldOuter & VT_ARRAY))
    {
        SAFEARRAYBOUND rgsabound[1];
        rgsabound[0].lLbound = 0;
        rgsabound[0].cElements = 1;
        SAFEARRAY *psa;
        psa = SafeArrayCreate(VT_VARIANT, 1, rgsabound);

        if(psa == NULL)
            return E_FAIL;

        VARIANT *pvarFirst;
        hr = SafeArrayAccessData(psa, (void**)&pvarFirst); ASH;
        pvarFirst->vt = vtInner;
        hr = VariantChangeType(pvarFirst, const_cast<VARIANT*>(&varOldValue),
                               0, vtInner);
        hr = SafeArrayUnaccessData(psa); ASH;
        varNewValue.vt = (VT_ARRAY | VT_VARIANT);
        varNewValue.parray = psa;
        return hr;
    }
```

Array to Simple VARIANT

Converting an array to a simple data type is a bit easier, since it's just a case of getting at the VARIANT inside the SAFEARRAY and running a VariantChangeType on it. This is the one case where we might legitimately fail – we need to make sure there is only one element in the array, otherwise we can't possibly convert it to a simple data type:

```
else if (!(vtOuter & VT_ARRAY) && (vtOldOuter & VT_ARRAY))
{
    varNewValue.vt = vtOuter;
    SAFEARRAY *psa = varOldValue.parray;
    if (psa->rgsabound->cElements != 1)
        return E_FAIL;
    VARIANT *pvarFirst;
    hr = SafeArrayAccessData(psa, (void**)&pvarFirst); ASH;
    hr = VariantChangeType(&varNewValue, pvarFirst, 0, vtOuter);
    SafeArrayUnaccessData(psa);
    return hr;
}
```

Array to Array

Finally, we need to deal with converting an array to another array. Note that there is an API function SafeArrayCopy that would have simplified this bit of code a lot. Except we can't use it, because SafeArrayCopy merely copies the SAFEARRAY. However, we have to allow for the possibility of having to do some data conversion, if the datatype contained in the VARIANT, vtOldInner, in the source differs from what we need in the destination.

```
else if ((vtOuter & VT_ARRAY) && (vtOldOuter & VT_ARRAY))
{
    SAFEARRAY *psaOld = varOldValue.parray;
    if (psaOld->rgsabound->cElements < 1)
        return E_FAIL;

    SAFEARRAYBOUND rgsabound[1];
    rgsabound[0].lLbound = 0;
    rgsabound[0].cElements = psaOld->rgsabound->cElements;
    SAFEARRAY *psa;
    psa = SafeArrayCreate(VT_VARIANT, 1, rgsabound);
    if(psa == NULL)
        return E_FAIL;

    VARIANT *pvarFirstOld, *pvarFirstNew;
    hr = SafeArrayAccessData(psaOld, (void**)&pvarFirstOld); ASH;
    hr = SafeArrayAccessData(psa, (void**)&pvarFirstNew); ASH;
    for (unsigned i=0 ; i<psaOld->rgsabound->cElements ; i++)
    {
        hr = VariantChangeType(pvarFirstNew + i, pvarFirstOld+i, 0, vtInner);
            ASH;
    }
    SafeArrayUnaccessData(psa);
    SafeArrayUnaccessData(psaOld);
```

```
            varNewValue.vt = (VT_ARRAY | VT_VARIANT);
            varNewValue.parray = psa;
            return hr;
        }

        ASSERT(false); // something's wrong - we should have covered all possibilities
        return E_NOTIMPL;
    }
```

Converting between Get and GetEx format

This is a task that might commonly need to be done. Recall that if you request a property value using GetEx(), it will always be returned as a VARIANT containing a SAFEARRAY of VARIANTs containing the required data type, irrespective of whether the value is multi-valued or not. If you request it using Get(), then you'll only get this complex format back if the data actually is multi-valued. Otherwise, you'll get a simple VARIANT back.

On occasions, it may be useful to convert between these forms. This is something that is easy to accomplish using the ConvertVariantType() function that we've just developed.

First up, going from Get() format to GetEx():

```
HRESULT GetToGetExFormat(VARIANT &varNewValue, const VARIANT &varOldValue)
{
    VARTYPE vtOuter = VT_VARIANT | VT_ARRAY;
    VARTYPE vtInner;
    if (varOldValue.vt == (VT_VARIANT | VT_ARRAY))
    {
        return VariantCopy(&varNewValue, const_cast<VARIANT*>(&varOldValue));
    }
    else
    {
        if (varOldValue.vt & VT_BYREF)
            return E_FAIL;
        vtInner = varOldValue.vt;
        return ConvertVariantType(varNewValue, varOldValue, vtOuter, vtInner);
    }
}
```

Then going the other way:

```
HRESULT GetExToGetFormat(VARIANT &varNewValue, const VARIANT &varOldValue)
{
    HRESULT hr = S_OK;
    VARTYPE vtOuter;
    VARTYPE vtInner = 0;
    if (varOldValue.vt & VT_BYREF)
        return E_FAIL;
    else if (varOldValue.vt == (VT_VARIANT & VT_ARRAY))
    {
        SAFEARRAY *psa = varOldValue.parray;
```

```
            if (psa->rgsabound->cElements != 1)
                return E_FAIL;
            VARIANT *pvarFirstInArray;
            hr = SafeArrayAccessData(psa, (void**)&pvarFirstInArray);

            if ((pvarFirstInArray->vt & VT_ARRAY) || (pvarFirstInArray->vt &
                                                      VT_BYREF))
                return E_FAIL;
            vtOuter = pvarFirstInArray->vt;
            return ConvertVariantType(varNewValue, varOldValue, vtOuter, vtInner);
        }
        else if (varOldValue.vt & VT_ARRAY)
            return E_FAIL;
        else
        {
            return VariantCopy(&varNewValue, const_cast<VARIANT*>(&varOldValue));
        }
    }
}
```

...and that's it! We've now filled in the holes you need to get ADSI's VARIANT-intesive mechanics working with C++.

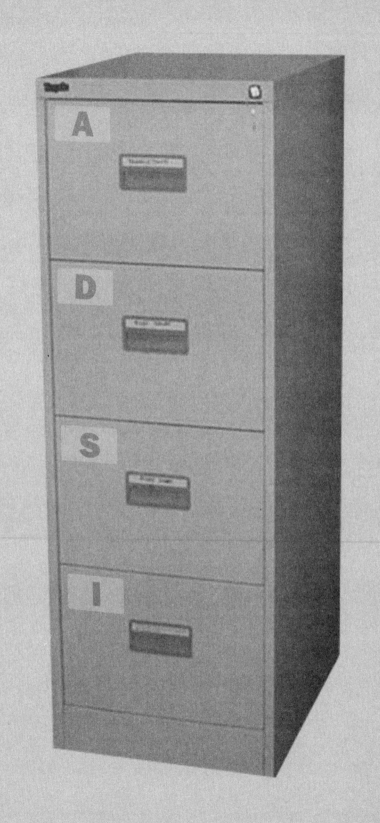

D

ADSI Interface Summary

This appendix lists all the properties and methods exposed by the different ADSI interfaces (excluding the NDS-specific interfaces).

Before we start on the interfaces, a quick recap on the different directory objects you're likely to encounter, and the interfaces you can usually expect them to expose.

Stuff Exposed by All Objects

All objects that are objects in the directory tree should implement IADs, IADsPropertyList, IDirectoryObject and IDirectorySearch. However, some providers may not support IDirectoryObject, and only providers that support searching will support IDirectorySearch.

In addition, all containers will expose IADsContainer. In some providers, objects will also implement IADsDeleteOps.

Obviously, it should go without saying that all objects will implement IUnknown and IDispatch.

Apart from these interfaces, directory objects that wrap particular types of object may implement the following.

> *You should be aware that this list describes what tends to happen in the Microsoft providers, notably WinNT and LDAP. However, it is quite possible that other providers may be written which do not follow this list.*

Access Control Entries

These are not part of the directory tree, and so will **not** implement `IADs`, etc. They will implement `IDispatch` and `IADsAccessControlEntry`. These objects are implemented by the ADSI runtime: there is no need for authors of ADSI providers to implement them.

Access Control Lists

These are not part of the directory tree and so will **not** implement `IADs`, etc. They will implement `IDispatch` and `IADsAccessControlList`. These objects are implemented by the ADSI runtime, so there's no need for authors of ADSI providers to implement them.

Computers

These will implement `IADsComputer`. However, in Active Directory, computers instead implement `IADsUser`.

Domains

These may implement `IADsDomain`.

Groups

These will implement `IADsGroup`.

The lanmanserver

This will implement `IADsFileService` and `IADsFileServiceOperations`.

Namespaces

These will *always* implement `IADSOpenDSObject`.

Print Jobs

These are not part of the directory tree and so will **not** implement `IADs`, etc. They will implement `IDispatch`, `IADsPrintJob` and `IADsPrintJobOperations`.

Print Queues

These will implement `IADsPrintQueue` and `IADsPrintQueueOperations`.

The ADSI Router

This object is implemented by the ADSI runtime. It implements `IADsNamespaces`.

Resources

These are not part of the directory tree and so will **not** implement IADs, etc. They will implement IDispatch and IADsResource.

Security Descriptors

These are not part of the directory tree and so will **not** implement IADs, etc. They will implement IDispatch and IADsSecurityDescriptor. As these objects are implemented by the ADSI runtime, there is no need for authors of ADSI providers to implement them.

NT Services

These will implement IADsService and IADsServiceOperations.

Sessions

These are not part of the directory tree and so will **not** implement IADs, etc. They will implement IDispatch and IADsSession.

File Shares

These will implement IADsFileShare.

Users or User Accounts

These will implement IADsUser.

The Interfaces

The interfaces are arranged alphabetically.

IADs

Derived from: IDispatch

This interface is implemented by all ADSI objects that exist in the directory tree. It contains read-only properties to give basic information about the object, and some methods to manipulate the property cache.

IADs properties and methods	Description
get_Name	Gets the object's relative name.
get_Class	Gets the name of the object's schema class.
get_GUID	Gets the GUID of the object as stored in the underlying directory store.
get_AdsPath	Gets the object's ADsPath that uniquely identifies this object from all others.
get_Parent	Gets the ADsPath string for the parent of the object.
get_Schema	Gets the ADsPath string to the schema class object for this object.
GetInfo	Loads the property values of this object from the underlying directory store.
SetInfo	Persists the changes on this object to the underlying directory store.
Get	Gets the value for a property by name.
Put	Sets the value for a property by name.
GetEx	Gets the value for a single or multi-valued property by name.
PutEx	Sets the value for a single or multi-valued property by name.
GetInfoEx	Loads specific property values of this object from the underlying directory store.

IADsAccessControlEntry

Derived from: IDispatch

This interface is implemented by access control entry (ACE) objects. These objects are implemented by the ADSI runtime: they are not provider-specific. Note that these objects do not exist in the directory tree, and so do not implement IADs. They are obtainable by enumerating on access control list objects.

IADsAccessControlEntry properties and methods	Description
get/put_AccessMask	Gets/sets the access mask for an ACE.
get/put_AceType	Gets/sets the ACE type.
get/put_AceFlags	Gets/sets ACE flag values.
get/put_Flags	Gets/sets flag values.

IADsAccessControlEntry properties and methods	Description
get/put_ObjectType	Gets/sets the object type.
get/put_InheritedObjectType	Gets/sets the inherited object type.
get/put_Trustee	Gets/sets the trustee.

IADsAccessControlList

Derived from: IDispatch

This interface is implemented by access control list (ACL) objects. These objects are implemented by the ADSI runtime: they are not provider-specific. These objects do not exist in the directory tree, and so do not implement IADs. They are obtainable as properties exposed by IADsSecurityDescriptor: DiscretionaryACL and SystemACL.

IADsAccessControlList properties and methods	Description
get/put_AclRevision	Gets/sets the ACL revision number.
get/put_AceCount	Gets/sets number of ACEs in the ACL.
AddAce	Adds an entry to the ACL.
RemoveAce	Removes an entry from the ACL.
CopyAccessList	Copies the ACL.
get__NewEnum	Gets a pointer to the enumerator object.

IADsClass

Derived from: IADs

This interface is exposed by class schema objects, which will usually exist in the schema container. It gives you access to a set of properties that describe a given class of object. Active Directory is an exception to this, in that it exposes the equivalent properties using the property cache, and IADs::Get(), IADs::Put(), etc.

Although all the properties are technically read/write, you will only be able to write to them in providers that support schema extension.

IADsClass properties and methods	Description
`get_PrimaryInterface`	Gets the identifier of the interface defining this schema class.
`get/put_CLSID`	Gets/sets the CLSID identifying application component that implements this schema class.
`get/put_OID`	Gets/sets the directory-specific object identifier.
`get/put_Abstract`	Gets/sets the flag in order to determine whether or not this schema class is abstract.
`get/put_Auxiliary`	Gets/sets the flag in order to determine whether or not this schema class is auxiliary.
`get/put_MandatoryProperties`	Gets/sets a list of names of mandatory properties an ADSI object must have.
`get/put_OptionalProperties`	Gets/sets a list of names of optional properties an ADSI object may have.
`get/put_NamingProperties`	Gets/sets a list of naming attributes for the schema object.
`get/put_DerivedFrom`	Gets/sets the immediate super class of this schema class.
`get/put_AuxDerivedFrom`	Gets/sets the immediate super auxiliary class of this schema class.
`get/put_PossibleSuperiors`	Gets/sets a list of classes that can contain instances of this class.
`get/put_Containment`	Gets/sets legal objects types that can be contained within this container.
`get/put_Container`	Gets/sets the flag to indicate whether or not this is a container object.
`get/put_HelpFileName`	Gets/sets the name of an optional help file.
`get/put_HelpFileContext`	Gets/sets the context identifier of an optional help file.
`Qualifiers`	Returns a collection of ADSI objects describing provider-specific qualifiers for the schema.

IADsCollection

Derived from: `IDispatch`

This interface is exposed by objects that need to manage collections of other objects, which are not part of the directory tree. For example, groups manage collections of members, while in the WinNT provider, print queues manage collections of print jobs, and file shares each manage two collections – of resources and sessions.

IADsCollection methods	Description
get__NewEnum	Gets an interface on an enumerator object.
Add	Adds an object to the collection.
Remove	Removes an object from the collection.
GetObject	Gets the specified item.

IADsComputer

Derived from: IADs

Exposed by ADSI objects in WinNT that wrap computers. These objects will also expose IADsComputerOperations.

IADsComputer properties and methods	Description
ComputerID	Gets and sets globally unique identifier for this machine.
Site	Gets and sets globally unique identifier for this site.
Description	Gets and sets description of this computer.
Location	Gets and sets physical location of this computer.
PrimaryUser	Gets and sets contact person for this computer.
Owner	Gets and sets licensed user of this computer.
Division	Gets and sets division to which this computer belongs.
Department	Gets and sets department to which this computer belongs.
Role	Gets and sets role of this computer (server, workstation, and so on)
OperatingSystem	Gets and sets installed operating system in use.
put_OperatingSystemVersion	Gets and sets version of installed operating system in use.
Model	Gets and sets make/model of this computer.

Table Continued on Following Page

IADsComputer properties and methods	Description
Processor	Gets and sets type of processor.
ProcessorCount	Gets and sets number of processors installed in this computer.
MemorySize	Gets and sets amount of RAM in MB.
StorageCapacity	Gets and sets size of disk space in MB.
NetAddresses	Gets and sets binding information.

IADsComputerOperations

Derived from: IADs

Exposed by ADSI objects in WinNT that wrap computers. These objects will also expose IADsComputer.

IADsComputerOperations methods	Description
Status	Returns the current operations status
Shutdown	Executes shutdown with optional reboot.

IADsContainer

Derived from: IDispatch

Exposed by all objects that can be containers.

IADsContainer properties and methods	Description
get_Count	Gets the number of directory objects in the container.
get__NewEnum	Get the interface on an enumerator object.
Get/put_Filter	Gets/sets the filter on the schema classes to use for an enumeration.
Get/put_Hints	Gets/sets properties to load.
GetObject	Gets interface on a named object.
Create	Requests creation of specified object.
Delete	Deletes a specified object.
CopyHere	Copies a specified object within a directory service.
MoveHere	Moves a specified object within a directory service.

IADsDeleteOps

Derived from: `IDispatch`

This a useful interface, which allows you to delete from the directory the object against which it is called and all its children in one go. This is in contrast with the `IADsContainer::Delete()` method, which must be called from the container of the object to be deleted, and which will only delete one object at a time.

IADsDeleteOps methods	Description
`DeleteObject`	Deletes the object from the directory.

IADsDomain

Derived from: `IADs`

This is implemented by domain objects – and it exposes some extra automation properties that may be useful in describing domains.

IADsDomain properties and methods	Description
`IsWorkgroup`	Checks if the domain is actually a workstation that is a member of a workgroup.
`MinPasswordLength`	Gets and sets minimum number of characters required.
`MinPasswordAge`	Gets and sets minimum age before allowing a password change.
`MaxPasswordAge`	Gets and sets age at which password must be changed.
`MaxBadPasswordsAllowed`	Gets and sets maximum bad password logins before lockout.
`PasswordHistoryLength`	Gets and sets number of passwords saved.
`PasswordAttributes`	Gets and sets password restrictions.
`AutoUnlockInterval`	Gets and sets the minimum time that can elapse before an account is automatically re-enabled.
`LockoutObservationInterval`	Gets and sets time window for monitoring account.

IADsExtension

Derived from: IUnknown

This interface should not be implemented by any object in a directory. Rather, it should be implemented by any other COM objects written by ISVs, which are intended to extend objects in another ADSI provider. Its methods will only ever be called up by the provider it is extending, never by ADSI clients – which is why it is derived from IUnknown rather than IDispatch. There is no need to support scripting clients.

It contains one method, Operate(), which allows the extension object to be initialized, and two methods that support IDispatch functionality, allowing the extension to give the appearance of merging its IDispatch with that of its aggregator.

IADsExtension methods	Description
Operate	Performs the specified extended functionality.
PrivateGetIDsOfNames	Maps the name(s) to a DISPID.
PrivateInvoke	Invokes methods of the extended object.

IADsFileService

Derived from: IADsService

This interface will be exposed by directory objects that wrap the lanmanserver file service. Such objects should also implement IADsFileServiceOperations.

IADsFileService properties and methods	Description
Description	Gets and sets the description of the file service.
MaxUserCount	Gets and sets the maximum number of users allowed to run the service concurrently.

IADsFileServiceOperations

Derived from: IADsServiceOperations

This interface will be exposed by directory objects that wrap the lanmanserver file service. Such objects should also implement IADsFileService.

IADsFileServiceOperations methods	Description
Sessions	Gets an interface pointer on a collection object that represents current open sessions on this file service.
Resources	Gets an interface pointer on a collection object that represents current open resources for this file service.

IADsFileShare

Derived from: IADs

This is exposed by file share objects.

IADsFileShare properties and methods	Description
CurrentUserCount	Gets the current number of users connected to this share.
Description	Gets and sets the description of the file share.
HostComputer	Gets and sets the ADsPath reference to the host computer.
Path	Gets and sets the file system path to shared directory.
MaxUserCount	Gets and sets the maximum number of users allowed to access a share at any one time.

IADsGroup

Derived from: IADs

This interface is exposed by group objects.

IADsGroup properties and methods	Description
Description	Gets and sets the description of the group membership.
Members	Gets an IADsMembers interface on the members object that is the collection of ADSI objects that represent the members of this group.
IsMember	Tests for membership.
Add	Adds an object to a group.
Remove	Removes an object from a group.

IADsLocality

Derived from: `IADs`

At present this interface is not implemented by any of the system providers. It is available in case it is useful in other providers in order to describe objects that wrap localities.

IADsLocality properties and methods	Description
`get/put_Description`	Gets/sets the description of the geographical region as represented by this object.
`get/put_LocalityName`	Gets/sets the name of this region.
`get/put_PostalAddress`	Gets/sets the main post office address of this region.
`get/put_SeeAlso`	Gets/sets any other information relevant to this region.

IADsMembers

Derived from: `IDispatch`

This is not normally implemented by any objects in the directory tree. Rather, it is available as the Members property on group objects. It implements methods to allow access to a collection of members. The reason why this is not exposed by any object in the directory tree is that its methods would otherwise get confused with the `IADsContainer` methods, which have the same name.

IADsMembers properties and methods	Description
`get_Count`	Gets the number of members.
`get__NewEnum`	Retrieves an interface on an enumerator object.
`get/put_Filter`	Gets/sets the filter for selection.

IADsNamespaces

Derived from: `IADs`

The only object that should expose this interface is the ADSI router.

IADsNamespaces properties and methods	Description
`get/put_DefaultContainer`	Gets/sets the default container name for the current user.

IADsO

Derived from: `IADs`

At present this interface is not implemented by any of the system providers. It is available in case it is useful in other providers, in order to describe objects that wrap organizations.

IADsO properties and methods	Description
`get/put_Description`	Gets/sets the description of the organization, such as the company name.
`get/put_LocalityName`	Gets/sets the name of the physical location of the organization.
`get/put_PostalAddress`	Gets/sets the postal address of the organization.
`get/put_TelephoneNumber`	Gets/sets the telephone number of the organization.
`get/put_FaxNumber`	Gets/sets the fax number of the organization.
`get/put_SeeAlso`	Gets/sets the other information relevant to this organization.

IADsObjectOptions

Derived from: `IADs`

This interface allows certain options to be set that govern how an ADSI object behaves. It is implemented by objects in the LDAP provider, where it allows improved performance by switching off certain rarely used security and searching features.

IADsObjectOptions methods	Description
`GetOption`	Get the option
`SetOption`	Set the option

IADsOpenDSObject

Derived from: `IADs`

This should be implemented by the namespace object in each provider. It allows the ADSI client to supply authentication credentials to the directory

IADsOpenDSObject method	Description
`OpenDSObject`	Binds to the specified object using the supplied username, password, and authentication flags.

IADsOU

Derived from: `IADs`

At present this interface is not implemented by any of the system providers. It is available in case it is useful in other providers in order to describe objects that wrap organizational units.

IADsOU properties and methods	Description
`get/put_Description`	Gets/sets the description of the organizational unit.
`get/put_LocalityName`	Gets/sets the physical location of the unit.
`get/put_PostalAddress`	Gets/sets the post office address of the unit.
`get/put_TelephoneNumber`	Gets/sets the telephone number of the unit.
`get/put_FaxNumber`	Gets/sets the fax number of the unit.
`get/put_SeeAlso`	Gets/sets the other information relevant to the unit.
`get/put_BusinessCategory`	Gets/sets the category of general business functions of the unit.

IADsPathName

Derived from: `IDispatch`

`IADsPathName` is implemented by a special pathname object. The pathname object is implemented by the ADSI runtime, and exists to provide a means of converting ADsPaths between different formats.

IADsPathname properties and methods	Description
`get_EscapedMode`	Retrieves the mode for escaping a path.
`put_EscapedMode`	Specifies the mode for escaping a path.
`Set`	Sets an object path with an `ADS_SETTYPE` option.
`SetDisplayType`	Specifies how a path is to be displayed.
`Retrieve`	Retrieves an object path with an `ADS_FORMAT` type.
`GetNumElements`	Gets the number of elements in the path.

IADsPathname properties and methods	Description
GetElement	Gets elements stored in the object with its index.
GetEscapedElement	Escapes an RDN string and returns the output.
AddLeafElement	Adds an element to the end of the path.
RemoveLeafElement	Removes the last element from the object.
CopyPath	Generates an object with the same path.

IADsPrintJob

Derived from: IDispatch

This is implemented by print jobs. Note that print jobs do not form part of the directory tree – at least in the WinNT provider in which they are implemented – hence they do not implement IADs. They are obtainable by enumerating the PrintJobs property in print queues that implement IADsPrintQueueOperations. Print jobs will also expose IADsPrintJobOperations.

IADsPrintJob properties and methods	Description
get_HostPrintQueue	Gets the ADsPath string that names the print queue processing this print job.
get_User	Name of user submitting the print job.
get_UserPath	Gets the ADsPath name for user to submit the print job.
get_TimeSubmitted	Gets the time when the job was submitted to the print queue.
get_TotalPages	Gets the total number of pages in the print job.
get_Size	Gets the size of the print job in bytes.
get/put_Description	Gets/sets the description of the print job.
get/put_Priority	Gets/sets the priority of the print job.
get/put_StartTime	Gets/sets the earliest time when the print job should be started.
get/put_UntilTime	Gets/sets the time when the print job should be stopped.
get/put_Notify	Gets/sets the user to be notified when job is completed.
get/put_NotifyPath	The ADsPath string for the user to be notified when the job is completed.

IADsPrintJobOperations

Derived from: `IDispatch`

This is implemented by print jobs. Note that print jobs do not form part of the directory tree – at least in the WinNT provider in which they are implemented – hence they do not implement `IADs`. They are obtainable by enumerating the `PrintJobs` property in print queues that implement `IADsPrintQueueOperations`. Print jobs will also expose `IADsPrintJob`.

IADsPrintJobOperations properties and methods	Description
`get_Status`	Status of print job.
`get_TimeElapsed`	Elapsed time in seconds since job started printing.
`get_PagesPrinted`	Number of pages completed.
`get/put_Position`	Numeric position of print job in print queue.
`Pause`	Pauses processing of this print job.
`Resume`	Resumes processing of this print job.

IADsPrintQueue

Derived from: `IADs`

This is implemented by print queues. Print queues will also implement `IADsPrintQueueOperations`.

IADsPrintQueue properties and methods	Description
`get/put_PrinterPath`	Gets/sets the path where a shared printer can be accessed.
`get/put_Model`	Gets/sets the name of the driver used by this print queue.
`get/put_Datatype`	Gets/sets the data type that can be processed by this print queue.
`get/put_PrintProcessor`	Gets/sets the print processor associated with this print queue.
`get/put_Description`	Gets/sets the description of this print queue.

IADsPrintQueue properties and methods	Description
get/put_Location	Gets/sets the administrator's description of the print queue location.
get/put_StartTime	Gets/sets the time when the print queue starts processing jobs.
get/put_UntilTime	Gets/sets the time at which the print queue stops processing jobs.
get/put_DefaultJobPriority	Gets/sets the default priority assigned to each print job.
get/put_Priority	Gets/sets the priority of this printer object's job queue for connected devices.
get/put_BannerPage	Gets/sets the file system path to the banner page file used to separate jobs.
get/put_PrintDevices	Gets/sets the names of print devices that this print queue uses as spooling devices.
get/put_NetAddresses	Gets/sets the binding information.

IADsPrintQueue

Derived from: IADs

This is implemented by print queues. Print queues will also implement
IADsPrintQueueOperations.

IADsPrintQueueOperations properties and methods	Description
get_Status	Current status of print queue service.
PrintJobs	Retrieve an interface pointer on a collection object that represents print jobs managed by this print queue.
Pause	Pause print queue processing of print jobs.
Resume	Resume print queue processing of print jobs.
Purge	Purge all jobs from a print queue.

IADsProperty

Derived from: `IADs`

This interface is exposed by property objects, which will usually exist in the schema container. It gives you access to a set of properties that describe a given property. Active Directory is an exception to this, in that it exposes the equivalent properties using the property cache, and `IADs::Get()`, `IADs::Put()`, etc.

Although all the properties are technically read/write, you will only be able to write to them in providers that support schema extension.

IADsProperty properties and methods	Description
`get/put_OID`	Directory-specific object identifier.
`get/put_Syntax`	Relative path of syntax object.
`get/put_MaxRange`	Upper limit of values.
`get/put_MinRange`	Lower limit of values.
`get/put_MultiValued`	Whether or not this is a property that supports multiple values.
`Qualifiers`	Optional additional provider-specific constraints on this property.

IADsPropertyEntry

Derived from: `IDispatch`

This interface is exposed by property entry objects. Property entry objects do not correspond to directory objects, and they do not exist in the directory hierarchy. They encapsulate one property, giving the name, value(s) and datatype, and are used by methods in the `IPropertyList` interface. They are provider-independent, and are hence implemented by the ADSI runtime.

IADsPropertyEntry properties and methods	Description
`get/put_Name`	Gets/sets the name of the property entry.
`get/put_ADS_Type`	Gets/sets the ADS data type of the property entry.
`get/put_ControlCode`	Gets and sets the operation to be performed on the named property
`get/put_Values`	Gets and sets the current values of a property entry.

IADsPropertyList

Derived form: IADs

IADsPropertyList should be implemented by all ADSI directory objects. It implements methods that allow direct access to an object's property cache, i.e. without going via the schema when looking up properties. This also means it is possible to use IADsPropertyList to enumerate through the properties without explicitly naming them.

IADsPropertyList properties and methods	Description
get_PropertyCount	Gets the number of properties in the property list.
Next	Gets the next item in the property list.
Skip	Skips a specified number of items in the property list.
Reset	Moves back to the start of the list.
Item	Gets a property that is specified by name or by index.
GetPropertyItem	Gets the value of a named property.
PutPropertyItem	Puts the value of a named property.
ResetPropertyItem	Resets the value of a named property.
PurgePropertyList	Deletes all properties from the list and, therefore, releases the property caches as well.

IADsPropertyValue

Derived from: IDispatch

This interface is exposed by property value objects. PropertyValue objects do not correspond to directory objects, and they do not exist in the directory hierarchy. They encapsulate one property value, giving the data type and value, and are used by methods in the IPropertyEntry interface. PropertyEntry objects store entire properties – the name and all values, and use PropertyValue objects to store each value. PropertyValue objects are provider-independent, and are hence implemented by the ADSI runtime.

IADsPropertyValue properties and methods	Description
Clear	Clears the PropertyValue object's current value.
get/put_ADsType	Gets/sets a property value's data type.
get/put_DNString	Gets/sets an object's distinguished name (pathname).
get/put_CaseExactString	Gets/sets the value of a case-sensitive string.
get/put_CaseIgnoreString	Gets/sets the value of a case-insensitive string.
get/put_PrintableString	Gets/sets the value of a printable string.
get/put_NumericString	Gets/sets the value of a string consisting of numeric characters.
get/put_Boolean	Gets/sets a Boolean value.
get/put_Integer	Gets/sets an integer value.
get/put_OctetString	Gets/sets the value of a string of eight-bit characters.
get/put_SecurityDescriptor	Gets/sets a security descriptor.
get/put_LargeInteger	Gets/sets a large-integer value.
get/put_UTCTime	Gets/sets a Coordinated Universal Time value.

IProperrtyValue2

Derived from: IDispatch

IPropertyValue2 has been designed to replace IPropertyValue. Instead of exposing separate automation properties for each possible data type the actual value can be stored in, it exposes one generic automation property which is accompanied by an integer to indicate what data type it represents.

IADsPropertyValue2 methods	Description
GetObjectProperty	Retrieves property values of an object.
PutObjectProperty	Sets property values of an object.

IADsResource

Derived from: IDispatch

IADsResource is exposed by Resource objects. These are resources, such as folders, which are currently in use by ADSI session objects. They do not form part of the directory tree, but are accessed by enumerating through the Resources collection implemented by IADsFileShare.

IADsResource properties and methods	Description
get_User	Gets the name of the user for the Resource.
get_UserPath	Gets ADsPath of the user object for the user who opened the resource.
get_Path	Gets the file system path of the opened resource.
get_LockCount	Gets the number of locks on the resource.

IADsSecurityDescriptor

Derived from: IDispatch

This interface implements a security descriptor. Security descriptors do not participate in the directory tree: instead they are usually accessed as one of the properties on the object to which they apply (nTSecurityDescriptor for Active Directory, NT-Security-Descriptor for the Exchange 5.5 directory). They are provider-independent, and so are implemented by the ADSI runtime.

IADsSecurityDescriptor properties and methods	Description
get/put_Revision	Gets/puts the revision number assigned to the security descriptor.
get/put_Control	Gets/puts the Security_Descriptor_Control flag.
get/put_Owner	Gets/puts the owner of the object associated with the security descriptor.
get/put_OwnerDefaulted	Gets/puts the flag that indicates if the owner information is derived by a default mechanism.
get/put_Group	Gets/puts the group that owns the object associated with the security descriptor.
get/put_GroupDefaulted	Gets/puts the flag that indicates if the group information is derived by a default mechanism.
get/put_DiscretionaryAcl	Gets/puts the discretionary ACL associated with the security descriptor.
get/put_DaclDefaulted	Gets/puts the flag that indicates if the DACL is derived from a default mechanism.

Table Continued on Following Page

IADsSecurityDescriptor properties and methods	Description
get/put_SystemAcl	Gets/puts the system ACL (SACL) associated with the security descriptor.
get/put_SaclDefaulted	Gets/puts the flag that indicates if the SACL is derived from a default mechanism.
CopySecurityDescriptor	Copies the security descriptor.

IADsService

Derived from: IADs

IADsService is implemented by directory objects that correspond to NT services. These objects will usually also implement IADsServiceOperations.

IADsService properties and methods	Description
get/put_HostComputer	Gets/sets the host of this service.
get/put_DisplayName	Gets/sets the display name of this service.
get/put_Version	Gets/sets the version information of this service.
get/put_ServiceType	Gets/sets the process type in which this service runs.
get/put_StartType	Gets/sets the type for how this service starts.
get/put_Path	Gets/sets the path and filename of the executable.
get/put_StartupParameters	Gets/sets the parameters passed at start-up.
get/put_ErrorControl	Gets/sets the actions taken in case of service failure.
get/put_LoadOrderGroup	Gets/sets the load order group for this service.
get/put_ServiceAccountName	Gets/sets the authentication account name.
get/put_ServiceAccountPath	Gets/sets the path to the user object to be authenticated.
get/put_Dependencies	Gets/sets the array of BSTR names of services or load groups that must be loaded in order for this service to load.

IADsServiceOperations

Derived from: IADs

IADsServiceOperations is implemented by directory objects that correspond to NT services. These objects will usually also implement IADsService.

IADsServiceOperations properties and methods	Description
get_Status	Gets the status of the service.
Start	Starts the service.
Stop	Stops the service.
Pause	Pauses the service.
Continue	Continues the service.
SetPassword	Sets password to be used by service manager to create security context.

IADsSession

Derived from: IDispatch

IADsSession is exposed by Session objects. A session corresponds to an open connection from another machine that is accessing a file share. Session objects do not form part of the directory tree, but are accessed by enumerating through the Sessions collection implemented by IADsFileShare.

IADsSession properties and methods	Description
get_User	Gets the name of user for the session.
get_UserPath	Gets the ADsPath of the user object.
get_Computer	Gets the name of the client workstation.
get_ComputerPath	Get the ADsPath of computer object for client workstation.
get_ConnectTime	Gets the number of minutes since the session started.
get_IdleTime	Gets the number of minutes the session has been idle.

IADsSyntax

Derived from: IADs

IADsSyntax is exposed by syntax objects in the schema container. Each syntax object describes the automation data type that is used to store data of the named syntax. Although the property implemented by IADsSyntax is marked as read/write, it is only writeable in providers that support schema extension.

IADsSyntax properties and methods	Description
get/put_OleAutoDataType	The Automation data type constant, VT_xxxx.

IADsUser

Derived from: IADs

IADsUser is exposed by ADSI objects that wrap users or user accounts. In the case of Active Directory, it is also exposed by computer objects. It has a large number of automation properties that may be used to indicate useful information about users and user accounts. However, be aware that all providers do not implement all properties.

IADsUser properties and methods	Description
Get_BadLoginAddress	Gets the address of the last node considered an "Intruder".
Get_BadLoginCount	Gets the number of the bad logon attempts since last reset.
Get_LastLogin	Gets the date and time of the last network login.
Get_LastLogoff	Gets the date and time of the last network logoff.
Get_LastFailedLogin	Gets the date and time of the last failed network login.
Get_PasswordLastChanged	Gets the date and time of the last password change.
Get/put_Description	Gets/sets the description of the user account.
Get/put_Division	Gets/sets the division within a company (organization).
Get/put_Department	Gets/sets the organizational unit within the organization.
Get/put_EmployeeID	Gets/sets the employee identification number of the user.
Get/put_FullName	Gets/sets the full name of the user.

IADsUser properties and methods	Description
Get/put_FirstName	Gets/sets the first name of the user.
Get/put_LastName	Gets/sets the last name of the user.
Get/put_OtherName	Gets/sets the additional name, such as the nickname, or the middle name of the user.
Get/put_NamePrefix	Gets/sets the name prefix, such as Mr., Ms. or Hon., of the user
Get/put_NameSuffix	Gets/sets the name suffix (Jr., III) of the user.
Get/put_Title	Gets/sets the user's title within the organization.
Get/put_Manager	Gets/sets the manager of the user.
Get/put_TelephoneHome	Gets/sets the list of home phone numbers of the user. In Active Directory the list has a single element.
Get/put_TelephoneMobile	Gets/sets the list of mobile phone numbers of the user. In Active Directory the list has a single element.
Get/put_TelephoneNumber	Gets/sets the list of work-related phone numbers. In Active Directory the list has a single element.
Get/put_TelephonePager	Gets/sets the list of pager phone numbers. In Active Directory the list has a single element.
Get/put_FaxNumber	Gets/sets the list of fax phone numbers. In Active Directory the list has a single element.
Get/put_OfficeLocations	Gets/sets the array of end-user locations. In Active Directory the array has a single element.
Get/put_PostalAddresses	Gets/sets the array of end-user post office addresses.
Get/put_PostalCodes	Gets/sets the array of zip codes for the Postal Addresses. In Active Directory the array has a single element.
Get/put_SeeAlso	Gets/sets the array of ADsPaths of other objects related to this user.
Get/put_AccountDisabled	Gets/sets the flag to indicate whether or not the account is disabled.
Get/put_AccountExpirationDate	Gets/sets the date and time that the user account expires.

Table Continued on Following Page

IADsUser properties and methods	Description
Get/put_GraceLoginsAllowed	Gets/sets the number of times the user can log on after the password has expired.
Get/put_GraceLoginsRemaining	Gets/sets the number of grace logins left before locking account.
Get/put_IsAccountLocked	Gets/sets a flag to indicate whether or not an account is locked.
Get/put_LoginHours	Gets/sets the time periods during each day of week indicating valid login periods.
Get/put_LoginWorkstations	Gets/sets the workstations and their net addresses for this end-user.
Get/put_MaxLogins	Gets/sets the maximum number of simultaneous logins.
Get/put_MaxStorage	Gets/sets the maximum amount of disk space allowed for the user.
Get/put_PasswordExpirationDate	Gets/sets the date and time when the password will expire.
Get/put_PasswordMinimumLength	Gets/sets the minimum number of characters allowed in a password.
Get/put_PasswordRequired	Gets/sets a flag to indicate whether or not a password is required.
Get/put_RequireUniquePassword	Gets/sets a flag to indicate whether or not a new password must be different from ones in the password history list.
Get/put_EmailAddress	Gets/sets the email address of the user.
Get/put_HomeDirectory	Gets/sets the home directory of the user.
Get/put_Languages	Gets/sets the array of language names for the end-user.
Get/put_Profile	Gets/sets the end-user's profile path.
Get/put_LoginScript	Gets/sets the end-user's login script path.
Get/put_Picture	Gets/sets the picture of the user.
Get/put_HomePage	Gets/sets the URL to the home page of the user.
Groups	Determines the groups to which this end-user belongs.
SetPassword	Sets the password.
ChangePassword	Changes the password from the specified existing value to a new value.

IDirectoryObject

Derived from: `IUnknown`

`IDirectoryObject` is designed for C++ ADSI clients that need fast access to the directory itself. It does not use the property cache, but sets and gets properties straight from the directory itself. It implements methods corresponding to some of the `IADs` and `IADsContainer` methods.

Note that not all providers implement `IDirectoryObject`. For example, LDAP does, but WinNT doesn't.

IDirectoryObject methods	Description
GetObjectInformation	Gets information about a directory service object.
GetObjectAttributes	Gets one or more attributes of a directory service object.
SetObjectAttributes	Sets one or more attributes of a directory service object.
CreateDSObject	Creates a directory service object.
DeleteDSObject	Deletes a directory service object.

IDirectorySearch

Derived from: `IUnknown`

`IDirectorySearch` is the interface that will allow searching against a directory. It is only directly accessible to C++ clients: Scripting clients which must use dual or disp-interfaces should use the ADO ADSI provider instead, which will indirectly call up `IDirectorySearch`.

Note that not all providers implement `IDirectorySearch`, since not all directories have the infrastructure to allow efficient searching. For example, LDAP does, but WinNT doesn't.

IDirectorySearch methods	Description
SetSearchPreference	Sets options for conducting a search.
ExecuteSearch	Executes an individual search.
AbandonSearch	Abandons a search already under way.
GetFirstRow	Gets the first row of the search result.
GetNextRow	Gets the next row of the search result.
GetPreviousRow	Gets the previous row of the search result.

Table Continued on Following Page

IDirectorySearch methods	Description
GetNextColumnName	Gets the name of the next column of the search result.
GetColumn	Gets the item in a specified column from the current row of the search result.
FreeColumn	Frees the ADS_SEARCH_COLUMN structure created by the GetColumn method.
CloseSearchHandle	Releases the search result from memory.

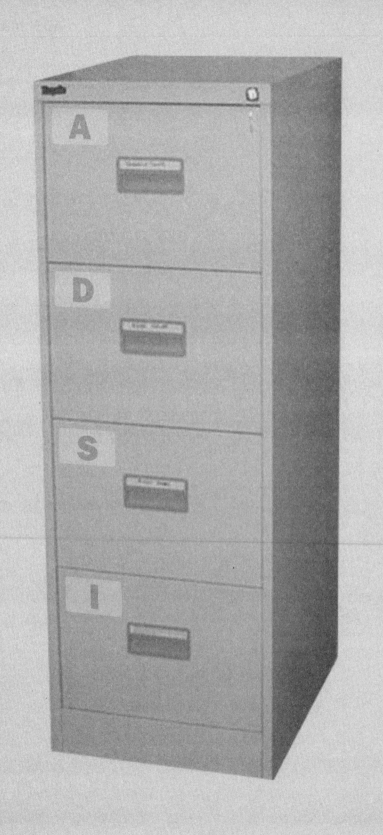

E

ADSI Error Codes

This appendix has been taken from MSDN. It lists those error codes that are specific to ADSI, and which may be returned from method calls to ADSI providers.

They have the facility code 5 with severity bit set either TRUE or FALSE. Setting the severity bit to TRUE results in error values of the form 0x80005xxx and error messages of the form E_ADS_*. When the severity bit is set to FALSE, the resulting error values are of the form 0x00005xxx and the error messages are of the S_ADS_* form.

Note that calls to ADSI objects may also return generic COM error codes, such as S_OK and E_FAIL, which are not listed here.

These error codes are defined in adserr.h.

Value	Code	Description	Corrective Action
0x80005000L	E_ADS_BAD_PATHNAME	An invalid ADSI pathname was passed.	Verify that the object exists on the directory server and check for typos in the path.
0x80005001L	E_ADS_INVALID_ DOMAIN_OBJECT	An unknown ADSI domain object was requested.	Verify the path of the domain object.

Value	Code	Description	Corrective Action
0x80005002L	E_ADS_INVALID_ USER_OBJECT	An unknown ADSI user object was requested.	Verify the existence of the user object, check for typos in the path name and the user's access rights.
0x80005003L	E_ADS_INVALID_ COMPUTER_OBJECT	An unknown ADSI computer object was requested.	Verify the existence of the computer object, check for typos in the path name and the computer's access rights.
0x80005004L	E_ADS_UNKNOWN_ OBJECT	An unknown ADSI object was requested.	Verify the name of and the access rights to the object.
0x80005005L	E_ADS_PROPERTY_ NOT_SET	The specified ADSI property was not set.	
0x80005006L	E_ADS_PROPERTY_ NOT_SUPPORTED	The specified ADSI property is not supported.	Verify the correct property is being set.
0x80005007L	E_ADS_PROPERTY_ INVALID	The specified ADSI property is invalid	Verify the parameters passed to the method call.
0x80005008L	E_ADS_BAD_ PARAMETER	One or more input parameters are invalid.	
0x80005009L	E_ADS_OBJECT_ UNBOUND	The specified ADSI object is not bound to a remote resource.	Make sure to call GetInfo on a newly created object after SetInfo has been called.
0x8000500AL	E_ADS_PROPERTY_ NOT_MODIFIED	The specified ADSI object has not been modified.	

Value	Code	Description	Corrective Action
0x8000500BL	E_ADS_PROPERTY_MODIFIED	The specified ADSI object has been modified.	
0x8000500CL	E_ADS_CANT_CONVERT_DATATYPE	The data type cannot be converted to/from a native DS data type.	Make sure that the correct data type is used and/or that there is sufficient schema information available to perform data type conversion.
0x8000500DL	E_ADS_PROPERTY_NOT_FOUND	The property cannot be found in the cache.	Make sure that GetInfo has been called (implicitly or explicitly). If the problem persists, the property has not been set on the server.
0x8000500EL	E_ADS_OBJECT_EXISTS	The ADSI object exists.	Use a different name to create the object.
0x8000500FL	E_ADS_SCHEMA_VIOLATION	The attempted action violates the directory service schema rules.	
0x80005010L	E_ADS_COLUMN_NOT_SET	The specified column in the ADSI was not set.	
0x00005011L	S_ADS_ERRORSOCCURRED	During a query, one or more errors occurred.	Verify that the search preference can be legally set and, if so, is properly set
0x00005012L	S_ADS_NOMORE_ROWS	The search operation has reached the last row.	Move on to the rest of the program.
0x00005013L	S_ADS_NOMORE_COLUMNS	The search operation has reached the last column for the current row.	Move on to next row.
0x80005014L	E_ADS_INVALID_FILTER	The specified search filter is invalid.	Make sure to use the correct format of the filter that is acceptable to the directory server.

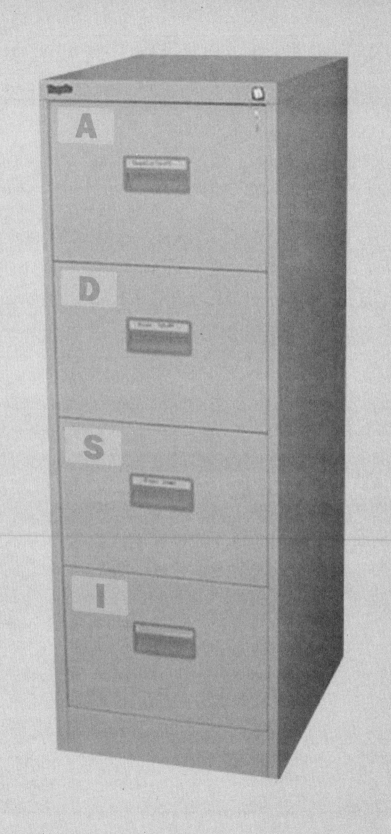

ADSI Constants and Structures

This appendix lists the various constants and structures (other than error codes) that are defined by ADSI.

The constants and structures are listed by their usual usage, and are divided into categories of constants and structures used by/for:

- ❑ Describing ADSI properties and values
- ❑ Security descriptors and access control lists
- ❑ Searching
- ❑ Extension objects
- ❑ Authentication
- ❑ Name conversions
- ❑ Groups (LDAP only)
- ❑ IADsObjectOptions methods
- ❑ Attribute schemas (LDAP only)
- ❑ Users
- ❑ IDirectoryObject methods

Note that in most cases the actual description of each constant is taken from MSDN, although the arrangement and other general notes aren't.

Describing ADSI Properties and Values

These constants can be divided into two categories: those that indicate how a value should be modified, and those that indicate how a value should be stored.

Modifying Values

Constants that indicate how a value should be modified are defined in the ADS_PROPERTY_OPERATION_ENUM enumeration, and are used by the IADs::PutEx() method, as well as by PropertyEntry objects. This enumeration is defined as:

```
enum {
        ADS_PROPERTY_CLEAR       = 1,
        ADS_PROPERTY_UPDATE      = 2,
        ADS_PROPERTY_APPEND      = 3,
        ADS_PROPERTY_DELETE      = 4
} ADS_PROPERTY_OPERATION_ENUM;
```

Name	Description
ADS_PROPERTY_CLEAR	Instructs the directory service to remove the property value(s) from the object.
ADS_PROPERTY_UPDATE	Instructs the directory service to replace the current value with the element(s) in the passed VARIANT array.
ADS_PROPERTY_APPEND	Instructs the directory service to append the new value(s) to the existing one(s).
ADS_PROPERTY_DELETE	Instructs the directory service to delete the specified value(s) of a property.

Storing Values

The IADs methods use VARIANTs, as explained in Appendix C.

IDirectoryObject has its own structures used to store the data, which are explained under the IDirectoryObject heading later in this appendix.

Here, we are interested in the ADSVALUE structure and related constants, which are used extensively by PropertyValue objects, as well as on some occasions by IDirectorySearch. The ADSVALUE can really be seen as *the* structure that holds a value of arbitrary data type where we are not referring to the schema.

It's defined as:

```
typedef struct ADSVALUE
{
    ADSTYPE   dwType ;
    union
    {
        ADS_DN_STRING                  DNString ;
        ADS_CASE_EXACT_STRING          CaseExactString ;
        ADS_CASE_IGNORE_STRING         CaseIgnoreString ;
        ADS_PRINTABLE_STRING           PrintableString ;
        ADS_NUMERIC_STRING             NumericString ;
        ADS_BOOLEAN                    Boolean ;
        ADS_INTEGER                    Integer ;
        ADS_OCTET_STRING               OctetString ;
        ADS_UTC_TIME                   UTCTime ;
        ADS_LARGE_INTEGER              LargeInteger ;
        ADS_OBJECT_CLASS               ClassName ;
        ADS_PROV_SPECIFIC              ProviderSpecific ;
        PADS_CASEIGNORE_LIST           pCaseIgnoreList ;
        PADS_OCTET_LIST                pOctetList ;
        PADS_PATH                      pPath ;
        PADS_POSTALADDRESS             pPostalAddress ;
        ADS_TIMESTAMP                  Timestamp ;
        ADS_BACKLINK                   BackLink ;
        PADS_TYPEDNAME                 pTypedName ;
        ADS_HOLD                       Hold ;
        PADS_NETADDRESS                pNetAddress ;
        PADS_REPLICAPOINTER            pReplicaPointer ;
        PADS_FAXNUMBER                 pFaxNumber ;
        ADS_EMAIL                      Email ;
        ADS_NT_SECURITY_DESCRIPTOR     SecurityDescriptor ;
    };
} ADSVALUE, *PADSVALUE, *LPADSVALUE;
```

Note that many of these values in the union are NDS-specific.

Name	Description
dwType	Data type to be used to interpret the union member of the structure. Values of this member are taken from the ADSTYPE enumeration.
DNString	String identifying the distinguished name (path) of a directory service object, as defined by ADS_DN_STRING, an ADSI simple data type.
CaseExactString	String to be interpreted case-sensitively, as defined by ADS_CASE_EXACT_STRING, an ADSI simple data type.
CaseIgnoreString	String to be interpreted without regard to case, as defined by ADS_CASE_IGNORE_STRING, an ADSI simple data type.
PrintableString	String that can be displayed or printed, as defined by ADS_PRINTABLE_STRING, an ADSI simple data type

Table Continued on Following Page

Name	Description
NumericString	Numerals to be interpreted as text, as defined by ADS_NUMERIC_STRING, an ADSI simple data type.
Boolean	Boolean value, as defined by ADS_BOOLEAN, an ADSI simple data type.
Integer	Integer value, as defined by ADS_INTEGER, an ADSI simple data type.
OctetString	An octet string, as defined by ADS_OCTET_STRING, an ADSI-defined data type.
UTCTime	Time specified as Coordinated Universal Time (UTC), as defined by ADS_UTC_TIME, an ADSI simple data type.
LargeInteger	Long integer value, as defined by ADS_LARGE_INTEGER, an ADSI simple data type.
ClassName	Class name string, as defined by ADS_OBJECT_CLASS, an ADSI simple data type.
ProviderSpecific	Provider-specific structure, as defined by ADS_PROV_SPECIFIC, an ADSI-defined data type.
pCaseIgnoreList	Pointer to a list of ADS_CASEIGNORE_LIST, an ADSI-defined data type that is mainly used for the NDS provider.
pOctetList	Pointer to a list of ADS_OCTET_LIST, an ADSI-defined data type that is mainly used for the NDS provider.
pPath	Pointer to the ADS_PATH name, an ADSI-defined data type that is mainly used for the NDS provider.
pPostalAddress	Pointer to the ADS_POSTALADDRESS data, an ADSI-defined data type that is mainly used for the NDS provider.
Timestamp	Time stamp of the ADS_TIMESTAMP type, an ADSI-defined data type that is mainly used for the NDS provider.
BackLink	A link of the ADS_BACKLINK type, an ADSI-defined data type that is mainly used for the NDS provider
pTypedName	Pointer to the ADS_TYPEDNAME name, an ADSI-defined data type that is mainly used for the NDS provider.
Hold	A data structure of the ADS_HOLD type, an ADSI-defined data type that is mainly used for the NDS provider.
pNetAddress	Pointer to the ADS_NETADDRESS data, an ADSI-defined data type that is mainly used for the NDS provider.
pReplicaPointer	Pointer to a replica pointer of ADS_REPLICAPOINTER, an ADSI-defined data type that is mainly used for the NDS provider.

Name	Description
pFaxNumber	Pointer to a fax number of ADS_FAXNUMBER, an ADSI-defined data type that is mainly used for the NDS provider.
Email	Email address of a user of ADS_EMAIL, an ADSI-defined data type that is mainly used for the NDS provider.
SecurityDescriptor	Windows NT/Windows 2000 security descriptor, as defined by ADS_NT_SECURITY_DESCRIPTOR, an ADSI-defined data type

Most of these member variables are simple data types or arrays. However, if a provider-specific data type is used, then another structure, ADS_PROV_SPECIFIC, should be used to hold this:

```
typedef ADS_PROV_SPECIFIC
{
    DWORD    dwLength ;
    LPBYTE   lpValue ;
} ADS_PROV_SPECIFIC, *PADS_PROV_SPECIFIC;
```

Name	Description
dwLength	The size of the character array.
lpValue	Pointer to an array of bytes.

Hence, ADSI defines provider-specific data to be an array of bytes. It's up to the provider to document the internal format and meaning of this array.

The individual data types defined in ADSI are themselves defined as an enumeration, the ADSTYPE enumeration.

```
typedef enum {
    ADSTYPE_INVALID = 0,
    ADSTYPE_DN_STRING ,
    ADSTYPE_CASE_EXACT_STRING ,
    ADSTYPE_CASE_IGNORE_STRING ,
    ADSTYPE_PRINTABLE_STRING ,
    ADSTYPE_NUMERIC_STRING ,
    ADSTYPE_BOOLEAN ,
    ADSTYPE_INTEGER ,
    ADSTYPE_OCTET_STRING ,
    ADSTYPE_UTC_TIME ,
    ADSTYPE_LARGE_INTEGER ,
    ADSTYPE_PROV_SPECIFIC ,
    ADSTYPE_OBJECT_CLASS ,
    ADSTYPE_CASEIGNORE_LIST ,
    ADSTYPE_OCTET_LIST ,
    ADSTYPE_PATH ,
    ADSTYPE_POSTALADDRESS ,
    ADSTYPE_TIMESTAMP ,
    ADSTYPE_BACKLINK ,
    ADSTYPE_TYPEDNAME ,
    ADSTYPE_HOLD ,
    ADSTYPE_NETADDRESS ,
    ADSTYPE_REPLICAPOINTER ,
    ADSTYPE_FAXNUMBER ,
    ADSTYPE_EMAIL ,
    ADSTYPE_NT_SECURITY_DESCRIPTOR ,
    ADSTYPE_UNKNOWN
} ADSTYPEENUM;

typedef ADSTYPEENUM ADSTYPE;
```

693

Name	Description
ADSTYPE_INVALID	The data is of an invalid type.
ADSTYPE_DN_STRING	The string is of the Distinguished Name (path) of a directory service object.
ADSTYPE_CASE_EXACT_STRING	The string is of the case-sensitive type
ADSTYPE_CASE_IGNORE_STRING	The string is of the case-insensitive type.
ADSTYPE_PRINTABLE_STRING	The string is displayable on screen or in print.
ADSTYPE_NUMERIC_STRING	The string is of a numeral to be interpreted as text.
ADSTYPE_BOOLEAN	The data is a Boolean value.
ADSTYPE_INTEGER	The data is an integer value.
ADSTYPE_OCTET_STRING	The string is of a byte array.
ADSTYPE_UTC_TIME	The data is of the universal time as expressed in Universal Time Coordinates (UTC).
ADSTYPE_LARGE_INTEGER	The data is of a long integer value
ADSTYPE_PROV_SPECIFIC	The string is of a provider-specific string.
ADSTYPE_OBJECT_CLASS	The string is of an object class.
ADSTYPE_CASEIGNORE_LIST	The data is of a list of case insensitive strings.
ADSTYPE_OCTET_LIST	The data is of a list of octet strings.
ADSTYPE_PATH	The string is of a directory path.
ADSTYPE_POSTALADDRESS	The string is of the postal address type.
ADSTYPE_TIMESTAMP	The data is of a time stamp in seconds.

Name	Description
ADSTYPE_BACKLINK	The string is of a back link.
ADSTYPE_TYPEDNAME	The string is of a typed name.
ADSTYPE_HOLD	The data is of the Hold data structure.
ADSTYPE_NETADDRESS	The string is of a net address.
ADSTYPE_REPLICAPOINTER	The data is of a replica pointer.
ADSTYPE_FAXNUMBER	The string is of a fax number.
ADSTYPE_EMAIL	The data is of an e-mail message.
ADSTYPE_NT_SECURITY_DESCRIPTOR	The data is of Windows NT/Windows 2000 security descriptor as represented by a byte array.
ADSTYPE_UNKNOWN	The data is of an undefined type.

Mapping Data Types to Syntaxes

While we are on the subject of data types, here's the list of standard ADSI syntaxes:

Syntax Name	Automation data type
Boolean	BOOL
Counter	LONG
ADsPath	BSTR
EmailAddress	BSTR
FaxNumber	BSTR
Integer	LONG
Interval	LONG
List	Array of BSTR
Interface Ptr	IDispatch*
NetAddress	BSTR

Table Continued on Following Page

Syntax Name	Automation data type
Octet String	VARIANT
Path	BSTR
Phone Number	BSTR
Postal Address	BSTR
SmallInterval	LONG
String	BSTR
Time	DATE
DN	BSTR
UTCTime	BSTR
ORName	BSTR
IA5String	BSTR
OID	BSTR
NumericString	BSTR

Security Descriptors and Access Control Lists

There are a number of enumerations that define the constants stored in various automation properties of the ADSI security objects.

Note that in addition to these, you should also check the constants used by IADsObjectOptions, since some of these constants enable or disable access to security information.

ADS_ACEFLAG_ENUM

The ADS_ACEFLAG_ENUM enumeration specifies how security may propagate along an inheritance path, and how the system generates audit messages. This enumeration should be used for interpreting the AceFlags automation property of IADsAccessControlEntry.

```
enum {
    ADS_ACEFLAG_INHERIT_ACE                 = 0x2,
    ADS_ACEFLAG_NO_PROPAGATE_INHERIT_ACE    = 0x4,
    ADS_ACEFLAG_INHERIT_ONLY_ACE            = 0x8,
    ADS_ACEFLAG_INHERITED_ACE               = 0x10,
    ADS_ACEFLAG_VALID_INHERIT_FLAG          = 0x1f,
    ADS_ACEFLAG_SUCCESSFUL_ACCESS           = 0x40,
    ADS_ACEFLAG_FAILED_ACCESS               = 0x80,
} ADS_ACEFLAG_ENUM;
```

Name	Description
ADS_ACEFLAG_INHERIT_ ACE	Child objects will inherit this access-control entry (ACE). The inherited ACE is inheritable unless the ADS_ACEFLAG_NO_PROPAGATE_INHERIT_ACE flag is set.
ADS_ACEFLAG_NO_ PROPAGATE_INHERIT_ACE	ADSI will clear the ADS_ACEFLAG_INHERIT_ACE flag for the inherited ACEs of child objects. This prevents the ACE from being inherited by subsequent generations of objects.
ADS_ACEFLAG_INHERIT_ ONLY_ACE	Indicates an inherit-only ACE that does not exercise access control on the object to which it is attached. If this flag is not set, the ACE is an effective ACE that exerts access control on the object to which it is attached.
ADS_ACEFLAG_INHERITED_ ACE	Indicates whether or not the ACE was inherited. The system sets this bit.
ADS_ACEFLAG_VALID_ INHERIT_FLAGS	Indicates whether the inherit flags are valid. The system sets this bit.
ADS_ACEFLAG_SUCCESSFUL_ ACCESS	Generates audit messages for successful access attempts, used with ACEs that audit the system in a system access-control list (SACL).
ADS_ACEFLAG_FAILED_ ACCESS	Generates audit messages for failed access attempts, used with ACEs that audit the system in a SACL.

ADS_ACETYPE_ENUM

The ADS_ACETYPE_ENUM enumeration specifies types of access-control entries (ACEs). These values should be used to interpret values of the AceTypes automation property of IADsAccessControlEntry. The enumeration is defined as:

```
enum {
    ADS_ACETYPE_ACCESS_ALLOWED          = 0,
    ADS_ACETYPE_ACCESS_DENIED           = 0x1,
    ADS_ACETYPE_SYSTEM_AUDIT            = 0x2,
    ADS_ACETYPE_ACCESS_ALLOWED_OBJECT   = 0x5,
    ADS_ACETYPE_ACCESS_DENIED_OBJECT    = 0x6,
    ADS_ACETYPE_SYSTEM_AUDIT_OBJECT     = 0x7
} ADS_ACETYPE_ENUM;
```

Name	Description
ADS_ACETYPE_ACCESS_ALLOWED	The ACE is of the standard ACCESS_ALLOWED type, where the ObjectType and InheritedObjectType fields are NULL.
ADS_ACETYPE_ACCESS_DENIED	The ACE is of the standard ACCESS_DENIED type, where the ObjectType and InheritedObjectType fields are NULL.
ADS_ACETYPE_SYSTEM_AUDIT	The ACE is of the standard system type, where the ObjectType and InheritedObjectType fields are NULL.
ADS_ACETYPE_ACCESS_ALLOWED_OBJECT	The ACE is of the ADSI extension of the ACCESS_ALLOWED type, where either ObjectType or InheritedObjectType or both contain a GUID
ADS_ACETYPE_ACCESS_DENIED_OBJECT	The ACE is of the ADSI extension of the ACCCESS_DENIED type, where either ObjectType or InheritedObjectType or both contain a GUID.
ADS_ACETYPE_SYSTEM_AUDIT_OBJECT	The ACE is of the ADSI extension of the system type, where either ObjectType or InheritedObjectType or both contain a GUID.

ADS_RIGHTS_ENUM

The AccessMask automation property of access control list objects should be interpreted according to the values in the ADS_RIGHTS_ENUM enumeration. This enumeration indicates which permissions are being granted, denied, or audited, by the access control entry.

```
enum {
        ADS_RIGHT_DELETE                  = 0x10000,
        ADS_RIGHT_READ_CONTROL            = 0x20000,
        ADS_RIGHT_WRITE_DAC               = 0x40000,
        ADS_RIGHT_WRITE_OWNER             = 0x80000,
        ADS_RIGHT_SYNCHRONIZE             = 0x100000,
        ADS_RIGHT_ACCESS_SYSTEM_SECURITY  = 0x1000000,
        ADS_RIGHT_GENERIC_READ            = 0x80000000,
        ADS_RIGHT_GENERIC_WRITE           = 0x40000000,
        ADS_RIGHT_GENERIC_EXECUTE         = 0x20000000,
        ADS_RIGHT_GENERIC_ALL             = 0x10000000,
        ADS_RIGHT_DS_CREATE_CHILD         = 0x1,
        ADS_RIGHT_DS_DELETE_CHILD         = 0x2,
        ADS_RIGHT_ACTRL_DS_LIST           = 0x4,
        ADS_RIGHT_DS_SELF                 = 0x8,
        ADS_RIGHT_DS_READ_PROP            = 0x10,
        ADS_RIGHT_DS_WRITE_PROP           = 0x20,
        ADS_RIGHT_DS_DELETE_TREE          = 0x40,
        ADS_RIGHT_DS_LIST_OBJECT          = 0x80,
        ADS_RIGHT_DS_CONTROL_ACCESS       = 0x100
} ADS_RIGHTS_ENUM;
```

Name	Description
ADS_RIGHT_DELETE	The right to delete the object.
ADS_RIGHT_READ_CONTROL	The right to read information from the security descriptor of the object, not including the information in the SACL.
ADS_RIGHT_WRITE_DAC	The right to modify the discretionary access-control list (DACL) in the object's security descriptor.
ADS_RIGHT_WRITE_OWNER	The right to assume ownership of the object. The user must be a trustee of the object. The user cannot transfer the ownership to other users.
ADS_RIGHT_SYNCHRONIZE	The right to use the object for synchronization. This enables a thread to wait until the object is in the signaled state.
ADS_RIGHT_ACCESS_SYSTEM_SECURITY	The right to get or set the SACL in the object's security descriptor.
ADS_RIGHT_GENERIC_READ	The right to read from the security descriptor, examine the object as well as its children, and read all properties.
ADS_RIGHT_GENERIC_WRITE	The right to write all the properties and write to the DACL. The user can add and remove the object to and from the directory.
ADS_RIGHT_GENERIC_EXECUTE	The right to list children of this object.
ADS_RIGHT_GENERIC_ALL	The right to create or delete children, delete a subtree, read and write properties, examine children and the object itself, add and remove the object from the directory, and read or write with an extended right.
ADS_RIGHT_DS_CREATE_CHILD	The right to create children of the object. The ObjectType member of an ACE can contain a GUID that identifies the type of child object whose creation is being controlled. If ObjectType does not contain a GUID, the ACE controls the creation of all child object types.
ADS_RIGHT_DS_DELETE_CHILD	The right to delete children of the object. The ObjectType member of an ACE can contain a GUID that identifies a type of child object whose deletion is being controlled. If ObjectType does not contain a GUID, the ACE controls the deletion of all child object types.
ADS_RIGHT_ACTRL_DS_LIST	The right to list children of this object.
ADS_RIGHT_DS_SELF	The right to modify the group membership of a group object.

Table Continued on Following Page

699

Name	Description
ADS_RIGHT_DS_READ_PROP	The right to read properties of the object. The `ObjectType` member of an ACE can contain a GUID that identifies a property set or property. If `ObjectType` does not contain a GUID, the ACE controls the right to read all of the object's properties.
ADS_RIGHT_DS_WRITE_PROP	The right to write properties of the object. The `ObjectType` member of an ACE can contain a GUID that identifies a property set or property. If `ObjectType` does not contain a GUID, the ACE controls the right to write all of the object's properties.
ADS_RIGHT_DS_DELETE_TREE	The right to delete all children of this object, regardless of the permission on the children.
ADS_RIGHT_DS_LIST_OBJECT	The right to list a particular object. If the user is not granted such a right, the object is hidden from the user.
ADS_RIGHT_DS_CONTROL_ ACCESS	The right to perform an operation controlled by an extended access right. The `ObjectType` member of an ACE can contain a GUID that identifies the extended right. If `ObjectType` does not contain a GUID, the ACE controls the right to perform all extended right operations associated with the object.

ADS_FLAGTYPE_ENUM

The `ADS_FLAGTYPE_ENUM` enumeration specifies values that can be used to indicate the presence of the `ObjectType` or `InheritedObjectType` fields in the access-control entry (ACE). These values should be used to interpret the `Flags` automation property of `IADsAccessControlEntry`.

```
enum {
    ADS_FLAG_OBJECT_TYPE_PRESENT            = 0x1,
    ADS_FLAG_INHERITED_OBJECT_TYPE_PRESENT  = 0x2
} ADS_FLAGTYPE_ENUM;
```

Name	Description
ADS_FLAG_OBJECT_ TYPE_PRESENT	The `ObjectType` field is present in the ACE, but `InheritedObjectType` is not.
ADS_FLAG_INHERITED_ OBJECT_TYPE_PRESENT	The `InheritedObjectType` field is present in the ACE, but `ObjectType` is not.

ADS_SD_CONTROL_ENUM

The ADS_SD_CONTROL_ENUM enumeration specifies control flags for a security descriptor. Values for the Control property of IADsSecurityDescriptor should be interpreted from this enumeration.

```
enum {
    ADS_SD_CONTROL_SE_OWNER_DEFAULTED         = 0x1,
    ADS_SD_CONTROL_SE_GROUP_DEFAULTED         = 0x2,
    ADS_SD_CONTROL_SE_DACL_PRESENT            = 0x4,
    ADS_SD_CONTROL_SE_DACL_DEFAULTED          = 0x8,
    ADS_SD_CONTROL_SE_SACL_PRESENT            = 0x10,
    ADS_SD_CONTROL_SE_SACL_DEFAULTED          = 0x20,
    ADS_SD_CONTROL_SE_DACL_AUTO_INHERIT_REQ   = 0x100,
    ADS_SD_CONTROL_SE_SACL_AUTO_INHERIT_REQ   = 0x200,
    ADS_SD_CONTROL_SE_DACL_AUTO_INHERITED     = 0x400,
    ADS_SD_CONTROL_SE_SACL_AUTO_INHERITED     = 0x800,
    ADS_SD_CONTROL_SE_DACL_PROTECTED          = 0x1000,
    ADS_SD_CONTROL_SE_SACL_PROTECTED          = 0x2000,
    ADS_SD_CONTROL_SE_SELF_RELATIVE           = 0x8000
} ADS_SD_CONTROL_ENUM;
```

Name	Description
ADS_SD_CONTROL_ SE_OWNER_DEFAULTED	A default mechanism provides the owner security identifier (SID) of the security descriptor rather than the original provider of the security descriptor.
ADS_SD_CONTROL_ SE_GROUP_DEFAULTED	A default mechanism provides the group SID of the security descriptor rather than the original provider of the security descriptor.
ADS_SD_CONTROL_ SE_DACL_PRESENT	The discretionary access-control list (DACL) is present in the security descriptor. If this flag is not set, or if this flag is set and the DACL is NULL, the security descriptor allows full access to everyone.
ADS_SD_CONTROL_ SE_DACL_ DEFAULTED	The security descriptor uses a default DACL built from the creator's access token.
ADS_SD_CONTROL_ SE_SACL_PRESENT	The system access-control list (SACL) is present in the security descriptor.
ADS_SD_CONTROL_ SE_SACL_ DEFAULTED	The security descriptor uses a default SACL built from the creator's access token.

Table Continued on Following Page

Name	Description
ADS_SD_CONTROL_ SE_DACL_AUTO_ INHERIT_REQ	The DACL of the security descriptor must be inherited.
ADS_SD_CONTROL_ SE_SACL_AUTO_ INHERIT_REQ	The SACL of the security descriptor must be inherited.
ADS_SD_CONTROL_ SE_DACL_AUTO_ INHERITED	The DACL of the security descriptor supports automatic propagation of inheritable access-control entries (ACEs) to existing child objects.
ADS_SD_CONTROL_ SE_SACL_AUTO_ INHERITED	The SACL of the security descriptor supports automatic propagation of inheritable ACEs to existing child objects.
ADS_SD_CONTROL_ SE_DACL_ PROTECTED	The security descriptor will not allow inheritable ACEs to modify the DACL.
ADS_SD_CONTROL_ SE_SACL_ PROTECTED	The security descriptor will not allow inheritable ACEs to modify the SACL.
ADS_SD_CONTROL_ SE_SELF_RELATIVE	The security descriptor is of self-relative format with all the security information in a continuous block of memory.

ADS_SD_REVISION_ENUM

The Revision property of access control lists should be interpreted using the ADS_SD_REVISION_ENUM enumeration:

```
enum {
    ADS_SD_REVISION_DS    = 4
} ADS_SD_REVISION_ENUM;
```

Name	Description
ADS_SD_REVISION_DS	The revision number of the ACE, or the ACL, for Active Directory.

Searching

The following are used for searching.

Returning Results of Searches

IDirectorySearch methods return columns of data via an ADS_SEARCH_COLUMN structure. A column is the set of values of one attribute on a given object (row). It needs to contain information on the name of the attribute, as well as the actual array of values.

It is defined as:

```
typedef struct ads_search_column {
    LPWSTR pszAttrName;
    ADSTYPE dwADsType;
    PADSVALUE pADsValues;
    DWORD dwNumValues;
    HANDLE hReserved;
} ADS_SEARCH_COLUMN;
```

Name	Description
pszAttrName	Pointer to a string that contains the name of the attribute whose values are contained in the current search column.
dwADsType	Value from the ADSTYPE enumeration that indicates how the attribute values are to be interpreted.
pADsValues	Array of ADSVALUE structures that contain values of the attribute in the current search column for the current row.
dwNumValues	Size of the pADsValues array.
hReserved	Reserved for internal use by providers

Details of the ADSTYPE enumeration and ADSVALUE structure are given above, under the section on structures and enumerations used in the property cache.

Expressing Search Preferences

A search preference is expressed using the ADS_SEARCHPREF_INFO structure, which contains details of which preference is being examined or set, what the value is, and a status that indicates whether the preference was successfully set. The value is contained in an ADSVALUE structure.

ADS_SEARCHPREF_INFO is defined as:

```
typedef struct  ads_searchpref_info {
    ADS_SEARCHPREF dwSearchPref;
    ADSVALUE vValue;
    ADS_STATUS dwStatus;
} ADS_SEARCHPREF_INFO;
```

Name	Description
dwSearchPref	One of the ADS_SEARCHPREF enumeration values.
vValue	Value of the search preference that uses the ADSVALUE structure.
dwStatus	One of the ADS_STATUS enumeration values.

In this structure, the type of data stored in the value depends on the search preference. The search preferences are:

```
typedef enum {
    ADS_SEARCHPREF_ASYNCHRONOUS       = 0,
    ADS_SEARCHPREF_DEREF_ALIASES      = ADS_SEARCHPREF_ASYNCHRONOUS + 1,
    ADS_SEARCHPREF_SIZE_LIMIT         = ADS_SEARCHPREF_DEREF_ALIASES + 1,
    ADS_SEARCHPREF_TIME_LIMIT         = ADS_SEARCHPREF_SIZE_LIMIT + 1,
    ADS_SEARCHPREF_ATTRIBTYPES_ONLY   = ADS_SEARCHPREF_TIME_LIMIT + 1,
    ADS_SEARCHPREF_SEARCH_SCOPE       = ADS_SEARCHPREF_ATTRIBTYPES_ONLY + 1,
    ADS_SEARCHPREF_TIMEOUT            = ADS_SEARCHPREF_SEARCH_SCOPE + 1,
    ADS_SEARCHPREF_PAGESIZE           = ADS_SEARCHPREF_TIMEOUT + 1,
    ADS_SEARCHPREF_PAGED_TIME_LIMIT   = ADS_SEARCHPREF_PAGESIZE + 1,
    ADS_SEARCHPREF_CHASE_REFERRALS    = ADS_SEARCHPREF_PAGED_TIME_LIMIT + 1,
    ADS_SEARCHPREF_SORT_ON            = ADS_SEARCHPREF_CHASE_REFERRALS + 1,
    ADS_SEARCHPREF_CACHE_RESULTS      = ADS_SEARCHPREF_SORT_ON + 1
} ADS_SEARCHPREF_ENUM;

typedef ADS_SEARCHPREF_ENUM ADS_SEARCHPREF;
```

Name	Description
ADS_SEARCHPREF_ ASYNCHRONOUS	Specifies that searches should be carried out in an asynchronous way.
ADS_SEARCHPREF_ DEREF_ALIASES	Specifies that aliases of found objects are to be resolved. Use the ADS_DEREFENUM enumeration to specify how this should be done.
ADS_SEARCHPREF_ SIZE_LIMIT	Specifies the size limit that the server should observe in a search. For Active Directory, the size limit specifies the maximum number of returned objects. The server stops searching once the size limit is reached and returns the results accumulated up to that point.

Name	Description
ADS_SEARCHPREF_ TIME_LIMIT	Specifies the time limit (in seconds) for the search that the server should observe in a search. When the time limit is reached, the server stops searching and returns whatever results it has accumulated up to that point
ADS_SEARCHPREF_ ATTRIBTYPES_ ONLY	Indicates that the search should obtain only the name of attributes to which values have been assigned.
ADS_SEARCHPREF_ SEARCH_SCOPE	Specifies the search scope that should be observed by the server. For the appropriate settings, see the ADS_SCOPEENUM enumeration.
ADS_SEARCHPREF_ TIMEOUT	Specifies the time limit (in seconds) that a client is willing to wait for the server to return the result. This option is set in an ADS_SEARCHPREF_INFO structure.
ADS_SEARCHPREF_ PAGESIZE	Specifies the page size in a paged search. For each request by the client, the server returns at most the number of objects as set by the page size.
ADS_SEARCHPREF_ PAGED_TIME_ LIMIT	Specifies the time limit (in seconds) that the server should observe to search a page of results (as opposed to the time limit for the entire search). When the limit is reached, the server stops searching and returns the result obtained up to that point, along with a cookie containing the information about where to resume searching.
ADS_SEARCHPREF_ CHASE_ REFERRALS	Specifies that referrals may be chased. If the root search is not specified in the naming context of the server or when the search results cross a naming context (for example, when you have child domains and search in the parent domain), the server sends a referral message to the client, which the client can choose to ignore or chase. For more information on referrals chasing, see ADS_CHASE_REFERRALS_ENUM.
ADS_SEARCHPREF_ SORT_ON	Specifies that the server sorts the result set. Use the ADS_SORTKEY structure to specify the sort keys.
ADS_SEARCHPREF_ CACHE_RESULTS	Specifies if the result should be cached on the client side. By default, ADSI caches the result set. Turning off this option may be more desirable for large result sets.

The status is defined as:

```
enum {
    ADS_STATUS_S_OK                         = 0,
    ADS_STATUS_INVALID_SEARCHPREF           = ADS_STATUS_S_OK + 1,
    ADS_STATUS_INVALID_SEARCHPREFVALUE      = ADS_STATUS_INVALID_SEARCHPREF + 1
} ADS_STATUSENUM;
```

Name	Description
ADS_STATUS_S_OK	The search preference was set successfully.
ADS_STATUS_INVALID_ SEARCHPREF	The search preference specified in the dwSearchPref field of the ADS_SEARCHPREF_INFO structure is invalid. Search preferences must be taken from the ADS_SEARCHPREF enumeration.
ADS_STATUS_INVALID_ SEARCHPREFVALUE	The value specified in the vValue member of the ADS_SEARCHPREF_INFO structure is invalid for the corresponding search preference.

For some of the search preferences, further enumerations or structures are used to interpret the possible values. If the possible value is a structure, then the type in the containing ADSVALUE structure should be set to provider-specific.

Sorting Results

The ADS_SORTKEY structure specifies how to sort a query.

```
typedef struct ADS_SORTKEY {
    LPWSTR  pszAttrType;
    LPWSTR  pszReserved;
    BOOLEAN fReverseorder;
} ADS_SORTKEY, *PADS_SORTKEY;
```

Name	Description
pszAttrType	Pointer to a stream that contains the type for the attribute.
pszReserved	Reserved for future use
fReverseorder	Reverse the order of the sorted results. In Active Directory, if TRUE, the fReverseorder parameter specifies that the sort results be ordered from the lowest to the highest.

Search Scope

The ADS_SCOPEENUM enumeration specifies the scope of a directory search.

```
typedef enum {
    ADS_SCOPE_BASE       = 0,
    ADS_SCOPE_ONELEVEL   = 1,
    ADS_SCOPE_SUBTREE    = 2
} ADS_SCOPEENUM;
```

Name	Description
ADS_SCOPE_BASE	Limits the search to the base object. The result contains at most one object.
ADS_SCOPE_ONELEVEL	Searches one level of the immediate children, excluding the base object
ADS_SCOPE_SUBTREE	Searches the whole subtree, including all the children and the base object itself.

Chasing Referrals

The ADS_CHASE_REFERRALS_ENUM enumeration specifies if and how referral chasing is pursued. When a server determines that other servers hold relevant information, in part or as a whole, it may refer the client to another server to obtain the result. Referral chasing is the action taken by a client to contact the referred to server to continue the directory search.

```
typedef enum {
    ADS_CHASE_REFERRALS_NEVER          = 0x00,
    ADS_CHASE_REFERRALS_SUBORDINATE    = 0x20,
    ADS_CHASE_REFERRALS_EXTERNAL       = 0x40,
    ADS_CHASE_REFERRALS_ALWAYS         = 0x20 | 0x40
} ADS_CHASE_REFERRALS_ENUM
```

Name	Description
ADS_CHASE_REFERRALS_ NEVER	The client should never chase the referred to server. Setting this option prevents a client from contacting other servers in a referral process.
ADS_CHASE_REFERRALS_ SUBORDINATE	The client chases only subordinate referrals, which are a subordinate naming context in a directory tree. For example, if the base search is requested for DC=ArcadiaBay, DC=Com, and the server returns a result set and a referral of DC=Sales, DC=ArcadiaBay, DC=Com on the AdbSales server, the client can contact the AdbSales server to continue the search. The ADSI LDAP provider always turns off this flag for paged searches.
ADS_CHASE_REFERRALS_ EXTERNAL	The client chases external referrals. For example, a client requests server A to perform a search for DC=ArcadiaBay, DC=Com. However, server A does not contain the object, but knows that an independent server, B, owns it. It then refers the client to server B.
ADS_CHASE_REFERRALS_ ALWAYS	Referrals are chased for either the subordinate or external type.

Dereferencing Aliases

The `ADS_DEREFENUM` enumeration specifies the behavior in which aliases are dereferenced.

```
enum {
    ADS_DEREF_NEVER        = 0,
    ADS_DEREF_SEARCHING    = 1,
    ADS_DEREF_FINDING      = 2,
    ADS_DEREF_ALWAYS       = 3
} ADS_DEREFENUM;
```

Name	Description
ADS_DEREF_NEVER	Does not dereference aliases when searching or locating the base object of the search.
ADS_DEREF_SEARCHING	Dereferences aliases when searching subordinates of the base object, but not when locating the base itself.
ADS_DEREF_FINDING	Dereferences aliases when locating the base object of the search, but not when searching its subordinates.
ADS_DEREF_ALWAYS	Dereferences aliases when both searching subordinates and locating the base object of the search.

Dialects Used in OLE DB and ADO Queries

This enumeration is not used directly in `IDirectorySearch`, but is passed by ADSI clients to OLE DB in order that OLE DB can correctly interpret the command string.

The `ADSI_DIALECT_ENUM` enumeration specifies query dialects used in the OLE DB provider for ADSI.

```
typedef enum {
    ADSI_DIALECT_LDAP    = 0,
    ADSI_DIALECT_SQL     = 0x1
} ADSI_DIALECT_ENUM
```

Name	Description
ADSI_DIALECT_LDAP	ADSI queries are based on the LDAP dialect.
ADSI_DIALECT_SQL	ADSI queries are based on the SQL dialect

Extension objects

Extension objects use a couple of constants passed to `IADsExtension::Operate` to indicate the purpose for which `Operate` has been called. There are also constants that define the range of Dispatch IDs that extensions can use. You're unlikely to need to go outside this range anyway, but doing so may cause problems with the DispID encoding algorithm used by the aggregator to distinguish your extension in `IDispatch` calls.

ADSI Constant	Value	Description
ADS_EXT_ INITCREDENTIALS	1	A control code that indicates that the custom data supplied to the `IADsExtension::Operate` method contains user credentials.
ADS_EXT_ INITIALIZE_ COMPLETE	2	A control code used with `IADsExtension::Operate` to indicate that extensions can perform any necessary initialization, depending on the functionality supported by the parent object.
ADS_EXT_ MAXEXTDISPID	16777215	The highest DispID an extension object can use for its methods and properties.
ADS_EXT_ MINEXTDISPID	1	The lowest DispID an extension object can use for its methods and properties.

Authentication

Authentication using the `IADsOpenDSObject::OpenDSObject()` method relies on an enumeration to indicate the security of authentication required. This is the `ADS_AUTHENTICATION_ENUM` enumeration, defined as:

```
typedef enum {
    ADS_SECURE_AUTHENTICATION  = 0x1,
    ADS_USE_ENCRYPTION         = 0x2,
    ADS_USE_SSL                = 0x2,
    ADS_READONLY_SERVER        = 0x4,
    ADS_PROMPT_CREDENTIALS     = 0x8,
    ADS_NO_AUTHENTICATION      = 0x10,
    ADS_FAST_BIND              = 0x20,
    ADS_USE_SIGNING            = 0x40,
    ADS_USE_SEALING            = 0x80
} ADS_AUTHENTICATION_ENUM;
```

Name	Description
ADS_SECURE_AUTHENTICATION	Requests secure authentication. When this flag is set, the WinNT provider uses NT LAN Manager (NTLM) to authenticate the client. Active Directory will use Kerberos, and possibly NTLM, to authenticate the client. When the user name and password are NULL, ADSI uses the credentials of the currently logged-on user.
ADS_USE_ENCRYPTION	Forces ADSI to use encryption for data exchange over the network.
ADS_USE_SSL	Encrypts the channel with SSL (Secure Sockets Layer). Data will be encrypted using SSL. Active Directory requires that the Certificate Server be installed to support SSL encryption.
ADS_READONLY_SERVER	For a WinNT provider, ADSI tries to connect to a primary domain controller (PDC) or a backup domain controller (BDC). For Active Directory, this flag indicates that a writeable server is not required for a serverless binding.
ADS_PROMPT_CREDENTIALS	User credentials are prompted when the authentication is initiated, if the selected Security Support Provider Interface (SSPI) provides a user interface to do so.
ADS_NO_AUTHENTICATION	Request no authentication. The providers may attempt to bind client, as an anonymous user, to the targeted object. The WinNT provider does not support this flag. Active Directory establishes a connection between the client and the targeted object, but will not perform any authentication. Setting this flag amounts to requesting an anonymous binding, which means "Everyone" as the security context.
ADS_FAST_BIND	When this flag is set, ADSI will not attempt to query the objectClass property, and thus will only expose the base interfaces supported by all ADSI objects instead of the full object support. A user can use this option to boost the performance in a series of object manipulations that involve only methods of the base interfaces. However, ADSI will not verify if any of the request objects actually exist on the server. For more information, see "Fast Binding Options for Batch Write/Modify Operations" in Active Directory Programmer's Guide.

Name	Description
ADS_USE_SIGNING	Verifies data integrity to ensure the data received is the same as the data sent. The ADS_SECURE_AUTHENTICATION flag must also be set in order to use the signing.
ADS_USE_SEALING	Encrypts data using Kerberos. The ADS_SECURE_AUTHENTICATION flag must also be set in order to use the sealing.

Serverless binding refers to a process in which a client attempts to bind to an Active Directory object without explicitly specifying an Active Directory server in the binding string, for example, LDAP://CN=jsmith,DC=ArcadiaBay,DC=Com. This is possible because the LDAP provider relies on the locator services of Windows 2000 to find the best domain controller (DC) for the client. However, the client must have an account on the Active Directory domain controller in order to take advantage of the serverless binding feature.

Name Conversions

The pathname object, which exposes the IADsPathName interface, uses a number of enumerations in order to specify different format types etc.

Pathname Portions

The ADS_SETTYPE enumeration specifies the available pathname format used by the IADsPathname::Set method.

```
typedef enum ADS_SETTYPE {
    ADS_SETTYPE_FULL       = 1,
    ADS_SETTYPE_PROVIDER   = 2,
    ADS_SETTYPE_NAMESPACE  = 2,
    ADS_SETTYPE_SERVER     = 3,
    ADS_SETTYPE_DN         = 4
} ADS_SETTYPE, *PADS_SETTYPE;
```

Name	Description
ADS_SETTYPE_FULL	Sets the full path, for example, LDAP://servername/o=internet/.../cn=bar.
ADS_SETTYPE_PROVIDER	Updates the provider only, for example, LDAP.
ADS_SETTYPE_NAMESPACE	The same as ADS_SETTYPE_PROVIDER.
ADS_SETTYPE_SERVER	Updates the server name only, for example, servername.
ADS_SETTYPE_DN	Updates the distinguished name only, for example, o=internet/.../cn=bar.

Displaying the PathName

The `ADS_DISPLAY_ENUM` enumeration specifies how a path name is to be displayed.

```
enum {
    ADS_DISPLAY_FULL       = 1,
    ADS_DISPLAY_VALUE_ONLY = 2
} ADS_DISPLAY_ENUM;
```

Name	Description
ADS_DISPLAY_FULL	The path name is displayed with both attributes and values. For example, CN=John Doe.
ADS_DISPLAY_VALUE_ONLY	The path name is displayed with values only. For example, John Doe

The Escape Mode

The `ESCAPE_MODE_ENUM` enumeration specifies how escaped characters are handled in a path name.

```
enum {
        ADS_ESCAPEDMODE_DEFAULT = 1,
        ADS_ESCAPEDMODE_ON      = 2,
        ADS_ESCAPEDMODE_OFF     = 3
    } ADS_ESCAPE_MODE_ENUM;
```

Name	Description
ADS_ESCAPEDMODE_DEFAULT	The default mode is ADS_ESCAPEDMODE_ON.
ADS_ESCAPEDMODE_ON	Display escaped characters in the path name string.
ADS_ESCAPEDMODE_OFF	Do not display escaped characters in the path name string.

Pathname Formats

The `ADS_FORMAT` enumeration specifies the available pathname value types used by the `IADsPathname::Retrieve` method.

```
typedef enum ADS_FORMAT {
    ADS_FORMAT_WINDOWS           = 1,
    ADS_FORMAT_WINDOWS_NO_SERVER = 2,
    ADS_FORMAT_WINDOWS_DN        = 3,
    ADS_FORMAT_WINDOWS_PARENT    = 4,
    ADS_FORMAT_X500              = 5,
    ADS_FORMAT_X500_NO_SERVER    = 6,
    ADS_FORMAT_X500_DN           = 7,
    ADS_FORMAT_X500_PARENT       = 8,
    ADS_FORMAT_SERVER            = 9,
    ADS_FORMAT_PROVIDER          = 10,
    ADS_FORMAT_NAMESPACE         = 10,
    ADS_FORMAT_LEAF              = 11,
} ADS_FORMAT, *PADS_FORMAT;
```

Name	Description
`ADS_FORMAT_WINDOWS`	Returns the full path in Windows format, for example, `LDAP://servername/o=internet/…/cn=bar`.
`ADS_FORMAT_WINDOWS_NO_SERVER`	Returns Windows format without server, for example, `LDAP://o=internet/…/cn=bar`.
`ADS_FORMAT_WINDOWS_DN`	Returns Windows format of the distinguished name only, for example, `o=internet/…/cn=bar`.
`ADS_FORMAT_WINDOWS_PARENT`	Returns Windows format of Parent only, for example, `o=internet/…`.
`ADS_FORMAT_X500`	Returns the full path in X500 format, for example, `LDAP://servername/cn=bar, …, o=internet`.
`ADS_FORMAT_X500_NO_SERVER`	Returns X500 format without server, for example, `LDAP://cn=bar, …, o=internet`
`ADS_FORMAT_X500_DN`	Returns only the distinguished name in X500 format. For example, `cn=bar,…,o=internet`.
`ADS_FORMAT_X500_PARENT`	Returns only the parent in X500 format, for example, `…,o=internet`.
`ADS_FORMAT_SERVER`	Returns the server name, for example, `servername`.
`ADS_FORMAT_PROVIDER`	Returns the name of the provider, for example, `LDAP`.
`ADS_FORMAT_NAMESPACE`	The same as `ADS_FORMAT_PROVIDER`.
`ADS_FORMAT_LEAF`	Returns the name of the leaf, for example, `cn=bar`.

Groups

In Active Directory, it is possible to specify the type of group an object represents. This is done through the `groupType` attribute on group objects, which takes values from the `ADS_GROUP_TYPE_ENUM` enumeration.

```
enum {
    ADS_GROUP_TYPE_GLOBAL_GROUP          = 0x00000002,
    ADS_GROUP_TYPE_DOMAIN_LOCAL_GROUP    = 0x00000004,
    ADS_GROUP_TYPE_LOCAL_GROUP           = 0x00000004,
    ADS_GROUP_TYPE_UNIVERSAL_GROUP       = 0x00000008,
    ADS_GROUP_TYPE_SECURITY_ENABLED      = 0x80000000,
} ADS_GROUP_TYPE_ENUM;
```

Name	Description
ADS_GROUP_TYPE_ GLOBAL_GROUP	Group that contains only accounts and other account groups from its own domain. This group may be exported to a different domain.
ADS_GROUP_TYPE_ DOMAIN_LOCAL_ GROUP	Group that can contain accounts and universal groups from any domains. It may not be included in either access-control lists of resources in other domains or groups other than global groups in the same domain
ADS_GROUP_TYPE_ LOCAL_GROUP	This flag is for the WinNT provider as the ADS_GROUP_TYPE_DOMAIN_LOCAL_GROUP flag is for the LDAP provider.
ADS_GROUP_TYPE_ UNIVERSAL_GROUP	Group that can contain accounts and account groups from any domains, but not domain local groups.
ADS_GROUP_TYPE_ SECURITY_ ENABLED	Group that is security enabled. This group can be used to apply an access-control list on an ADSI object or a file system.

IADsObjectOptions

IADsObjectOptions allows the setting of options that are provider-specific. This means that you are perfectly at liberty to define your own constants for options in providers that you write. However, for the benefit of the LDAP provider, the following are defined by the ADS_OPTION_ENUM enumeration:

```
enum {
    ADS_OPTION_SERVERNAME       = 0,
    ADS_OPTION_REFERRALS        = 1,
    ADS_OPTION_PAGE_SIZE        = 2,
    ADS_OPTION_SECURITY_MASK    = 3
} ADS_OPTION_ENUM;
```

Name	Description
ADS_OPTION_SERVERNAME	Specifies that the host names of servers are to be set or obtained in a query.
ADS_OPTION_REFERRALS	Specifies that referral chasing is to be performed in a query
ADS_OPTION_PAGE_SIZE	Specifies that page sizes are to be set or obtained in a paged search.
ADS_OPTION_SECURITY_MASK	Specifies that security information, including the system access-control list (ACL), of an object is to be examined. This element takes any combination of the bit-masks as defined in the ADS_SECURITY_INFO_ENUM enumeration

This last option refers to an ADS_SECURITY_INFO_ENUM enumeration.

ADS_SECURITY_INFO_ENUM

The `ADS_SECURITY_INFO_ENUM` enumeration specifies the available options for examining security information of an object. This enumeration is defined as:

```
enum {
    ADS_SECURITY_INFO_OWNER   = 0x1,
    ADS_SECURITY_INFO_GROUP   = 0x2,
    ADS_SECURITY_INFO_DACL    = 0x4,
    ADS_SECURITY_INFO_SACL    = 0x8
} ADS_SECURITY_INFO_ENUM;
```

Name	Details
ADS_SECURITY_INFO_OWNER	Reads or sets the owner information.
ADS_SECURITY_INFO_GROUP	Reads or sets the group information.
ADS_SECURITY_INFO_DACL	Reads or sets the discretionary access-control list (DACL).
ADS_SECURITY_INFO_SACL	Reads or sets the system access-control list (SACL).

Attribute Schemas

The `ADS_SYSTEMFLAG_ENUM` enumeration defines the values that can be assigned to the `systemflags` attribute of the `attributeSchema` object in Active Directory, as well as other objects, such as `domainDNS` objects. The flags specify the types of attributes (also known as properties) represented by an `attributeSchema` object. For example, for the user object, there are three types of attributes: Domain-replicated and stored properties, Non-replicated and locally stored properties, and Non-stored and constructed properties.

```
typedef enum ADS_SYSTEMFLAG_ENUM {
    ADS_SYSTEMFLAG_DISALLOW_DELETE          = 0x80000000,
    ADS_SYSTEMFLAG_CONFIG_ALLOW_RENAME      = 0x40000000,
    ADS_SYSTEMFLAG_CONFIG_ALLOW_MOVE        = 0x20000000,
    ADS_SYSTEMFLAG_CONFIG_ALLOW_LIMITED_MOVE = 0x10000000,
    ADS_SYSTEMFLAG_DOMAIN_DISALLOW_RENAME   = 0x08000000,
    ADS_SYSTEMFLAG_DOMAIN_DISALLOW_MOVE     = 0x04000000,
    ADS_SYSTEMFLAG_CR_NTDS_NC               = 0x00000001,
    ADS_SYSTEMFLAG_CR_NTDS_DOMAIN           = 0x00000002,
    ADS_SYSTEMFLAG_ATTR_NOT_REPLICATED      = 0x00000001,
    ADS_SYSTEMFLAG_ATTR_IS_CONTRUCTED       = 0x00000004
}
```

Name	Description
ADS_SYSTEMFLAG_DISALLOW_DELETE	The attribute cannot be deleted.
ADS_SYSTEMFLAG_CONFIG_ALLOW_RENAME	The configuration property can be renamed.
ADS_SYSTEMFLAG_CONFIG_ALLOW_MOVE	The configuration property can be moved.
ADS_SYSTEMFLAG_CONFIG_ALLOW_LIMITED_MOVE	The configuration property can be moved with restrictions.
ADS_SYSTEMFLAG_DOMAIN_DISALLOW_RENAME	The domain property cannot be renamed.
ADS_SYSTEMFLAG_DOMAIN_DISALLOW_MOVE	The domain property cannot be moved.
ADS_SYSTEMFLAG_CR_NTDS_NC	Naming context is in NTDS.
ADS_SYSTEMFLAG_CR_NTDS_DOMAIN	Naming context is a domain.
ADS_SYSTEMFLAG_ATTR_NOT_REPLICATED	The attribute is not to be replicated.
ADS_SYSTEMFLAG_ATTR_IS_CONTRUCTED	The attribute is a constructed property.

Users

The ADS_USER_FLAG enumeration defines the flags used for manipulating various user properties in the directory.

```
typedef enum ADS_USER_FLAG {
    ADS_UF_SCRIPT                           = 0x1,
    ADS_UF_ACCOUNTDISABLE                   = 0x2,
    ADS_UF_HOMEDIR_REQUIRED                 = 0x8,
    ADS_UF_LOCKOUT                          = 0x10,
    ADS_UF_PASSWD_NOTREQD                   = 0x20,
    ADS_UF_PASSWD_CANT_CHANGE               = 0x40,
    ADS_UF_ENCRYPTED_TEXT_PASSWORD_ALLOWED  = 0x80,
    ADS_UF_TEMP_DUPLICATE_ACCOUNT           = 0x100,
    ADS_UF_NORMAL_ACCOUNT                   = 0x200,
    ADS_UF_INTERDOMAIN_TRUST_ACCOUNT        = 0x800,
    ADS_UF_WORKSTATION_TRUST_ACCOUNT        = 0x1000,
```

```
      ADS_UF_SERVER_TRUST_ACCOUNT           = 0x2000,
      ADS_UF_DONT_EXPIRE_PASSWD             = 0x10000,
      ADS_UF_MNS_LOGON_ACCOUNT              = 0x20000,
      ADS_UF_SMARTCARD_REQUIRED             = 0x40000,
      ADS_UF_TRUSTED_FOR_DELEGATION         = 0x80000,
      ADS_UF_NOT_DELEGATED                  = 0x100000
  } ADS_USER_FLAG_ENUM;
```

Name	Description
ADS_UF_SCRIPT	The logon script will be executed.
ADS_UF_ACCOUNTDISABLE	The user's account is disabled.
ADS_UF_HOMEDIR_ REQUIRED	The home directory is required.
ADS_UF_LOCKOUT	The account is currently locked out.
ADS_UF_PASSWD_NOTREQD	No password is required.
ADS_UF_PASSWD_CANT_ CHANGE	The user cannot change the password.
ADS_UF_ENCRYPTED_TEXT_ PASSWORD_ALLOWED	The user can send an encrypted password.
ADS_UF_TEMP_DUPLICATE_ ACCOUNT	This is an account for users whose primary account is in another domain. This account provides user access to this domain, but not to any domain that trusts this domain. Sometimes it is referred to as a local user account.
ADS_UF_NORMAL_ACCOUNT	This is a default account type that represents a typical user.
ADS_UF_INTERDOMAIN_ TRUST_ACCOUNT	This is a permit to trust account for a system domain that trusts other domains.
ADS_UF_WORKSTATION_ TRUST_ACCOUNT	This is a computer account for a Windows NT Workstation/Windows 2000 Professional or Windows NT Server/Windows 2000 Server that is a member of this domain.
ADS_UF_SERVER_TRUST_ ACCOUNT	This is a computer account for a system backup domain controller that is a member of this domain.

Table Continued on Following Page

Name	Description
ADS_UF_DONT_EXPIRE_ PASSWD	Represents the password, which should never expire on the account.
ADS_UF_MNS_LOGON_ ACCOUNT	This is an MNS logon account.
ADS_UF_SMARTCARD_ REQUIRED	When set, this flag will force the user to log on using smart card.
ADS_UF_TRUSTED_FOR _DELEGATION	When set, the service account (user or computer account), under which a service runs is trusted for Kerberos delegation. Any such service can impersonate a client requesting the service. To enable a service for Kerberos delegation, you must set this flag on the userAccountControl property of the service account.
ADS_UF_NOT_DELEGATED	When set, the security context of the user will not be delegated to a service, even if the service account is set as trusted for Kerberos delegation.

IDirectoryObject

IDirectoryObject uses two structures to return or set information about an object. ADS_OBJECT_INFO gives information about the name, parent, ADsPath, class, and schema. ADS_ATTR_INFO stores the value of one attribute.

ADS_OBJECT_INFO

This is defined as:

```
typedef struct _ads_object_info {
    LPWSTR pszRDN;
    LPWSTR pszObjectDN;
    LPWSTR pszParentDN;
    LPWSTR pszSchemaDN;
    LPWSTR pszClassName;
} ADS_OBJECT_INFO;
```

Name	Description
pszRDN	Relative distinguished name (relative path) of the directory service object.
pszObjectDN	Distinguished name (path) of the directory service object.
pszParentDN	Distinguished name of the parent object.
pszSchemaDN	Distinguished name of the schema class of the object.
pszClassName	Name of the class of which this object is an instance.

ADS_ATTR_INFO

This structure contains an ADSVALUE structure, described earlier.

```
typedef struct _ads_attr_info {
    LPWSTR pszAttrName;
    DWORD dwControlCode;
    ADSTYPE dwADsType;
    PADSVALUE pADsValues;
    DWORD dwNumValues;
} ADS_ATTR_INFO;
```

Names	Attributes
pszAttrName	Pointer to a string containing the name of the attribute.
dwControlCode	One of the ADS_ATTR_* constants that control what operation to be performed on the attribute. For more information on the ADS_ATTR_* constants, see ADSI Constants
dwADsType	Data type of the attribute as defined by ADSTYPE.
pADsValues	Pointer to an array of ADSVALUE structures that contain values for the attribute.
dwNumValues	Size of the pADsValues array.

When setting an attribute, the ADS_ATTR_INFO structure makes use of the following values to indicate the action that should be taken.

Name	Value	Description
ADS_ATTR_APPEND	3	Instructs the directory service to append the new value(s) to the existing attribute(s). The attribute and this constant are specified in an ADS_ATTR_INFO array.
ADS_ATTR_CLEAR	1	Instructs the directory service to remove attribute value(s) from an object. The attribute and this constant are specified in an ADS_ATTR_INFO array.
ADS_ATTR_DELETE	4	Instructs the directory service to delete the named attribute value(s) as specified in an ADS_ATTR_INFO array.
ADS_ATTR_UPDATE	2	Instructs the directory service to update the named attribute value(s) as specified in an ADS_ATTR_INFO array.

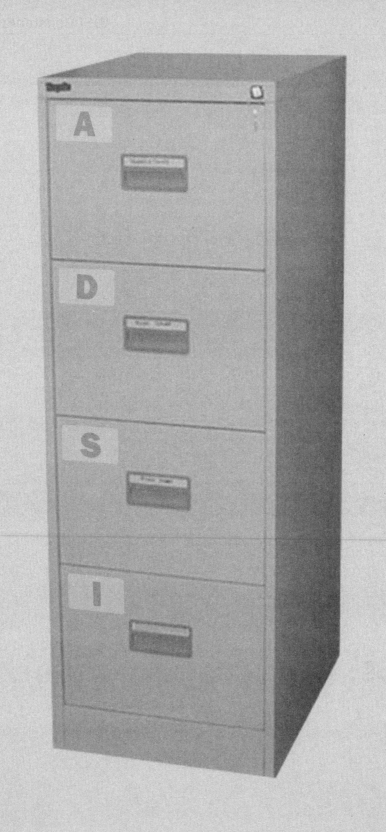

G

ADSI API Functions

This appendix lists the ADSI API functions.

Function	Description
ADsGetObject	Binds to an ADSI object using the current credentials.
ADsOpenObject	Binds to an ADSI object using specified credentials.
ADsGetLastError	Retrieves the last error code value of the calling thread.
ADsSetLastError	Sets the error code value of the calling thread.
ADsBuildVarArrayInt	Builds a variant array from an array of DWORDs.
ADsBuildVarArrayStr	Builds a variant array from an array of Unicode strings.
ADsBuildEnumerator	Creates an enumerator object for the specified ADSI container object.
ADsEnumerateNext	Populates a variant array with elements retrieved from the specified enumerator object.
ADsFreeEnumerator	Frees an enumerator object previously created by ADsBuildEnumerator.
AllocADsMem	Allocates a block of memory.

Function	Description
FreeADsMem	Frees the memory allocated by AllocADsMem.
ReallocADsMem	Assigns the existing memory content to a newly created memory location.
AllocADsStr	Allocates memory for a given string.
FreeADsStr	Frees the memory allocated for the given string.
ReallocADsStr	Replaces an existing string with a new one.
ADsEncodeBinaryData	Converts a blob of binary data to the format suitable for a search filter.

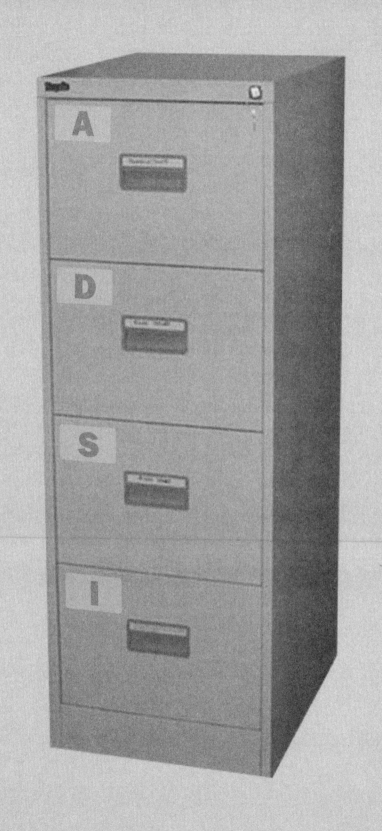

ADSI Providers Currently Available

IIS:
Access the Internet Information Server metabase and configuration data.

LDAP:
Access any LDAP directory service, including Active Directory, the Exchange Directory, the Site Server Membership Directory and Netscape Directory Server.

NDS:
Use this to access Novell Directory Services

NWCompat:
To get to Novell Netware.

WinNT:
Accesses data about computers on the local network.

Sample:
The Microsoft sample provider.

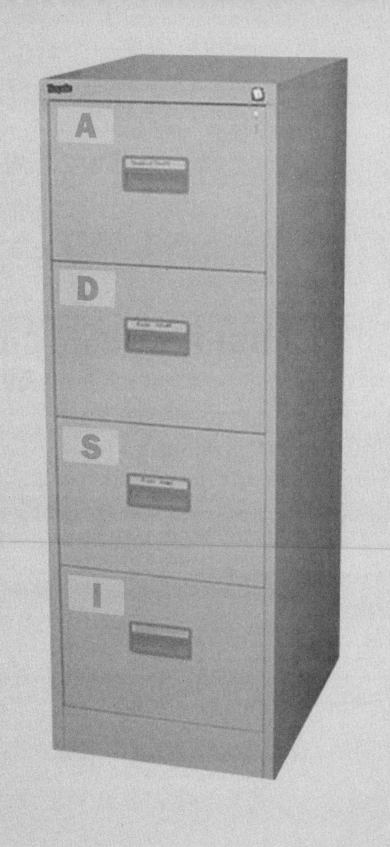

Microsoft Samples

Originally, I envisioned this appendix as being a comprehensive guide to all the Microsoft ADSI samples that were available with the ADSI SDK. Unfortunately, Microsoft has kept adding and adding to the samples, until now it's just not practical to give a comprehensive guide. There's stuff to do everything: Active Directory specific samples, Exchange Server specific samples. Stuff in every language: C++, VB, ASP, Java. All I can really do is tell you to go and explore them.

In this appendix, I'll just mention what I regard as the most important samples – the ones that I found most useful in the course of my ADSI travels.

dsbrowse

This is significant because it is a general purpose ADSI browser. It is moderately useful, although it doesn't have as many features as `adsvw.exe`. You can find it in the General samples. I won't say anything more about it here as we already covered it in Chapter 1.

ADQI

This is the Quest for Interfaces. It's one of the few samples that was written using MFC. It's quite useful for showing which ADSI objects expose which interfaces. We talked a bit about ADQI in Chapter 3.

Extension Tutorials

I mention these because, not only are the complete samples there, but there is also a set of documentation that explains all the steps you have to go through to create them. There are two samples, each of which creates an ADSI extension. The first sample doesn't support `IDispatch`, the second does – and I'd suggest you head straight for the second sample.

Sample Provider

This is in the Provider folder in the samples. It is an ADSI provider that gives you a registry-based directory of people in two towns. It's written in raw C++ rather than ATL, so you can use it to get an idea of how to write the COM interfaces without all the ATL boilerplate code, if you want a super-efficient provider.

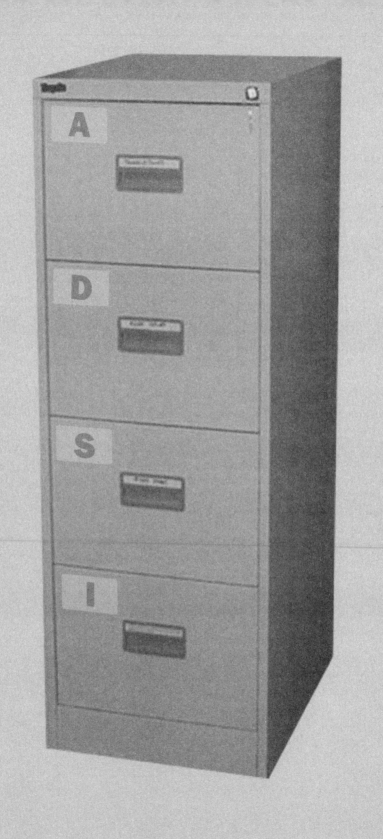

Support and Errata

One of the most irritating things about any programming book is when you find that bit of code you've just spent an hour typing simply doesn't work. You check it a hundred times to see if you've set it up correctly and then you notice the spelling mistake in the variable name on the book page. Of course, you can blame the authors for not taking enough care and testing the code, the editors for not doing their job properly, or the proofreaders for not being eagle-eyed enough, but this doesn't get around the fact that mistakes do happen.

We try hard to ensure no mistakes sneak out into the real world, but we can't promise that this book is 100% error free. What we can do is offer the next best thing by providing you with immediate support and feedback from experts who have worked on the book and try to ensure that future editions eliminate these gremlins. The following section will take you step by step through the process of posting errata to our web site to get that help. The sections that follow, therefore, are:

- ❑ Wrox Developers Membership
- ❑ Finding a list of existing errata on the web site
- ❑ Adding your own errata to the existing list
- ❑ What happens to your errata once you've posted it (why doesn't it appear immediately)?

There is also a section covering how to e-mail a question for technical support. This comprises:

- ❑ What your e-mail should include
- ❑ What happens to your e-mail once it has been received by us

So that you only need view information relevant to yourself, we ask that you register as a Wrox Developer Member. This is a quick and easy process, that will save you time in the long-run. If you are already a member, just update membership to include this book.

Wrox Developer's Membership

To get your FREE Wrox Developer's Membership click on **Membership** in the top navigation bar of our home site – http://www.wrox.com This is shown in the following screenshot:

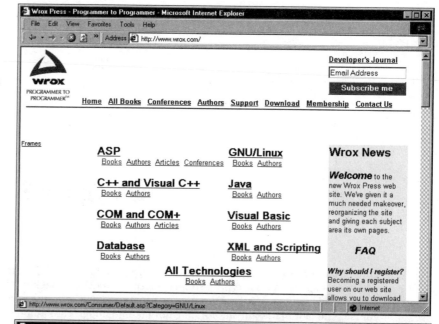

Then, on the next screen (not shown), click on **New User**. This will display a form. Fill in the details on the form and submit the details using the **Register** button at the bottom. Before you can say 'The best read books come in Wrox Red' you will get the following screen:

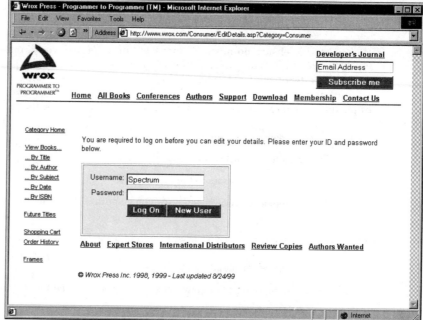

Type in your password once again and click Log On. The following page allows you to change your details if you need to, but now you're logged on, you have access to all the source code downloads and errata for the entire Wrox range of books.

Finding an Errata on the Web Site

Before you send in a query, you might be able to save time by finding the answer to your problem on our web site – http:\\www.wrox.com.

Each book we publish has its own page and its own errata sheet. You can get to any book's page by clicking on Support from the top navigation bar.

Halfway down the main support page is a drop down box called Title Support. Simply scroll down the list until you see Professional ADSI Development. select it and then hit Errata.

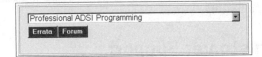

This will take you to the errata page for the book. Select the criteria by which you want to view the errata, and click the Apply criteria button. This will provide you with links to specific errata. For an initial search, you are advised to view the errata by page numbers. If you have looked for an error previously, then you may wish to limit your search using dates. We update these pages daily to ensure that you have the latest information on bugs and errors.

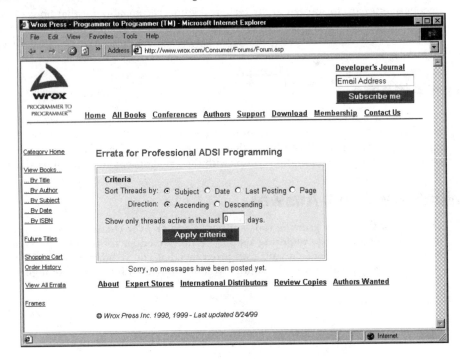

Add an Errata : E-mail Support

If you wish to point out an errata to put up on the website or directly query a problem in the book page with an expert who knows the book in detail then e-mail `support@wrox.com`, with the title of the book and the last four numbers of the ISBN in the subject field of the e-mail. A typical email should include the following things:

- ❑   The **name, last four digits of the ISBN** and **page number** of the problem in the Subject field.

- ❑   Your **name, contact info** and the **problem** in the body of the message.

We won't send you junk mail. We need the details to save your time and ours. If we need to replace a disk or CD we'll be able to get it to you straight away. When you send an e-mail it will go through the following chain of support:

Customer Support

Your message is delivered to one of our customer support staff who are the first people to read it. They have files on most frequently asked questions and will answer anything general immediately. They answer general questions about the book and the web site.

Editorial

Deeper queries are forwarded to the technical editor responsible for that book. They have experience with the programming language or particular product and are able to answer detailed technical questions on the subject. Once an issue has been resolved, the editor can post the errata to the web site.

The Authors

Finally, in the unlikely event that the editor can't answer your problem, s/he will forward the request to the author. We try to protect the author from any distractions from writing. However, we are quite happy to forward specific requests to them. All Wrox authors help with the support on their books. They'll mail the customer and the editor with their response, and again all readers should benefit.

What We Can't Answer

Obviously with an ever growing range of books and an ever-changing technology base, there is an increasing volume of data requiring support. While we endeavor to answer all questions about the book, we can't answer bugs in your own programs that you've adapted from our code. Do tell us if you're especially pleased with the routine you developed with our help, though.

How to Tell Us Exactly What You Think

We understand that errors can destroy the enjoyment of a book and can cause many wasted and frustrated hours, so we seek to minimize the distress that they can cause.

You might just wish to tell us how much you liked or loathed the book in question. Or you might have ideas about how this whole process could be improved. In which case you should e-mail feedback@wrox.com. You'll always find a sympathetic ear, no matter what the problem is. Above all you should remember that we do care about what you have to say and we will do our utmost to act upon it.

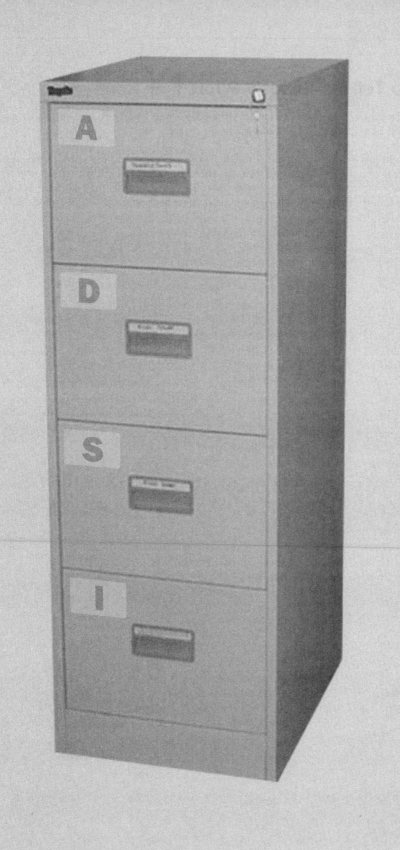

Index

Symbols

$ character, hidden file shares, 239
.chm help files, snap-ins, 539
  implementing, 541
.msc files, MMC snap-ins, 54, 537
  ATL Object Wizard, 550
.msi files, Windows Installer, 587
  writing, 600
_asm, assembly language, 552
_ATL_NO_UUIDOF
  defining in StarRaiders provider, 414
_Copy<VARIANT>
  replacing class for enumeration, 435
_NewEnum property
  access control entries, 363
  enumerators 221, 458
  COM interfaces, looping in VB, 95
  IADsCollection interface, 142
  IADsContainer property, 100
  VB, invisible to, 97
-> syntax, C++, 76

A

AbandonSearch, IDirectorySearch method, 319
About box, disabling, MMC snap-ins, 552
abstract classes, 133, 425
Abstract, IADsClass, 132, 133
Access allowed object, 351
access control entries, 349
  _NewEnum property, 363
  inheritance, 350, 365
  use of, 352
access control lists, 238, 349
  Active Directory Browser, accessing, 373
  use of, 352
Access flags, 350
  conversion function, 361
  displaying as property, 357

Access Mask, 350
  displaying as property, 357
Access Tokens, 386
AccessControlEntry, COM object, 352, 405
AccessControlList, COM object, 352, 404
AccessExecute, 271
AccountDisabled, IADsUser property, 206
AccountExpirationDATE, IADsUser property, 206
accounts
  disabling, 210
  locked out, 210
  modifying, 365
  moving, effect on distinguished name, 345
ACEFlags, 350
  conversion functions, 361
  inheritance, 365
AceMask, 350
  conversion function, 358
ACEs see access control entries
AceType
  conversion function, 358
ACLs see access control lists, 349
Action menu, 571
  All Tasks submenu, 572
Active Directory, 1, 23
  + signs, objects that contain objects, 178
  access control entries, 350
  ADSI, difference from, 8, 33
  ADSI, investigating using breakpoints, 509
  ADsPath, 197
  auditing, 374
  authentication, 336, 344
  defined, 47
  directory for whole domain, 186
  directory structure, extending, 200
  DIT objects, 193
  DNS names as domain names, 169
  domain forests, 48
  domains, 167

Index

Orca, 591
.msi files, writing, 600
components, 594
core tables, 595
FeatureComponents table, 594
installer databases, structure, 595
installing, 591
relational databases, 592
tables, linking, 593
Organization, Exchange Server, 275
OtherName, IADsUser property, 208
OutputDebugString() statements, in investigating ADSI, 509
overriding functions, 455
advantages, 459

P

pADsValues, 322
page size, search preference, 318
paged time limit, search preference, 318
pagefiles, 384
pages, locking privilege, 384
Parameter Object
ADO, 309
parameters, IADsUser property, 210
ParseDisplayName()
code, 471
PasswordExpirationDATE, IADsUser property, 208
PasswordLastChanged, IADsUser property, 208
PasswordMinimumLength, IADsUser property, 208
PasswordRequired, IADsUser property, 209
passwords, 210
changing, 215
in C++, 73
in VB, 72
encryption, 388
Kerberos security, 390
setting, 107
setting on users, 215
trapdoor functions, 397
path names, 37
pAttrInfo, 154
pchEaten, monikers, 472

pComponent
notifications, 562
pComponentData
notifications, 562
Performance Monitor provider, WMI provider, 613
PerlDAP, 479
permissions, 360, 382
permissions, file shares, 238
persistent object interfaces, 106, 184
Picture, IADsUser property, 209
pointer monikers, 468
Polish notation, 302
PossibleSuperiors, IADsClass property, 41, 132
PostalAddresses, IADsUser property, 209
PostalCodes, IADsUser property, 209
ppMonikerToLeft parameter, moniker composition, 467
ppViewType, 569
options, 569
preferences, setting, 314
prefix notation, 302
primary key, relational databases, 593
primary snap-ins, 539
required extensions, 541
PrimaryGroupID, IADsUser property, 210
PrimaryInterface, IADsClass property, 133, 137
print jobs, 250
deleting, 253
status numeric codes, 252
print queues, 248
status, 253
printableString property, IADsPropertyValue, 120
PrintQueue objects, 248
enumerating, 249
private keys, public key encryption, 397
PrivateGetIDsOfNames method, IADsExtension interface, 517
implementing, 528
late binding, 518
PrivateInvoke method, IADsExtension interface, 517
implementing, 528
late binding, 518
privileges, 382

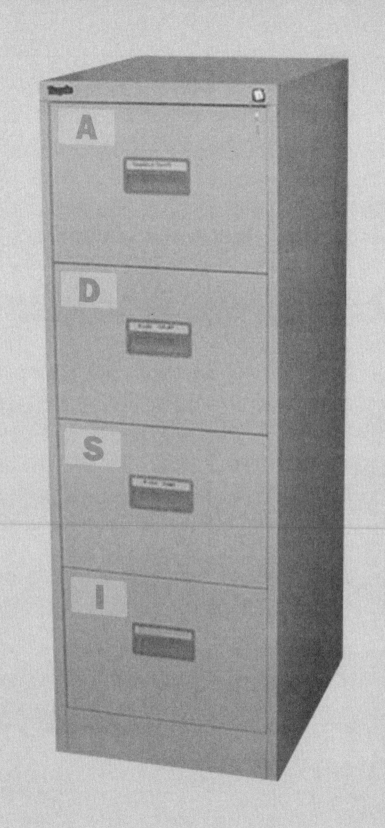

wrox

PROGRAMMER TO PROGRAMMER™

Wrox writes books for you. Any suggestions, or ideas about how you want information given in your ideal book will be studied by our team. Your comments are always valued at Wrox.

Free phone in USA 800-USE-WROX
Fax (312) 893 8001

UK Tel. (0121) 687 4100   Fax (0121) 687 4101

Professional ADSI - Registration Card

Name _____

Address _____

_____

_____

City _____ State/Region _____

Country _____ Postcode/Zip _____

E-mail _____

Occupation _____

How did you hear about this book? _____

☐ Book review (name) _____

☐ Advertisement (name) _____

☐ Recommendation _____

☐ Catalog _____

☐ Other _____

Where did you buy this book? _____

☐ Bookstore (name) _____ City _____

☐ Computer Store (name) _____

☐ Mail Order _____

☐ Other _____

What influenced you in the purchase of this book?

☐ Cover Design

☐ Contents

☐ Other (please specify) _____

How did you rate the overall contents of this book?

☐ Excellent   ☐ Good

☐ Average   ☐ Poor

What did you find most useful about this book? _____

What did you find least useful about this book? _____

Please add any additional comments. _____

What other subjects will you buy a computer book on soon? _____

What is the best computer book you have used this year? _____

Note: This information will only be used to keep you updated about new Wrox Press titles and will not be used for any other purpose or passed to any other third party.

Check here if you DO NOT want to receive support for this book ☐

wrox

PROGRAMMER TO PROGRAMMER™

NB. If you post the bounce back card below in the UK, please send it to:

Wrox Press Ltd., Arden House, 1102 Warwick Road,
Acocks Green, Birmingham B27 6BH. UK.

——————— *Computer Book Publishers* ———————